T3-BOQ-665

BUSINESS & MANAGERIAL COMMUNICATION

COMMUNICATION

NEW PERSPECTIVES

CO-AUTHORS

Cliff Atherton, President, The Emprise Group, and Lecturer in Finance, Graduate School of Administration, Rice University

Steve Barnhill, President, Steve Barnhill & Company

Donald A. Clayton, Certified Management Consultant, Business Systems Group

Linda Driskill, Associate Professor, Graduate School of Administration, Rice University

June Ferrill, President, Ferrill and Associates

William Howell, Chief Scientist, Air Force Human Resources Laboratory, and Professor of Psychology, Rice University

Kathryn McAllister, Staff Editor and Communication Specialist, Graduate School of Administration, Rice University

Albert Napier, Associate Professor, Management Information Systems, Graduate School of Administration, Rice University

R. J. Phillips, President, Texas Commercial Realtors

Peggy Shaw, Reference Librarian, Graduate School of Administration, Rice University

David Shields, Associate Professor of Accounting, University of Houston

Marda Nicholson Steffey, President, Career Development, Inc.

Francis D. Tuggle, Dean, Kogod College of Business Administration, The American University, Washington, D.C.

Wilfred C. Uecker, Associate Dean, Graduate School of Administration, Rice University

Ed Williams, Henry Gardiner Symonds Professor of Administrative Science, Graduate School of Administration, Rice University

Duane Windsor, Associate Dean, Graduate School of Administration, Rice University

BUSINESS & MANAGERIAL COMMUNICATION

NEW PERSPECTIVES

Linda P. Driskill
Rice University

June Ferrill   Marda Nicholson Steffey
Editors

The Dryden Press
Harcourt Brace Jovanovich College Publishers

Fort Worth   Philadelphia   San Diego   New York   Orlando   Austin   San Antonio
Toronto   Montreal   London   Sydney   Tokyo

Copyright © 1992 by Harcourt Brace Jovanovich, Inc.

All rights reserved. No part of this publication may be reproduced or transmitted in any form or by any means, electronic or mechanical, including photocopy, recording or any information storage and retrieval system, without permission in writing from the publisher.

Requests for permission to make copies of any part of the work should be mailed to: Permissions Department, Harcourt Brace Jovanovich, Publishers, 8th Floor, Orlando, Florida 32887.

ISBN 0-15-505589-5

Library of Congress Catalog Card Number: 90-82385

Printed in the United States of America

☐ PREFACE

Sixteen authors collaborated on this book. We all believed that communication was central to our work, but we represented a variety of management specialties and we had different perspectives. Through a process of learning from one another, we began to find the links between our ideas about communication. These points of connection finally became the book's central themes.

We wanted to develop a comprehensive account of communication within organizations and to provide a model for interpreting what writers and speakers do. Our consulting work testified to the diversity of communication in business. We believed that the impersonal "transportation" models (which describe senders encoding a message that travels over noisy channels to be decoded by a receiver) short-changed the complex reality of business communication. To address this problem, we developed a theoretical framework that would account for differences in communication in different companies. We considered it essential that many often overlooked factors—such as the size and structure of the company, its technology, its corporate culture, and the legal environment in which it operates—be incorporated into an understanding of business communication.

We also wanted to help students develop strong communication skills. The first three parts of this book emphasize a core of communication skills, such as defining the situation and participants' roles, analyzing complex audiences, managing long-term relationships, creating communication strategies, generating and organizing ideas, planning meetings, creating graphics, tailoring styles, and designing appropriate page layouts. From our point of view, fundamentals consist not only of words, sentences, and paragraphs, but also of situations that account for so many differences and the collectively understood means of handling them.

The section called "Communicating in Special Situations" responds to global changes that have increased the importance of international communication and personal career management. The emergence of new democracies and the consolidation of the European Economic Community make it imperative that students be aware of intercultural and international communication challenges; meeting these challenges is the focus of two chapters. Changing career patterns also force students to learn how to direct their own careers. The Job Search chapter helps students with the various communications needed in finding the right job; it also contains a special feature on résumé preferences in other countries.

The set of chapters called "Specialists' Perspectives" focuses on communications requiring knowledge or special skills in marketing, finance, performance evaluation, accounting, strategic planning, real estate, or consulting. These chapters help students develop an insider's understanding of how experts in various business specialties apply their knowledge. Some of the authors commented that they were writing the chapter they wished their students had read before writing papers.

Each business specialty or discipline interprets situations in particular ways because of its own assumptions, definitions, and procedures. These differences result from the ethos or standards taught in professional schools and partly from the cultures that develop in departments or groups that share common tasks and problems. Sometimes the preferred communication styles of these specialists may even interfere with communication beyond their own groups. Some accountants have been accused of "speaking in footnotes," and some lawyers are charged with "writing legalese." When appropriately used, however, the techniques of analysis, argument, and problem solving developed in special disciplines can be crucial to a company's success.

The book's final section features perspectives from executives from a variety of firms. Their accounts of situations in their businesses, the strategies followed, and the communications required describe the authentic challenges that communications must address—product decisions, international agreements, human relations, rapid business expansions, starting a new venture, keeping in touch with clients, and forging a company identity. Their views convincingly illustrate concepts presented in other chapters.

Business and Managerial Communication: New Perspectives differs from many others in its emphasis on the importance of analyzing the specific communication context of an organization. While particular communication skills such as graphics, organizing, or style may be studied independently, they must be used strategically in specific contexts. This book brings together the resources for systematically developing business savvy and for understanding how to communicate special knowledge.

This book is organized so it can be used effectively in a variety of ways. Instructors may choose chapters to suit the educational levels and experiences of their students, and different course plans have been suggested. Chapters include a range of assignments, so students who have more educational or business experience, such as MBA students, will have opportunities to try more challenging assignments. At the same time, other assignments require no more technical knowledge than that discussed in the chapter.

We also hope that this book will offer many benefits for business communication instructors. First, we want this book to make the value of communication courses readily apparent to the communication instructors' colleagues. Second, we want students to recognize clearly the relationship between their work in business communication and what they are learning in their other courses, so

that instructors will enjoy greater student interest and cooperation. Third, we hope to advance the discussion of the role of communication in business disciplines.

We would like to thank those colleagues who were kind enough to review some or all of our manuscript. They are W. Clark Ford, Middle Tennessee State University; F. Lynn Galbraith, Rutgers University—The State University of New Jersey; Robert D. Gieselman, University of Illinois at Urbana-Champaign; John H. Hagge, Iowa State University; Melinda Kramer, Purdue University; Brenda M. Larkin, Louisiana State University; Lee Odell, Rensselaer Polytechnic Institute; Jone M. Rymer, Wayne State University; and Jeremiah J. Sullivan, University of Washington.

In addition, we owe thanks to many other people for making this collaborative book project possible. Reviewers Jone Rymer, Bob Gieselman, and Lee Odell provided thoughtful commentaries that helped us address the key problems of teaching people who are not already members of a discourse community how to find their place in an organization. The core approach in Chapters 1 through 5 owes much to their suggestions. Deborah Barrett also provided a useful outside perspective on the core chapters.

During their respective tenures, the deans of the Jesse H. Jones Graduate School of Administration at Rice University, Francis D. Tuggle and Benjamin Bailar, and associate deans, Wil Uecker and Duane Windsor, integrated communication as a subject throughout the school's MBA curriculum. They thereby fostered much of the collaboration that led to our chapters in the Specialists' Perspectives section. The Jones School has also generously supported this project through a reduced teaching load for the senior author and through the expert help of staff members Dru Vail and Suzanna Ramos.

Producing a text with so many new features took courage and foresight from the decision makers at Harcourt Brace Jovanovich. We clearly broke the safe "80/20 Rule" of 80 percent old material, 20 percent new. We thank William Barnett, Marlane Miriello, Marcus Boggs, Thomas Thompson, and Karen Allanson for their support for this project. We owe the cover to Steve Lux, design chief at HBJ. John Wright, world's best agent, gave us crucial advice. Cece Munson coordinated the extraordinarily complex production process.

Our enthusiastic coauthors and consulting clients were generous in supplying materials from companies and helping develop cases for teaching. Their examples and feedback enabled us to test and confirm insights about differences in communication scenarios at various firms. Jeannine Klein, Fiona Tolhurst, and Amy Barber assisted with proofreading, indexing, and question writing for the instructors' manual—which, on a project of this size, are formidable and important tasks.

Our encouraging and patient families enabled us to devote hundreds of hours to this project. We declare special gratitude to them: George P. Jones; Robert Burnside; Melba and David Nicholson; Michael, Nicholas, and Drew Steffey; Robert Eddy; Frank, Gladys, and Lorinda Driskill; Jason Hadley; and Bob Phillips. As always, the faults that remain with this book we claim as our own.

Linda Driskill

June Ferrill

Marda Steffey

□ CONTENTS

PART TWO
MASTERING THE LANGUAGE OF BUSINESS   125

PART THREE
PRODUCING COMMUNICATIONS   193

PART FOUR
COMMUNICATING IN SPECIAL CONTEXTS 441

PART SIX
EXECUTIVES' PERSPECTIVES 763

BUSINESS
&
MANAGERIAL
COMMUNICATION

NEW PERSPECTIVES

PART ONE

COMMUNICATING IN BUSINESS CONTEXTS

COMMUNICATION AND YOUR CAREER

OBJECTIVES

This chapter will help you to

- appreciate the value of communication skills in your career

- understand the principal differences between the academic writing you do now and professional writing

- understand the relationship between general problem-solving skills and communication

- use this book

PREVIEW

Your success in business depends on how well you communicate. Researchers, managers, and students who work all agree that your ability to write, speak, participate in meetings, interact with people from other cultures and countries, and use computers and other media will affect whether you are hired and promoted. Businesses will no longer tolerate employees who are not productive, and the person who cannot communicate the results of his or her work cannot compete with the person who communicates well. Furthermore, the ability to analyze communication situations can help people adapt to new jobs and changing business circumstances.

Students sometimes do not realize how business communication differs from academic communication. Business writers must achieve complex purposes, use different techniques, play different roles, write for complex audiences, and produce results. Because of ongoing changes, they must communicate in a complex legal, economic, and technical environment.

This book was planned to help you know what to expect on the job—not by suggesting that all businesses are alike, but by showing you how to decide what is important about the communication in any business situation you face. It offers many avenues to learning about communicating in business situations: a coherent approach to analyzing situations and audiences, narratives about how people communicate at work, and communication planning forms and checklists. The preliminary exercises in each chapter will help you solidify your understanding of whatever related experience you may already have, but you need not have business experience to use this book. Cases and exercises will give you a chance to play roles in a safe and friendly environment. A section called "If You Would Like to Read More" offers suggestions for independent study.

Preparing for, carrying out, and evaluating business transactions are mostly problem-solving processes; therefore many communications activities are concerned primarily with solving problems. This chapter reviews the combination of problem solving and communication in ten commonly used steps. Part 1, the first five chapters of the book, teaches you to develop your own solutions to communication challenges in many situations. Parts 2 and 3 help you master the language of business and produce different types of communications. Part 4 discusses special communication situations and emphasizes skills needed for investigating another culture, preparing international correspondence, and finding a job. Part 5 contains nine chapters on communicating in special areas of business, such as accounting, marketing, and personnel management. Guest commentaries from executives on communication situations in their companies comprise Part 6.

❏ YOUR SUCCESS DEPENDS ON LEARNING TO COMMUNICATE

This book has been written through the collaboration of sixteen authors who are experts in different areas of business, most of whom also are professors in various business fields. The students in our communications and management courses over the years have come from diverse backgrounds and have had a wide variety of career goals. One thing they have had in common: high hopes for a successful career. Regardless of their majors or concentrations, our students realize that their ability to communicate their ideas and knowledge to others affects their opportunities and achievements. We assume that you, too, have set your sights ambitiously. To reach your goals, you will need skill in communication, because at every stage of the career ladder, communication is essential.

What Is Business and Managerial Communication?

Business and managerial communication may be defined as the use of language or graphics in business. Such communication includes telephone conversations, interviews, meetings, oral presentations, speeches, letters, memos, electronic mail, press releases, proposals, reports, studies, videotaped programs, videoconferences, and films.

Almost all business situations involve communication. Advertising new jobs; soliciting bids from vendors and suppliers; applying for licenses; consulting with lawyers, financial institutions, or advertising media; selling products and services; announcing a company picnic; or recommending a change in the accounting treatment of an expense—all involve communication. Language interprets the numbers of the accountant's spreadsheets, embodies agreements in contracts, describes products, conveys terms in real estate deals, interprets and compares risk and reward possibilities, explains the significance of customers' responses in marketing surveys, details union grievances, and presents the results of scientific or engineering work.

Furthermore, language organizes business life. Language creates shared interpretations of what people will do and how they will do it, which is what we mean by "being organized."

You must learn both oral and written communication skills. Although you sometimes can handle business communication tasks simply by talking "one-on-one," you will face many situations in which you cannot meet with the people who will use your information. You will have to write a memorandum or a report, and that document will remain in the company files as legal evidence that you hired and reviewed people fairly, evaluated the hazards of products with concern for human safety, negotiated honestly, or proposed specific types of work. Likewise, you cannot hide behind your word processor; there will be times when speaking on your feet or participating in meetings is the only way you can convey your message. You must be ready to meet both kinds of circumstances.

How Business and Managerial Communication May Affect Your Career

Your communication skills may win your first job for you. Many personnel managers use applicants' performance in a communication course to select job candidates from otherwise academically qualified students. Once hired, your communication skills may determine whether you are promoted. In a survey of *Harvard Business Review* readers and other executives, 98.7 percent of respondents gave "the ability to communicate" as the top-ranked criterion for managers.[1]

In an entry-level job, communication skills associated with a company's fundamental transactions will be important. For example, if you are an engineer, your ability to explain technical problems and write persuasive reports will determine whether the company's engineering problems are solved. If you are in retail sales, your skills in sizing up customers and using oral persuasion will affect your sales record. Later on, as you move into management positions, you will need communication skills to direct new employees to do the tasks you and others used to do: conduct meetings; negotiate among departments; write plans, proposals, and progress reports; and resolve conflicts.

As a top-level manager, you will be perceived as a company spokesperson for outside audiences, you may represent the company's products on television, you will affirm and motivate others to follow the central tenets of the company culture, and you will need to articulate plans and goals with great clarity.[2] Ronald J. Naples, Chief Executive Officer for Hunt Foods, told business college deans and other executives that the primary job of business leaders is "to communicate a vision and get people to share it and contribute to the vision."[3]

Studying Communication: It's the Right Thing to Do!

Everywhere, the message is the same. Managers, researchers, and students who are already employed say communication is important—perhaps even the single most important skill you can acquire.[4] The presidents and chief executive officers of major corporations such as Chrysler, Coca Cola, and Nabisco have gone on record to recommend that students prepare for a career in business by studying communication.[5] They are not alone. Over 1000 executives ranked business communication higher than any other course taught in the business school curriculum.[6] If you're enrolled in a communication course, you're in the right place.

How the Challenges of Communication Have Changed

While people have consistently ranked the value of communication skills extremely highly over the last thirty years, the challenges of communicating in business have changed dramatically. As companies have grown larger, expanding to serve international as well as national markets, and as communication technologies have become more sophisticated, new aspects of communication have become important. In addition to writing, listening, and speaking, people have had to learn to use telecommunications and graphics. Negotiation, persuasion, and other "people skills" have turned out to be critical in a service economy. Everywhere, the legal context for communication has become more complex.

Understanding intercultural and international communications is now mandatory; as you look around your classrooms today, you see people from other cultures and nations. As people change careers more frequently and new hires are given less time to become productive, knowing how to adapt to new communication environments has become a crucial survival skill. "A new employee coming here has to pick up on how the whole place works, fast. They're not here to write term papers," one audit supervisor remarked.

How These Changes Affect You

These changes have several implications:

- Whatever means you have used to obtain information and prepare communications in the past, you now must learn to work with electronic media, because these systems will become increasingly prevalent in the future. Electronic media include telephones, facsimile (FAX) machines, photocopiers, video, and spreadsheets, graphics, databases, and word processing software for computers.

- These electronic media will continue to change rapidly. For example, entering words into a computer by speaking aloud probably will be one of the most important changes in communication to occur by the turn of the century. You must understand how to learn about technology, because keeping up with technological change is an ongoing process. Your first word processing program will not be your last.

- You must accept the idea that you will do your own writing, because these systems tend to eliminate people who used to serve others by answering phones, sending out routine memos, and entering or keystroking messages and documents. By the turn of the century, a larger proportion of this drudgery will be handled by machines.

- You will communicate with many people from other cultures and nations. The unification of the European Common Market and the political revolution in central European countries will accelerate the creation of global markets and international business.

- You will have to rely less on communication *rules* and more on your own *analysis* of situations, because no professor can tell you, any more than Polish professors in 1985 could have told European students, exactly what situations and problems will arise in careers a decade from now.

- You must learn to adapt to new business communication situations because businesses will no longer tolerate employees who are not productive. You must be able to communicate the results of your work to compete effectively. The trend toward changing jobs more frequently will intensify the importance of adaptation skills.

❑ BUSINESS COMMUNICATION DIFFERS FROM ACADEMIC COMMUNICATION

New graduates need to understand the difference between the purposes of business communication and academic communication. They must be able to analyze and respond to new situations. In college, students write primarily to demonstrate their mastery of academic subjects such as political science or economics, to interpret literary works, and to express their feelings about personal experiences. Students sometimes are asked to advocate an idea and support it with reasons and information, but they seldom write to cause action. After reading students' papers, professors rarely use or act upon the information students have presented.

When students take positions in business, the purpose of their communication must change. In business, people seek to create meanings that serve business purposes—produce sales, cooperation, approval, compliance, or agreement; their communication is *instrumental*. Business people may draw on academic knowledge as they write or speak, but their effectiveness depends largely on how they shape their knowledge to the demands of particular situations—*on the results they produce*.

To fulfill your responsibilities in the organization, you have to understand what your fellow employees expect you to do and how they interpret situations. Individuals represent situations and their transactions to themselves as *scenarios*: abstract stories about who will be involved, when, and in what way. Employees' scenarios prescribe the roles of the people involved; the sequence of steps in the situation; the types of documents, meetings, or presentations that are part of the situation; and the values, preferences, rules of etiquette, technological considerations, and criteria pertinent to the interactions. They use phrases such as "This is one of those situations where . . ." or "In this kind of situation . . ." that describe recurring events in terms of the company's goals or their department's routines. Figure 1-1 illustrates the relationship among the situation, the scenario, and the communications required.

You already understand many experiences according to this model. For example, if you walked into a restaurant and a waiter immediately presented you with a bill, you would probably say, "Wait a minute, I haven't even ordered yet." You expect particular people in a restaurant to do particular things in a specific order. This common understanding of how people behave in restaurants can be called "the restaurant scenario." Business people have similar scenarios that insiders know.

As a customer, you have certain expectations about employees and they have expectations about you. If you walk up to the teller's window in a bank, the teller expects you to present a check for deposit or to request that a check be cashed. If you want to make a loan, the teller will send you to a loan officer, because that's how loans are made (the loan scenario) in a bank. As a college student, you probably are familiar with the check-cashing scenario, but you may or may not have applied for a bank loan. In order to encourage people to apply for loans, one bank posted brochures about how to come in to apply for a loan and how to tell in advance whether the application was likely to be approved. In

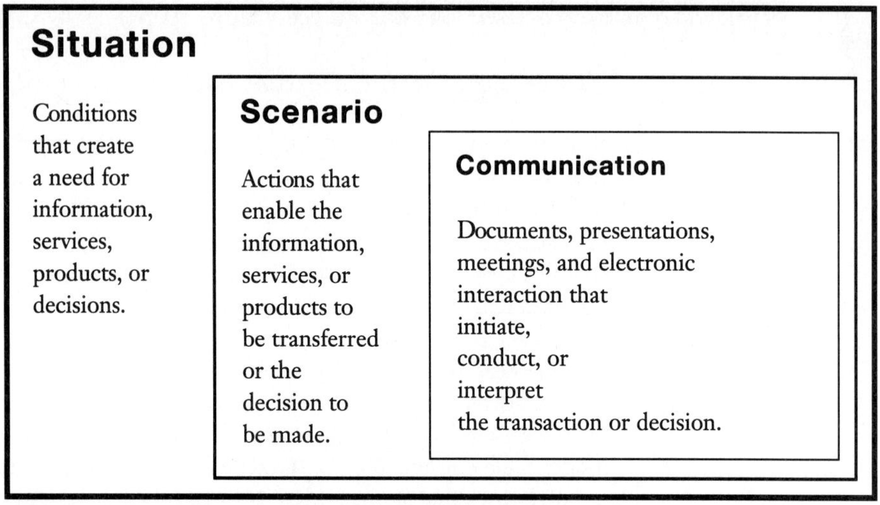

```
┌─────────────────────────────────────────────────────────────────┐
│ Situation                                                         │
│                                                                   │
│ Conditions   ┌───────────────────────────────────────────────┐   │
│ that create  │ Scenario                                      │   │
│ a need for   │                                               │   │
│ information, │ Actions that  ┌─────────────────────────────┐ │   │
│ services,    │ enable the    │ Communication               │ │   │
│ products, or │ information,  │                             │ │   │
│ decisions.   │ services, or  │ Documents, presentations,   │ │   │
│              │ products to   │ meetings, and electronic    │ │   │
│              │ be transferred│ interaction that            │ │   │
│              │ or the        │ initiate,                   │ │   │
│              │ decision to   │ conduct, or                 │ │   │
│              │ be made.      │ interpret                   │ │   │
│              │               │ the transaction or decision.│ │   │
│              │               └─────────────────────────────┘ │   │
│              └───────────────────────────────────────────────┘   │
└─────────────────────────────────────────────────────────────────┘
```

FIGURE 1-1.   Relationship of Situations, Scenarios, and Communication

addition, the employees of the bank would have had an even more detailed version of this scenario than the one customers knew.[7]

Business situations often involve familiar scenarios, but at the heart of a business situation is a problem that must be solved. The transaction is the solution to the situational problem. For example, a manufacturer uses up raw materials in producing goods. When the supply of a particular raw material decreases, new quantities must be obtained. A manufacturer will see this as a routine situation and routine purchase procedures will be used to solve the problem unless something such as an unusual shortage of raw material forces additional, nonroutine problem solving. Communication helps determine what transaction will occur, and it may be part of carrying out and interpreting the transaction by means of reports, memoranda, and accounting records.

The word "problem," used in a business sense, does not necessarily mean something dreadful or emotionally distressing. If customers are wildly enthusiastic about your chocolate pecan ice cream and the stores want more than you are currently producing, you actually have an opportunity, not something to worry about. Nonetheless, in business terms, your company will have to solve the "demand problem" by ordering more chocolate and more pecans, reorganizing the production schedule so that more chocolate pecan ice cream is manufactured, and calculating the increased profits. From the plant manager's perspective, your company has a production problem; from the purchasing manager's perspective, there is an inventory draw-down problem; and from the accountant's perspective, the company may have a tax problem.

In business, the word "problem" usually means the kind of business challenges everyone faces. There are times, however, when "problem" means "crisis," just as it does in everyday life. Problem-solving processes are used to tackle both sorts of circumstances.

❏ PROBLEM SOLVING AND COMMUNICATING

How Problem Solving and Communication Are Related

It is common to talk about the relationship between problem solving and communication with metaphors such as: managers wear two hats, one for business activities and one for communication activities; or communication is a tool that can be used to distribute the results of problem solving to others. The "hat" metaphor rests on the idea that people behave according to their dress. The metaphor doesn't explain why there's a difference, just that the difference occurs. The "tool" metaphor makes communication sound inert; as unlikely to influence what it delivers as a shovel is to interact with the dirt it carries. These metaphors disguise something much more exciting and fundamental.

Language habits are deeply embedded in every professional group's ways of thinking and acting. Language influences how a group or specialty defines its members, what it studies, what is possible in situations, and how to resolve differences among specialists. To see what we mean, think back to a time when your parents still referred to you as "a boy" or "a girl," even though you had begun to think of yourself as "a man" or "a woman." Surely there were moments in your conversations when they spoke of what was proper "for a boy your age." The words they used affected what they perceived, their reasoning about the situation, and the course of action they would consider. So long as they perceived you as a juvenile, certain actions were impossible and certain solutions couldn't be tried.

You will be intellectually rewarded for studying how language functions in all of the specialties you study and all of the situations you encounter on the job. For example, watch how individuals represent themselves in documents. The financial accountant strives for an utter impersonality in tone that implies, "I have no vested interest in this matter; I'm simply showing you how these standards or rules apply to this transaction." The financial analyst, on the other hand, must deal with future events and must convince the reader that he or she is trustworthy, reasonable, and likely to make good predictions in several areas: future interest rates, the competence of management, and the future of the industry. The financial analyst must display his or her character in order to generate trust. The differences between other specialties hinge on other factors, but all of them are fascinating, and the chapters at the end of the book will explore some of them. This is the first text, so far as we know, that brings together a variety of specialists to tell you how language works in their specialties and the critical factors to consider when dealing with situations in these areas.

Problem Solving and Communication: Combined Steps

Communication and problem-solving functions, which are discussed in the final part of this chapter, are closely—even inextricably—linked. Problem solving involves communication in defining the problem, summarizing and analyzing information, generating alternatives, and negotiating the evaluation of these alternatives. Furthermore, communication is an essential part of developing support for any solution. Communication also involves problem solving: analyzing the need for communication and the audience that must be addressed, generating alternatives, and making choices. Because problem solving and communicating are so closely linked in business situations, many chapters in this book refer to problem solving and communication steps in combination. You should, therefore, become familiar with these steps.

The steps used to solve a particular problem depend on the nature of the problem and the training of those solving it. Some company problems are routine and well-defined; others are unanticipated and ill-defined. The processes used to address routine problems and select a transaction are often a compressed subset of the processes that should be used to handle nonroutine problems. However, both compressed or full-scale processes break down into understanding and solving phases.[8] Keep in mind that any list of steps describing a process is a simplified version of something complex and variable. When solving a complex problem, typical successful problem solvers use the following steps:

UNDERSTAND THE PROBLEM

1. State the problem
2. Obtain and review necessary information
3. Perform the appropriate analysis or task
4. Scrutinize the problem from additional perspectives
5. Redirect the focus from symptoms to causes of the problem

SOLVE THE PROBLEM

6. Generate alternative courses of action
7. Define objective criteria
8. Select a course of action
9. Communicate the plan and motivate others
10. Carry out and interpret the transaction

We will review a full set of problem-solving steps, mentioning in the discussion how these steps may be collapsed when the problem is routine. The discussion will stress both the communication and problem-solving functions of the process.

1. State the Problem

Identifying the problem at the outset may not seem necessary in a routine situation. However, it is always a good exercise to name your task. If you are addressing what appears to be a nonroutine situation, then problem definition is necessary. Giving a name to the problem will help you be aware of your perceptual biases and their effect on problem definition. Obviously, you can only solve the problem you define, so appropriate definition is essential.

Some of the problems that must be solved are communication problems: how to inform clients, how to build goodwill for the firm, how to attract media attention, how to explain the risks or hazards associated with the company's business to the surrounding community, how to persuade employees to work safely, how to reduce sexism or racism in the workplace, how to train everyone in the use of a new system, or how to announce company decisions to employees scattered around the globe. In addressing these problems, communication and problem solving can scarcely be separated.

Your perception that a problem needs to be solved and the statement of the problem usually derive from the scenario. The scenario determines whether circumstances are typical, and if they are typical, what comes next.

2. Obtain and Review Necessary Information

The sources of information pertinent to routine problems may be well known; however, for nonroutine problems, research may be necessary. For most routine problems, well-defined scenarios exist; nonroutine situations may elicit a wide range of definitions. When confronted with something unusual, do not be surprised if other people offer you what appears to be extraneous information about apparently separate issues. What appears to be one type of problem to you may have another character altogether to someone else because of his or her technical background, position in the company, or personal or departmental objectives. You can learn about research strategies for retrieving published information in print or electronic form in Chapter 12.

3. Perform the Appropriate Analysis or Task

Once you have sufficient data or resources, begin your analysis. The method you use will depend on the type of technical or professional problem you have identified in step 1. Step 3, the analysis, is where the procedures of different business specialties vary. Marketing specialists will use one type of analysis; accountants, another. If step 2 has produced additional information that seems unfit for the appropriate analysis or tasks, include step 4 in the process.

4. Scrutinize the Problem from Additional Perspectives

Before concluding that the results of your analysis are unequivocally correct, consider other external and internal factors that may affect the situation and reanalyze the data with other methods.

For example, what appears to be a labor problem may have multiple definitions. Looked at from a financial perspective, labor's demands for higher wages may affect the profitability of the company and investors' willingness to invest; looked at as a product pricing problem, prospective increases in labor costs may drive up prices and affect the company's ability to compete. Looked at from a labor relations perspective, labor's demands may reflect employees' need to contribute to decision making and a broader need for more participative management. Additional information from these other fields may offer new ways to solve the original problem and account for other issues that have been uncovered.

5. Redirect the Focus from Symptoms to Causes

Before moving on to the solution of the problem, review the original problem definition. A problem incorrectly defined at the outset may need to be restated after some analysis has been performed. The most common discovery is that the problem as first stated described a symptom rather than a root cause. The re-definition of a problem is often necessary, because at the outset you simply do not know enough about the situation.

6. Generate Alternative Courses of Action

When using a full-blown problem-solving process, invent as many alternative solutions as possible without stopping to criticize or evaluate any of them. Creativity and criticism flourish separately, not together. Keep telling yourself (and others) that at this stage, there are *no bad ideas*. Try to invent options for mutual gain: Each solution should attempt to provide benefits to all parties affected by the course of action. In routine situations, the alternatives may be well known, but do not accept them too quickly.

Many examples can be cited in which people too quickly accepted the idea that a routine situation lay ahead and proposed a traditional (and inappropriate) solution. In the early 1970s, the Swiss watch industry expected to continue dominating the market with traditional mechanical watches and failed to develop electronic watches and sophisticated marketing strategies. As a result, Swiss watch manufacturers lost much of their market share to Japanese companies.

7. Define Objective Criteria

How will you recognize a good solution when it is offered? Define a set of criteria that can be applied with objective measures. Unless the options can be tested against specific criteria, people may evaluate options with different standards and reaching a consensus will be hard. One university department announced a position for an economics scholar, but the members found themselves dead-locked between two prominent candidates. Half of the voting members preferred a candidate with an excellent teaching record who would be appealing to undergraduate students; the other half, interested in the graduate program and the department's national reputation, favored a scholar with an acceptable but rather mediocre teaching record but an outstanding record of research and publication. Debate over the "quality" of each candidate was fruitless because of the underlying disagreement about criteria. Without defining objective criteria, the members could not move forward in their problem-solving process.

In all organizations, problem solvers must adopt criteria that take implementation and the company environment into account. Models are widely used in generating business options. People sometimes expect the real world to act as a model does, and they ignore implementation problems. Any change to a model implies that people perform tasks differently and respond differently to standard business situations. Before accepting any single option produced by a model, you should analyze whether people can or will change their behavior to conform to the model.

The process of communicating often helps you to discover solutions. For some people, saying whatever comes to mind causes fresh ideas to bubble up. For others, writing brings about the bright ideas. Researcher Lee Odell comments that insight occurs while a person writes because some of the mental processes that enable the person to understand a subject also enable him or her to formulate and support the assertions in writing.[9] During planning or drafting, you may come to see the problem in a different light and redefine the problem and its solutions. The writing and problem-solving processes work together, as the act of articulating perceptions creates new connections among pieces of evidence or modifies routine habits of thinking.

Specialists frequently solve problems during the report writing or communication phase, because much of the data-gathering and analysis go on under conditions that allow little time for reflection. Thinking about communication often forces closure on a problem. The creative part of your work may begin as you sit down to interpret data in light of the audience and the situation.

8. Select a Course of Action

There may be no clearly superior course of action, although something must be done. One of the alternatives that appears to be superior in one respect may be accepted as the dominant alternative if it is not clearly inferior in another respect. The objective at this stage is to develop a consensus, either by means of a document or through presentations and meetings. Even if the decision is to be made by one person, it is almost certain that many other people will in some way be affected. The course of action may involve one transaction or many, depending on the size and importance of the problem.

9. Communicate the Plan and Motivate Others

Once a solution has been chosen, one or more people must communicate the decision to others and motivate them to cooperate. This stage of the process may be more important than all the others, because unless people are motivated to cooperate, the solution may not be implemented. If those who must implement the decision were involved in the earlier stages of problem solving, it may be easier to convince them to cooperate and to implement the decision.

10. Carry Out and Interpret the Transaction

This phase almost always involves communication, as the transaction must be completed to solve the problem. Even if the transaction is electronic (sale of shares) or mechanical (production of 2000 units of a product), the transaction must be recorded in some way. Later, the usefulness or value of the transaction will be interpreted in an operations report, accounting report, briefing, closure report, or some other form of communication. This interpretation will, in turn, affect the organization's perception and definition of other situations in the future.

Communication and problem solving are not identical, for all of their interconnections. Some studies of problem solving show that people may use non-linguistic cognitive processes in analyzing problems or in generating solutions. Visual thinking (such as the perception of shapes or three-dimensional spatial perception), musical perception, or calculation can be used to interpret information or design solutions. Even these analyses and solutions must usually be explained, in language, to other people. On the other hand, some language processes do not seem aimed at resolving differences. People use language to entertain one another, to provide emotional solidarity, and to create works of art. Some of the components may be the same, but the purposes differ. Because business focuses on dealing with situations and attaining goals, a great deal of time is spent preparing for, carrying out, and evaluating transactions to solve problems; therefore the language of business is dedicated, in large part, to problem solving, as well.

❑ THIS BOOK'S APPROACH

In this chapter we have talked about two underlying constructs in business communication: the relationship between problem solving and communication, and the importance of understanding scenarios. This book's approach makes use of both of these ideas.

How You Learn Scenarios

How have you learned the multitude of scenarios appropriate to the many situations in your life? How did you learn how to act, what to do? The answer is that you have doubtless used many learning methods, some more efficient than others. First, you observed others; if you did not have the opportunity to observe, you may have plunged in and learned by trial and error. You may have taken a class, read a book, asked advice, watched films or videos, read manuals, and talked with friends and coworkers. You surely looked back over past experience and generalized, and you kept matching your results against your hopes and goals.

It is possible to become an outstanding business communicator with the "plunge in" method, but it is also risky and inefficient. Business rewards communication success, but it likewise punishes communication failures. Trial and error can be hazardous on the job. You may intuitively try something that works, but you may try something that doesn't. Communicating shouldn't be like rolling dice.

Some books set out a single set of rules based on assumptions that these will fit whatever company you join. Because business situations are so diverse and companies vary so drastically, the "one size fits all" approach to business communication doesn't work much better than it does in clothing. One document format, one document preparation procedure, and one writing style may not stretch to fit the situation. Therefore, we are going to teach you how to analyze communication situations so you can think for yourself. We will, of course, recommend strategies for solving communication problems, but we won't tie you to a single set of solutions.

We want you to have tools for analyzing many different situations and problems that will emerge in the future. We have created a theoretical framework that could account for the differences in situations and scenarios. We consider it essential that many overlooked factors, such as the size, structure, and culture of a company, be incorporated into the model.

Although your business experience may all be in the future, you don't have to be employed to learn about business scenarios and communication. If you are employed or have been employed, that will be helpful but it isn't a prerequisite. In this book, you will learn from examples. Wherever possible, we have tried to enhance your understanding of business with narratives about how people work and interact. We have created an approach you can use to analyze situations and audiences and plan persuasive communication strategies. The preliminary exercises in each chapter will help you solidify your understanding of whatever related experience you may already have.

Cases and exercises will offer you a chance to play roles in a safe and friendly environment. If you have to invent motivations and ascribe attitudes to others in a case from time to time, you'll only be doing what people do on the job anyway. The level of information people have about real audiences and real problems is always less than perfect. Because business documents may be taken from the files and used years after they were written, it is always hard to anticipate all the readers to whom you may eventually be accountable. Professor Arn Tibbetts, acknowledging the limits of writers' knowledge about all their audiences, recommends: "Always write as if there were at least one ghost looking over your reader's shoulder." [10]

The chapters written by specialists in nine business fields and the executives' guest commentaries in Part 6 will give you the benefit of their experience and guidance. Furthermore, we've added special features in most chapters on trends in business communication, the legal context, and "document spotlights" that explain how a particular document fulfills the requirements of a particular situation. Gradually, you will analyze and react smoothly to new situations, rather like a pilot dealing with the ever-varying combinations of weather in a cross-country flight. Pilots never make quite the same trip twice; that's true for business communicators as well.

How This Book Is Organized and Why

If you've glanced at the table of contents, you've seen that this book has six parts:

Communicating in Business Contexts

Mastering the Language of Business

Producing Communications

Communicating in Special Situations

Specialists' Perspectives

Executives' Perspectives

Part 1, "Communicating in Business Contexts," contains chapters on analyzing situations, managing relationships with audiences, and developing persuasive communication strategies. These chapters contain the book's basic advice on analyzing and planning. Your application of this advice should produce many different specific plans for different types of situations.

Part 2, "Mastering the Language of Business," invites you to consider seriously the skills of choosing words, structuring sentences, creating coherence, and developing a personal style in writing, listening, and participating in meetings. Part 3, "Producing Communications," tells what to do once you've developed a strategy and need to write a letter, memo, report, or presentation, putting those language skills to use. Part 4, "Communicating in Special Contexts," teaches you how to investigate and understand another culture, prepare international correspondence, and use your communication skills to find the right job.

Part 5, "Specialists' Perspectives," contains chapters on communication for consulting, real estate, marketing, performance evaluation, financial and managerial accounting, finance and financial analysis, strategic planning, and new ventures. Several of the specialists who wrote the chapters in Part 5 undertook the job of writing "the chapter I wish my students had studied *before* they took my course."

Part 6 contains executives' perspectives on communication situations in their companies. Seven executives in companies large and small explain the function of communication in a variety of important situations, ranging from deciding to discontinue an enormously successful but environmentally damaging product to keeping in touch with clients in a small insurance agency.

If you are taking a communication course as a sophomore, you may wish to return to this book as a junior or senior and read some of these chapters as you advance in your studies. You may also return to this section once you're on the job. Each of these business specialties uses basic problem-solving processes as well as special techniques of analysis and argument and particular kinds of documents and presentations. In any case, understanding these specialized communications will enable you to read or listen to them astutely and to employ techniques needed on the job.

❑ HOW TO USE THIS BOOK

Chapters 1 through 5 support all of the rest of the book, so study these chapters first. These chapters cover analyzing situations, recognizing scenarios, building relationships with audiences, and developing communication strategies (purpose, persuasive appeal, contents, and organization). Chapters in the rest of the book refer to these chapters and the checklists and forms (for analyzing situations and audiences and planning documents) in them.

Look at the organization of the book as shown in the table of contents. You may wish to use chapters out of order. You may need to know how to find information about a company before you reach Chapter 12, or you may need to start your search for a summer job before you reach Chapter 19. You might want to read what an executive had to say about a certain type of business situation by reading selectively in Part 6, the Executives' Perspectives. You could read the chapter on managerial accounting communications before writing a report in an intermediate accounting or tax class. If you have a feel for the resources, you can use this book for special projects in other courses and for developing your own career.

Skim the preview of each chapter. Having an overall idea of the chapter's contents can increase your comprehension on your first reading by up to 50 percent.

Skim the marginal notes in the chapter. These short commentaries tell you where the ideas are discussed and they may distill the point of the paragraph or section to help you remember it. The headings reinforce the marginal notes.

Use the preliminary exercises to tie your personal experience to the concepts in the text. Even if your instructor does not assign them, these preliminary exercises create mental links between what you've done in the past and the kinds of tasks required by the exercises and cases. If you've ever been involved in track events, you know that it's easier to run high hurdles if you've first run low hurdles. You have less apprehension and you enjoy it more.

❑ COMMUNICATION CHALLENGES

PRELIMINARY EXERCISE 1 If you have worked in a company, choose an employee or manager whom you consider a good communicator. Write a one- or two-page description of this person's communication activities and explain why he or she performed them especially well.

PRELIMINARY EXERCISE 2 Describe in one to two pages the oral and written communication responsibilities that you have had in a job. How did these activities affect the success of people in similar positions? Were any of these skills prerequisites for promotion to another job?

PRELIMINARY EXERCISE 3 Identify and briefly describe three routine problems that you solve frequently or regularly. Identify one nonroutine problem that you have had to solve. Compare these problems with regard to their complexity, clarity of definition, or ease of solution.

EXERCISE 1

You are a manager for a small printing company. Three months ago, you hired Ray Denton, a man about 23 years old, as a client representative. Client representatives talk with firms about their printing needs, solicit orders, spot check the printing runs (perform "press checks," to make sure the ink is applied smoothly, the colors are true, and all is as the customer has ordered), and seek new business. It's time to decide whether to keep Ray or let him go. Ray does understand the printing business, so he knows what he's selling. While he was a college student, he worked in a printing shop as a printer's helper.

You've had two calls from clients who were unhappy with the jobs your company delivered. Ray hadn't listened carefully, they said, and the job came back with errors in ink color or paper choice. His notes on his call book were pretty sketchy, and if it had only happened once, you might think that the customers had changed their minds without notifying you. Furthermore, even though Ray understands the technical processes, he doesn't explain them very well. You went along on one call and it was clear he was using jargon the customer didn't understand, and he didn't bother to explain it.

He's a nice person, though. You only have one other client representative, and if she has to take back the clients who don't like Ray, she won't be able to work on attracting new business. That's another thing. Ray doesn't like "cold calling," dropping by to tell prospective clients about your services. He hasn't brought in one new client. Perhaps he needs some communications training. Perhaps you should just hire someone else. *What are you going to do about Ray and why?* Jot down notes that you can use in a discussion about Ray with the company owner.

As your instructor directs, compare your conclusions in class with those of other students.

EXERCISE 2

Make a list of communication tasks that you handle well. Which of these is most likely to win you a promotion? How do they relate to the job you are now holding or to one that you intend to seek? What communication skill would make you even more promotable if only you could improve it?

EXERCISE 3

The president of your college has appointed you to a committee that will invite a nationally prominent speaker to the campus for the president's lecture series. The committee decides that one speaker should be invited to speak about communication. Each member is supposed to recommend one person who might be invited. Which person would you recommend that the committee invite? The college funds this program, so you need not worry about the size of the speaker's fee or honorarium.

a. *Choose the subject area for the address.* Considering what you have read about business communication and your knowledge of your college, select an area of communication change that would be provocative and interesting to an audience of your peers.
b. *Choose the speaker.* Go to the library and use the directory of organizations to find the head of a national organization interested in this topic. Another possibility is to use *INFOTRAC* or *The Reader's Guide to Periodical Literature* to identify someone who has written an article on communication in a particular field. By looking up the article, you could see whether this person's ideas are stimulating. Or, read about business in the *Wall Street Journal* and choose the president of a company whose communications problems interest you (trouble with customers, an indictment for pollution, product recalls—these difficulties mean the company *has* to communicate).
c. *Write a one-page recommendation to your committee chair, Tracy Tarkington.* This recommendation should include two points: what subject you think is most interesting and why, and which speaker should be invited to discuss this subject and why.

Be prepared for a class discussion of all the students' recommendations.

EXERCISE 4

Interview someone who now holds a job similar to the one you hope to have after you graduate in order to find out some of the communication responsibilities of an entry-level position. Ask what kinds of situations require communications, whether there are both written and oral communications involved with the job, and how these activities affect performance evaluations.

EXERCISE 5

Interview someone who now holds a job similar to the one you hope to have about five years after graduation. The objective is to find out some of the communication responsibilities of a person in an advanced position. Ask what kinds of situations require communications, whether there are both written and oral communications in the job, and how these activities affect performance evaluations. Also ask about the kinds of communication competence the person you interview expects in the people who work for him or her.

EXERCISE 6

Prepare for a class or panel discussion, using the short reports you prepared for either Exercise 4 or Exercise 5. Discuss the differences in the communication requirements at different stages of career development and in different parts of organizations. Pick out three or four points from your report that would be valuable to the other members of the class.

EXERCISE 7

Select some decision you intend to make in the near future, such as purchasing a computer or car, choosing an apartment, deciding on further professional training, or buying expensive season tickets for a favorite activity.

Sketch the process necessary for effectively making this decision. What kinds of information will you need and where will you get it? What kinds of evaluation or analysis will be necessary? What kinds of choices could you make that would satisfy your needs? What criteria will you apply? What choice are you likely to make in real life? Will this choice be an ideal one, or will it be constrained in some way? Will communication be involved in this choice? How?

EXERCISE 8

Select a problem experienced by a group to which you belong. If the problem occurred in the past, compare the process used to solve the problem with the problem-solving steps explained in this chapter. How did the actual process differ from the process recommended in the text? Can you now identify any alternatives or strategies that might have resulted in a more satisfying solution? If this is a current problem, write a sketch of the process the group should use, suggesting what types of information are needed, the types of analysis that should be used, possible options you anticipate, and criteria for a solution. What solution do you now believe would be best? What solution do you think the group is actually likely to adopt? Why is this outcome probable? How is communication involved in this process?

NOTES

1. G. W. Bowman, "What helps or harms promotability?" *Harvard Business Review, 42* (1964, Jan.–Feb.), 6–26. This study, conducted over twenty years ago, was affirmed in W. J. Heisler, "Promotion: What does it take to get ahead?" *Business Horizons, 21* (1978), 57–63.

2. N. B. Sigband, "Changing role of the CEO." *The Bulletin of the Association for Business Communication, 48* (1985)2, 1–8.

3. Touche Ross roundtable discussion. *The business of a business education.* New York: Touche Ross (1986).

4. J. H. Stegman, "The importance of managerial communication: An annotated bibliography." *The Bulletin of the Association for Business Communication, 51* (1988)3, 25–26. See the similar responses of recent graduates randomly selected from Fortune 500 Companies in A. S. Bednar & R. J. Olney, "Communication needs of recent graduates." *The Bulletin of the Association for Business Communication, 50* (1987), 22–23. A similar evaluation of the importance of communication skills can be found in C. G. Storms, "What business school graduates say about the writing they do at work: Implications for the business communication course." *The Bulletin of the Association for Business Communication, 46* (1983)4, 13–18.

5. Letters from executives are included in J. J. Stallard, E. R. Smith, & S. E. Price, *Business communication: A strategic approach.* Homewood, IL: Irwin (1989), 10–15.

6. H. W. Hildebrandt, F. A. Bond, E. L. Miller, & A. W. Swinyard, "An executive appraisal of courses which best prepare one for general management." *Journal of Business Communication, 19*(1982), 5–15.

7. Many academic fields including sociology, linguistics, speech communication, psychology, philosophy, and anthropology use concepts similar to schema theory to explain how humans perceive and interpret the world. Recognition of pattern in events is central to all of them and to the argument of this book. Although there are differences among the specific definitions and theories of these fields, the terms *situation*, *context*, and *scenario* are sufficiently flexible to build a solid approach to business and managerial communication.

8. The grouping of steps into "understanding" and "solving" phases is based on J. R. Hayes's analysis in *Cognitive psychology: Thinking and creating*. Homewood, IL: Dorsey Press (1978), 177.

9. C. L. Odell, "Teaching writing by teaching the process of discovery: An interdisciplinary enterprise," in L. W. Gregg & E. R. Steinberg (Eds.), *Cognitive processes in writing*. Hillsdale, NJ: Lawrence Erlbaum Associates (1980), 145.

10. A. Tibbetts, "What are the most useful principles for teaching business writing?" *The Bulletin of the Association for Business Communication*, 47 (1984)1, 19.

ANALYZING BUSINESS SITUATIONS AND THE COMMUNICATIONS THEY REQUIRE

OBJECTIVES

This chapter will help you

- analyze business situations
- recognize scenarios for dealing with situations
- identify communications used in these scenarios

PREVIEW

When you join a firm as an employee, you must learn to recognize the situations that occur as the firm conducts its business. You must also understand the ways people are expected to act in these situations and learn strategies for playing your part. A *situation* requires a transaction of some kind: an exchange of goods, services, or information. Most people in a company have a common understanding, rather like an abstract story, about how to carry out a particular transaction; this common understanding is called a *scenario*. Both large-scale situations, such as a national sales campaign, and smaller-scale situations, such as a meeting with a client, have scenarios.

Situations and the scenarios for handling them are shaped by factors outside and inside the firm. Outside the firm, government regulations, competitors, news media, labor unions, consumers, suppliers, and trade organizations affect the way the company conducts business and communicates. Inside the firm, the organization's mission, size, structure, technology, and culture define situations and scenarios. All of these factors will affect the choice of actions, words, and media involved in a particular scenario, but the personalities and experience of the firm's employees are also important.

The scenarios for dealing with situations require various types of communications. A scenario might include writing a letter, making a presentation, or gathering information for a report. These communication requirements may vary from company to company. Understanding the scenarios for different types of situations in a specific company can help you decide which communication medium to select and what communication strategies will be effective.

❑ ## UNDERSTANDING SITUATIONS AND SCENARIOS

Sizing Up Situations in a New Job

All new employees must become familiar with the recurring situations in their jobs.

A new employee must be a good detective, paying attention to details and putting together many clues. Over its history, each company develops special meanings for words. Familiar words, such as *secretary*, can have a range of meanings. In some companies, secretaries make coffee and take dictation. In other companies, secretaries prepare budgets, oversee a wide range of functions, and act as special kinds of managers. New employees have to discover the ways words are used in their company so they can interact appropriately with others and carry out their responsibilities.

The opening story of "In Search of Excellence," a videotape adapted from a management best-seller of the early 1980s, illustrates this process of discovery. A training director at Disney World, talking to new employees, explains that the park has one purpose and one purpose only: to make visitors happy. To accomplish this purpose, the park hires only one class of employees, "hosts and hostesses," to "perform" for the millions of visitors. Disney World has no job titles such as "janitor," "waitress," "dancer," or "security guard." Naturally, the park has to be swept, food must be served, visitors must be entertained, and traffic must be supervised. However, the employees whose roles include these tasks have the job title of "host" or "hostess," which reminds them of the most important element of their work, "making the customer happy."

Your coworkers' language contains many clues about situations, roles, and communication.

The Disney World trainer's language constantly invokes the world of the stage. He notes that each of these hosts or hostesses has been hired by "central casting" for "a particular role in the show." Disney World has "attractions," not "rides." Each attraction's host learns a "spiel," a word for the script of a carnival barker. Employees, the trainer says, must refer to areas of the park where visitors go as "on stage." Areas off-limits to visitors are referred to as "backstage." Uniforms are called "costumes," and are picked up each day from the "wardrobe department."

The faces of Disney World's new employees who are hearing these language clues reflect both confusion and pleasure. They have to figure out how they will fit into this "magic kingdom." The trainer warns that he can't sprinkle "pixie dust" over them to enable them to handle their roles. Each employee must learn to cope with carrying out his or her tasks while being a friendly "host or hostess" to the park's visitors. However, Disney employees receive several days of training, during which they rehearse the situations they are likely to encounter. Mentors advise them on what to say, how to act, what body language to use, and what tone of voice to employ. The elaborate training system at Disney World is more extensive than in many other companies, but all new employees in every company must go through this process of becoming familiar with the company's situations and the roles they must play.

Defining Situations and Scenarios

Communication may initiate, conduct, or interpret a business transaction.

A situation is a set of conditions that requires a *transaction* (an exchange of goods, services, or information). Employees may use communication to initiate, conduct, or interpret the transaction. For example, a machine in a small firm producing custom metal fabrications broke down, causing a delay on the project because the company did not have an extra machine of that type. These conditions required a transaction (obtaining a new part and repairing the machine).

An employee called the manufacturer about the broken part and followed up with a purchase order sent by FAX machine. The phone call and the purchase order *initiated* the transaction. The manufacturer responded the same day, sending the part by overnight courier. The invoices and receiving forms used in delivering and accepting the replacement part helped *conduct* the transaction. The same employee who initiated the transaction later wrote a memorandum to the boss about the malfunctioning machine. He explained that although the part had been replaced, a new machine should be included in next year's budget, because this machine had become badly worn and additional delays and repairs were likely. This memorandum *interpreted* (explained the significance of) the transaction (replacing the broken part) between the two companies. The memorandum also set up the conditions for a new situation: a budget decision.

Figure 2-1, first introduced in Chapter 1, illustrates the relationship between the situation, the scenario, and the communications required.

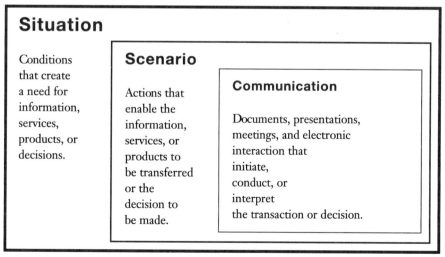

FIGURE 2-1.   Relationship of Situations, Scenarios, and Communication

Scenarios tell who does what and how.

To discover the situations and scenarios in a company, listen thoughtfully to informal office conversations, such as the following examples, which often reveal scenarios.

SAMPLE SCENARIO 1

Head of Customer Support in a Software Company "Our company develops software for banks. My job is customer support, so frequently a customer wants to do something slightly different with one of our large standard programs. Well, then she calls me to see if these modifications are possible. In that situation, I'm the one who has to determine whether we can respond. First, I write a note to the client documenting her requested changes. We have a form for preparing this kind of note on the computer. It prints out one copy and sends it to the client. Another copy goes by electronic mail to the Software Engineering department.

"Engineering replies by electronic mail, saying whether we can do the kind of modification the customer wants. If the answer is yes, I send Scheduling a personnel request to find out when programmers can be sent to the client's site and when work can begin. I call the client, giving her the estimated price and the dates for the project. If the customer agrees, I confirm the conversation in writing and then give Project Management the go-ahead. I also monitor the job and follow up, keeping the project records."

SAMPLE SCENARIO 2

Group Supervisor in a Public Utility Firm "In our business, we have to comply with OSHA (Occupational Safety and Health Administration) regulations. They require us to go over safety rules once a month with each work crew that installs electrical equipment. Over time, things had become pretty lax around here, so my boss gave me the job of coming up with a good way of complying with this regulation. Now, in November, I make out a list of topics for the next year, so that all the safety categories are covered. I present a talk to the crews on some aspect of safety each month. I ask questions of each worker, and at the end of the year I write a report to my boss."

How External Factors Affect Situations

Both the computer software company's head of customer support (Sample Scenario 1) and the public utility company's group supervisor (Sample Scenario 2) describe situations caused by factors outside the companies. In the public utility company, OSHA regulations require that the safety meetings be held. In the software company example, the customer initiated the situation. This example also illustrates the narrative or story element in most scenarios, because the manager recites the sequence of transactions in the order in which they occur. Figure 2-2 illustrates some of the elements of a firm's external environment.

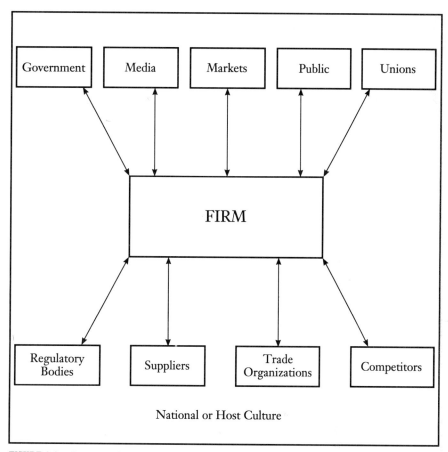

FIGURE 2-2. Interaction Between External Environment and Firm

Business people are usually well aware that they must be sensitive to the external environment and to the internal environment of the company. For example, a business cannot name a new product without considering what names competitors have given their products, the legal requirements for offering products of certain types, and the ways customers will react to a product name. A few years ago, General Motors was troubled when Puerto Rican dealers initially showed no enthusiasm for the new Chevrolet Nova. Although the literal translation of *nova* is "star," the spoken pronunciation sounds like *no va* in Spanish, which means "doesn't go." To restore consumer confidence in the vehicle, General Motors quickly renamed the automobile Caribe, and Puerto Rican sales increased.[1]

External factors must be taken into account in naming products and companies.

This example demonstrates that the culture and language of groups in the external environment must also be taken into account. Note that the culture of the host society is shown as part of the company's external environment in Figure 2-2. Many costly communication failures have occurred when the language and culture of prospective customers were not taken into account. To avoid such problems, Standard Oil Company (New Jersey) undertook a million-dollar research project in 1972 to discover a word that had no negative connotations in English or any other language before renaming its worldwide corporation Exxon. Chapter 17, "Communicating in International Contexts," introduces ways to become sensitive to cultural differences and to anticipate their effects on communication.

External audiences often have a stake in company actions.

A company's environment may include suppliers, prospective employees, customers, unions, competitors, governments, trade organizations, financial markets, consumer rights organizations, and the media. These entities not only affect the company, but are affected by it. Consequently, they have a "stake" in the company. Management experts call these entities *stakeholders*. (Stakeholders are not necessarily *stockholders*—people who own shares of stock in a public company.) Society as a whole can also be thought of as a stakeholder, since company actions such as resource depletion or toxic waste dumping can affect everyone's welfare and safety. Regulatory bodies are supposed to protect society's stake by controlling the ways companies do business.

Sometimes these controls include governing the marketing language companies may use to inform prospective customers about their products. If a company is part of a heavily regulated industry (such as investments), certain laws and organizations will be important that may have only a minor effect on a company in a different industry (such as a yogurt manufacturer). Features of the company itself will also affect its situations, scenarios, and communication.

How Company Characteristics Affect Situations

Company characteristics reflect industry turbulence.

The structure, size, and technology of the organization, created in part as a response to external conditions, may affect the roles people play and definitions of situations (see Figure 2-3). In rapidly changing industries such as electronics and software, information about new products and innovations is vital. Companies adapt their internal structure in response: communication paths are short, meetings are called as needed, and information usually is transmitted rapidly. In contrast, companies in static industries, such as tobacco products, may reduce reports to forms and schedule ritualistic formal meetings well in advance. A firm's characteristics (discussed more fully in the following section) may be interdependent, as some of the arrows in Figure 2-3 show.

Once again, coworkers' conversations may reveal what factors inside the company affect its situations and the communications they require. In the next two sample scenarios taken from employees' conversations, factors *inside* the company strongly affect the situation. The holding company in Sample Scenario 3 conducts its budget review process as it does because the company is structured into four divisions. No division can adopt a budget without the parent company's review and approval. In Sample Scenario 4, the Park Service analyst's work depends on understanding the technical issues of administering state park lands as well as the agency's routines and individuals' roles.

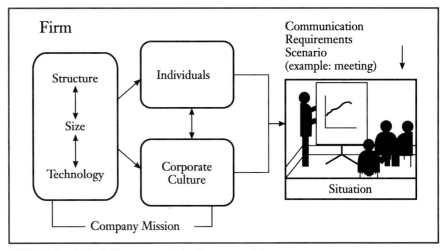

FIGURE 2-3.   A Firm's Characteristics Define Situations and Scenarios

SAMPLE SCENARIO 3

Divisional Controller in a Holding Company   "The new budgets for this division are due the first week of December each year. I review each department's budget proposal with the department manager before the budgets go to headquarters. We go over the department's runs from the last quarter, review the runs from earlier quarters, and try to anticipate new needs. I write up an explanation of how this budget will support our division's strategic plan and explain exceptional items."

SAMPLE SCENARIO 4

Park Service Staff Analyst   "When new bills are proposed in the state legislature, the Department of Parks and Wildlife (DPW) has to anticipate their impact on the agencies' offices and the parks we manage. I'm an analyst and my job is to report on legislative proposals to the agency director. Essentially, we must prepare to implement a proposed bill or fight its passage.

"I meet with the staff of the legislator backing the bill, and I may meet with other DPW people if I think that's necessary. I usually meet with our legal counsel and then I write a report for the director. I may follow up with a report for the legislator's staff if we think changes are needed, but sometimes I write that report for the director's signature (instead of my own), and he sends it to the sponsoring legislator. Internally, I also write a proposed action plan describing changes we would have to make as a result of the bill's passing. I send notices to our offices if the legislation passes, telling them to implement these plans."[2]

Size, Structure, and Technology

Structure dictates the formal communication system.

The effects of companies' size, structure, and technology have been studied for many years.[3] Obviously, size affects the knowledge employees have about one another. Communication in most large firms is more likely to be written, indirect, and less personal than communication in a small firm, where all the employees know one another fairly well. A large company is more likely to have a complex structure than a small company. A company's structure is the organized system of jobs defined by titles and responsibilities. By defining the reporting paths, this system provides formal communication routes in an organization.

Technology affects communication in a variety of ways. If the technology used in the company's primary business activities has the potential to be dangerous, as in nuclear power plants, people may be physically separated from one another and may have to rely less on face-to-face interaction and more on telephones or electronic mail. Some technology requires operators who have extensive technical education, thus affecting the backgrounds of individuals who must communicate. Advanced electronic systems, such as computer networks, may enable people at distant locations to feel they know one another, even though they seldom meet face to face. Thus, technology may either bring people together or keep them apart.

Individuals in the Firm

Individuals can alter scenarios and communication processes.

In most business situations, the professional roles of writers and readers, their powers of action, and their expertise as members of the organization are more important than other aspects of their personal identity. Nevertheless, the individual still has creative power to develop original solutions to organizational problems. In the utility company example mentioned in Sample Scenario 2, the supervisor devised new communication steps. Her boss had become aware that over the years, supervisors had begun to neglect safety training, and he had asked her to come up with a plan. The supervisor developed new procedures to ensure that her group met the OSHA requirement. Her method for meeting the agency's requirement was recommended to other supervisors, and it quickly became a standard company procedure (a scenario).

Furthermore, powerful executives' communication preferences tend to become maxims of the company culture and thus shape many scenarios. William Sick, president of Primerica and former executive at Texas Instruments (TI), was believed to favor short documents and presentations. One associate at TI related, "Bill always said that an idea is no good if it can't be explained in the space of an elevator ride on the way to lunch." No wonder that "Is it short enough for an elevator ride?" became a rule of thumb for judging explanations at Texas Instruments. Thus, individuals do have the power to modify old scenarios and to create new ones.

Corporate Culture

In the late 1970s and early 1980s, management consultants began to pay attention to such stories as this one from Texas Instruments, noting the power of shared values, norms, roles, rituals, and "the company way." They gave the name *corporate culture* to the system of shared and meaningful symbols manifested in the company's image, myths, ideologies, values, and multiple cultural artifacts.[4] These aspects of culture reflect a company's technical and social codes.

A company's image re-
flects its culture.

Company's Image   Like individuals, companies communicate an image to audiences both inside and outside the firm. A company may represent itself as "leading edge," traditional, sensitive to social issues (such as apartheid, women's issues, or housing for the homeless), committed to employee benefits of wellness or safety, or dedicated to protecting the environment. Such an image melds many values of a company's culture and presents them symbolically. The company's image may be manifested in dress, talk, and relations with customers and suppliers. Visiting a company's headquarters or offices and noting carefully the decor, employee dress, and general atmosphere of the place can be very revealing.

Technical Code   A group's culture prescribes attitudes about the physical plant and technology of the group, sometimes called the *technical code*. This code usually reflects some values of the host (national) culture and especially embodies the values of the corporate culture. In Japan, where the work of the group is highly valued, few individuals have private offices. To American visitors, the undivided Japanese work spaces seem disorganized and cluttered. To the Japanese observer there is no disorder as he looks across the room filled with employees seated at tables. The person of greatest authority in any group is seated at the end of each table, flanked by his closest associates. The rank of people on either side of the table is proportional to their distance from the manager or executive.[5]

Although a few U.S. industries, such as newspapers, have traditionally used the "bull pen" open space approach to organizing workers, most U.S. businesses prefer to divide workspace into offices. The executive of highest rank usually has the largest, most attractively furnished office, with one or more windows, which are considered to be status symbols. U.S. executives consider corner offices plum locations. A few years ago the "open office concept" was heavily promoted by modular furniture manufacturers. Companies that adopted this space plan generally have gone back to the separate office concept, which is more compatible with American attitudes toward space, privacy, and individual work.

The technical code contains attitudes about facilities and equipment.

Within a single industry, however, the technical codes of two companies may differ considerably. One company may value prestigious accommodations; another company, pursuing a low-cost strategy, may occupy no-frills facilities. One company may pride itself on possessing the latest in high-tech equipment; another may prefer doing things in an old-fashioned way. Understanding the technical code can help a writer or speaker choose appropriate reasons for persuading an audience in the company. For example, in a company that prides itself on using advanced technology, technical innovation might be accepted as a reason for a proposed solution.

Social Code or Code of Etiquette   Each person in a group has ideas about how he or she would like to be perceived by others. Each person tries to demonstrate selected qualities, such as leadership, ability to foresee the future, friendliness, and technical competence. This projected impression is sometimes called an individual's *persona*, which comes from the word for the mask an actor wore in ancient Greek theaters. This mask helped the audience identify the character he was playing (such as the king, queen, or messenger). Individuals choose to project their personae, or particular qualities that they want the group to associate with them in their roles.

The social code governs interaction of individuals as well as groups.

A group's social code dictates how the organization's members are supposed to interact. In one company, supervisors may be allowed to enter the offices of managers without an appointment; in another company all such visits may be formally scheduled. If an organized subgroup, such as a union, exists in a company, the social code may become complicated by the competing social codes of the company and the union. A new employee must watch for evidence of the prevailing social code in a company, because companies are not alike.

A company's social code also governs the expression of individuals' private personalities. In one organization, tyrants may be free to upbraid subordinates in public and subordinates may be without recourse. In another company, tyrants may be reprimanded. Some cultures allow for the expression of a broad range of emotion regardless of the social status of the individuals; in others, feelings must be repressed. These differences obviously affect what emotions one may express in letters and conversations, the motivating strategies that may be used, and the formality or informality of the language.

When preparing to communicate in an unfamiliar situation or when events have occurred that seem to have changed the situation, you should take a few minutes to jot down the factors shaping the situation. You can use the form in Figure 2-4 to identify these factors.

Type of Situation: _____

Note any aspects of the external and internal environment that may affect this situation.

External

Customers

Competitors

Regulatory standards

Professional standards

Suppliers

Host culture

Media

Other

Internal

Company structure

Corporate culture

Departmental culture

Size of company

Mission of the company

Technology used

Position in company

Employee's personality

Professional training

Other

FIGURE 2-4. Form for Analyzing Influences on Situations

Corporate Culture Affects Communication

Both corporate structure and culture help to define situations, affecting who speaks to whom and who listens to whom, when, and why. Nevertheless, structure and culture may have quite different effects on communication practices.[6] A company's structure affects the formal communication channels (reporting system), whereas corporate culture affects informal communication routes and contributes many of the standards that guide a writer's choices of content, persuasive approach, and words. A company president told one of this book's authors to delete *hope* from a draft of a letter she had written for his signature, included in a consulting project. "We don't *hope* for anything around here," he advised her. "We decide what we want and then we make it happen." She checked her file of documents from that company; the word "hope" did not appear even once.

Coworker conversations will demonstrate cultural values, beliefs, and attitudes toward communication.

As you listen to your coworkers, note their attitudes toward the following topics:

1. The importance of the group versus the importance of individuals
2. Personal status
3. Goals
4. Work intensity
5. Socializing
6. Gift giving
7. Status of women
8. Agreements
9. Rules
10. Negotiations

These attitudes will provide you a profile of your department. Within a large organization, departments or divisions may develop subcultures—variations of the large organization's culture. One department may be much more formal than another or show more respect for people of high rank. Listening closely to the cultural values expressed in the language of other employees can help you in several ways. You will learn to recognize the values and beliefs your coworkers share and account for different attitudes toward communication. When you analyze communications, you will discover preferences for modes and genres, types of analogies and anecdotes, types of arguments, and roles of writers and readers. Eventually, you should be able to determine how your department's culture varies from that of other departments and from the culture of the company as a whole.

How Corporate Cultural Values May Differ

ATTITUDES TOWARD	ONE POSSIBILITY	CONTRASTING POSSIBILITY
Individualism/group	Team comes first	Individual most important
Time/punctuality	Be on time, always	Be flexible about schedules
Status	Egalitarian	A person is entitled to privileges
Goals	Group goals all-important	Individuals will work hardest on the goals they set for themselves
Work intensity	Come early, stay late	Set your own schedule
Socializing	Must be friends outside to work together well on the job	Work and play don't mix
Gift-giving	No gifts needed	Gifts demonstrate esteem
Women	If they're team players, we need women	Women are special; not well-suited for this work
Agreements	Agreements must suit the parties, be flexible	An agreement is permanent
Rules or policies	Results, not rules, count	Policies are necessary to allow individuals to make decisions for themselves
Negotiations	Negotiations are never over and are pleasurable	Negotiations should be short so we can get on to the important thing, work

Some strong cultures inhibit communication. A British researcher who worked as a consultant for seven years with several companies reported that the tenets of some strong cultures repressed communication about problems ("better to let sleeping dogs lie"), prevented naming individuals who were the source of trouble ("better not to name names"), resisted cooperative problem solving ("go it alone if you don't want a knife in the back"), and forbade the expression of emotions ("hide your feelings; don't get out of hand"). Communication and participation could be improved only by attacking the pervasive beliefs of the companies' cultures—not an easy task.[7]

Corporate culture shapes employees' understanding of the firm's economic history, which in turn strongly affects the way they interpret the environment, situations, and their own performance. A company's management and employees often perceive its environment and future plans through economic

CULTURAL VALUES USED AS REASONS FOR REFUSALS

The values of a company's culture are often revealed when someone's request is denied. Researchers have found that when a reason must be given for a decision, a manager is apt to choose a reason that higher-level executives and employees alike will accept as valid. As a result, the reasons offered may differ widely from company to company. Look at the two messages from Mr. Caxton and Mr. Rogers and imagine how the cultures of these two firms differ.

January 4, 1991

FROM THE DESK OF HANK CAXTON

Bill,

I can understand that you'd like to schedule your vacation so that you can attend your sister's wedding on June 10th. Unfortunately, that week we will be having the national sales conference and all of our key sales reps will be in town, so every one of us will have to be available during the conference. We just can't spare you from the team, Bill. Please call your sister and let her know right away, so that perhaps she can reschedule the big event for the following week. It's still six months away, so there may be time to work things out. I'm sorry I can't let you go at that time.

Hank

The informal tone and the helpful suggestions for accomplishing Bill's goal to attend his sister's wedding suggest that this company values the individual's wishes and needs. However, in this company's culture the good of the team takes precedence over the wishes of the individual. This manager must reconcile individual and group needs, and the group's needs are more important. The informal note and personal signature are consistent with the informal culture.

January 4, 1991

TO: W. K. Rogers
          Assistant Manager, Marketing

FROM: C. C. Connerly
          Manager, Marketing

SUBJECT: Vacation Schedule Request

Your request for vacation from June 7 through June 11, 1991 was received on January 3, 1991. I regret that I cannot approve this request. Requests of senior members of the firm have priority, and no more than 4 percent of the staff of any department can be away on vacation at any one time. District Manager Larson and Project Manager Rawlins have already requested that week. These considerations preclude your absence on the week you requested. Please select a new vacation period and resubmit your request.

The formal heading, the use of individuals' last names, full initials, and titles, plus the opening of the memorandum with the date on which the request for vacation time was received, signal that in this organization formal procedures are more important than the reader's feelings. The writer first justifies his refusal by referring to two rules that make Bill ineligible for the vacation date he requested. The company's culture is bureaucratic; an impersonal adherence to rules is considered the highest good.

COMPANY CULTURE AND COMMUNICATION

In *Corporate Culture*, Deal and Kennedy proposed that the nature of the company's mission usually determined the proportion of resources (principally money or people) committed to typical projects and the length of time required for results to be known (feedback time). Different combinations of these two factors produced four types of corporate cultures: the bet-your-company culture; the macho, or tough-guy, culture; the work hard/play hard culture; and the process, or bureaucratic, culture. A summary of these four types of cultures and their influence on communication features follows.

The *bet-your-company culture* is common among industries in which long-term projects require a high proportion of company resources, such as research and development or resource development costs. Examples include high-technology companies, an oil company investing in coal liquefaction, a real estate developer acquiring land for development, or an aircraft manufacturer relying on government contracts. Because of their impact on potential profits, perhaps even on the survival of the company, big projects are viewed seriously. Proposals for such projects are often lengthy and contain extensive analyses and appendices that will be reviewed by different types of experts. The time required for feedback on project outcomes is long, perhaps from three to fifteen years. The situations in which "bet-your-company" employees communicate tend to be planned, to follow written agendas, and to demonstrate seriousness and formality.

In contrast, the *macho, or tough-guy, culture* involves big projects with relatively short-term feedback horizons. These projects depend on much shorter working documents plus long technical documents, such as contracts. The entertainment business, advertising, and some property transactions may be conducted on the basis of short, "to-the-point" proposals or presentations backed by long contracts prepared by lawyers. The brief working documents contain specifics of the deal or project and lead to a handshake between wealthy principals; the legal contracts may contain much "boiler plate" (standard clauses that vary only a little from document to document).

The situations in macho cultures tend to convey the momentousness of the occasion by dramatic symbolic gestures rather than by seriousness and formality. The lawyers and support staff handle the serious or formal part; the major players focus attention on themselves and their power by means of lavish settings and impressive details (for example, a gold signing pen for the letter of intent, champagne toasts, and multimedia presentations).

Work hard/play hard cultures emphasize meeting short-term deadlines, require high energy and lots of client contact, and usually involve only a fraction of the company's resources in any one deal. Selling is usually the dominant activity of such firms; success depends on the number of contacts made.

Situations in these firms meld ritual and short-term utility. Typical situations are sales meetings, sales calls, and follow-up paperwork sessions. Although ritual paraphernalia is common (such as incentive gifts, accessories, and promotional gifts), the pens used in work hard/play hard companies are plastic emblazoned with product slogans, not gold signing pens. Documents in this culture are brief and routine: solicitation letters, prospecting letters, large mailings, sales reports, campaign proposals, sales literature, and monthly or quarterly summaries. Where the industry is regulated, as is the case in the mutual funds industry, the cultures are constrained by regulatory requirements, even though the basic attitudes of the culture persist.

Bureaucracies or process cultures such as universities, government agencies, hospitals, and credit card companies rarely receive feedback on their success; each transaction tends to be relatively unimportant. Process cultures rely on forms, ritualistic formal reports, and policy statements. Many memoranda are written "to the file," as a kind of insurance in case a complaint is ever received. Since performance is judged by adherence to codes and procedures, compliance may be recognized only by a challenge: when a candidate claims discrimination in admissions, a policy holder challenges claims handling, or a citizen complains that due process was not followed.

As these examples illustrate, companies' resource commitments and feedback times strongly shape situations and their communication requirements, affecting what kinds of communication media are used, the length and tone of documents, the style of presentations, and the audiences for particular documents.

assumptions that have been used to make judgments about the past. The members of the firm value some ways of seeking information more than others; they may value interest rates, for example, more than other economic indices, or the number of repeat clients, or some other sign that has seemed significant in the past. Employees recognize present situations according to the features of prototypical situations from the past.

Scenarios learned from the past guide the perceptions of both individuals and organizations. Some theorists have gone so far as to talk about organizational intelligence and organizational learning behavior, as though the network of scenarios known by employees, along with their knowledge of company history and culture, constituted the knowledge base for coordinated company action.

❑ EXTERNAL AND INTERNAL FACTORS CONVERGE TO CREATE SITUATIONS

Routine situations require typical problem solving.

When external and internal factors regularly converge in the same way, the resulting situation is routine and the scenario for dealing with it is likely to be standard. The actions in the scenario may be called "standard operating procedures" or SOPs. In routine situations, the problem seems so well-defined and the SOPs become so familiar that employees may scarcely spend any time at all analyzing the situation or imagining other scenarios.

This familiarity may sometimes lead employees into a complacency that undermines the company's objectives; what is a routine situation for an employee may not seem at all routine for a customer. The employee may use form letters filled with jargon the customer does not understand, or may completely fail to recognize what the customer needs to know, believe, and feel about the transaction. One company that has been vigilant about such complacency is Compaq Computer Company, whose quality campaigns stress dedication to understanding the customer's point of view in every transaction, telephone call, and business letter. For an insider's account of how this focus on quality was emphasized throughout the company, see Lee Murdy's comments in Part 6, Executives' Perspectives.

Problems in non-routine situations may be complex and ill-defined, or they may simply be unfamiliar to the organization.

Nonroutine situations may demand extensive problem solving. The problems presented in a nonroutine situation may be clearly defined but unfamiliar to the people in a particular company. For example, acquiring a client in a foreign country may present new problems in freight forwarding for a company that has always produced for domestic markets. In an exporting company, freight forwarding would be a well-defined problem. In contrast, nonroutine situations may present ill-defined and complex problems.

Scenarios tell how to go about solving a problem.

As discussed in Chapter 1, problem solving involves an *understanding process* and a *solving process*.[8] In the understanding process, people try to comprehend the gap that separates them from their goal or to recognize what is different or unfamiliar in the situation, the kind of effort one makes when playing,

"What is wrong with this picture?" In the solving process, people imagine and select procedures to bridge that gap or cope with uncertainty, often choosing the solutions implicit in the scenarios they know without searching extensively for new solutions.

Different researchers have identified several possible steps in these problem-solving processes, which may number as few as four to as many as eight. A nonroutine situation may require several steps; a routine situation may allow a person to collapse the processes into only a few steps. Later chapters in this book will explain some of the steps used in various scenarios. Scenarios, as problem representations, imply a method of solving the problem: they tell who does what to solve the problem and achieve the desired goal. In most cases, both external and internal factors converge to define situations and the scenarios people develop in response. The combination of external and internal influences on situations is shown in Figure 2-5.

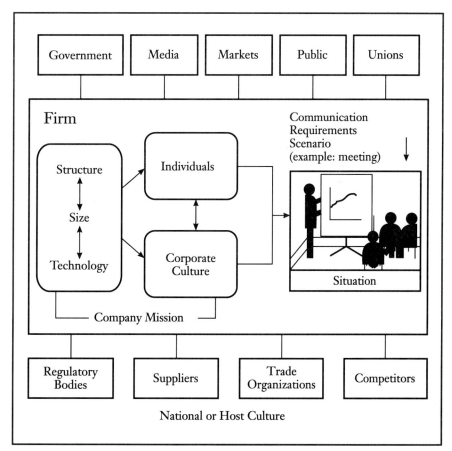

FIGURE 2-5.   Model of How External Environment and Firm's Characteristics Define Business Situations and Communication Requirements

The Atherton Jordan Case: Creating a New Scenario for a Changed Situation

In a research report presented at the 1988 international meeting of the Association for Business Communication, two researchers from Santa Clara University, Claudia McIsaac and Mary Ann Aschauer, reported a case study that described a scenario of proposal preparation at an engineering firm whose disguised name is Atherton Jordan, Inc.[9] Their report illustrates many of the claims of this chapter.

Changes in the company's environment had dramatically changed its situation for obtaining new work. Formerly, Atherton Jordan had been a sole supplier to the Department of Defense. While the company had that status, engineers worked closely with Pentagon personnel to develop proposals, sending them the rough drafts for feedback. In this situation, Atherton Jordan engineers knew intimately what was wanted and could informally suggest improvements or substitutes for features specified in the formal Request for Proposal (RFP). Fraud and mismanagement at certain sole suppliers, such as General Dynamics, prompted Congress to require competitive bidding, which put former sole suppliers under extreme pressure.[10] Now they had to compete for contracts by writing proposals (new communication requirements).

Managing the proposal-writing process well was extremely important, because proposals for contracts worth $30 to $50 million might cost up to half a million dollars to prepare. If a proposal did not capture the contract, the company submitting the proposal would lose the money spent preparing it. At that rate, companies such as Atherton Jordan could not afford to lose often. In the months after the Pentagon switched to competitive bidding, Atherton Jordan, like other former sole suppliers, found it more difficult to win contracts.

To deal with the competitive stress, Atherton Jordan created a Proposal Operations Center (POC) and developed a new scenario for proposal writing that their writers now use. For the duration of proposal-writing projects, all engineers move to the POC from their various sites. Writers often work twelve or more hours a day, seven days a week, for a month or more. The POC staff members prepare and distribute a plan for each proposal project task force. The plan contains an analysis of the RFP, an analysis of anticipated competitors' strengths and accomplishments, and competitive themes called "Win Strategies" that the writers might use (for example, a "Win Strategy" might be the availability of experienced designers or state-of-the-art technology). Proposal Operations Center staff and engineers work on the project. POC staff help writers emphasize comparative analysis and persuasion, rather than simple description of work to be done.

The setting for this scenario is a large room with walls covered with bulletin board material. Working at tables in the center of the room, participants fill out big sheets of paper called Scribblesheets (see Figure 2-6).

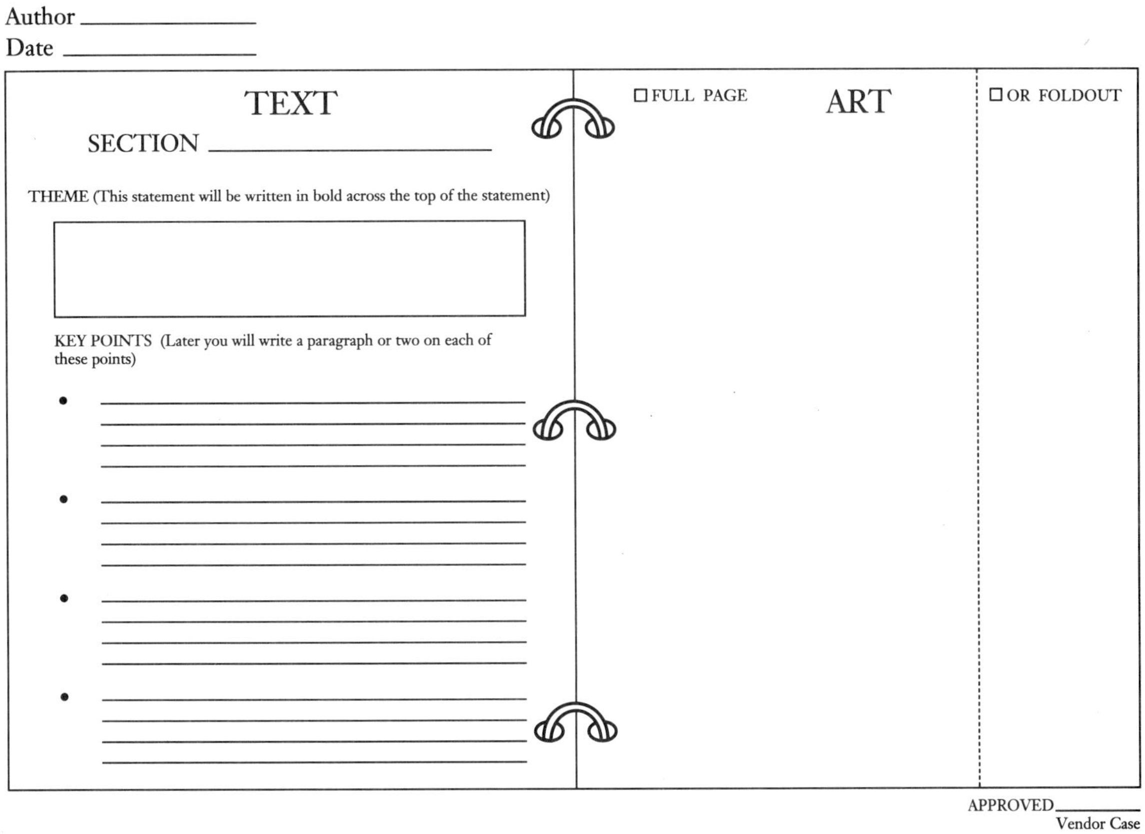

Author _____
Date _____

FIGURE 2-6. **Proposal Scribblesheet**

Individuals suggest ways of developing different parts of the proposal on the scribblesheets, then post them on wall space reserved for their work. Comment sheets are tacked beside the big scribblesheets, and task force members walk around the room reading other members' ideas and writing comments for their colleagues. After discussion, individuals draft parts of the proposal to which they have been assigned. These activities force engineers to take on a reader's role and to get a sense of other team members' ideas. Later, the first draft of the proposal is given to an elite group called a "Red Team" drawn from a variety of specialties, to review the draft and provide extensive feedback. The Red Team's function is to analyze the draft from the Pentagon's perspective. Serving as a Red Team member confers high status at Atherton Jordan.

Case Comments   The changes produced by the introduction of competitive bidding (an event in the external environment) were a loss of knowledge about the audience's views and a change in the reader's activities. Instead of comparing the proposal's offer with the requirements of the formal request as they had under the old system, the Pentagon readers under the new system had to compare the design Atherton Jordan proposed with those of several other bidders. The new scenario involved a change in the internal structure of the company, new roles for participants, and new physical circumstances (bulletin boards, scribble-sheets, working at a single location, etc.). The "win rate" or proportion of successful proposals created with this strategy has caused most engineers to prefer the new scenario, even though individuals have had to modify their writing processes. Atherton Jordan's new scenario both ensures continuation of its primary business activity and copes with pressure generated by changes in the external environment. For an account of how Cray Research, Inc. adapted to changes in its external environment, see Jim Sheehy's comments in Part 6, Executives' Perspectives.

Learning about Situations and Scenarios on the Job

As suggested earlier in the chapter, you must discover the situations in which you will participate. Situations serve different purposes, and some are easier to learn about than others. A situation may be used to

1. Conduct the company's primary business activities, such as producing ice cream;
2. Maintain the organization, such as hiring new employees;
3. Cope with pressure, such as getting out a large rush order; and
4. Deal with internal conflict, such as reducing employees' dissatisfaction with a new office manager.

There will be typical situations and scenarios for each of these four functions. A few companies have corporate manuals that specify types of transactions and situations, show how work is to be done, and describe communication requirements. These manuals are more likely to describe the first two types of functions than the last two. A checklist for taking notes and analyzing situations and scenarios is shown at the end of the following guidelines.

Learn about Primary Business Activities

Highly regulated companies, such as banks, that have high turnover in personnel and decentralized facilities often have employee handbooks or training manuals. Companies that are not regulated but need a high degree of consistency in work routines also have manuals (for example, auto parts stores, national chain restaurants, auto rental agencies). Companies that desire uniform work procedures often express this preference symbolically as well, by requiring employees to wear uniforms and by decorating all their offices in the same way. If you join this type of company, request permission to read their manuals as soon as possible, or sign up for training programs. Reading manuals may be boring, but learning how the company operates will enable you to see how your work fits into the much larger picture and will help you communicate well from the beginning.

In some companies, it is hard to find out how work is supposed to be done. If most employees have been with the company for a long time, or if the company is small (and especially if it is privately owned or run by family members), no one may have thought it necessary to produce written guidelines. Furthermore, withholding information about work procedures is a means of controlling others, so people may hoard information to increase their own power. If appropriate work procedures have not been written down in the company you join, you have several choices. As a first step, try to find out whether your immediate supervisor will take some time, either during work hours or at lunch, to tell you about the company.

If your supervisor seems to want to withhold information to emphasize the distance between your positions ("You're just a salesperson; you don't need to know that"), look for a company "storyteller" (not a gossip) to recount the company's success stories. Often such a person will have been with the company for a long time and will have firsthand memories of important events in the firm's history. In order to get the information you need, ask about how the company got started and about some of the most successful projects or periods the person remembers. Identify the factors that seem to have made the projects successful. Ask questions about the work of people who formerly held the job you now hold: "How did the account executive persuade the bank to give us the contract?" "What kind of presentation did we use then?" "Did we have to meet with them several times before we got the account?"

Look for personal contacts and friendships (evidence of an old-boy or old-girl network) that may have influenced procedures. You may not have such contacts, and you may have to discover other means of accomplishing your tasks. Look through the available files to learn the history of client relationships, evidence of which information is needed for different types of projects, and the sequence in which transactions occur in typical projects.

Teach yourself and *write down* what you learn. Later on, you may be able to delegate effectively by turning your notes into guidelines for employees who report to you. Your group may achieve high productivity goals because you have saved employees the trouble of learning procedures for themselves. Furthermore, you can prevent mistakes likely to be made by those new employees who don't bother to learn how work ought to be done. Growing companies, especially, often do not have procedures written down, but still need to manage new employees efficiently. Being the account executive, marketing supervisor, or sales manager who can quickly train subordinates will make you productive and successful.

Learn about Maintaining the Group

Some situations and scenarios keep the group ready to perform its principal business activity. Such maintenance scenarios include hiring new employees, training them, evaluating performance, and keeping accounting records. Such activities usually have regular procedures and occur in well-defined situations according to standard scenarios. Some of these functions, such as recruiting and hiring personnel, are governed by laws and will be highly standardized. Others, such as a mentor's coaching or "bringing along" a new engineer, may be dictated by custom in the organization.

Learn about Coping with Pressure

Not only must companies do routine work, they also must cope with pressure. Pressure may originate outside the group: for example, a client might request an extraordinarily large order and demand an early delivery. As a result, the group might have to work nights and weekends to meet the deadline. On the other hand, the company might adopt a new strategy that creates intense pressure, such as a decision to open a new branch or introduce a new product. Non-routine communication is usually necessary to cope with pressure. Sometimes an informal meeting must be held to organize or adjust work routines. At other times, formal communication such as a press release or news conference is necessary. You may have to pursue information about such procedures casually. Ask such questions as, "What happens when a rush order comes in?" or, "How do we handle really big orders?" or, "Do we ever have to write proposals on very short notice?"

Learn about Managing Internal Conflict

Many companies have formal grievance procedures for handling the most serious conflicts between employees (such as sexual harassment) or disagreements between unions and management. Most organizations do not have standard scenarios for informally managing internal conflict, although more companies have begun to offer training in conflict management and negotiation. Conflict (sometimes referred to as *agitation* in the management literature) is upsetting precisely because it does not fit into the regular routines.

Scenarios for conducting regular business activities and maintaining the organization are usually acknowledged publicly. The scenarios for coping with pressure or dealing with conflict may be covert and may vary from department to department. All four kinds of situations involve written and spoken communication. *Understanding situations and scenarios for information exchange and document creation is the primary component of "learning the ropes" in your company.* To identify these situations and scenarios, use your skill at "reading" work settings, employee dress, and dialogue among your fellow workers. Think about the conversations you hear as though they had been scripted for the occasion. Imagine the scenario that underlies the conversations. What values and beliefs do the scenario and the dialogue represent? After you have become familiar with your company's processes, you may be able to spot weaknesses in old ways and help develop more successful scenarios, such as the one created at Atherton Jordan to win government contracts. Any new scenario must take into account both the external and the internal influences that act upon the firm and its employees.

A Form for Analyzing Situations, Scenarios, and Communications

One way to analyze communication systematically in your job is to fill out a situation and scenario analysis form (see Figure 2-7) when you discover something new occurring. Naturally, you might fill these forms out frequently when

Situation/Scenario Form	
Type of Situation	**Problem or Condition**
Who Does What and in What Order?	
Communications Required:	
Relevant External Factors:	
Relevant Internal Factors (size, structure, culture, image, mission, individuals):	
Criteria Used to Evaluate Success:	
Situation ( ) addresses primary business activities, ( ) maintains the organization, ( ) copes with pressure, ( ) copes with agitation. (check one or more)	

FIGURE 2-7.   Analysis of Situations and Scenarios

you are first beginning a job, but use them only occasionally after you become quite familiar with the company. Don't forget about these forms, however. Pulling out your forms for a periodic review every three months or so can help you keep abreast of communication changes and provide insight into communication processes. If the forms no longer describe the way things have been working lately, you will be able to detect shifts in the roles of people involved or detect the impact of other factors, such as new office equipment. You may discover that much of your communication has shifted from oral to written communication, or vice versa. Further, these notes can be extremely valuable to others who have to fill in for you when you're on vacation or when you have to train new employees.

❑ COMMUNICATION CHALLENGES

PRELIMINARY EXERCISE 1   You can prepare to analyze business situations by analyzing what you already know about clubs and organizations. For example, a club might sponsor a fundraising event such as a fall festival, haunted house, or 10-K fun run. Club members would know this situation and the roles different members play in carrying out the event. *Choose an organization you know well and write a short description of such an event, telling*

- the purpose of the event
- the kind of transaction that is central to the event (what kind of goods, services, and/or information is transferred?)
- who does what to make the event take place

PRELIMINARY EXERCISE 2   If you are already employed, look back over your date book or other records and try to recognize business situations that occur repeatedly. For example, are there people that you had to meet with on certain times or on recurring kinds of projects? Choose one of these situations and write a short description of it, telling

- the purpose of the situation
- the roles of people involved
- who does what to make the transaction occur
- the kind of transaction that is central to the situation (what kind of goods, services, and/or information is transferred?)

PRELIMINARY EXERCISE 3   The software firm's customer support manager and the utility company's group supervisor describe scenarios for situations in their companies (see Sample Scenarios 1 and 2). What transaction is most important in each scenario?

EXERCISE 1

If you have worked for a company, describe its external environment, using the form in Figure 2–2. What government agencies, competitors, suppliers, or other groups affected communication in that company? Make up a simple diagram and be prepared to explain it. Alternatively, you might choose a company that you have targeted for a future job search and prepare a diagram for that company.

EXERCISE 2

Choose an organization in which you have been active for a long time, preferably one that has a strong identity and history. What were some of the major events sponsored by or involving the group? Did it have colors, a motto, uniforms, or a mascot? What were some of the important slogans or beliefs of that club, team, or group? What were some of the sayings that pertained to its major purpose? What did people say about handling routine matters? What did people say when the organization was under pressure? How did the organization cope with agitation from dissatisfied members? How did those slogans or beliefs affect what the group did? Write a paragraph or more explaining the way the culture of the group affected what it did and how it communicated.

EXERCISE 3

Like most American television viewers, you probably watch the major national news and some sportscasts. If so, you may have seen 1989 news reports on the oil spill in Alaskan waters caused by the Exxon tanker, *Valdez*.

You may also have watched reports about fan dissatisfaction with a coach or professional team. Read the following articles from the May 19, 1989 *Houston Chronicle* and prepare a diagram indicating the factors affecting the chief officer's situations in each case. Then, write about one to two pages, following whatever format your instructor recommends, comparing these two executives' situations. Consider both external and internal factors contributing to the situations.

Exxon protesters grill chairman

By BILL MINTZ
Houston Chronicle
Washington Bureau

PARSIPPANY, N.J. — Robin Dexter of Bellingham, Wash., and John Schimelpfenig of Oradell, N.J., represented the sharply contrasting attitudes of the 2,000 persons attending the Exxon annual meeting here Thursday.

Dexter is a fisherman who makes his living off the fisheries of the Prince William Sound, where the Exxon tanker Valdez ran aground and spewed 11 million gallons of crude oil into the once pristine waters.

Dexter said he bought Exxon's stock after the March 24 spill, and he plans to return to future annual meetings to measure the company's performance "until my livelihood is restored."

His comments were mild compared to those of environmental activists inside the meeting and about 400 protesters outside in the parking lot.

Schimelpfenig, though, seemed more in touch with the majority of shareholders at the meeting who appeared willing to accept Exxon Corp. Chairman Lawrence Rawl's repeated pledges that Exxon will live up to its promise to clean up the oil-soaked sound.

Explained Schimelpfenig, "Sure, they deserve some flak. But I really think Exxon is a responsible company. They are doing everything that can be done."

In the end the protesters' motions had little effect.

Asked for his resignation by a Washington activist, Rawl was applauded when he responded, "The answer is no, I won't. It's anti-productive to consider that."

The nomination of actor and environmental activist Robert Redford for a seat on Exxon's board of directors was greeted with groans. The incumbent board, including Rawl and four other Exxon executives, was elected with about 78 percent of Exxon's 1.3 billion shares.

Exxon officials had hired more than half of Parsippany's 111-person police force with the expectation of far more fireworks than the meeting produced.

About 400 protesters conducted a noisy rally outside the Aspen Hotel Manor as the meeting dragged on inside. None of the banners criticizing Exxon or calling for a boycott of the company was allowed inside.

The activists—a far younger crowd than the predominantly gray-haired stockholders—sang protest songs, cut up Exxon credit cards, and chanted "Exxon must pay."

Exxon officials said since the March 24 spill, 18,000 credit cards have been returned to the company by protesting customers out of about 5 million "active" accounts.

"We are here to pass judgment on a crime—a crime against nature and the American people," said Barry Commoner, a well-known environmental activist. "Our duty is to punish that crime.

"The proper punishment is not adding one environmentalist to the board of directors," he said. "The proper punishment is to replace every one of them."

Under pressure from public employee pension funds, Exxon officials announced last week plans to appoint a new outside director with environmental background to the board. Rawl said Thursday that he hoped to submit a list of nominees to the board soon.

Despite the costs—which already have reached $115 million—Rawl said he was "confident that Exxon's traditional financial strength will not be impaired by this major accident." He also said Exxon had a good financial year in 1988, with net income of $5.3 billion and earnings per share up 15 percent to a record high of $3.95.

Several shareholders and environmental critics scoffed at the company's 10-minute videotape that claimed that three-quarters of the spilled oil had evaporated, dispersed or been cleaned up. The film was filled with praise for Exxon's efforts but showed no pictures of dead otters or birds.

"That film will not end the outrage," said Dorothy Edinburg of Brookline, Mass., who suggested that top Exxon managers should, at the very least, forgo their bonuses or stock options for the year. "Some heads have to roll."

After another criticism of the company's cleanup efforts, Rawl asked, "What would make you happy?"

Rawl also said the company is putting in place a random drug and alcohol testing program for 4,000 to 5,000 employees in sensitive transportation jobs. The captain of the tanker Exxon Valdez had a record for drunken driving and reportedly had been drinking the night his ship struck the Bligh Reef.

The Exxon chairman also said a committee of three non-employee members of Exxon's board has been appointed to evaluate the management's reaction to the spill.

He said the committee, chaired by Lomas Financial Corp. Chairman Jess Hay of Dallas, is authorized to hire its own legal counsel and has broad authority to investigate the company's performance in the disaster.

Source: *Houston Chronicle*, Section B, May 19, 1989. Reprinted with permission.

McMullen stink will get worse, Astros fans warn

By JULIE MASON
Houston Chronicle

Disgusted Houston Astros fans Thursday promised reprisals for this week's Astrodome incident in which two spectators were ejected after displaying signs critical of the team's owner.

The president of the area's largest Astros fan club warned the Houston Sports Association, owner of the Astros, that it should expect more signs—and worse—during a network-televised home game against the Pittsburgh Pirates Saturday.

"People are mad," said Michael Griffin, president of Grif's Astro Army. "They'll be bringing all sorts of signs out.

"What if they show up in T-shirts with the same message? How are the security folks going to deal with that?"

Spokesman Ethan Cartwright said HSA does not plan to re-evaluate its policy banning signs considered "in bad taste." He said the two spectators were ejected after refusing to relinquish the signs and disturbing play.

"It doesn't say much about the mentality of Houston fans if a reactionary stance is their forte," Cartwright said. And "as far as HSA is concerned, we refuse to comment on plans (to change the policy), because we have none. It's business as usual here."

Griffin said fans are unhappy about losing pitcher Nolan Ryan and catcher Alan Ashby, and they suspect owner John McMullen is trying to sell the Astros to another city.

"It would be different if this involved ugly language," Griffin said. "These people lost their heroes. The fans are disgusted, and I think (HSA) handled it poorly."

The dispute arose Tuesday night during a game against the St. Louis Cardinals when two fans displayed signs that read, "McMullen stinks, Ryan and Ashby fans."

When ushers asked the two to relinquish the signs, one fan tore his in half and passed it to his female companion, who passed it to others. In the ensuing fracas, fans pelted security officers with beer and popcorn. A woman was charged with two felony counts of aggravated assault on a police officer, and her brother was charged with misdemeanor disorderly conduct.

Some witnesses said security guards—including off-duty police—were unnecessarily rough.

But Cartwright said the incident was handled correctly.

"We simply enforced our long-standing stadium policies and . . . enforced the rules and regulations in place for 25 years," he said.

Meanwhile, the director of the Houston chapter of the American Civil Liberties Union Wednesday advised McMullen and County Attorney Mike Driscoll in separate letters that HSA's sign policy probably violates fans' right to free speech.

Driscoll said Thursday his office is studying the issue and will discuss it with HSA officials.

"I personally don't think negative signs have a place," Driscoll said, "but that's tempered by what the Constitution says you have the right to do, and that I have not researched."

Driscoll was reluctant to comment because he would defend the county—which owns the stadium and leases it to HSA—in any lawsuits resulting from the incident.

ACLU attorney Bruce Griffiths said in his letters that a policy of censoring non-obscene, non-commercial signs in the Astrodome on the basis of their content violates the federal and state constitutions.

"The Astrodome is a publicly owned facility, and it is clear that fans with signs do not interfere with the ballgame, since the Astros have permitted signs to be displayed by fans since 1965, when the stadium opened," the letters said.

Janie Nathans, a season ticketholder who witnessed the sign fracas, said, "They (HSA) don't have any right to take signs away, as long as they're not obscene.

"I'm not much for people breaking the law, but I don't think those people broke the law. I certainly don't want the Astrodome to turn into Shea Stadium (home of the New York Mets)."

Teresa Letson, 33, a delivery service owner who was charged with the assault counts, said she may not go back to see the Astros again this season.

"I like the Astros and I've always followed them, but I just don't know," she said after a brief court appearance Thursday. Her attorney, Bruce C. Zivley, urged her not to comment.

"The person who brought the sign just handed it to her

as he was being escorted out," Zivley said. "She's going to be arraigned June 1, and she'll enter a not-guilty plea."

But Letson said the Astros' letting Ryan and Ashby go distresses her.

"We're going to miss Nolan," she said. "He's always been one of my favorites."

Letson's brother, Jeff, 24, was charged with the misdemeanor count.

Chronicle reporters Rad Sallee and John Makeig contributed to this story.

Source: *Houston Chronicle*. Reprinted with permission.

EXERCISE 4

Read the following transcription of a manager's answer to the question, "What has made your company a success?" In a one-page statement, answer the following questions: What are the key beliefs of this company's corporate culture? What behaviors does the manager admire? What are some of the reasoning or argument techniques that he prefers? Make up a short list of rules that you think managers in this company are likely to follow in their weekly Monday meeting.

> We did our homework before we made the business decision to offer the new investment service. The empirical evidence was so powerful that it made the business decision relatively easy; it was a powerful combination of conclusions.
>
> In a sense, the thing that is going to make this company succeed is the same thing that makes an individual succeed, extensive information and competent analysis. We were the first there to see the changes going on, interpret them correctly, and find a business opportunity.
>
> There's no such thing as luck. You have to analyze and plan and practice and prepare. You make your own luck. I think a lot of people out there are myopic; they don't work at seeing. I think we're structured to get every possible perspective on what's going on. Without teamwork, you can't get the range of perspectives you need to see what's really going on and to develop a powerful analysis.
>
> Some people in this industry are narrow, terribly narrow in focus. We're consciously

different; we're not going to be myopic. We hire people with the ability to analyze and the power to communicate. It's no good having an insight if you can't communicate it. When we get together for the weekly meeting, everybody has to speak up and put their ideas on the table. There can't be any holding back.

EXERCISE 5

Suppose that you are the person who was interviewed in Exercise 4. You have been with the company for nearly eight years and your group has hired a new manager, Janet Chess, who will soon attend her first weekly meeting of the investment committee. She has been asked to investigate and report on the effect of product liability suits that have been filed against major companies, such as R. J. Reynolds, that own cigarette manufacturing units. Your management group will be reviewing its investments in tobacco companies, which traditionally have been "cash cows" (highly profitable firms).

> What do you think I should do? So far, the cigarette manufacturers have not lost one single product liability case. In case after case, the presence of the Surgeon General's warning has been enough to show that the people who got cancer have been adequately warned. I have thoroughly researched the legal situation, but I've heard from a friend, a lawyer in New York City, that in the present case a consumer advocates' group has successfully forced the companies to turn over years and years of files. Something damaging might be turned up against the companies.

I want to make a good impression, and I'm thinking of opening my presentation with this new possibility my friend told me about. It's hot news and I'd like to show I have contacts in both the investment and the legal community. In fact, I might not go into the legal history much, because the legal stuff is pretty dry, just years and years of cases in which the companies have been using the same set of defenses.

What advice should you give Janet? How good is her scenario for this situation? How well suited is her proposed argument to the ways of thinking this group prefers? Does it suit the corporate culture? How will her presentation be received if she proceeds as she has planned? Write your comments.

IF YOU WOULD LIKE TO READ MORE

To learn more about scenarios and related concepts in various disciplines, you may want to read some of the following articles.

Anderson, J. R., & Kosslyn, S. M. (Eds.). (1984). *Tutorials in learning and memory: Essays in honor of Gordon Bower.* San Francisco: W. H. Freeman. This book is especially valuable to people new to the field because Bower's former graduate students have written the chapters as tutorials or introductory lectures that summarize particular topics. Well worth reading are Black's "Understanding and remembering stories" (pp. 235–56) and Thorndyke's "Applications of schema theory in cognitive research" (pp. 167–92).

Anderson, R. C., & Pikert, J. W. (1978). Recall of previously unrecallable information following a shift in perspective. *Journal of Verbal Learning and Verbal Behavior, 17,* 1–12. People who were asked to describe a house were then asked to imagine they were burglars. They were then able to recall information they had not been able to remember earlier.

Borisoff, D., & Victor, D. A. (1989). *Conflict management: A communication skills approach.* Englewood Cliffs, NJ: Prentice Hall. Explains communication techniques for fostering creative conflict and minimizing hostile or nonproductive conflict.

Houston, J. P. (1986). *Fundamentals of learning and memory* (3rd ed.). San Diego, CA: Harcourt Brace Jovanovich. This basic undergraduate textbook explains the function of schemata in memory and learning. A schema or frame refers to the organized body of information an individual has about some action, concept, or other segment of knowledge. The schema organizes the information, and causes people to perceive and even distort incoming information accordingly.

NOTES

1. Dozens of these errors are reported in D. Ricks, *Big business blunders.* Homewood, IL: Dow Jones-Irwin (1983).

2. Apparently this function is common in state agencies. C. L. Odell reports a similar role for staff analysts in a New York agency dealing with transportation in "Beyond the text: Relations between writing and social context," In L. Odell & D. Goswami (Eds.), *Writing in non-academic settings.* New York: Guilford Press (1985), 249–280.

3. Effects of size, structure, and technology have been studied for over thirty years, especially by the Tavistock group in England and by the contingency theorists at Harvard. The sociotechnical models can be useful for analyzing patterns of communication, but other sources of meaning must be considered as well. T. Burns & G. M. Stalker, *The management of innovation.* London: Tavistock Publications (1961); J. Woodward, *Industrial organizations: Theory and practice.* London: Oxford University Press (1965); P. R. Lawrence & J. W. Lorsch, *Organization and environment.* Boston, MA: Harvard Business School (1967). For an historical review, see H. Mintzberg, *The structuring of organizations: A synthesis of the research.* Englewood Cliffs, NJ: Prentice Hall (1979).

4. For a review of anthropological theories of culture and their parallels in concepts of corporate culture, see Y. Allaire & M. Firsirotu, "Theories of organizational culture." *Organization Studies, 5* (1984)3, 193–226. T. Deal & A. Kennedy developed a theory of the interaction of key influences that affect corporate culture in *Corporate culture: The rites and rituals of corporate life.* Reading, MA: Addison-Wesley (1982). Many systems have been devised for describing the structure and dynamics of groups. The 7-S model presented in Chapter 27 of this book links culture and structure.

5. *Japan*, presented by Jane Seymour. Produced by WTTW/Chicago and Central Independent Television (1987). The first videotape in the series of eight, "The electronic tribe," illustrates this Japanese way of organizing space in businesses, seating patterns, and the roles of men and women in business, among many other topics.

6. A. Wilkins & W. Ouchi, "Efficient cultures: Exploring the relation between culture and organizational performance." *Administrative Science Quarterly, 28* (1983)3, 468–481.

7. P. Bate, "The impact of organizational culture on approaches to organizational problem solving." *Organization Studies, 5* (1984)1, 43–66.

8. J. R. Hayes, *Cognitive psychology: Thinking and creating.* Homewood, IL: Dorsey Press (1978), 177.

9. C. McIsaac & M. Aschauer, "Engineers and persuasion: An ethnographic study." Association for Business Communication Convention, Indianapolis, IN (1988, October). Also "Proposal writing at Atherton Jordan, Inc.: An ethnographic study." *Management Communication Quarterly, 3* (1990), 527–560.

10. McIsaac & Aschauer do not mention this background information.

YOU AND YOUR AUDIENCES: MANAGING RELATIONSHIPS

OBJECTIVES

This chapter will help you

- understand your responsibilities
- analyze the needs of your readers and listeners
- build good relationships

PREVIEW

You will communicate with people who have very different reasons for reading or listening to what you have to say. Some of them will be decision makers; some will be affected by whatever decision is made; others will pass along your message to other people. Each of these people has different needs, and your communication must satisfy all of them. At the same time, your communication must accomplish your own purposes in the situation.

You should view these audiences (readers and listeners) as long-term partners. Too many times writers or speakers focus only on the current interaction and fail to look at the effect their communication will have on a long-term relationship. A successful relationship makes business transactions smooth; provides legitimate rewards for all parties; helps participants cope with differences, pressures, and agitation; and erects no barriers to future interaction. Such a relationship should always be your goal.

❏ YOUR ROLE: WHAT OTHERS EXPECT YOU TO DO

Understanding Your Roles

Scenarios include roles.

A *scenario* tells who performs necessary actions and how. Each scenario includes a set of expectations about people's behavior, called *roles*. In most cases, these expectations are related to the kind of transaction that must take place.

Scenarios for transactions vary from company to company.

Although the scenarios for a particular kind of situation usually vary from company to company, some situations and scenarios may be conducted almost uniformly because of government regulations or other constraints. Banking, real estate, and hazardous waste disposal spring to mind as examples. In some other industries, such as resorts and specialty clothing stores, each company strives to provide a distinctive experience for its customers. This variation means you will have to discover the scenarios in your company; a textbook cannot present exact rules or descriptions that will fit all circumstances.

One Job Title, but Different Communication Roles in Two Companies

The way people in your company expect you to handle your job may differ from the way you learned to perform it in school or in another company. For example, when Harrison Marks, an investment portfolio manager from a large metropolitan bank, joined a small investment management company (a company that directs the investment portfolios of clients such as wealthy individuals and corporations with employee retirement plans), his role changed. Both the bank and the investment management company held weekly meetings of the portfolio managers.

In the bank, the investment strategy was planned by a single individual (a vice president) who supervised several securities analysts. This individual set the investment policy for the week, deciding what portion of a portfolio should be invested in various types of securities: common stocks, fixed income securities, cash equivalents, and so on. During the meeting, the vice president set out his investment strategy and called on some of the analysts to back up his decisions by explaining their research. The portfolio managers listened, asked questions, and then implemented this policy by buying and selling investments in the portfolios they managed. The portfolio managers did not say much in these meetings, but instead listened and thought about the implications of the vice president's decisions for the portfolios they managed.

The scenario for the investment company meetings was substantially different. In the investment management company, portfolio managers shared the responsibilities for securities analysis, investment strategy planning, and implementation.

After Harrison had joined the investment management company and had attended two of the weekly meetings, one of the senior executives took him aside and said, "Look, Harrison, what's the matter? You've hardly said anything in these meetings the last two weeks. We expect everyone to contribute, to speak up in these meetings. You may not always be right about what you say, but you've got to contribute. You know more about bank stocks than many of us, and you've got to make that expertise available. Didn't you expect to pull your weight around here?" Harrison hadn't fully recognized the difference in the way he was supposed to perform his new job.

Company structure, culture, and other factors affect scenarios and roles.

The difference *in roles* resulted partly from differences in the two companies' sizes. The bank had several hundred employees in various branches; the investment management company had a total of only twenty-four employees in one large suite of offices. Moreover, the different roles reflected different structures and corporate cultures. The bank's structure assigned securities analysis, strategy planning, and portfolio management to different individuals or groups. The investment management company combined these tasks, expecting portfolio managers to specialize in such areas as U.S. bank stocks, Japanese investments, or Federal Reserve policy; to contribute their views in strategy planning sessions; and to implement the investment strategy. The culture of the bank prized individual expertise and valued specialization and separation of duties. The culture of the investment management company believed markets were too complex for any one individual to know everything that was relevant, and it valued teamwork and collaboration ("pulling your weight"). These differences directly affected Harrison's communication role and caused him some difficulties in adjusting to the scenario.

Discovering Your Own Roles

Like Harrison, you will find that external and internal factors affect your company's scenarios and roles. Use the form introduced in Chapter 2 and repeated here (Figure 3-1) to note the influences that affect your company's situations and scenarios. *A review of these factors can help you understand the scenario and play your part, or, if things seem to be going wrong, to identify the problem in your performance or in the scenario itself.* The form below has been filled out to emphasize Harrison's new job. As you become more and more aware of these influences, you will need to refer to such forms less often. However, a fresh analysis can help you prepare for an important situation. You should also keep in mind that scenarios change as key factors change, a truth illustrated by the Atherton Jordan case in Chapter 2.

Analyzing Specific Roles

To analyze your role in a specific scenario, consider what part you play in the transaction. The form in Figure 3-2 will help you to answer the following questions. Are you performing a service, arranging for the exchange of goods or payments, transmitting information, or reaching a decision? What communication

Type of Situation: _Weekly policy meeting_

Note any aspects of the external and internal environment that may affect this situation.

External

Customers   Clients' requests; level of sales and redemptions in the accounts

Competitors   New products; institutional investor behavior

Regulatory standards   Securities and Exchange Commission

Professional standards   Chartered Financial Analyst standards

Suppliers   Analysts' reports, purchased research

Host culture   Wall Street, investment industry, United States

Media   Wall St. Journal, trade publications, newsletters

Other   World economy, political developments

Internal

Company structure   Flat, managers are equals

Corporate culture   Everybody does his share; egalitarian. No one knows it all

Departmental culture   Collaboration leads to good strategy

Size of company   Small

Mission of the company   Service and performance for clients in investment management

Technology used   High tech (on-line electronic information)

Position in company   Portfolio Manager

Employee's personality   Quiet but confident

Professional training   M.B.A. with concentration in finance

Other   Group history: Frequency of meeting developed close ties among portfolio managers.

FIGURE 3-1. Analyzing Influences on Situations

Situation: _____

<u>Circle</u> the actions and media/types needed for your role. Write the initials of the scenario's other participants in the space beside their actions. List the audiences for each type of event below.

FUNCTION	ROLE		MEDIA
	Lead	**Respond**	**Type**
Initiate	_____ Seek info	_____ Provide info	Letter
	_____ Tell, relate	_____ Listen	Memo
	_____ Analyze	_____ Prepare resources	Hand-written note
	_____ Plan	_____ Schedule	In-person request
	_____ Persuade	_____ Refuse/Approve	Meeting
	_____ Present	_____ Decide	Presentation
			Phone call
Conduct	_____ Supervise	_____ Count	Standard form
	_____ Collect data	_____ Test	Report
	_____ Negotiate	_____ Manufacture	Electronic mail
	_____ Request	_____ Deliver	Teleconference
	_____ Order	_____ Purchase	Advertising
	_____ Advertise	_____ Record	Computer presentation
	_____ Interview	_____ Process	Presentation handout
	_____ Offer	_____ Provide data	Videotape
			Audio tape
Interpret	_____ Analyze	_____ Confirm	
	_____ Report	_____ Approve	
	_____ Request	_____ Question	
	_____ Recommend	_____ Reject/Deny	
	_____ Publicize	_____ Seek more info	
	_____ Support	_____ Persuade	

List the names of participants, audiences, or readers for the various communications here:

FIGURE 3-2.   Role Analysis Form

EVENT OR ACTION	AUDIENCES	GENERAL SPECIFICATIONS OF LOCATION OR DOCUMENT
I send notice of meeting	Service Committee	Memo
I chair meeting	same	3rd floor conference room, 3–4:30 P.M., date
We review employees' proposals	same	Helen presents them
Bill Lane writes minutes of meeting	same	Minutes
I send out Bill's minutes	same	Minutes
I send approval or rejection notices	Proposal writers	Letters
I ask controller to dispense funds	Controller	Memo
I tell Public Relations	Public Relations	Memo
Public Relations announces awards	Reporters, editors	Press release

FIGURE 3-3.   Sample Scenario Profile

responsibilities do you have in the situation? Will you use communication to initiate, conduct, or interpret the transaction? What results must you achieve? You can use the list of communication functions and media in the scenario analysis form (Figure 3-2) to identify both the leading and responding roles in a scenario. This would be a good time to complete Preliminary Exercise 1 in the Communication Challenges at the end of the chapter to analyze a familiar role.

If the scenario is quite simple, you may find that a scenario profile, a "who does what" list, is handy. It will show the most important tasks and will also serve as a checklist as you complete various responsibilities. The sample here (see Figure 3-3) has been filled in by the chairman of a company's community service committee. Such a simple list may not reveal the important psychological functions that are indeed part of your role, such as reassuring people, reducing anxieties, inspiring their cooperation, and acknowledging their importance. These considerations will be part of your communication strategy, which is the subject of the next two chapters. Before developing a strategy, you must think more about your audiences.

Understanding Your Audience

Communicators must write for decision makers.

"Know your audience" is one of the most common maxims in communication. "Keep your audience constantly in mind," your teachers have doubtless advised you. It isn't easy to know the audience, especially if you are new in the organization. Many new employees believe they are writing for their immediate supervisors. After all, the supervisor is the one who requests the reports. Nevertheless, he or she may not be the person who will make the decision your work is intended to support. It is important to know what decision will be based on your work and who will make the decision.

Misunderstanding the Audiences

The difficulty of recognizing the actual decision maker frustrated one of my clients, an insurance executive. Several of his recent proposals had failed. He explained: "I can't see why we lost that contract. We had the best rates. Every number they needed is right there—bam–bam–bam! (He thumped the various columns vigorously.) Their president got involved in making that decision. The problem is that people who don't know what they're doing are getting mixed into the decision process."

The insurance executive unwittingly had put his finger on the source of the problem, although he had defined the problem incorrectly. The first six pages of the proposal he held in his hands, after the title and the date, consisted solely of numbers and table headings. By not explaining the significance of these numbers, the insurance executive failed to convince the actual decision maker, the client company's president. It is much easier to explain numbers than to exclude presidents of corporations from decisions. The insurance company needed to modify its proposal format. By explaining for the decision makers, both in words and graphs, why their policy was better than others, the insurance company provided the information needed for both specialists and nonspecialists who might become involved in decision making. Once these changes were adopted, the company and the executive won several contracts.

Multiple Audiences: Primary, Secondary, and Transmitting Audiences

Communication may involve multiple audiences.

This insurance company's problem illustrates another important point about audiences: most business situations today involve *multiple audiences* for both written and oral communications. A person trying to understand a scenario should consider how these audiences will respond. The *primary audience* for any communication makes decisions or takes action on the basis of the communication. Those who will be affected by the decision or the idea presented in the document are the *secondary audience* (for example, the insurance and benefits coordinator in the company to which the insurance company was making the proposal). Since most companies keep documents in their files for at least four years (and often for seven), it may be helpful to think of future audiences as another secondary audience: one composed of people likely to need additional help when they eventually read the document. The *transmitting or intermediate audience*, the third type of audience, may only review and pass along the report. If members of the transmitting audience have to sign the document, they become responsible for the document along with the actual author, and thereby gain some authority over its content or form.[1] The first two types of audiences, decision makers and people affected by the decision, may be inside or outside the company. The third type, the transmitting audience, usually is internal.

Audiences as "Stakeholders"

Audiences, both inside and outside the company, are stakeholders.

Both external and internal audiences usually are *stakeholders*.[2] A "stakeholder" is an individual, group, or organization whose interests are affected by the goals and activities of a particular company. The internal stakeholders of the company are its executives, managers, and employees. The firm's primary external stakeholders—owners (and the directors who represent their interests to management), customers, suppliers, and competitors—are directly affected by its goals and activities. Thus, a writer or presenter must take into account these people's particular vested interests. Their sense of what is important in any situation will reflect the kind of stake they have in the company and their probable involvement as the scenario is played out.

The U.S. airline industry is particularly rich in external stakeholder constituencies. It is regulated for safety purposes by the Federal Aviation Administration and the National Transportation Safety Board, both subunits of the U.S. Department of Transportation. Environmentalists are concerned with airport noise pollution. Consumer action groups complain about lost baggage and late departures and arrivals. The media publicize accidents and "near-misses." Community groups lobby in response to proposals to expand existing airports or to construct new ones. International and domestic airplane manufacturers have a large say in the future economics and operating details of airline companies. Almost every city in the nation has a commercial airport; several very large cities have more than one. Hundreds of millions of passengers travel annually on airlines.

Kinds of stakes affect audiences' concerns.

Although not all businesses face such a complex array of stakeholders as those of the airline industry, any business communicator must sometimes address the concerns of complex audiences whose reasons for being interested in the situation may differ substantially. Further, these interests or stakes may extend far beyond the bounds of a single transaction. Your understanding of the roles that primary, secondary, and intermediate audiences inside and outside the firm play in various situations will affect how you see yourself and others. Analyzing your own role and those of your audiences will enable you to complete transactions successfully. Moreover, you can use your understanding of roles to develop lasting relationships. This would be a good time to complete Preliminary Exercise 3 at the end of the chapter to consider your role as a stakeholder in your college.

❑ ANALYZING AUDIENCE NEEDS USING THE CONCEPT OF UNCERTAINTY

Audiences experience *uncertainty*, the discrepancy between what they know, feel, and believe now and what they must know, feel, and believe to take action.

One way to nurture relationships is to analyze audience needs thoroughly every time you communicate. Your goal is to reduce and manage uncertainties—both your own and the audiences'—through language. People generally need more than just information. Even if they possess appropriate facts, they may not have the requisite beliefs, attitudes, or emotions to take the action the writer or speaker desires. They may know what to do and how to do it but lack sufficient confidence or perceived authority, saying, "That's not my job; headquarters—or someone else—ought to handle it." Imagine calculating audience uncertainty with a formula:

Information, beliefs, feelings needed for task
Minus Information, beliefs, feelings already possessed
Equals UNCERTAINTY

Driskill and Rymer defined "uncertainty" in communication situations as *the perceived lack of information, knowledge, beliefs, and feelings—whatever must be supplied for accomplishing both the organization's task and the personal objectives of the communicators.*[3] Earlier, Galbraith had defined uncertainty only in terms of information.[4] It would be wrong, however, to think of "uncertainty" only as the emotional aspect of an audience's readiness to respond. Uncertainty is made up of all three elements. Most situations don't call only for information or only for persuasion, and most people don't completely separate feelings and thinking. The checklist in Figure 3-4 can be filled in for each person or group in your audience.

Uncertainties may be corporate (pertain to the company as a whole), departmental, or individual.

As you plan to manage your audience's uncertainties in a particular situation, you should review three levels of uncertainty: corporate, departmental, and individual uncertainty. *Corporate uncertainty* refers to issues in the situation that affect the company as a whole, such as, "Will the government pass the law requiring 60-day notice of plant closings?" Although all departments share some of the corporate uncertainties, each unit also has its own *departmental uncertainties* related to its goals, values, standard operating procedures, structure, and communication patterns. For example, mastering and following a new tax code might be a CPA firm's crucial corporate concern because the tax code is the foundation of its business and a serious concern to its tax department, but its personnel department would see the new tax code only as a knowledge requirement for certain jobs.

As a member of a department, an employee assumes that certain levels and kinds of uncertainties are typical for his or her particular job. Many employees also identify with a profession or a craft by virtue of education or testing ("I am a CPA"). These affiliations typically cause the person to expect certain kinds and degrees of uncertainty. For example, a real estate agency typically spends many hours preparing information for a client and showing the client properties. If the client does not purchase any of these properties, the agency is paid nothing.

Situation: _____

Audience: _____ Action Writer Desires: _____

Primary _____ Secondary _____ Transmitting _____

| Information needed | Information possessed | Uncertainty |

| Feelings needed | Feelings now | Uncertainty |

| Beliefs needed | Beliefs held now | Uncertainty |

Corporate uncertainties:

Departmental uncertainties:

Individual uncertainties:

FIGURE 3-4. Uncertainty Analysis Form

Situation: Renovation Project, Carpet Installation Planning

Audience: Members of the Retail Tenants' Association

Desired Results: Suggestions for project from enthusiastic, involved tenants

Stake: Profits affected by project

Primary __✔__   Secondary _____   Transmitting _____

Information needed	Information possessed	Uncertainty
Dates for project	Sometime in fall	Exact dates?
Length of disruption in front of each store	Guesses	Interruption of traffic flow to my store?
Knowledge that business losses will be small, if any	Guesses	Facts on which to base estimate

Beliefs needed	Beliefs held	Uncertainty
Benefits will derive from project	Some enthusiasm	What are the benefits?
Project can attract customers	Project would deter shoppers	How many customers will be lost?
I can help make this a success	Management is deciding everything	Management is open to ideas

Feelings needed	Feelings now	Uncertainty
Cooperation, hope, enthusiasm	Not sure it will help; may lose customers	Whether I can help by thinking about my customers, my store's needs
I'm included; I have a say	Management may exclude me	Are my ideas wanted?

FIGURE 3-5.   Shamrock Mall Uncertainty Analysis Form

In contrast, an advertising agency expects to be paid for time spent discussing a possible project, whether the project is authorized and executed or not. Thus, the real estate agency expects and must cope with greater financial uncertainty than the advertising agency.

Individual uncertainty usually is related to the internal processes of the organization; the processes that determine membership, roles, rewards, and prestige. Personal uncertainty can involve whether a job will be performed differently under changed conditions or—the ultimate uncertainty—whether it will be performed at all.

Another way to figure out the uncertainties in the right-hand column of Figure 3-4 is to think of them as the things your audience should know, believe, and feel at the end of your presentation, meeting, or document. By comparing these items with what the audience already knows, you can isolate the audience issues (uncertainties) that must be addressed. The form shown in Figure 3-5 was prepared by the marketing director of the management company for a large urban shopping mall, the Shamrock.

Situation. The Shamrock needed new carpeting. Once the management company's executive committee had selected the carpet and placed the order for its installation, the members of the tenants' retail association needed more information. The management office of the Shamrock also wanted to involve the tenants by soliciting their ideas.

Scenario. Kent Brickle, the marketing manager, had presented the overall renovation plan at the August 1991 monthly meeting of the retail tenants' association, but now the tenants need to know specific dates for the various parts of the project.

Role. Kent's role causes him to act as a liaison between the retail tenants and the management company. He generally proposes ideas to the executive committee of the property management company, and he reports its decisions and plans to the tenants. Therefore, when he addresses the tenants he speaks for the company. Anything he says can be taken as an unofficial contract to perform, so he has to be careful that he doesn't promise more than he can deliver. On the other hand, he's also responsible for generating enthusiasm and for conveying the message that the management company supports the aims of the merchants who lease space in the Shamrock. In this letter to the head of the tenants' association, Brickle must provide information, inspire enthusiasm for the project, and request suggestions, while expressing a commitment to shared goals. Brickle uses the tenants' stake in the project—the effect the renovation can have on their profits—to increase their commitment to the project. He reduces their uncertainties about loss of business by explaining that the recarpeting will take place without interrupting the flow of traffic to their stores. He even explains plans to increase business during the project. The letter that he wrote on the basis of this analysis is shown in the example.

Shamrock Property Management Co.
Shamrock Center
Meridian, Texas 77099

September 3, 1991

Mr. Gerald Raspberry
President, Shamrock Retail Tenants' Association
Raspberry World Gift Boutique
Shamrock Mall, 340 East Leaf
Meridian, Texas 77099

Dear Mr. Raspberry:

The property management team is interested in attracting as many customers as possible to the Shamrock, not only throughout the holiday season but also during the renovation period October 1–11. The Shamrock's program to refurbish the entrances, install new signage, and recarpet all the common areas will enhance the image of the complex. We intend to keep access to your stores fully open during the recarpeting, as I explain below. We would like to invite additional suggestions from your members about how we can help them get through the project with their profits high.

We plan to turn the renovation into a customer attraction for you. Our advertising slogan during this ten-day period will be "At the Shamrock, we're rolling out the carpet for you!" This phrase will emphasize what we're doing for customers and will invite them to see the transformation as it occurs. People love seeing change in progress.

Putting in 40,000 square feet of carpet will take nearly ten days, beginning 10 P.M. October 1. The installers will work from 10 P.M. to 2 A.M. to remove old carpet. Then they will return at 6 A.M. and install until 10 A.M. when most stores in the mall open. The carpet installers believe they can lay approximately 4,000 square feet per day, and no disruptions will occur during business hours.

We're looking for good ideas about anything Shamrock management could do to make this project proceed even more smoothly while building for a more profitable fall and winter season. For instance, Mrs. Quinn at the New Directions Training Center let me know that she is holding a Saturday seminar for personnel directors that will begin at 9:30 A.M. on the first Saturday of the project. We'll make sure the installation people will not interfere with their arrival. If there are any other special situations we should take into consideration, I would be pleased to know about them. I have sent a copy of this letter to your members. Please call me at ext. 2788 to discuss the project.

Sincerely,

Kent Brickle

Kent Brickle
Marketing Manager

cc: Tenants' Association members

Formal and Informal Communication: A Case of Mismanaged Uncertainties in a Manufacturing Company

Driskill and Rymer discuss a situation that had the possibility of creating serious departmental and individual uncertainty among the employees of a mid-sized manufacturing company. Its management had decided to close one of the company's distant plants. Management needed to manage the long-term relationship with its employees, not just deal with a single event or decision.

Because of union negotiations aimed at an orderly shutdown, the company could not announce the closing unilaterally for several months. Once the negotiations were concluded, however, management met with the workers at that plant to inform them about the conditions of the closure. But at headquarters, employees in certain departments learned about the impending shutdown informally, and some who worked as the liaison staff with the plant that was to be closed became concerned that their own jobs might be affected. After a few days of delay, management—hoping to quell the discussion—responded by officially reporting the plant closing through a formal bulletin posted in the headquarters office. The company's bulletins have been reproduced here with the names of specific people, products, and locations deleted:

Bulletin 1

During meetings with both salaried and hourly employees of the "Z" plant on Wednesday (month, day), the employees were informed that it has been decided to close the "Z" plant because of economic and other business decisions. No specific closing date has been determined, but it is anticipated that the shutdown will occur during fiscal year 198_. No other details were announced.
(signed)
Human Resources Manager

Not surprisingly, this bald announcement of the plant's closing increased rather than reduced uncertainties among headquarters staff members. The notice confirmed the truth of the rumored shutdown but did not give a cause, vaguely suggesting "economic and other business decisions." Moreover, by using sentence structures that do not show *who* is deciding or announcing ("it has been decided") and by indicating unwillingness to share information ("no other details were announced"), senior management sounded as if it were refusing to acknowledge its responsibility.

Eventually, the pressures from the underground network for some answers became so intense that management felt compelled to respond a second time. Although the formal communication system was an awkward way to convey information about departmental restructuring and certain staff members' future employment, management chose to write a second bulletin.

Bulletin 2

Reference is made to the previously posted notice regarding the announced shutdown of the "Z" plant. The announcement raised some questions as to why this action was necessary and whether we would sustain a loss of business as a result of the shutdown.

The reason for the announcement is not a loss of business. The underlying reasons for the decision are:

1. The plant is not equipped with the equipment, systems, or trained people to assure consistent "world class" quality.
2. The new computer system will allow our marketing and materials group to forecast needs for [name of finished products] and eliminate the assembly and packaging requirements now filled by the "Z" plant.
3. The location [of the plant] for distribution of shipments from [foreign country] is not proper.
4. We will find there are residual requirements for "Z" plant type work. However, the basic facilities would not support the quality requirements.
5. Approximately 40 percent of the "Z" plant workload is in "G" plant and "R" plant products. Both plants are establishing systems to cost-effectively handle these small lot requirements and therefore eliminated the need for the "Z" plant.

The closing of the "Z" plant, therefore, will result in a more efficient, cost-effective distribution of higher quality products.
(signed)
Manager, Human Resources

This second bulletin, posted less than a week after the first, aimed to allay employees' uncertainties expressed through informal channels. Unfortunately, it defined those uncertainties mainly in corporate-level terms, whereas individuals were primarily concerned with potential loss of jobs, an individual-level uncertainty. The CEO's immediate staff perceived the announcement to be a candid explanation of the solid business reasons behind the shutdown—the aging plant's shortcomings, the projected effects of new technology, and the availability of alternative facilities within the company. The memo reassured department heads and middle managers that loss of business was unlikely and addressed departmental questions about who would do what work.

The professional staff read the bulletin far more critically and expressed many personal anxieties. Some noted that management seemed concerned only about the company, not about the "people who work here." The new computer control system, which had just come on line, was already displacing plant personnel. Could the lower-level corporate staff in the materials department be far behind? Many of them, not surprisingly, translated this general possibility into the specific possibility of losing their own jobs.

The style of the announcement also exacerbated these individual uncertainties. The announcement was signed by the head of personnel, not by a director or vice president of manufacturing or materials. In the choice of a spokesperson, management hinted that jobs were at stake. This spokesperson then began the announcement in a depersonalized, detached manner ("Reference is made to the previously posted notice"), explicitly targeting the informal network as the reason for this further explanation ("The announcement raised some questions . . ."), but ignoring the people who constituted that network and their individual concerns. Instead, he represented all those rumors and the staff members' questions in corporate-level terms ("whether we should sustain a loss of business") and created an image of management dissociated from its corporate community. Altogether, the uncertainties created by this plant closing, a typical event in a time of vigorous competition in the marketplace, were neither alleviated nor managed by company communications.

How to Use the Concept of Uncertainty

To achieve positive results, follow these guidelines to analyze audiences and plan documents:

1. *Use the concept of uncertainty to identify and analyze the multiple needs of your audiences.* Ask what feelings, beliefs, and information would potential readers need in order to feel motivated in the particular situation. Use the form for analysis shown in Figure 3-4. Review the corporate, departmental, and individual uncertainties for each audience. If the audience is likely to have no problems of belief or feelings, then stress information. If the audience needs only a little information but has personal uncertainties, address those concerns. Address the uncertainties that are of greatest concern to your readers.

2. *Select the most appropriate forms in the formal and informal communication networks to reduce or manage the uncertainties of your audiences.* Ask what combination of forms would be most effective. Follow oral presentations or telephone conversations with written notes or memos, where appropriate. Follow general announcements with personal calls to key members of the informal network. Since the grapevine is such an active conduit of information, you may decide to put out the word there and later reinforce that message with formal communication.

3. *Design communications by using the projected uncertainties of all the stakeholders as a guideline.* In your planning, acknowledge your own uncertainties and develop a dialogue about them with the audiences. Then, design the text with your readers in mind. Imagine their probable reactions, given their uncertainties, sentence by sentence. The next two chapters will discuss ways of creating communication strategies to address uncertainties. The uncertainty analysis in Figure 3-6 could have made the preparation of an appropriate memorandum much easier.

<u>Situation</u>: Announcement of Plant Closing

<u>Audience</u>: Employees at company headquarters

<u>Desired Results</u>: Reduced anxiety, constructive action

<u>Stake</u>: Jobs, retirement plans

Primary ___✔___   Secondary _____   Transmitting _____

Information needed	Information possessed	Uncertainty
How company will handle personnel matters	Rumors	Fear of job loss
Effects on departments	Rumors	Fear changes in depts.
Effects on company as whole	Rumors	Is company in trouble?
A rational plan has been established	It's all a mystery	How will this be handled? What do I need to do?

Beliefs needed	Beliefs held	Uncertainty
Company chooses experienced workers for alternate positions	Jobs are on the line	Will I be fired?
Company resists firing people without good reason		
Action is being taken for a reason	Not known	Why is this being done?

Feelings needed	Feelings now	Uncertainty
Company stands behind its people	We may be fired	Will I still have a job?
I have a reasonable chance	I'm at risk	What chance is there?

Corporate uncertainties:	How does closing impact the company's future?
Departmental uncertainties:	Will any departments be closed? Which ones?
Individual uncertainties:	Will I lose my job? What do I have to do now?

FIGURE 3-6.   Uncertainty Analysis Form for Plant Closure

The following hypothetical memorandum from the president to the employees of the manufacturing company, based on the analysis, could have achieved a much more positive result:

TO: All Employees

FROM: Derek Drake
         President

DATE: April 5, 1990

SUBJECT: Effects of Reorganization

At Drover Manufacturing, we've never dismissed anyone because of reorganization. Our employees' training, experience, and knowledge of our business have always made them the best new staff for new plants and reorganized offices. Although we are indeed going to close the Zenado Plant, we will find alternative positions for Zenado employees. I'm sure you must wonder what implications this action will have for you and your departments, and I want you to know that I share your concern for providing jobs for Drover people.

The aging equipment in Zenado is no longer able to provide the quality of packaging and shipping that we need for distributing our air conditioning systems. Furthermore, since we began integrating Swedish thermocouples and fans, Zenado's location has increased our shipping costs. The more conveniently located plants of our competitors have recently begun to enable them to price their products below ours. Drover's Greenbay and Rockland plants just outside of Portland, Maine, will be able to provide transportation savings that we can turn into competitive advantages.

I have asked Human Resources to prepare a list of openings that will be created by our reorganization, anticipated retirements, and other attrition. This plan has the approval of Zeke McAllister of our union. On the 15th of this month, Peter Reynolds, the Human Resources Manager, will distribute information about these opportunities so that people can learn the details of the plans. Peter will have a team of people ready to assist Zenado employees at that time. If you are one of the people eligible to redirect your career at Drover because of the reorganization, please read his report carefully so that you can begin discussions with the team about your future assignment and the transition process. The reorganization will make Drover a stronger company for all of us.

CHECKLIST FOR MANAGING UNCERTAINTIES

_____ Search for the uncertainties audiences face by comparing what they must know, believe, or feel with what they already know, believe, or feel.

_____ Look for corporate, departmental, and individual uncertainties.

_____ Rank these uncertainties and consider the stakes that different audiences have in the situation.

_____ As you plan your communication strategy, acknowledge your own uncertainties and think of a dialogue.

_____ Imagine the readers' or listeners' questions (based on uncertainties) and answer them.

_____ Transform readers' or listeners' feelings, beliefs, and information from an initial state of uncertainty to readiness for action by addressing a person who has power to act, believe, and know.

Derek Drake's memorandum helps readers understand the corporate level concerns about competition and plant limitations in concrete terms, but he doesn't address *only* corporate uncertainties. He affirms the corporate culture's values as they apply to individuals' uncertainties and explains opportunities for employees affected by the plant's closing. In the third paragraph he explains how employees can use the information to guide their own futures, giving them an empowered role at the end of the document, even though the change he announces at the beginning cannot be avoided.

Communications should address the audiences' uncertainties.

The scenarios of your company may require a variety of communication roles and involve multiple forms of communication. Search for the uncertainties audiences face. Then, as you plan your communication strategy, think of a dialogue. Imagine the readers' (or listeners') questions, and answer them. Arrange your answers according to a communication strategy (described in Chapters 5 and 6) that will transform the reader's feelings, beliefs, and information from an initial state of uncertainty to readiness for action. Moreover, a solid understanding of roles can help you build a relationship with your audiences.

You may wish to read how the public relations staff of Vista Chemical Company (earlier, DuPont Chemicals Company) carefully selected media for complex audiences (in Part 6, Executives' Perspectives).

BUILDING RELATIONSHIPS WITH YOUR AUDIENCES

Relationships often determine the outcome of communications.

In *Getting Together*, Roger Fisher and Scott Brown of the Harvard Negotiation Project point out that the outcome of a particular transaction depends not only on a person's negotiation skills, but on the relationship between the people who are negotiating.[5] All communication works more easily when the participants have already established a good relationship. One of the purposes of understanding your communication role is to use that role to build good relationships with your audiences.

Roles may cause individuals to view a situation narrowly and adopt a single solution or position too quickly. To seek the best solution, force yourself to see positions and people separately. If you have analyzed your audiences' roles, you will have become aware of some of the pressures these people face. Try to keep in mind their interests and the things they value, not just their initial position on a particular point.

Separate People from Negotiating Positions

Fisher and Brown point out that people sometimes make damaging assumptions that are revealed by the questions they consider.

Question: Should I give in or sweep a problem under the rug?
Damaging Assumption: Avoiding disagreement will build a better relationship.

Question: Should I risk the relationship to get what I want, or should I sacrifice my interests for the sake of the relationship?
Damaging Assumption: There is a tradeoff between substantive interests and a good relationship.

Question: Should I take the first step to improve the relationship, hoping the other person will reciprocate, or should I wait and see what he does and respond accordingly?
Damaging Assumption: Reciprocity of some kind is a good guideline for how to treat people.[6]

Faulty assumptions cause people to mismanage relationships.

These damaging assumptions rest on a faulty definition of "good relationships." Fisher and Brown advise that having a good business relationship doesn't mean that all the participants will always see things the same way, share the same values, or approve one another's every action. A good business relationship produces good transactions, inner peace for the participants, and an ability to deal with differences. Handling differences, they advise, depends upon a few basic elements: balancing emotion with reason, consulting and listening before making a decision, and being trustworthy without being wholly trusting.

In Chapter 2, we distinguished between primary business activities and activities that maintain the group. Fisher and Brown say that relationships, too, involve both substantive and maintenance issues. They recommend that people address maintenance issues in a relationship separately from substantive issues. For example, if the testing laboratory in a pharmaceuticals company frequently is asked to interrupt regularly scheduled work to divert personnel to special "rush" research and development (R&D) department work, the testing laboratory people will become frustrated. Angry about R&D's lack of consideration for the laboratory's schedule and other projects, they may resist cooperation.

Instead of waiting until the next time R&D shows up with a "rush" project and refusing the order, the testing manager should treat the scheduling problem in a special meeting. There the relationship problem can be separated from the substantive business activity of supplying answers to particular testing questions. If the testing laboratory manager tries to deal with the scheduling problem and a particular work request simultaneously, the communication process will become complicated. The two departments are unlikely to focus appropriate time and attention on solving both problems simultaneously.

Treat business activity issues separately from relationship issues.

A well-established relationship provides a good climate for business transactions. The goodwill, trust, and memory of previous interactions will contribute to the success of communication. Therefore Fisher and Brown claim that the *relationship*, much more than the *reasons* given in a particular communication episode, may govern a specific outcome.[7]

Some people expect to "buy" a relationship, implying, "If I give you this big order, then you should like me and my company." Such people expect that reciprocity will drive the relationship. The big order is a business transaction; it doesn't necessarily create a relationship agreement.

Invent Options That Satisfy Mutual Needs

Often you and your audiences will share goals and needs. Even if your departmental or individual needs differ, you may be able to base your relationship on corporate goals that overarch your differences. Given the specific situation and the type of transaction that seems necessary, look for solutions that serve mutual needs or goals. The more options you create, the better the chances you will find a solution both parties can accept. According to psychologists, people too often settle for the first, often routine, solution that springs to mind. To put your relationship on firmer ground, try to maximize the returns on every solution so that everyone has the most satisfying option. Draw a circle with your options that is big enough to take in the needs of all parties, or at least most of the needs of all parties.

Learn How to Disagree

People perceive circumstances differently. A set of circumstances may constitute an emergency situation for one department but not for another. For example, a potential shortage of a raw material may appear critical to a purchasing officer and to those in production, but accounting or marketing may not readily notice trends in availability of materials. Therefore, accounting may not see a need to rush contract arrangements with a second supplier, but if there is a good relationship between accounting and purchasing, accounting may be willing to accept the other department's priorities. A good relationship helps both parties see the other's point of view.

To deal with differences in perception and yet maintain a good relationship, you need to learn communication tactics that can balance emotion with rationality. Here, Fisher and Brown suggest tactics for communicating about differences:

Balance emotion and reason to tolerate disagreements.

1. Be explicit and specific without blaming others.
2. Double-check before proceeding.
3. Provide an easy way out.
4. Accept responsibility and apologize.

Being explicit and specific means acknowledging emotions and describing the basis of these feelings. Saying "I feel very angry about the delays that occurred last week" gives the other party information about your feelings and the reason for your anger. In contrast, saying "You guys just figure that you'll get the work out to us whenever it damn well suits you, don't you?" invites the other parties to defend themselves against a much more general accusation against their character and diverts attention from the specific events that are causing trouble. If you describe the problem, then you and the other people in the situation can discuss the causes and the responsibility for the problem. In a separate meeting, you can work on the relationship and try to develop procedures that will prevent the problem in the future. Although some negotiators recommend emotional detachment, such a stance is unconvincing. Talk with feeling, but focus on the problem rather than the person. It is quite possible to like a person without liking what they have done.

If you *double-check before proceeding*, you enable everyone to work with the same set of data or understanding of the issues. Give people a chance to correct your misperceptions by asking whether you have heard them incorrectly or received wrong information. *Providing an easy way out* makes it easy for the other person to accept an idea; it's much easier to step over a line than a fence. Wherever possible, think about a possible process for resolving the problem that the other side can accept without reservation. Finally, *accepting responsibility* means to accept a measure of control and to take active steps toward setting things right. Apologizing for a mistake or error is much easier than "stonewalling" stubbornly. An apology can allow courtesy to prevail in the relationship. Fisher and Brown further recommend being trustworthy without being gullible (too trusting) in all transactions.[8]

CHECKLIST FOR BUILDING RELATIONSHIPS

Test the past relationship by asking whether this relationship

____ allowed everyone to complete business transactions smoothly.

____ provided legitimate rewards for all parties.

____ coped well with differences, pressures, and agitation.

____ erected barriers to future interaction.

If you answer no to any of these questions, it is time to apply steps 1 through 3 to your relationship with your audiences.

Step 1: Separate people from negotiating positions.

Step 2: Restate the other person's views before presenting your own.

Step 3: Disagree constructively.

____ Be explicit and specific without blaming others.

____ Double-check before proceeding.

____ Provide an easy way out.

____ Accept responsibility and apologize.

Restate the Other Person's Views

Restate others' views. Perhaps the single most useful communication rule in negotiating is: "Restate what you think you've just heard the other person say before expressing your own views." First, it shows respect for the other person's contribution to the dialogue. Second, it enables the other person to detect whether you've heard him or her correctly. Third, expressing someone else's viewpoint enables you to internalize and remember, even to understand the issues in a different light. Acquiring an additional perspective may enable you to imagine solutions or possibilities for mutual gain that you otherwise would not have considered. It certainly will help you define critical uncertainties that must be addressed.

While negotiating often takes place face-to-face, written communications also affect relationships. The principles described above apply to your writing as well as to your meetings with others. A good relationship produces a successful transaction, maintains the possibility of future transactions, and provides emotional and intellectual benefits to all. One aspect of the situations presented in Chapter 2 is the relationship among the parties that must communicate. A relationship exists over time; it is part of, but more than a momentary element in, a transaction.

An Exxon refinery manager's letter to employees, especially directed at those who have supervisory responsibilities over others, encourages readers to develop positive relationships through communication. Examine his practical advice and compare it with the ideas presented in this chapter. Studying later chapters on communication strategies (Chapters 4 and 5) and developing a professional style (Chapter 9) will extend your understanding of how to play a professional role and maintain positive relationships.

Manager's Corner

Sherman Glass, Refinery Manager

Frequently I am asked by fellow employees, "What types of traits do we expect our supervisors to display on the job?" "How should they act?" "How should they treat subordinates?" "What supervisory skills are most valued by the Company?" After reflecting on these questions, I have concluded there is another, more basic question being asked. That is, "As an Exxon employee, how will I be treated on the job?"

Clearly, there are several traits that supervisors need to have to be effective, many of which I would like to see all employees display. Foremost is a predisposition that all Exxon employees—whether in the role of co-worker, supervisor, or subordinate—are valuable resources that should be treated with courtesy, respect, and in a helpful manner enabling them to maximize their productivity and contributions. I am convinced the vast majority of Baytown Refinery employees come to work each day wanting to contribute. The more each of us can do to unencumber our co-workers' progress by removing obstacles and providing assistance as needed, the more progress we'll make in getting out in front of competition. A simple rule of treating other employees as we ourselves would like to be treated is generally a good test in trying to fulfill this need.

Supervisors should also be model employees. They need to earn the respect of subordinates and co-workers by displaying attitudes and practices that are beyond reproach. Supervisors should not put on airs or be arrogant or pompous. They need to come across as "regular people,"

approachable and receptive to suggestions on how to maximize their effectiveness and the effectiveness of their work group. Supervisors should take a genuine interest in employees' welfare and development, and willingly help when employees have problems or need assistance.

Further, all of us need to be better communicators. One of the biggest shortages in a large operation such as the Baytown Refinery is the time to adequately communicate what we are trying to accomplish at all levels. Those who take time to both inform people about our expectations and, perhaps more importantly, listen and understand what problems people are encountering tend to get the most done. Understanding where the obstacles to our progress exist enables each of us to strike them down and pave the way for further achievements by the entire organization.

Supervisors also need to be decisive. They should take the time to gather input from all levels—seeking out the best ideas. Once they have gathered the available data, they need to make good, sound business judgments even though it may involve taking some risks. These risks should have a higher probability for success than failure and possible negative consequences should be lower than the potential gain. When things start to go awry, quick action is needed to minimize possible negative consequences. Further, once a decision is made, supervisors and subordinates alike need to make sure they are willing to explain their decisions and, just as importantly, "follow through" with what they have committed to in a timely, efficient manner.

Finally, supervisors and subordinates should not be hesitant to either praise or point out areas for improvement when appropriate. Praise should be open, honest, and genuine. I still believe we are not taking enough time to stop and thank people for doing a good job. When corrective comments are needed, this should be done in private only with those people who need to be involved—not in public.

These are some of the key traits I think are helpful in being an effective supervisor and are traits that will be rewarded at the Baytown Refinery—not only because they are the right things to do; but just as important, these bring out the best in people. In fact, these are the traits that we expect from all employees. I would like to ask each employee to think about how they measure up in each of the performance categories discussed above and decide for themselves if there are things they can do differently that will positively impact our work force. People who feel good about their interactions with others on the job are ultimately more productive and more satisfied in their work. There is no question that Exxon Baytown employees are an exceptional group of people. If each of us takes the time to be a little more careful with the interactions we have with each other, I'm convinced that each of us can "make a difference in '88" and improve both our individual and collective contributions to this fine organization.

Source: *Baytown Briefs*, September 1988. Reprinted by permission of Exxon Company, U.S.A.

Communication, whether written or oral, whether a memo, letter, phone call, videoconference, or face-to-face meeting, has a structure and a dynamic character. Communication may begin by picking up a pen or a phone, but it involves simultaneously locating oneself and one's audience with respect to a relationship. Making the assumption that people must collaborate side by side to solve problems and resolve differences enables you to forego "tit for tat" reciprocity and "give up something to get something" strategies that characterize temporary relationships. Business needs relationships that make future interaction possible. You can practice the principles of building effective relationships as you complete the exercises at the end of the chapter and in your daily interactions with students and professors.

❏ COMMUNICATION CHALLENGES

PRELIMINARY EXERCISE 1 *In about one page, analyze your role in a specific scenario.* Choose a role that you play frequently because you are a member of a social group—a club, your family, your college dormitory, or church. Use a scenario profile or a role analysis form to prepare this assignment. Consider what part you play in the transaction that occurs in a specific situation. Are you performing a service, arranging for the exchange of goods or payments, transmitting information, or reaching a decision? What communication responsibilities do you have in the situation? Do you use communication to initiate, conduct, or interpret the transaction? What results must you achieve? You can use the list of communication functions and media in the scenario analysis form (Figure 3-2) to identify both the leading and responding roles in a role analysis. Do you consider your present role successful? Can you identify any factors that suggest a different role or a different scenario would produce better results?

PRELIMINARY EXERCISE 2   Choose a situation that occurred in a company where you worked or in a club to which you have belonged; perhaps one of the situations you analyzed in the preliminary exercises for Chapter 2. *Analyze the roles in the scenario for that situation, using the scenario profile form shown in Figure 3-3. Then, using the uncertainty analysis form (Figure 3-4), analyze the knowledge, beliefs, and feelings of the audiences in that situation.* Were the procedures used for communication in that group well suited for resolving those uncertainties? *Write one page explaining your analyses and your evaluation of the communication procedures used.*

PRELIMINARY EXERCISE 3   Think about your role as an internal stakeholder in your school. How would you react if the administrators or governors of the institution announced a 10 percent tuition increase and a 15 percent increase in other fees? Who would be the other stakeholders, both internal and external, who would be affected in such a situation? What would their "stakes" in the situation be? What range of possible actions might you and your constituents consider taking? How much might you be able to influence the outcome of the situation? What other stakeholder groups might you be able to gain support from? What media or regulators could you appeal to? *Write a one-page analysis of your role as a stakeholder in this situation.*

PRELIMINARY EXERCISE 4   *Practice a negotiation mediator's role.* Everyone has belonged to a group in which a serious disagreement occurred. Think back to some disagreement in a club or organization to which you belonged.

1. List the positions and the names of people who held them (or at least their initials). What was the central conflict?
2. Make a list of the common goals or interests that these people had.
3. Make up a list of solutions that might have accomplished at least one mutual goal and have resolved the central issue.
4. Regardless of the actual outcome of the negotiations in the real situation, rank the solutions according to their ability to solve the greatest number of differences while accomplishing mutual objectives or satisfying conditions important to all parties. Be prepared to discuss your case with other class members.

THE SHAMROCK CASE

It really does look like the Emerald City, you say to yourself, coming along the curving avenue toward the Shamrock. The green glass geodesic domes atop the three "leaves" of the mall and the reflecting green glass spires of the twin office towers, the O'Donnell and the Belfast, glisten in the sun like a set from *The Wizard of Oz*. You feel just a little giddy working at the Shamrock, too, even though you didn't travel a yellow brick road to get here. Putting yourself through four years of school has been a long haul. Your new job as assistant to one of the senior managers in the development company, Kelly Abelman, seemed the perfect reward for all your hard work. Recently you've been taking on some assignments for Kent Brickle, the marketing manager, as well.

After four months, you're beginning to get a feel for the business, you think. Your boss has let you deal with important issues, and she's very constructive when discussing new ideas. Kent Brickle has been very congenial, also. When you look down from your office on the eleventh floor of the O'Donnell Tower into the retail pavilions of the east leaf, you can see the tiny figures skating around the ice rink and you feel like royalty surveying the palace.

The Shamrock is the brainchild of an Irish immigrant, Kevin O'Malley, who began with a small shopping center in the Midwest and went on to develop a string of investments in the United States, Canada, and Mexico. The Shamrock was started in 1970 in the center of a fifty-mile stretch between two expanding U.S. cities. In the following two decades both cities have grown so that the

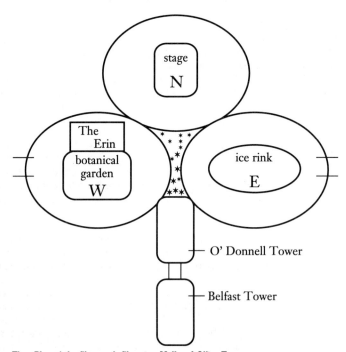

Floor Plan of the Shamrock Shopping Mall and Office Towers

Shamrock now is surrounded by prime suburban commercial, retail, and residential areas. The Shamrock managers report to O'Malley Corporation headquarters in New York.

In the beginning the Shamrock was a single circle of stores, three stories high, around an ice rink marked with a giant cloverleaf beneath the ice. A geodesic dome formed a bubble roof high above the rink. As his wealth increased, O'Malley decided to expand the Shamrock. Taking his cue from the complex's name, he built two more circular additions or "leaves" that give the entire place an architectural shape resembling a clover leaf. In the center of the second "leaf" is a dance and entertainment pavilion, and in the third is a botanical garden filled with exotic plants. At the nexus of the three circular retail "leaves," two office towers form the stem of the Shamrock. From the air the whole complex is a dazzling geometric symbol, much of which is visible from your office window in the O'Donnell Tower.

Behind you, out of sight in the west leaf, the rooms of the Erin, a luxury hotel, overlook the botanical garden. In the mid-1980s, a downturn in the economy made business conditions much worse for the retail shops on the first floor of the west leaf. Two of the restaurant locations had repeated failures. The turnover rate in the retail rental areas was much higher than in the other two leaves, where the entertainment and the skating arena attracted a higher volume of pass-through traffic. Lately, the retail traffic in the east leaf has slumped as well. The Italian-made escalators that lead to the ice rink break down frequently, and people don't seem as interested in the skating. The Shamrock is still popular, however, because early on O'Malley attracted leading fashion stores to the mall and their presence has continued to define the Shamrock as a style leader and fashion center. Now the Shamrock is beginning a major renovation project, including the recarpeting discussed earlier in the chapter.

Since June, you have worked full time preparing special reports for Kelly Abelman. The accountants prepare most of the routine reports, but the executive committee has needed more exploratory reports as they searched for a viable strategy to cope with the business downturn. Your day consists of a juggling act, balancing the demands of whatever special projects Kelly has assigned you. Each project has its own schedule, based on its priority and the difficulty of obtaining information. You send weekly progress reports to let Kelly know where you are on each project.

SHAMROCK CASE: EXERCISE 1

Part of the renovation project negotiated by Kelly Abelman and Rob Kurtle with the O'Malley Corporation in New York last summer was the repair of the short escalators that transport people from one balcony to another going to and from the bottom floor of the Shamrock Center's east leaf, where the skating rink is located. Earlier you worked with the manager of the skating rink to prepare a report for Abelman on the relationship of the number of people skating at the rink, the turnover of retail rental property, and the time these escalators were out of service. Using an appropriate statistical technique, you showed that when the escalators were out of service, the number of people skating, as well as the pass-through traffic, declined. It also seemed likely that more businesses failed or moved out during months when the pass-through traffic declined, although you couldn't show statistically that the traffic figure was the causal factor.

The escalator motors are the source of the problem, and the only repair solution appears to be to send them back to the Italian company that originally manufactured them. Labor strikes in Italy have caused the manufacturer to be quite slow, and the company can't promise you when the motors will be returned. Dave Schmidt, the property manager for the complex, received the following letter from one of the tenants, which he discussed with Abelman this morning:

October 30, 1991

Mr. Dave Schmidt
Property Manager
Shamrock Property Management Company
Shamrock Center
Meridian, Texas 77099

Dear Mr. Schmidt:

Several of the merchants on the Rink Level are very dissatisfied with the escalators' being continually out of service, I among them. The escalator that usually delivers people less than a hundred feet from my door has been out of service for four days. The customers are all being diverted to the escalator on the west side of the balcony. I haven't noticed you in my shop either.

My sales have been nearly 28% lower this week than last week, and this is usually one of the busiest times of the year, when people are eager for the smell of fall in their homes. I have seen similar variations over the past three months as these ancient escalators have been in and out, in and out of service. This is not the kind of business environment I imagined when I chose to locate my shop in this complex. When are these escalators going to be fixed so we can rely on them?

I would like to receive a prompt reply.

Clara Bowden,
Manager
Scent of Heaven Potpourri

Abelman hands it to you, saying, "Dave Schmidt has been in this morning. The escalators are turning into the biggest problem in the renovation. Look at this letter. We have money in the budget to rebuild those escalators. He's got to move that project fast. Dave is planning to send King O'Connor to New Orleans to talk with that consulting company that helped us out once before. We must have something we can tell the tenants. In the meantime, please draft a reply to Clara Bowden, acknowledging her complaint. Try to buy us a little time. King O'Connor will be back from New Orleans tomorrow with ideas about how to proceed. Dave will revise the letter if necessary and sign it, of course, but it has to state the company position, so you may as well start a draft for him. He has his hands full right now."

In planning your draft, follow the steps for coping with differences: double-check information before proceeding, restate the other person's views before presenting your own, be explicit and specific without blaming others, accept responsibility and apologize, and provide an easy way out. You double-check with Tom Tarvey in the Property Management office and discover that in the four days Clara Bowden mentions, the escalator was out of service for two hours on the first day, three hours on the second day, only one hour on the third day, and thirty minutes on the fourth day. Tarvey thinks the repair people worked as fast as they could, but you think, listening, that Tom isn't seeing this problem from a retailer's perspective. *Prepare the draft.*

THE SHAMROCK CASE: EXERCISE 2

When O'Connor came back, he gave Schmidt the following report, which Schmidt attached to his own memo to Abelman. *Read through the trip report and write out the answers to the following questions:*

1. What were Schmidt's uncertainties and the corporate-level uncertainties for the Shamrock Management Co.?
2. Did O'Connor address Schmidt's uncertainties in his report?

3. Read the memo sentence by sentence, imagining what the property manager would have felt at each point. How would you describe the series of changes in your information, beliefs, and feelings? How could O'Connor have improved his memo, based on your reactions as a stand-in for Schmidt?
4. Given the information in O'Connor's memo, can you now revise the response from Dave Schmidt to Ms. Bowden? What are her uncertainties in this situation?

Shamrock Property Management Co.
Shamrock Center
Meridian, Texas 77099

November 3, 1991

TO: Dave Schmidt
FROM: K. K. O'Connor
SUBJECT: Trip to New Orleans

I got the 5:30 P.M. flight on Tuesday to New Orleans to talk with International Equipment Supply (IES). It was a very rough trip, largely because of that tropical depression out in the Gulf. When we hit the runway, I didn't think I would be able to eat dinner, and I'd been looking forward to that, especially since you and Nick told me about the great food they have at the Commander's Palace. But Jim Corbett, their head of engineering, met me at the airport, and it's clear that even though they've gone through this leveraged buyout and all, they still want to retain Texas customers and do the kind of work we want. They have a really good attitude, and when I first came down here, you know, I had heard so much about the Southern approach to business that I didn't think engineers would push projects the way I wanted them.

Jim has a lot on the ball, very competent, and he seemed familiar right away with the problem we're having. He said that the possibility of sending those large escalator motors back to Italy is simply not cost-effective. When we had the problem with the big escalator in the north leaf in 1982, the exchange rates were quite different, and even though oil prices have gone down since then, the transportation costs would be about the same. It seemed to him that we couldn't get the repairs completed in less than six months, either, which would mean that we would have two of the six escalators out during both the Christmas and Easter promotions, which would cause the tenants' association to give us a lot of trouble. Jim says they can order us two new motors from a manufacturer in St. Louis, modifying the motors to work with the rest of the Italian assembly. IES will oversee the modifications, flying over here on Monday, if you approve, to get measurements and flying on up to St. Louis Monday afternoon. By rushing the production, we could have the two motors here on the 19th and complete installation by the 21st, in time for the big after-Thanksgiving rush. I think the tenants' association would like that. The cost of sending the motors to Italy and having them rebuilt and repaired at the original factory that built them would be $82,000. All this would need your approval, and I told Jim I would call him as soon as I heard from you and tell him to make his plane reservations to get over here ASAP Monday. The cost of having IES oversee the modification of new motors here in the U.S. would cost $102,000, which is indeed more, but we wouldn't have to wait six months and we could keep our tenants happy during the biggest retail periods. I'm glad you sent me over to see them.

THE SHAMROCK CASE: EXERCISE 3

If you have access to a computer, locate O'Connor's memo on your computer disk for this course and rewrite it, putting the answers to Schmidt's uncertainties first and deleting un- *necessary statements in the memorandum.* Use "Cut" and "Paste" (or "delete" and "insert") commands, along with any insertions you consider necessary.

IF YOU WOULD LIKE TO READ MORE

Brown, L. D. (1983). *Managing conflict at organizational interfaces.* Reading, MA: Addison-Wesley. Stresses analysis of conflicts between departments within an organization as well as conflicts between organizations and external stakeholders.

Driskill, L. P., & Rymer, J. (1986, Summer). Uncertainty: Theory and practice in organizational communication. *Journal of Business Communication, 23*(3), 41–56. Expands the concept of "uncertainty" proposed by Jay Galbraith, a specialist in organization theory, as a means of audience analysis. Galbraith had defined the uncertainty an organization faces as the difference between the amount of information it needs to accomplish its tasks and the amount of information it already has. Driskill and Rymer contend that uncertainty involves more than lack of information. See also Galbraith, J. (1977). *Organization design.* Reading, MA: Addison-Wesley.

Ede, L. (1984, May). Audience: An introduction to research. *College Composition and Communication, 35*(2), 140–154. A coherent review of changing definitions of audience in rhetorical theory and the research done to support various views.

Ede, L., & Lunsford, A. (1984, May). Audience addressed/audience invoked: The role of audience in composition theory and pedagogy. *College Composition and Communication, 35*(2), 155–171. Some people allow the perceived attributes of the specific audience addressed to direct and even limit their sense of what may be said, whereas others regard the actual audience only a little and emphasize the role they want to suggest for the audience. Ede and Lunsford argue for a balanced view in writing. Slavish adherence to what is known about an audience might prevent the writer from inducing an audience to play a beneficial and desirable role the audience can imagine.

Fisher, R., & Brown, S. (1988). *Getting together: Building relationships that get to YES.* Boston, MA: Houghton Mifflin. An excellent resource on negotiating.

Mathes, J. C., & Stevenson, D. (1976). *Designing technical reports.* Indianapolis, IN: Bobbs-Merrill. Opening chapters review the relationship of the professional to others in an organization. Distinguishes among primary, secondary, and transmitting audiences.

Thomas, G. P. (1986, October). Mutual knowledge: A theoretical basis for analyzing audience. *College English, 48*(6), 580–594. Proposes categories that could be used by researchers or ordinary writers to understand an audience. The concept of "mutual knowledge" describes the knowledge that both writer/speaker and readers/listeners know they share. Certitude that both parties are aware of one another's knowledge allows them to exploit conventions, information, and world knowledge in sophisticated ways.

Zurcher, L. A. (1983). *Social roles: Conformity, conflict, and creativity.* Beverly Hills, CA: Sage Publications. Discusses role development and change in a variety of social institutions.

NOTES

1. This classification of audiences originated with J. C. Mathes and D. Stevenson, *Designing technical reports: Writing for audiences in organizations.* Indianapolis, IN: Bobbs-Merrill (1976).

2. R. E. Freeman, *Strategic management: A stakeholder approach.* Boston, MA: Pitman (1984).

3. L. P. Driskill and J. Rymer expanded the concept of "uncertainty" as a means of audience analysis in "Uncertainty: Theory and practice in organizational communication." *Journal of Business Communication, 23* (1986)3, 41–56.

4. R. Fisher & S. Brown, *Getting together: Building relationships that get to YES.* Boston, MA: Houghton Mifflin (1988), xiii.

5. Fisher & Brown, p. xii.

6. Fisher & Brown, pp. 9–15.

7. Fisher & Brown, pp. 107–131.

8. Fisher & Brown, pp. 107–131.

CREATING SUCCESSFUL COMMUNICATION STRATEGIES: PURPOSES AND PERSUASION

OBJECTIVES

This chapter will help you

- define a comprehensive purpose
- choose a persuasive approach
- select productive social processes
- choose appropriate media

PREVIEW

A communication strategy transforms a general scenario into specific plans. An effective strategy includes an analysis of the audience, a comprehensive purpose, a persuasive approach, a productive social process, appropriate media, relevant content organized into issues, and criteria for evaluating the success of your communication. This chapter deals with purposes and persuasion in a communication strategy.

The challenges in developing communication strategies will vary, depending upon a number of circumstances: the amount of information the participants already have, the degree of conflict between their perceived goals, the deadlines involved, the available resources, and what is at stake. Sometimes the available strategies will be few, sometimes many. Business communicators often work in a routine situation that predetermines many factors: whether the report will be written, oral, or both; what types of exhibits or visual aids will be appropriate; and whether the information will be delivered in person, or by telephone, electronic mail, facsimile transmission (FAX), delivery service, or regular postal service. Even within routine situations, however, fully recognizing all the participants' purposes and carefully choosing a persuasive approach can increase communication effectiveness.

❑ PLANNING COMMUNICATION STRATEGIES

An effective communication strategy turns the general communication requirements of a scenario into plans for specific documents, presentations, or meetings. A communication strategy should include

- an analysis of the audience
- a comprehensive *purpose*
- a *persuasive approach*
- productive *social processes*
- appropriate *media and visual aids*
- *content* organized to address the audiences' beliefs and feelings as well as their need for information
- *criteria* for judging the success of the communication

In routine situations, the major task in developing a communication strategy may be to locate the important pieces of information and organize the issues and information appropriately. More complex situations may make information much less important than persuasion, and the proper location, spokesperson, and media for a message will be crucial.

Use a heuristic, a structured but flexible approach, to develop a communication strategy.

Effective communicators make the most of their own ways of thinking and style of communicating by using a *heuristic technique*. As Richard Young explains, "a heuristic procedure provides a series of questions or operations whose results are provisional. Although more or less systematic, a heuristic search is not wholly conscious or mechanical; intuition, relevant knowledge, and skill are also necessary. A heuristic is an explicit strategy for effective guessing." [1] The six elements of a communication strategy constitute a heuristic, a flexible means of achieving a specific goal.

You learned about analyzing audiences in Chapter 3. The rest of this chapter is devoted to the following elements of a communication strategy: developing a comprehensive purpose, choosing a persuasive approach, envisioning a social process, and choosing an appropriate medium.

Define a Comprehensive Purpose

First, identify *purposes*. The audiences discussed in Chapter 2 will have different stakes in the situation. Some will be decision makers (the *primary audience*). Others will be affected by the decision (the *secondary audiences*). Transmitting audiences review and sometimes approve documents. Because participants tend to ask, "What's in this for me?" you must develop a comprehensive purpose that unites (as far as possible) the goals of all interested parties.

Defining Purposes in a Simple Situation

In fairly simple situations, the goals of all the participants may be complementary. The publishing company editor who wrote the letter in Figure 4-1 faced a

Blackstone Publishing
220 Orange Avenue
Glenoaks, CA 92150

August 11, 1990

Ms. Beverly Saxon
Mr. Don Carr
Ms. Paula Heatherton
P.O. Box 1289
Culbertson, NE 69001

Dear Beverly, Don, and Paula:

With Beverly's letter I am enclosing all copies of the contract. Once you have had time to review it, please have everyone sign each copy and return the batch to us. We'll have them signed in-house and return one to each author for his or her records.

If any questions come up at the signing session, please call me for clarification.

Thank you all once again for agreeing to sign with Blackstone. I am very much looking forward to our liaison.

Sincerely,

Suzanne Armani
Acquiring Editor

SPA/dp

FIGURE 4-1. Letter Written in a Simple Situation

routine situation. The editor, Suzanne Armani, wrote many similar letters each year, inviting authors who had submitted proposals or manuscripts to sign an enclosed contract. She enjoyed the advantage of being able to convey good news to a receptive audience: a primary audience (the three author-editors to whom the letter is addressed) and a secondary audience (Blackstone Publishing management and the coauthors who collaborated on the book), whose goals were almost identical.

Organization: Blackstone Publishing wanted the author-editors and the co-authors to sign a publishing contract.

Writer: Ms. Armani wanted to
- get the contract signed
- establish a sense of teamwork with the authors
- maintain open communications and stress her availability for further communications
- maintain a tone of goodwill and encouragement.

Readers: The editors and authors needed
- the contract, so they could sign it
- information about how to execute the contract properly
- reassurance that Blackstone was committed to the project.

Ms. Armani sought a combination of results that formed a comprehensive purpose for the document.

- To cause action (sign and return the contracts)
- To inform (the contracts are enclosed; I am available to answer questions)
- To affect beliefs and feelings (we are working as a team; we have established a liaison)

Defining Purposes in Complex Situations

Becoming aware of multiple purposes is a complex, continuing process.

Longer documents and more complex situations may require a more complicated analysis of purposes. See the chapters in the Specialists' Perspectives section for examples of how managers use these steps and apply them to the communication process. People (and textbooks) often talk about purposes in a simplistic way; however, discovering your purposes in a complex situation is not an easy, straightforward task. Linda Flower, who has studied writers' "thinking aloud" transcripts for over a decade, says the process of setting up goals is anything but simple:

> The goals writers construct in working memory do not form a chain of ideas, organized by the order of appearance, by associations, or by the serendipity that generated an idea. Rather this web of information has first the character of a network. That is, an individual idea can have multiple links to multiple other nodes or ideas. . . . Second, this network has the character of a hierarchy . . . certain goals from the top-level structure of the network subsume and integrate other goals, plans, and criteria within their compass. As a result, the network that emerges over time is not a temporal log left by the process of invention, but is, to varying degrees, a purposeful, goal-directed structure.[2]

The writers Flower observed sometimes changed their purposes as they went along. Because of the complex, dynamic, interlinked character of a network of purposes, a preliminary statement may be incomplete. Defining your purposes will be a complex, continuing process.

In the following transcript, you will see that many purposes emerge as Elaine, a new employee in the corporate finance department of a securities firm, gets ready to write the second valuation report she has prepared in this job. She's not too certain of the complete situation, but she knows the scenario—her firm's process—because she's been through it once. The situation is as follows. The wife of a local newspaper owner/publisher is suing for divorce and wants to make sure she gets a fair property settlement. Since the newspaper (disguised as the *Terhune Tribune* in the transcript) is owned by her husband's family, she wants to make sure that she receives her half of the value of the stock in the newspaper.

The stock does not trade on the open market, and so it does not have an obvious market value, as a publicly traded stock would have. The wife's lawyers, therefore, requested that the husband's lawyer have the stock appraised. The task of the corporate finance department is to produce a report on the newspaper company's stock that can be used in the divorce proceedings in court. The divorce is bitterly contested, and since the stock constitutes a large part of the couple's property, the conclusions of the report are almost certain to be challenged. Elaine has never been in court during such a case, but it is not uncommon for the firm to prepare this kind of report. In the weeks since she joined the firm, she has heard conversations about these cases and has had access to similar reports.

The scenario in the company is that younger employees are assigned to research cases and to write the first draft. These drafts are circulated to five or six people in the department. Then one of the two senior department members leads a meeting in which the drafts of junior members are criticized—a "roast 'n toast," as the juniors call these meetings. Afterwards, junior members revise their drafts. The senior members complete the final editing and send the reports under their own names to the clients. Subsequently, the senior members might appear in court on behalf of the clients to explain and justify their conclusions. Since the senior members are accountable for the contents of the reports, they are highly critical of all drafts. The groups understand that it is much better for a report to be attacked in-house and improved than to be sent on with a flaw that other experts might criticize.

Look at the transcript of Elaine's comments as she makes notes for getting started on her report. The term "comps" stands for "stock price information on comparable companies."

I've got to write a valuation report for the *Terhune Tribune* Company; I've been working on this for . . . ah . . . since the first week in August, and . . . Mrs. K (the publisher's wife) will want to prove the value was very high so that she will be able to demand a lot . . . that was what Carmen (another junior staff member) had to deal with . . . present an objective case that would be hard to inflate . . . I've got to sound very unbiased. Where is her report? Oh, yes . . . yes, she begins by citing the statute here . . . (reads the first line aloud). . . . Yes, I could do that, so that it sort of sets up the standard as not mine but the law's . . . that's unbiased . . . and I need to give Mr. K's lawyers something to quote, and they could use that, refer to it, and then I could follow that with the comps that I found. No, I'd better put the *Tribune*'s figures first and work the value out, . . . hmm . . . Carmen didn't do it in that order, but I've seen another report that did, . . . oh, well, . . . I'll find out whether it's ok when we have the roast . . . I'd rather not get roasted . . . but I think I will put the comps afterward, sort of to reinforce and justify my conclusions instead of really using the comps to derive my figures . . . or, well, . . . yes, I could use some of the comps to help work out the appropriate value and then take these that aren't in the same industry and use them as a confirmation, to show I was being as reasonable as I could by the kinds of other industries I looked at. . . . What would Mrs. K's lawyers make of that? . . . I don't know. . . . I want Mr. K to think we did a good job for him. Hmm. . . ."

Multiple purposes form a web or network. Some purposes include or dominate others.

The transcript shows a complex web of purposes. The primary audiences for the report are the lawyers and the judge, who will decide whether the value presented in the report was fair. The secondary audiences (who will be affected by the report) are Mr. and Mrs. K, whose settlement in part will be influenced by the report. The transmitting audience, the senior member of the department whose name will appear as author, will present the report in court, if necessary. Figure 4-2 simplifies but highlights the relationships in the writer's comprehensive purpose. The higher-level or more inclusive goals have been outlined with heavy lines.

You may find that creating a network of your own—drawing circles around notes, finding the connections between your goals, and locating the highest ranking or most inclusive goals—helps you establish a complex purpose. On the other hand, you may be able to work from an analysis of your audiences' uncertainties, as Mark does in the case on page 88.

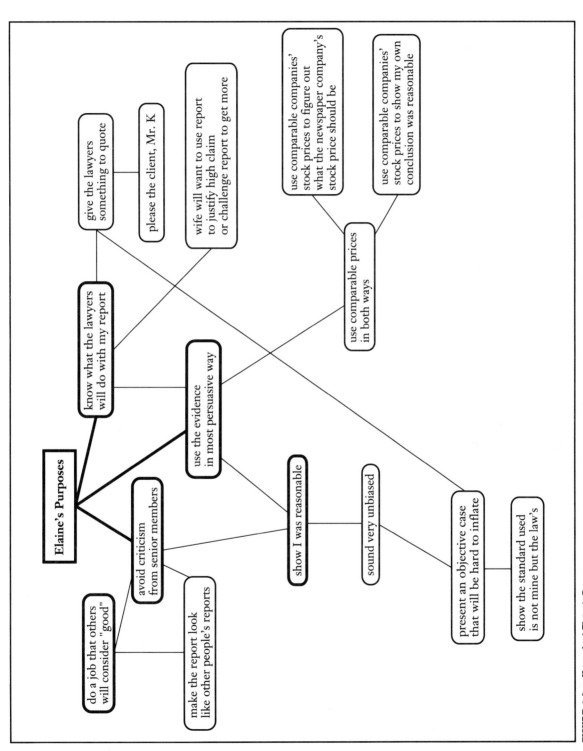

FIGURE 4-2. Network of Elaine's Purposes

Case: A Presentation for the Technology Conference

Mark, a technical manager in a large engineering firm, was invited to give a presentation at an international conference on the industrial use of computer technology. He was asked to prepare an oral presentation and a hard-copy report to accompany it, and to give the presentation four times during the one-week conference in Boston. Mark had not made a conference presentation before, so the situation was unfamiliar.

Mark talked with his vice president and with the conference coordinator to establish more specific goals for everyone involved. The vice president approved Mark's plan to focus on robotics and pointed out other potential benefits to the company. The conference coordinator gave Mark more information about the scenario: the time available for the presentation, the kind of room that would be used, the number of people likely to attend, the reasons his presentation had been requested, plus information about the visual aids equipment that could be made available. The coordinator also explained this was the first time the annual conference had included a session on this topic, and she wanted participants to find the addition useful. Figure 4-3 presents Mark's analysis of each participating group's uncertainties.

Mark then wrote a comprehensive purpose for his presentation (see Figure 4-4). Mark's purposes are limited almost exclusively to the results he wishes to obtain; they are not as closely tied to the communication he is preparing as Elaine's purposes were. The list of results nevertheless helped Mark make decisions about his persuasive approach.

Audiences	Uncertainties	Goals
Mark's Company	Can we attract more customers? Can we increase prestige in industry?	four new clients receive comments
Mark's Department	Can we obtain new projects?	four projects
Mark	Can I gain a forum for ideas, increase prestige, and perform well?	recognition no errors
Oil and gas firms	Is this new technology less expensive? How can we be more effective than our international competitors?	reduce costs increase productivity
High-tech computer firms	Are advances being made in our field?	new information leading to recommendations for future business
Conference planner	offer a new topic, improve conference	satisfy participants gain credit for planner

FIGURE 4-3. Analysis of Uncertainties and Goals

> to demonstrate the technical superiority and cost-effectiveness of our robotics application; to explain how robotics works in the field, so that its capability is credible; to attract four new clients who will recognize the cost advantages of our technology and four new projects for my department; to cause participants to recognize our firm as a leader; to cause at least one to send us a referral for robotics applications; and to spark discussion and questions after each session.

FIGURE 4-4.   Comprehensive Purpose

Choose a Persuasive Communication Strategy

Mark's desire to explain the advantages of his company's robotics technologies to people in the oil and gas industries involved him in persuasion, one of the oldest human concerns. For nearly 2000 years, people have continued to follow the advice of classical rhetoricians such as Aristotle, who emphasized discovering substantive issues (called *invention*), organization (called *disposition*), style, and presentation. For the most part, textbooks today turn these methods into formulas or rules. Annette Shelby sees a problem with such formulas, however: "Despite its comprehensive approach to persuasion, the classical paradigm becomes skewed when presented simply as a formulary without emphasizing the given case. Every case is different; the audience, the situation, the goal, the message sender, and the channel all combine to drive persuasive choices. The unique interrelationships of these variables determine which messages will be effective and which will not." [3]

Your organization, style, and presentation must be based on your understanding of the situation. The checklists and forms for analyzing situations, scenarios, roles, and audience uncertainties (introduced in Chapters 2 and 3) enable you to form an in-depth picture of your communication context. Furthermore, by using the heuristic approach and tools such as mind mapping (presented in the next chapter), you will learn to explore your own ideas and to achieve your comprehensive purpose.

Careful analysis of the situation, scenario, and audiences will enable you to choose a persuasive approach.

At this point, you're ready to learn about choosing a persuasive approach; you can draw on the perspective of several research traditions, as well as the classical paradigm, in making your choice. We've incorporated the views of several disciplines in the following section and suggested additional sources at the end of the chapter.

To choose a persuasive approach, you should consider several questions:

- How easy will it be to influence my audience?
- What should be the basis of the persuasive appeal?
- How can I increase my personal effectiveness?

Almost all communications involve persuasion. Even when you are exchanging information, showing the information's relevance to the situation at hand means interpreting the information and motivating your audience to agree with that interpretation.

How Easy Will It Be to Influence My Audience?

An overdone or excessively ardent appeal will be suspect, and one that is too mild or routine may not receive attention. So you should ask yourself, "How easy will it be for my audience to say yes?" Your first clue should come from your analysis of the scenario.

- Do you share a mutual understanding of the scenario?
- Has the audience done this or felt this before?
- Is the audience predisposed to do what you request?
- Is your relationship with this audience strong?

If the action or belief you're requesting is familiar, especially if it is something that the person has done before or is positively predisposed to accept, you can rely on your past relationship to gain acceptance. A great deal of research shows that people are likely to repeat actions they have already performed or to carry out those that they have already committed themselves to fulfilling.

When you and your audiences both understand and agree to a scenario, you may be able to persuade the reader or listener primarily by describing the situation, pointing out the key issues, and explaining your comprehensive purpose. Such a communication might begin, "It's time to prepare the third quarter report. Please prepare a summary of your work on automating the billing procedures. I need a draft by next Thursday." On the other hand, if you and your audiences do not share an understanding of the situation, or if you request a new task, you must choose the basis of your appeal carefully, giving further thought to the predispositions of the audience. If possible, take advantage of any other attitudes your audience already holds that may be applied to your request. For example, if your audience already strongly values efficiency, you might justify a proposed change in procedure by explaining its superior efficiency.

On the other hand, if the audience already holds contrary beliefs, your request will cause dissonance: a pressure to adjust feelings. This reaction can increase an audience's sense of the necessity to act, or it can predispose them to resist or ignore you. Once you have decided the strength and direction of this reaction, you are ready to choose the basis of your persuasive appeal.

What Should Be the Basis of the Persuasive Appeal?

If you face a difficult persuasive task, choose a powerful persuasive appeal. You may wish to think about the culture of your organization in determining which appeal will be most suitable for your situation. You may consider any of the following choices:

Shared goals or mutual needs	Credibility of the medium
Mutual benefits	History of the relationship
Benefits for the audience only	Corporate values
Audience's desire to be part of the group	Preferences of powerful people
	Power or coercion
Audience's desire to lead group	Policies or laws
Audience's desire for personal appreciation	Cultural value associated with request
Writer/speaker's credibility	Fear of punishment, loss of esteem, or other penalties
Writer/speaker's expertise	

The circumstances of a particular situation and the personality of a particular audience may elevate any one of these factors. In a company that values status and hierarchy, the opportunity to work directly with the president on a project might be more attractive than any order or legal injunction.

Combine appeals to suit multiple audiences or intensify persuasive effects.

Naturally, an appeal that combines several of these bases into a single argument becomes increasingly powerful. However, your goal should not be to create the most powerful appeal possible, but to create an appropriate appeal that will further your relationship with the audience and still accomplish your comprehensive purpose. Overkill is unnecessary and, over time, ineffective. Furthermore, negative appeals such as threats of punishment, loss, or other penalties must be chosen with care.

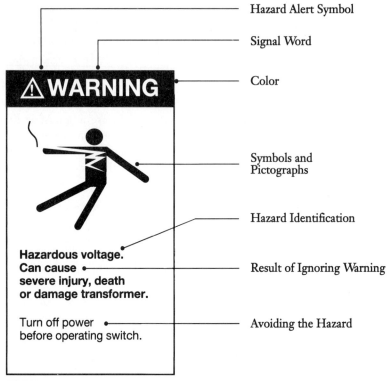

FIGURE 4-5. Warning Label

Source: *Danger Warning Caution* (A Public Safety Handbook).
Reprinted by permission of Westinghouse Electronic Corporation.

Use negative appeals only when you must elicit a response right away. An anxious person is likely to respond more compliantly to a strong threat, whereas a confident person is likely to respond more favorably to a mild threat. In both cases, a negative appeal exerts more force when combined with other supporting appeals and specific instructions about how to take the recommended action.[4] The warning in Figure 4-5 sets forth a negative appeal, presenting the nature and severity of the hazard, the consequences of not following the warning, and specific instructions for avoiding the hazard.

If you prefer a moderate to mild appeal, you might choose mutual goals, benefits to the audience, and values that the corporation ranks highly. For example, if your scenario is familiar and your audience likes you, looking forward to the results of your joint effort may be a perfectly satisfactory appeal.

Match persuasive appeal with audience uncertainties and predispositions.

Look carefully at the list of possibilities and think of your audiences' uncertainties in the situation. Given their needs for information, beliefs, and appropriate feelings, which of these bases are suitable? An appeal that corresponds to their most severe uncertainty is likely to be influential. Often you can combine different bases, so the complete document or presentation motivates the audiences in several ways. A combination may also enable several audiences with different concerns to respond favorably.

To review,

- If you can recommend a response that will alleviate an important uncertainty, emphasize the effectiveness of the desired response.
- If you can associate your request or proposal with something the audience already values or feels strongly about, you can use that association to encourage the same attitude toward your request.
- If you can create a feeling of discrepancy or dissonance that suggests a need for action, then the audience will be more motivated to reduce the dissonance through the action you request.

These ideas form the basis for strategic patterns that contrast the ideal with the actual, a goal with the present condition, or a problem with its possible solution.

In the case of Mark's robotics presentation, he combined several bases in his persuasive appeal. He pointed out the benefits of the technology for the audience, such as the superior efficiency and cost-effectiveness of the technology. His ideas alleviated the audience's fear of falling behind in a technical field. He used the computer in his presentation, and asked for suggestions during the demonstration so he could solve certain problems for his audiences on the spot. By allowing interested individuals to try the robotics simulations right there after the presentation, he gave prospective customers experience with the products, so they might later agree to view a full-scale sales presentation.

How Can I Increase My Personal Effectiveness?

Some audiences respond more to the person sending the message than to the message itself. Many studies have been done to identify the traits that influence audiences most. Some media consultants insist that in the age of video, the image of the speaker is more important than any other factor. In *You Are the Message: Secrets of the Master Communicators*, Roger Ailes (whose clients have included both President Bush and President Reagan) says today's television audiences require that communicators be prepared, committed, interesting, and able to make others comfortable.[5]

Audiences respond to four perceived characteristics. Which is your strength?

Sherron Kenton also has proposed a four-trait model of speaker influence that might be applied to writers as well as speakers. Kenton's model is interesting not only because it synthesizes earlier work on speaker traits, but because it attempts to account for gender differences as well. The four dimensions are

- *Goodwill and fairness*—speaker's perceived concern for the audience
- *Expertise*—speaker's knowledge and intelligence
- *Prestige*—power attributed to the speaker
- *Self-presentation*—the audience's perceptions of the speaker's platform personality and presentation skills.

Audiences expect men and women to differ on these key traits.

Kenton points out that earlier studies suggest women tend to rank higher on the goodwill and fairness dimension and men tend to rank higher on the expertise, prestige, and self-presentation dimensions. These results occur when the women are equally experienced and even, in experimental situations, where the women read the same speech that men read. Kenton concludes that since societal expectations about male superiority in expertise and prestige are slow to change, a woman will produce few results by trying to be more expert or more prestigious—that is, by basing her primary appeal on knowing more ("I know more than you do, so do it my way") or having more clout ("I'm at a higher rank or I'm better known in this field than you are, so do what I say"). She notes, on the other hand, that since self-presentation consists of many skills that can be learned, "women who acquire these skills . . . might raise perceptions of their expertise and prestige, as well, and therefore raise the perceptions of their overall credibility."[6]

Learn ways to establish and increase audience perceptions of key traits.

Both men and women can work on their documents and presentations to convey fairness and goodwill, can demonstrate their knowledge of situations and their understanding of the issues in them, and can work on self-presentation in both writing and speaking. The checklist for building credibility (Figure 4-6) offers tactics for implementing a strategy. Chapter 16, "Preparing and Delivering Presentations," contains advice for both men and women on enhancing credibility. For maximum persuasiveness, your goodwill, fairness, prestige, expertise, and visible image must be suited to the social processes and media you use.

Increase Your Personal Effectiveness

FACTOR	TO ESTABLISH	TO INCREASE
■ **Goodwill and fairness**	compliment audience, mention values shared by audience, look forward to achievement of audience's goals	use audience's values in your arguments; refer to shared goals, benefits audience wants
■ **Expertise**	describe experiences, attach your résumé	link yourself to someone or some organization your audience respects; quote, paraphrase, tell anecdote.
■ **Prestige**	mention your title or offices held	affirm values, goals and results that audience seeks; take a leadership position
■ **Self-presentation**	prepare and practice your talk, or evaluate your document before sending it	be flexible, recover quickly, keep yourself visible in the message; emphasize your relationship with your audience

FIGURE 4-6.   **Communication Guide**

Envision the Social Process

Imagination can help you envision social processes.

Communication is a social process that occurs moment by moment. Participants are influenced by events of the past and by prospects for the future. In planning a communication strategy, you must anticipate how the audiences will experience your ideas. Sometimes the scenario allows for a sequence of events, not just a single document. Think about the effect that different sequences will have. If you will not be able to combine events in sequence, at least compare the possible impacts of different types of events or media. Your options include the following choices.

Document before Discussion   If you face a complex, unfamiliar subject or problem, sending a document (report, proposal, memorandum) in advance will help the audience understand more before the discussion. A document distributed in advance also can help form positive attitudes toward a previously neutral subject.

Discussion before Document   When personal uncertainties grip the audience or when the audience feels strongly negative about a subject, then meeting with individuals before preparing a document can ensure that the final document will reflect audience expectations. Negotiations commonly precede the writing of a contract, although a draft of a contract or proposal may be used during the discussion. Face-to-face, one-on-one meetings allow for the expression of any dissent or concern *before* the official meeting.

Such meetings are essential in companies where consensus is highly valued and open conflict during group meetings is suppressed. Some national cultures, such as the Japanese, value consensus and dislike confrontation; therefore small face-to-face meetings are very common. This process allows formal group meetings in Japan to be short and ritualistic, a rubber-stamping of an agreement reached before the meeting began. In contrast, certain other national cultures are famous for flamboyant disagreements and dramatic meetings. You must use the cues of the corporate and national culture to consider what kinds of events will be suitable.

Group Meeting   The usefulness of a group meeting, in comparison with other events, varies from company to company. In a formal, hierarchical culture, the person with the greatest power will dominate the meeting. In an informal, egalitarian culture, a meeting may be the best place to share expertise, develop a common definition of the problem, and generate many options for solving it.

Electronic Conferencing   When delays must be minimized and face-to-face contact is impossible, an electronic conference may be a good choice. Telephone conferencing, video teleconferencing, and computer conferencing are all possible options, discussed in more detail in Chapter 7.

Going through Superiors   In some organizations, only people of a particular rank can make certain decisions or negotiate certain issues. Therefore, if the scenario requires people of a higher rank, involve your superiors in solving the problem.

Sometimes you must evaluate the social processes of your company's typical scenarios. If decisions have traditionally been handled by circulating a written proposal but your particular proposal is controversial or sensitive, a meeting where people can express their feelings and concerns might be valuable. If you are proposing the purchase of a new piece of equipment, an oral presentation where you can demonstrate the equipment in action might be more persuasive.

If the meetings you hold seem ineffective because people cannot absorb all the information and come to a consensus, would circulating a memorandum or summary of the issues before the meeting move things along? If people have taken some aspect of their work (perhaps involvement in community affairs) too lightly, would scheduling a formal presentation or special event change people's attitudes? Would involving additional people improve implementation of your plan or solution? Envisioning possible social processes is always a good idea; although you may rarely make changes in the scenario, remember that people love a little variety.

Select a Medium and Choose Visual Aids

The medium of communication itself has the ability to persuade. The medium is therefore part of your persuasive approach as well as your communication strategy. People hold definite attitudes about different media. Some hate talking on the telephone; others delight in receiving letters. Before you assume that you must use the same medium of communication typically used in a particular scenario, take a moment to consider whether a change of media would accomplish your purpose more effectively for a particular audience. A conference call may be superior to a circulated memorandum because it allows people to ask questions and develop a sense of group commitment. The budget limits and the availability of people also will influence your choice of media.

Choose a medium and visual aids that make your most important points easy to grasp and easy to remember.

Because seeing is believing, graphics or visual aids can affect your persuasiveness. Sometimes something as simple as color, graphic aids, or sound effects can turn a humdrum presentation into a satisfying experience. For example, a management consultant who stresses prioritizing and planning uses two identical square plastic containers as visual aids to convince managers to complete the high-priority items first. The first container is about two-thirds full of rice, dried peas, and beans, which represent the easy, low-priority tasks. The second container is about two-thirds full of walnuts, which represent the difficult tasks people would rather avoid or delay. If the easy tasks are completed first, too little space remains to pile in all the walnuts (difficult tasks). However, if the difficult, high-priority tasks are completed first, the low-priority tasks can be poured on top of the walnuts and both kinds of items can be held in the same container. This visual analogy is highly persuasive. A visual aid can not only persuade, it can increase the memorability of an idea. Graphics for presentations and reports are discussed in Chapter 15.

In the presentation project for the technology conference discussed earlier, Mark decided to develop a slide presentation, and he arranged for computing equipment and a monitor projector in the presentation room, so that people could see some robotics simulations and even try them later. As he gave the presentation (four times), he was able to adjust his delivery and content based on the reactions of his audience. Mark's choices of media were closely linked to his persuasive approach and the results he wanted.

In your own situations, you will need to consider how media are related to your objectives. A formal printed announcement has a different impact than a memo tacked on a bulletin board; a videotape or computer graphics can make an unobservable process explicit and interesting; laser-printed documents have different aesthetic properties than dot-matrix printing. "I know the minute I touch the paper whether something belongs in my life," one executive remarked. While this claim is probably an exaggeration, your audiences will notice the quality of production in any medium. Moreover, they will judge you by the medium you use. In the Executives' Perspectives section (Part 6), June Holly discusses how the quality of the brochures and advertisements used in promoting the first season of the Da Camera Society's concerts affected the public's perceptions of the group.

The Strategy Planner Form (Figure 4-7) will help you to incorporate all the elements of a successful strategy into your communications. The strategy planner not only allows you to analyze uncertainties, it encourages you to think through the scenario and come to terms in advance with possible outcomes of your plan. Specifying the minimum acceptable outcome as well as the desired outcome will help you design a strategy that will lead at least to the minimum acceptable result. Thinking beforehand about how to measure and test the success of the communication will prevent rationalizing afterward. Figures 4-8 and 4-9 present completed strategy planners for Mark, the technical manager giving the robotics presentation, and Elaine, who needed to prepare the stock valuation report for the divorce trial. The next chapter will present specific techniques to help you formulate organizing patterns and evaluation criteria for your communications.

Event		Date Time	
		Audience Issues: Uncertainties	
Location			
Contact:			
Primary Audiences			
Secondary Audiences		Comprehensive Purpose	
Transmitting Audiences			
Preferred Response		Lowest Acceptable Response	
Persuasive Strategy			
Organizing pattern: fulfill purpose, answer questions, create emphasis			
Media and Channels			
Visual Aids			
Criteria for Evaluation			

FIGURE 4-7.   Strategy Planner

Event	Conference on Industrial Computer Technology	Date Feb. 2-5 Time 11: Am each day	
Location	Boston Convention Center	**Audience Issues: Uncertainties** 1º. Costs, effectiveness, new developments	
Contact:	Marsha Williams	2°. potential for new customers and increased prestige	
Primary Audiences Oil & Gas firms, High-Tech companies			
Secondary Audiences My boss, his boss, my department		**Comprehensive Purpose** Demonstrate superiority of robotics, explain how the technology works, attract 4 new clients.	
Transmitting Audiences Marsha Williams, conference planner			
Preferred Response 4 new projects for our department		**Lowest Acceptable Response** Inquiries from 6 potential clients	

Persuasive Strategy Highlight problems audience currently deals with that can be eliminated by the use of robotics.

Organizing pattern: fulfill purpose, answer questions, create emphasis 1. Gain attention by highlighting human and economic costs of refinery accident near ship Channel 2. Preview benefits of learning about robotics.
3. Present benefits 4. Demonstrate product
  a) cost savings   (video, then computer simulation)
  b) time savings
  c) safety

Media and Channels slide presentation, video demonstration of robotics applications, hands-on demonstration.

Visual Aids 35 mm slides
video
computer simulation of robotics in action

Criteria for Evaluation Responses of my department members to practice sessions, comments and evaluation forms from audience members, projects generated as a result of the presentation

FIGURE 4-8. Strategy Planner for Mark's Robotics Presentation

Event	Divorce trial preliminary review	Date *Meeting Thursday* Time *10:00 am*
		Audience Issues: Uncertainties
Location	County Courthouse	Judge & lawyers: is value of stock well justified?
Contact:	Corp. finance department conference room	Mr. K's lawyer: is this the lowest justifiable price?
Primary Audiences	Husband's lawyer; Wife's lawyer; judge	Mrs. K's lawyer: can this price be increased? Is this writer biased? Does this report meet professional standards?
Secondary Audiences	Mr. & Mrs. K, other corporate finance juniors	**Comprehensive Purpose** To write an unbiased, professionally sound valuation argument whose conclusions can be defended
Transmitting Audiences	Senior members of the corporate finance department	successfully in court, bringing credit to my firm.
Preferred Response	Wife's lawyers accept valuation without contesting it.	**Lowest Acceptable Response** Report can be successfully defended during the divorce proceedings

Persuasive Strategy

Follow legal standards and use stock prices of comparable companies to derive stock price and justify its reasonableness. Expertise & fairness.

Organizing pattern: fulfill purpose, answer questions, create emphasis ← Contents to be covered
Review of pertinent legal code
Summary of financial information about the Terhune Tribune
Justification of companies selected as comparable
Analysis of comparable companies' stock prices
Application to Terhune Tribune stock value
Conclusions

Media and Channels Word-processed draft for "Roast 'n Toast."
Final bound copies for lawyers.
Oral discussion in "Roast."

Visual Aids Large poster exhibits for court of comparable stock prices.

Criteria for Evaluation Court allows decision to stand.
Senior Members' standards are met.

FIGURE 4-9.   Strategy Planner for Elaine's Stock Valuation Report

❑ COMMUNICATION CHALLENGES

PRELIMINARY EXERCISE 1   Examine a business letter, memorandum, or advertising circular that you have received in the last month. Were you the primary decision maker or a secondary audience for the document? Make a photocopy of the document so you can make marginal notes. What seems to have been the comprehensive purpose of this document? Circle the sentence or clause that expresses this purpose. Was the statement explicit enough for you to understand the purpose clearly, or was the document rather ambiguous? Were any potential readers' needs omitted from this purpose? Did you wonder why the writer expected you to read the document?

What is the persuasive strategy of the document? Note in the margins why you think so. What are the bases of the appeal? How is the writer trying to persuade you? What transaction is the writer trying to influence? At the bottom of the page, describe the scenario into which this document fits.

PRELIMINARY EXERCISE 2   You wish to replace one of the required courses in your major with another course that would be directly related to your career goals. Select such a course. Plan an approach for persuading the person who must approve this curriculum change. What social process will you use? What medium? How can you make the most of your personal effectiveness? *Fill out a strategy planner.*

THE STROHMEYER MANUFACTURING CASE

Strohmeyer Manufacturing Company produces gasoline-powered appliances: lawnmowers, riding mowers, rotary tillers for gardens, small riding vehicles, a full range of construction tools, and similar products. Founded in 1957, the company has remained a mid-sized manufacturing firm with plants in four states. The firm is privately owned and the Strohmeyer family members hold a variety of positions. Earl Strohmeyer, the head of the company, likes to involve his children, nieces and nephews, and their spouses in the company, but he believes in the merit system. As a result, some family members hold positions of power, but many high-level positions are held by people outside the family who came up through the ranks.

Two years ago, the family of a former employee, Bertie Wilson, filed suit against the company. The employee died of lung cancer, and the complaint charges Strohmeyer Manufacturing Company with having provided a hazardous work environment. The employee's family alleges that Wilson, a nonsmoker, was forced to inhale the fumes of fellow workers' cigarettes in the small supervisors' office near the assembly line. The room overlooking the large assembly area was heated but not air conditioned, and contained three occupants and their desks in a small space (15 feet by 20 feet square).

You work in the Human Resources Department as the Assistant Manager. Since the suit was filed, the company has undertaken a major study of workplace safety, applying Occupational Safety and Health Administration (OSHA) standards to conditions in all its plants. Your responsibility over the past fourteen months has been to chair the task force reviewing plant safety.

The Surgeon General's report declaring smoking to be addictive (May 1988) and Japanese studies showing smokers' families are at higher risk of lung cancer than nonsmokers' families have convinced Mr. Strohmeyer that smoking on company property must be limited. He is a determined man and used to having his commands obeyed. His solution is to permit smoking within private offices (occupied by one person), but to banish smoking in common areas.

You realize, however, that implementing such a policy would cause a rebellion. Union negotiations will open in less than six months, and a survey of union workers showed that a majority smoke and object to being unable to smoke at work. The union has contended in a New York case that the private office rule is discriminatory, since very few union workers have private offices and since the majority of private office holders are white. Most of the union employees are minorities (Hispanic in the New Mexico plants, Cuban in the Florida plant, and black in the Georgia plant). Announcing Mr. Strohmeyer's plan as a company policy will cause negative repercussions when negotiations begin.

In a series of plant trips you have met with the union chiefs at each plant to discuss possible ways of making the plant safe, especially for non-smokers, without creating undue resentment. In the New Mexico plants, rooms near the assembly lines that were originally part of the training area have been identified as convenient smoking areas. Both are large enough to be partitioned so that a smoking lounge and a nonsmoking lounge can be created. Originally, these rooms were used as classrooms to teach English to workers who did not speak it, but remodeling can turn them into attractive rest areas. Training programs in English as a second language are now conducted at other facilities near the plants. (See Figure 4-10.)

The problems in the Florida plant and the Georgia plant are less easily solved. There are no large spaces that can be turned into lounges at either location. A lounge two blocks away, across a parking lot, or in another building would not be

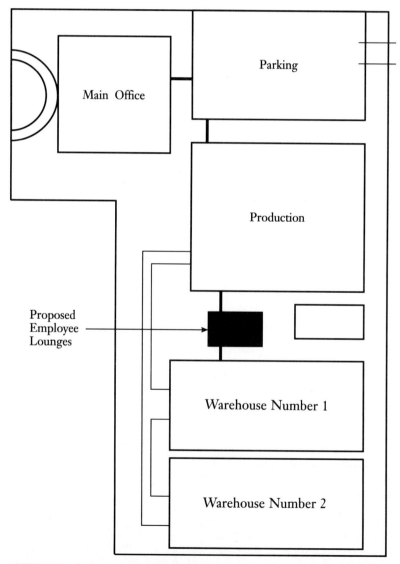

FIGURE 4-10. Strohmeyer's Florida Plant Site

used. Alternative ventilation systems have been investigated; new partitions and "smokers' shifts" have been discussed. Nothing seems likely to work. Mr. Strohmeyer, however, insists that action be taken: "I can do nothing about the past. We will have to accept the judgment we get in court, although we have hired the best attorneys we can find to defend us. Nonetheless, I do not intend to harm any other innocent employee. I myself do not smoke. It's just a lack of will that causes employees to persist. It will do them good to have an environment in which their weakness will not be tolerated."

One possibility for the Georgia plant has occurred to you. Although in all the other plants the Quality Control and Publications departments are located in the headquarters building, in the Georgia plant these two large departments have remained in the manufacturing building. Mr. Strohmeyer's niece, Rhoda Strohmeyer, is head of publications and works with an advertising agency. The Public Relations Department, on the other hand, is located in the new headquarters building, and it has space to accommodate several additional staff members and their equipment.

If publications were merged with the Public Relations Department, the old publications office in the Georgia plant would be available for remodeling into two large employee lounges.

One question remains: Who would head the consolidated department?

In Florida, an addition will have to be made to the building to provide a lounge immediately adjacent to the assembly lines. You have identified an area between the production building and Warehouse Number 1 where a connecting structure could be built.

STROHMEYER CASE, EXERCISE 1

Plan a communication strategy to persuade Mr. Strohmeyer. You intend to convince him that adding a low-cost building for smokers' and nonsmokers' lounges in the Florida plant will be in his interest. Union unrest and discrimination charges would be bad for the company in several ways. Will you seek a meeting, or will you give your explanation in a letter? Who will be your intermediate audience? Your secondary audiences? *Complete a strategy planner for these audiences.*

STROHMEYER CASE, EXERCISE 2

Plan a communication strategy for a meeting with your boss, Mercuria Marden, Manager of Human Resources, about your idea for the Georgia plant. Is moving the Publications Department into the headquarters feasible? *Prepare a flexible agenda for your discussion.*

IF YOU WOULD LIKE TO READ MORE

Cooper, L. (1932). *The rhetoric of Aristotle: An expanded translation with supplementary examples for studies of composition and public speaking.* New York: Appleton-Century-Crofts.

Fisher, R., & Ury, W. (1981). *Getting to YES: Negotiating agreement without giving in.* New York: Viking Penguin.

French, J. R. P., & Raven, B. (1959). The bases of social power. In D. Cartwright (Ed.), *Studies in social power* (pp. 150–167). Ann Arbor, MI: University of Michigan Institute for Social Research.

Gilsdorf, J. W. (1986). Executives' and academics' perceptions on the need for instruction in written persuasion. *The Journal of Business Communication, 23*(4), 55–68.

Kenton, S. B. Speaker credibility in persuasive business communication: A model which explains gender differences. *Journal of Business Communication, 26,* 159–176.

McCroskey, J. C., & Young, T. J. (1981). Ethos and credibility: The construct and its measurement after three decades. *Central States Speech Journal, 32,* 24–34.

Shelby, A. N. (1986). The theoretical bases of persuasion: A critical introduction. *Journal of Business Communication, 23*(1), 5–30.

Smith, M. J. (1982). *Persuasion and human action: A review and critique of social influence theories.* Belmont, CA: Wadsworth.

Young, R. (1982). Concepts of art and the teaching of writing. In *The rhetorical tradition and modern writing* (pp. 130–141). New York: Modern Language Association.

NOTES

1. R. Young, "Concepts of art and the teaching of writing," in *The rhetorical tradition and modern writing.* New York: Modern Language Association (1982), 130–141.

2. L. Flower, "The construction of purpose in reading and writing." *College English, 50* (1988), 528–550.

3. A. N. Shelby, "The theoretical bases of persuasion: A critical introduction." *Journal of Business Communication, 23* (1986)1, 6.

4. M. J. Smith, *Persuasion and human action: A review and critique of social influence theories.* Belmont, CA: Wadsworth (1982), 150–151.

5. R. Ailes, *You are the message: secrets of the master communicators.* Homewood, IL: Dow Jones-Irwin (1988).

6. S. B. Kenton, "Speaker credibility in persuasive business communication: A model which explains gender differences." *Journal of Business Communication, 26* (1989), 155.

CREATING SUCCESSFUL COMMUNICATION STRATEGIES: IDENTIFYING AND ORGANIZING ISSUES

OBJECTIVES

This chapter will help you

- generate relevant content
- organize information to meet audience needs
- set criteria for evaluating your success

PREVIEW

An effective strategy includes an analysis of the audience, a comprehensive purpose, a persuasive approach, a productive social process, appropriate media, relevant content organized into issues, and criteria for evaluating the success of your communication. This chapter focuses on the last two parts of a communication strategy.

Once you have developed a comprehensive purpose and chosen a persuasive strategy, you must select relevant content and organize it appropriately. Because your needs will vary from situation to situation, this chapter suggests several ways of completing an appropriate communication strategy. It includes some new techniques that can help you discover what you know and how you feel about a particular situation, and it recommends some traditional techniques of invention and arrangement that you will find especially useful when you already possess ample information and ideas for a given scenario.

Just as the most successful companies demonstrate a continuing commitment to quality products, you—as a writer or speaker—must maintain your own quality controls. Unless you plan how you will obtain feedback and compare it with criteria chosen in advance, you will find it easy to rationalize the outcome, justifying whatever results occur. Also you need to develop your own sense of your abilities and your own criteria for performance, so you will not be at the mercy of instructors and supervisors. Keeping records can provide valuable evidence, both of your effort and your progress, when performance evaluations are conducted.

ACHIEVING YOUR PURPOSE AND IMPLEMENTING A PERSUASIVE STRATEGY

If staring at a blank page (classic writer's block) is among your nightmares, you will be glad to know that there are many techniques to help you at that crucial moment when you must turn from analyzing to creating your message. The techniques for generating ideas, organizing them, and implementing your strategy are active, creative, and rewarding. Having experience in using these techniques is like knowing you have a friend or a ride home—a way to accomplish your goals.

One aspect of "blank page terror" is the sense that something should have happened before you sat down to fill the page, and that instinct is right. Too many people think of "communicating" as what happens when you begin typing or stand up and walk to the podium. Nothing could be further from the truth. Communication begins long before you begin speaking or writing the words. Some of the crucial knowledge exists long before the communication event: in your understanding of the company, its situations, and your relationships with audiences. Other crucial knowledge comes from exploring your own ideas and shaping them to accomplish your purposes. This chapter is about that exciting, creative part of the communication process.

Use Creative Techniques to Identify and Organize Issues

Choose creative techniques that fit your situation.

Different creative techniques can help you in different ways. Mind mapping or puzzle solving helps you discover ideas about your subject. If you already have a great deal of information, you may want to use a technique that helps you relate your information immediately to your audiences' goals and needs: filling in the blanks, coding, or issue trees.

This section presents a range of creative techniques that focus on

1. The subject
2. Audience questions and feelings
3. Logic and professional arguments and genres

Techniques That Focus on the Subject: Mind Mapping and Puzzle Solving

Mind mapping and puzzle solving help you discover ideas and their connections.

Two approaches, *mind mapping* and *puzzle solving*, are especially effective for capturing accumulated information and identifying relationships among items. You will be able to apply these techniques in virtually every writing situation you encounter. You will almost certainly want to apply them when you complete the exercises in this book's "Job Search" and "Marketing Communications" chapters (19 and 20).

Mind Mapping The technique of mind mapping (also known as "clustering," "bubbling," or "webbing") shows you what you think. It is especially useful for recalling interview data, ideas from multiple sources, or ideas that have been stored away over a long period of time and that are not immediately available in your memory. Even when you are dealing with routine information, mind mapping can help you decide upon the key issues you need to emphasize within a given scenario.

Mind mapping side-steps many obstacles to creative thinking.

Mind mapping helps you to expand beyond the limits of professional training because it enables you to use both sides of your brain—not just the linear, left-brain function that handles outlining and technical detail, but also the creative right side. You write down everything that pops into your head; thus, wild ideas are encouraged and many ideas are likely to emerge. You withhold judgment, evaluating the ideas later. You are free to be at your most creative, to discover how much you know, and find out what you really think about the topic at hand.

To create a map, take a large piece of paper, write the central issue in the middle of it, and draw a circle around that issue. Then write down the next thing that pops into your head, circle it, and so on. Some people like to draw lines between the circles as they create the map. Others prefer to wait until the map is complete and then draw lines to connect related issues and specific details. The key is to plop ideas out randomly, not as a list or an outline. Mind mapping should allow you to see your thoughts on paper, in a specific and creative form, *before* you impose any linear organization upon them. See Figure 5-1 for an example of a mind map.

In addition to helping you see what you think, mind mapping can help you to eliminate the unnecessary background and get straight to what your reader needs to know. The sample mind map shown in Figure 5-1 presents the thoughts of an office manager planning the introduction to a no-smoking policy statement. After mapping her ideas about the issues, she can eliminate unnecessary background that would bore her readers, then look for the angle that will get their attention in the most positive light. The entire process can take less than ten minutes, but can save an hour of false starts and rewriting later on.

After the map is made, you can organize your ideas.

1. Code groups of ideas that are related to your goals, to the audience's goals, or to the organization's goals.
2. Code ideas that are related to specific issues.
3. Look for ideas that suggest feasible solutions to problems.
4. Identify any new topics or possibilities about which you need additional information.
5. Imagine how your audience's mind map would look, in order to compare your audience's views with your own.
6. Mark out or throw away the unusable ideas.
7. Apply either or both of the next two techniques, puzzle solving or issue tree analysis, to structure the ideas.

FIGURE 5-1. **Mind Mapping the Introduction to a No-Smoking Policy**

Puzzle solving helps you identify missing pieces and see the "fit" among items of information.

Puzzle Solving   The "jigsaw puzzle" technique is particularly useful in technical situations, when the information you need is already recorded in a data base, in lab reports, in survey reports, on a mind map, or elsewhere. It is a method for transforming detailed information into a congruent, purposeful unit. The term *puzzle solving* implies that there is an implicit picture in your data, an interpretation that you must find and convey. Having gathered all your data—the puzzle pieces—you need to establish a clear sense of direction that leads inevitably to the final picture. What picture does your audience seek? You will save time if you imagine this shape before you begin to piece the puzzle together. Are you dealing with problems and solutions, with steps in a process, or with a hierarchical situation? Having a clear image in mind is like seeing the picture on the jigsaw puzzle box—it gives you a vision of your ultimate goal.

One way to arrive at that final picture is to begin with your audience's questions, then go through your data and record the answers to those key questions. If you do not know what your audience's questions are, you can use your data review to decide upon the key issues. Write each key issue (or the answer to each question) as a short sentence, preferably with an active verb. Using the nosmoking mind map, for example, you might decide to focus on the lower right quadrant. You would then write:

- Smoking infringes upon the rights of others.
- A nonsmoking office environment will increase our productivity and profits.
- A nonsmoking environment ensures cleaner air and a healthier working environment.

You can write each sentence on a separate index card (color-coded to facilitate adding and organizing details later on), or you might enter each sentence in your computer's outlining program or on a separate page in your word processor. The next step is to look for the picture in the key ideas. Do you have a cause/effect relationship, are you making comparisons, is there a geographical order to your data, or will a simple hierarchy work best?

Because each key issue is recorded separately, you are free to regroup your ideas to achieve the most useful organization. If you are writing a lengthy report, you probably will have a great deal of detailed information to back up your key issues. At this point, therefore, you must group the details under your main topics and arrange them in logical order. Again, you can use colored index cards (a separate card for each detail), your outlining program, or your word processor. When certain details don't seem to fit your main issues, it can mean one of two things: Either the detail is unnecessary and you can discard it, or you haven't identified all the key issues and you need to reevaluate your picture. If one key issue lacks adequate supporting details, or if one of the key issues has much more support than any of the other issues, your final picture will be out of proportion. Again, you should reevaluate the key issues. Perhaps you need to find more support for an issue, eliminate an issue, combine minor issues, or divide a major issue into component parts.

No doubt you have learned how to prepare a formal outline of topics and details, but if you have already organized your key issues and added support for each of them, you can probably skip the formal outline. At this point, you will only need to add transitions and edit for sentence structure, style, and grammar. The following section will present some alternatives to the standard outline that you can apply to other writing situations.

Techniques to Address Audience Questions and Feelings:
Filling in the Blanks, Issue Trees, and Coding

"Filling in the blanks" helps you follow the reader's guidance.

Filling in the Blanks You may already be familiar with "boiler plate" memos, form letters, and standard formats for reports. When used with discretion and not abused, these old standbys offer valuable shortcuts. They are suited to routine scenarios in which audience, purpose, structure, and media are predetermined. The problem with standardized formats is that they tend to be organized around the needs of the writer or, at best, around the needs of a stereotypical reader. Efficient fill-in-the-blanks writing is organized around the needs of your particular, *individual* reader.

Consider, for example, this correspondence between a manager in a title company (Mary) and a loan officer in a bank (John).

Jones Title Company
441 Copper Canyon Drive
Oakwood, CA 91505

November 22, 1991

John Baker, Loan Dept.
First National Bank
100 S. Elm St.
Oakwood, CA 91505

Dear John:

Before we can complete the follow-up documentation on the title policy for Allen Baker (Loan number 123456), I will need a copy of the deed of trust with the revisions you require. Please note your changes in red ink on the original deed of trust.

As soon as we have incorporated your changes into the original, I will send a copy for your approval.

The closing is scheduled for January 24, 1992, so we need to receive your revisions by January 14.

Sincerely,

Mary Adams
Manager

This is a standard scenario; therefore, John chooses a simple communication strategy. His purpose is to comply with Mary's request and to be open to any further communications that would facilitate her work. The issues can be organized as Mary's letter has presented them, filling in the "blanks" she has created. With this strategy, John can quickly organize his response as follows:

Introduction: State that his revisions are enclosed.

Body: Tell how he's complied with her suggestions:
"I've marked the insertion points with red ink and attached a typewritten version of the exact wording we require for each insertion. Deletions and brief changes in wording are noted in red ink on your original."

Mention that his revisions should reach her ahead of schedule, and maintain open communications by inviting questions.

Conclusion: Stress action by saying that he looks forward to receiving a copy of the revised original.

As a general organizing principle, filling in the blanks works as well when you respond to a lengthy Request For Proposal (RFP) as it does when you write a one-page letter. Address your reader's concerns in the order your reader has expressed them.

Issue trees organize information needs *in a hierarchy and help you meet them.*

Issue Trees   When you lack the luxury of responding to your reader's written request, you will need another means of focusing on the major issues and organizing them to maintain your audience's interest. Several of the techniques you can use are discussed and illustrated with examples from a sales situation. The situation involves Al Gomez, national sales manager for International Motor Company (IMC), who must inform the dealers about a price increase for 1992 Sunrizer models.

Al Gomez already has created a comprehensive goal for the letter's readers:

Action: Dealers will change prices on these models and participate in the sales campaigns.

Information: Dealers will know what the changes are and understand why they had to be made.

Feelings and beliefs: Dealers will understand that we have their best interests in mind, that we are supporting them, and that we appreciate their continued success with the Sunrizer.

He must now analyze his audiences to determine the key issues surrounding the price increase (*from their perspective*), the major subissues, and how his message should be adapted. One way of structuring this analysis is an issue tree.

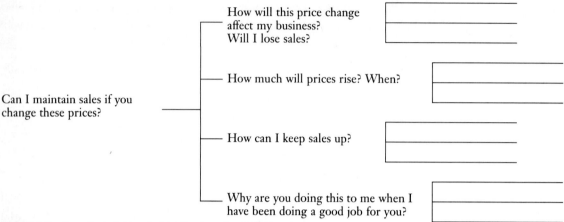

FIGURE 5-2. Issue Analysis Tree: Dealers' Questions about Price Increase

The answers to the dealers' key questions would then appear in the introduction, and individual elements would be developed more fully in subsequent paragraphs. The answers to each subordinate question can become topic sentences. In a longer document, the key issues would become the major headings and subheadings; the answers to subordinate questions would be developed from supporting detail.

Coding creates order without imposing restraints during idea generation.

Coding to Address Audience Needs   You can also explore what you know and determine what you think about an issue through a technique known as "freewriting" or "stream-of-consciousness." If you sometimes fear that you must capture your thoughts in complete phrases or lose them, freewriting presents an alternative to mind mapping. This nonstop method of drafting allows you to get started without previous organizing. Afterward, you can use coding to select information useful to your audience.

Although this method is more time-consuming than mind mapping, it presents another alternative if you seem to suffer "blank page paralysis" during a particular project. If Al Gomez had encountered a mental block in trying to organize the key issues and details surrounding the Sunrizer price increase, he might have formulated the following freewriting draft.

FREEWRITING DRAFT

We have been watching the production costs closely for several months, and they keep going up. The costs of the parts we're using from Japan, Germany, and other European countries have risen over 8% in the past year. Although the labor costs are lower than they would be if the parts were made here in the U.S., the continued fall of the U.S. dollar against the currencies of these countries has caused parts prices to rise. We want the joint venture with DGM Group of South Korea to do well, but we can't sell these vehicles at a loss. We finally had to face up to raising prices. We've given a lot of thought to the way that the Sunrizer has been selling this year, and we're very grateful to all of you dealers for moving so much inventory. It still means that we've got to raise the base price for 1992 Sunrizer models. The SE Sedan will increase 7.1%, or $600, to $9050. The basic Sedan will rise 2.8%, or $224, to $8224. The average increase across the models will be 4.9%, or about $400. This price change will go into effect on January 1, 1992. To offset possible impact on our dealers, we will begin a national advertising campaign for the Sunrizer the third week in February. The campaign will run through the end of March. This will be a comprehensive campaign, with flights of ads scheduled in all major metropolitan newspapers and commercials on two national television networks. You will soon receive more information on this campaign from your regional marketing supervisor. We regret that we must raise prices, and we intend to support your sales efforts. You must change prices on January 1, 1992. Mickey Tallefaro will also send you materials for a year-end "buy before the price change" sales promotion. We have a newspaper insertion that state dealers' associations can sponsor jointly. We hope to maintain both your profits and IMC's with the Sunrizer.

This "freewriting draft" is chronologically organized. Al Gomez first writes about his own experience—keeping track of production costs. Next he deals with the response to rising production costs—the price increase. Only then does he deal with the marketing campaigns for maintaining sales despite the price hike. Interspersed throughout the draft, however, are comments that show Al is thinking about his audience's response to the higher dealer price.

While freewriting is a powerful tool for delivering what your memory has stored, it is usually egocentric, focusing on issues of greatest concern to the writer and presenting them in a chronology that makes sense only to the writer. Using a system of codes, however, you can quickly assign a meaningful organization to the document, identifying the elements according to the audience's interests and needs. To produce an appropriately organized document, Al Gomez could

1. List reader's questions or concerns.
2. Code similar ideas with colors or symbols that correspond to the readers' concerns.
3. Group similar colors or symbols together into paragraphs.
4. Give the paragraphs and the letter itself a useful order.

The first paragraph should describe what the situation is, what the key message is, and what the reader must do. The most useful order for the body answers the reader's questions, beginning with the most important one. Upon learning about the price change, the dealers probably would ask the following questions:

1. How will this price change affect my business? Will I lose sales?
2. Just how much are you raising prices and when will this happen?
3. How am I going to keep sales up?
4. Why are you doing this to me when I've been doing a good job for you?

The numbers from this list of questions, plus "X" for irrelevant, can be used to code the content of each sentence:

CODED VERSION OF FREEWRITING DRAFT

④We have been watching the production costs closely for several months, and they keep going up. ④The costs of the parts we're using from Japan, Germany, and other European countries have risen over 8% in the past year. ⊗Although the labor costs are lower than they would be if the parts were made here in the U.S., ④the continued fall of the U.S. dollar against the currencies of these countries has caused parts prices to rise. ⊗We want the joint venture with DGM Group of South Korea to do well, but we can't sell these vehicles at a loss. ⊗We finally had to face up to raising prices. ⊗We've given a lot of thought to the way that the Sunrizer has been selling this year, and ① we're very grateful to all of you dealers for moving so much inventory. ②It still means that we've got to raise the base price for 1992 Sunrizer models. ②The SE Sedan will increase 7.1%, or $600, to $9050. ②The basic Sedan will rise 2.8%, or $224, to $8224. ②The average increase across the various models will be 4.9%, or about $400. ②This price change will go into effect on Monday, January 1, 1992. ③To offset possible impact on our dealers, we will begin a national advertising campaign for the Sunrizer the third week in February. ③The campaign will run through the end of March. ③This will be a comprehensive campaign, with flights of ads scheduled in all major metropolitan newspapers and commercials on two national television networks. ③You will soon receive more information on this campaign from your regional marketing supervisor. ③We regret that we must raise prices, ①and we intend to support your sales efforts. ②You must change prices on January 1, 1992. ③Mickey Tallefaro will also send you materials for a year-end "buy before the price change" sales promotion. ③We have a newspaper insertion that state dealers' associations can sponsor jointly. ①We hope to maintain both your profits and IMC's with the Sunrizer.

Coding works well with freewriting or discovery drafts.

Electronic Coding   When a project involves revising a document (for example, editing an employee handbook or reorganizing a training manual), the best and quickest method is a system of codes. If you are working with a computer, you can insert symbols into the text that a Search or Find command can identify later. Some software programs feature electronic "buttons" that mark and sort information, images, and phrases. Even with a basic word processing program, you can insert seldom-used symbols such as @, $, or § in your text as flags. When you reorganize, you can find flags using the "search" command. If Al Gomez had done his brainstorming at the keyboard, he could reorganize using % = price increases, @ = cost increases, # = marketing campaigns, $ = dealer support information. He would then type @ at the beginning of each sentence that described cost increases. Some word processing programs and personal computers now have accessories that allow you to use these techniques to organize and (if necessary) reorganize your document while you are in the planning stages. Later, you can delete all the symbols, leaving clean copy. More information about these techniques can be found in the chapter on the technological context for communication.

Color Coding   If you are working with hard copy, you will find that color coding is handy. Gather several colored pens, then color-code passages that deal with a single idea or topic. Color coding can also be particularly useful for revising documents that have been dictated. After color coding, group the coded segments and give the segments a logical order.

Techniques That Focus on Professional Argument Structures and Document Types (Genres)

All professional disciplines, such as accounting, strategic planning, law, economics, and marketing, have methods of analysis and reasoning that set them apart from other fields. Lawyers have procedures for discovery; strategic planners isolate decision factors and apply models of industry competition; marketing researchers use conjoint analysis; finance professionals evaluate risk and reward. If your audience is trained to follow the logic or argument structure of a particular specialty, that structure may provide an organizing pattern for your communication strategy. If your audience does not share your background, adapt your pattern of logic to your audience's perspective; interpret the conclusions in light of the organization's problem, and, wherever possible, present the expert findings in meaningful exhibits. You might also provide additional explanations in appendices or in another medium.

In some situations the document or presentation types (genres) are fixed, either by tradition or by law. If that is the situation you face (for example, if you are writing a contract or an environmental impact statement), the conventional organization of the document type may help you plan your communication. Several of the applications chapters explain the structure of fixed genres—financial reports, for example.

On the other hand, some established genres are not particularly helpful; they represent, instead, the staleness that too often accompanies routine communications. For example, the traditional research report contains sections usually entitled "Background," "Equipment," "Methods," "Results," "Discussion," and "Conclusions." Such titles do little or nothing to guide the writer or the readers into a meaningful discussion of issues. What should be included as background? How should results be discussed? In an academic situation, a student report on desalination might well begin with the practices of the ancient Greeks. An engineer considering desalination to provide drinking water on an offshore rig would probably limit her review to current practices.

Three frequently used written genres are the letter, memorandum, and report. Other chapters in this book discuss these types in greater detail. Although each pattern uses a different format, they all require you to answer three questions:

1. What do I want the reader to do?
2. What must the reader know in order to do this?
3. What must the reader feel or believe to do this?

The introduction usually identifies the participants (writer, readers, and sponsoring organization), the situation, and the communication purpose, letting the readers know what they are expected to do. The body paragraphs supply the detailed information and motivation for taking action. The conclusion provides specific details about carrying out the action (such as telephone numbers, places, and dates) and looks forward to the mutual benefits of the reader's having carried out the action.

Al Gomez could have turned his coded freewriting draft into a letter by filling out the Strategy Planner shown in Figure 5-3. The first paragraph explains the situation and states the central point, which answers the dealers' main questions, "How will this price change affect my business? Will I lose sales?" The next three paragraphs answer questions 2, 3, and 4, which were listed earlier ("Just how much are you raising prices and when will this happen?" "How am I going to keep sales up?" and "Why are you doing this to me when I've been doing a good job for you?"). The letter concludes with a restatement of the shared goal, which is the persuasive basis of the writer's appeal: maintaining profits.

Event	*Informing dealers about price increase*	Date Time *November 1991*	
		Audience Issues: Uncertainties *How will price change affect my business? How much will prices rise? How can I keep sales up? Why doing when I've done a good job?*	
Location	*all dealerships*		
Contact:	*Dealers*		
Primary Audiences	*Dealers*		
Secondary Audiences *None known*		**Comprehensive Purpose** *Dealers will change prices and participate in sales campaign while understanding reasons and believing we support them.*	
Transmitting Audiences *None known*			
Preferred Response *Sales continue at present or even higher rates*		Lowest Acceptable Response *Sales fall by no more than 10 percent.*	

Persuasive Strategy
Appeal to shared goals and desire for personal appreciation and logic based on situation of increased costs.

Organizing pattern: fulfill purpose, answer questions, create emphasis
Briefly answer dealers' questions in introductory paragraph and elaborate in succeeding paragraphs. Reinforce common goal in last chapter.

Media
Letter

Visual Aids
None

Criteria for Evaluation   *Evidence of positive support which regional supervisors relay about their dealers.*

FIGURE 5-3.   Strategy Planner for IMC Price Increase Letter

International Motor Company
1800 IMC Boulevard
Detroit, Michigan 48225

November 15, 1991

(inside address)

Dear (Dealership Owner's Name):

The costs of imported parts have continued to increase, driving up our production costs. To cover these costs, we must raise the base prices on all Sunrizer models, effective January 1, 1992. You have been selling Sunrizers very successfully, and we intend to support your future sales efforts with increased advertising and a special end-of-the-year promotion to ensure your continued success.

The average increase across the models will be 4.9%, or about $400. The SE Sedan model will increase 7.1%, to $9050. The Sedan model will rise 2.8%, to $8224. You should change list prices in your inventory on January 1.

To help prevent any negative impact on our dealers, we will conduct two special promotions. First, Mickey Tallefaro will send you materials for a year-end "buy before the price change" sales promotion. We have a newspaper insertion that regional dealers' associations can sponsor jointly. Second, we will begin a national advertising campaign for the Sunrizer the third week in February. The campaign will run through the end of March. This comprehensive campaign will include flights of ads scheduled in all major metropolitan newspapers and commercials on two national television networks. You will soon receive more information on this campaign from your regional marketing supervisor.

Although we regret raising prices, we had no choice. Production costs have been going up for nearly two years. The costs of the parts from Japan, Germany, and other European countries have risen over 8% because of the continued fall of the U.S. dollar against the currencies of these countries. With these price changes and our national campaigns, we hope to maintain both your profits and IMC's with the Sunrizer.

Sincerely,

Al Gomez
National Sales Manager

When Al writes for an in-house audience, he will probably choose a memorandum (memo) format, and he will present the message a little differently. The in-house nature of memos often contributes to informality. The subject of the memo is introduced in the subject line (a useful heading on letters, as well), and the readers and writer are introduced in the headings "To" and "From." A memo usually will go quickly to the point, announcing the key information and immediately supplying the most important details. In the following example, the action details are presented in the first paragraph and other details follow in a hierarchy from most to least important. Many readers do not read memos all the way to the end, so vital requests for action or details about the time or place should not be saved for last. Memos often lack a formal concluding paragraph.

SAMPLE MEMORANDUM TO MARKETING AND SALES DEPARTMENTS

November 20, 1991

TO: Marketing and Sales Department Personnel

FROM: Al Gomez
            National Sales Manager

SUBJECT: Price Increases and Sales Campaigns for 1992 Sunrizer
            Models (Sedan, SE Sedan)

On January 1, 1992, we will increase the retail prices of Sunrizer models and initiate campaigns to maintain sales levels. Since dealer sales of the Sunrizer have been high, we must work hard to help dealers continue to move these models.

Two campaigns have been developed to maintain high sales levels for these models. The first will be an "end-of-year, buy-before-the-price-change" promotion to attract price-sensitive buyers. The second, beginning January 21, will emphasize quality and engineering. You will receive campaign summaries and sample kits later this week. If you have questions about these campaigns, call Sara Malachnik at ext. 4779.

These new prices result from continuing cost increases tied to the devaluation of the dollar. The average increase across the models will be 4.9%, or about $400. The SE Sedan model will increase 7.1%, to $9050. The Sedan model will increase 2.8%, to $8224.

A full price schedule for all models and accessories is attached.

Different types of documents impose different requirements.

The memo answers different questions in a different order from the letter, beginning with the information most important to the reader and ending with the least important. Since the price schedule is attached, the reader will find it in any case.

Different document types have different degrees of flexibility. A periodic report, such as a status report or a 10K form, will have a preestablished structure and, to a large extent, standard content. The response to a Request For Proposal (RFP) must answer the needs expressed by the potential client, but the context permits a degree of creativity and it *requires* a persuasive strategy. Your invitation to appear as a keynote speaker for a local club will allow for even greater flexibility of content and structure, but you will certainly be required to work within specific time constraints. Effective business communications require a balance between the constraints of generic expectations and individual creativity.

Establish Criteria for Success

When you prepare your strategy planner (explained in Chapter 4), you need to do more than set goals—you need to establish objective criteria for judging your success. The first step is coming to terms with the minimum acceptable response to your message (the lowest level of audience reaction that would still accomplish the most important purpose of the communication). This standard must be operational; that is, it must be measurable, testable, or demonstrable. For example, your most important goal in sending a direct mail letter might be to increase market awareness of your product. How can you tell whether that awareness has increased? If, for example, the average number of unsolicited calls in a month is 20, you might set as a goal increasing the number of calls to 24, with the criterion that 4 of the 20 must be from your mailing list.

General goals make measurement hard. Create operational goals.

You may need some practice turning general goals into operational criteria. In the list below, three of the five general goals have been turned into operational criteria. What would you suggest for the other two?

Communication	General Goal	Minimum Acceptable Response
Request for information	Get prices for copiers	Receive price information on three copiers before 9/15
Announce employee B-B-Q	Create interest, generate employee attendance	_____
Proposal to client	Increase market share	Receive invitation to discuss proposal
Ad for new sales staff members	Increase number of sales representatives	_____
Compliance report to Environmental Protection Agency	Meet regulations	Obtain EPA approval

Control the quality of all your professional work, including communications.

Once you have formulated the minimum response standard, you can specify other criteria that you consider reasonable tests of your success. In addition, you should establish quality control criteria to ensure that you make a good impression and develop a positive relationship with your audience. These criteria could include standards for document appearance, slide quality, gestures and eye contact in a presentation, expressions of goodwill toward customers, and proportion of active verbs in a document. When you establish criteria in advance, you can combat the very human tendency to be satisfied with whatever results you get.

Using these criteria must be an active process. Seeking feedback and checking it against your criteria will help sharpen your communication performance. Feedback won't appear by magic; you must plan to solicit feedback. For example, you might ask a member of your audience (in advance) to watch for certain things and give you comments afterward, or you might prepare an evaluation sheet for the end of the meeting or conference. Taking this formal step will convince your audience that you care about them, their ideas, and the quality of your service to them, and will increase their perception of your goodwill as a communicator.

Your criteria and your evaluation files can help you in another way as well. You need to develop your sense of your abilities and performance so you will not be at the mercy of instructors and supervisors. Your records can provide valuable evidence, both of your effort and your progress, when performance evaluations are conducted or end-of-semester conferences with instructors are held.

❏ COMMUNICATION CHALLENGES

PRELIMINARY EXERCISE 1 *Write a paragraph describing the creative processes you like best.* How do you come up with ideas? Have you used any of the tools listed in the chapter, such as mind mapping or freewriting, previously? Do you keep a journal? Do you like to work visually or do you prefer a formal outline? What would be the most important change that would improve your creativity?

PRELIMINARY EXERCISE 2 Think of a change you've wanted to make in your college or in some organization. No doubt at some time or other you've said to yourself, "If only they'd _____, things would be a lot better around here." Suppose that you magically have been put in charge of implementing that very change. *Create a mind map exploring your own feelings and ideas about this change,* similar to the mind map on the no-smoking policy. Now, suppose you are someone

who does not want this suggestion implemented. *Create the person's mind map.* The difference between these two maps is a fair indication of the persuasive challenge you would face.

EXERCISE 1

Use the Strategy Planner form to devise a communication strategy for informing employees of the new no-smoking policy. Assume this is a local accounting firm with 26 employees. The choice of media, locations, and other variables within the plan are yours. Make your strategy realistic, viable, and appropriate to the constraints of the situation.

Event	*No-Smoking Policy Announcement*	Date Time
Location		Audience Issues: Uncertainties
Contact:	*Arch Tucker, ext 2909*	
Primary Audiences		
Secondary Audiences		Comprehensive Purpose
Transmitting Audiences		
Preferred Response		Lowest Acceptable Response

Persuasive Strategy

Organizing pattern: fulfill purpose, answer questions, create emphasis

Media

Visual Aids

Criteria for Evaluation

STRATEGY PLANNER FOR EXERCISE 1

STROHMEYER CASE (CONTINUED)

If you have not read the general case description of the Strohmeyer company in Chapter 4, go now to pages 101–103 and review the general situation of the case before completing these exercises.

EXERCISE 2, STROHMEYER CASE

In your role as Assistant Manager for Human Resources, plan a communication strategy to announce the renovation project for employee lounges at the New Mexico plant. *Use mind mapping, an issue tree, or freewriting to help you plan. Describe the scenario you expect and the document or presentation you will use.*

Complete a Strategy Planner. What audience attitudes must be addressed? How will you organize the issues? What is the lowest level of response you will consider acceptable? How will you evaluate the success of your announcement?

Write out the first paragraph of your introduction (document or speech).

EXERCISE 3, STROHMEYER CASE

A. Plan a communication for the Properties Committee. This committee, which is composed of four staff executives, is responsible for all construction, leasing, and renovation. *Prepare a strategy planner to explain the following:*

- Needs at the four plants differ.
- The Florida plant needs to hire an architect to estimate project costs for the new construction.
- No decision has yet been reached about the Georgia plant.
- The building and maintenance groups will be able to handle the minor renovations and partitioning in the New Mexico plants.

The Properties Committee will also need some background explanation because this problem has been seen as simply a policy decision.

Decide what medium or media you should use to present your information.

B. *Prepare your oral or written presentation.*

IF YOU WOULD LIKE TO READ MORE

Bruffee, K. A. (1983). Writing and reading as collaborative or social acts. In Hayes, J. N., Roth, P. A., Ramsey, J. R., & Foulke, R. D. (Eds.). *The writer's mind: Writing as a mode of thinking.* Although we often think of writing and reading as acts people do alone or independently, Bruffee shows how both our writing and reading depend on social experience.

Flower, L. (1989). *Problem-solving strategies for writing.* (3rd ed.). San Diego, CA: Harcourt Brace Jovanovich. The chapters on idea generation and analyzing one's own writing process are excellent.

Graesser, A., Hopkinson, P. L., Lewis, E., & Bruflodt, H. (1984). The impact of different information sources on idea generation: Writing off the top of our heads. *Written Communication, 1,* 341–364.

McClelland, B. W. (1984). Discovering and inventing ideas. In *Writing practice* (pp. 24–56). Longman Series in College Composition and Communication. New York: Longman. Contains a wide variety of methods to stimulate thinking processes.

PART TWO

MASTERING THE LANGUAGE OF BUSINESS

❏ CHOOSING WORDS

OBJECTIVES

Studying this chapter will help you choose appropriate words by

- appreciating the precision of English

- choosing the proper level of formality for the situation and participants

- adopting a positive tone

- using business jargon sparingly in written documents

- avoiding slang and clichés in written documents

- using nonsexist terms

PREVIEW

As you choose words, sensitivity to precision, tone, and sexist language will help you expedite transactions and manage your relationship with your audience. These considerations are especially important in preparing messages that give negative information about a transaction.

❏ ENGLISH AS A LANGUAGE FOR BUSINESS

A Heritage for Precise Usage and Complex Tone

The large number of words in English enables business writers to express precise meanings and complex connotations.

English arguably has the richest vocabulary. It contains nearly 500,000 words, compared to 185,000 in German and 100,000 in French. Because English has borrowed heavily from Latin, French, German, Spanish, Old Norse, Danish, and other languages, it contains many words with similar but not identical meanings. The wide diversity enables writers to choose words that precisely express their exact meanings. For example, a business writer might describe someone in the company by choosing among

manager (from Latin, "hand"),

executive (from Middle English and Latin, "performed"),

chief (from French and Latin, "head"),

decision (from Latin, "what is chosen or determined"); *maker* (from Old English, "do" or "construct"),

officer (from French and Latin, "one responsible for duty or work"),

division (from Latin, "part") *head* (from Old English, "head"),

leader (from Old English and German, "one who leads, guides"),

honcho (Japanese, "squad leader"), or

vice president (Latin and French, "deputy," "one who sits before and presides").

These choices denote different things about a person. A *manager* allocates resources and oversees operations. A *honcho* leads a small group to produce specific results. An *executive* executes policies. A *chief officer* is at the head of a group of executives and controls duties and activities. The term *vice president* describes a person's rank in a company.

Not only do these choices have different specific meanings (denotations), they also carry many overtones or suggestions called connotations. Literally, *connotation* means "noted or expressed together." *Honcho* is informal; *vice president* carries ideas of official status; *manager* might connote one who only manages—one who takes care of what he or she is given to do, not one who leads. The combined connotations of words in a passage reinforce one another, creating its *tone.*

English accumulated an enormous store of words because English speakers developed a philosophy of borrowing and adapting. Unlike the French, who created an intellectual academy to minimize linguistic change and decide which words are legitimate, the English accepted all words that people commonly spoke. The first great English dictionary builder, Dr. Samuel Johnson, scorned the idea of permanence in language, and claimed in the preface to his 1755 *Dictionary* that change was inevitable. Business writers today must also expect changes as English spreads to new communities around the globe.

Indeed, English is now the language of business across the world. It is used as a first or second language by over 750 million people, as the authors of the television series, *The Story of English*, report:

> The statistics of English are astonishing. . . . Three-quarters of the world's mail, and its telexes and cables, are in English. So are more than half the world's technical and scientific periodicals: it is the language of technology from Silicon Valley to Shanghai. English is the medium for 80 percent of the information stored in the world's computers. Nearly half of all business deals in Europe are conducted in English. . . . English is the official voice of the air, of the sea, and of Christianity. . . . [and] five of the largest broadcasting companies in the world.[1]

Today people learn English as a second language because it is the language of trade and technology.

Before the middle of the twentieth century, English was spread primarily as other languages have been spread in the past: by military conquest and political dominance. Today, in contrast, business, trade, and technology induce people to learn English. Its ability to link people in global markets and friendly political communities supplies dramatic momentum, although no conquerors impose it.

To become a master of English you must learn how to make choices, and that means discovering your options. All great writers have collected phrases or passages from other great writers; you should do the same. How you do that is up to you. Some people photocopy good pages and file them. Others color-code book and report pages with stick-on notes. Some writers have a personal "phrase maker" diary on their word processor and type in pleasing sentences so that they can peruse them in a second window while composing at the computer.

As you become more aware of the options available, concentrate on choosing appropriate words, making your sentences easy to read, creating coherence, and developing your own professional style. The first of these skills is discussed in this chapter. Choosing words has been separated into three functions: (1) choosing words appropriate to the scenario and the people involved, (2) maintaining a positive relationship with the reader even when you are delivering a negative message, and (3) avoiding sexist language.

CHOOSE WORDS APPROPRIATE TO THE SCENARIO AND THE PEOPLE INVOLVED

People interpret the words of a message not only according to the denotative meanings of the individual words, but according to many other kinds of mutual knowledge that the writer and readers share. This mutual knowledge encompasses similar situations, company culture, other company documents, company policies, trends in the industry, and the roles and personalities of the people involved. From a linguist's point of view, this mutual knowledge makes up specific frames of reference that apply to the communication at hand.

Frames of reference guide writers' word choices and readers' interpretations.

If you've followed the guidelines in Chapters 2 through 5, you already have made many decisions that will influence your choice of words. For example, you know whether the situation is related to a primary business activity, a maintenance matter, pressure, or agitation. You know whether the transaction is a policy decision or a transfer of information, goods, or services. You know whether the role you are playing initiates, conducts, or interprets the transaction. You know whether you are leading or responding in the situation. You have analyzed the various audiences' roles and you've pinpointed their uncertainties: the issues in the organization and the department, as well as their own personal uncertainties. You've used these analyses to create a communication strategy with a comprehensive purpose, a persuasive approach, and an organizational plan. In short, you're not starting from square one when you think about word choice.

Choose words that (1) expedite the transaction and (2) manage your relationship with your reader.

Nonetheless, the choices are not simple; you have two tasks in front of you. You must simultaneously play your role in the transaction and manage the relationship with your readers. That means you have to think about conveying content, but you also have to compete for the readers' attention, help them feel committed to your ongoing relationship, and motivate action. Fortunately you've already planned a persuasive approach, and that early decision will spark your imagination and guide many of your moment-to-moment choices.

In Chapter 4, an engineer named Mark planned a presentation on robotics for a technical conference. The transaction was an exchange of information, and his role was to conduct the presentation. His comprehensive purpose was to demonstrate and explain the technical superiority and cost effectiveness of his company's robotics application to attract new clients. In his communication strategy, Mark combined several persuasive appeals. He stressed the benefits for the audience (superior efficiency and cost effectiveness). He planned to alleviate the audience's fear of falling behind in a technical field, and he demonstrated that he could solve certain problems for his audience on the spot. He hoped that his goodwill, fairness, and expertise would also persuade them. He organized his talk by explaining two important problems in the field and demonstrating how his product could solve them. These intentions and preliminary decisions were powerful guides for word choice.

First, since the problems he chose were well-known (even chronic) problems, he believed that most of the conference participants were aware of them. He could refer to a well-publicized accident to heighten his audience's conviction that the problems could be serious and to induce some fear about not properly solving them. Although the participants were familiar with the terminology of the problem, they were not familiar with the robotics technology that Mark's company had developed. Therefore, Mark carefully included definitions of key terms about his own product. Offering definitions increased the audience's perception of Mark's expertise. He also compared functions to familiar actions, making them more memorable. For example, Mark called an automatic act of selection "cherry picking," which created images of choosing the best fruit and evoked connotations of skill and delicate handling. By asking for questions and demonstrating some solutions in front of the audience, he demonstrated his concern for their problems and his ability to solve them.

Your Choices: Level of Formality

Formal and informal terms may vary in their connotations as well as their precise meanings.

In addition to considering the audience's level of knowledge, you must consider the *degree of formality* appropriate to the situation. Your choice will depend on whether the communication is oral or written and on the company norms (standards). Furthermore, you should consider the kind of relationship you have with these readers. Is your relationship competitive, casual, friendly, or correct but cool? The words should reflect both the formality of the situation and the relationships among the participants.

Formal words convey approximately the same meanings as informal words, but their connotations are more serious and status-conscious. Formal words are often Latin or French in origin, and they are generally known by educated people. Informal words are more likely to be Old English (Anglo Saxon) in origin; the 100 most common words in English come from Old English. In the list that follows, the formal term *authorize* seems to say that the person has the power of initiation; the informal term *approve* says the person has power to decide, but seems to imply someone else may have initiated or proposed an action this person has agreed to.

FORMAL	INFORMAL	SLANG
request	ask	hit up
authorize	approve	give the go-ahead
announce	tell	put out the word
evaluate	judge	size up
inquire	ask	check it out

Your Choices: Business Jargon

Ask yourself: "Does this jargon term have the advantages of both precision and conciseness? Will *all* the readers understand what it means?" Unless you can answer yes to both, replace the term.

Business jargon consists of terms used in an unusual way that only a limited group of people know, such as "value-added products," or "economies of scale."

- *Value-added products*, unlike commodities such as wheat or rice, have been processed to increase their value to consumers.
- *Economies of scale* are cost advantages a big company has because of its size. A big company can purchase supplies at lower prices than a small company because the big company purchases very large quantities; the big company also is likely to have specialized equipment and trained personnel that can be used more efficiently than the small company's multipurpose or limited equipment.

Business jargon can serve a useful purpose—if it provides a short way of saying something and if everyone concerned understands it.

DOCUMENT SPOTLIGHT

LEVELS OF FORMALITY

A public company's annual report consists of several distinct sections that routinely follow a standard order, as explained in the chapter on financial accounting communications. An advertising agency or an in-house publications officer usually writes the management letter and the description of the company's business activities. The financial reports section is written or at least reviewed by the outside auditors.

The Quaker Oats Company's 1988 Annual Report uses approximately 1600 words to explain the activities of the U.S. Foods Group's Diversified Grocery Products and Pet Food divisions, which had acquired two other companies. This acquisition is also discussed in the footnotes of the financial reports section. The complete footnote on the acquisition takes about 150 words.

Aimed at investors and creditors, both accounts of the acquisitions are quite readable, but the words in the business activities section are generally less formal than the words of the footnote, as you can see. For example, the activities section contains informal phrases, such as "well-known national brands," actual brand names, and "is now number one . . . number two . . . and number three." This ranking statement is familiar from the Olympics and other sports contests, where winners are numbered. In contrast, the footnote phrases "value-added rice and pasta products" and "completed the acquisition of all the outstanding shares" are more formal; "value-added" can also be considered management jargon.

From the business activities description:

> Quaker's pet food products include a broad line of dog foods in addition to cat food products. . . . The Gaines acquisition added the well-known national brands of *Gravy Train* and *Cycle* dry and canned dog foods as well as *Gaines-Burgers* and *Top Choice* semi-moist dog food to the Quaker pet food line. . . . Quaker is now number one in the semi-moist category, number two in dry dog food, and number three in canned dog food.

From the footnotes of the financial reports section:

> Note 2
> Acquisitions
> Two major acquisitions were made in fiscal 1987, both in the U.S. Grocery Products group. In August 1986 the Company purchased the Golden Grain Macaroni Company, manufacturer of value-added rice and pasta products for $275 million, and during October 1986 the Company completed the acquisition of all the outstanding shares of Anderson, Clayton Co. (Anderson Clayton), manufacturer of *Gaines* pet food products and several unrelated consumer and industrial lines for $801 million. Both were accounted for as purchase transactions.

Source: *The Quaker Oats Company 1988 Annual Report.* Reprinted by permission of the Quaker Oats Company.

Your Choices: Business Clichés

A cliché is a sign that you made no conscious choice.

In contrast, a *business cliché* is tired language; it puts your readers at a distance by telling them that you could have said this to anyone. Clichés indicate boredom and a lack of creativity in the way you approach your work. Business clichés include familiar words, phrases, and clauses that can be replaced with less hackneyed equivalents.

CLICHÉS	SUBSTITUTES
acknowledge hereby receipt of yours	Thank you for your letter (or move directly to describing the situation)
are in receipt of	we received . . .
as a matter of fact	(delete, no need to replace)
at an early date	soon
due to the fact that	because
for your information	(usually unnecessary)
in due course	soon (or, if possible, on a specific date)
in regard to	about
in terms of	as
in the event that	if
in the near future	soon
meet with your approval	satisfy you, are satisfactory
please be advised that	(delete, or state the point)
prior to	before
same (referring to an earlier item; for example, "send same to this address")	this + (noun)
take this opportunity	(delete; no substitute needed)
we regret to inform	we are sorry that

Your Choices: Slang

Save slang for informal conversations.

Slang phrases are the least formal of your choices. They often combine very general terms with prepositions. Slang usually is unacceptable in a written document.

Jeannette Gilsdorf asked 120 top-level managers of Fortune 1000 companies about the use of slang and buzzwords in business. Their comments indicate how you might be perceived in their companies if you used business slang heavily. These executives were likely to label someone who used slang heavily as not being an original thinker. Although people sometimes think that using buzzwords makes them sound like insiders, these executives disagreed. Gilsdorf concluded, "Respondents felt they did not wish to see, and were not likely to use, business slang expressions in formal written reports. However, few respondents made any objection to hearing business slang in informal business discussions, and most considered themselves quite likely to use business slang in such discussions."[2]

Therefore, you should be aware that words you choose to speak in a meeting may not necessarily be perceived as appropriate for written documents. In general, you will choose appropriate words if you analyze the situation, note the kind of language used in other documents produced in similar situations, and look at the transaction from your reader's perspective.

Choose Words by Taking the Reader's Perspective

Readers should not be expected to muse over your business document or presentation, nor should they be forced to spend time deciphering long, complex words if simple ones will do just as well. When you write in business, use your vocabulary wisely.

- Replace long words with short ones that mean the same thing.
- Use concrete terms.
- Avoid technical phrases unless your readers use them in daily conversation.
- Insert definitions of unavoidable technical terms if you are writing for an audience of both specialists and nonspecialists.

According to Walter Weintz, author of *The Solid Gold Mailbox*, he doubled the circulation of *McCall's* magazine—from 4 to 8 million—by adopting the perspective of the magazine's readers when he solicited subscriptions. Key to this effort was a change in the renewal offer from "Your subscription is about to expire," to "You can have your subscription continue without interruption so long as you wish." To write from the reader's perspective, search for the aspect of the topic that interests the reader and choose words that have positive connotations for that reader.

Mr. Weintz studied his current and potential readers to determine what would motivate them to read *McCall's* magazine, to buy a subscription, and to renew that subscription. The power to have one's way and to control the arrival of the magazine was the key to renewals. Then he framed his offers in the most positive terms possible, replacing the negative word "expire."[3] To obtain a positive response, replace negative words with positive words in your drafts.

WORDS WITH NEGATIVE CONNOTATIONS

claim	misrepresented
complain	mistrust
complaint	misunderstood
dissatisfied	must
fail	neglect
failure	uncalled-for
inconvenience	unfair
misconception	unfortunately
misinformed	unreasonable
misled	unsatisfactory

DOCUMENT SPOTLIGHT

THE READER'S PERSPECTIVE

When you compare the language from the two telephone book notices, you can readily see the difference between the words that belong to the world of law and words familiar to most telephone users.

California

"California Penal Code section 384 makes it a misdemeanor for any person to willfully refuse to immediately relinquish a telephone party-line when informed that such line is needed for an emergency call to a fire department or police department or for medical aid or ambulance service. Also, any person who shall secure the use of a telephone party-line by falsely stating that such line is needed for an emergency call, shall be guilty of a misdemeanor."

New York

"New York State law requires you to hang up the receiver of a party line telephone immediately when told the line is needed for an emergency call to a fire department or police department or for medical aid or ambulance. It is unlawful to take over a party line by stating falsely that the line is needed for an emergency."

CALIFORNIA	NEW YORK
California Penal Code Section 384 makes it a misdemeanor	New York state law requires
for any person who	you
shall willfully refuse to immediately relinquish a telephone party line	to hang up the receiver of a party line telephone immediately
when informed that such line . . .	when told the line . . .

The New York example targets a party-line telephone user. The words are specific and personal ("you" versus "any person who"), and the concrete terms "hang up the receiver" help the reader conjure a mental image more easily than "willfully refuse to immediately relinquish."

Source: David Mellinkoff, *The Language of the Law*. Boston: Little, Brown and Company, 1987, p. 430. Reprinted with permission.

Choose Words That Maintain a Positive Relationship

Describe both the transaction and your relationship in positive terms whenever possible.

According to a proverb, "An optimist looks at a glass and sees it is half full; a pessimist sees the glass is half empty." In most business situations, you should write as an optimist. Unless your communication strategy is to threaten, a positive tone will present you and your ideas in the best light. A positive tone helps the reader perceive your relationship as empowering, active, and rewarding. In the example from the *McCall's* renewal notice, the sentence "Your subscription is about to expire" implies that the action is out of the reader's control: The expiration will occur. In the revision, the reader is the empowered agent or actor: "You can have your subscription as long as you wish." Compare the following positive and negative phrases.

GLASS HALF FULL	GLASS HALF EMPTY
what is	what is not
what you have	what you lack
what will be	what won't be
what you have done	what you haven't done
what you can do	what you can't do
what you will do	what you won't do

Suppose you are a credit manager and you receive a letter from a customer who is behind in her payments. Imagine that she writes, "I can bring my account up to date on June 15th. I hope you can bear with me three more weeks." Now imagine that instead she wrote, "I can't pay anything until June 15th. Don't expect anything until then." If you are like most managers, you will be more pleased with the first message. The first not only says what she can do, but may lead you to think of what *you* can do with the money once the payment is received. Employees and managers will react to your negative or positive messages in much the same way.

Negative Messages

Negative message about the *transaction*? Make sure your message about the *relationship* is positive.

When you must deliver a negative message, be courteous. Sarcasm, flattery, hostility, or an uncaring tone may endanger your relationships and future transactions. *Even though the message about the transaction in question may be negative, the message about your relationship with the reader should be positive.*

Choose a positive personal message in spite of the negative information. The positive message may be "I enjoyed working with you on this project," or "you had several very creative ideas," or "I appreciated the effort you put into this task," or "your product is very versatile." In addition, try to deliver the negative message without blocking the possibility of future interaction. You might want to suggest what the person could do to achieve his or her goal eventually, although it is not possible right now.

The following two-sentence termination notice was sent to a large number of Braniff Airways employees. It is a classic example of a message that bars future interaction.

Effective with the close of business on Wednesday, September 10, 1980, your job will be abolished and no further work will be authorized on that position.

Your support and assistance of Braniff in its sales efforts have been most appreciated.

Create no bars to future interaction.

Each sentence has a distinctively different tone.[4] The first sentence is harsh and impersonal. The reader can't tell who has abolished her job or why no further work will be authorized. The opening phrase, "Effective with the close of business on Wednesday," rings with finality. "Abolished," "authorized," and "position" are all formal in tone. The second sentence, in contrast, uses positive words—"support," "assistance," and "appreciated"—but once again, no person is mentioned who might be "most appreciative." The praise sounds false. Since readers process written text a few words at a time, not all at once, the negative announcement has already affected the reader when the claim of appreciation is read.

Don't forget the effect of culture on readers' interpretations.

We should note, however, that differences in culture may affect how readers understand the tone of a passage. In U.S. culture, sincerity is highly valued and exaggerated humility is not trusted. In Japanese culture, exaggerated humility and modesty are accepted and even expected. Choose words suited to the national culture and the corporate culture of your audience. Target your reader.

Use Nonsexist Language

Sexist language is off target; it skews people's perceptions of themselves and others. Sexism harms everyone by linking opportunity and responsibility with gender rather than ability. A company that persists in sexist policies harms itself, because presumably the company with the most talented people, regardless of gender, will compete most successfully in the marketplace. Adopt the following guidelines for nonsexist communication and learn techniques for following them.

Sexism shows up in documents when a writer links a job function with a male or female pronoun that does not refer to any specific person, as though all persons with a specific job were also a particular gender. Always saying "the secretary . . . she" or "the engineer . . . he" is sexist unless a specific woman or man is meant.

Avoid gender stereotypes in pronoun choice.

To avoid this practice, sometimes link job types with nonstereotypical gender pronouns. Say, "a secretary . . . he" or "an engineer . . . she." By varying the pronouns, you indicate awareness that such roles can be filled either by men or women. If you begin by saying "a secretary . . . he," then continue to use male pronouns as long as you are talking about the secretary in that specific instance. Later on, in another part of the discussion, you can change gender in the pronouns. Of course, if there are no male secretaries in the company, then use the female pronouns when you refer to the secretaries in your company, but vary gender when you talk of secretaries in general.

Substitute plural nouns for *anyone* and similar pronouns.

Anyone, Anybody: Everybody's Problem   English treats as singular several frequently used pronouns: anyone, everyone, and anybody. When a writer wishes to use a pronoun to refer to these terms, only gender-specific singular pronouns (he, she, or it) will match. By choosing either "he" or "she," the writer labels

GUIDELINES FOR NONSEXIST COMMUNICATION

The changes that will ensure equal opportunity and fair treatment for all require both awareness and commitment. Bobbye D. Sorrels, author of *The Nonsexist Communicator, Solving the Problems of Gender and Awkwardness in Modern English*, proposes the following guidelines for replacing entrenched habits with positive communication.

1. Commit yourself to removing sexism from all your communication.
2. Practice and reinforce nonsexist communication patterns until they become habitual. The ultimate test is your ability to carry on a nonsexist private conversation and to think in nonsexist terms.
3. Set a nonsexist communication example and direct or persuade others to adopt your example.
4. Use familiar idioms whenever possible, but if you must choose between sexism and the unfamiliar, use the unfamiliar term until it becomes familiar.

5. Take care not to arouse negativism in the receiver by using awkward, cumbersome, highly repetitious, or glaring revisions. A sufficient variety of graceful, controlled, sex-positive, dynamic revisions exist so that you can avoid bland or offensive constructions.
6. Use the full range of techniques for correction of sexist communication, including reconstruction, substitution, and omission.
7. Check roots and meanings of words to be sure that the words need to be changed before changing them.
8. Check every outgoing message—whether written, oral, or nonverbal—for sexism before sending it.

Source: Bobbye Sorrels. *The Nonsexist Communicator.* Englewood Cliffs, N.J.: Prentice-Hall, 1983, p. 17. Reprinted by permission of the publisher.

"anyone" as either male or female. Some people have chosen to treat "everyone" and similar words as plural terms, but many others, especially older managers who have learned grammar rules thoroughly, strongly resist this use. To solve this problem, choose one of the following solutions:

- Substitute a plural noun for the singular "anyone," "everyone," or "anybody"; match the plural noun with "they," "them," or "their."
  Instead of saying "Did everyone bring his or her calendar?" substitute
  "Did all the members bring their calendars?" or
  "Did all of you bring your calendars?"
- Use the constructions "his or her," "he or she," or "him or her" sparingly.

When faced with a choice of words that make women seem ineffectual imitations of males, choose the male term. Choose "director," not "directress," "singer," not "songstress," "executor," not "executrix." Where the suffix "-man" traditionally has been used to indicate that men usually hold a particular job, replace the suffix with the neutral suffix "-person" or substitute a word that pertains to the job function. Thus, use "company spokesperson" rather than "company spokesman," "chair" or "chairperson" rather than "chairman," and "flight attendant" rather than "stewardess." "Manager," however, is not a sexist term. Manager has nothing to do with maleness; the term comes from the Latin word "manus," for "hand" (preserved in our term "manual labor"). The hand that guides the corporation can be either male or female.

☐ CHECKLIST FOR WORD CHOICE

_____ Are the words appropriate to the scenario for this situation?

_____ Are the words appropriate to the knowledge and uncertainties of people involved?

_____ Do the words precisely denote your meaning?

_____ Is any jargon you've used likely to be understood by all present and future readers?

_____ Do the connotations of the words create an appropriate tone for the piece?

_____ Have you searched for and replaced clichés?

_____ Have you used slang only where the situation is informal enough to tolerate it?

_____ Have you chosen words that suit your reader's perspective?

_____ Have you emphasized a positive relationship with the reader even when the message about the transaction (policy or exchange of goods, information, or services) is negative?

_____ Have you identified and replaced all sexist language?

_____ Have you chosen words appropriate to your communication strategy?

The attempt to eliminate sexist language has even led businesspeople to create new titles for certain jobs. Instead of chairman (or the impersonal *chair* or rather awkward *chairperson*), such titles as *team leader, champion, head, captain,* and even *product evangelist* focus on active functions.

☐ COMMUNICATION CHALLENGES

PRELIMINARY EXERCISE 1   *In a paragraph, identify and discuss business jargon or other jargon from your own work experience or from a class you've taken.* Jargon expresses an idea in a kind of shorthand. Everyone in the group should understand it—otherwise, the jargon won't work. For example, a few years ago Detroit auto makers decided to "downsize" their cars to make them proportionally smaller. A second example occurs in marketing, where customers often are classified on the basis of characteristics that make them probable buyers of certain kinds of goods: "dinks" are "dual-income, no kids" families likely to have more discretionary income; "yuppies" are "young urban (or upwardly-mobile) professional people." In a political science course, "oligarchy" is the professional term for a government or political institution run by a small, elite, powerful faction, and in economics an "oligopoly" is an industry domi-

nated by a few, large, powerful companies. Think back to coffee breaks at work, class discussions, or study sessions. What words did you and your friends use as shorthand when you were "talking shop?"

PRELIMINARY EXERCISE 2   *Circle the word that is more precise (has a more restricted meaning) in each pair.*

lease	deal
employee	receptionist
Nintendo®	electronic game
absenteeism	personnel problem
product	radiator
talk to	counsel
persuade	present

PRELIMINARY EXERCISE 3   *Complete the following table of words.*

FORMAL	INFORMAL	SLANG
inspect	check	look over
inadequate	poor	shoddy
excellent	fine	_____
compensated	_____	_____
superior	_____	_____
strive	_____	_____
pursue	_____	_____

EXERCISE 1

First, decide upon a likely reader for each of the sentences below. Then revise the sentences, using positive expressions to improve tone and clarity.

a. We have acquired the technology to dispose of dangerous drill cuttings without harming the environment.

b. We don't think the changes you've asked for will be too much trouble.

c. We have started four new projects in Europe because we were pretty weak there, having plants only in Portugal and Switzerland.

d. No one produces more carpet fiber than we do, and our patented product "Stainaway" has only one major competitor.

e. If you had filled out your order form correctly, we wouldn't have sent you material you didn't want.

f. We cannot fill your order before March 20th.

g. We have a hiring freeze on accountants until after January 1. Write us then.

h. (Orally) "He's in a meeting. Try again later."

i. We found no evidence to indicate the amount of inventory of the specific items claimed was inconsistent with the previous physical inventory.

j. Our evidence shows that the company's compensation system is not as effective as it should be.

k. Any failure in planning, coordination, and execution of the project will undoubtedly result in failure to meet the completion schedule and the likelihood of bringing in the project at higher costs than had been initially envisioned.

l. If we can help, don't hesitate to call.

EXERCISE 2

Deliver a negative message, but give a positive message about the relationship. Write a short letter or note.

You work in a bookstore that mostly serves people who live near a small university. Your store is not affiliated with a large national chain, so all your ordering must be handled by the order clerk and the owner. At 4:30 P.M. you received a request for a children's book, *Herschel and the Hannekuh Goblins*, that is published by a small independent press. You call the wholesaler before she leaves the store, and the wholesaler confirms that the book was in stock as of 8 A.M. that morning. The order clerk places the order the next day, but when the order arrives three days later, the book is not included and the invoice shows the book marked "out of stock."

You have the customer's phone number, but she doesn't answer any of your calls during the morning. You decide to send her a brief note in the afternoon mail, letting her know of your problem obtaining the book through the wholesaler. She has already paid for the book and is a fairly good customer. You can order from the publisher by telephone, but the store owner requires that the customer pay for the call in advance or that the customer allow the call to be charged to her home telephone number. The book is a holiday gift for a child and the holiday is only three weeks away. You cannot be sure that the book will be received in time, even if you telephone the publisher.

Draft the note, making sure that you explain the problem and the possibility that you cannot obtain the book she ordered, and let her know that she is a valued customer. The customer's name is Hilda Zolnick. The name of your bookstore is Riverway Books; the store owner is Tony Cache.

EXERCISE 3

Revise the sexist terms in the following sentences to reduce stereotyping and awkwardness.

a. Complete the workmen's forms and send them to Payroll.

b. The supervisor must approve any requests for a secretary's time that go beyond her normal duties. He must fill in the overtime form with the number of hours he has approved the girl's working.

c. If an employee leaves after 7 P.M., she may request that the night watchman accompany her to her car.

d. During the holidays, the mailmen in the company will have five days off. Each department should appoint a mailboy to pick up packages and mail that arrive during that period, starting December 26th.

e. If anyone wants his or her name attached to the condolence card for Mrs. Henry Hammond, he or she should come by the office and deliver his or her check for $4 for the funeral spray for her husband and sign his or her name to the card. I know she will appreciate our support.

f. According to the Probate Department, Mrs. Hammond is the executrix of her husband's will.

g. Has everyone in the customer group received their copies of the program evaluation form? Good. Don't anybody forget to put his name at the top of the form.

EXERCISE 4

Tape record a meeting or dinner conversation, or any event where people who know one another well are talking (ask permission first). Transcribe about ten minutes' conversation and look for the words that seem suited to the level of formality, the status of the individuals, the seriousness of the transaction, and the culture of the group. Go through the transcript and underline high-content nouns, adjectives, or verbs (not prepositions, pronouns, or articles). What do they tell you about the nature of the occasion, the group's sense of propriety, and the seriousness or casualness of the members? Do the people use much slang?

EXERCISE 5

Read through the following notice that the Harry and David Company inserts in its boxes of pears. Harry and David is an Oregon fruit and specialty food products subsidiary of a large corporation, but the company perpetuates the memory of the two men who founded it. *Make a photocopy for your assignment. Mark on the copy those words that seem formal and those that seem informal. Underline the opening and closing phrases of each paragraph. At the end of the page, answer the following questions:* What kind of overall tone does this combination produce? What purpose does the tone serve? Do you see any jargon or slang? If so, what is its purpose? What ideas do the words at the beginnings and ends of paragraphs emphasize? Finally, would you like someone to send you a box of these pears?

ROYAL RIVIERA PEARS: AMERICA'S MOST CELEBRATED FRESH FRUIT

Get set to enjoy one of life's purest luxuries . . . a hallmark of living well. We call them Royal Riviera Pears—highly prized, extremely rare, truly magnificent.

They were first grown in the Angers region of France in the 1840s. Those early crops were chancy and difficult to bring to harvest, but the taste and texture of the few pears that survived were so clearly superior, the entire crop was reserved for the exclusive enjoyment of European nobility.

Royal Rivieras are still temperamental about soil and light and climate—so much so that they're really at home in only a few places in the world: a couple of small valleys in the South of France and here in the "South of Oregon" where a few pioneering orchardists began planting them in the 1800s.

It takes nearly 20 years for a Royal Riviera Pear tree to hit its productive stride—and some of the trees here at Bear Creek Orchards are over 90 years old now. For all those years they've been pruned and watered and fed and just generally pampered into producing fruit of the size and quality you'll find here.

The pears in this gift box have been nurtured through spring frosts, summer hailstorms, autumn winds—and the harvest itself. (Royal Rivieras are so thin-skinned they're actually more difficult to handle than hen's eggs.) They're a scarce commodity—available only a few brief weeks each year—with rarely enough to go around.

In an age when mass merchandising is the rule, and supermarket produce is often a disappointment, it's a real pleasure to provide you with the exception. We believe our Royal Riviera Pears represent a level of quality and enjoyment you'll find truly luxurious.

(Reprinted with permission.)

IF YOU WOULD LIKE TO READ MORE

About the history and future of English:
McCrum, R., Cran, W., & MacNeil, R. (1986). *The story of English*. New York: Viking. Available also as a video series.

About the use of slang:
Gilsdorf, J. (1983). Executive and managerial attitudes toward business slang: A *Fortune*-list survey. *Journal of Business Communication*, *20*(4), 29–42.

About sexism and language:
Sorrels, B. D. (1983). *The nonsexist communicator: Solving the problems of gender and awkwardness in modern English*. Englewood Cliffs, NJ: Prentice-Hall.

About questions of usage:
Bernstein, T. M. (1985). *The careful writer: A modern guide to English usage*. New York: Atheneum.

Fowler, H. W. (1983). *A dictionary of modern English usage* (2nd ed., rev.). Revised by Sir Ernest Gowers. New York: Oxford University (Second edition first published 1965).

NOTES

1. R. McCrum, W. Cran, & R. MacNeil, *The story of English*. New York: Viking (1986), 19–20.

2. J. Gilsdorf, "Executive and managerial attitudes toward business slang: A *Fortune*-list survey." *Journal of Business Communication*, *20* (1983)4, 204.

3. W. Weintz, *The solid gold mailbox*. New York: Wiley (1987), 195.

4. A copy of this notice was given to Linda Driskill by an employee who was fired.

STRUCTURING SENTENCES

OBJECTIVES

Studying this chapter will help you make sentences easy to read by

- structuring sentences to reflect the relationships among ideas

- placing modifying phrases close to the words they modify

- structuring sentences to express action

- choosing strong verbs to control the sentence

- reducing the number of passive voice constructions

- using progressive forms only when the condition of being in action matters

- eliminating unnecessary words and prepositional phrases

- placing high-content words in power positions

PREVIEW

Sentences structured for easy reading and comprehension help persuade readers to accept ideas. The reason is simple: people tend to like ideas they can understand better than those they cannot grasp readily. Sentences structured to reflect the relationships of ideas are easy to comprehend. This chapter explains techniques that help create highly readable, plain but graceful sentences.

❏ MAKING SENTENCES EASY TO READ

What is readable prose? Ewald and Stine claim that business style is "context-dependent," varying according to specific situations.[1] It follows that readability is also context-dependent. Readers can have different expectations in different reading situations; these expectations affect *how* they read. Think about the factors that affect your own reading, such as your motivation (are you reading because this text was assigned, or for your own purposes?) and the conceptual difficulty of the topic. You probably also react to the way the document is organized, the length of the sentences, the familiarity of the words, the beliefs and experiences you and the writer have in common, your mutual knowledge of document types and writing conventions, the format (use of headings, bulleted lists, and so on), and the type of print. A document that might be readable in leisurely circumstances can be frustrating in an emergency.

The Limitations of Readability Formulas

The popularity of readability formulas depends on ease of use, not validity.

Various formulas have been created to test the readability of documents. All of the common ones rely on only two of the many factors just listed: the number of words per sentence and the number of multisyllable words. The creators of these formulas generally seem to assume that physiological limitations on image processing are the only elements that really matter.[2] At some time or other you may have to use such a formula, because some businesses require them. Some state legislatures require the use of readability formulas in certain contracts and insurance policies. Several word processors will calculate one or more for you automatically. If the law requires you to check your document with a readability formula, find out which one you must use. The "Fog Index" explained here is one of the most common formulas.

Scores of twenty or more are considered too difficult for all readers. However, in industries that use many Latin words, such as pharmaceuticals, electronics, and oil exploration, such scores are found fairly often and the specialists can read the documents with few complaints. The reader's familiarity with the words matters a great deal in how rapidly he or she can process the information. The ease of using readability formulas, not their usefulness to the writer, seems the main reason for their popularity.[3] Readability formulas are useful only after you've written a draft; they don't tell you how to produce good prose.

Readability and the Plain Style

Too often business students are taught to write a skeletal style of monosyllables and short sentences, a "Dick and Jane go to the office" style of writing. This type of writing may be simple, but it is inefficient for explaining complex ideas. The "skeletal style" associated with a low fog index (short sentences and one- or two-syllable words) may be easy to process but uninteresting and inefficient for expressing complex meanings, Michael Mendelson argues.[4] Mendelson is inter-

FOG INDEX PROCEDURE SHEET

To find the Fog Index of any writing, mark out a sample 100–125 words long. Put down the number of words in successive sentences (12-17-6-21-10-29-10 = 105). This is the total word count.

(1) Total word count _____

Count number of sentences in passage.

(2) Number of sentences _____

Divide (1) total word count by (2) the number of sentences to get average sentence length. Semicolons, colons, and dashes count as periods in counting the sentences.

(3) Average sentence length ___

Count the number of words in the passage with three syllables or more. Omit, in your count, all words that are capitalized; are combinations of short easy words like "book-keeper," or verb forms made into three syllables by adding "-es" or "-ed" (such as "trespasses" or "created"). This gives you the count of multisyllable words.

(4) Number of long words _____

Divide (4) the number of long words by (1) the total word count, to get the percentage of long words.

(5) Percent of long words _____

ADD: (3) Average sentence length and
      (5) Percentage of long words

$$(6) \; \underbrace{}_{(3)} + \underbrace{}_{(5)} = \underbrace{}_{(6)}$$

MULTIPLY: (6) by 0.4 to get the Fog Index of the passage you are testing.

$$(7) \; \underbrace{}_{(6)} \times 0.4 = \underbrace{}_{\text{Fog Index}}$$

Eliminate the digits following the decimal point. The result gives you the number of years of schooling required for easy reading of the passage you have tested.

NOTE: Since most readers do not have more than a college education, any Fog Index above 17 is called "17-plus," meaning hard reading for any college graduate.

_____

Source: FOG INDEX is a service mark of Gunning-Mueller Clear Writing Institute, Inc., Santa Barbara, CA 93110. This material adapted from *How to Take the Fog Out of Writing* by Robert Gunning and Douglas Mueller, 1985, Chicago, IL. Dartnell Corporation. Used with permission.

Reading Level

FOG INDEX STUDIED	BY GRADE	BY PUBLICATION
17	College graduate	(No popular magazine is this difficult.)
16	College senior	
15	College junior	
14	College sophomore	
13	College freshman	
Danger Line		
12	High school senior	*Harper's, The Atlantic*
10	High school sophomore	*Time, Newsweek*
9	High school freshman	*Reader's Digest*
8	Eighth grade	*Ladies' Home Journal*
7	Seventh grade	*True Confessions*

ested in the principles of the classical "plain style," defined by Demetrius of Alexandria in the third century B.C.[5] Think of "plain" as "clear or lucid," not "without ornament." Mendelson's goal is not merely to imitate classical orators, but to give credit to someone whose insights are valuable in our own time, especially as a counter to the simplistic use of readability formulas.

Principal goals of the plain style: clarity and vividness.

The heart of Demetrius' program is a plan for creating clarity using different methods that are appropriate to different situations. Other rhetoricians, such as Cicero and Aristotle, also argued that one style would not work for all audiences. Demetrius tried to define a style that had the same goals of clarity and vividness but achieved them in different ways suited to the particular demands of specific situations. His method exploits word choice and sentence structure. Demetrius encourages the writer to choose words the audience knows and to vary the diction to suit the subject, occasion, audience, and personality of the author (see Chapter 6, "Choosing Words"). Although he likes leanness and simplicity in sentences, Demetrius also sees that simple styles can become ambiguous. He therefore recommends variation in word order if the variations make the essential idea more lucid. Demetrius' emphasis on clarity, precision, and vividness are especially applicable to modern business communication.

Consider the skeletal style of the following passage, which a readability scale would rate as *very* easy to read. Compare it to the revision in a modern plain style. For a full effect, read both aloud.

SKELETAL STYLE

The travel and tourism industry has changed a lot recently. It is now the world's largest employer. Much more must be done. Then it can have its full economic potential. Some airlines still can't use certain airports. Air service agreements with the United Kingdom are outdated. Air service agreements with Japan are also outdated. They have various bad restrictions. . . . World airlines must be able to act freely. They must meet demands if they are to grow bigger and make money. The flag they fly does not matter. (88 words; Fog Index, 3)

PLAIN STYLE

Despite many recent changes, much more must be done to unshackle the full economic potential of the travel and tourism industry—now the world's largest employer. Substantial barriers continue to bar airlines' access to many destinations abroad. Outdated bilateral air service agreements with the United Kingdom and Japan impose a variety of restrictions inappropriate for an increasingly global economy. . . . Regardless of whose flag they fly, international air carriers must be able to respond to market demands if they are to expand and prosper. (86 words; Fog Index, 8.4)[6]

The version written in skeletal style is less successful in conveying the idea that international airlines, now unfairly restricted, should be able to compete on equal terms in an industry that serves global markets. The notion that the industry is now restrained does not appear in the first version until the fifth sentence (at the thirty-second word rather than at the eleventh word). Although the words and the sentences are shorter, the type of harm is ambiguous in the first version: "bad restrictions" is imprecise. The short, direct sentences are repetitive and blunt, unrelated to the meanings they are supposed to convey. Before you accept a very low fog index as proof of clear communication, look at the way the sentences express your ideas.

Meaning and Structure: The Key to the Plain Style

In a plain style, the sentence structure should reflect the relationships among the ideas, which are the heart of meaning.

CONDITION	ACTION CLAIMED NECESSARY	RESULT/PURPOSE OF ACTION	JUSTIFYING ASPECT
Despite many recent changes,	much more must be done	to unshackle the full economic potential of the travel and tourism industry,	now the world's largest employer.

The sentence begins by setting aside a possible objection: that many changes have already occurred. Next, the main clause makes a claim about action; the agent noun (the actor) is unnamed because the action itself and not the agent matters. The result or goal of the action appears next. The final modifier about the size of the industry shows that the industry has demonstrated its potential. You can look at the elements of your thought and arrange them straightforwardly without being a linguist or English teacher. What you do need is a clear view of how your ideas relate to one another.

In a plain style, phrases and clauses that modify or expand ideas should be placed close to those ideas. In the sentence below, the modifying phrase "with the United Kingdom and Japan" follows immediately after "agreements"; "inappropriate for an increasingly global economy" follows the phrase "a variety of restrictions."

AGENT	MODIFYING PHRASE	ACTION	OBJECT	MODIFYING PHRASE
Outdated bilateral air service agreements	with the United Kingdom and Japan	impose	a variety of restrictions	inappropriate for an increasingly global economy.

This sentence has the basic agent/action/object form, expanded at two key points to give the reader extra information about the agent and the object. These phrases give examples of limiting agreements and support the judgment "inappropriate." The details in these modifiers increase the persuasiveness of the sentence.

Improving Sentences with a Computer

Work on sentence structure *after* you write your first draft.

When you first draft a sentence, it may tumble from your head in a jumbled form, but you can deliberately reshape your sentence to convey its meaning more clearly. If you write with a computer, the changes are very easy to make. Suppose that you want to compare the sales of two products. You initially write this sentence: "It seems to me from these figures that I can conclude Tylenol® has sold better in Philadelphia than Advil® has." Think through your ideas when you edit for sentence structure. Use a "new line" command to break the sentence into chunks:

> "~~It seems to me~~
>
> ~~from these figures~~
>
> ~~that I can conclude~~
>
> Tylenol® has sold better in Philadelphia
>
> than Advil® ~~has sold~~."

The main idea is the comparison, not your thinking about the subject. Delete the unnecessary words. Positioning the names of the two products at opposite ends of the sentence and linking them with a comparative claim offers the reader a structure that illustrates the message:

> Product X (comparative claim) Product Y (base claim)
> Tylenol® has sold better in Philadelphia than Advil® has.

Similarly, if you want to explain that two causes produced a result, a sentence with a compound subject made up of the two causes and a single predicate will illustrate the message:

> X and Y produced result Z.
> Lower costs and higher productivity enabled the company to pay off its debt early.

Most readers can understand actions easily if they are expressed in "who does what" (agent/action/result) sentences: "The city of San Antonio bid for the Democratic Political Convention in 1996."

When modifying phrases shift the main message into unimportant positions in the sentence, the meaning is harder to recognize. Look at padded versions of the sentences you have just examined.

The earlier than expected retirement of its considerable debt by the company was possible because of lower raw materials' costs, which were helped by higher productivity as well.

In order to attract the Democratic Political Convention in 1996 to the city, it was necessary that a bid be put in by the city of San Antonio.

Sales were somewhat better for Tylenol® in Philadelphia than for Advil®.

In the padded versions, additional low-content words have been added to each sentence. High-content verbs (sells, enabled, and bid) have been replaced with a linking verb, *was*, whose only power as a verb is to convey that the terms on each side are equal: X *was* Y. This substitution makes the sentence harder to read because the controlling linguistic element in a sentence is the verb. The verb determines how much guidance readers have in understanding the nouns of the sentence.

How Verbs Control Interpretation

Verbs specify required features of nouns and thus govern sentence meaning.

Take a moment to read the following sentence: "Sincerity cooked pancakes for breakfast." Your first reaction is probably that the sentence is somehow wrong. Probe to think why you have that reaction. Tucked away in your head, linguists believe, is a set of conditions associated with each verb. These conditions govern which words can appear with the verb as agents, objects, or nouns of other types. The most frequently used meaning of "cook" requires an agent noun that is both living and human, such as "Ralph" or "the chef." Sincerity, an abstraction like truth and intelligence, is not alive. However, many young women have been named for abstract virtues: Faith, Hope, and Chastity, for example. If you accept the premise that Sincerity is one of these women, then you can make sense of the sentence. Furthermore, *cook* tells your mind that the object cooked must be concrete, not abstract. Sincerity may cook, but she can't cook "justice" for breakfast.

Thus, a strong verb actively specifies a great deal about the meanings of and relationships among the nouns in the sentence, and the action or idea the verb represents. Linking verbs and low-content verbs such as "get," "do," and "make" don't tell the reader much about these relationships. These low-content verbs are imprecise because they are used to mean so many different things that they offer little interpretive guidance about the nouns in the sentence. Consider how different the meanings of *get* are in the following phrases: "get together," "get children," "get a raise," "get the flu," "get some groceries," "get the machine to work," "get by on my income," "get going," "get it from the boss." If your sentences are dull and imprecise, try transplant surgery. Pick a strong verb as a transplant. Strip away strings of prepositions and nouns so your active verbs will govern livelier clauses.

The precision English offers because of its immense vocabulary can be lost when sentences are poorly structured. Since English no longer has word endings that mark the syntactic function of nouns (only possessives, singulars, and plurals are marked), word order and sentence structure must be managed carefully. Verbs and prepositions help you show the connections among sentence parts.

English offers three types of verbs: linking verbs and two kinds of action verbs (transitive and intransitive). A linking verb makes a claim about a state of being and sets up an equation between the nouns on either side of the verb or between the noun and some modifier (adjective): Mary *is* toastmaster; George *was* late again. "Seem," "appear," "become," and "resemble" are also linking verbs. "Charles is young" and "Charles seems young" both link the proper noun with an attribute. In contrast, "Charles negotiated the contract" describes an action that affects an object; in this case, "negotiated" is a transitive verb. You can remember the meaning of "transitive" by recalling that "trans" means "across." A transitive verb carries the action across to some object. "Charles negotiates" also describes an action, but without showing an object affected by the action. In this case "negotiates" is an *in*transitive verb (*in* means "not"). These three types of verbs form the basis of the three basic sentence patterns:

Subject	linking verb	predicate noun or adjective
Charles	*is*	*a negotiator.*

Subject	transitive action verb	object of action
Charles	*negotiates*	*contracts.*

Subject	intransitive action verb	(no object)
Charles	*negotiates.*	

In addition to tense (present, past, future, and so on) and number (singular or plural), verbs also show voice and mood. Verbs can be in an active or passive voice. When you use a transitive verb in the active voice, the agent will be the subject. For example,

Active voice:
Harlen Klinger founded the
   (agent)   (action)
   museum   in 1911.
(object of action)

In the passive voice, the object of the action becomes the subject and the preposition "by" precedes the agent.

Passive voice:
The   museum   was founded by
   (object of action)   (action)
Harlen Klinger in 1911.
   (agent)

If the agent is unimportant, it may be deleted.

Passive voice (agent deleted): The museum was founded in 1911.

To review, a verb phrase in the passive voice consists of a form of "to be" and a past participle (usually ending in -ed). The object that receives the action moves to the beginning of the clause (it takes the subject position) and the agent or actor is deleted or appears after a preposition. Some passive voice constructions eliminate the agent altogether. You will always find a linking verb (some form of "to be") as part of a passive verb phrase: It *was decided* by the finance committee that more money *would be spent* on the training of new employees. (Active version: The finance committee decided to spend more money training new employees.) Strings of nouns and prepositional phrases deprive your prose of momentum; you can usually replace them with a simple noun or short noun phrase ("the finance committee") and an active verb ("decided").

You should use the passive voice with discretion, usually under the following conditions.

1. When you have bad news to convey,
2. When the agent is unknown, or
3. When the thing being acted upon is more important than the agent.

VERBS AND PREPOSITIONS (*continued*)

In the sentence "Charlene Jacobson was named president of ABC Electronics last Tuesday," Charlene Jacobson is obviously the most important person, and who named her president is unimportant.

Writers and speakers also have a choice of indicative, interrogative, imperative, or subjunctive mood.

Imperative mood: Please *send* the sales report to me on Friday.

Interrogative: *Will* you *send* your report by Monday?

Indicative mood: Advil® *has lost* market share.

Subjunctive mood: *If I were president*, I would fire the sales department.

The imperative mood expresses an order or request; the interrogative mood asks a question; the indicative mood describes what actually is; the subjunctive mood expresses what is contrary to fact, what is wished, or what is hypothetical.

The progressive form shows an action that is in progress at some particular time; for example, "Rex *will be meeting* with clients most of the morning." This form is used much too frequently, when the state of being in action is irrelevant to the main idea of the sentence. *Use the progressive form only when the state of being in progress matters.* Do not say, "I will be sending you a letter on Saturday." You will not be in the process of sending a letter all day Saturday. You will swiftly complete this action. Instead, write: "I will send you a letter on Saturday." Many naive writers begin their letters, "I am writing this letter . . ." How obvious, the reader thinks, I know that already! I wouldn't be sitting here reading it if you, at some past time, hadn't been in the process of writing.

Subjunctive mood forms, which were used frequently in Latin and still are used to express subtle nuances of meaning in Spanish, are not often used in everyday English. The subjunctive form was meant to call attention to claims that were hypothetical, conditional, or uncertain.

Present subjunctive	*Example*
be	Unless the husband be dead, the wife cannot inherit.

Future or hypothetical subjunctive	
were	If he were in Tulsa, I would invite him to the office.

Prepositions connect vital parts of sentences. English couldn't get along without prepositions, since most of the endings that once told whether a noun was a subject, object, means, source, goal, location, or some other type have long since been dropped. A prepositional phrase is a short group of words that begins with a preposition and ends with a noun or pronoun.

aboard	below	like
about	beneath	of
above	beside	off
across	between	on
after	beyond	since
against	by	through
along	down	to
among	during	toward
around	for	under
at	from	until
before	in	with
behind	into	without

We need prepositions to say, "by the door," "from the bookcase," or "to the moon." On the other hand, a sentence that links prepositional phrases together in long lines seldom produces a string of pearls. Look at this limp, winding sentence:

The new company *of* former employees *of* NASA intends to offer shuttle services *for* small payloads *of* companies *in* the Southwest *on* its missiles *in* the spring *of* 1991.

Some of these prepositions are essential, but others can be removed:

Former NASA employees announced their new company will shuttle Southwestern companies' small payloads aboard its missiles after March, 1991.

Power Positions in Sentences

The beginnings and ends of sentences are power positions.

As you shape your sentences to reflect your thoughts, remember that the beginning and end of a sentence or paragraph are positions of special power. When you begin with a modifying phrase, make sure it presents information that the readers must grasp before they consider the main idea. Readers notice the beginning and the end, just as they notice the caboose and engine of a train, but they pay less attention to the middle. Whoever remembers boxcars, right?

In the following example, the main ideas are tucked into the middle. The power positions contain low-content phrases and clauses: "it is necessary in the method called" and "first." Springing key terms out to more powerful positions changes the emphasis of the sentence.

It is necessary in the method called morphological analysis for *the marketing specialist* to *identify the structural dimensions of a problem* first.

The marketing specialist, using morphological analysis, first *identifies the problem's structural dimensions*.

The first version emphasizes the nature of the method; the second version emphasizes what the market specialist does. The second version places the words about method in a modifying phrase, "using morphological analysis."

Parallel Placement and Structure

Place similar ideas in similar forms (use parallel structure).

In addition to using the power positions at a sentence's beginning and end, you can help readers see similarities or equivalencies in ideas by using another positioning technique, parallel placement and structure. Parallel structure means simply that you use similar grammatical structures to present similar ideas. Suppose that you want your assistant to do three things. Since these are actions, you can express those tasks as three verbs: "Please *ask* Roger for the performance summary, *review* the marketing layout, and *set up* a meeting with the facilities committee." "Ask," "review," and "set up" are similar or "parallel" in form. If one action is being performed for two purposes, combine the purposes in a single compound phrase:

Harrison met with a tax consultant to save time and meet the tax deadline.

The structure (form) of the following sentence does not properly emphasize its key idea (what an approval sheet does).

The idea behind this approval sheet would be to provide you with proof substantiating that the contract has been reviewed by the appropriate parties in the region and that approval has been obtained prior to your signing a similar document that comes from the corporate contracts department.

This sentence should have an agent/action/result structure to reflect its ideas. Instead, the writer begins with an abstract subject (*idea*), followed by a weak linking verb (*would be*). Next comes a string of phrases:

behind this approval sheet

would be to provide you

with proof substantiating

that the contract

has been reviewed

by the appropriate parties

in the region [and]

that approval has been obtained

prior to your signing a similar document

that comes

from the corporate contracts department

Prepositions string the words together without parallel constructions.

The sentence needs to point out that before the reader signs the sheet, two things have happened: (1) the right people have reviewed the contract, and (2) they have approved it. In the revised version *approval sheet* is the agent, and the action *will prove* is the verb. The parallel constructions *have reviewed* and *have approved* combine to show off their similarity: *have reviewed and approved*. The repeated verb *have*, which shows action completed before the present time (perfect tense), can be deleted before *approved*. Readers will recognize that *have* applies to both *reviewed* and *approved*.

This approval sheet will prove that the appropriate regional authorities *have reviewed* and *approved* the contract before you sign it.

The new version limits the number of prepositional phrases, expresses similar ideas in similar forms, and includes phrases of varied length in the "results" section.

Eliminating Unnecessary Words

Make meanings plain by pruning clutter.

Even a properly structured sentence can be obscured if unnecessary words are loaded to its frame. According to William Zinsser, "Clutter is the disease of American writing. We are a society strangling in unnecessary words, circular constructions, pompous frills and meaningless jargon."[7] The following phrases should raise a red flag in your subconscious. Whenever you see them, edit:

at some future time

at this point in time

due to the fact that

☐ CHECKLIST FOR SENTENCE STRUCTURE

_____ Are relationships among your ideas clearly reflected in the structure of your sentences?

_____ Are the initial and final positions of paragraphs devoted to important terms?

_____ Are similar ideas placed in parallel constructions (forms)?

_____ Have you limited passive voice constructions to appropriate uses?

_____ Have you used progressive tense only where being in progress matters?

_____ Have you looked for and revised long strings of prepositions?

_____ Have you eliminated unnecessary words?

> I am of the opinion that
>
> in the amount of
>
> in the event that

You probably have some pet deadwood of your own; other candidates are "there are" and "it is." These are useful clauses when your main intent is to claim the existence of something, but they usually should be pruned. The goal is to let the important words stand out, to make your sentences easy to read. Your main tools are sentence structure that reflects the structure of your ideas, strong verbs, power position within the sentence, and high-content words. These tools help you achieve Demetrius' principal goals in the plain style: clarity and vividness.

☐ COMMUNICATION CHALLENGES

EXERCISE 1

Change the following passive voice constructions to active voice. Make sure the tone of the sentence is positive.

a. Your reservation on June 12th at the White House Bed and Breakfast in Portland, Oregon has been confirmed by me.

b. An order was placed by Herring Associates for $4340.

c. The Carson Award was won by Harry Goldberg.

d. _Big Business Blunders_ was written in 1983 by David Ricks.

e. Maximum sales cannot be achieved by our company without preserving and enhancing goodwill.

EXERCISE 2

Revise the progressive form (a helping verb plus a verb ending in "-ing") _in those sentences that should emphasize a completed action rather than an action in progress._

a. Our sales manager will be sending you a reminder on June 18th.

b. I am writing this letter to welcome you to Rodgers Brothers Manufacturing.

c. While Mr. Cassidy is recovering from his car accident, I will be handling his accounts.

d. I regret that I cannot attend your presentation on Tuesday at 4 P.M. I will be picking up a client at LAX airport at that time, and I am the only person in the office who knows this client.

e. We will be dealing with that problem at the November meeting. I will be reporting to you about the committee's solution shortly thereafter.

EXERCISE 3

Revise the samples below to place similar ideas in parallel structure. The first one has been completed for you.

1. The boss wants him to arrive on time, print out the electronic mail, and typing his correspondence. Change "typing" to "type." The boss wants him to arrive on time, print out the electronic mail, and type his correspondence.
2. Our company offers friendliness of service, helpful advice and reasonable fees.
3. Chuck's reasons for not writing the report are

   ■ not enough time
   ■ too little help
   ■ He didn't have all the data he needed.

4. Mr. Fesque wants his speech to be entertaining, informative, and inspire his audience.

5. An effective speaker should

   ■ consider the audience's needs and expectations
   ■ provide verbal and visual signposts to highlight organization
   ■ keep the audience's attention
   ■ use strategic repetition of key points

EXERCISE 4

Rewrite the four sentences below, placing the most important words at the beginning and/or end of the sentence. You may delete unnecessary words, change passive to active voice, or make any other sentence structure changes you consider appropriate.

a. From model to model, the power of a microwave varies, with confusion resulting.
b. In regard to personal property losses away from home, most general homeowners' policies pay except in the state of New York.
c. Losses due to unauthorized use of your credit cards are limited by federal law to $50 per card.
d. The time is sometimes lacking for parents to guide their children how to cope with the intense commercial pressure to buy products advertised on children's programs and both parents often work.

IF YOU WOULD LIKE TO READ MORE

About readability formulas:
Redish, J. C. (1980). Readability. In D. B. Felker (Ed.), *Document design: A review of the research* (pp. 73–75). Washington, DC: American Institutes for Research.

Courtis, J. K. (1987). Fry, Smog, Lix and Rix: Insinuations about corporate business communications. *Journal of Business Communication, 24*(2), 19–28.

Selzer, J. (1981). Readability is a four-letter word. *Journal of Business Communication, 18*(4), 23–4. An indictment of readability formulas.

About business prose style:
Mendelson, M. (1987). Business prose and the nature of the plain style. *Journal of Business Communication, 24*, 3–19. Sees Democritus' "plain style" as a model for contemporary business writing.

Smith, C. K. (1974). *Styles and structures.* New York: Norton. This book argues that style enacts patterns of thinking. It shows how different thought processes are embodied in different styles.

Williams, J. (1985). *Style: Ten lessons in clarity and grace* (2nd ed.). Glenview, IL: Scott, Foresman. Not necessarily for business, but a classic for people who believe in a single appropriate style.

Zinsser, W. (1985). *On writing well* (3rd ed.). New York: Harper & Row. Contains a chapter of invective against bureaucratic, impersonal business prose.

NOTES

1. H. Ewald & D. Stine, "Speech act theory and business communication conventions." *Journal of Business Communication, 20* (1983) 2, 17.

2. To learn about the research that has been done on readability formulas, check J. C. Redish, "Readability," in D. B. Felker (Ed.), *Document design: A review of the research.* Washington, DC: American Institutes for Research (1980), 73–75. To find out how these formulas differ in application, see J. K. Courtis, "Fry, Smog, Lix and Rix: Insinuations about corporate business communications." *Journal of Business Communication, 24* (1987) 2, 19–28.

3. Readability formulas are reviewed and indicted in J. Selzer, "Readability is a four-letter word." *Journal of Business Communication, 18* (1981) 4, 23–24.

4. M. Mendelson, "Business prose and the nature of the plain style." *Journal of Business Communication, 24* (1987) 3–19.

5. The convenient source of Demetrius' treatise is G. M. A. Grube, *A Greek Critic: Demetrius on Style.* Toronto: University of Toronto Press (1961), 39–56.

6. These two examples are based on a passage on page 22 in the *1988 AMR corporation annual report,* AMR Corporation, P.O. Box 9616, Dallas/Fort Worth Airport, Texas 75261-9616.

7. W. Zinsser, *On writing well* (3rd ed.). New York: Harper & Row (1985), 7.

CREATING COHERENCE

OBJECTIVES

This chapter will help you create coherent documents by

- sequencing given and new information

- using patterns of inclusive and particular terms

- leading the reader with titles, headings, and forecasting sentences

- adding words and phrases that point to relationships among sentences

PREVIEW

Business communicators must abide by an unwritten contract that says everything in a document should be related to a comprehensive purpose. Writers must make clear how the document relates to the situation in which they and the audience are involved. The document also must make it easy for readers to understand the document as a whole and the connections among its parts. Obvious devices such as titles, headings, page layout, forecasting sentences, repetitions of words and pronouns, sequencing of old and new information, patterns of inclusive and particular terms, and other devices can explicitly point to the unifying themes of the discourse. Several of these devices can be used simultaneously to reinforce and provide alternative guides to the reader's attention. Nonetheless, these devices should not be overused. Mutual knowledge of the situation can allow writers to communicate without too many explicit devices.

❏ THE BUSINESS COMMUNICATORS' CONTRACT

An unwritten "contract" exists among business communicators. Your colleagues will expect your communications to be related to the situations and transactions in which you all participate. All document parts should relate to the comprehensive purpose you defined in your communication strategy. You must signal these connections so that the reader can find the appropriate links between what he or she already knows and the new information or ideas in the communication.

Mutual Knowledge: The Basis for Communication

Writers and readers use mutual knowledge to create and interpret documents.

Knowledge of the situation provides writers and readers (or speakers and listeners) with mutually held beliefs and references. This mutual knowledge is organized into sets, or frames of reference. By writing something that triggers a frame of reference in the reader's mind, writers signal how to interpret their words. One of the most commonly used verbal triggers, *as you requested*, calls up a memory of a past event in which the reader requested the writer to take some action.

Linguists have begun to develop theories about how writers and readers build on a foundation of mutual knowledge. Barbara Glatt explains:

> Any given utterance typically communicates on several different levels at once. The most general level is the extent of world knowledge shared by conversants— relevant critical beliefs, assumptions, experiences, and so on, that neither party needs to explain but are nonetheless essential to their mutual understandings. Another, less general level is the context of the immediate moment—shared perceptions of the environment or circumstance. Both of these contexts are situational, in effect, essential things unsaid that give meaning to words actually said.[1]

Your analysis of business situations, the transaction involved, participants' roles and uncertainties, and your relationship with your audience will identify many frames of reference that you can invoke to make your meanings clear.

Placing known information before new information helps the reader follow the argument.

Over the course of a document or conversation, a pattern of old and new information is constructed.[2] Typically, old information (from a frame of reference known to both writer and reader) precedes new information. These patterns help make the document or presentation easy to follow. H. H. Clark and E. V. Clark, two of the leading researchers in this field, conclude that this pattern occurs because communicators have an implicit agreement. The writer or speaker is pledged to begin with information she thinks the listener can uniquely identify from what he already knows and to follow this with information she believes to be true but thinks the listener does not yet know.[3]

In a single pair of sentences, the given and new information can be combined in predictable patterns, identified by the sequence of the alphabet. Each time a particular idea occurs, it is given the same letter. Some of the patterns that might occur in a pair of sentences, illustrated in the examples, include: AB-AC, AB-BC, AB-CA, or AB-CB.

AB-AC A <u>Mac II</u> has been installed in the word processing office.
The <u>Mac II</u> is easy to use.

(A = Mac II; B = has been installed in the word processing office;
C = is easy to use.)

AB-BC <u>The Country's Best Yogurt®</u> is a very successful dessert product.
　　　　　　A　　　　　　　　　　　　　　　　　　　B
<u>Today's successful desserts</u> have little saturated fat.
　　　　B　　　　　　　　　　　　C

AB-CA <u>The Country's Best Yogurt®</u> is a very successful dessert product.
　　　　　　A　　　　　　　　　　　　　　　　　　　B
<u>Twenty-one franchise locations</u> now offer <u>it.</u>
　　　　　　C　　　　　　　　　　　A

AB-CB <u>The Country's Best Yogurt®</u> is a very successful dessert product.
　　　　　　A　　　　　　　　　　　　　　　　　　　B
<u>Swiss Chalet Yogurt</u> is also <u>a very successful dessert product.</u>
　　　　C　　　　　　　　　　　　B

This system can be used to trace ideas in longer series of sentences.

AB　The manager trained the new employees.

BC　The new employees are Canadian.

BD　They misunderstood his instructions.

"Given information" refers to information that can be recovered from the previous linguistic or nonlinguistic context. At the beginning of a communication, only situational or general knowledge can supply the meaning of the topic (in this case, "the manager") and the comment made about it ("trained the new employees"). New information is the opposite of given information. New information represents concepts that the reader cannot infer from the context and that have not been explicitly mentioned in the previous lines of text. The statement that the new employees are Canadian might seem not to belong to the series of statements. It would make sense, however, if the reader had shared situational knowledge that these Canadians spoke French as a native language and their language experience made it difficult to comprehend the manager's Alabama English dialect.

In some documents, a large portion of the information may be new; for example, the tutorial for a new software product may contain a great deal of new information. In contrast, nearly all the information in some documents may be old, known to both the writer and reader. In these documents, the logic of the claims may be the most important part of the message; the writer may review information both people know in order to reach a new conclusion.

Other Provisions of the Business Communicators' Contract

Readers want to know right away how the document pertains to them, what the overall message is, and how the parts are related.

Although the desire to build on old information seems logical, most readers and listeners want to know right away what is going to be "new" in the document. In the business communicators' contract, the writer agrees to disclose within the introductory component a topic and a new claim he or she will support. Furthermore, this claim is expected to relate to the situations in which both writer and reader participate and the kinds of transactions they conduct. A document or presentation that does not fulfill these conditions may be perceived as irrelevant or misdirected (not sent to the right office or person).

Indeed, an audience that knows the general topic and the context may comprehend and remember up to twice as much as an audience that does not.[4] Once the writer or speaker has made the proper connections between the topic, the claim, and the organizational situation, readers will usually agree to read (either fully or selectively) until they are convinced that they know what action is expected.

There is no provision in the business communicators' contract that readers will read any document in its entirety. This surprises people used to academic situations, where professors expect students to read all of the assignments and professors are expected to read all of each student's paper. Failures to do so may result in low grades or poor teaching evaluations. In business you cannot be sure that anyone will read to the end. Writers must make the overall message easily available right away.

A document is a linking device that uses multiple signals to help readers and writers connect their ideas.

Therefore, instead of thinking of a document or presentation as being complete in itself, think of a document as a linking device—a skillet with many handles. The document has to present the writer's argument in such a way that the reader will notice and react to the right points or threads in the argument. The amount of known information you should specify depends on many factors: how much your readers are likely to remember concerning the topic at hand, how many future readers with less mutual knowledge may read your document, and the amount of time you have to prepare the document. You must emphasize your main points so they will be obvious, persuasive, and memorable.

Many conventions can reinforce one another, such as information arrangement, word choice, layout, headings, and graphics.[5] The artistry of writing consists in deciding which and how many techniques to use and how much repetition or variety will attract without distracting. The degree of coherence needed depends on the situation and the participants.

To sum up, the coherence of a text or utterance is determined by emphatic or foregrounding aspects of the document:

Titles and introductory headings

Introductory summary or abstract

Headings and subheadings throughout the document

Thesis statement and forecasting sentences in individual paragraphs

Marginal notes

Graphic hierarchies (fonts, point size, position on the page, underlining, upper and lower case letters, italics, and other devices)

Illustrations, graphs, or photos

Position in paragraph (beginning and ending positions are most prominent)

Repetition of nouns or pronouns to remind readers of the subject

Sequencing of old information before new information

Words and phrases that "point" to relationships among sentences

Footnotes

These conventions are for print or written electronic communication. Other conventions apply to spoken discourse.

Inclusive-to-Particular Patterns

Inclusive terms introduce or summarize ideas. Particular terms give examples or support general claims.

Another coherence device is the pattern of related inclusive and particular terms. English contains some terms whose meanings are so broad that they can refer to many particular examples. In the sentence "Wilson Company is a leading meat producer," the word "meat" could refer to many products (beef, pork, ham, veal, drumsticks, or sausage). Imagine a vertical continuum or ladder from *inclusive* at the top to *particular* at the bottom. By choosing an inclusive term to introduce or to sum up the main ideas, a writer can usually select a term that all of the readers will understand—that will be old information or mutual knowledge. In the body of the paragraph, these inclusive terms can be discussed, expanded, illustrated, and analyzed with modifiers and more particular terms.

This communication technique corresponds to deep-seated mental processes that people use very frequently to link old and new ideas. When confronted with unfamiliar inclusive terms, readers will try to imagine the particular terms and the particular situation that would make sense of the inclusive terms. For example, people who were asked to read insurance policies aloud and comment on them often tried to come up with examples, saying to themselves something like the following: "Well, I guess that means, for instance, that if I ran my car into a post and dented the fender, I would have to pay the first $100 and the company would pay the rest of the bill." On the other hand, when confronted with new specific events, readers will try to generalize and relate the instance to a general category.

Inclusive and particular terms are used in the outlines and issue trees that organize documents.

Writers can plan documents with issue trees whose trunks are labeled with inclusive terms and whose branches are concerned with specific aspects of the topics, as shown in Chapter 5. A presentation recommending the company discontinue unprofitable meat products would no doubt illustrate what these *unprofitable meat products* (inclusive term) were: *turkey roast, venison sausage, and game hens* (particular terms).

GIVEN-TO-NEW PROGRESSION

The Quaker Oats Company 1988 Annual Report uses the given-to-new progression in informing readers about recent achievements. The excerpt that follows contains a pattern of old and new information that will be analyzed for you with topic symbols. As you read, look for new ideas as they are added and repeated as "old" information.

Hot Cereals

Hot cereals are Quaker's oldest, best-known, and most profitable products. Quaker holds the top share (66 percent) of the $600 million hot cereal market, with Old Fashioned and Quick *Quaker* Oats the leading "long-cooking" hot cereals, and Instant *Quaker* Oatmeal the best-selling brand in the "instant" segment. Fiscal 1988 saw substantial growth in the hot cereals category—the first increase in six years—fueled by Quaker's aggressive advertising and merchandising programs, in addition to a greater awareness of oatmeal's health benefits. Studies have found that adding soluble fibers to a fat-modified diet leads to lower serum cholesterol levels, thereby decreasing the risk of heart disease. *Quaker* Oatmeal and Oat bran are good sources of soluble fiber. In addition, *Quaker* Oatmeal is an excellent source of protein and vitamins.

The version below shows the repetition of old or given terms and the introduction of new information. Old information is boldfaced. When an old idea is repeated as a modifier or component of a new idea, the old information's letter is shown in parentheses.

Hot Cereals

Hot cereals are Quaker's oldest, best-known, and
    A   B

most profitable products. **Quaker** holds the top
    C   B

share (66 percent) of the $600 million **hot cereal**
 D   (A)

market, with Old Fashioned and Quick *Quaker* Oats
 E   F   G

the leading "long-cooking" **hot cereals,** and Instant
        H   A   I

Quaker Oatmeal the best-selling brand in the
 B   J   K

"instant" segment. Fiscal 1988 saw substantial
 L(E)   M

growth in the **hot cereals category**—the first in-
 N   A   (E)

crease in six years—fueled by **Quaker's** aggressive
 O   B

advertising and merchandising programs, in addi-
 P

tion to a greater awareness of **oatmeal's** health
 Q   (J)

benefits. Studies have found that adding soluble
 R   S   T

fibers to a fat-modified diet leads to lower serum
         U

cholesterol levels, thereby decreasing the risk of
 V(R)   W

heart disease. *Quaker* **Oatmeal** and Oat bran are
      (B)   J   X

good sources of **soluble fiber.** In addition, *Quaker*
 Y   T   (B)

Oatmeal is an excellent **source** of protein and
 (J)   Y   Z

vitamins.

Source: *The Quaker Oats Company 1988 Annual Report.* Reprinted by permission of the Quaker Oats Company.

INCLUSIVE AND PARTICULAR TERMS

These paragraphs are from Chapter 8, "Persuasion, Not Coercion," of a book by two leaders of Harvard's Negotiation Project. The headings and paragraph structure lead the reader from high-level inclusive terms to particular examples and explanations.

Attacking the Individual vs. Attacking the Problem

¶1 *Attacking an individual is psychological coercion.* A standard negotiating ploy is to direct *ad hominem* criticism at the person with whom I am negotiating. I may believe that by focusing my attention on you rather than on our substantive differences, I will coerce you into giving in. I may try to play on your fear or insecurity: "You obviously don't know what you are doing. I wouldn't want to be in your shoes when your boss hears about this."

¶2 It is often easy indeed to attack your actions, your judgment, your honesty, and your character in general. I may even do so without fully realizing it. A clue is when I find myself using *you* frequently, telling you what you really think, what you really want, and what your secret motives may be. Personal attacks are designed to focus psychological pressure on the will of the negotiating partner. All such tactics will feel coercive and tend to damage the ability of the people to work together in the future.

¶3 *Attack the problem.* In every negotiation there are two set of issues: "people" issues of the kind to which this book is directed (such as rationality, understanding, communication, honesty, and acceptance), and "substantive" issues (such as price, terms, specifications, dates, numbers, and conditions). It helps to disentangle these two issues—to separate the people from the problem—and deal separately with each. Too often negotiators are hard on the people and somewhat fuzzy on the problem. In this way, difficulties with the problem need not cause difficulties in the relationship.

¶4 One way to make it easier for me to attack a problem without attacking you is for us to sit more or less side by side facing a flip chart, a map, a list of issues, a draft, or some other physical representation of the substantive problem. I can jot down points, figures, or arguments and disagree with them forcefully, without criticizing you in any way that is likely to be taken personally and to damage our working relationship.

Source: Roger Fisher and Scott Brown. *Getting Together: Building a Relationship That Gets to Yes.* (Boston: Houghton Mifflin, 1988), pp. 139–140.

Attacking an individual — *Inclusive*

Direct ad hominem criticism — at the person with whom I am negotiating — *Particular*

Psychological coercion — *Inclusive*

Focus attention on person rather than on substantive differences

Play on person's fear or insecurities

"You obviously don't know what you are doing. I wouldn't want to be in your shoes when your boss hears about this." — *Particular*

Titles, Headings, and Forecasting Sentences

Titles should distin-
guish a document from
others in the file.

Titles, like subject lines, are part of the introductory headings of some documents, especially reports and proposals. A title concisely expresses the topic and principal message of the document. A title or subject line should do more than tell only the general topic; the title should enable the reader to select this document from among many other documents likely to be filed in the same system.

TOO GENERAL AND VAGUE	MORE PRECISE
Cooling System Modifications	Chiller Redesign and Installation Proposal, Conestoga Tower Building
Marketing Results	Sales to New and Existing Clients during the Impact Campaign for Models 200 and 201
New Sales Force	Hiring Plan for Custom Software Sales Force

Marketing reports are written frequently. A report titled "Marketing Results" would be only one among many in the company files. Similarly, during a renovation project, many different reports might deal with the cooling system; during an expansion, several documents might discuss the new sales force.

As the negotiations example shows, headings and subheadings can serve both to indicate the ladder of inclusive-to-particular terms in the discourse and to advance the pattern of given and new information.

Attacking the Individual vs. Attacking the Problem

Attacking an individual is psychological coercion.

old information   new information

Attack the problem.

old information

The boldface heading, **"Attacking the Individual vs. Attacking the Problem,"** shows the claim of opposition that will be argued in the passage. Usually, communications instructors advise using parallel structure in subheadings. This shift in structure in this series, from a complete claim to a command or verb phrase, does not fulfill the reader's expectations. The reader has been led to expect another full sentence with both old and new information.

Forecasting sentences
create a skeleton of the
argument and sum up
paragraph messages.

A forecasting sentence appears near the beginning of a paragraph and directs the reader's attention to the main idea of the paragraph. Such sentences are sometimes called "lead sentences," "topic sentences," or "guide sentences." The first subheading is a forecasting sentence: *"Attacking an individual is psychological coercion."* Several researchers have pointed out that people who write articles for prestigious magazines and scholarly articles do not use forecasting sentences very often, although business communication texts recommend that they be used frequently or even always. A common-sense resolution to this disagreement is that a forecasting sentence is one of many ways to create coherence in discourse. By guiding the reader's attention to the paragraph's main point, the forecasting sentence increases the obviousness of the message and enables the reader to connect details to the main idea more quickly. Forecasting sentences also suit the practical circumstances facing many business readers.

Many executives skim or speed-read business documents. If you know that your document will receive only a few seconds of your reader's attention, you should use devices that make its importance and meaning stand out. To test your document for speed readers, pull out the headings and the opening (forecasting) sentences of each paragraph. The result should be a skeleton form of your argument. If the reader can read only this frame without missing any key points, the speed readers should be able to use your document easily.

Logical Perspectives

Use "you" only when directly addressing the reader.

The excerpt on negotiating also illustrates another aspect of the business communicators' contract, the obligation to use logical perspectives consistently. Unfortunately, it offers a negative example. The ideas are important, but readers have to work hard to keep the references straight. To begin with, the two authors refer to themselves in the first person singular, "I." This is only the beginning of the confusion.

The first sentence after the first subhead in paragraph one seems to be about the writer and some person other than the reader: "the person with whom I am negotiating." Most readers would not think of themselves as people with whom the writer is negotiating. Suddenly, in the next sentence, the writers begin to talk to the reader as "you," and now the reader seems after all to be across the negotiating table: "I may believe that by focusing my attention on you rather than on our substantive differences, I will coerce you into giving in." A few sentences later, in paragraph two, the writers switch back to talking about people who are not the readers: "Personal attacks are designed to focus psychological pressure on the will of the negotiating partner. All such tactics will feel coercive and tend to damage the ability of the people to work together in the future." Readers are likely to ask, "Why don't the writers continue in the same manner as before by writing something like, 'Personal attacks focus psychological pressure on your will'?"

The logical perspective continues to shift in the rest of the passage. The next sentence is ambiguous: "All such tactics will feel coercive. . . ." This first part of the sentence might be directed to the readers or might be spoken about negotiating partners generally. If the writers hadn't reverted to the third person, readers would think they were still being told how they would feel in such circumstances. However, the second part of the last sentence makes it appear the writers are *not* talking directly to the readers anymore, because the object of the verb "affects" is "the ability of *the people* to work together in the future." The third paragraph is not about readers as negotiating partners; it is written entirely in the third person. The final paragraph, however, shifts back to "readers as negotiating partners" and addresses the readers in the second person (you).

Readers expect more coherent treatment than this passage gives them. A practical rule of thumb is to use "you" only when the readers are supposed to apply the comment to themselves. In a textbook such as this one, the authors do shift from general discussion to specific advice, and when they do, they often address the reader as "you." Such shifting should be less frequent in business documents than in a textbook, unless the document is a set of instructions or an operating manual.

Pointers

Use pointers when the change in topic might otherwise be abrupt or when the relationship is important to the argument.

Along with forecasting sentences, writers can show relationships among sentences with *pointers* (phrases that identify the type of relationship that exists between sentences). An example is the word *obviously*, in the sentence, "Obviously, pointers tighten the logic in a sentence." These are useful when the link between the sentences might otherwise be confusing. The words that describe a specific example, for instance, might seem unrelated unless a pointer helps the reader through the jump.

The following list shows types of relationships between sentences that pointers can bring to the reader's attention. The list is representative and not exhaustive.

RELATIONSHIP	POINTERS
Elaboration or addition	and, again, besides, further, furthermore, moreover
Parts or sequence	first, second, third, initially, then, finally, next
Time relationships	before, later, earlier, formerly, soon, then, immediately
Comparison	but, however, in contrast, on the other hand, nevertheless
Exception	although, nevertheless, conversely, however
Illustration	for example, in illustration, for instance, to demonstrate
Emphasis	indeed, obviously, in fact, remarkably, unfortunately
Summary	in conclusion, in short, in other words, in summary
Logical conclusion	therefore, accordingly, consequently, thus, as a result, hence

Some of these pointers (boldfaced) can be seen in Philip Kotler's discussion of product life cycles, highlighted in the Document Spotlight below. In addition to pointers, this discussion uses many of the devices for directing the reader's attention listed earlier: headings, illustrations, key words, forecasting

There are three categories of product life cycles that should be distinguished from the others, those pertaining to styles, fashions, and fads.

A *style* is a basic and distinctive mode of expression appearing in a field of human endeavor. **For example,** styles appear in homes (colonial, ranch, Cape Cod); clothing (formal, casual, funky); and art (realistic, surrealistic, abstract). Once a style is invented, it may last for generations, going in and out of vogue. A style exhibits a cycle showing several periods of renewed interest.

A *fashion* is a currently accepted or popular style in a given field. **For example,** jeans are a fashion in today's clothing, and "country western" is a fashion in today's popular music. Fashions pass through four stages. In the *distinctiveness stage,* some consumers take an interest in something new to set themselves apart from other consumers. The products may be custom-made or produced in small quantities by some manufacturer. In the *emulation stage,* other consumers take an interest out of a desire to emulate the fashion leaders, and additional manufacturers begin to produce larger quantities of the product. In the *mass-fashion stage,* the fashion has become extremely popular and manufacturers have geared up for mass production. **Finally,** in the *decline stage,* consumers start moving toward other fashions that are beginning to catch their eye.

Thus fashions tend to grow slowly, remain popular for a while, and decline slowly. The length of a fashion cycle is hard to predict. Wasson believes that fashions come to an end because they represent a purchase compromise, and consumers start looking for missing attributes. **For example,** as automobiles get shorter, they get less comfortable, and then a growing number of buyers start wanting longer cars. **Furthermore,** too many consumers adopt the fashion, thus turning others away. . . .

Fads are fashions that come quickly into the public eye, are adopted with great zeal, peak early, and decline very fast. Their acceptance cycle is short, and they tend to attract only a limited following. They often have a novel or capricious aspect, as when people start buying "pet rocks" or run naked and "streak."

Source: Philip Kotler. *Marketing Management: Analysis, Planning, Implementation, and Control,* Sixth Edition (Englewood Cliffs, N.J.: Prentice-Hall, 1988), pp. 353–354. Reprinted with permission of the publisher.

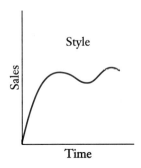
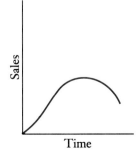
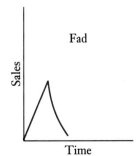

Style, Fashion, and Fad Life Cycles

sentences, and an inclusive-to-particular pattern of related terms. This would be a good time to do Preliminary Exercise 3, which asks you to trace these devices in Kotler's discussion.

Repetition of nouns and pronouns focuses attention on the subject of the paragraph.

Readers need to keep track of the particular topic about which claims are being made. In the explanation of product life cycles, Kotler repeats the term "style" and he uses pronouns to focus the reader's attention on fads, the topic of the last paragraph: "*Their* acceptance cycle is short, and *they* tend to attract only a limited following. *They* often have a novel or capricious aspect. . . ." When readers are given more of these pointers than they need, the prose is said to be wordy or not concise. The demand for coherence and the need for brevity force writers into difficult decisions.

Overuse of pointers causes wordiness. Exploit mutual knowledge to create implicit coherence.

Richard Haswell suggests that when possible, experienced writers strive for cohesive elegance by drawing on their readers' mutual knowledge.[6] The following example relies on readers' general knowledge and shared culture as well as knowledge of a specific type of situation. The example is a note to be tucked in the boxes of graduate students who voluntarily met after class on Thursday evenings for informal soup suppers during which they viewed films about Japanese culture. The students' expectations make it unnecessary to state explicitly, "a meeting will be held."

Menu for Thursday, June 12th

Southwestern Bean Soup   *Tortilla Vegetable Soup*

Jalapeño Corn Bread

An episode on the next phase in Japanese industrial

development.

Fruit and Mexican Wedding Cookies

Iced Tea

☐ CHECKLIST FOR COHERENCE

_____ Is the title or subject line worded in such a way that the specific issue is obvious? Can the document be recognized among others in the file?

_____ Do the introductory headings to the document clearly indicate the source of the document, the intended readers, the date, and any other information necessary for the reader to grasp quickly the situation and transaction to which this document pertains?

_____ Is there a summary or introductory paragraph that makes the situation, the issues (questions or tasks), and the purpose of the communication obvious?

_____ Are there sufficient "answer" headings and subheadings to help readers who need to read only a portion of the document?

_____ As you read through the document, does old or given information precede new information?

_____ Can you identify a pattern of inclusive and particular terms that illustrate or prove the claims in the document?

_____ Are there enough repeated terms to remind the reader of the subject being discussed?

_____ Are there pointers to identify for the reader the crucial relationships in the argument? Such relationships as grouping based on commonalities, opposition or contrast, and conclusions should be identified with transitional phrases.

_____ Does the document maintain a coherent, logical perspective, switching from third to second person only when the actual reader is being addressed?

_____ Can you identify some of your readers' expectations that might enable you to use high-content words to establish coherence without overusing explicit devices?

_____ When you read the document aloud, can you imagine any questions the reader might ask that your document does not answer?

The film and the food are both listed as menu items. Only a person who knew about this group's meetings would be likely to make sense of the unusual combination. Furthermore, this combination shows that the students themselves are not Japanese, for Japanese people do not mix coursework and eating. A visitor used to Japanese ways who met with the class was quite surprised. In addition, the foods are not Japanese.

The "menu" note is not necessarily elegant, but it conveys information as efficiently as a notice reading: "The informal group studying Japanese business culture will meet on Thursday evening, June 12th, after Accounting 503 at 6:30 P.M. in the conference room to view film four in the series. During the meeting a light meal of soups, corn bread, fruit, cookies, and iced tea will be served. Members of the group are expected to attend or call Linda at ext. 2633 before noon on Thursday." The more you and your readers share expectations about the situation and the transaction, the more such unstated expectations can be counted on.

❑ COMMUNICATION CHALLENGES
▬

PRELIMINARY EXERCISE 1   *Select a passage from a textbook, advertising circular, or letter that you have received recently. Photocopy one page of the document and trace the progression of given and new topics by assigning letters to new information. Draw lines between numbers to trace the development of the pattern.* Are there any new topics introduced that are not tied to known information? Would you say that the reader has sufficient old information at each point to interpret the new information correctly and easily?

PRELIMINARY EXERCISE 2   *Read this excerpt from the Quaker Oats Company annual report and make a diagram of inclusive-to-particular terms.* The diagram should be similar to the one for the first paragraph of the negotiations excerpt in the Document Spotlight on page 163.

HOT CEREALS

Hot cereals are Quaker's oldest, best-known, and most profitable products. Quaker holds the top share (66 percent) of the $600 million hot cereal market, with Old Fashioned and Quick *Quaker* Oats the leading "long-cooking" hot cereals, and Instant *Quaker* Oatmeal the best-selling brand in the "instant" segment. Fiscal 1988 saw substantial growth in the hot cereals category—the first increase in six years—fueled by Quaker's aggressive advertising and merchandising programs, in addition to a greater awareness of oatmeal's health benefits. Studies have found that adding soluble fibers to a fat-modified diet leads to lower serum cholesterol levels, thereby decreasing the risk of heart disease. *Quaker* Oatmeal and Oat bran are good sources of soluble fiber. In addition, *Quaker* Oatmeal is an excellent source of protein and vitamins.

PRELIMINARY EXERCISE 3   *Make a photocopy of the Kotler excerpt shown in the Document Spotlight on page 167. Use marginal notes to identify the coherence devices he uses,* including word repetition, sentence pattern repetition, patterns of given and new information, patterns of inclusive and particular terms, headings, and graphics.

PRELIMINARY EXERCISE 4   *Select a passage from one of your textbooks and photocopy one page. Circle the words or phrases that point out a relationship for the readers. Revise one paragraph to increase the coherence.*

increase repetitions and pronouns

take out unnecessary transition tags

add transition tags

EXERCISE 1

Add forecasting sentences to each of the following paragraphs.

Thesis: Although the business graphics function in integrated business software can produce impressive presentation aids, its "picture power" also can sharpen your decision skills.

_____ Some people say they bought their integrated software, such as Lotus 1-2-3, Excel, Symphony, or Supercalc3, primarily to do analysis. The spreadsheets crunch numbers and the database on these programs blends, extracts, and selects them. Some people say that because their jobs don't require presentations, they never use the graphics part of the program. Still others hold that "real managers don't need pictures" and argue that anyone who wants to look at pretty graphics should transfer to the art department.

_____ Were the graphics features meant just for making pretty pictures? For people who spend half their time explaining things to numbskulls? Depending on the sort of work you do, the exact capabilities of your program, and your level of involvement with the world of numbers, graphics could be just your ticket to clarity and insight. Indeed, as close as a couple of key strokes.

_____ Business graphics can capture the essence of a complex collection of data, distill the relationships between different numbers, and present them instantly and dramatically. In analytical use, it is important to minimize the interruptions in your train of thought. With an on-line graphing function, you can quickly move from the intimate details of a spreadsheet to a meaningful overview of the data, its distribution, frequencies, and parts. Having two views, spreadsheet and graphics, at your fingertips can stimulate your thinking and speed your ability to draw conclusions.

_____ Michael Mizen, a special projects coordinator at a medical products marketing research and consulting company in Chicago, often uses graphs as an integral part of his analytical process. Mizen prepares market analyses and projections for a number of pharmaceutical companies. "When you can get a graph with just two keystrokes," he says, "graphics become a decision tool you can change as fast as you can think of ways to analyze the data."

_____

Source: Based on C. Rubin, "Visual decision support." *Personal Computing*, February 1985, 101–103.

EXERCISE 2

Trace the progress of the given-to-new pattern in the selection from Getting together: Building a relationship that gets to YES *on page 163.* The Document Spotlight points out inclusive and particular terms. How are the given-new pattern and the inclusive-to-particular pattern related?

EXERCISE 3

The paragraph below is taken from a memorandum written by a college's security chief to the head of academic affairs. Using letters of the alphabet, mark the progression of new and old information. Look for a point where the writer jumps from old information to a sentence containing only new information. *Write a sentence that will close the gap by linking the old subject with the new information.*

For the past several years we have scheduled the three-day fall break for the first week of November. Faculty and students have expressed no dissatisfaction with this schedule, but I believe it should be changed. In the security reports for 1988, 1989, and 1990 (copies are in your files), the incidence of vandalism rises slowly but steadily from the first week of September, when students arrive on campus, until the third week of October. Thereafter, the numbers of incidents remain virtually constant until fall break. After break the weekly number for all three years drops back to about half the previous rate and stays there until the Christmas holidays. Apparently the tension the break is intended to relieve has already built up to its full force by the third week of October. I recommend that next year we schedule the break two weeks earlier and observe whether we can lower the amount of mischief accordingly.

EXERCISE 4

Draw inclusive-to-particular ladders for paragraphs 2, 3, and 4 of the Document Spotlight on negotiations tactics on p. 163.

EXERCISE 5

Choose an important concept or theory from a course that you are taking this year. Write an explanation of this theory or concept for Bob, another student in the class, who has been away from school. Assume that Bob was away from school at the time the lecture and readings about this concept were assigned and he needs a concise explanation that will enable him to pass the test on Friday. *Write a one- to two-page account of this idea, building on the old information Bob would have known from being in the course up to the point this topic was presented.* Although your audience is a student, do not rely heavily on campus slang in preparing this summary.

IF YOU WOULD LIKE
TO READ MORE

Aulls, M. (1975). Expository paragraph properties that influence recall. *Journal of Reading Behavior, 7,* 391–400.

Clark, H. H., & Haviland, S. E. (1977). Comprehension and the given-new contract. In R. O. Freedle (Ed.), *Discourse production and comprehension* (pp. 1–40). Norwood, NJ: Ablex Publishing.

Glatt, B. S. (1982). Defining thematic progressions and their relationship to reader comprehension. In M. Nystrand (Ed.), *What writers know: The language, process, and structure of comprehension* (pp. 87–103). New York: Academic Press.

Kent, T. L. (1984). Paragraph production and the given-new contract. *Journal of Business Communication, 21*(4), 45–66.

NOTES

1. B. S. Glatt, "Defining thematic progressions and their relationship to reader comprehension," in M. Nystrand (Ed.), *What writers know: The language, process, and structure of comprehension.* New York: Academic Press (1982), 87.

2. Linguists refer to the pattern of given and new information as a "contract." Because several other sorts of agreements also seem to exist between business communicators, I have called the larger set of agreements a "contract" and the use of given-new sequences only a "pattern."

3. H. H. Clark and E. V. Clark, *Psychology and language.* San Diego, CA: Harcourt Brace Jovanovich (1977), 92.

4. Based on research reported by J. D. Bransford & N. S. McCarrell, "A sketch of a cognitive approach to comprehension," in W. Weiner (Ed.), *Cognition and symbolic processes.* Hillsdale, NJ: Erlbaum (1974).

5. A similar notion of the effects of reinforcement on poetry readers' perception, called "coupling," was proposed by Samuel Levin in *Linguistic structures in poetry, Janua Linguarum, 23* (1961), The Hague.

6. R. H. Haswell, "Textual research and coherence: Findings, intuition, application." *College English 51,* (1989), 311.

DEVELOPING A PROFESSIONAL COMMUNICATION STYLE

OBJECTIVES

This chapter will help you develop your own professional communication style in

- writing
- listening
- conversing
- participating in meetings

PREVIEW

Students must learn to create communication styles appropriate to their professional roles. Knowing some of the written language patterns that mark typical student and professional roles will make it easier to select those techniques that best suit your own personality and circumstances. Naturally, there are many professional styles and you are a unique personality, so your professional style will not copy anyone else's and will vary to suit different situations.

You must also develop the listening and conversational styles that are important for business meetings. Your listening style will affect your ability to obtain information from others and develop good relationships. Your body language, gestures, stance, and voice also embody your professional role during meetings. All these aspects of language use will affect the way others perceive you as a professional.

Meetings are essential in many business situations. People must work together to analyze problems, plan work, resolve differences, and share information. Planning for meetings and understanding communication functions can make your participation as a team member successful.

A role is more than formal authority or a title on your door. A role is a way of being in specific social circumstances. This chapter discusses your communication style: turning your knowledge, authority, and purposes into oral and written language behavior that can help you fulfill your role.

❏ ADOPTING A PROFESSIONAL STYLE

Changing from a Student's to a Professional's Communication Style

Your goal: to develop your own professional communication style in writing, listening, speaking, and participating in meetings.

For the most part, our communication roles are made up of the language and gestural conventions we have observed or used in the past. When we take up a new role, whether in business or in personal life, generally we imitate the language and behavior of others we have seen in the role. Sometimes we catch ourselves sounding like our parents, our teachers, or our bosses when we try to write a memorandum or speak on a formal occasion for the first time. We may be unaware of our imitation.

Although people often rely on imitation when playing a role, they also can create new roles for themselves. The human dilemma of not knowing what to say in order to play the right part has been illustrated in many movies and plays. In the movie comedy *Big Business*, a character played by Bette Midler suddenly finds herself in a company crisis, mistaken for a twin sister who is a corporate executive. Bette's character rises to the occasion by imitating Joan Collins in the television soap opera "Dynasty." We are more than people speaking others' lines, however. Human beings also create novel language; it is the clearest mark of being human that we can speak thousands of sentences we never heard anyone else speak and create new roles for ourselves. You don't want to sound like a carbon copy of another person. As you develop your own professional style, you will want to remember the high value business people place on communication styles that reflect the individual's personal ways of thinking.[1]

Creating a Professional Written Style

As a professional, your style must reflect your knowledge, ability, and personality.

When students join companies, they must adjust to the role of the knowledgeable professional whose information, reasoning, and judgment justify audiences' belief and action. Gordon Cain, a distinguished leader in the leveraged buyout field and president of the Sterling Group, once remarked to me, "The only person worth promoting is a person with the courage to say, 'I think,' 'I recommend,' or 'I will.'" In academic situations, students may adopt language techniques that are acceptable in student roles but not appropriate for professional roles. Students nearly always know less about the subject than the teachers who grade their papers, and as we mentioned in Chapter 1, they seldom write to cause action; their role is mostly passive. Students sometimes insert many qualifying phrases and clauses that deny responsibility for the truth, accuracy, or validity of their statements. For example, students may use clauses like "it seems that" or "statistics show that" instead of clauses that express their own claims, such as "I noticed that" or "my analysis shows."

In conversations or class discussions, students may "swallow" the ends of their sentences, making statements seem uncertain or tentative, or they may add tag clauses such as "I *think* that's right. . . ." Sometimes students refuse to say "I" or "we" when discussing a business case and present every fact or opinion as the position of someone else in the case, eventually showing one person or another as having the better position. Another passive tactic is to discuss the case or problem as though telling a story: "Mr. Baxter has a problem, because his company's market share is declining. . . . He could consider this. . . . He could consider that. . . . Mr. Baxter is likely to. . . ." Another tactic is to present the discussion entirely in the passive voice (for example, "losses were experienced") as though disembodied events occurred without anyone's agency—least of all the student writer's.

The student who wants to develop a professional writing style must adopt new tactics. The examples that follow concern a case about Brand Pipe Company.[2] The students who wrote them were asked to take the role of a member of the management committee, read the case, and write a report to the management committee. Some of the students succeeded in enacting a professional role; others sounded more like students. After reviewing all five, you should complete Preliminary Exercise 1 in the Communication Challenges at the end of the chapter. This exercise asks you to select one of the weaker versions and enact a more professional role by changing the style.

EXAMPLE 1

Our advantage over our competitors springs from two distinctive competencies: our technically advanced equipment, which leads the industry, and our location in the midst of our customers. Our superior technology provides us the opportunity to produce pipe with a minimal amount of raw material wastage. Our plant location gives us an opportunity for a price advantage, because of reduced freight costs, on approximately 47.5% of the total market demand. Unfortunately, we're using up profits manufacturing some products that these customers have shown they don't want. We have to face up to the problem of overcapacity. Using our capacity doesn't make sense if we can't sell the products we manufacture.

Comments: This student succeeds in selecting the information that an audience within the company would think important to review. He also elicits favorable attitudes by stating things the audience would agree with and take pride in. He then uses this initial agreement to lead the reader into rethinking the consequences of the production policy. He enacts the role of the audience's equal. Nouns modified by the first-person possessive pronoun *our* (as in "Our plant location gives us") serve as subjects in three of the six sentences. *We*, which unites the audience and writer, is the subject of two more. Naturally, if every sentence in the document began with such subjects, it quickly would become boring. Used judiciously, this technique can foster unity.

EXAMPLE 2

The management at Brand Pipe, particularly Mr. Buford, is faced with a very difficult and very broad task for the upcoming years. The parent company, Arnol, having sent down the proclamation that Buford must come up with a specific marketing plan to improve company profits "as quickly as possible" and come up with a plan for the long term, is now set to back off and see if he lets the business continue to flounder or if he manages to pull it up out of the quagmire of stagnant unprofitability into which it has sunk. Buford must very quickly and very efficiently pull together his resources and analyze the nature of his organization and its environment to formulate a plan and save his job. What should he do? The excess capacity in the plastic pipe industry creates a formidable barrier to all manufacturers. Brand Pipe cannot expect dramatic success in the face of this problem, but Mr. Buford can reduce its operating losses by reducing the number of products it offers.

Comments: Some of the details this writer has chosen are quite relevant to the decision the company faces, such as the total sales for the preceding year. On the other hand, the student writes *about* the company and its management, referring to them in the third person. He includes company information that every manager would know and that is not relevant to the decision. In general, a professional does not restate to audience members what they know unless this information is directly involved in the conflict or problem that must be solved.

The principal decision maker, Mr. Buford, is talked about in the third person. Although those who are making a decision may be mentioned indirectly, this writer treats Buford as a character in a story, not as a listener. The writer says, "Buford must very quickly and very efficiently pull together his resources and analyze the nature of his organization and its environment to formulate a plan and save his job. What should he do?" A manager writing to a group in which Buford was a member would be more likely to write, "Our success depends on formulating and implementing an appropriate strategic plan without delay. I recommend that the president appoint a full-time strategy task force to develop a plan during the next two weeks." The company's code of etiquette would not allow the manager to discuss the possibility that the president might lose his position.

EXAMPLE 3

Brand Pipe Company is the second largest producer of plastic pipe in the Pacific Northwest. It is owned by the Arnol Corporation, a large company in an unrelated field. It produces pipe from four types of plastic resins: polyvinyl chloride (PVC), styrene, acrylonitrile butadiene styrene (ABS), and polyethylene (Poly). Brand Pipe produces two hundred different sizes and styles of pipe from these four resins. Brand Pipe has over $2 million invested in plant and equipment. Its pipe is of standard quality as compared with the rest of the market's pipe. Company sales last year totaled $1.6 billion, but the company has been operating at a loss for the past year and a half.

Comments: The beginning of this student's report seems quite uninvolved with the audience. The student positions himself well away from the scene of the action, describing one fact at a time in static prose whose sentences have the structure "X is" or "It produces." Note the timid, factual sentence structure: "Brand Pipe Company is . . . . It is . . . . It produces . . . . Brand Pipe produces. . . . Brand Pipe has. . . . Its pipe is. . . . Company sales last year totaled $1.6 billion, but the company has been operating at a loss for the past year and a half." Only the last sentence, whose structure contrasts the total sales and the net losses, sets ideas in relation to one another and thereby makes the writer seem more assertive and authoritative.

EXAMPLE 4

I believe our problem is a misconception of our products and our customers. We need to sell the right products to the right people. From the chart below, we can see that Poly and ABS are unprofitable (a discussion of styrene is on page 6). Our assumption that we can reach all the end-use segments in order to use our plant capacity has led us into losses. Our high variable costs for ABS and Poly are eating up our margin for covering fixed costs. We have to ask, "Why produce these products when they are undermining our financial situation?" Overcapacity and low sales are also caused by the sales approach we have taken. Our sales representatives should concentrate on distributors rather than end-users. I believe we can solve the sales problem, and the rest of this report evaluates the feasibility of changing our sales strategy.

Comments: This writer feels able to enter into a dialogue with the readers. He claims that both he and the audience are asking the same question. It is true that he hedges in the beginning by starting out "I believe" and by ending the paragraph with another "I believe" sentence, instead of declaring "We can solve the sales problem" straightforwardly. What follows, he seems to say, is only his belief. However, he shares responsibility for what has been happening by referring to "our assumption." Furthermore, he juxtaposes the problem to his solution, which shows some confidence.

EXAMPLE 5

There are several causes for Brand Pipe's poor performance over the last two years. Industry conditions have deteriorated due to the entrance of Japanese firms and "garage shops." Inefficiencies in production have gone uncorrected due to insufficient manpower or inadequate management. Excessive changeover costs were incurred in chasing small-volume purchases. Other small-volume purchases have been lost due to insufficient and uneconomic inventory levels.

Comments: This writer has distanced herself from the problems by stating them in the passive voice. She thus avoids blaming anyone. Further, she is not quite certain whether "insufficient manpower" or "inadequate management" has caused the problem. She implies criticism through her word choice: "*chasing small volume purchases.*" She also creates a negative tone by using many words that have negative prefixes: *insufficient, uneconomic,* and *inefficiencies.* This critical but distanced role makes it more difficult for the audience to identify with her. On a mechanical level, her use of "due to" would be condemned by most experts; according to many grammar and style manuals, "due to" should only follow a linking verb.

This would be a good time to complete Preliminary Exercise 1 at the end of the chapter.

To plan your style, you must know yourself.

How can you make your writing convey your professional role? Consider the reasons you were hired or are going to be hired for the job: your knowledge of some technical function in the business (such as accounting, marketing, sales, engineering, or finance), your ability to interpret trends in the business, your ability to lead others and motivate high performance, your ethical character, your attention to detail, your ability to foresee the future, or your sensitivity to social issues.

Choose your three principal strengths and plan how your style will convey them.

Make a list of your professional qualities and rank the three most important as the hallmarks of your professional style. Make a second list of ways that each of these traits can be shown in a document. At first, you may think of only a few strategies. Begin looking for evidence of these traits in other people's writing. How do they convince you they're reliable, detail-oriented, trustworthy, knowledgeable about market trends? Add their methods to your list and imitate those features in your own prose as often as possible. For example, people who are farsighted usually include something, however brief, about the consequences of an action or proposal, perhaps something about implementation or benefits of a particular strategy. Or, people who are considerate of others take note of other people's efforts and praise them. A statement that acknowledges another person or group's progress, such as "I noticed you've already started the installation of the new crane," or "Thanks for sending the sales figures to me last Thursday" may be no more than descriptions, but they show the reader that his or her work is recognized. Consistent embodiment of your most important traits will create a professional reputation.

Developing a Professional Listening Style

You're very familiar with listening in the classroom, but you must prepare for different listening situations on the job. In school, you're supposed to listen for information, ask questions, take notes, and be prepared to demonstrate that you've grasped the material. Sometimes you also must demonstrate that you know how to apply the concepts or techniques presented when you take tests or answer the instructor's questions in class. In general, you can only influence in a limited way what the instructor tells you.

Active listening produces power.

On the job, you need a more active listening style. "Active listening" on the job is more than remaining silent; it involves planning, listening with a purpose, helping people provide what you need to hear, interpreting what others say, and responding in ways that facilitate the transaction. Meada Gibbs, a communications researcher, and her associates point out that the person who possesses real power is not the person who dominates by talking constantly, but the person who is able to "*listen* carefully, *understand* thoroughly, *evaluate* logically,

CHECKLIST FOR WRITTEN STYLE

Mark Y for yes or N for no. Use the checklist as a guide for revisions.

_____ Are situations and conditions described with positive words wherever possible?

_____ Do you speak as a member of the organization, using "I" and "we" occasionally?

_____ Do you take responsibility for your professional judgments, using the active voice?

_____ Have you made your ideas or information relevant to the situation?

_____ Have you evaluated the impact of your recommendations on the larger community (assessed ethical consequences)?

_____ Do the word choices, metaphors and other comparisons reflect pertinent aspects of your personality? Does this language sound like you? Can you read it aloud smoothly?

_____ Can you point out elements of the document that reflect the three characteristics you want readers to remember about you?

and *react* intelligently." Effective listening, Gibbs says, requires that listeners "(1) consciously exert effort in listening; (2) resist distractions, (3) seek areas of interest in what the speaker is saying, (4) exercise their minds by not avoiding difficult material, (5) judge content, (6) listen for central themes, not isolated facts, (7) maintain open minds, (8) defer evaluation of the speaker's remarks until comprehension is complete, (9) be flexible and selective in note taking, and (10) capitalize on their thought speed."[3]

Planning for Listening

Before you go in to talk with your manager or with an associate, jot down or at least think about the following questions:

What aspects of the transaction require obtaining new information from this person?

What facts or instructions must I learn?

What feelings should I listen for?

What future steps must we agree on?

Use the same analysis and planning for situations requiring listening that you would use for situations requiring writing.

Create a comprehensive purpose for the conversation and jot it beside the appointment in your calendar or schedule: "See Taylor about new inventory control procedure. Are they on schedule? Does he need any help from us? New problems? Does he like it?" A comprehensive purpose, of course, involves your own purpose, the other person's purpose, and the company's purpose. As the conversation occurs, begin by reviewing with the other person the points you both want to cover during the conversation. Setting the stage for the conversation will help ensure that its purposes are accomplished.

TWO VIEWS ON PROFESSIONAL STYLE

The first of the following passages is from Ralph Wanger's speech at the Financial Analysts Federation Annual Conference, June 18, 1986. Wanger is talking directly to the financial analysts who write the kinds of reports he is discussing. He argues that the competitive information environment means the financial analysts must compete for readers' attention. Reinforcing the idea that financial analysts' style should differ from that of some other professions, he recommends a style that, by itself, causes readers to read the report.

The second excerpt is Marda Steffey's advice to executives in one of her communication seminars. Steffey is president of Career Development, Inc., a consulting firm that serves corporations such as Compaq Computer Corporation and Cray Research, Inc. Unlike Wanger, she is speaking broadly about all types of communication, not just a single kind of report.

ADVICE TO FINANCIAL ANALYSTS FROM RALPH WANGER
"WILL YOUR REPORT GET READ?"

Too Much Paper

How does my firm handle research material? My firm is Harris Associates, a medium-sized investment counseling firm running about $2.5 billion in assets, evenly split between individual and institutional money. We have six portfolio managers and nine securities analysts. . . . As the firm has grown, the amount of research we get into our mail room has grown in spectacular fashion. The body of research material far exceeds anyone's ability to read it. Our mail room sorts the material and publishes a daily index. On the June 6 list, the index ran four full double-column pages and a little on page 5, which is about 400 separate items.

Each analyst and portfolio manager gets a copy of the index each day, and marks the items he or she wants to see. The mail room then delivers those reports. One must be careful not to order so many items that the whole day is spent just in studying reports! In summary, we have a lot of people, a lot of input, and a few systems to fight clutter, but not enough. We are undoubtedly typical of a whole lot of institutions today. If you have a suggestion on how to improve our report-handling system, we would love to hear it.

Style

I have stressed how the user of your reports is overwhelmed with material. You have to grab his attention in order to get your report in the "5 percent pile" which actually gets read and will help boost your firm's brokerage allocation. Your report must be clear and interesting.

Clarity can be enhanced by the use of standardized formats, so I know where to find the cash flow exhibit in your firm's reports. A summary at the front of the report will help. A table of contents is good in a long report. Spreadsheets are fine, but label the rows and columns very clearly. Try to figure out how to include some graphs (pertinent to the report and well-labeled) even if it is just a Mansfield price chart. If you can add diagrams, pictures or cartoons, great. An economic forecaster, Siff, Oakley & Marks, always includes some

BUSINESS COMMUNICATION TRENDS

TWO VIEWS ON PROFESSIONAL STYLE (*continued*)

cartoons in their material, sometimes *The Wizard of Id,* sometimes drawn by one of their own staff people. I can tell you that the cartoons get read first.

Humor, vivid writing, and clear style are very helpful. Strategists such as Barton Biggs at Morgan Stanley and Eric Miller at DL&J are reasonable and thoughtful people, but their high reputation is due in large part to their witty and incisive writing style. . . .

Have I left you with the impression that style is more important than substance? Good—it is, if you are trying to get to the top of our profession. Every analyst makes some good forecasts and some bad forecasts, but wit gets remembered, and so a well-written report is more likely to get the reader to take action than a dull report. . . . We are CFA's, not accountants, so let's be interesting characters.

ADVICE ON STYLE FOR ETHICAL COMMUNICATORS FROM MARDA STEFFEY, COMMUNICATIONS CONSULTANT

Fulfilling the needs of all interested parties (audience, organization, outside interests and self) is not always simple; fulfilling these needs while maintaining ethical integrity can require personal courage as well as the ability to communicate effectively. The choice of an appropriate writing style does not always depend upon what will best serve the interests of the company or the individual writer. That choice also depends upon what will best

serve the interests of the reader and the population as a whole. As you strive to achieve ethical integrity, you should write with strong verbs, a confident tone (few, if any, weasel words such as "possibly," "should," and "perhaps"), and a clear request for action. Ethical writers go beyond these stylistic elements, however, to take action themselves.

ETHICAL WRITERS

- Are clear, accurate, and concise
- Put important information in important places
- Use simple lists and exhibits to make information accessible
- Ask for specific action from specific individuals
- Follow through with phone calls and visits when necessary

This last tenet is one of the most difficult to follow, especially for individuals who have recently emerged from academic settings, where writing is an end unto itself. It can be difficult to accept this new, but undeniable reality: Writing something brings no guarantee that anyone will read it, much less act upon it. Assertive writers go beyond the mere creation of a document; they do what it takes to ensure results.

Source: The full text of Wanger's speech was reprinted in the *1986 Semi-Annual Report of The Acorn Fund, Inc.*, 120 South La Salle Street, Chicago, IL 60603-3596. Reprinted with permission.

Active Listening

Listen with a purpose and identify central themes, not isolated facts.

Listen to organize and understand what you hear. The average person speaks about 125 words per minute, but the average listener can process about 500 to 600 words per minute. Some listeners shift part of their attention to other topics: tonight's dinner, the color of the walls, last night's game. Some merely put their mind in neutral and doodle on their notepad while waiting to say something. Instead, the extra processing time should be used to summarize what the person is trying to say, to make connections among points and facts, and discover new issues or questions that need clarification. While you are thinking, you have the advantage because you have the time to understand the nature of the arguments offered, separate fact from opinion, and listen for central themes, not isolated facts.

During the conversation, begin your turns by acknowledging the main point of the other person's comments. Restating the main point will make the other person feel important and gives that person a chance to correct you if you misunderstood. Paraphrasing what the other person has said may seem to take up vital time you need to express *your* ideas. In the long run, however, the increased accuracy of the communication and the relationship that develops will more than make up for any delays. Besides, if you have agreed on an agenda for the conversation at the beginning, you should not have to worry about covering what is necessary.

Listen to prevent misunderstandings. Listen for words that the other person seems to be using in a different way. Sometimes people with different backgrounds associate different ideas with a single term. For example, people trained in the social sciences tend to think of "openness" and "open systems" in a positive way; they view an open system as one that interacts readily with its environment and open people as flexible, adaptable, and outgoing. Electrical engineers, on the other hand, see an "open system" as an unworkable or disabled system. Unless a system is closed, the current can't flow through it and no work can be done. Acknowledging differences and exploring them can help individuals understand one another and cooperate more easily.

Taking notes is good business; it shows you care about remembering what was said.

Take notes selectively. Note all dates and amounts. Keep track of the major points of the conversation. Be sure to write down your responsibilities and any specific steps others will take. These notes can be the basis for a memorandum to the file or a memorandum to the other person to confirm your agreements.

Before concluding the conversation, check for mutual understanding. Many phrases can lead into this part of the conversation:

"Before I go, let me make sure we agree on the next steps."

"Let me go over the key points to make sure we understand them the same way."

"I'd like to run through what we've decided. I don't want to leave out anything."

Follow Up to Increase Listening Effectiveness and Goodwill Don't forget to follow up conversations with memos or letters. A written record reminds everyone of the group's agreements, provides guidance in the future, and motivates people to carry out the group's decisions. Thank-you notes or memos also build goodwill and cement relationships.

Developing a Professional Conversation Style

What people see is as important as what they hear.

People remember and are profoundly influenced by body language and eye contact as well as by voice qualities and words. "Body language" includes head position, stance, and gestures. You can no doubt read the body language of your friends and teachers almost automatically; you know when someone is irritated, happy, anxious, or angry without hearing a word. Body language is a system of cultural signs, and you know how to read the signs of your own group. You probably expect that your business associates from foreign countries will have a different system of gestures, but you may not realize that people in business organizations also develop distinctive systems of nonverbal communication. Assume that when you join a company you will have to modify your body language somewhat to suit the new social context.

Head Position and Facial Expression In most companies, head position is interpreted as being related to your confidence and your interest in issues and other people. Stand in front of a mirror and imagine you are talking about an important idea. What is your head position? If you usually keep your head down, you will look less confident and attentive, perhaps even bored or indifferent. To change your habits and convey more confidence, try the following four-minute exercise daily for a couple of weeks. Read a paragraph aloud to your mirror every day with a fist placed under your chin. Then read the paragraph again with your chin up (fist removed). Note the look of authority and confidence that results from a higher chin position.

People may take their cues from your expressions; smile often.

Your facial expression, especially your willingness to smile, can have a wonderful effect on others. People often take their cues from others' facial expressions. If you are excited about an idea, enthusiastic about another person's work, or eager to work on a new project, your facial expression alone may influence your listeners' views of the subject. It is sometimes the responsibility of a person who proposes a new idea or a solution to a problem to bear the group's anxiety about making a change. If you don't believe in an idea yourself and express that concern, why should anyone else be enthusiastic?

Stance To give your posture a professional look, imagine a string coming from the top of your head and keeping your body erect—the effect is "uplifting." Stand comfortably with your feet four to six inches apart. You can't maintain a stable stance if your feet are touching one another. If you're sitting, make sure that your posture is energetic and open. Don't cross your arms across your chest defensively or slump in your seat. You may relax, but stay alert. Keep your head and chin up, attentive to other people in the group.

Videotape can help
you see yourself as
others see you.

If possible, be videotaped during a meeting or project group work session. Analyze your gestures and body language. Rolling hand gestures and palms-up gestures generally are thought to be conciliatory and even uncertain; vertical and horizontal gestures are thought to be decisive. Which do you use most? Are your gestures concept related? Do you use gestures that suggest contrast, extent, sequence, and time order appropriately? Are there "pointless" gestures—hand bouncing or rolling, shrugs, or nervous mannerisms? Leading a gesture with the fingertips is thought to be masculine; leading with the wrist is thought to be feminine. Women can sometimes counteract patronizing attitudes by adopting more decisive horizontal and vertical gestures. When you aren't making a gesture, let your arms hang at your side. Don't hide them behind you, military style, or cross them across your chest (considered a defensive gesture) or hold your hands together over your lower abdomen like an usher or an undertaker. This last gesture is thought to be too deferential or obsequious.

Eye contact says "This
message is meant for
you."

Eye Contact   If you avoid looking at your audience, you will seem deferential, anxious, or indifferent. Looking into another person's eyes not only conveys your interest in that person, it gives you information that you can use in the conversation. If you sweep your eyes rapidly across the room, you won't be able to focus on your listener's response. On the other hand, you don't want to stare and make him or her feel uncomfortable. In general, you want to look at a person long enough to give that individual a sense of personal involvement; this usually requires that you address a complete clause to the person before looking elsewhere.

Voice Quality   Finally, your voice will give others many cues about you. If your voice shakes, others will infer you are nervous or afraid. Nervousness often results in a higher pitched voice, too, which sounds anxious and quarrelsome. To develop more control, learn to slow down your breathing. The body has a wonderfully complex automatic system that you can use to your benefit. Slow breathing alters the ratio of gases in the blood, which in turn controls your heart rate and the rate the nerves fire along the intercostal muscles of your ribs. When your heart rate slows and your muscles along the rib cage relax, suddenly you will be able to breathe deeply. There will be sufficient air to prevent your vocal chords from wavering. The effect will last for at least five minutes, by which time you will have become engaged in the meeting or conversation and will feel more at ease. For most people, four to seven minutes of very slow breathing will put them in control of their voice (and perhaps of their emotions, too). Practice at home to find out how long it takes your body to put itself in a calm state.

Audio tape recording
will help you develop
greater expressive
range.

Few of us know how we sound to other people. Your pronunciation may keep people from taking you seriously. People associate pronunciation styles with images of social status and authority. If you speak without sounding final consonants ("gonna" instead of "going to," "meetin'" instead of "meeting," "ax" instead of "ask," and so on) you should correct those habits. Speak into a tape recorder for ten to fifteen minutes every day. Play back the tape and make a list of words that you pronounce imprecisely. During the next day's talk to the recorder, keep the list in front of you and use those words again if you can. Buy a tape recording of a famous man or woman reading a book and listen to the passage on your tape player. Then record yourself reading the same passage. Compare the differences. Continue recording and comparing daily. The goal is not to teach you to impersonate the actor but to give you greater control over your own voice, using that famous person as a model. You might watch a videotape of Martina Navratilova's tennis serve to improve your serve; in a similar way, you can compare your reading to that of a professional reader.

In addition to pronouncing words clearly, you need to give yourself greater control over the variety in pitch and pacing in your voice. Women who have very high-pitched, chirpy, "Minnie Mouse" voices often are dismissed as having nothing important to say; many women executives work on lowering their voices and controlling the pacing to increase the authority of their voices. Similarly, men can increase the authority of their speaking voices. Pitch is the highness or lowness of your voice, rather like tones in music. Pacing is the speed of your delivery. Analyze your tape recording to see whether you habitually raise or lower your voice when you want to emphasize a word. Most people use one or the other of these patterns. Say out loud: "Perhaps you think a tax reduction is important, Harry, but I don't think so." Did you raise your voice when you said "you" and "I," or did you lower it? This sentence will usually reveal your natural pattern of pitch change.

A person who has a very narrow range of pitch is usually thought to be diffident or uncertain. To sound more confident and outgoing, you may need to practice more exaggerated changes of pitch on key words. The goal is to increase the expressiveness of your voice so that it embodies your natural enthusiasm and confidence.

Pacing and pitch create emphasis and direct listeners' attention.

Pacing, like pitch, emphasizes words. The general rule is: *Slow down for important ideas; pick up the pace on less important ideas.* Tiny pauses are like the white spaces surrounding a title or heading; they call attention to the words in the center. Likewise, your changes in pace will alert your listeners to important points. Some people naturally speak much more quickly than others. If you and your colleagues have different speaking styles, be aware that these differences may be irritating. If you habitually speak quickly, especially if people often ask you to repeat what you've said, you may need to vary the pacing more so that your listeners can pick up the key ideas more easily. On the other hand, if the other people around you speak considerably more quickly, try to increase the pace of your supporting remarks even though you "slow down for the lowdown."

Differences in conversational styles can create dissonance.

In addition, there are differences in people's conversational sentence structure. Some people ask many questions; some people think questions are rude. Some people make direct requests, "Please get me those files by Tuesday," while others make only indirect requests, "I need those files by Tuesday." Notice the conversational style of the groups with which you work, because conversational styles are culturally learned. Indirect requests and evasive answers are typical of Japanese speakers, who believe it is impolite to ask for something directly or to obligate the other person.

Think about how your body language, voice qualities, and listening style can convey the three most important qualities you selected as the hallmark of your professional style. Plan ways to reinforce this impression with the other aspects of your communication style.

Finally, remember that in conversation people need more restatement, more summarizing, and more previewing than they need with a written document. Listeners cannot refer to an earlier statement for clarification. If your eye contact with your listener makes you think he or she is "lost," take a minute to review. In oral communication, use additional examples to illustrate your ideas. As a result, you will seem more in control, more competent, more knowledgeable, more professional. Chapter 16, "Preparing and Delivering Oral Presentations," will help you prepare for occasions when you are responsible for a briefing, sales presentation, or proposal at a meeting or conference.

Participating in Meetings

Meetings are essential in many business situations. People must work together to analyze problems, plan work, resolve differences, and share information. Planning for meetings and understanding communication functions essential to group problem solving can make your participation successful.

Use a Strategy Planner for meetings, too.

Plan for participating in a meeting as you would plan for any other business situation. Analyze the transaction and the roles of people involved. Develop a comprehensive purpose for your participation in the meeting and plan a persuasive approach for presenting your most important issues. Build consensus with others informally, if possible, before the meeting takes place. Such conversations will help you anticipate problems that might come up in the meeting. Check the office files to find minutes of similar meetings, just to get a feel for what has gone on at these sessions.

Talk with the person who is setting the agenda if you have an item that you want the group to discuss. If you are leading the meeting, begin by going over the agenda with the group and establishing any ground rules. Go to the meeting prepared with a copy for every person of any data you believe might be essential for decision making. If you do nothing else, determine in advance what time the meeting will end, and no matter what, end at that time. If you become known as a person who begins and ends meetings on time, people will be more willing to attend and participate. People dread and despise going to meetings that last well past their scheduled close.

Communication functions include initiating, maintaining, and blocking.

As the meeting progresses, specific communication functions may be necessary. These functions have been grouped into types: those that lead the group, maintain the group, and block the group. *Lead the group* means to initiate new topics or to adopt particular decisions or opinions; *maintain the group* means to move the group ahead in solving problems, accumulating sufficient information to infer generalizations or reach conclusions, reconciling opposing viewpoints, etc., but not initiating new work or decision making. *Block the group* means to impede either maintenance or leadership. Described by Hensleigh C. Wedgewood more than twenty years ago, these functions have proved fruitful for analyzing others' roles and directing one's own behavior.[4] When you are working in a group, it is important to be able to detect when your group's scenario requires that people carry out certain functions. The following table summarizes the functions and illustrates the kinds of comments that embody them.

TYPICAL COMMENTS OF COMMUNICATION ROLE FUNCTIONS

ROLE FUNCTION	ACTION	TYPICAL COMMENT
Role Functions in Work Activities		
Initiator	suggests new or different ideas, proposes new approaches	"Perhaps we should consider X" "What would happen if we Y?"
Opinion Giver	states pertinent beliefs about what group is considering and others' suggestions	"I think Rona's ideas will boost sales in St. Louis because average personal income has been rising there."
Elaborator	builds on suggestions made by others	"If we combined Rona's ideas with Fred's plan to decentralize, we would have more flexibility."
Clarifier	gives relevant examples offers rationales probes for meaning restates problems	". . . like the plant in Del Rio, right?" ". . . consistent with the sales plan." "Does that mean raising prices?" "In other words, the deductions would offset costs."
Tester	raises questions to "test out" whether group is ready to decide	"Does anyone see any problems with going ahead with this?"
Summarizer	Reviews or tries to pull together the discussion content	"So what we're saying here is that if interest rates fall, we should begin buying back shares as soon as possible."

TYPICAL COMMENTS OF COMMUNICATION ROLE FUNCTIONS

ROLE FUNCTION	ACTION	TYPICAL COMMENT
Group Maintaining Role Functions		
Harmonizer	mediates differences of opinion	"We certainly want both divisions to meet their budgeted profit margins, but not at the expense of the profitability of the corporation as a whole."
	reconciles points of view	"Terry's view gives a good short-term option, whereas Loni's plan takes the life of the contract into consideration."
Encourager	praises and supports others in their contributions	"It's really good that you mentioned last year's problem, Karl. We've got to be prepared for that possibility."
Compromiser	is willing to yield when necessary for the purposes of the group	"Although I would like to renovate this office, we need to put the funds into replacing and upgrading the incinerator."
Tension Reliever	draws off negative feelings with humor calls for a break at appropriate times	"Ease up, Harry! This isn't a yacht in our budget." "Let's see how we feel after lunch."
Gate Keeper	keeps communications open	"Although we can't review that now, let's have a report on it before we decide on the budget."
	creates opportunities for others to participate	"Since Will's new here, he may be able to give us a new perspective on this issue."

Learn to recognize communication functions as you would recognize steps in a dance. Timing is critical: make the right move at the right time.

The blocking role functions Wedgewood identifies are the familiar ones that keep groups from attending to their principal tasks: disagreeing aggressively, criticizing, withdrawing, dominating the discussion, using the group's time to draw attention to one's own concerns, and continually changing the subject. While you surely recognize these unpleasant and difficult behaviors, you may be less aware of the positive role functions that need to be played. Blocking roles can usually be overcome by studying communication processes and by using positive role functions to discourage blockers. If you analyze situations in advance, as suggested in Chapter 2, you often can identify the kinds of communication roles that are required.

❑ COMMUNICATION CHALLENGES

PRELIMINARY EXERCISE 1   Choose either Student Example 2, Example 3, or Example 5 in this chapter and *revise the passage to help the writer enact a professional communication role.*

PRELIMINARY EXERCISE 2   Read the advice about professional writing styles in the Business Communication Trends feature on pages 180–181. These two professionals do not fully agree on the most desirable features of a professional style. How do they differ? What ideas do they share? What elements in Wanger's situation may cause him to value certain aspects of style more than others? What aspects of style do you value most? *Be prepared to discuss these excerpts in class.*

PRELIMINARY EXERCISE 3   *Write a one- to two-page account of an incident in which you either listened very effectively, or failed to listen effectively.* What were the causes of your success or failure? What specific procedures could change the outcome in a similar situation in the future? Avoid broad general answers, such as "listen better" or "pay more attention." *Be prepared to discuss your experience and views in class.*

EXERCISE 1

Revise the memorandum at the right, written by a student intern. Use a professional style that makes the student seem more of an insider, more confident, and more assertive.

EXERCISE 2

Plan to meet with four other people to discuss some possible change or a solution to a problem that now occurs on your campus. Parking arrangements and the quality of the food are a perennial problem at most campuses; try these topics if you can't think of another. The group should discuss the nature of the problem and what solutions might be implemented. The group should try to imagine as many solutions as possible before evaluating them. The meeting should last fifteen minutes. Ask two other people from your class to observe your meeting or videotape your group if your school has audiovisual support services. Ask each of the observers to note features of body language, stance, posture, eye contact, and voice for two of the group members, using the form at the top of page 190. After the meeting, watch the video and ask for feedback from the observers. Return the analysis forms to your instructor.

December 18, 1990

TO: Sam Nussbaum

FROM: Henry Peterson

SUBJECT: Request for Information

My supervisor, Dalia Stokes, asked whether the heat will be on in the offices on Saturday the 22nd and perhaps on Sunday the 23rd. Our department has to send out a proposal by Federal Express on Monday, December 24th, to our office in Buenos Aires, and the people in the department may have to work on the 22nd and maybe even on the 23rd. This proposal is very important and everyone has been working on it for nearly a month now. If you have not ordered heat and other services for this department, like if you were going to have everything on reduced temperatures as you usually do, thinking nobody would be here on a holiday weekend, Ms. Stokes needs you to know that her people will be working and will need support, including the large photocopying machines on the 18th floor, and would you please check to see the printer cartridges have been changed on the laser printers if it isn't too much trouble.

EXERCISE 3

Make arrangements to visit a meeting held by a city or county agency or governing body, or ask to visit a directors' meeting of a charitable organization, such as the Red Cross, the Girl Scouts, the YMCA, or the United Way. Explain that you are studying how groups interact to make decisions. Make a tape recording if the group will give you permission. Analyze the communication role functions of the participants, using the list of role

	Group member 1 (name)	**Group member 2** (name)
head position		
posture or stance		
gestures		
eye contact		
voice		

functions on the chart. How many can you recognize? Did you notice any blocking roles? Who was in charge of the group? *Prepare a two- to three-page memorandum report on this meeting for your instructor.*

EXERCISE 4

Eye contact requires deliberate coordination of your eyes and your speaking, and anything deliberately done must be practiced. To make the nerves and muscles familiar with this task, practice giving numbers to the furniture in your room. The following exercise sounds strange, but it teaches your brain to coordinate your voice and your eyes. Say "I want the desk to take 1, 2, 3, and 4; then if the computer will take 5, 6, and 7; I will give the chair 9, 10, and 11; please let the picture on the left have 12, 13, and 14; the mirror needs only 15," and so on. You may feel a bit silly, but you'll gain considerable control with this exercise. Demonstrate this ability in class and compare your performance with that of other students.

EXERCISE 5

Divide your class into several project groups of four people each. Let each project group choose a company that has an office or a plant in your town. It is all right to have different groups interviewing companies in the same industry. *Write a letter or call the manager or president of the company and ask permission to interview four employees about listening and its importance in that business.* Most executives appreciate the need for students to learn how businesses actually work and will honor your request. (An alternative is to interview people who hold

administrative positions on your campus—people from admissions, personnel, buildings and grounds, central kitchens, and so on.) If possible, interview people who hold the kinds of jobs you would like to have. If that is not possible, try to interview people in different roles in the company. Begin by explaining that you are trying to learn about listening as part of a person's job and how it affects the work of a department or company. Some of the questions you might ask are listed below:

- In what situations do you have to listen to people?
- If the person you are interviewing hasn't told you the kinds of people who participate in those situations, ask, "Who are the people to whom you have to listen?"
- What do you do when people don't want to tell you the information you need?
- How does good listening affect your success?
- What prevents people from listening well?
- What are the risks or problems of not listening well in the situations you've described?
- How would you define a "good listener?"
- Is there anyone in your company that you would describe as a really good listener? Would you tell me about that person?

After the interview, send a thank-you letter to the individuals with whom you met, as your instructor may direct. Meet with your project group to compare notes. *Write a short memorandum report to your instructor summarizing your findings and nominate one of your group to present your findings to the class. Or, form panels representing similar companies and let the panels present their find-*

ings to the class. You may be surprised to find that different companies in the same industry may be organized differently and use listening in different ways. People in different professions or at different levels of a company may prize different qualities in speakers. A good listener in one company may be a person who can take action and make changes quickly. A good listener in another company may be a person who is sensitive to the feelings of others, even though he or she can do little or nothing about the complaint.

EXERCISE 6

Prepare notes for a three-minute talk on an idea from an unusual course you have taken. As your instructor directs, meet with two other students for fifteen minutes. Each person should take three minutes to talk about the course he or she has chosen. Each time, one of the people should be the listener and the other should be the observer. Only the observer can take notes; the observer also should act as timekeeper. After the presentation, the listener has 90 seconds to summarize what he or she has heard. The observer then takes one minute to note any points in the presentation that the listener has overlooked. Afterward, another person makes the presentation and the other two people act as observer and listener. Each person should have an opportunity to play each role.

If the members of your class do not know one another, each of you may choose to talk about yourself and your background.

EXERCISE 7

Plan to attend a meeting of a club or organization to which you belong. Ask in advance to interview two of the people immediately after the meeting, explaining that you are completing an assignment for a communications class. If possible, also get permission to tape record the meeting. Interview each person separately; the interview should take no more than ten minutes. Ask the following questions, and others of your own choosing:

■ Please summarize the meeting; review what happened today (tonight).

■ From your point of view, what was the most important thing that happened?

■ Why do you consider that important?

■ How did people feel about this meeting? Is there any dissension here?

■ What would make these meetings more effective, from your experience with this group?

Write a comparison of the two people's answers, referring to your tape recording or notes. Did the two people generally remember the same things? Did they view the same things as important? Do you agree with their interpretation of the meeting? What does this project tell you about the ways that people listen to the same information?

Case: Children's House of Hope

You are a board member of Children's House of Hope (CHH). The board is having a meeting to discuss how to improve interaction with the local office of the state child protective services agency. The director and staff of Children's House of Hope must deal with this agency often. Although Children's House of Hope is a private, nonprofit organization that primarily cares for abused children whose parents bring them in voluntarily, sometimes these children become involved in the state agency's investigations.

a. The meeting has just gotten underway, and Tim Boucher, the director of CHH, has just described how the caseworkers at the state agency do not return phone calls and do not read the detailed records kept by the professional staff at CHH. These failures cause them to make inappropriate recommendations to the court. How, Boucher asks, can CHH ensure the safety of these children when the records of their physical and psychological condition at the time the children came to CHH are not read or considered? Geraldine Fontenot, a board member, proposes that the board send the governor a formal declaration of complaint. She already has had her friend, a family practice lawyer, draw up such a declaration and offers to pass it around for signature.

Since no other board members have had a chance to ask any questions of the director or to consider any other solutions, what communication roles should you and other board members now play? Look at the list of communication functions on pages 187 and 188 to refresh your memory about possible roles. List the roles, and suggest a sentence opener that would announce that role.

b. Later in the meeting, several proposals have been offered:

1. The board could send a formal declaration of complaint to the state governor.
2. A preliminary meeting could be requested between the advisory board for the state agency and CHH's board of directors.
3. A meeting could be requested between the executive committee of the CHH board of directors and the three county judges who hear child abuse and custody cases to discuss how the court would like to receive information.
4. The board could invite the local director of the state agency to attend one of its meetings and to discuss communication problems from her point of view.
5. A reporter for one of the city newspapers could be contacted about doing a story on the trage-

dies that occur when caseworkers from the state agency do not seek full information about the children involved in litigation.

The fifth option provokes lots of strong feelings. You have plenty of information to release; only last week, a child that the court returned to a father that CHH knew to be the abuser was found beaten to death. The state agency caseworker had refused to meet with the CHH staff, who had photos of the child at the time of placement at CHH, conversations with the father, and other evidence. None of that evidence was used in the custody hearing.

Now that five proposals have been suggested, what roles could you play? Name the roles and write the sentence openers for those roles. This time, suggest the order in which these roles should be played by board members to ensure a good decision. Compare your plans and sentences with those of others in your class or group. How would each comment be likely to shape the interaction of the group?

IF YOU WOULD LIKE TO READ MORE

Ailes, R. (1988). *You are the message: Secrets of the master communicators.* Homewood, IL: Dow Jones-Irwin.

Harris, T. E. (1982). Understanding listener reception. *Supervision, 44,* 6–7. Explains styles of listening that lead to problems.

Henze, G. (1985). *From murk to masterpiece: Style for business writing.* Homewood, IL: Richard D. Irwin.

Montgomery, R. L. (1981). Are you a good listener? *Nation's Business, 69*(10), 65–66, 68.

Montgomery, R. L. (1981). *Listening made easy: How to improve listening on the job, at home, and in the community.* New York: AMACOM.

Williams, J. (1985). *Style: Ten lessons in clarity and grace* (2nd ed.). Glenview, IL: Scott, Foresman.

NOTES

1. C. K. Smith demonstrates that different styles enact different patterns of thinking in *Styles and structures,* New York: Norton. Although published in 1974, this book remains an excellent introduction to the wide variety of styles in both fiction and nonfiction prose and their relation to different thinking processes.

2. These papers were based on a case by S. U. Rich in R. A. Kerin & R. A. Peterson (Eds.), *Strategic marketing problems: Cases and comments.* Boston: Allyn & Bacon (1984), 232–242.

3. M. Gibbs, P. Hewing, J. E. Hulbert, D. Ramsey, & A. Smith (Teaching Methodology and Concepts Committee of the Association for Business Communication). "How to teach effective listening skills in a basic business communication class." *The Bulletin of the Association for Business Communication, 48* (1982)2, 30.

4. H. C. Wedgewood, "Fewer camels, more horses: Where committees go wrong." *Personnel, 44* (1967)4, 62–67.

PART THREE

PRODUCING COMMUNICATIONS

THE TECHNOLOGICAL CONTEXT FOR BUSINESS COMMUNICATION

OBJECTIVES

This chapter will help you

- analyze the effects of technology on communications processes and productivity

- communicate with voice mail, electronic mail, videoconferencing, FAX, and other equipment in the electronic office

- use word processing programs and other software to improve your writing

PREVIEW

Historically, improvements in technology have repeatedly changed communication patterns and affected competition among companies. Companies with advanced information technology may compete more effectively and efficiently than other firms. Greater productivity and competitiveness usually mean greater job security for employees, so using technology well is important to individuals as well as to companies.

The pace of technological change has quickened in the last decade. Today, high-performance workstations give people access to a wide variety of information and enable them to compile and analyze information with calculations and visualizations. Telecommunications can link them with coworkers and others around the world. Technological innovation will continue to change communication processes and business situations, rapidly making textbook descriptions of the technological context, such as this one, obsolete.

Technological innovation has transformed the *experience* of communication as well as its *speed* for workers throughout an organization. Many innovations in the electronic office have allowed workers to spend less time on routine jobs and more time interacting with clients, solving problems, and being creative. Employees also can have more independence and flexibility in scheduling their work.

Word processing software programs have enabled writers to create, revise, and produce high-quality documents easily. Word processing enhances the information gathering, planning, drafting, and editing in composing communications. Although special software is available for many of these steps, the trend is toward more and more powerful word processing programs that include a comprehensive range of features. Properly used, this software (and other equipment in the electronic office) allows people to manage their relationships with others and to work productively and efficiently.

❑ COMMUNICATION TECHNOLOGY AFFECTS PRODUCTIVITY

Why should you care about your company's communication technology? The answers are simple: communication technology affects your ability to be effective, efficient, and productive and your company's ability to compete. If you work for a company that can't compete, you may soon be out of a job. Therefore, you have a stake in how well communication technology is used in your company. We will take a little time to show you how technology, communication, and productivity are linked, but most of this chapter is devoted to demonstrating how to use the electronic office to be an outstandingly productive person. Among the technologies you may have at your disposal are equipment and systems for obtaining and analyzing information; communicating with others; and preparing documents (including writing, editing, and producing them).

❑ TECHNOLOGY, COMMUNICATION, AND A COMPANY'S ABILITY TO COMPETE

Improvements in technology often have been related to changes in the communications patterns of organizations and individuals. For example, telegraph lines that connected points on the east coast of the United States with points on the west coast replaced the Pony Express and led to the destruction and financial ruin of the Pony Express Company. Telephones, which became available at the

FIGURE 10-1.   Electronic Office

turn of the century, continued to improve the speed of communications and allowed many messages that would have been transmitted in written form to be communicated orally. The introduction of the telephone also reduced the telegraph industry's importance and profitability. When mechanical typewriters began to be used in the early twentieth century, some businesspeople claimed these machines would never replace beautifully handwritten correspondence and business documents. However, the greater productivity that could be achieved through the mechanical typewriter, carbon copies, and other mechanical devices such as adding machines meant that businesses could not afford to be without them.

Computers are replacing older technologies because they can give companies competitive advantages.

Computers, first introduced to business, government, and other organizations during the 1950s, are now pervasive. Computers have enormously improved information processing and communications. Computers allow employees to simulate processes, store and retrieve information, manipulate huge data sets, and compose and distribute documents with unprecedented ease. Today, most employees working in offices have access to a computer as well as many other electronic devices, including voice mail, recorders, video, photocopiers, FAX machines, and other equipment. These resources now are used as competitive tools. Many organizations have gained an advantage by using information and communications technologies more effectively than their competitors.

❏ SCENARIOS IN THE ELECTRONIC OFFICE

The electronic office changes the way people manage their work and interact with one another. In one sense, electronic equipment has enabled people to maintain ties despite physical distances in ways that were impossible a half century ago. The availability of this technology has helped make the modern large corporation possible. Even small companies can benefit enormously.

The Components of the Electronic Office

With electronic office equipment, people can obtain and process information as well as create, transmit, and store oral and written messages.

Today, the electronic office combines computers with communications technology (telephone lines and other cables, satellites, and equipment). Most businesses are connected to their environment with telecommunications that include ordinary telephones as well as FAX (facsimile) machines that send electronic photocopies of documents over phone lines to similar machines in other offices, which print out the transported copy. They usually also have modems, small electronic devices that connect computers through telephone lines with computers in other businesses or in employees' homes. Customers can place orders, and businesses can receive information, via modems. In addition to microcomputers (personal computers), many electronic offices now have workstations that combine access to computers with access to telecommunications. Workstations usually contain the following types of hardware and software components.

COMPONENTS OF THE ELECTRONIC OFFICE

HARDWARE

Component	Description
CPU	Central processing unit
Monitor	Display unit; may have color or monochrome screen; usually has color capabilities
Keyboard	Device used to communicate with CPU; usually includes a number keypad
Mouse	Manipulates data or items appearing on the screen
Printer	Creates hard copy of reports; may be a dot matrix, letter quality, or laser printer
Plotter	Produces high-quality graphs; usually makes color as well as black and white graphs
Secondary storage	Stores data and software programs; usually floppy or hard disk
Communications	Connects workstation to local area, regional, or international networks.

SOFTWARE

Type	Purpose
Document preparation	Letters, memos, and reports
Presentation graphics	"35mm slide" quality screens that can be projected on a large screen using a computer and a projector. Transparencies, 35mm slides, and handout materials also can be prepared.
Spreadsheets	Financial projections
Decision support	Analyses of specific decision-making situations; may include expert systems or other advanced information technology
Graphics	Graphs for reports
Database management	Software used to assist the worker in storing, retrieving, and analyzing data
Communications	Software used in conjunction with computer hardware that facilitates the movement of information between individuals and organizations
Personal time management	Program(s) used to schedule individual as well as group activities

The way you use these resources will affect your efficiency, productivity, and job satisfaction. The following sections offer advice on how to make the most of your electronic office equipment.

Organizing Schedules

Many workstations and personal computers have time management programs that allow the user to list activities day by day, along with times, places, phone numbers and other information. Some of these systems will send an alarm to remind users that it is time to go to a meeting or call a customer. Some programs can store telephone numbers of individuals and automatically dial the number when a call has been scheduled. When all the people in an office use the same time management programs, secretaries can schedule meetings by checking these schedules for mutually convenient times without having to contact each individual personally, a task that takes up a great deal of time in many organizations. Other programs, called project management programs, allow employees to enter and display all the tasks in a complex project, such as target dates, project group members' names, and resources needed.

Interacting with Managers, Coworkers, and Customers through Technological Systems

Videoconferences

The videoconference is the most dramatic form of electronic communication. Videoconferencing involves transmission over cables or satellites of black and white or color pictures taken with videocameras. Additional equipment, such as electronic "blackboards" on which words written with a light pen are transmitted to a similar display in another location, also may be involved. Once prohibitively expensive, the cost of video and videoconferencing has dropped dramatically. Cost alone should not be the determining factor in your decision to use this technology. Some situations and scenarios benefit from videoconferencing, while others do not.

Three conditions are necessary for successful video teleconferencing.

Use videoconferencing when the personal relationship among the participants is essential to the transaction. Wal-Mart uses videoconferencing to link the more than a thousand stores for the chairman's announcements, fostering a feeling of a close personal relationship between the company's charismatic founder and people spread across the company. Exxon used this method during the Valdez oil spill, when employees needed to hear top management's account of what was being done, how much was being spent, and how sincerely the company was acting in the face of the disaster. These sessions also were recorded and replayed for employees in other time zones and for employees who worked other shifts. Sales announcements are especially suited to this format, because both the object to be sold and the speaker who motivates others with enthusiasm, gestures, and expression, can be seen at once. Ford Motor Company uses teleconferencing for this purpose.

When relationships have been managed in the positive ways recommended in Chapter 3, "You and Your Audiences: Managing Relationships," productive decision making can be facilitated by videoconferences. When people are interested in a productive relationship (as described in Chapter 3), videoconferencing can support the ongoing negotiation process. If the corporate culture

HOW TECHNOLOGY AND COMMUNICATIONS HELPED FIDELITY INVESTMENTS COMPETE

Partly through its strategic use of computers and communication systems, Fidelity Investments has become the largest mutual fund management company in the United States. By 1988, Fidelity Investments managed 52 mutual funds and operated the country's second-largest discount brokerage business. Its 1986 ad, a reproduction of which is shown on the facing page, invites the reader to review the strategic milestones in the company's history.

Some of these milestones were financial product innovations (1946, 1981, 1983, 1985), but many others involved changes in communication that simultaneously were changes in services:

"Toll-free access to salaried representatives. These phone reps will revolutionize the way individuals invest money, making your investment decisions easier, quicker, and less expensive to execute" (1976);

"Convenient, walk-in investing centers" (1978);

"Home computer trading at discount brokerage prices. With Fidelity Investors Express, the active investor can initiate trades even when the market is closed" (1984); and

"24-hour toll-free sales and service lines let you call anytime to get information, transfer from one fund to another, or check account balances. Hourly pricing introduced for sector portfolios, the only mutual funds with hourly pricing" (1986).

By 1987 Fidelity had invested heavily in a computerized system that enabled investors to obtain price quotes, buy shares, sell shares, or exchange their investments from one fund to another twenty-four hours a day by means of touch-tone telephones. No conversation with telephone representatives was required.

In many other mutual fund companies, requests to buy or sell shares had to be submitted in writing, accompanied by a bank officer's signature guarantee. To obtain a signature guarantee, the investor had to write a letter, go to a bank to meet with the bank officer, and then mail the letter. In many cases, the price of the shares bought or sold depended on when the postal service delivered the request.

Fidelity's automated system gave investors a much greater sense of control over their investments, ensuring that their purchases or sales would be executed at the closing price on the day they called the FAST system. A large number of sales assistants, also available twenty-four hours daily, could take care of transactions that could not be executed automatically.

By shifting inquiries about prices, account balances, and exchanges to the automated system, the company was able to make better use of employee time. Thus, the technological innovation changed the *pattern* as well as the *speed* of communication. The technical innovations also changed the *experience* of communication for customers and Fidelity employees. The ability to conduct many transactions without talking with anyone gave customers a greater sense of control and satisfaction; the elimination of the many routine calls made the telephone salespeople's jobs more varied and interesting. Thus, the new systems changed feelings about communication as well.

Share the Vision of Fidelity

What has made Fidelity Investments one of the largest and fastest-growing money managers in the world? In a word, *vision.* Over the years, Fidelity has aimed to provide you with the best.

For four innovative decades, Fidelity has had the vision to combine new ideas with a tradition of outstanding money management.

Fidelity gives you the same kind of state-of-the-art, professional management that once only the wealthy could afford . . . and the kind of service and choice few others can provide.

Extraordinary Portfolio Management—Fidelity's commitment to superior money management is second to none. The result —funds like Fidelity Magellan Fund, America's #1 performing fund for the past 5- and 10-year periods.[1] And Fidelity Overseas Fund, the nation's top international fund.[2]

Extraordinary Service—Only Fidelity gives you 24-hour toll-free access to our own representatives—call any time to ask a question, check your account balance, or transfer funds. Or just walk into any Fidelity Investor Center, in 36 locations to serve you coast to coast.

Extraordinary Choice—Come to Fidelity for over 65 funds to suit practically any investment need, including the nation's largest selection of tax-free funds and sector portfolios. Fidelity offers money market funds, taxable and tax-free bond funds, growth funds, growth and income funds, sector portfolios, and more.

The Innovations You Need

The investments you need, with the features you need—they're all at Fidelity. Consider Fidelity's 40-year track record of investment innovation and improvement:

1946—Income-oriented stock market investing in a mutual fund, pioneered by Fidelity Puritan Fund.

1974—Free checkwriting on a money market fund, first offered to the public through Fidelity Daily Income Trust.

1976—Tax-free investing with no sales charge, available for the first time with Fidelity Municipal Bond Fund.

1976—Toll-free access to salaried registered representatives. These phone reps will revolutionize the way individuals invest money, making your investment decisions easier, quicker, and less expensive to execute.

1978—A money market fund for everyone, with its low $1000 minimum, Fidelity Cash Reserves.

1978—Discount brokerage services. Fidelity offers commissions savings for the self-directed investor.

1978—Convenient, walk-in investing centers: as the first of today's 36 local Investor Centers is established.

1980—Tax-free income from a money market fund . . . another Fidelity innovation that won quick popularity.

1981—Tax-deferred IRAs become widely available for the first time. Today, Fidelity manages more IRA money than any other fund company.

1981—Sector Investing. Fidelity Select Portfolios," the first multi-portfolio sector fund, creates a new standard for sector investing convenience. Today with 35 targeted industry sectors!

1982—A cash management account with discount brokerage, Fidelity USA, with unlimited checkwriting and Gold MasterCard.

1983—Double and triple tax-free funds for your state. A new era in tax-free investing begins with Massachusetts Tax-Free Fund. Fidelity now offers specialized tax-free funds for *eight* states.

1984—Home computer trading at discount brokerage prices. With Fidelity Investor's Express, the active investor can initiate trades even when the market is closed.

1985—Fidelity Overseas Fund and Fidelity OTC Portfolio, introduced in Dec. '84, become America's Number One and Number Two performing funds.[3]

1986—24-hour toll-free sales and service line let you call anytime to get information, transfer from one fund to another, or check account balances. Hourly pricing introduced for sector portfolios, the only mutual funds with hourly pricing. More new funds and sector portfolios introduced.

Fidelity offers today's investor a world of opportunity. Why not find out more? No matter when you have a question, need an account balance, or want to make a purchase, Fidelity service is there to help. All day and all night. Just pick up a phone, make a quick toll-free call, and a Fidelity representative will be there.

Call us now to discuss one of our funds, or for a free issue of *Investment Vision*, the magazine written by Fidelity for its investors. Call 24 hours a day, toll-free, at **1-800-544-6666.** (In Mass. or Alaska call collect 1-617-523-1919).

Fidelity offers opportunities in all these areas:

**Money Market Funds
Bond Funds
Tax-Free Bond Funds
Growth Funds
Sector Portfolios
Growth and Income Funds
International Funds
State Tax-Free Funds
IRAs, Keoghs
Discount Brokerage**

For more information on Fidelity funds, including management fees, expenses, and applicable sales charges, call or write for a free prospectus. Read it carefully before you invest or send money. Fidelity Distributors Corporation, General Distribution Agent. P.O. Box 660603, Dallas, TX 75266.

1. Source: Lipper Analytical Services, Inc., which currently ranks over 1,000 mutual funds. Rankings are for the 5- and 10-year periods ended 9/30/86.
2. Source: Lipper. For the 12-month period ended 9/30/86.
3. Source: Lipper. For the 12-month period ended 12/31/85.

Past performance is no guarantee of future results.

Fidelity Investments

Corporate Headquarters
The Fidelity Building
82 Devonshire Street
Boston, MA 02109

**24 hours
1-800-544-6666**

▢ V I D E O C O N F E R E N C I N G   C H E C K L I S T

____ Are the situation and scenario suitable for videoconferencing?

    ____ Does the transaction depend on relationships?

    ____ Can video enhance product perception?

    ____ Can all participants be present at locations simultaneously?

____ Are the participants suitably dressed (not distracting)?

____ Is there a *short* agenda?

____ Do participants use animated facial expressions?

is negative and fosters distrust, or if people turn to negotiation as a power game of compromise, money as well as time may be wasted in videoconferences.

Finally, in deciding whether to use videoconferencing, consider whether you will be able to assemble the participants at the various properly equipped locations simultaneously. Choose participants carefully. If someone who is new to the organization must participate, brief that person as fully as possible on the scenarios and problem-solving processes usually used in the group and on the facts of the situation. If all of these preliminary factors are positive in a particular situation, you should go ahead with the videoconference.

Dress for the camera; do not let accessories or patterns direct attention away from your face or your message.

For the most part, videocameras can operate in natural light, so that problems of glare and contrast that once affected television actors' costume choices no longer worry businesspeople. Nonetheless, choose your outfit sensibly. Busy geometric patterns such as herringbone in bright contrasting colors, dangling jewelry, or exaggerated clothing designs will draw attention away from your face. Your message may be lost in the motion of your accessories.

A limited agenda improves interaction and satisfaction.

Prepare an agenda. A restricted, sensible agenda will allow the business to be completed on time and without a sense of pressure. Since the technology will create some psychological stress for anyone unfamiliar with it, a complicated agenda will sabotage your transaction. Make sure someone is designated as leader at each location, so that interaction can proceed smoothly and someone will take charge if there is a problem. Pay attention to your body language during the videoconference: be as relaxed as you possibly can, keep your chin up (not buried in your notes), smile often, and let your facial expressions reinforce what you say.

Voice Mail Systems

Going to the manager's office to get an assignment frequently is unnecessary today. Videoconferencing, voice mail, and electronic mail now supplement more traditional oral and written interaction. Others may leave comments or questions for you on the voice mail system (sometimes called phone mail), a recording system that enables people to leave messages at any time of the day or night. You, too, can leave messages for others. Voice mail has the advantages of

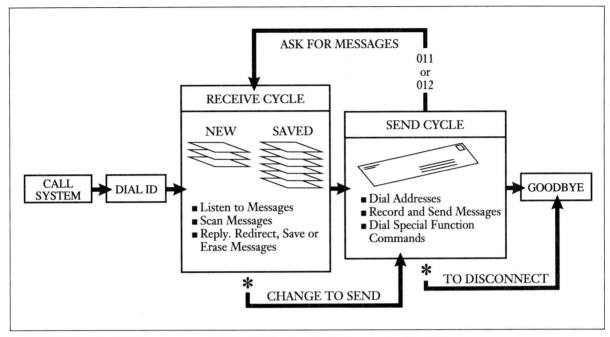

FIGURE 10-2. Voice Mail Diagram from the 3M Voice Mail Handbook. Used with permission of the 3M Company.

conveying the personalities we associate with individual voices, just as a telephone can. Figure 10-2, from an award-winning voice mail manual, illustrates these concepts.

On voice mail, prepare daily welcoming messages and plan messages for others carefully.

To make the most of this system, you should record welcoming messages for your callers and you should carefully plan the messages you leave for others. Some callers are hesitant to leave messages because they dislike speaking directly to a machine. Many phone messages are too abrupt and impersonal and do not support good relationships with callers. Changing your message every morning and recording a message when you are going out of the office may seem like extra work, but it is actually a highly professional gesture. It reassures the hesitant caller and tells your listener that you truly care about the call. The familiar sound of your voice provides some of the reassurance that the listener might have received if you had been there to take the call personally.

At first, you may need to write down the message you are going to leave. As you become more familiar with the system, you can jot notes and dictate your message from the notes. Compose your message to:

- respond to the other person's effort to reach you,
- provide information about why you cannot receive the call and any other information likely to be helpful to the caller,
- tell when you will return the call, if possible,

- invite the caller to leave a message, and
- explain other options of the system, such as pressing another number to return to an operator, if your system contains such options.

The wording of your message should minimize the caller's anxiety about talking to a machine. Compare the following messages:

POOR VOICE MAIL MESSAGES

Hello. I can't take your call now, but if you want, you can leave a message at the sound of the tone. Don't forget to wait for the tone.

You've reached 661-4191. No one is here now. Leave an order for landscaping services at the tone.

The party you have dialed at extension 2369 is not available. Leave your name, phone number, and a very brief message at the tone. Don't start talking before the beep.

This is the voice-mail service. The recorder for extension 2639 is not accepting messages. Have a nice day.

GOOD VOICE MAIL MESSAGES

Good morning, this is Gretchen Fields at Westbrook Dairy. I'm in meetings this morning, Tuesday the 19th, until ten o'clock. I'm sorry to have missed your call, but if you will leave your name and number, I will return your call between 10 and 11 o'clock. I look forward to talking with you then.

Hello, this is Bob Smallwood. I won't be in town today, Thursday, February 28th, but I will return your call promptly tomorrow morning, March 1st. Please leave your name and your phone number at the sound of the tone, or press 7 to reach my secretary, Tom Stallings, if you'd like Tom to recommend someone else who could help you.

Good afternoon, you've reached Carter Plumbing Services. Thanks for calling us. I'm Milt Carter, and I'm sorry that all of us are out of the office on calls this afternoon. However, I'll be checking in for messages at 3 P.M., and if you will leave your name and phone number, I'll return your call then. If you have a plumbing emergency, dial my pager number at 887-4041. Otherwise, I'll talk with you soon after 3 o'clock.

The poor messages are too negative ("I can't take your call," "don't start talking") and provide too little information to motivate the caller ("The recorder for extension 2639 is not accepting messages." Why not, the caller wonders). Goodwill clichés such as "Have a nice day" seldom convince the listener. The good messages help maintain the relationship, provide the caller with specific information that explains the situation, and motivates the caller to leave a message. This would be a good time to turn to the end of the chapter and try preliminary exercise 1 on composing voice mail messages.

In addition to your own welcoming messages, you should plan the messages you leave for others. Many times you will know in advance that the person you are contacting will not be in the office to answer. In such cases plan your message before dialing, using the form below.

VOICE MAIL MESSAGE PLANNER

Statement that identifies the person recording the incoming message:

The situation is:

I want the listener to _____

In order to do that, he or she must know _____

Key points:

He or she needs to feel _____

The tone I want to maintain is:

Many executives may receive anywhere from a dozen to two dozen messages during a morning away from the office. Imagine how you would feel if you needed to listen to and respond to that many messages. You, too, would want callers to get to the point quickly and indicate what they want you to do.

Here is a brief but efficient message: "Linda, this is Davis. I'm calling about the shipment to my client, the Gallery Company in Pierre. I need your help in finding out the shipment status. They hadn't received it by 5 P.M. Wednesday. I need an update on the status of that shipment, order number AW-2119, so that I can call and assure them they'll have it before Friday noon. Please call me back at extension 2881." The message gives the information that Linda needs to track the order: the client's name and the order number, plus the deadline for receipt. The message motivates her to respond by explaining the caller's need and the nature of the problem. Finally, it tells the number to call to respond.

☐ VOICE MAIL WELCOMING MESSAGE CHECKLIST

_____ Do you change your message every morning?

_____ Does your current message

    _____ respond positively to the other person?

    _____ provide information about why you cannot receive the call?

    _____ provide any other information likely to be helpful to the caller?

_____ tell when you will return the call, if possible?

_____ invite the caller to leave a message?

_____ explain other options of the system?

_____ minimize the caller's anxiety about talking to a machine?

Electronic Mail (E-mail)

Electronic mail, or E-mail, uses computers linked by a network. A blinking symbol on the computer screen alerts the user to the presence of messages. The computer stores all the messages that others have sent to a person and allows him or her to review, save, or discard them later. In some offices an inexpensive printer attached to the reader's computer can print out those messages the reader wants to save. However, if people print out all their messages, they may increase the amount of paper-handling in the office—an inefficient use of technology.

E-mail has advantages, but it is not necessarily more efficient than other forms.

Although E-mail lacks the intimacy of hearing a person's voice, it has advantages. Written information is more easily recognized than orally delivered information. For example, a telephone number or a price estimate displayed on the screen is more easily recognized than a series of numbers heard on a voice mail recording. In voice mail the person may speak too quickly, mumble, or fail to enunciate clearly, causing errors in the transmission of information.

Research studies on E-mail show that E-mail affects the communication system of the organization as a whole, changing what people know and how they come to know it. Because E-mail messages seem fleeting and immediate, they also seem informal and personal. Messages among coworkers tend to be information exchanges and social remarks: questions, replies, and comments. The overall effect is a heightened sense of collaboration; knowing what someone else is working on, how he or she feels about it, and what the group thinks about it.

E-mail makes people depend more on peers, less on superiors.

When people share information openly, they tend to rely on themselves rather than on authority figures, affecting people's sense of who is in control of information. Bulletin boards and E-mail on students' networks have had similar effects; students frequently teach each other rather than wait for a professor to answer questions. Coworkers who use electronic mail value creativity in messages and use informal punctuation, such as dashes, more frequently than in memos or letters. They create sideways smiling faces with a colon, dash, and right parenthesis :—), and add jokes, wry comments, and exclamations. These features outside the conventions of ordinary syntax and punctuation have been described as "electronic paralanguage." However, paralanguage is problematic when it causes people to notice the way you've said something and not what you've said. Substituting "U" for "you," "B4" for "before" is unnecessary and distracting.

HAVE A HAPPY THANKSGIVING!
JASON

Example of Electronic Paralanguage

Only well-organized, relevant E-mail messages are likely to be read to the end.

E-mail readers tend to be less committed to reading entire messages than letter or memo readers. If a subject line or a first paragraph is ambiguous or not clearly relevant, the reader may not finish reading the message. To present a message effectively, explain the situation in the first sentence, then explain the issue, problem, or question in the following sentence. Use a subject line that makes the purpose of your message clear and relevant to the receiver. To ensure that your E-mail correspondence does you credit, take time to proofread your message. However much people say that they value spontaneity and freshness, many still laugh at grammatical errors and use incorrect usage as a basis for negative judgments about writers.

The following E-mail message is complete and friendly.

(date)

TO: Design Department Members«DESIGN.ALL»
FROM: Hugh Mosell, Office Manager«H.Mosell.ADMIN»
SUBJECT: Air Conditioning Interruption for Design Department Offices
           July 4.

Although several of your department members will be working over the holiday to finish the Douglas proposal, the management company must interrupt air conditioning for six hours (noon to 6 P.M.) on July 4th to make necessary repairs. Other electrical systems will be working during that time. Six large cooling fans will be available in the reception area for your use. In addition, I've scheduled the catering company to deliver iced drinks and snacks at 3 P.M. to give you a break. If there are any other adjustments that could help you survive the interruption, please reply.

The next example begins with a narrative detail, the time the person arrived for work. The message doesn't tell what the situation is. Why is the situation "pretty bad?" Why does it matter that Pat hasn't seen them either? There is an accusatory implication in the final sentence. What is the reader to do?

SUBJECT: Branning Account

OK, I came in the office at 9:30 A.M. and I couldn't find the Branning Account files. This is pretty bad. Furthermore, Pat hasn't seen them either. I don't appreciate this at all.

Local Area Networks (LAN)

Local area networks allow the electronic transmission of documents; people need not wait for interoffice mail to share information. Networks bring documents directly to the computer or terminal on the desk. A LAN allows other computing equipment to function more productively. For example, a sales representative for an office products company might return from visits to clients' offices, take a small disk out of his portable computer, place it in the disk drive of his office computer, and send orders and other information directly over the LAN to the warehouse for processing.

Dictation Systems

Planning is the key to dictating well.

Many companies still compensate for employees' lack of keyboarding skills by providing dictation systems and word processing pools. In this arrangement, people speak into dictation units, some of which are tiny hand-held devices, and their words are recorded on a tape that a secretary transcribes on a word processor or a personal computer with word processing software. The draft copy then is sent to the person who dictated the document for editing.

Since oral speech is very different from written language, many people have trouble at first with these systems. One problem is a lack of training in dictation skills, and another problem is that voice data entry is still about ten to twelve years behind keyboard entry on computers. In 1990, computers able to recognize 40,000-word vocabularies and trained to recognize an individual's voice were available for approximately $10,000 to $12,000. In 1980, microcomputers with 256k memories cost about the same. Eventually, keyboarding skills may become less important and dictation skills may become more important. Therefore, even if you are an excellent typist, you should practice dictating.

To dictate, use a planner and speak aloud all punctuation, paragraphing, and format instructions.

The same steps you have practiced for organizing voice mail and E-mail messages are used in dictation. In addition, you must learn the habit of spelling out all unusual words and proper names, such as the names of streets, companies, and individuals. If you use the forms for analyzing situations and audience uncertainties, plus the voice mail planner, you can organize your dictation

---

ELECTRONIC MAIL CHECKLIST

_____ Does your message explain the situation in the first sentence?

_____ Does the second sentence explain the issue, problem, or question?

_____ Does the subject line specifically identify your request and show the relevance of your message for this person?

_____ Is the language vivid and friendly (not slangy or ungrammatical)?

_____ Does the message use paralanguage appropriately to express emotion and friendliness?

---

of most short documents quite successfully. You should also remember to speak out loud the format instructions you want the typist to follow, such as "new paragraph," and "heading in initial caps, boldfaced." In addition, you must specify all punctuation, saying aloud the commas, periods, quotation marks, and semicolons. Most typists and secretaries understand that if you have said "period," they should start a new sentence; few people insert the instruction "New sentence." To edit your draft when it has been returned from word processing, follow the guidelines on word choice, sentence structure, and coherence in Chapters 6, 7, and 8.

Unlike voice mail and E-mail, the communication process in dictation requires the mediation of a third person. You must learn to work with the person who transcribes your tapes. Begin the tape by addressing remarks to the person doing the typing. Explain the situation to the person, noting any special considerations in paper, format, or deadlines at the beginning. Be considerate. If you build a good relationship, you will get more assistance when you actually do have an emergency. This is a good time to stop and complete the preliminary exercise on dictation at the end of the chapter.

Using Word Processing and Other Software to Prepare Documents

If the tools of the electronic office sound magical, come down to earth. Computers are tools that extend human capabilities, but they don't write for you. Their great advantage is reducing irritating and repetitive tasks such as recopying and retyping. You will have to dedicate some time to learning how to use the equipment. This chapter will not substitute for instruction in word processing or desktop publishing, but it will alert you to good ways to use the available programs and encourage you to find new uses for the features of your own program. In most companies, you will not have a choice of word processing programs or of equipment on which to use them. Most companies want all employees to use the same programs so that all the messages will be transportable over the networks and readable on all computer screens. If you do have a choice of software, test it thoroughly before purchasing it.

Many programs are available for writing and editing documents on microcomputers (also called personal computers) and larger computers. These software programs, called word processing programs, are a system of electronic commands that tell the computer what to do with the information you enter and how you want the information to appear on the page when it is printed. The computer records the keystrokes you make on the keyboard as an electronic record that can be saved with a document title, retrieved, changed, printed, copied into another document, or moved into another computing program such as a desktop publishing program.

Professionals value word processing because making changes is very easy.

You can compose at the computer or you can write out your document by hand and then type the manuscript on the computer keyboard. Although it seems awkward at first, composing on a word processor is more efficient in many ways than handwritten drafting, because much of your drafting can become part of the final document. You probably had some trouble getting used to writing with a pencil long ago. Adjusting to this new technology will take time until your muscular actions are semiautomated. If you don't type, there are software programs called "typing tutors" that help you learn to use the keyboard quickly.

Word processing makes it very easy to change what has already been written, and students therefore generally are very positive about writing papers and revising them with word processors. Professionals value word processing for the same reason: Very often someone in an organization will want "just a few changes" to a document before it is sent. With word processing, letters, words, or whole paragraphs can be inserted, deleted, or reformatted without retyping the whole document. Furthermore, many word processing programs will check the spelling of each word in a document against a list of 40,000 or more correctly spelled words and identify any words not on the list—a feature that speeds up proofreading.

The word processing programs available today are not identical, but most of them will accomplish the basic composing tasks described in this chapter. Superior programs will allow you to have more than one window open on the screen at a time. They also will allow you to look at the page as a whole before printing, not just at fifteen or so lines (see Figure 10-8 on page 221).

The form shown in Figure 10-3 is designed to allow you to write in the specific commands for the word processing program you use alongside the writing tasks discussed in this chapter. The commands for Microsoft® Word 4.0 for the Macintosh computer are shown in the column on the right as an example. By photocopying the form, filling it in, and posting it near your computer, you can use it as a reference guide during your writing. If you are not using Microsoft® Word, you can fold under the information about that program when you copy the form.

Planning Your Document

Analyzing Situations, Scenarios, and Audience Uncertainties with Computer Forms

Analyze situations and audiences with stored forms or "templates."

All of the forms for analyzing situations, scenarios, roles, and audience uncertainties that have been shown in this book can be created as form documents on your data disk. After you have opened your word processing program, you can

WRITER'S ACTION	YOUR PROGRAM'S COMMANDS	MICROSOFT® WORD COMMANDS
Planning		
Analyzing Audience		File menu, *open* (doc name)
with forms		Open Microsoft Word and choose files
with database		Open Microsoft Works or other database and choose files
Idea generating		
outlining		Command U
multiple windows		File menu: *new* or Command N
commercial programs		Acta, Learning Tool, Think Tank
Freewriting and organizing		
delete		select and *delete key*
place or move		Edit menu, *paste*
copy		Edit menu, *copy*
cut		Edit menu, *cut*
insert		put pointer at desired space; click mouse button, Edit menu, *paste*
Drafting		
Writing from sources with double windows		Open two documents, size windows, margins
Form letters		See manual, form letters
Revising		
Identifying key ideas with boldfacing		outlining function; Command U
		select phrase, Format menu, *bold*
Support ideas by underlining evidence		select phrase, Format menu, *underline*
Perfecting formats		
Creating a hierarchy of headings		Outlining commands or, save second copy and delete ordinary text (not key ideas)
Placing headings		File menu, *Print preview*
Checking paragraph size		File Menu, *Print preview*
Indenting paragraphs		Format menu, *show ruler*
Space between paragraphs		Format menu, *show ruler*
Adding footnotes		Command key and E
Viewing footnotes		Shift, Command, Option, S

FIGURE 10-3.   Guide to Writing with Your Word Processor

Prepared with an Apple® Macintosh II® using Microsoft® Word 4.0 and Capture©, by Mainstay, Agoura Hills, CA.

WRITER'S ACTION	YOUR PROGRAM'S COMMANDS	MICROSOFT® WORD COMMANDS
Perfecting formats		
Special effects		
italics		Command key, shift, I
other types		Format menu, select choice
Importing graphics		Document menu, *insert graphics*
Lines, boxes, and drop shadows		Format menu, or command key and M, click on *borders*
Table of contents		Document menu, choose *TOC entry*
Using styles		Format menu, choose *Styles*
Editing traces or redlining		Available for PC version, not Macintosh. See manual.
Multiple columns		Section break, Format menu, *section*

FIGURE 10-3 (*continued*)

open any one of these forms, such as the audience uncertainty form, and copy or save it with a different title appropriate for the audience you are analyzing. A basic form used in this way is sometimes called a "template."

Place the insertion point on your computer screen beside a heading and type in your comments. If you complete a thorough analysis of an audience on one occasion, you can reopen the analysis on other occasions, renaming the document and altering the analysis to fit the uncertainties of a new situation. If your company writes documents that require specific kinds of information in a specific order, you can create a template or form for that kind of document (say, a weekly report) and call it up whenever you must prepare such a report.

Multiple windows allow you to see your analyses and your document at the same time.

Many of the word processing programs available today allow you to have more than one document open at a time, so you can have your audience analysis, situation analysis, and new document windows open simultaneously. Different programs have different methods for moving from one window to another. Some programs use a function key; others use a click of the mouse, and still others have a menu at the top of the screen that controls movement between windows. On Macintosh computers, you can see more than one window at a time by sizing the windows so that one is wider but shorter than the other. This arrangement allows you to move back and forth by clicking the mouse to think about the audiences' needs, the situation, and the document you are writing. Figure 10-4 shows a screen on which two windows are open. Those shown are sized vertically, but you may decide that you prefer having horizontal windows open one above the other, as shown in Figure 10-5.

You can control the width of the document in your window by controlling the margin settings. Use the means appropriate to your word processing program to change the margin setting for the entire document to approximately half your screen width if you are working with windows that are narrower than they are high. Then change window shape with the "size" box.

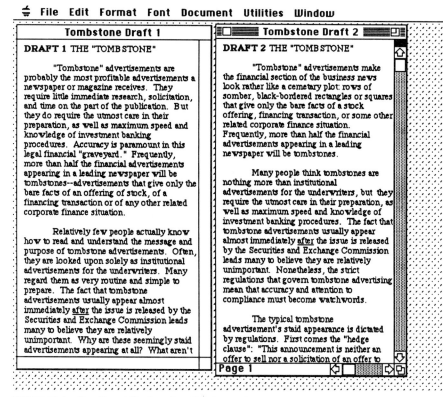

FIGURE 10-4.   Two Vertical Windows Open Simultaneously

Prepared with an Apple® Macintosh II® using Microsoft® Word 4.0 and Capture©, by Mainstay, Agoura Hills, CA.

Another way to use your computer to store and retrieve information about particular audiences is to prepare a database with different categories of information about your audience's uncertainties. These can be printed out or combined and printed out to give a composite picture of all the individuals who are likely to receive copies of a certain document. If you must communicate with people you see only infrequently, such as personnel at other company offices, keeping a database can help you recall personal details about various individuals that you might otherwise forget over time. Customers often are impressed when a businessperson remembers key information about them in sales or renewal letters. Computers make it easy to keep this information handy.

Generating Ideas

You can use your word processing and editing software in several ways to help you generate ideas. Most of the techniques mentioned in Chapters 4 and 5 can also be used with a computer. You can freewrite or jot ideas into a new document. When you have finished, you can use commands to delete those that are irrelevant to your purpose, move others to new positions in the document, and

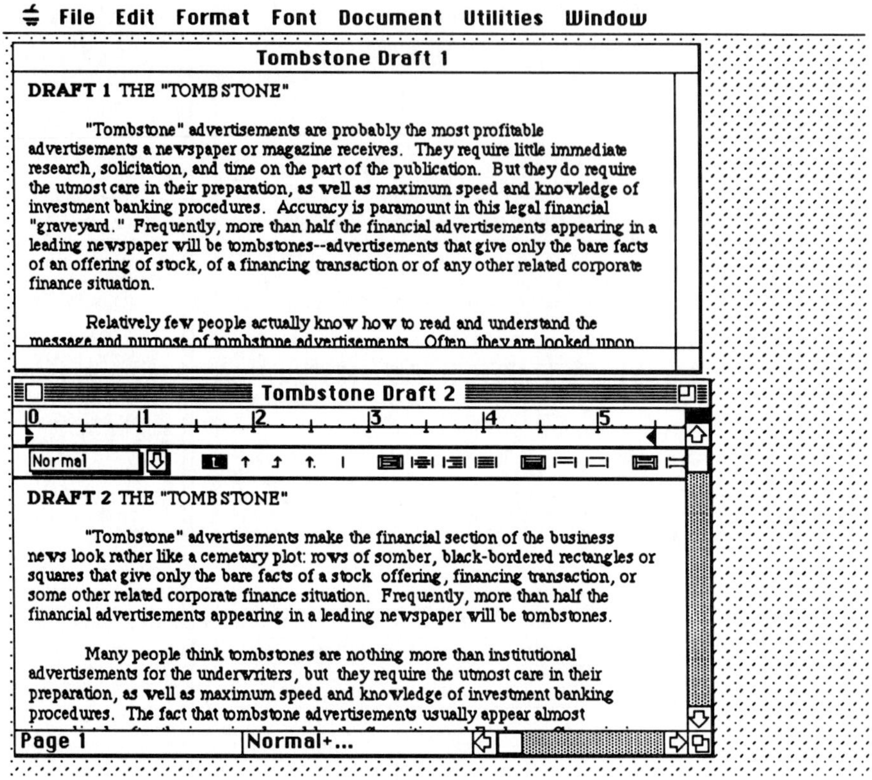

⏚ **File   Edit   Format   Font   Document   Utilities   Window**

Tombstone Draft 1

DRAFT 1 THE "TOMBSTONE"

"Tombstone" advertisements are probably the most profitable advertisements a newspaper or magazine receives. They require little immediate research, solicitation, and time on the part of the publication. But they do require the utmost care in their preparation, as well as maximum speed and knowledge of investment banking procedures. Accuracy is paramount in this legal financial "graveyard." Frequently, more than half the financial advertisements appearing in a leading newspaper will be tombstones--advertisements that give only the bare facts of an offering of stock, of a financing transaction or of any other related corporate finance situation.

Relatively few people actually know how to read and understand the message and purpose of tombstone advertisements. Often, they are looked upon

Tombstone Draft 2

Normal

DRAFT 2 THE "TOMBSTONE"

"Tombstone" advertisements make the financial section of the business news look rather like a cemetary plot: rows of somber, black-bordered rectangles or squares that give only the bare facts of a stock offering, financing transaction, or some other related corporate finance situation. Frequently, more than half the financial advertisements appearing in a leading newspaper will be tombstones.

Many people think tombstones are nothing more than institutional advertisements for the underwriters, but they require the utmost care in their preparation, as well as maximum speed and knowledge of investment banking procedures. The fact that tombstone advertisements usually appear almost

Page 1   Normal+...

FIGURE 10-5.   Two Horizontal Windows Open Simultaneously

Prepared with an Apple® Macintosh II® using Microsoft® Word 4.0 and Capture©, by Mainstay, Agoura Hills, CA.

build an outline or set of organized notes. There are also special programs for generating ideas, such as Acta, Think Tank, and Learning Tool. Learning Tool, available through Kinko's educational software, enables you to use two open windows simultaneously. One is a conventional list or outline format; the other is a graphics space in which small pictures of cards can be moved about. By double clicking, you can open these cards to full size and enter notes in them. By dragging one on top of another, these cards can be organized in stacks and connected with lines that indicate various kinds of relationships. When you move a card from one stack to another, the information is moved simultaneously in the outline window. The outline plus the content of the cards can then be printed out.

Several word processing programs allow outlines to be created that can then be expanded into paragraphs. MindWrite© and Microsoft® Word both offer this feature. At any time, you can view only the outline portion of headings instead of the entire document. If your word processing program does not have a built-in outlining feature, you can write an outline, then copy it and instantly move the entire outline and notes into a new blank document. Keep only the outline on view in the other window so that you can view the expanding document and the outline simultaneously. If you have taken notes from a source, you can use a copy and paste command (or copy and move command, depending on the program) to transfer notes to your document and turn them into quotes without having to retype.

Freewriting and Organizing

Coding allows you to plan and reshape a draft efficiently.

As was suggested in the chapter on communication strategies, you can code items in a freewriting draft that answer different types of audience questions. Then, by cutting and pasting (or copying and moving), you can reorder the ideas you wish to keep or expand and you can cut or delete those parts that don't fit in your final draft. Use the highlight, delete or cut, and insert commands to accomplish these changes.

Drafting and Revising Your Document

Drafting Freely, Saving Time

Without worrying about whether your spelling is right or whether you're choosing exactly the best word, you can draft freely on a word processor. In a sense, not having to give part of your attention to correct spelling and other aspects of the final document enables you to use more of your focusing power on generating ideas and supporting them. Spelling, format choices, and page layout can be delayed until later. If you've ever "lost" a good idea because you had to stop and correct a typing mistake, you'll appreciate word processing.

If you "get stuck" trying to find a word that fits your idea exactly, several word processing programs contain a thesaurus that can help you evaluate synonyms. Dictionaries also are available in software form, and some computers can search compact disks that contain books of quotations, ZIP code lists, all the works of Shakespeare, and many other reference tools.

Creating Form Letters

Create your own bank of form letters suited to your situations.

Some word processing programs allow you to create form letters that can be sent to several people simultaneously. For example, you might send a marketing announcement, such as news of a sale or special promotion, to people in ZIP codes near your store. Or, you might have to send a notice to all people who have not paid their accounts after 30 days. With word processing, you can create your own folder of form letters that suit your most routine situations. However, these should not be sent out without thinking about possible revisions or adaptations for specific individuals.

To create a form letter, you write the letter, leaving a coded space for any information that is specific to a particular reader. The program you have will explain the kind of code you should enter. The most common kind of form letter uses a mail-merge function that combines the form letter with the names, addresses, and greetings to individuals on a list. A form letter on Microsoft® Word, before the specific details have been added, is shown in Figure 10-6.

Revising

Naturally, your first test of a draft should be to check whether you said what you wanted to say. Second, you need to determine whether the document needs more adaptation for your audience. Are topics in the right order for these readers? Would one more example or piece of information be more persuasive? Have you rambled when you should have been more concise? Are there any words that the audience won't understand? By moving the insertion point according to your program's method to the place where changes should be made, you can insert additional words, delete unnecessary passages, or cut out and move sentences or paragraphs in your document.

Identifying Key Ideas

In business writing, it is important for readers to be able to find your main points quickly. Often, executives skim a document by reading the first and last sentence in each paragraph; sometimes only the first sentence. You can check whether an executive using this method would get your points by boldfacing the first sentence in each paragraph of your draft and reading through these sentences. If you have a long document, you may wish to print out a draft in this form. If your key ideas are not in these sentences but tucked in the middle of paragraphs, rearrange the sentences so that key ideas stand out. In moving sentences, "cut and paste" or "delete and insert" them. Moving sentences may force you to adjust their wording. You might have moved an antecedent away from the pronoun. Recheck to be sure your pronoun reference is clear.

Supporting Ideas with Evidence

You can check your first draft to determine whether you have supported all your major ideas by underlining the phrases that provide evidence or support for your claims. Simply highlight and change the format of the supporting phrases to produce a clearly visible pattern of boldfacing, italics, and underlining that shows the pattern of the argument. A marked sample is shown in Figure 10-7.

Editing with Software, Including Traces or Redlining

Sometimes when you are writing with other people it is useful to have a record of the changes that have been made to a document. Some programs have a feature called "redlining" or "editing traces." Check your manual to see whether your program has this feature. The command causes a line to be drawn through

«FUDGE PROMOTION LIST» (list of names to be merged)

SWENSEN'S FLAGSHIP CHOCOLATES, INC.
Number 7 Harbor Drive
Northport, Michigan

June 5, 1991

«Title»«F Name»«Last Name»
«Address»
«Town», MI«ZIP»
Dear «Title»«Last Name»:

This summer the flag will be flying every morning above the cottage at Number 7 Harbor Drive. When you look across the village and see the chocolate chef's crimson banner on the horizon, you'll know the first batch of fresh fudge is ready for you at Swensen's Flagship Chocolates. The chef makes butter fudge every day, but he also makes special varieties that seem suited to the weather, his moods, or your special requests. Sometimes he sprinkles the fudge with nuts, flavors it with a variety of liqueurs, melts it to a glacée and dips in fresh strawberries, cherries, or pineapple chunks, or tucks fudge strips inside Swensen's Flagship Ice Cream Bars.

Bring this letter with you, and we'll tip our flag to you by giving you 40% off whatever you buy. That way, you decide what's on sale and chef Swensen concentrates on the chocolates. It's a perfect recipe for a sweet summer in Northport. Our flag usually will fly by 10 a.m., and we will take the flag in at sunset. Come see us often.

Sweetly,

Sonia Swensen

FIGURE 10-6. **Basic Form Letter to Be Merged with Mailing List by Computer**

The Hudson Company
No. 2 Red Oak Boulevard
Corpus Christi, TX 77921

<u>For Immediate Release</u>
Contact: Barry Burnett
(512) 439-7211

<u>New Apartments</u> Planned for Inner Loop Property

The Hudson Company has contracted to buy 8 acres inside Loop 510 for an <u>English-style apartment complex.</u> The property is part of a 140-acre project contracted by Corpus Christi businesswoman Sophia Dominguez.

To be called the Hudson Mews Garden, the complex <u>will imitate the English custom of building apartments above the stables (or mews) in a palace or estate. Such stables are usually arranged around a courtyard for exercising royal steeds.</u> The Hudson Mews Garden will feature a courtyard with a fountain and <u>English gardens in the center.</u> Residents will have automatic membership in the Hudson Riding Club, whose riding paths are part of the larger property.

The property on which the complex will be built was formerly Shaws' Nursery for ornamental trees, shrubs, and roses. <u>"The excellent soil and well-established trees here will make the property ideal for our English garden,"</u> Ms. Dominguez said. The Hudson Company expects the inner loop location close to the central business district to be attractive to business executives.

The Hudson Company has engaged in real estate development in the Southwest since 1959.

# # #

FIGURE 10-7. Press Release Marked to Show Development of Key Idea, "New Apartments," with Pattern of Specific Details

any letter or phrase in the document that you wish to delete and boldfaces all newly inserted words. The document can be printed out in this way and other people in your group can immediately see what changes will be made.

Showing this form of a document to a manager can allow the manager to see the document "before and after," without using two documents, the old version and the new version, to determine whether the changes are desirable. After you've received approval or additional suggestions, using one more command will remove all the characters that were marked for deletion and put new characters into the same style as the surrounding text, ready for printing or electronic transmission.

Quantitative Analysis of Document Style

Quantitative analysis can identify overlooked writing features: very long sentences, clichés, many abstract words.

In addition, you can use style or grammar checking programs on your documents. You can ask these programs to check several features of your documents, such as number of sentences per paragraph, number of words per sentence, spelling, use of clichés or unfamiliar words, and other stylistic features. The useful feedback includes the number of linking verbs, such as forms of "to be," advice on words frequently misused, the percentage of abstract words used, and a list of negative words that might influence the reader's perception of your message.

Although it is possible to revise primarily on the screen, revising long documents is much easier if you print out a draft version. Possibly because the computer screen can display only a small portion of most documents, most writers find they can recognize different sorts of problems by reviewing a printed draft than they can recognize on the screen. When you have typed the wrong word (you have typed *thesis* and you meant to type *these*, or you have typed the word *the* twice in a row), you can locate these mistakes much more easily by reading aloud from a printed copy. A spelling checker is a wonderful aid, but it cannot distinguish *thesis* from *these*, except to tell you if either one is incorrectly spelled.

Perfecting Formats

Creating a Hierarchy of Headings

Readers expect documents to be broken into parts and marked with headings. To check whether your system of headings forms an orderly hierarchy, save your document. Then use a "Save as" command, probably shown on the "File" menu, to create a second copy with a slightly different name. Then delete the paragraphs, leaving only the headings. You will be able then to check quickly whether you have treated all the headings in the same way, creating a logical graphic hierarchy. The chapter on graphics discusses graphic hierarchies in detail. You may find that in one place you underlined a heading and at an equivalent place you boldfaced a heading, or that at one point you used letters and at another point you used numbers to identify headings. By opening up the document in a second window, you can go back and correct any of these problems.

In the list of headings below, you will see the uncorrected and corrected versions of headings in the opening section of a proposal to relocate Tellexstar, Inc.

RELOCATION PROPOSAL	TELLEXSTAR RELOCATION PROPOSAL
SUMMARY	SUMMARY
Background	*Why Tellexstar Must Select a New R&D Facility*
Satcom Lease	*Satcom Lease Expires Soon*
Importance of R&D Facilities	*Importance of R&D Facilities to Tellexstar's Strategic Plan*
LOCATION AND SITE	*Conclusion: Relocate in Charleston*
Factors Used by the Committee	DISCUSSION
Site Selection Process	

Placing Headings

By using the "print preview" function of a word processing program, you can see how the full page will look when it is printed. The small version of the pages, side by side, will help you see whether you have long stretches of text without any headings or pages in which every paragraph has a heading, as shown in Figure 10-8. If you do not have this function in your program, print out a draft and lay the pages out on a table so you can compare the distribution of headings throughout the document.

Paragraphing

The print preview command will also allow you to see long stretches of unbroken text that might need to be broken into separate paragraphs. If you are using double spacing between lines, indenting the beginning of paragraphs will help the reader find new paragraphs. Some people prefer to imitate book publishing style and not indent the first paragraph after a heading. If you are using single spacing, the page may look too dense unless you separate paragraphs with an extra line of blank space. Many programs allow you to request blank space between all paragraphs by pressing a single function key. Check your word processing manual to see how this effect is created with your program.

Although business writing uses far fewer footnotes than academic writing, occasionally you still will need footnotes in a business document. You can add these and keep track of their numbers very easily with a word processing program. Check your manual for the specific command that creates automatic footnote placement and numbering in your text. If you need to add an extra footnote later, the program automatically will renumber all the footnotes—a great time-saver for writers.

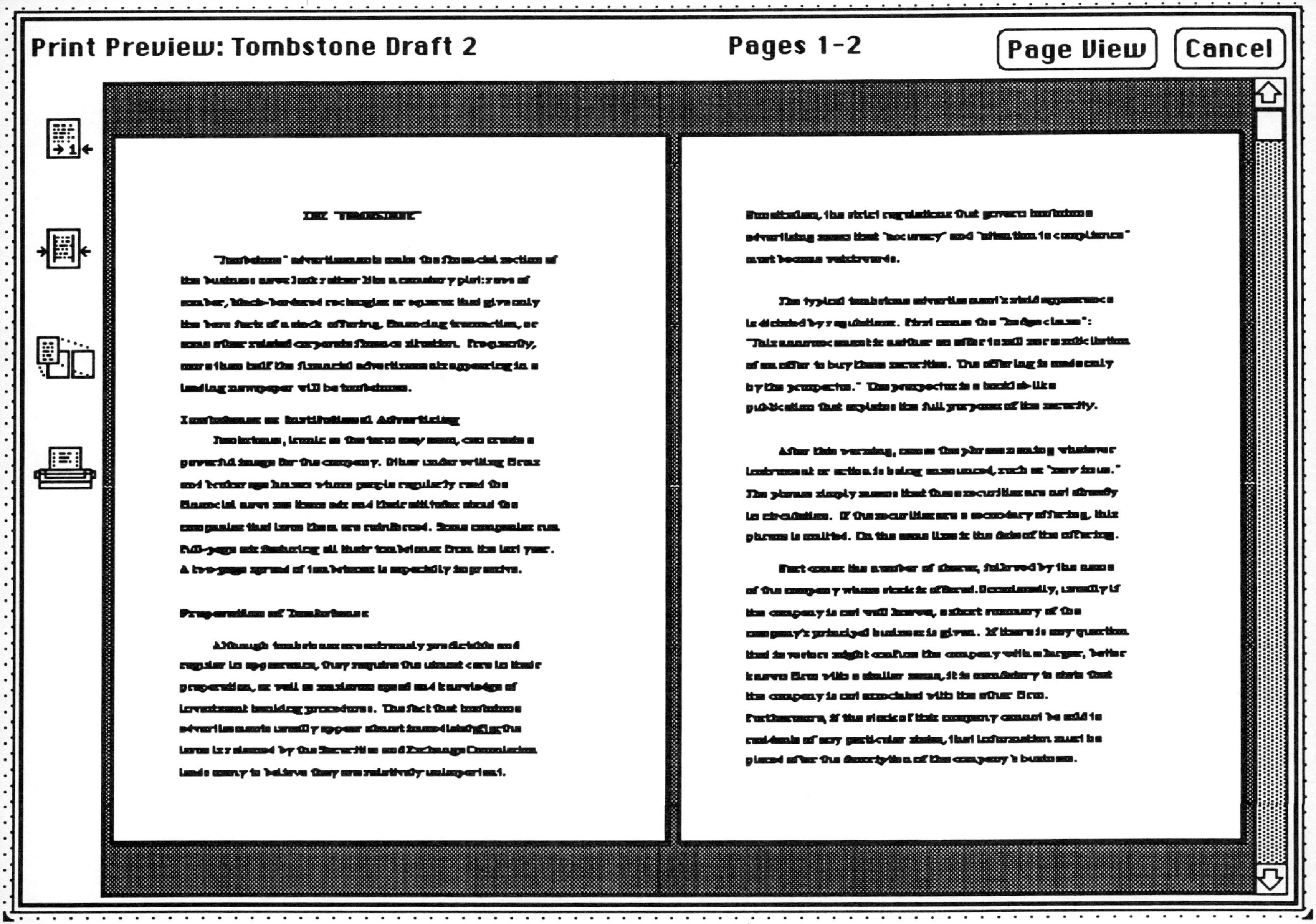

FIGURE 10-8.   Print Preview

Most programs will allow you to look at your footnotes whenever you wish by pressing a combination of keys or making a menu choice. Check your manual for this feature and enter it in the Guide to Writing with Your Word Processor form (Figure 10-3).

Using Multiple Columns

Word processing enables writers to use multiple columns almost automatically. Some programs will show all columns simultaneously on the screen; some versions will only show multiple columns in the printer preview screen. Narrow columns are easier to read than columns that cover the entire page. You sometimes can make a document more appealing if the line of text contains only five or six words.

Creating Special Effects

Use special effects for a purpose; use them sparingly.

The number of special effects available varies from program to program. Among the most common are underlining, boldfacing, and italics. Macintosh computers also offer outlined characters and shadow characters. While these effects are not likely to be used often, they can be handy in announcements and title pages. Perhaps their most useful function is in checking for patterns of development, as shown earlier in the section on revising. In addition, word processing programs for Macintosh computers can offer a variety of fonts, from traditional typewriter fonts, such as Courier, to modern-looking fonts, such as Geneva or Helvetica. By selecting or highlighting the entire document and changing the font setting, an entire document can be shown in a new typeface.

<u>underlining</u>   Courier font

boldfacing   Geneva font

italics   Times font

Importing Graphics

Some programs allow you to import line drawings, diagrams, and scanned images. The command for accomplishing this function will vary from program to program. This feature is useful in preparing sales letters, catalogues, and reports. Graphics programs are discussed in Chapter 15: "Graphics: Visual Persuasion."

Emphasizing with Lines, Boxes, and Drop Shadows

Advanced programs enable you to place lines above or below headings or paragraphs to give visual emphasis to a section of your document. They may also give you the choice of single or double lines, thin or thick lines. In addition, some programs allow you to place boxes or drop shadows around special elements such as headings, warnings, price lists, and other material.

Creating a Table of Contents

Some programs allow you to create a table of contents as you write your document. To create a table of contents entry, you have to tell the program what you want to use as the entry. Generally, you simply add a contents code before the entry. When you choose this code, the program compiles the entries and automatically calculates the correct page number.

Presenting and Distributing the Document

Different types of printers offer different combinations of advantages in cost, speed, and aesthetic quality.

Documents may be distributed electronically (over networks) or printed out. In the electronic office you may have a choice of printers. Dot matrix printers are the cheapest printers, but the quality of the document is not very attractive. Dot matrix printing is great for draft copies, and the cost of printing is cheaper. The letters of a dot matrix printer are made up of tiny ink dots, which don't quite create a solid outline for the letters. Plotters use multiple colors, which are very helpful in making graphs and maps. Letter-quality printers print documents that resemble professionally typed documents, using a device such as a daisy wheel or thimble that strikes a carbon ribbon.

Laser printed documents resemble those that have been typeset and printed. When you give the "print" command and send a document to a Postscript-based laser printer, the computer sends a description of each page to the printer. The laser printer uses this description to build a picture of the page in its memory. The laser in the printer then draws that picture on a rotating, light-sensitive drum by "neutralizing" the spots where black should be, leaving the surrounding areas positively charged where white should be. When the drum rolls through toner, the positively charged toner sticks to the zero-charged dots. The printer then transfers the picture from the drum to paper and heat-seals the page.

In addition, you can display the document to a group with a monitor projector. This small device attaches directly to the computer and sits on top of a conventional overhead projector. The image projected on the screen is the same as the one shown on the computer monitor. This device can be useful in collaborative writing, so that everyone working on the document can see it easily.

Once printed, a document may be distributed through the mail or by courier service, or it may be sent over a FAX (facsimile) machine. A facsimile machine sends an electronic copy of the printed version of the document over the telephone lines to another FAX machine, which prints out a copy that looks like a photocopy of the original document. The printer will also attach a line documenting the date and time of transmission. Facsimile copies are treated as acceptable legal records of transactions, unless original signatures are required. Telex communications, which are not facsimiles and use only capital letters, also are acceptable as legal documentation. The telex, which comes from "telegraph exchange," transmits messages that have been typed in on a special machine. The immediacy of the transmission, only a few seconds from point to point, is more satisfying even than air mail.

When sent internationally, both FAX and telex copies are more costly than when they are sent in the United States. Some people who write international documents for immediate transmission sometimes try to save money by using a cryptic, terse style similar to that used in telegrams. The lack of civility and the possibility for ambiguity and misunderstanding make such a style a dubious savings. Especially if your audience is from a culture that values status, relationships, and formality, pay the additional charge and send a courteous message.

Photocopying is so familiar a technology that it scarcely needs description, but these machines are clearly the backbone of many organizational communication systems. Providing copies of documents to all people who need them has indeed improved information flow and has contributed much to the efficiency of companies. Communications, whether electronic or paper, must be easy to access and easy to use if technology is to support the productivity of individuals and the competitiveness of companies.

❏ COMMUNICATION CHALLENGES

PRELIMINARY EXERCISE 1 Prepare voice mail messages for each of the situations described below. Write out the message.

a. You are the buyer for the men's sportswear department of Connally's Department Store. Your job, in addition to purchasing, is to maintain contact with the sales supervisors, find out customer reactions, and provide information about new merchandise deliveries. You will be out of town for three days while attending the fashion previews for the spring lines at the market showing in Dallas. While you are gone, Lajuana Osborne will take important inquiries for you, but Lajuana is not located in the same building. To reach her, a caller would have to dial 471-2970. Your phone is part of the voice mail system. *Compose a message to leave on your telephone* beginning Wednesday, September 3rd. You will be back in the office on Monday.

b. You manage Timberlife Tree Service, the largest nursery in northwest Oregon. A major storm that swept into the area over the weekend downed many trees and caused a great deal of damage. The city and county road crews are taking care of debris on the roads and highways, of course, but your company is swamped with requests from people who have damaged trees on their property. Every crew at your disposal is working this morning and your secretary is off on vacation until Tuesday. You haven't been able to reach her and you need to be out supervising crews. You have a recorder in the office and a pager, 787-1121, by which people can call you if there's an emergency. You have a cellular telephone in your car from which you can return pager calls, but people can't call you on the car phone unless the motor is running. You don't want everyone to call you on the pager, so set a time for returning calls. It is now 5:45 A.M. on Monday the 12th and you're getting ready to send out your crews. *Prepare a message to leave on your recorder.*

c. You are getting ready to meet with the property manager to review additional space that your company needs to lease in the building where your company now has offices. You expect the meeting to last about 45 minutes, so you will be back by 10:30 A.M. Your company is Wickham Insurance Associates. If any people have an urgent call, Terry Granville in the adjoining office can advise them. They can either leave a message for you or press 637 at the tone to reach Terry. *Prepare a message for your voice mail system.*

PRELIMINARY EXERCISE 2   Make an inventory list of the office equipment you already know how to use and could discuss in a job interview with a prospective employer. Do you know how to type? Have you ever used a photocopier, calculator, telephone message recorder, voice mail system, video player, video conference equipment, or computer? Which brands, models, or systems do you know? Which word processing programs, spreadsheets, outliners, editing tools, or graphics programs have you used? Mark on the list the degree of familiarity you have with each piece or program. Your experience may range from "I've seen one" to "I've used one frequently" to "I can repair one."

PRELIMINARY EXERCISE 3   You are a student who has to be away from the campus for a good reason and will miss class on the day of a one-hour examination. There is no stated policy in the course syllabus about make-up examinations. Plan a message to leave on the professor's recorder requesting permission to take the examination on a different day, either before or after the regularly scheduled date. Record this message on a tape recorder. Bring the message to class with you for analysis.

EXERCISE 1

You and three friends have decided to split the cost of having a computer for the next two years of your college work. Your task is to compare two word processing programs and to recommend one of them. Your audience is your friends. Although you would doubtless present such a report to them orally, for this assignment you must make up a handout of information about the two programs that shows you understand their needs and did your best to select the most suitable program. Talk to your three friends and make notes about the kinds of writing they want to do with a word processing program. What do they need to be able to do with a program? Will it need to be able to import sections of spreadsheets, graphics, and other data? Will they write long papers or short papers? Are they already familiar with any word processing programs? Do they know how to type?

EXERCISE 2

Imagine that you have been denied admission to this class on the grounds that this section of the course is limited to 25 people and that 29 people enrolled. The administration has given seniors and graduate students

priority in this plan. If you are a senior or graduate student, pretend that you are a junior. *Plan and dictate a letter to the instructor requesting special permission to enroll in the class in spite of this situation.* Assume that you would want to take the course in spite of this rejection. Use a tape recorder to dictate your letter. Transcribe your own letter and bring it to class for a discussion about editing drafts.

EXERCISE 3

Read the following draft of a memorandum or enter it in a word processor if you have one. Identify the key claim in this memorandum. This claim will have two parts: a topic and an idea about the topic. Change the phrase expressing the idea to boldface. Underline supporting details for this idea, making a visible pattern of boldfacing and underlining that shows the pattern of the argument.

TO: All Staff Members
FROM: Harold Carson
SUBJECT: Carson Brothers' Employees Trip

We'd like to celebrate your success in a historic way! For the past five years, Carson employees have operated the plant without a lost-time accident either on or off the job. That's a wonderful record. So, on May 8th, the commemorative train will leave Sacramento for the trip to the Golden Spike National Historic Site, Utah. We'd like as many Carson employees to yell "All aboard" as possible. The train will return to Sacramento on May 11th, arriving at 6 P.M. on May 12th. Invite your family to join us in the old-fashioned sleeper cars for an historic reenactment of the Union Pacific's drive across 1,775 miles of desert, rivers, and mountains. They set a record; you've set a record. It's time to celebrate.

See the attached form for instructions on signing up.

IF YOU WOULD LIKE TO READ MORE

Communications technology and productivity

Benson, D. H. (1983, December). A field study of end user computing: Findings and issues. *MIS Quarterly*, 35–45.

Beswick, R. W., & Williams, A. B. (1983). *Information systems and business communications*. Urbana, IL: Association for Business Communications.

Brown, D. S. (1987). *Management's hidden enemy—and what can be done about it.* Mt Airy, MD: Lomond Publications. Argues that while many of the dysfunctional effects of introducing unfamiliar technology are minor and easily fixed, others are long-lasting, hurtful, and debilitating—even intolerable. Emphasizes people's roles, values, and strengths. Says we must change way management thinks about people to cure problems.

Clemons, E. K., & McFarlan, F. W. (1986, July–August). Telecom: Hook up or lose out. *Harvard Business Review, 64*, 91–97.

Davis, G. B., & Olson, M. H. (1985). *Management information systems: Conceptual foundations, structure, and development* (2nd ed.). New York: McGraw-Hill.

Halpern, J. W. (1985). How do the new technologies affect composing on the job? In L. Odell & D. Goswami (Eds.), *Writing in non-academic settings* (pp. 158–179). New York: Guilford Press.

Lesko, M. (1986). *Lesko's new tech sourcebook: A directory to finding answers in today's technology-oriented world.* New York: Harper & Row. Extremely easy to use book; helps reader figure out where to begin a search. Also lists sources on artificial intelligence. Complete with phone numbers and addresses. Good cross-reference list.

Lucas, Jr., H. C. (1989). *Managing information services.* New York: Macmillan.

McFarlan, F. W. (1983). *Corporate information systems management: The issues facing senior executives.* Homewood, IL: Richard D. Irwin.

Porter, M. E., & Millar, V. E. (1985, July–August). How information gives you competitive advantage. *Harvard Business Review, 63*, 149–160.

Sprague, Jr., R. H., & McNurlin, B. C. (1986). *Information system management in practice.* Englewood Cliffs, NJ: Prentice-Hall.

Writing with computers in the electronic office

Alderman, E., & Lawrence, J. M. (1987). *Advanced Word Perfect®: Features and techniques.* Berkeley, CA: Osborne McGraw-Hill.

Beacham, D., & Beacham, W. (1985). *Using Wordperfect®.* Indianapolis, IN: Que.

Brownstein, M. (1987). *Advanced Microsoft® Word.* Berkeley, CA: Osborne McGraw-Hill.

Edwards, Jr., B. L. (1987). *Processing words: Writing and revising on a microcomputer.* Englewood Cliffs, NJ: Prentice-Hall.

LETTERS AND MEMOS

OBJECTIVES

This chapter will help you

- implement a communication strategy using the conventions of letters and memos

- understand the principles behind these conventions

- use the conventions of special-purpose letters to create goodwill, convey negative messages, increase sales, and respond to complaints

PREVIEW

Letters are sent to individuals and companies outside the firm; memos are sent to people within the firm. These two types of short documents have a common origin, but today the business letter and the business memo have different formats and different conventions of content organization.

Letters are involved in many situations: promoting products, answering complaints, building goodwill for the firm, communicating with prospective employees, and handling transactions with vendors, regulators, and trade associations. Memos are primarily tools for managing the company, used for everything from meeting announcements to proposals and short reports. Memos and letters are often retained for future use, and they may have several political (and sometimes legal) benefits to the writer.

❏ LETTERS

Do You Need to Write a Letter?

When you consider writing a letter, think about the specific situation and the way it is usually handled. Is a letter the best medium for the transaction? Do you need a written record of your spoken communication? A letter preserves the interaction, confirming spoken agreements. Do you want to congratulate or recommend someone? A letter has a more official status than a phone call. In some situations, however, a telephone call is more immediate and effective than a letter. Face-to-face, you can assess and respond to the other person's feelings; sitting at a desk composing a letter, you can only imagine that person.

Chapter 5 suggested that a document is part of a social process. Is this letter a prelude to discussion, or do you need to hold a discussion before you write the letter? In some corporations, letters are written *after* matters have been resolved. Is this a situation that requires one-on-one communication, or is a group meeting necessary? Can the issue be resolved by sending a letter to one person or must a group act on it? Should this letter have your name on it, or would the issue be taken care of more easily if you write the letter for your boss's signature? Make certain that a letter is the most effective way of carrying out the function before you spend time writing.

Planning a Letter

Planning letters ensures their effectiveness.

Plan your letters as you would any other communication. Answer four questions by jotting a few phrases on a worksheet or in your Letter Planner (Figure 11-1).

1. What do I want the reader to do?
2. What information will the reader need to take action?
3. What feelings would motivate the reader to do what I want? Or, how should the reader's feelings have changed by the end of the letter?
4. What is my relationship to this reader?

Consider future as well as present readers.

Naturally, some letters are likely to have multiple readers, so you should think about other people who might later read the letter in the file, who might be given the letter as a source of instruction, or who might scrutinize the letter for legal reasons. Plan for these secondary readers as well. Assess the reader's uncertainties and develop a comprehensive purpose. Review your purpose with the following questions:

- Does the purpose include my intentions toward each of my readers?
- Does the purpose address the most important uncertainties of each reader?
- Does the purpose reflect my personal objectives, the company's objectives, and my department's objectives?

Develop a persuasive appeal, even for informative letters.

Evaluate your knowledge of your readers and choose a persuasive appeal appropriate to them in the situation by answering the following questions:

HOW EASY WILL IT BE TO INFLUENCE MY READERS?

Do the reader and I share a mutual understanding of the scenario?

Has the reader done this or felt this before?

Is the reader predisposed to do what I request?

Is my relationship with this reader strong?

WHAT SHOULD BE THE BASIS OF THE PERSUASIVE APPEAL?

Benefits for the reader	Credibility of the letter medium
Mutual benefits	History of the relationship
Corporate values	Preferences of powerful people
Shared goals or mutual needs	Desire to be part of the group
My credibility	Desire to lead the group
My expertise	Personal appreciation
Power, coercion	Cultural values
Policies or laws	

Given the appeal that seems appropriate for the degree and kind of persuasion needed, you have several choices.

- If you can recommend something that will alleviate an important uncertainty, emphasize how the action can effectively address the uncertainty.

- If you can associate your request or proposal with something the subject already values or feels strongly about, you may be able to convince the reader to hold the same attitude toward your request.

- If you can create a feeling of discrepancy or dissonance that suggests a need for action, then the reader will be more motivated to reduce the dissonance through the action you request.

- If you and the reader have a good relationship, the reader may agree simply on the strength of your association.

- Every reader is thinking, "What's in this for me?" Respond to that interest by stressing benefits to the reader whenever possible.

You may also persuade the reader by demonstrating your *goodwill and fairness* (concern for the reader), *expertise* (knowledge and intelligence), *prestige* (attributed power), and *self-presentation* (writing skills). If you need to review how you can demonstrate these qualities, review Chapter 4, page 94.

Now you need to define the topics you will discuss. The content of the letter should address the readers' beliefs and feelings, satisfy their need for information, and be organized into logically related strategic issues. You may want to use a mind map, as explained in Chapter 5, to plan the types of issues and information you will use.

Use mind maps, issue trees, and other heuristic tools to plan and organize the content of your letters.

Your letter's communication strategy has four major elements: a comprehensive purpose, a persuasive approach, relevant content organized into issues, and criteria for evaluating success. A special strategy planner for letters follows (see Figure 11-1). The planner is a place to jot key words that will enable you to draft efficiently. Don't short-change yourself or your reader by failing to prepare.

Situation: Date:		Reference:

Primary Audiences
 	
Relationship
 	
Action wanted
 	
Information reader needs
 	
Motivating feelings
		Uncertainties
		
		  Information
		
		  Beliefs
		
		  Feelings
		
		Reader Benefits

Secondary and Transmitting Audiences
 	
Relationship
 	
Action expected
 	
Information reader needs
 	
Motivating feelings
		Uncertainties:
		
		  Information
		
		  Beliefs
		
		  Feelings
		
		Reader Benefits

Comprehensive Purpose	Persuasive Strategy	
Preferred Response	Lowest Acceptable Response	
Organizing Pattern		
Opening paragraph situation, motivation, purpose Body paragraphs: information and reasons Closing paragraph: benefits + details		
Criteria for Evaluation		

FIGURE 11-1.   Letter Planner

Letter Organization Conventions

Place content where readers expect it.

Next, adapt your communication strategy to the conventions of the letter form. Business letters usually have a familiar three-part organization: an introductory paragraph, body paragraphs, and a closing paragraph.

- The *introductory paragraph* explains the situation and your purpose in writing. Sometimes it mentions your existing relationship with the reader. The introductory paragraph also begins motivating the reader to do what is requested.
- The *body paragraphs* provide information and reasons that justify the reader's taking action.
- The *final paragraph* looks forward to the benefits of the reader's taking the desired action. It also supplies additional details relevant to that action: telephone numbers, times, directions (such as, "deliver the shipment to Gate 3 if you arrive after 5 P.M.").

The common-sense justification for these conventions is that readers must know the general situation and your purpose before they can make much sense of your message. Occasionally, advertisers begin sales letters with shocking or unexpected information (for example, "Americans observe themselves nude for thirty minutes each month") in order to gain the reader's attention, but the usual business letter does not require shock treatments.

The Opening Paragraph

Explain the situation and imply how your reader should feel.

One way to begin the first paragraph is to explain the situation while making the reader feel a motivating emotion. For example, you might ask yourself, "How can I talk about this situation while making someone feel like helping me?" This procedure sounds mechanical, but because of the enormous variation in situations and persuasive approaches, it seldom produces routine openings. The document spotlight illustrates some letter openings. Since the opening of your letter creates expectations and feelings that affect the reader's interpretation of the rest of the letter, work on the opening carefully.

Body of the Letter

Body paragraphs of your letter should contain the information the reader needs to take action. They also should continue to motivate the reader. The issue tree or outline you created in developing your communication strategy will guide your organization of the body of your letter.

The Closing Paragraph

Use a goodwill close.

The final paragraph looks forward to the *benefits* of the reader's taking the requested action or changing his or her attitude. The final paragraph also is the place for providing performance details: telephone numbers, hours for calling, and other special instructions. Although thanking the reader in advance for taking action used to be common, such anticipated gratitude has little persuasive force and most writers have abandoned the practice. Thanking in advance is

OPENING PARAGRAPHS

LETTER OPENING ONE: AN INQUIRY

Dear _____:

    For the first time, our company is introducing a product that must carry a warning. At a Society for Technical Communication meeting last week, a friend told me that Westinghouse has developed a very efficient system for designing effective product warning labels and that I might obtain a handbook and layout kit through your department. Since I want to prepare the most effective label possible, I would appreciate your telling me whether you still offer such a handbook for sale.

Comments: The first sentence sets out the circumstances that led the writer to send the letter: because his company is about to produce a hazardous product, the writer needs a product that Westinghouse has created. The reference to Westinghouse's efficient system compliments the reader. The opening invites the reader to play the role of an expert in an outstanding company. The writer's assertion that "I want to prepare the most effective label possible" expresses a commitment to standards that the reader presumably shares, creating a professional relationship between the writer and the reader. The last sentence in the introductory paragraph expresses the writer's purpose.

LETTER OPENING TWO: A COMPLAINT

Dear _____:

    After receiving your August catalog, I purchased six TR1000 portable computers for our insurance representatives, expecting them to be able to use the computers in demonstrating policy benefits to clients. Although the computers live up to TR's reputation in other ways, the plain reflective LCD screen is so faint that a client sitting beside the representative often cannot see it, and the screen scarcely can be adjusted so that someone can view it when sitting across a desk. This screen does not live up to the description in your catalog. Will you modify these computers to give us satisfactory performance or replace these with computers that have more visible screens?

Comments: This writer begins by explaining the situation: The catalog for the office equipment company created expectations that were not fulfilled. The computers do not serve the function for which they were purchased. By mentioning the catalog first, the writer attempts to make the reader feel responsible for the claims in the catalog. After pointing out the discrepancy between the advertisement and the level of performance, the writer poses the principal question: asking for modification or replacement of the unsatisfactory items, which is his purpose in writing the letter. By phrasing the question as a choice between two acceptable alternatives, the writer attempts to limit the reader's response.

(Continues)

DOCUMENT SPOTLIGHT

OPENING PARAGRAPHS (*continued*)

LETTER OPENING THREE:
A GOODWILL LETTER

Dear _____:

We received many compliments last week on the landscaping and signage your company prepared for the clinic's grand opening. The topiary animals on the lawn drew many positive comments; one child visitor told her mother she wanted to bring Snowball, her kitten, to see "the big green kitty." We are looking forward to having Westwood Landscaping as our grounds maintenance company. Your care and imaginative landscaping will make Vincent's Veterinary Clinic a landmark in Westwood.

Comments: The veterinarian begins with an aspect of the situation (visitor compliments) that should motivate the reader (the owner of the landscaping service) to feel goodwill toward the writer and his clinic. The anecdote about the little girl who wants to bring her kitty to see the topiary cat makes the compliment vivid. The writer's purpose—to motivate the reader to continue providing high-quality service during the contract for lawn care and maintenance—is well-grounded in the persuasive appeal: Keep doing something you've already done. The reader may also infer that the clinic's reputation is his reputation as well, but the writer doesn't directly mention this benefit.

presumptuous, indicating that the writer assumes the reader *must* do as asked. Instead, the closing paragraph should build goodwill. The following example illustrates the subjects often included in a letter's conclusion.

> We will guarantee delivery of your specially wrapped gifts to everyone on your list by December 24th if you call us by December 15th. UPS priority service delivery is like a visit from Santa. Just dial 1-800-435-9888 and have your Visa, Mastercard, or American Express number handy. The people you love will be impressed by the special consideration that our absolutely fresh, premium quality fruit symbolizes at holiday time.

Letter Format Conventions

In addition to subject matter conventions, letters also follow format conventions. In most companies, all employees are expected to use the same format. Most companies choose one of these four formats: *block format* (Figure 11-2), *modified block format* (Figure 11-3), *indented format* (Figure 11-4), or *Administrative Management Society Simplified* (AMSS) *format* (Figure 11-5). Most company correspondence is prepared on letterhead (stationery printed with the company name, address, telephone number and electronic mail address, plus other identifying information such as the department name). Important executives have special letterhead with their names and titles on the stationery as well. Individuals writing without letterhead stationery may use one of the four formats shown in Figures 11-2 through 11-5. Figure 11-6 shows an example of a student's letter in block format without a letterhead.

McNabb Accounting Associates
4887 Fondren Road
Shelby, Texas 77280

25 February 1991

Ms. Amy Nettleson
Winston Corporation
5634 West Loop South, Suite 234
Houston, Texas 77027

Dear Ms. Nettleson:

xxxxxxxxxxxxxxxxxxxxxxxxxxxxxxxxxxxxxxxxxxxxxxxxxxxxxx
xxxxxxxxxxxxxxxxxxxxxxxxxxxxxxxxxxxxxxxxxxxxxxxxx
xxxxxxxxxxxxxxxxxxxxxxxxxxxxxxxxxxxxxxxxxxxxxxx.

xxxxxxxxxxxxxxxxxxxxxxxxxxxxxxxxxxxxxxxxxxxxxxxxx
xxxxxxxxxxxxxxxxxxxxxxxxxxxxxxxxxxxxxxxxxxxxxxxxxxx
xxxxxxxxxxxxxxxxxxxxxxxxxxxxxxxxxxxxxxxxxxxxxxxxxxx
xxxxxxxxxxxxxxxxxxxxxxxxxxxxxxxxxxxxxxxxx.

xxxxxxxxxxxxxxxxxxxxxxxxxxxxxxxxxxxxxxxxxxxxxxx
xxxxxxxxxxxxxxxxxxxxxxxxxxxxxxxxxxxxxxxxxxxxxxxxxxx
xxxxxxxxxxxxxxxxxxxxxxxxxxxxxxxxxxxxxxxx.

Sincerely,

Royce Carmichael

Royce Carmichael
Audit Manager

FIGURE 11-2. Block Format

McNabb Accounting Associates
4887 Fondren Road
Shelby, Texas 77280

February 25, 1991

Ms. Amy Nettleson
Winston Corporation
5634 West Loop South, Suite 234
Houston, Texas 77027

Dear Ms. Nettleson:

xxxxxxxxxxxxxxxxxxxxxxxxxxxxxxxxxxxxxxxxxxxxxxxxxxxxxx
xxxxxxxxxxxxxxxxxxxxxxxxxxxxxxxxxxxxxxxxxxxxxxxxx
xxxxxxxxxxxxxxxxxxxxxxxxxxxxxxxxxxxxxxxxxxxxxxx.

xxxxxxxxxxxxxxxxxxxxxxxxxxxxxxxxxxxxxxxxxxxxxxxxx
xxxxxxxxxxxxxxxxxxxxxxxxxxxxxxxxxxxxxxxxxxxxxxxxxxx
xxxxxxxxxxxxxxxxxxxxxxxxxxxxxxxxxxxxxxxxxxxxxxxxxxx
xxxxxxxxxxxxxxxxxxxxxxxxxxxxxxxxxxxxxx.

xxxxxxxxxxxxxxxxxxxxxxxxxxxxxxxxxxxxxxxxxxxxxxx
xxxxxxxxxxxxxxxxxxxxxxxxxxxxxxxxxxxxxxxxxxxxxxxxxxx
xxxxxxxxxxxxxxxxxxxxxxxxxxxxxxxxxxxxxxxx.

Sincerely,

Royce Carmichael

Royce Carmichael
Audit Manager

Enclosure

FIGURE 11-3. Modified Block Format

McNabb Accounting Associates
4887 Fondren Road
Shelby, Texas 77280

25 February 1991

Ms. Amy Nettleson
Winston Corporation
5634 West Loop South, Suite 234
Houston, Texas 77027

Dear Ms. Nettleson:

xxxxxxxxxxxxxxxxxxxxxxxxxxxxxxxxxxxxxxxxxxxxxxxxxxx
xxxxxxxxxxxxxxxxxxxxxxxxxxxxxxxxxxxxxxxxxxxxxxxxxxx
xxxxxxxxxxxxxxxxxxxxxxxxxxxxxxxxxxxx.

xxxxxxxxxxxxxxxxxxxxxxxxxxxxxxxxxxxxxxxxxxxxxxxxxxx
xxxxxxxxxxxxxxxxxxxxxxxxxxxxxxxxxxxxxxxxxxxxxxxxxxx
xxxxxxxxxxxxxxxxxxxxxxxxxxxxxxxxxxxxxxxxxxxxxxxxxxx
xxxxxxxxxxxxxxxxxxxxxxxxxxxxxx.

xxxxxxxxxxxxxxxxxxxxxxxxxxxxxxxxxxxxxxxxxxxxxxx
xxxxxxxxxxxxxxxxxxxxxxxxxxxxxxxxxxxxxxxxxxxxxxxxxxx
xxxxxxxxxxxxxxxxxxxxxxxxxxxxxxxxxxxxxxxxx.

xxxxxxxxxxxxxxxxxxxxxxxxxxxxxxxxxxxxxxxxx.

Sincerely,

Royce Carmichael

Royce Carmichael
Audit Manager

Enclosure

FIGURE 11-4. Indented Format

McNabb Accounting Associates
4887 Fondren Road
Shelby, TX 77280

February 25, 1991

Ms. Amy Nettleson
Winston Corporation
5634 West Loop South, Suite 234
Houston, Texas 77027

REFUND DUE ON 1990 TAXES

xxxxxxxxxxxxxxxxxxxxxxxxxxxxxxxxxxxxxxxxxxxxxxxxxxx
xxxxxxxxxxxxxxxxxxxxxxxxxxxxxxxxxxxxxxxxxxxxxxxxxxx xxx
xxxxxxxxxxxxxxxxxxxxxxxxxxxxxxxxxxxxxxxx
xxxxxxxxxxxxxxxxxxxxxxxxxxxxxxxxxxxxxxxxxx.

1. xxxxxxxxxxxxxxxxxxxxxxxxxxxxxxxxxxxxxxxxxxxxxxx
   xxxxxxxxxxxxxxxxxxxxxxxxxxxxxxxxxxxxxxxxxxxxxxxxxxx
   xxxxxxxxxxxxxxxxx.

2. xxxxxxxxxxxxxxxxxxxxxxxxxxxxxxxxxxxxxxxxxxxxxxxxxxx
   xxxxxxxxxxxxxxxxxxxxxxxxxxxxxxxxxxxxxxxxxxxxxxxxxxx
   xxxxxxxxxxxxxxxxxxxxxxxxxxxxxxxxxx.

xxxxxxxxxxxxxxxxxxxxxxxxxxxxxxxxxxxxxxxxxxxxxxxxxx xx
xxxxxxxxxxxxxxxxxxxxxxxxxxxxxxxxxxxxxxxxxxxxxxxxxxx
xxxxxxxxxxxxxxxxxxxxxxxxxxxxxxxx.

ROYCE CARMICHAEL, C.P.A.
Audit Manager

Encl.

FIGURE 11-5. Administrative Management Society Simplified (AMSS) Format

4545 Newbury Street
Hampton Heights, VA 22911
March 5, 1991

Mrs. Margaret Newton, Executive Director
Phillips Foundation
747 West Douglas Street
Charlottesville, VA 22902

Dear Mrs. Newton:

Thank you for awarding me the Phillips Foundation Scholarship in communications. Because I have enrolled in the independent video course at the School of Public Health this semester, I needed additional money for videotape and editing studio rental fees. Your generous gift will help me cover these expenses.

My project this semester is to prepare a videotape about AIDS for use in businesses. I am interviewing doctors and clinic staff as well as AIDS patients and lawyers. The videotape will focus on two topics: the rights and needs of AIDS patients and how to help coworkers who have AIDS. I would be pleased to show the board members of the Phillips Foundation my film when it is finished.

Electronic communication is an exciting field. After graduation I want to use video to help educate Americans about health problems. I hope my future success will justify your confidence in me.

Sincerely,

Amelia Swift

Amelia Swift

FIGURE 11-6. Block Format without Letterhead

How Letter Formats Differ

These formats differ in page design, use of greetings and close, punctuation, and signposts.

- **Page design.** All four formats use single spacing within paragraphs and double spacing between paragraphs. *Block format* and *The Administrative Management Society Simplified (AMSS) format* line all elements along the left margin, approximately 1" to 1 1/2" from the left edge of the paper. When company letterhead is used, the first typed element is the date. When there is no letterhead, the page begins with the writer's address, not the writer's name (see Figure 11-6). *Modified block format* lines up all elements except the date and signature block on the left margin. The date and the signature block are placed on an axis approximately in the center (or slightly to the right of center) of the page. *Indented format* also places the date and signature block on a centered axis, and it indents paragraphs five spaces (or one-half inch).

- **Use of greetings and close.** The block format, the modified block format, and the indented format use greetings and a complimentary close. The close is followed by the writer's typed name and title. The writer signs his or her name above the typed name. Writers using the block format or the modified block format may choose to write either their first name or initial before their last name. The AMSS omits the greeting and the complimentary close. The AMSS includes the writer's name typed all in capital letters after the last paragraph, but no handwritten signature is required.

- **Punctuation.** Two types of punctuation may be used, mixed or open. Mixed punctuation requires a colon after the greeting and a comma after the complimentary close. Open punctuation uses no punctuation after either the greeting or the complimentary close.

- **Signposts (elements that direct attention to specific information).** *Subject or reference lines.* AMSS format always uses a subject line; the other formats allow (but do not require) a subject line. *Initials, enclosures, and distribution lists.* All four formats allow the use of words or abbreviations to show that other materials are supposed to accompany the letter and to inform the reader that other people have been sent copies.

The choice of a letter format depends primarily on aesthetic and cultural values. Each format conveys a different image of the company. The AMSS format implies that efficiency and simplicity are valued more highly than any other quality. Ostensibly, the AMSS format requires less time for typists. Omitting the greeting and close also suggests that this company has no time for courtesy rituals. On the other hand, omitting the greeting avoids awkwardness when the gender of the reader is not known. The subject line replaces the "Dear Mr." or "Ms." The block format is efficient because the reader can skim the left margin to find topics without jumping to the center of the page, but the sense of ruthless efficiency is softened by the greetings and close. The indented format is the most social of the four images, reminding the reader more of the format of the informal personal letter.

Parts of the Letter

Writer's Address   The company's name, address, and zip code. Optional: logo, company motto, telephone number, FAX number, or electronic network address. Note that the writer's name does not appear in the address block unless the writer is a high-ranking officer in the company and has personalized company stationery. Individuals who are doing business in their own names as companies and have filed with the state for such purposes may also have letterhead that begins with their names. The writer's name also appears in the signature block.

Dateline   The date on which the letter was written, typed below the writer's address in one of the following three ways:

March 10, 1991	Most common in U.S. businesses
10 March 1991	Used in some U.S. firms
1991 03 10	International style; reader may not know which number represents the month

Receiver's Address (also called the inside address)   The name of the person to whom you are writing and his or her title, the company's department, branch, or division; the company name, the street number and name; the city, followed by the state or province abbreviation; and the zip code.

Greeting   In the block, indented, or modified block formats, an introductory phrase followed by the receiver's name and a colon: for example, "Dear Mr. Smith:" or "Dear Ms. Brown:"

Body   The message, divided into paragraphs.

Complimentary Close   A phrase that signals the end of the message in block, modified block, and indented formats. Once, very flowery phrases such as "your most humble and obedient servant" were in vogue. Such sentiments are no longer in style in the U.S., but in some other countries they are still employed. Even thanking the reader in advance for his time or attention is considered boorish and presumptuous in the U.S. Business writers end with a simple "Sincerely yours" or "Sincerely." If you are writing in the language of another country, you should try to adapt to their formalities. If you write a letter in English as the employee of a U.S. company, a foreign reader will expect you to follow U.S. conventions, but will feel comfortable with some adaptation to his or her cultural principles of propriety, reasoning, and tone (see Chapter 18, "International Correspondence").

Signature Block   The handwritten signature, the typed signature, and the writer's title (position in the company). In AMSS format, the signature is typed in capital letters and is not signed by hand. Courtesy titles such as Mr. or Ms. may be typed, but should not be handwritten. For example, above the name

"Ms. C. J. Fitzpatrick" a woman might write either "C. J. Fitzpatrick" or "Carolyn Fitzpatrick." Married women who prefer to call attention to their marital status may have "Mrs." typed before their name, but should not use "Mrs." in the handwritten signature. This matter is discussed in Chapter 6, "Choosing Words," under avoiding sexism in language.

Optional Letter Parts

Subject or Reference Lines   The subject line indicates the topic of the letter. Subject lines are also used to help future readers find a particular letter in the file. The difficult part of writing subject lines is selecting a phrase of fewer than twelve words that (1) identifies the specific issue and (2) cannot be confused with other letters in the same file. For example, in a large construction project many letters may be written about the lighting system, so the phrase "lighting system" would not be a sufficient entry in the subject line. If possible, explain the nature of the problem and the communication purposes of the document in the subject line. For example, "Request for design change approval in the Moskowitz Project CL-210 valve" shows the communication purpose (to request approval) and the problem addressed (the design change in the valve).

Attention Line   When the letter is addressed to a company, the position of the person who should read the letter (or the name of that person, if the name is known) may be indicated as follows:

Attention: Accounts Payable Clerk   or   Attention: Mr. Sam Gunderson

Page Headers   A line naming the person to whom the letter is addressed, the date of the letter, and the page number; for example, *Ms. Raelle Frost, Nov. 3, 1991, page 3.* Use a header at the top of all but the first page when the letter is more than one page long.

Company Name in the Signature Block   When the letter represents the company as a legal entity, the letter is said to be from the company. Type the name of the company two spaces below the close. The person sending the letter may then sign his or her name below the company name; for example:

Sincerely,

Heston Hotels, Inc.

Julian Firestone

Julian Firestone
Manager

Sometimes a line is typed three spaces below the company name followed by the words, "for the company." The individual signs his or her name on the line.

Distribution List   A list headed by the word *distribution* or the abbreviation for copies, then a colon (cc:), followed by the names of the people who will receive copies of the letter. In electronic mail, the distribution information is part of the transmission information at the head of the document. Names on a distribution list may be alphabetized or may be shown according to rank or seniority:

LPD: nep	LPD: nep
enclosures	encl.
Distribution	cc:
W. Taylor	H. Wells, President
H. Wells	W. Taylor, Senior Vice-president
T. Windsor	T. Windsor, Production Manager

Postscript   Literally, *postscript* means "written afterward." This notation, usually abbreviated as P.S., introduces a comment added to the rest of the text at the bottom of the letter. Sometimes the comment is an afterthought. It is used principally in informal personal letters and in sales letters. In sales letters, the postscript is often a pointed comment designed to provoke immediate action, call attention to an enclosure, or drive home the main point.

How to Prepare Envelopes

The condition of the envelope may determine whether the reader opens your letter.

The first thing your reader sees is your envelope. If the envelope is sloppily prepared, your letter may go unopened into the trash. For that reason, make sure your envelope creates a good first impression.

Choose a standard 9-1/2 inch by 4-1/8 inch envelope (known as a No. 10) of good quality paper. Most businesses have the company name and address printed in the upper left hand corner, three spaces or 3/8 inch down from the top of the envelope and 1/2 inch or five spaces in from the left edge of the upper left corner. When the envelope is headed in this way, the last name of the sender may be typed above the company name (if desired). When the envelope is not preprinted, type the return address (name of sender, company, street address, city, state, and zip code) in the upper left hand corner, in the same place where a printed address would go.

Type the name and address of the person or company to whom the letter is being sent (identical to the inside address) 2-1/2 inches from the top of the envelope and 4 inches from the left edge. Positioning the name and address in this way enables the U.S. Postal Service's optical character readers to read the address and speed your letter to its destination.

If your company uses smaller envelopes for some purposes, the recipient's address should begin 2-1/2 inches from the left margin. If your company uses window envelopes, the return address should be printed or typed in the usual space, but the inside address on the document enclosed will show through the window of the envelope. The standard size and the smaller size business envelopes are shown in Figure 11-7.

The state should be typed using the standard abbreviation. Additional mailing instructions, such as "Air Mail," "Registered Letter," or "Hold for Arrival," may be placed three spaces above the person's address and to the right. A letter addressed to a company may have an attention line directing the mail to a particular person. The attention line goes in the lower left-hand corner of the

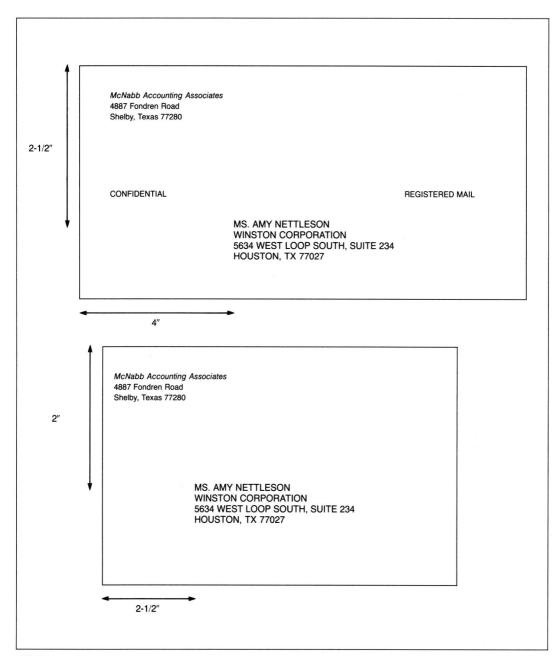

FIGURE 11-7.   Addressed Business Envelopes

envelope, three spaces below the address. The bottom margin for an envelope should be at least 5/8 inch. The following two-letter abbreviations should be used for addressing envelopes:

Alabama	AL	Louisiana	LA	Ohio	OH
Alaska	AK	Maine	ME	Oklahoma	OK
Arizona	AZ	Maryland	MD	Oregon	OR
Arkansas	AR	Massachusetts	MA	Pennsylvania	PA
California	CA	Michigan	MI	Rhode Island	RI
Colorado	CO	Minnesota	MN	South Carolina	SC
Connecticut	CT	Mississippi	MS	South Dakota	SD
Delaware	DE	Missouri	MO	Tennessee	TN
Florida	FL	Montana	MT	Texas	TX
Georgia	GA	Nebraska	NE	Utah	UT
Hawaii	HI	Nevada	NV	Vermont	VT
Idaho	ID	New Hampshire	NH	Virginia	VA
Illinois	IL	New Jersey	NJ	Washington	WA
Indiana	IN	New Mexico	NM	West Virginia	WV
Iowa	IA	New York	NY	Wisconsin	WI
Kansas	KS	North Carolina	NC	Wyoming	WY
Kentucky	KY	North Dakota	ND		

Sales letter envelopes often have "teasers" printed on them to gain attention and to prevent readers from discarding the envelope without reading the letter.

CONVENTIONS FOR SPECIAL-PURPOSE LETTERS

Although formula letters are sometimes ineffective, some special-purpose letters often follow typical conventions that you may consider when writing. The special purposes identified for letters include delivering good news, delivering bad news, promoting sales, and making adjustments. In the comprehensive purpose we have recommended, each of these special purposes would constitute only one of your objectives, and pretending that one of these is the only one worth paying attention to would surely sabotage your overall success. Therefore, we recommend that you consider the following suggestions as components of your plan, not as alternatives to developing a thorough communication strategy.

Good News Letters

Announce good news immediately.

Saying yes to requests, applications, and orders is a pleasure. Announce the good news early in the letter, and follow the news with justifications, details, or pleasant comments.

Read the two paragraphs below and compare the effects the two versions are likely to have on the reader.

EXAMPLE 1

The regular meeting of the management committee was held last Thursday to consider requests for additional space. The Johnson account that your department handles means substantial increased profits for the firm. The expanded responsibilities created by the Johnson account, the committee realizes, have overtaxed the space available on the west wing. Larry Hand, the property manager, has agreed to lease additional space and to renovate it to suit our needs. The committee therefore approved your request to expand into the four offices that have recently been vacated on the east side of the elevator.

EXAMPLE 2

Your request for expanded space to work on the Johnson account has been approved. When the management committee met today, we agreed that work for this new account has overtaxed your current office space. The Johnson account means a great deal to the firm, and the committee appreciates your hard work and high quality of service. You should meet immediately with the property manager, Larry Hand, to discuss any renovation that may be necessary for your people.

The second version places the good news in a high-impact position, where the pleasure of reading the first statement will color the reader's perception of the rest of the message.

Bad News Letters

Announce bad news after affirming the relationship with the reader.

Inevitably, you will face situations that require you to deliver bad news to people: the answer to their request is no; they will receive smaller raises than they expected; and so on. Chapter 6, "Choosing Words," discusses conveying negative news. Its main point is that even when the news about the transaction is bad, the message about the relationship should be positive.

To achieve that objective, say something positive about your relationship (for example, thanking a customer for taking time to send a letter of complaint) before you deliver the bad news about the transaction. Also, describing the situation before announcing the bad news will help you and the reader to share a perspective whose outcome is not what was wanted. Your opening, however, should not create false expectations. Such expectations would make bearing the bad news even harder. In your explanation of reasons why the outcome was necessary, be sure to separate issues from people. That is, talk about the ideas or information or options as though they were separate from the people who presented the ideas, so that rejection of the idea is not tantamount to rejecting the individual who proposed it. The close of your letter should make future interaction possible.

NOT: Your wish to reserve parking spaces for employees near the north entrance can't be approved.

BUT: Thanks for suggesting a new way to solve the problem with employee parking. We've monitored the use of the north lot the past two weeks to determine whether we could implement your change. So many patrons use the north lot that reserving spaces for employees would excessively inconvenience our customers.

Sales Letters

Plan to Write for a Real Person

Sales letters promote a product or service to prospective buyers. Learn as much as you can about these people. Sometimes you will have extensive marketing information about the target market: the age range, income group, educational level, and other characteristics. While this information will alert you to certain attitudes or probable actions of the readers, try to go beyond these demographic characteristics.

Build a complete picture of a reader before you write a sales letter.

Talk with sales people about the customers who buy the product. What do they say about the product when they purchase it? Why do they need it? Why do they choose it over competitors' products? What benefits do they get from the product? Try to understand the situations that lead a real person to purchase the product, attend the sale, or request the service. Then prepare to write for that real person; imagine him or her vividly and think which of his or her possible uncertainties this product addresses. What are its biggest benefits? Choose the most powerful benefit as your main selling point.

Capture the Reader's Attention

Capture attention with the unusual, the personally relevant, and other emotional content.

The opening of the sales letter must motivate the reader to continue reading as well as to take the recommended action. One popular formula for sales letters, AIDA (attention, interest, desire, and action) requires that the opening of the sales letter capture attention. Questions (such as, "Could you afford to be ill for two months?"), striking or unknown facts ("While you read this letter, two Americans will die of lung cancer. . . ."), or other arresting statements are common in sales letter openings. At other times, a compliment such as "Because you are one of our best customers, we'll let YOU decide what's on sale at Myer Brothers this week" will command attention.

Give New Information

New information motivates potential buyers to act.

Give your reader new information that makes the principal benefit more accessible than ever before. Perhaps the new information will be about an easier way to obtain the product. Or it may include prices, sale dates, or special discounts. In order to prompt action, people generally need some new information or a good reason to change from being a potential customer to being an actual customer. Many sales letters use a "feature/function/benefit" strategy in the body of the letter to explain the product's features, how they work, and how they produce the benefits claimed in the opening of the letter.

Close with a Positive Request for Action

Avoid negative ideas ("If not," "Why not") when you request action.

Close the sales letter with a positively stated request for action. Include details that will enable the reader easily to do what you want. Look forward to the benefits the reader will enjoy after doing as you request. Lively, readable sentences and vivid words are especially important in painting a picture of the product and its benefits. People may be unwilling to read sales letters to the end, so your writing must motivate them to continue. The planner in Figure 11-8 and sample letter in Figure 11-9 show how these ideas are implemented.

Adjustment Letters

Adjustments are often based on warranties, negligence, strict liability, and claims about the product.

Why does a business respond to customer complaints? It might seem mere common sense to keep the customer satisfied, but the discourse about complaints is firmly embedded in a legal context. First, the manufacturer or company has an implicit contract with the buyer, even if there is no expressed warranty. Advertising and labeling usually are enough to demonstrate an implied warranty that the product is fit for the ordinary purposes for which such goods are used. There may also be an implied warranty of fitness for a particular purpose, even if that use exceeds the general, ordinary uses of the product. Customers who suffer from breach of warranty may recover direct economic loss (the cost of the product) or consequential damages (losses caused by defective goods). Companies may also have to make adjustments when the customer suffers a *tort* or "wrong" because of strict liability, the company's negligence, or misrepresentation. Under tort law, customers may recover direct personal and property damages, and, if the manufacturer has been reckless, exemplary damages as well.[1]

The implications of these legal considerations are (1) that writers should adjust claims with the legal basis of the relationship between customer and company in mind; and (2) that adjustment letters should avoid statements that will bias future legal action. The writer should not admit a breach of warranty, negligence, or misrepresentation in an adjustment letter. A letter that says "We are sorry that the handlebars were not secured to the frame, causing your accident," is an admission of negligence in manufacture. Without inspecting the bicycle, the writer cannot know that the company is at fault. Given this legal context, what can a claims adjuster do?

Avoid admitting blame before the evidence has been examined.

No single set of rules will suffice. Write thoughtfully, and review and revise your letter before mailing. Ask your corporate attorney to hold a workshop for writers in your Customer Service or Customer Complaints department. Do not exaggerate the benefits of the product (boasting creates new and more rigorous standards of expressed warranty) and do not accuse the customer or increase hostility. Do not commiserate with the customer or describe his or her distress in a way that would make the company guilty in advance.

Preserve goodwill; look to the future.

Try to preserve whatever goodwill remains in the relationship. Thank the customer for past patronage; thank the customer for bringing the problem to your attention. Write as though you expect the customer to continue to do business with you.

Offer the adjustment that seems reasonable, given the legal basis of the customer's claim, even though the customer may not present the complaint in legal terms. For example, in most cases offering a replacement product will only meet the standard of direct economic damage that the customer would be entitled to under contract theory. Therefore, this is a reasonable gesture, and the

Situation:	Date:	Reference:

<u>Primary Audiences</u> *Women lawyers, accountants and executives*	<u>Uncertainties</u>
Relationship *cordial, have women's view in common*	Information *We offer plays by women*
Action wanted *Buy tickets, send back order card*	Beliefs *women are overlooked*
Information reader needs *How to use card, what plays offered, why she should attend*	Feelings *Women's work should be shown*
Motivating feelings *Women are overlooked*	<u>Reader Benefits</u> *Supporting other women, Enjoyable performance*

<u>Secondary and Transmitting Audiences</u> *Readers' daughters, girls*	<u>Uncertainties</u>:
Relationship *New*	Information *There are plays about girls*
Action expected *Ask mother to go to play*	Beliefs *seeing these would be fun*
Information reader needs *names and dates of plays*	Feelings *want to see plays about girls like them*
Motivating feelings *interest in other girls, plays*	<u>Reader Benefits</u> *Ego satisfaction, self esteem*

Comprehensive Purpose *To induce women professionals to buy season tickets to the theater and bring their daughters and young friends to children's series. Good feelings about our theater.*	Persuasive Strategy *Intro. question. Transfer feelings about women being neglected to conviction that they should attend women's plays.*

Preferred Response *Send back order form*	Lowest Acceptable Response *Adopt positive attitude about D.M.T.*

Organizing Pattern   *need satisfaction, info needed to act*

Opening paragraph situation, motivation, purpose	*Leading question. Need a season with women's plays. Del Mar needs women's plays and new subscribers.*
Body paragraphs: information and reasons	*list of plays, comments discount until sept. 30.*
Closing paragraph: benefits + details	*Fun! Benefits: complete season, being included in a good cause*

Criteria for Evaluation *Percentage of response should increase among this group by 10%.*

FIGURE 11-8.   Sales Letter Planner

DEL MAR THEATER

September 2, 1991

Dear Ms. Miller:

What's wrong with a new season that has William Shakespeare, Henrik Ibsen, and Edward Albee? *Two* things are missing. The world's best *women* playwrights and *you.*

As a professional, you know that women don't always get the attention they deserve. That's been especially true in the theater. Women today are writing wonderful plays. We must make sure that these plays are produced and enjoyed, so that later generations will be able to answer that opening question immediately. *Producing* is where we come in; *Enjoying* is your starring role. At Del Mar Theater, you will enjoy

William Shakespeare	*Taming of the Shrew*	Oct. 1–Nov. 13
Beth Henley	*Crimes of the Heart*	Nov. 15–Dec. 30
Henrik Ibsen	*The Doll's House*	Jan. 5–Feb. 10
Tina Howe	*The Art of Dining*	Feb. 12–March 30
Edward Albee	*American Dream*	April 2–May 14
Mary Gallagher	*¿De Donde?*	May 16–June 28

As you can see, our lineup features three plays by women, plays that will deserve a special niche in your memory because they tell stories of women's lives from a woman's point of view. And there's Shakespeare, Ibsen, and Albee, too, for comparison. Give women playwrights a fair chance to be heard; give yourself the pleasure of seeing their works.

Until September 30, you can buy six plays for the price of four. That's only three weeks away, so peel off the address label on the envelope and attach it to the enclosed order form. Fill in the number of season tickets you need and your credit card number (or enclose a check). We'll have *a complete season—great plays, great performances, and YOU.*

Sincerely,

Brenna Cutrer
Artistic Director

P.S. Our young people's series includes plays about girls as well as boys, featuring favorites such as *Nancy Drew* and *Little House on the Prairie.* Show your daughter, niece or young friend the enclosed brochure.

FIGURE 11-9. *Sample Sales Letter*

customer may even be pleased with uncontested replacement. The writer must avoid writing something that will be used to prejudge the case without a fair test of the evidence, something that would be used as an admission of negligence or harm, should the matter come to trial.

Strive to preserve the relationship, even if your adjustment message is negative. Use the suggestions on good news and bad news messages presented earlier in the chapter to guide the preparation of the adjustment letter. The planner in Figure 11-10 and sample adjustment letter in Figure 11-11 show these ideas in application.

❑ MEMOS

Memos or memoranda (Latin plural of *memorandum*), the most frequently written business documents, are essential to productive operations. The memo is a type of internal correspondence used to initiate, conduct, or interpret transactions *inside* a company. The reasons memos differ from letters have not been understood very well and deserve more attention, especially because many technological innovations, such as electronic mail (discussed in Chapter 10) are likely to prompt further changes in this form of communication. The "Trends in Business Communication" feature explains the key to this development.

Memo Headings

The headings of a memo replace the letter's inside address, salutation, and closing. Both letters and memos give the date. Since both the memo writer and readers work for the same company, there is no need for street and local addresses. However, since different departments may be involved, titles or department affiliations are sometimes added beneath or beside the names. Whatever is routine in the situation may have a regular place in the form. The subject line, project number, and other reference information identify the situation. (In most U.S. companies the word "SUBJECT" has replaced the letters "RE"—Latin for "about" or "concerning.") Therefore, the writer can begin the first paragraph of the memo with information relevant to the reader's response.

Memo headings identify the situation.

By putting the same types of information in the same place each time, the writer can help the reader find information more quickly. Once a reader becomes familiar with the format used in a specific company, retrieving information can be efficient. Since most memos are related to other documents in the firm, the subject line must be worded precisely, so that both the larger category and the specific transaction and related documents can be identified.

If the company does not have special printed letterhead for memos, you may type the word "memorandum" centered or flush left, usually in all capital letters, above the heading. When the company has special letterhead for memos, you may choose to make the left margin line up with the names of the writer and readers to simplify the typing (see Figure 11-12 on page 253). Ordinarily, the left margin would be aligned with the headings. The memo in Figure 11-12 pertains to training employees to manage their time more efficiently.

Situation:	Date:	Reference:

Primary Audiences *Bert Carey*	Uncertainties
Relationship *Repeat Customer*	Information *Is there another book? Can he get it?*
Action wanted *Commit to return; accept book*	Beliefs *Store owes me.*
Information reader needs *That he'll have his book for vacation*	Feelings *Dissatisfaction, frustration*
Motivating feelings *Desire for justice; good service wanted*	Reader Benefits *Needs relief. Has what he needs because of us.*

Secondary and Transmitting Audiences *Carey's friends, acquaintances*	Uncertainties:
Relationship	Information *Info. about Store's commitment to service*
Action expected	Beliefs
Information reader needs	Feelings *Stores don't care*
Motivating feelings	Reader Benefits *I can get what my friend got*

Comprehensive Purpose *To reassure customer and restore his confidence; relieve his frustration*	Persuasive Strategy *Thank him for notifying us; demonstrate we listened, care about him and his trip.*

Preferred Response *Tells his friends, Carey returns as customer.*	Lowest Acceptable Response *Carey says nothing bad about us.*

Organizing Pattern

Opening paragraph situation, motivation, purpose *Thank him, explain what we'll do.*
Body paragraphs: information and reasons — *all in first paragraph*
Closing paragraph: benefits + details *Benefits to him of having book. Ask for his continuing business.*

Criteria for Evaluation *No further complaints from Bert Carey*

FIGURE 11-10. Adjustment Letter Planner

Pickwick Book Shop
12 Tangle Lane
Los Angeles, CA 90078

January 12, 1991

Mr. Bert Carey
Apt. A-25
433 Wilforce St.
Los Angeles, CA 90076

Dear Mr. Carey:

Thank you for calling us about the missing pages in the copy of *The Outdoor Traveler's Guide: Caribbean* you purchased last Saturday. I appreciate your choosing Pickwick to purchase your travel materials, and to ensure that you have a complete copy to take on your trip tomorrow, I am sending you a new copy (complete pages—I checked!) by courier today.

Zella Silveman's advice on the best natural features of each island—the coral reefs, coves, and the best trails—should make your trip a wonderful vacation. When you return, please visit our store again to select guides for your next adventure.

Sincerely,

Tonia Squires
Manager

FIGURE 11-11. Sample Adjustment Letter

CHECKLIST FOR LETTERS

FOUR QUESTIONS TO ASK ABOUT EVERY LETTER

____ 1. Does the letter strengthen the writer's relationship to this reader?

____ 2. Is it clear what the writer wants the reader to do?

____ 3. Does the letter contain all the information the reader will need to accept the argument of the letter and take action?

____ 4. Does the letter encourage a change in the reader's feelings? What is this change?

GOOD NEWS CONSIDERATIONS

____ Is the good news announced immediately?

____ Is the news supported with details, justifications, or positive comments?

____ Is the tone sincere and friendly?

BAD NEWS CONSIDERATIONS

____ Does the letter describe the situation before announcing the bad news?

____ Does the opening avoid creating false expectations?

____ Do details and explanations establish the grounds for the decision?

____ Does the close of the letter sustain the relationship (make future interaction possible)?

____ Does the letter separate people from positions? (See Chapter 3)

SALES LETTER CONSIDERATIONS

____ Does the opening of the letter capture the reader's attention?

____ What aspects of the letter suit the demographic characteristics of prospective readers?

____ What personal appeal does the letter use to encourage readers to take action?

____ Do you feel the letter is written for a real person?

____ Is the biggest benefit obvious right away?

____ Does the letter give the reader new information? What is it?

____ Does the letter make it easy for the reader to act? How? (Prices, sales dates, how to claim discounts.)

____ Does the letter explain the way different features provide benefits?

____ Are the sentences lively and readable?

____ Does the letter use vivid words?

____ Does the letter motivate people to continue reading?

____ Does the sales letter close with a positively stated request for action?

(Continues)

☐ CHECKLIST FOR LETTERS *(continued)*

ADJUSTMENT LETTER CONSIDERATIONS

____ Does the letter have a respectful, courteous, and sincere tone?

____ Was the letter written thoughtfully, then reviewed and revised?

____ Does the letter exaggerate the benefits of the product or do anything that would increase the customer's hostility?

____ Does the letter try to preserve whatever goodwill remains in the relationship? (thank the customer for past patronage; thank the customer for bringing the problem to attention)

____ Does the letter offer an adjustment that will be legally defensible?

____ Are there any phrases or admissions that could be used to prejudge the case—something that would be used as an admission of negligence or harm should the matter come to trial?

TRENDS IN BUSINESS COMMUNICATION

THE MEMO: A DOCUMENT TYPE RESULTING FROM TECHNOLOGICAL CHANGE AND MANAGEMENT THEORY

Memorandum, today shortened to *memo*, originally meant "a note to oneself, a memory aid." If memos are notes to ourselves, why send them now to others? Changing technology and management theory produced this change in American business communication.[2] Before the turn of the century, American businesses used letters for both internal and external correspondence, and managers wrote "memoranda" to themselves as reminders. As the size of businesses increased and companies began operating stores and plants in several locations, businesses needed to coordinate their operations.[3]

"Systematic management" was the solution proposed as a correction to inefficiency. This method relied not on the knowledge of craftsmen, but on planning and instructions by top managers, who monitored and reviewed the work of those responsible to them. This method meant that the managers' systems had to be communicated to workers and workers had to report their progress to managers. As people began documenting their plans, de-

scribing their performance, and requesting information and action, the number of internal documents produced within companies expanded drastically. The elaborate courtesy language of formal correspondence (for example, "Being now in receipt of yours of the 18th, I beg . . .") was unfit for this efficiency-driven communication, and a crisis of communication management ensued.

Technological innovations, including typewriters and filing systems, offered one solution. As typewriters replaced steel-tipped pens, correspondence took less time to prepare. Filing systems, which seem commonplace today, had been introduced in the 1890s as another means of managing the flurry of communication. Tabbed folders containing copies of all incoming and outgoing correspondence on a single subject could be kept together.

A simplified form of internal communication was another solution. JoAnne Yates, a communication scholar, describes the growth, after 1910, of

(Continues)

THE MEMO: A DOCUMENT TYPE RESULTING FROM TECHNOLOGICAL CHANGE AND MANAGEMENT THEORY (*continued*)

more efficient formats and a less formal style: "The form and style of internal correspondence began to diverge from that of external letters in ways intended to make it more functional to read and handle."[4] Yates quotes two versions of a single document discussed in a 1913 study by DuPont's High Explosives Operating Department. According to the study, the difference in the two versions illustrated the efficiency benefits of adopting proposed reforms in internal correspondence.

AS ORIGINALLY WRITTEN

August 16, 1913

Copy to Chemical Department

Mr. C. A. Patterson, Supt.

Gibbstown, N. J.

Dear Sir:

OUR FILE OH-1129. Referring to your letter of June 11, in regard to the deposit of so-called "Triton Whiskers" in your weak nitric acid tube lines, we are sending you herewith copy of letter of August 15th from the Chemical Department on this subject which is self-explanatory.

You will note that Mr. Chickering expects to be at Repauno on Monday or Tuesday of next week to discuss this matter with you. From the estimate given in the Chemical Department's letter, the apparatus which it is proposed to install can be put in under a Minor Construction Notice.

Yours very truly,

(Sgd.) W. C. Spruance, Jr.,

J.T. B. (118 words)

By eliminating the polite but wordy stylistic conventions, writers could produce internal correspondence that was shorter (118 words versus 49 words), easier to read, and easier to type, as well. Note that the new revision's headings highlight the roles of people involved, the nature of the problem that has caused the situation, and all the documents pertaining to this situation. After scanning the headings, a reader is ready to make sense of the two main pieces of information. The transaction handled in this instance is an exchange of information about how a problem can be solved and who will help solve it.

(Continues)

THE MEMO: A DOCUMENT TYPE RESULTING FROM
TECHNOLOGICAL CHANGE AND MANAGEMENT THEORY (*continued*)

SAME LETTER REVISED

Copy to Chemical Dept.

SUPT. REPAUNO.

> OUR FILE: OH-1129. TRITON DEPOSITED IN WEAK NITRIC GLASS LINES.
> Your letter 6/11/13
> Enclosure Chemical Department letter 8/15/13

Mr. Chickering will discuss this with you Monday or Tuesday.

The apparatus proposed can be put in under a Minor Construction Notice.

(Sgd.) J. Thompson Brown

(49 words)

At about the same time, long informational letters were modified to create the report form.

The changes that led to the memo and the report forms in the early part of the century have implications for business writers today. Now, as then, many companies have become much larger, with today's firms growing by acquisitions, mergers, and joint ventures. Many businesses operate in several countries. Their increased size creates a need for new layers of communication, and once again, electronic technologies have been developed to help us cope with the information flow. Like our counterparts in the first decade of the century, we must find efficient ways to communicate with others in our organizations. Two types of memos, it has been suggested, are likely to emerge: fixed and interactive documents.

Fixed memos will contain rules, instructions, policies, and price lists. Interactive documents will invite a response or offer information for manipulation. These documents will be created with "templates" or partially designed document formats stored on computer file servers. The writer will be able to modify these forms to create special memo forms appropriate to the situation.

At first, most of these communications will be similar to today's printed memos, but eventually new forms are likely to emerge. The trend toward electronic communication among members of an organization is already clear. As more writers begin to have access to electronic office technology, they will be able to structure memos either to deliver information or to help the reader send them information with an interactive document.

The two versions of the memo are reproduced in Yates's article on pp. 501–2. Reprinted with permission.

tells who is affected

indicates the type of action that is requested

indicates the date of session

puts the most important information first

puts least important information last

Red Willow County Department of Human Services
Red Willow County Courthouse
P.O. Box 7299
Harmon, Kansas

MEMORANDUM

DATE: May 2, 1991

TO: Client Counselors
            cc: Alice Benjamin
                Sidney Greenblatt
                Elaine Nusbaum
                Trevor Parks

FROM: Carol Estevan, Director

SUBJECT: Making reservations to attend time management seminar
            on June 12, 1991

Renée Wright, a consultant in time management, will present a two-hour seminar on Wednesday, June 12th in the training conference room from 3 to 5 p.m. Reply to Jackie Armand at ext. 2369 by May 15, so she can make arrangements to have others cover your regular case appointments.

The first half of the seminar will help participants identify time management problems and the second half will focus on three time management techniques. Some time will be devoted to participants' work on their own time management plans.

Renée Wright has served as a consultant to other county agencies for the past five years and has earned very high ratings from past participants in her seminars. In addition to time management seminars, Ms. Wright offers other career planning and personal development seminars through the Personnel Office of Red Willow County.

FIGURE 11-12. Memo on Printed Letterhead

Legal Uses of Memos

A long life in the file means memos may have many readers.

Most companies keep on file for four to seven years all the letters, reports, and memos that have been written. Therefore, although a memo often is related to only a small part of a larger transaction or situation, it may be read and used for several years. A memo is legal evidence of the decision-making processes in a company. Memos may be subpoenaed in product liability suits to determine whether a company making a hazardous product gave balanced consideration to the hazards of the product during its design, manufacturing, and testing phases.[5] Carol Estevan's memo in Figure 11-12 could be reviewed by a plaintiff's attorney in a discrimination suit to see whether the plaintiff's name was listed among other employees of equal rank, indicating whether he or she received equal opportunities for training and advancement. Memos also may be cited in other legal proceedings.

Political Uses of Memos

Memos ensure an account of responsibility.

Memos also have a political function within a company. Memos create "paper trails" that document an individual's attempts to produce results, motivate others, or protest conditions. When performance is evaluated, the person who has written the memos can show evidence that he or she tried every reasonable means to obtain results and that any blame for shortcomings rests with those who were urged but did not respond. Used to excess, such memos are rightly condemned as "covering your tail."

Negative Political Uses Carla Butenhoff, a communication researcher, has argued that the routing of memos has at least as much impact as their contents. The significance of routing probably varies a good deal in different organizations. In a company with a complex hierarchical structure and a formal, competitive, militaristic culture, people are expected to "go through the chain of command." Therefore in such an organization, routing would make a great deal of difference. For example, Butenhoff points out that if the writer addressed a memo to both his boss and to someone perceived to be of higher status in the organization, the immediate boss might infer that the writer was being insubordinate by addressing both ranks at once. On the other hand, if the writer sent the memo only to the immediate boss, the immediate boss could later take credit for the writer's idea without anyone else's knowledge. In contrast, in a loosely structured organization with a short hierarchy, memo routing in itself might have much less significance. It is always important that people who must know and approve an idea be kept informed so that they do not feel surprised or threatened.

Butenhoff also claims that peers do not send memos to one another. In some organizations that may be true, but in other organizations, especially ones operating in turbulent industries (electronics or media, for example), memos and electronic mail help people pass information along quickly. In a static bureaucracy, a memo to a person of the same rank may imply that the sender is empowered to make judgments about the reader. Sly uses, such as putting a covering memo on another person's work, can seem to give the writer credit for the work attached.[6]

Like other communications, memos are used according to the tenets of the company's culture.

Political processes of competition for power and status vary from organization to organization. Any common form of communication, such as memos, weekly meetings, or presentations can become a means of enacting that competition. Continually analyzing the situations in your organization is your best defense and your best method of discovering new opportunities for effective communication.

Memos can have a positive effect on others.

Positive Political Uses   Memos can have a positive political effect on morale when they are used to give recognition and praise for outstanding service, performance, and effort. Many people would value a memo of praise more than a small salary increase. Memos can help build positive relationships among coworkers. To the extent that "business is always more than business," timely memos of sympathy, congratulations, and encouragement can be the "something extra" that makes one group outperform another.

The Memo's Purpose Is Management

As the origins of the memo point out, the purpose of internal communication is efficiency, cooperation, and productivity in the organization. The memo format is intended to accomplish those purposes. The lean system of headings helps orient readers to the situation. The body of the memo is organized according to the management purpose it serves. The memo may transmit information, it may initiate action, or it may comment on or interpret actions already complete.

Memos can be part of the main business activity of the company, involved in the manufacture or sale of products or delivery of services. Memos also can be part of the maintenance functions, personnel, training, benefits, accounting, and so forth. Memos set policy and address grievances. Chapter 3, "You and Your Audiences: Managing Relationships," presents memos used very poorly to quell employee anxiety about a plant closing.

Variety in tone, format, and length reflects the many possible functions of memos in a company.

Memos vary in tone, length, and style to reflect these differences. The memo form also may be used for short reports and proposals up to eight or ten pages. The body of these reports may follow the argument structure of any of the disciplines discussed in the specialists' chapters later in the book: marketing, accounting, finance, and other specialties.

Memos can be the lifeblood or the embalming fluid of the corporation. Therefore they should be written with care. Because memo purposes vary, you must work extra hard to ensure that the purpose of the memo is obvious and clear. Good memos reflect the writer's thinking processes and concern for detail.

Well-written memos will enhance your image in the company; poor memos will sabotage it.

Don't undervalue the memo just because it is familiar. Quality control and attention to detail can be as important in a memo as in a letter going outside the firm. Mistakes in spelling or grammar may be noted and even posted on bulletin boards, much to the chagrin of the writer. Use the memo checklist to ensure the quality of your memos.

CHECKLIST FOR MEMOS

_____ Is the subject line complete and informative?

_____ Do the headings plus the first sentence orient the reader to the situation?

_____ Are the most important details in the headings and first paragraph?

_____ Is the information placed in descending order of importance?

_____ Does the memo contain enough information to enable a future reader to make sense of what is going on?

_____ Does the memo contain any language that might cause legal problems later on? Does it reveal prejudice, bad faith, lack of concern for customer or worker safety, or inattention to product quality?

_____ Does the memo serve your interests politically? Will it show you in a positive light?

COMMUNICATION CHALLENGES

PRELIMINARY EXERCISE 1 Check your files for a business letter you have received from an institution, organization, or company. What format conventions does that organization employ? Make notes in the margin to show whether the information follows the content conventions explained in the letter checklist. How good is this letter and why do you think so? _Write your comments in a paragraph._ If your instructor directs, compare the letter you selected with those chosen by other students in a group.

Restaurant Equipment Manufacturing

TO: Chandler Wells	**SUBJECT:**
FROM: Ted Kirkpatrick	Promotion in August and September
DATE: May 28, 1991	

I have noted the following points in my analysis of prospects for marketing the Pizza Doughboy mixer:

- No other manufacturer is offering a machine comparable to the Pizza Doughboy mixer at a competitive price.
- Competitors' machines cannot match PD's wide variety of batch sizes.
- Demand for pizza increases during the fall and winter months, creating greater need among pizza restaurants and manufacturers.
- The potential for sales to large pizza chains makes the PD a much more promising product than any other item on our list.
- Our current client list offers few opportunities to sell the PD.

We should promote the Pizza Doughboy mixer (PD) with a direct mail campaign to large pizza restaurants. Direct mail beginning the third week in August followed by representatives' calls is the best strategy at this time for the following reasons. . . .

PRELIMINARY EXERCISE 2 How would you alter the heading and first paragraph of the memo at the bottom of page 258 to make it easier for the reader to understand its purpose and contents?

EXERCISE 1

Another student, Bob Barnfield, wants to obtain funds for attending a summer program in England. He has just finished writing a basic letter to send to people and foundations that have contributed to the business school in the last two years. Bob studies hard, and he has a very high grade point average. He comes to you

---

Apt. A25
2030 Avenue H
Lincoln, NE 68510

January 3, 1991

Mr. Sam Sherwood
Suite 1418, Markham Tower
Chicago, IL 60430

Dear Mr. Sherwood:

I am writing concerning the Denvers Foundation that you oversee. I have a unique opportunity to study at Oxford University at Oxford, England, next summer. Tuition, transportation, books, food, and rent will cost $4,000. The credits will transfer to the University of Nebraska, where I am currently a junior with a 3.95 grade point average.

I am trying to find funds to let me take advantage of this opportunity. I am unable to pay much from my own finances as I pay for all my expenses for school already. I need a $550 down payment by January 15. I ask that you consider my request for funds. Any amount would be appreciated. If you have any questions feel free to write or call me or Dean Rogers at his number, (402) 471-2300.

Sincerely,

Bob Barnfield

---

with his draft and asks you to look it over. *Use the checklist and the concepts developed in this chapter to evaluate Bob's draft.* What exactly does Bob want the reader to do? Suggest what's missing and indicate anything that a reader might need before agreeing to take the action he suggests. If you had received this letter, would you give Bob $550? Why or why not?

EXERCISE 2

Late Sunday night you watched the Quarterback's Corner on Channel 7. The primary guest was J. R. Mason of Mason Protective Equipment Company, a company that makes pads, braces, and other equipment for the Houston Oilers and various professional and amateur teams. The originality of the designs was impressive. It was amazing that the quarterback could play with cracked ribs and an injured shoulder, apparently without too much pain, while wearing the custom-designed braces.

On Monday morning, as you arrived at your job as administrator of Golden Oaks Nursing Complex, a light went on in your brain. Several of the women in the nursing home suffer from osteoporosis. This disease, caused by calcium loss from the skeleton, robs women of the ability to hold themselves erect. Many of the braces now provided are painful and the design of the chest portion does not accommodate a mature woman's figure. It occurs to you that Mason's design skill might solve this problem. Unlike the athletes, these women cannot look forward to a quick recovery and they cannot afford to pay the kinds of prices a professional football team pays. Your office is at 1226 Savoy Drive, Houston 77019. *Write a letter to Mason to inquire whether his company now makes or would consider making protective braces for women who suffer from osteoporosis.* You are not actually placing an order, however, because you suspect that the price may be prohibitive. Perhaps Mason's generosity will prompt him to assist these women. Your primary purpose is to request information, but also you want to set up a relationship that might later result in price reductions for patients. His company's address is 2456 Sensat Road, Houston, TX 77016.

EXERCISE 3

Select one of your favorite clothing stores, a place you really like to shop. Plan a promotional letter the store could send to college freshmen at your school. What could be the main selling point for visiting the store? What benefits does this store have for freshmen? What is the primary benefit? What reason would they have for coming to the store? *Prepare a letter for the store manager's signature.* You may invent any sale, discount, or other event that you think would be truly effective in achieving this purpose. The letter will be judged according to its fitness for the purpose described. For extra credit, imagine a teaser message that could be printed on the envelope.

EXERCISE 4

Select a nonprofit organization whose work you admire and *draft a letter that would cause people who do not now contribute to the organization to join.* Some possible candidates are the National Public Radio or Public Broadcasting Company in your area, the United Way, the Sierra Club, or an organization that fights disease either through research or treatment programs. Exclude religious and political organizations. List the types of readers to which you would send your letter. You may invent details of a campaign or fund-raising event as support in your letter. You are likely to write a more realistic, convincing letter if you choose an organization and a problem you know well.

EXERCISE 5

Assume that lecture series are a special priority at your university. The most prestigious of these series is the President's Lecture Series. Several other series, sponsored by the provost or the deans of the various schools, supply outstanding speakers from around the country, who address anywhere from 350 to 1000 people. Unfortunately, there has never been a students' lecture series: a series of invited speakers who talked on subjects of great importance to students. The Student Council has voted to recommend such a series, and the chancellor, Stan Wells, who is in control of the budget for lecture series, has invited the council to make a proposal. As secretary of the council, *write a memo explaining why the student council would like to sponsor a students' lecture series.* Propose four speakers who could be invited and explain why each of them would be suited to students' interests. Suggest dates when you think the lectures should be held and explain your choices. Use information about your own college's students and schedule in preparing this memo.

IF YOU WOULD LIKE TO READ MORE

Bielawski, L., & Parks, A. F. (1987). *Organizational writing.* Belmont, CA: Wadsworth.

Holcombe, M. W., & Stein, J. K. (1987). *Writing for decision makers: Memos and reports with a competitive edge* (2nd ed.). Belmont, CA: Lifetime Learning Publications.

NOTES

1. R. J. Aalberts & L. A. Krajewski, *The Bulletin of the Association for Business Communication,* 50 (1987)3, 1–5.

2. J. Yates. "The emergence of the memo as a managerial genre." *Management Communication Quarterly,* 2 (1989), 485–510.

3. A. D. Chandler, Jr., *The visible hand: The managerial revolution in American business.* Cambridge, MA: Belknap Press of Harvard University Press (1977).

4. The legal precedent usually cited is the case of *Barker* v. *Lull Engineering,* California Supreme Court, 1969. This decision shifted the burden of proof to the manufacturer of a hazardous product. Maintaining a complete communication record has become the recommended method of preventing product liability judgments against a company.

5. C. Butenhoff, "Bad writing can be good business." *The ABCA Bulletin,* 40 (1977)2, 12–13. Quoted in K. O. Locker, *Business and Professional Communication.* Homewood, IL: Dow Jones-Irwin (1989), 28.

RESEARCH STRATEGIES FOR BUSINESS REPORTS

OBJECTIVES

This chapter will help you

- define a research problem
- plan a research strategy
- select appropriate information resources
- use databases as well as print resources to locate information
- conduct searches for information about public or private companies

PREVIEW

Because business situations differ, the reports they require vary enormously in length, format, organization, and types of evidence. Nonetheless, nearly everyone thinks of "reports" as documents that contain information. The information they contain will come from many sources: management information systems, earlier reports, and public information stored in print resources and databases. In some cases, you will already have on hand all the information you need to prepare your report. A few situations will require that you accumulate information with the methods of special disciplines, such as market research or financial analysis. Other situations will require you to obtain information in public information sources. Obtaining public information requires a research strategy.

The rapidly growing number of databases available through vendors gives business librarians, students, and businesspeople access to a vast array of information about companies and other business topics. By understanding the most convenient print and electronic tools, students can expand their knowledge of the companies they study in their courses. They also can obtain information about companies with which they want to interview in a job search. Later, as employees, they will be able to use these same resources as they conduct research on other business topics.

❏ RESEARCH STRATEGY: A BASIC MANAGEMENT SKILL

Even though most businesspersons are not considered analysts or researchers, they must base their decisions, plans, or policies on information. As a business professional, you sometimes will be asked to obtain information for others, sometimes you will gather information for your own use, and sometimes you will supervise others who conduct research. In each of these situations, you should be able to

- define a research problem,
- plan a search strategy,
- select appropriate information resources, and
- use databases as well as print resources.

Many times the hardest part of doing research is figuring out exactly what to look for or deciding what the report is to be about. Confusion can arise because of how the request was phrased (usually very general in nature), what terms were used (words mean different things to different people), or even how the request was sent (verbally, by memo, by electronic mail, or delivered second or third hand). No matter how clear a request seems to you, there is always room for misunderstanding. This is as true of a school assignment as a request at work. Therefore, you must not omit the first step of developing a research strategy: defining the research problem.

❏ DEFINE THE RESEARCH PROBLEM

Create a Tentative Definition and Project Outline

Defining the research problem early enables you to perform the search the organization needs.

No matter how certain or confident you feel, *write down what you believe the report is about and what information is needed.* This step allows you to crystalize ideas, imagine questions to answer, and pinpoint information needs. You even may discover you are unsure about what was requested. Often this step helps you recognize that the request you were given was too general or that your view of the request requires a great deal more time and work than the person making the request thought. This is the time to get it right.

Either outline the report or list the major questions to answer. Next, if at all possible, list the statistics that may be needed. Are they needed daily, monthly, yearly? How far back must they go? How current must they be? Are there any calculations needed? What format will be used? Realize that at first you may not be able to determine everything that will be needed. Also, don't go into exacting detail. Just write down enough to give you an idea of what must be done.

If the topic is completely foreign to you, do a little background reading, but don't go into too much depth. If you take too much time with this step, your manager will think you are well into the project and may not be pleased when you turn in only an outline. Don't do extensive research until you know that you are on the right track.

Also, give an estimate of the time that will be needed to complete the project. Time can become a major issue on any project, so be realistic. As the project is clarified and refined, time schedules may need to be changed. The sooner your manager knows that the schedule must be adjusted, the more likely he or she will approve a change. If you come in after a week's work and say, "I can't have the report tomorrow; I need at least another three days," you may cause serious inconvenience to others and start a great deal of trouble for yourself as well.

Get Feedback on Your Project Definition

Feedback will clarify or confirm your research project definition.

The next step is to have the outline or list reviewed, because the request may have been flawed. If at all possible, take the outline or list to the person requesting the information. If you are working on a school assignment, take the outline to a professor; if you are working on a job search, take it to a placement officer. Many times people know exactly what they want, but when they speak or write the request for someone else, they miscommunicate. The following sentence is an example of a typical inexact request:

> "I need all the information you can find
> on how deregulation has affected the airline
> industry."

Detecting a vague research assignment helps avoid wasted effort.

This supervisor actually wanted to know how deregulation has affected regional airlines. The original request contains two clues that the request is inexact. Watch out when the request contains

- the term *all* (most people don't want or can't assimilate *all* the information on most topics; usually they want information on a certain aspect of a topic), or
- a very general phrasing of the topic (the very general, overwhelming nature of the request should act as a warning that it needs to be more clearly defined).

If there are no limits on time, sources, or types of information stated in the request, realize that the project very likely will have to be redefined.

If you are right on target, the person may be able to help to refine points more. If you are off-base, he or she can tell you so and help you refine your project description. This process may help the person requesting information as much as it helps you. Keep asking questions until you are certain of what is required.

Define the research problem to identify which information the situation requires.

Once the request has been clarified, you know what information and type of response would be appropriate. Varying levels of research call for different levels of responses. Don't mistake a short answer question for one that requires a formal report. Overloading people with information they do not want or need just to glean a small fact is very frustrating for everyone involved. For example, the managers making the requests below need short answers.

"Terry, I need the prime rate for the last ten years."

"Karen, collect sales figures from the Greenspoint unit and calculate the percentage of increase or decrease over the last five years."

Both examples require the person to look in one or maybe two sources and copy the information; in the second example, the person must also make a simple calculation.

DEFINING THE RESEARCH PROBLEM

- Write down the research problem.
- List the questions to be answered and points to be covered.
- List information needed to answer these questions.
- Describe the statistics needed. Are they needed daily, monthly, yearly? How far back must they go? How current must they be? Are there any calculations needed? What format will be used?
- Estimate time needed for the entire project.
- Review this project outline/list with your manager, supervisor, or professor.
- Revise the project outline.

❑ PLAN THE RESEARCH STRATEGY

Planning your research strategy is the next step. Unfortunately, most students are not taught how to plan a research strategy. They simply start collecting data and then are unable to use some of it because it does not pertain to their topic. In business and even in a job search, people can't afford the luxury of collecting information that isn't needed. Planning research is essential. The procedures you choose for conducting research will depend on whether a group or just one person is working on the project.

RESEARCH STRATEGY GUIDE

1. If the subject is unfamiliar, do some general reading or interview people who work in that area.
2. Try to write a one- or two-sentence research objective. This objective should be a refinement of your project definition. If writing this objective is hard, then you may have to go back to step one and define your research project more.
3. Find out whether a similar report has been done before (public, private, or in-house). Do not reinvent the wheel if the person requesting information is satisfied with the wheel that is available. If a report has been done before and if the format serves your purposes well, use the same format and sources.
4. Outline major questions with subcategories. The number of subcategories will vary according to your familiarity with the subject material and how well defined the search is.

5. Determine what type of information is needed to answer the questions:
   a. *Statistical information.* (In what form, for how long, calculations required, and so on.)
   b. *Expert opinions.* (Who are the experts? Are there experts in-house? How will they be interviewed?)
   c. *Primary information such as interviews, surveys, or questionnaires.* To collect this kind of "first person" data, questionnaires, surveys, and interviews must be carefully developed and distributed. Developing valid surveys, questionnaires, and interview questions is a highly technical skill. If you have never done this type of work, use already-developed test instruments, combine the good points of several, or consult with an expert. Your courses in marketing and other disciplines will teach you many applicable methods. Poor preliminary information can lead to seriously flawed reports.
   d. *Data in the company's internal records.* Be mindful that departments or individuals within a company may be very wary of giving out information. Go through proper channels, get whatever permission is needed, and be cooperative. If you are not sure that the company collects data, think of who would need such information. Contact the computer support department to see if they have written a program for or suggested software for a departmental database with this information.
   e. *Secondary information.* (Information located in journals, books, online databases, and usually found in a library)
6. *Set up a method of data collection and documentation.* You or your team must cite sources and document the search in a uniform manner so that anyone picking up the work can tell what has been done. **Always cite information completely.** Complete citations can save a great deal of time, especially if you must go back to the source to recheck something or need information to be included in a report. Some people use index cards. I use a log in which I give dates, times, citations, and people's names and phone numbers. Whatever system is used, make sure it is adopted by everyone in the research group.
7. *Set up a time schedule for research, compilation of information, and writing the report.* Divide work into appropriate segments. Try to build in time for unexpected delays. Try to complete the report or assignment ahead of schedule so you can go back and correct problems.
8. *Report your progress.* You may be required to report progress as you go along. If not, you may want to do so on an informal basis; reporting your progress acts as an incentive to stay on schedule, and it reminds the person who requested the report of your diligence.
9. *Increase the long-term usefulness of your research.* If you think the information is likely to be asked for again or if you think you will need to go back to that source for some reason, either enter the source on a mechanical index or reference file or create a database for the information on your computer.

❏ SELECT INFORMATION SOURCES

Choose a Library

Choose a library that has a strong collection in the fields of interest.

The strategy for obtaining information from library resources may not be as obvious as the strategy for finding primary source information or information from internal company documents.

First, there are several types of libraries:

1. *Public libraries* are general in nature, collecting for a broad user population. However, public library systems in large metropolitan areas often have one library with a strong research collection.

2. *Academic libraries,* such as college or university libraries, have strong research collections that support student and faculty research. Often they have strong collections in certain areas but not in others.

3. *Special libraries* serve a very distinct clientele. Special libraries include the libraries of companies, trade associations, professional associations, institutes, or research agencies. They are usually narrow in focus but offer a great deal of depth in their specific areas. Their librarians are often subject specialists. Many special libraries are not open to the public, but can give advice or help with questions over the phone.

No matter what type of library you use, most have distinct components:

1. A *reference section* with such sources as guides, handbooks, dictionaries, directories, indexes to journals, online data bases, and much more. Reference librarians, often with subject specialties, are there to help library patrons. Besides answering questions, they often do the online searching.

2. A *separate journal section* where journals are arranged alphabetically or in call number order.

3. A *circulating collection* containing books that can be checked out.

4. A *government documents section* that houses federal or state data.

5. An *archive or rare book collection* for special items. Not all libraries collect government documents or have a rare book section.

In most business research, the reference sources, journals, government documents, and online sources will be the most useful. You will most likely need the most current information available. Most disciplines (including business) have specialized reference sources such as guides, handbooks, encyclopedias, almanacs, dictionaries, statistical sources, directories, journals, and online databases. These sources usually are updated regularly and are well respected. Just because you are doing a report for a business does not mean your information will come from traditional business sources, however.

Compile the Information

Remember: you must not only find the data, you must evaluate it. You need to be confident of your data. Common-sense rules can help compile your information reliably. The following checklist can guide your collection process.

☐   CHECKLIST FOR EVALUATING INFORMATION

AUTHOR

____ Who is the author? Is he or she a recognized expert?

____ Is the author affiliated with some agency or company? Is this organization respected?

____ Is the author cited in other works?

____ Does the author depend on only one source for information? If so, watch out.

____ How did the author collect the information? The source should give some idea of primary research or origin of the information.

____ What is the source for any statistics?

PUBLISHER

____ Is the publisher well known? (Many publishers specialize in certain areas and publish under their own name, such as Dun & Bradstreet and Standard & Poors.)

____ Does the publisher have a bias? (Certain trade associations are publishers, and there can be built-in bias.)

____ Can the publisher be trusted?

____ How was the information collected? (Statistics, especially, need a source.)

INFORMATION QUALITY

____ Is the information timely? (If information is old it may not be useful; look to see who did the research or where the information was found originally. Find out if there is an update.)

____ Is the format of the information useful? (This can be particularly important with statistics.)

____ Does the information make sense? (Just because it's in print doesn't mean it's correct.)

____ What discrepancies do you expect? (Differences of opinions by experts; differences between information from several sections of the country, consumer groups, companies of different sizes, and so forth)

____ What does the preface or introduction tell you about how data were collected and what mathematical formulas were used in calculations?

☐   USE COMPUTER INFORMATION SERVICES

How the Technological Revolution Has Changed Information Searching

Technological advances have created extremely fast and efficient methods of storing and retrieving information. The online database industry has grown rapidly in the past decade. In 1979 there were just 400 databases; in 1989 there were more than 4000. While you are in school, you can use these databases to help you in your job search or in gathering information about companies you study in your courses.

"JUST GET ME WHAT I NEED. NOW."

"Don't just sit there.

"We've got 15 minutes to put together a complete dossier on the competition—annual report info, company vs. industry figures, current company announcements, stock quotes, everything. Let's *move* . . . ."

I hear myself asking a lot of my staff; and others asking a lot of me. It's not unreasonable, not if you want to come out on top. But nobody said it was going to be easy.

The fact is, I recently made our job easier. I subscribed to Dow Jones News/Retrieval.

It's the premier source of online business and financial information from Dow Jones & Company, Inc., publisher of *The Wall Street Journal*. It's up to the minute, accurate, easy to use. And all you need to get it is a personal computer and modem.

Using their QuickSearch service I'll get that complete dossier within 15 minutes, maybe less. With their 40 other services I can get everything from today's business news as it breaks and the full text of the *Journal*, to current stock quotes, insider trades reported to the SEC and detailed financials on thousands of companies and their industries.

I can get *exactly* what I need this minute. No fluff. No waste.

Make the job easier on yourself, and your people—call or mail the coupon at right today for more information on Dow Jones News/Retrieval.

Get what *you* need, NOW.

For more information, or a free trial, call 1-800-221-7700, Ext. 294E today.

Or fill out this coupon and mail to the address below.

Name _____
Title _____
Company_____
Address _____
City/State/Zip _____
Daytime Phone _____

Dow Jones News/Retrieval, Post Office Box 186, Drexel Hill, PA 19026-9973

DOW JONES NEWS/RETRIEVAL
From Dow Jones & Company, Inc.

The information that powers today's business.

4H770   294E

© 1988 Dow Jones & Company, Inc. All Rights Reserved. Dow Jones News/Retrieval is a registered service mark of Dow Jones & Company, Inc.

FIGURE 12.1   The Importance of Research Skills

Source: Reprinted by permission of *The Wall Street Journal*, December 18, 1987. © Dow Jones and Company, 1987. All rights reserved worldwide.

On-line searching con-
nects you with main-
frame databases.

Typical online database users include librarians, information specialists, economists, financial analysts, investment bankers, business planners, engineers, chemists, researchers in the social sciences, executives, educators, lawyers, and other professionals. A person doing a search sits at a computer terminal in a library, laboratory, office, or home and dials a local phone number that links his or her computer to a vendor's host computer. Using a password, the user is able to access the host computer and choose from among a wide variety of databases. These systems have been designed so users do not have to be computer programmers. However, most online searchers find it valuable to attend training sessions both on the particular system and on the databases to be searched. Most vendors and database producers offer classes, and some include the cost of training in their startup or monthly fees. If you are not familiar with a particular system or database, you could spend a great deal of money for less-than-satisfactory results. The need for instruction may be eliminated as more and more vendors develop user-friendly systems.

Types of Computer Databases

There are two types of computer databases: reference databases and source databases.

Reference databases refer users to other sources. Reference or bibliographic databases contain citations or citations and abstracts of journal articles, reports, patents, conference proceedings, books, or newspapers. Many of the bibliographic databases offer full-text retrieval of articles.

Source databases, the other type of database, contain original source data. The data can be anything from a full-text report to numeric data like that found in the income statements contained in annual reports. Source databases will be more expensive to use.

Most users have contracts with one or more of the major database vendors. The vendor selects the database that will go on the system, develops the hardware and software, trains the user, and bills the user for time spent. Costs and billing methods will vary from vendor to vendor, but the user can expect to be charged for time online, telecommunication costs, and printing. For some databases, the user must deal directly with the database producer. A good source of information about available data is the *Directory of Online Databases*. Some vendors have special discounts for educational institutions and students. While you're in school, you can use reference tools to find additional information about cases and companies studied in your courses and to prepare for your job search.

The next section lists vendors, bibliographic databases, and reference databases that you can use electronically. This list is not complete, but it gives an idea of what is available. The final section deals with how to conduct a company search, because many of the searches you are likely to make in student projects and in your job search will involve finding information about both public and private companies.

VENDORS

BRS Information Technologies
1200 Route 7
Latham, NY 12110
(518) 783-1611
(800) 345-4277

BRS AFTER DARK (reduced rates at nonpeak times)
1200 Route 7
Latham, NY 12110
(518) 783-1611
(800) 345-4277

Dialog Information Services, Inc.
3460 Hillview Avenue
Palo Alto, CA 94304
(415) 858-3785
(800) 334-2564

Knowledge Index (Dialog—reduced rates at nonpeak times)
3460 Hillview Avenue
Palo Alto, CA 94304
(415) 858-3785
(800) 334-2564

Dow Jones News/Retrieval
Dow Jones & Co., Inc.
P.O. Box 300
Princeton, NJ 08543-0300
(609) 520-4000

Data Resources (DRI)
Data Products Division Headquarters
1750 K Street, N.W., 10th Floor
Washington, DC 20006
(202) 663-7720

DataStar
D-S Marketing Ltd.
Plaza Suite
114 Jermyn St.
London, SW1Y 6H
England
44 (1) 930-5503
(800) 221-7754 (in U.S.)

DATATIMES Corp.
Suite 450
14000 Quail Springs Parkway
Oklahoma City, OK 73134
(405) 751-6400
(800) 642-2525

Information USA, Inc.
4701 Willard Avenue, Suite 1707
Chevy Chase, MD 20815
(301) 657-1200

Mead Data Central, Inc.
P.O. Box 933
Dayton, Ohio 45401
(513) 865-6800
(800) 227-4908

VU/TEXT Information
Service Inc.
325 Chestnut Street, Suite 1300
Philadelphia, PA 19106
(215) 574-4400
(800) 323-2940

WestLaw
West Publishing Co. (WESTLAW)
50 West Kellogg Blvd.
P.O. Box 64526
St. Paul, MN 55164-0526
(612) 228-2500
(800) 328-0109

DATABASES

Reference Databases (Bibliographic)

ABI/INFORM. Contains citations with abstracts to journal literature in the areas of business and management. Good source of current company information.

LEGAL resources index. Contains citations to legal and law related periodical literature. Covers journal articles, letters to the editor, case notes, reviews, and commentaries.

ERIC. Contains citations and abstracts for journal and report literature in the field of education.

MEDLINE. Covers almost every aspect of the area of biomedicine. Indexes over 3000 journals and other literature. Worldwide in scope.

Source Databases

COMPUSTAT. Contains income, balance sheet, source and use of funds, line of business, and market information for publicly held U.S. and selected non-U.S. companies.

DISCLOSURE. Contains information on 12,500 publicly owned companies that file reports with the SEC.

LEXIS. Offers a legal database with subfiles ranging from the admiralty and maritime law to state law.

NAARS. Financial statements with footnotes and auditors' reports for over 4200 companies filing annual reports.

❏ CONDUCT COMPANY INFORMATION RESEARCH

This section explains how to search for basic company information as an example of business research. This is only a small aspect of business research, but one that becomes very important when you are looking for an internship or job. This section will teach you how to search for information about a company's present situation, its relationship to its industry, and its ownership and management. If you do the proper research, you will be able to tell the interviewer how you fit the company's needs. Similarly, you can write more sophisticated and pertinent letters of application or inquiry.

A typical company information research project requires that a person

- conduct an industry survey;
- research a particular company's role in the industry;
- identify the issues and trends affecting the company and industry;
- learn the names of the chief executive officer and directors;
- identify the major divisions within the company;
- know where to find information that reflects the company's debt, growth, and profitability;
- possibly learn about the nonbusiness involvement of the company in other areas.

In the Communication Challenges at the end of this chapter, you will search for information on both a public company and a private company. It is easier to find information about public companies because of government requirements concerning disclosure of information—there is more information available on public companies. Don't despair. There are ways to collect information on private companies and to compensate for lack of information.

ADVICE FROM A SEASONED RESEARCHER: A FEW THINGS TO CONSIDER

■ Determine if the company is public or private. If public, is it the parent company or a subsidiary or division? This will determine how much information you can find.

■ Skim over the various reference sources. Instructions on how to use them are usually in the front. Many can be used in a variety of ways.

■ Realize that there is a time lag of several months to a year in publishing many of the traditional business sources.

■ Because of the need for current information, include a search of the periodical literature, either paper or online sources.

■ Private companies pose a real problem. They usually do not have an annual report and if they do, its distribution is limited. Periodical literature is the best source of information. Be realistic about what you can find!

■ Industry information is always important and becomes critical when you are dealing with a private company.

Company Information Search Process

The diagram in Figure 12-2 can serve as an outline of steps to take when searching for information about a company. Usually, you begin by choosing the company. However, you also can begin a search by looking for all the companies in a certain industry or geographic location. The search paths for public and private companies differ. Private companies and subsidiaries and divisions of public companies pose a real challenge to anyone wanting information. Private companies do not have to file annual reports with the SEC (which is where most business services get their information), and subsidiaries and divisions of public companies are often included in the parent company's report with no separate breakout. Industry information and periodical information may be all you can find. Therefore, on the path for private companies, the search moves directly from the directories to current public information rather than to information published by the company.

Use the steps already explained in the chapter to define your search problem. For example, you might set the following objective: "to find information on company X (chief executive officers, directors, major divisions, company's growth, debt, profitability) and its industry (survey of industry, trends and issues affecting the industry and the company, company's role in the industry, competitors)." Next, plan the search, using information sources from the bibliography at the end of the chapter.

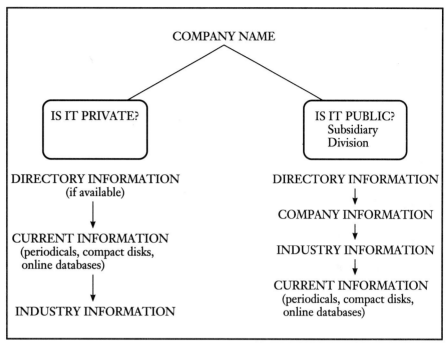

FIGURE 12-2.   Company Information Search Process

BIBLIOGRAPHY OF INDUSTRY, COMPANY, AND CAREER INFORMATION

I. Industry Information

Industry information is vital to those who apply for jobs; naturally, you should make sure the industry is healthy. Furthermore, what goes on in the industry directly affects companies in that industry. Also, you should know competitors. This information can help substantially when you interview with private companies, where company information may not be available. You may have to make inferences about the company based on industry information.

A. Books

U.S. industrial outlook. Washington, DC: U.S. Department of Commerce.

Government publication that surveys 350 industries in the U.S. Real emphasis is in manufacturing but more and more service industries are being included. Each section has a brief introduction, discussion of the current situation, outlook for the year, and long-term prospects. At the end of each section, additional sources of information are given. No companies are mentioned. Annual.

PUBLIC COMPANY RESEARCH STRATEGY SHEET

INDUSTRY INFORMATION

Current situation:

Outlook for future, long- and short-term:

Compelling issues or problems:

Industry leaders:

COMPANY INFORMATION (If the current annual report is not available in a paper copy, check to see who takes annual reports on microfiche.)

Full name of the company:

Location of headquarters:

Phone number: Address:

Other major locations, if any:

Name of chief executive officer:

Name of chairman of the board of directors:

Net income: current year _____ last year _____ choose earlier date _____

List major divisions in the company and their heads (this may not be available):

Read management's letter and write a brief synopsis of how you think the company is doing. Are there any problems, major or minor? What are the highlights of the past year of operation?

FIGURE 12-3.   Researching a Public Company

CURRENT INFORMATION (This can be obtained from printed or online sources, but there will be a charge for online information.)

Use the company name as your "key word." See whether you can find a listing of several recent articles and note their titles and sources:

Using the company's industry as your "key word," list several recent articles you think would be most pertinent to your company. Give titles and sources:

Read at least one article about the company or its industry and note important points about the company and/or its industry here.

FIGURE 12-3. (*continued*)

PRIVATE COMPANY RESEARCH STRATEGY SHEET

<u>CURRENT INFORMATION</u> (This can be print or online sources. There will be a charge for online information.)

Using the company name as your "key word," see whether you can find a listing of several recent articles and note their titles and sources:

<u>INDUSTRY INFORMATION</u> (This can be industry information either from sources in the bibliography or from current periodical articles on a particular industry.)

Using the company's industry as a "key word," list several recent articles you think would be most pertinent to your company. Give titles and source:

Does your company's industry show up in any of the traditional industry sources? If so, answer the following:

Current situation:

Outlook for future, long- and short-term:

Compelling issues or problems:

Industry leaders:

Read at least one article concerning either company or industry information and note the important points here.

FIGURE 12-4.   **Researching a Private Company**

Standard & Poor's industry surveys. Standard and Poor's Corporation. New York: McGraw-Hill, Inc.

Two-volume set, divided among twenty-two major industrial groups with various divisions within each major group. There is a basic analysis and current analysis for each of the twenty-two groups. The basic analysis gives background information, trends, and any major or developing issues. The current analysis gives more timely information on emerging issues. Information on companies is also given. Look within the two sets of analyses and in the back section where companies are grouped by major business line and compared financially. If you want to know the leaders in a field, this is a good place to find them.

The Value Line investment survey. (Value Line Ratings and Reports) New York: VALUE LINE, INC.

This service does give industry information. Each issue is devoted to six industries. In each section there is an introduction to the industry, giving basic statistics for the past year plus projections. Many times, you can pinpoint major trends or problems in the industry section. Following the general industry information is a discussion of companies within that industry, giving financial and stock information or forecasts. Information varies from company to company. This is a good place to identify leaders in a field.

Encyclopedia of associations. Detroit, MI: Gale Research Inc.

Many industries have at least one association specifically for that industry. Some are very good sources of industry information.

B. **Periodicals**
   Articles on industries can be found by using indexes. Some good indexes are:
   Accountants' index
   Business index
   Business periodicals index
   Predicast indexes
   On-line database searches in a variety of databases
   Compact disk products (*ABI/Inform,* for example)
   Certain journals service particular industries. Skimming these can be helpful.

Uhlan, M. (Ed.). (1985). *Guide to special issues and indexes of periodicals* 3rd ed. Washington, DC: Special Libraries Association.

Can lead to special issues dedicated to a certain industry or forecasts for a certain industry.

Remember: CIRR (Corporate Industry Research Reports). Microfiche service of industry and company reports done by various research firms and investment banks.

II. Company Information

(Because of the large number of sources in this section, only selected sources will be annotated.)

A. Directories

Most of these directories can be accessed in a number of ways, such as by type of industry or by geographic location. Many of the standard business directories are now online.

America's corporate families. Dun's Marketing Services, Inc. Parsippany, NJ: Dun and Bradstreet Corporation.

Two-volume set. First volume is U.S. companies; second volume is international affiliates. Several special indexes: alphabetical, industry, and geographical.

Consultants and consulting organizations directory: A reference guide to concerns and individuals engaged in consultation for business, industry, and government. Detroit, MI: Gale Research Inc.

Two-volume set. First volume is divided along general industry lines with alphabetical list of consultants or consulting firms under each industry. Volume 2 is an index. Annual.

The corporate finance sourcebook—1986. Wilmette, IL: Macmillan Directory Division.

Can act as a directory. Has sections on commercial banks, investment banks, and other financial institutions. Gives address, corporate headquarters, department heads, and direct phone numbers for certain key personnel. Annual.

Directory of corporate affiliations. Wilmette, IL: National Register Publishing Company.

Includes directory information on parent companies and their subsidiaries and divisions, using table of contents.

Directory of management consultants. Fitzwilliam, NH: Kennedy & Kennedy, Inc.

Alphabetical list of management consulting firms. Each citation gives address, brief description of firm, contact person, areas served, revenues, services offered, and industries of specialization. Helpful indexes are included.

Million dollar directory: America's leading public and private companies. Parsippany, NJ: Dun's Marketing Services, Inc.

Cross-indexed volume can give you access by SIC (Standard Industrial Classification) number or geographic location. List of major U.S. companies with address, phone number, officers, type of business. Annual.

Standard & Poor's register of corporations, directors, and executives. New York: Standard and Poor's Corporation.

List of U.S. companies (private/public), with address, phone number, type of business, and officers. Several special indexes so information can be accessed by type of business or geographic area. Annual.

Standard & Poor's security dealers of North America. New York: Standard & Poor's Corporation.

Directory of security dealers in U.S. Arranged by state, then by cities within each state. Annual.

Thomas register of American manufacturers. New York: Thomas Publishing Company.

Multivolume directory of manufacturers. Volumes 1–12 are companies listed according to what they produce; volumes 13–14 have company information; volumes 15–21 include examples of certain company catalogs. Annual.

Ward's business directory of U.S. private and public companies. Detroit, MI: Gale Research, Inc.

A comprehensive guide to 90,000 companies. Complete information in alphabetic and geographic arrangements. Gives rankings of top companies, employers and companies within the SIC (Standard Industrial Classification). Annual. (Volume 1) *Over 11.5 million in sales;* (Volume 2) *.5 to 11.5 million in sales;* and (Volume 3) *Ranked by sales within industry.*

Macmillan directory of leading private companies. Wilmette, IL: National Register Publishing Co., Macmillan Directory Division.

Basic directory information on leading private companies in U.S. Excellent alphabetical cross-reference index in front of book, plus industry and geographic index in back.

B. Company Information

Moody's Manuals. New York: Moody's Investor's Service, Inc. (Dun & Bradstreet).

Several different manuals organized along broad industry lines. Fairly extensive company information in one place. Each of the six sets (Industrial, Banking and Finance, Transportation, Public Utility, International, Municipal) has "current news" section. One place where company history can be found.

Standard & Poor's corporation records. New York: Standard & Poor's.

Multivolume set arranged alphabetically. Each volume is set up with three sections, except volume T–Z. Company table of contents (yellow), subsidiary affiliate section (blue), and company section (white). Volume T–Z has a section on mutual funds and a stock and bond section (green). Last volume is "Daily News."

Standard & Poor's stock record. New York: Standard & Poor's.

Primarily used for investment purposes, it can give a capsule view of events that are affecting the company. This information can be found in periodical literature also, but can sometimes be found here if major events are identified before you go to indexes.

Remember: Standard & Poor's industry surveys, Value Line, Inc., Annual reports, *CIRR.*
Periodical Indexes:
Accountants' Index
Business Index
Business Periodicals Index
Predicast Indexes
InfoTrac
Newspaper Index
Online databases (variety)
Compact disk products

Local newspapers can be very helpful and many are indexed with full text retrieval online. *Index of Corporate Changes* is online. It should always be part of your search because it gives *current* information.

C. International Company Information

Information on foreign companies can be hard to find. Locating the information you want may require going to more than one library.

Directory of American firms operating in foreign countries. New York: Uniworld Business Publications, Inc.

First volume of 3-volume set is alphabetical listing of American firms. Each entry gives address, officers, type of business, name of parent, number of employees, countries in which they do business. Volumes 2 and 3 are arranged by country.

Directory of foreign manufacturers in the United States. Atlanta, GA: Georgia State University Press, College of Business Administration.

Alphabetical list of foreign manufacturers, with just address information. Each citation includes the manufacturer in the U.S., foreign parent company, and product lines. Good indexes.

Principal international businesses. Parsippany, NJ: The World Marketing Directory, Dun's Marketing Services, Inc.

Arranged by country, then alphabetically by name of company. Degree of information given can vary. Two good indexes: SIC or industry index, alphabetical index.

International directory of corporate affiliation. Wilmette, IL: National Register Publication Company, Macmillan Directory Division.

Directory of major foreign companies arranged alphabetically. Gives information on divisions and subsidiaries. Good cross-index in front. Very surprising the number of U.S. companies now owned by foreign companies.

The Rand McNally international bankers directory.

Three-volume directory. Volumes 1 and 2 are arranged by states; third volume is international, arranged by country. Gives basic directory information.

Remember: Periodical literature (use index either paper or online), Moody's Manuals (Moody's Investors Services, Inc.), annual reports.

D. Biographical Information
Biographical information can be very hard to find.

Reference book of corporate managements: America's corporate leaders. Parsippany, NJ: Dun's Marketing Services, Inc., The Dun & Bradstreet Corporation.

Company listings with brief biographical information on officers. Cross-reference volume is useful.

Standard & Poor's register of corporation directors and executives. New York: Standard & Poor's Corporation.

This set has two main volumes with an index volume. First volume is alphabetical listing of companies with limited company information. Volume 2 is alphabetical listing of directors and executives with basic biographical information. Index volume has five sections that allow access to the service in various ways.

Who's who in finance and industry. Wilmette, IL: Marquis Who's Who, Macmillan Directory Division.

Alphabetical list of people in various fields of business. Each has a short biography.

Search periodical literature, especially local newspapers and the *Wall Street Journal* index.

E. Regional/Local Information

Most areas of the U.S. have information sources that pertain only to that area. They tend to pick up smaller companies. The examples given below are for Texas or Houston.

Texas or Houston information sources (similar guides are available for most states and metropolitan areas).

Directory of Texas manufacturers. Austin, TX: Bureau of Business Research, Graduate School of Business, The University of Texas at Austin.

Two-volume set. One volume has companies arranged by SIC number and the other by geographic location. Annual.

Harris County business guide. Houston, TX: Business Extension Bureau.

List of large and small public and private companies in the Harris County area. Table of contents indicates major industrial categories and there is also an alphabetical company index. Similar services exist for Dallas, Tarrant, and Travis Counties.

Houston international business directory.

Alphabetical listing of firms and organizations in Houston involved in international business. Several ways to use this directory.

Houston 1000: A corporate directory. Houston, TX: Corporate Directories of America.

Alphabetical list of Houston companies. Depth of information given varies. Includes names and titles of officers and key personnel.

Texas top two-fifty.

Profiles on the state's leading public and private companies and financial institutions.

F. Compact Disk Resources
Company Information
Dialog on Disc
Disclosure
Moody's
Journal articles on companies and industries
ABI/INFORM
PAIS (Public Affairs Information Service)

G. Online Resources
Disclosure
S&P Corporate Descriptions
Moody's Corporate Profile
Media General Plus
Dun & Bradstreet's International Dun's Market Identifier
ABI/INFORM
Businesswire
Business Dateline
McGraw-Hill News

III. Career Information
There are special sections in most libraries for career information. Many libraries put at least some career information in the reference area. A sampling of titles is listed below:

A. Books
Directory of executive recruiters. Fitzwilliam, NH: Kennedy & Kennedy, Inc. Annual.

Great deal of information in this book. Main section is a directory list of recruiters, divided according to type. Lists recruiters who require a fee for introductions separately from those who work on contingency. Differentiates recruiters who seek individuals in a few special fields from recruiters who handle candidates in many fields. Cross indexes can help in using main volume in different ways.

Dun's employment opportunities directory. Parsippany, NJ: Dun's Marketing Services, Inc. Annual.

Set up in four sections, alphabetically by company name, geographic, standard industrial classification code, and by branch offices (geographic location). In alphabetical section, the following is given for each company: overview, disciplines hired, career development, additional locations, benefits, summer internships.

The national job bank. Boston, MA: Bob Adams, Inc. Annual.

Alphabetical list of employers, arranged by states. Each entry gives address, contact, type of company, and product line.

Each year there are new books on career development and job search techniques. Some are very general and others are extremely specific. Go through several and find one you like. Many have tests or activities to help you with your plan. Some are listed below as examples.

Arnold, J. D. (1984). *Trading up: A career guide. How to get ahead without getting out.* Garden City, NJ: Anchor Press.

Bly, R. W., & Blake, G. (1983). *Dream jobs: A guide to tomorrow's top careers.* New York: Wiley.

Clawson, J. G., & Ward, D. D. (1986). *An MBA's guide to self-assessment & career development.* Englewood Cliffs, NJ: Prentice-Hall.

London, M., & Strumpf, S. (1982). *Managing careers.* Reading, MA: Addison-Wesley.

Rosenthal, D. W., & Powell, M. A. (1984). *Careers in marketing.* Englewood Cliffs, NJ: Prentice-Hall.

Salzman, M., & Marx, N. (1985). *MBA jobs: An insider's guide to companies that hire MBAs.* New York: AMACOM.

Souerwine, A. H. (1980). *Career strategies: Planning for personal achievement.* New York: AMACOM.

Encyclopedia of Associations
Three-volume set of national associations. Volume 3 has key word index that leads into other two volumes. Each entry gives addresses, officers, purpose, who joins, publications, and annual meeting dates. Some associations have excellent career information and even employment services.

B. Periodicals

Periodical indexes such as *Business index, Business periodical index*, or *Accountants' index* often carry information on careers.

Uhlan, M. (1985). *Guide to special issues and indexes of periodicals* (3rd ed.). Washington, DC: Special Libraries Association.

Lists journals and their regular special issues. Many professional journals have special issues on careers or salary survey. Professional journals often have employment sections.

COMMUNICATION CHALLENGES

PRELIMINARY EXERCISE 1 Select four tools, one from each of the categories: (1) locating company information in books, (2) locating company information in periodicals, (3) international company information, and (4) local or regional information. *Make notes on the kind of information included in the tool, the way the tool is organized, how frequently it is published or updated, and other features that you would like to remember.*

PRELIMINARY EXERCISE 2 Look up the name of the same famous business leader in each of the biographical information sources. Take some notes from each source. *Write a paragraph comparing the kinds of information you were able to obtain in each.* The objective of this exercise is to help you anticipate the kinds of information you might be able to obtain in the future by using each of these resources.

PRELIMINARY EXERCISE 3 Go to your college library and obtain a map of the library. Also obtain a handout on its business information resources or talk with one of the reference librarians. *Make a list of five or six resources that seem likely to be useful to you in the future,* such as compact disks that can be searched for business information, and hours in which students can do online searches at a reduced rate. Locate these resources and annotate the map, showing where to find each one. Turn in the list and the map together.

EXERCISE 1

Use the *Encyclopedia of associations* to identify a professional organization in a field that interests you. *Write a letter to the president or membership chairperson of the organization requesting information about the organization and asking whether they have student memberships.* Turn in a copy of this letter to your professor.

EXERCISE 2

Obtain one of the sources on careers and look through the table of contents. Pick a chapter that interests you. Read the passage and *write an abstract of the chapter for the use of other students in the class.* An informative abstract or summary should be approximately one-tenth the length of the whole piece. If you have a thirty-page chapter, a three-page double-spaced summary would be about right.

EXERCISE 3

Choose a private or public company, either from the list in this chapter or from your own list of companies for which you would like to work. Remember that your search path will depend on whether the company is public or private. Private companies, subsidiaries, and divisions of public companies will pose a greater challenge. Private companies do not have to file annual reports with the SEC (which is where most business services get their information) and subsidiaries and divisions of public companies often are included in the parent company's report with no separate breakout. Industry information and periodical information may be all you can find on private companies or on subsidiaries.

Use the appropriate worksheet and the bibliography in this chapter to prepare a short report of three to five pages on the company, its industry, and other interesting details. To obtain industry information, use one or more of the sources under Industry Information in the bibliography. Read the industry information about your company's industry and fill in the worksheet.

EXERCISE 4

Write a letter to the company you chose for Exercise 3, explaining your interest in the company and the potential value of your capabilities to that firm. Ask whether you could obtain an appointment for an informational interview. Review the advice on letters of application in Chapter 19, "Job Search Communications," if necessary.

TYPICAL COMPANIES THAT MIGHT BE CHOSEN FOR RESEARCH PRACTICE

Public Companies	Private Companies
AMR	Arthur Andersen & Co.
AT&T	Bain & Co.
Amerada Hess Corp.	Coopers & Lybrand
American General Corp.	Deloitte Haskins & Sells
Bank of Boston	Ernst & Young
Bankers Trust New York	Goldman, Sachs & Co.
Borg Warner Corp.	Hyatt Corp.
Coca-Cola Co.	Jack Eckerd Corp.
Exxon U.S.A.	McKinsey & Co.
Federal Express	Mary Kay Cosmetics
May Dept. Stores, Inc.	MONY Financial
Merrill Lynch & Co.	Services
Pennzoil Co.	Peat, Marwick & Main
Pepsico, Inc.	Peterson & Co.
Procter & Gamble Co.	Price Waterhouse
Prudential Capital	
Quaker Oats Co.	
Randall Stores, Inc.	
Salomon Bros.	
Texas Instruments, Inc.	
Transco Companies, Inc.	
Wal-Mart Stores, Inc.	

IF YOU WOULD LIKE TO READ MORE

Business researcher's handbook: The comprehensive guide for business professionals. (1985). Washington, DC: Working Researchers, Ltd.

How to find information about companies: The corporate intelligence source book. (1985). Washington, D.C.: Working Researchers, Ltd.

Daniels, L. (1985). *Business information sources* (rev. ed.). Berkeley, CA: University of California Press.

WRITING REPORTS

OBJECTIVES

Studying this chapter will help you

- understand various types of reports, including proposals and progress reports

- design a formal report and prepare the accompanying documents

- implement a communication strategy in a report

- use an efficient preparation process

PREVIEW

Variations in reports reflect differences in business situations and differences in information needs. The features of routine reports satisfy predictable content needs of well-defined audiences. Less routine reports call for specially designed structures and formats. Many elements may be combined in long reports to make information readily accessible to many different users.

Writing reports well can establish your reputation, so set your standards high. An excellent report tells readers something new, embodies a communication strategy, emphasizes the argument, distills recommendations, and subordinates analytical machinery. Time constraints make efficient report preparation essential.

❑ REPORTS: INFORMATION FOR BUSINESS

Why Reports Vary

Reports vary enormously in length, format, organization, and types of evidence. These variations reflect differences in business situations. The reports used in routine situations are typically nothing more than completed forms, such as credit approval forms, sales summaries, and job applications. The information in these routine reports helps managers monitor and control the company's transactions. Periodically, more complex reports are needed for decision making, especially in nonroutine situations where the level of information necessary for carrying out a new task is much greater than the level of information available from past experience. Reports may perform many different functions in different situations.

Differences in situations and their transactions cause reports to vary in length, format, complexity, and content.

Report Functions and Types

REPORT FUNCTION	REPORT TYPE	DEFINITION
Transmit information	Annual report	Informs outside stakeholders about company achievements and financial performance
	Compliance report	Compares actions taken with pertinent regulations or laws
	Audit report	Summarizes and interprets accounting information
	Sales report	Summarizes sales and compares results with goals; may explain results
	Performance report	Evaluates individual or organizational accomplishments for a specific period
	Trip report	Presents information obtained by visiting a site or meeting
Contribute to decision making	Analytical report	Describes and evaluates components, causes, and trends; interprets patterns in data
	Testing report	Explains results of tests; describes standards applied and procedures used

Report Functions and Types (*continued*)

REPORT FUNCTION	REPORT TYPE	DEFINITION
	Advisory report	Applies concepts or theories to available data to reach conclusions and make recommendations to decision makers; often prepared by staff members or outside consultants
	Strategic plan	Describes goals, objectives, and tactics for an organization
	Industry report	Describes the size, level of competition, number of competitors, barriers to entry, and level of activity in businesses that provide the same types of products or services
	Feasibility report	Evaluates the probable level of success of some course of action
Monitor or control some aspect of the company's operations	Progress report	Describes the work on tasks or topics intended to achieve some goal during a specific period
	Operating report	Like a progress report, presents the results of work in a department or division of a company entrusted with resources and charged with producing goods or delivering services
Evaluate need for action	Problem analysis	Interprets facts about a problem and defines its extent, causes, and importance
Propose action	Proposal	Establishes a need for action and criteria for solutions, evaluates alternatives, recommends an alternative that meets criteria

This list of report types is not complete. Many other report names derive from their functions in specific but less common situations. For example, the kind of report that requests individuals or companies to submit proposals to satisfy some need is called an RFP (request for proposal). Closure reports, as you might guess, explain the reasons for having "closed" or terminated a research project.

Report Length Affects Format

Short reports are usually written as letters or memos, but reports over eight pages are typically designed as formal reports.

Most situations require only short reports: *memo reports* to those inside the company or *letter reports* to people or companies outside the firm. Short memo and letter reports, illustrated in the Document Spotlight features, will usually be no more than six to eight pages, and many will be shorter.[1] Some situations, however, require long reports, which may run from ten to several hundred pages. When readers must manage more than eight pages of text, the report should be carefully organized and formatted to help them find appropriate information fast. When a great deal of information must be presented, when the analysis is complex, or when a report may be used over a long period of time, a formal report is appropriate.

The Parts of a Formal Report

Different parts of a formal report serve different audiences' needs in specific ways. Decision makers usually need answers to only a selection of the questions, and they don't necessarily need to read all the technical support. People likely to carry out recommendations or those likely to be affected by the report in other ways usually read the summary and some parts of the discussion or appendices.

Over the past two decades, the vast majority of U.S. companies seem to have shifted from a report structure that places the conclusions last to a two-part report structure that places conclusions and recommendations near the beginning of the report.[2] The *opening component* (written in concise, condensed general terms), plus the figures or tables, should stand alone so that the decision maker has a clear general picture of the situation and critical information for decision making. The *discussion component*, on the other hand, contains the full analyses and descriptions that support the opening component. The discussion component, usually at least twice as long as the opening component and directed mostly to secondary audiences, thoroughly discusses the problem, the technical or professional issues, tasks undertaken, and proposed solutions. Appendices further serve the interests of special subgroups of readers. The list at the top of page 291 compares the parts of a formal and an informal report.

Both long formal reports and short informal reports indicate at the beginning the report's subject, date, source, and the recipients of the report. Sometimes the person who signs the report is not the person who wrote the document. Employees frequently write for their bosses' signatures. If the report is prepared by one company to be read by another company, the presidents of each company may be designated as the source and recipient. If questions are to be directed to

PARTS OF A FORMAL REPORT	PARTS OF AN INFORMAL REPORT
Opening Component	**Opening Component**
Letter of transmittal	Headings (including title, source, receiver, data, and other information)
Title page	
Abstract	
Table of contents	
Table of illustrations	
Introductory summary	Introductory summary
Discussion Component	**Discussion Component**
Tabbed dividers	Body headings
Discussion section	Discussion section
Appendices or attachments	
Bibliography	
Index	

the writer rather than to the executive signing the document, the name and position of the writer or "contact person" should be included in the introductory headings.

The title and any subtitles or subject lines should identify the subject or problem the report addresses. Reference numbers may indicate the contract, project, file or customer associated with the report. Letters of request and letters of agreement pertaining to a project may be incorporated in the appendices of a report. Figures 13-1 to 13-4 illustrate a letter of transmittal, title page, table of contents, and table of illustrations.

Abstracts

Although abstracts usually are included in the report, they also are incorporated in various printed and electronic bibliographies and databases. Two principal types of abstracts have developed over the years: descriptive abstracts and informative or summary abstracts. Descriptive abstracts are available in many printed reference tools. They tell what the report is about, but do not give the conclusions or recommendations of the report (see Figure 13-5 on page 296). The verbs in a descriptive report usually include terms such as "discusses," "examines," "investigates," "analyzes," and "suggests."

In contrast, the *informative or summary abstract* includes the conclusions and recommendations in addition to the topics of the report (see Figure 13-6 on page 296). Some (but not all) summary abstracts present the recommendations in the first sentence and support these with statements summarizing the principal reasons for the recommendations. This is common in a company's internal report. One approach to preparing a summary abstract is to write a summary

Commercial Real Estate Advisors, Inc.

3400 South Post Oak
Houston, TX 77098

December 18, 1991

Mr. R. J. Mackleigh, President
R. J. Mackleigh Fabricators
24 Sterling Drive
Minneapolis, MN 55430

Ref. No. TTX 2867-91

Dear Mr. Mackleigh:

You have two excellent choices for your new fabrications plant in north-west Houston. These two sites meet all the criteria described in the needs analysis we prepared earlier. Copies of all the proposals received, as well as comparative computer analyses of these offers, are attached in the appendices.

I look forward to our meeting Friday to discuss these properties and to tour both sites. My assistant, Ralph Tendrick, will meet your flight at Intercontinental Airport at 10:30 a.m. Friday.

Sincerely,

Stennis Hollowell

Stennis Hollowell, Realtor®
President

FIGURE 13-1. Sample Transmittal Letter

sentence for each of the major sections of the report. Another approach is to condense or miniaturize the executive summary.

Any business abstract should contain a "stand alone" message. An abstract that contains unexplained jargon prevents the reader from knowing whether he or she should read the report. Insert short (one- to three-word definitions) for unavoidable technical terms rather than violate the reader's trust.

Abstracts must be very concise. Many publications and databases have

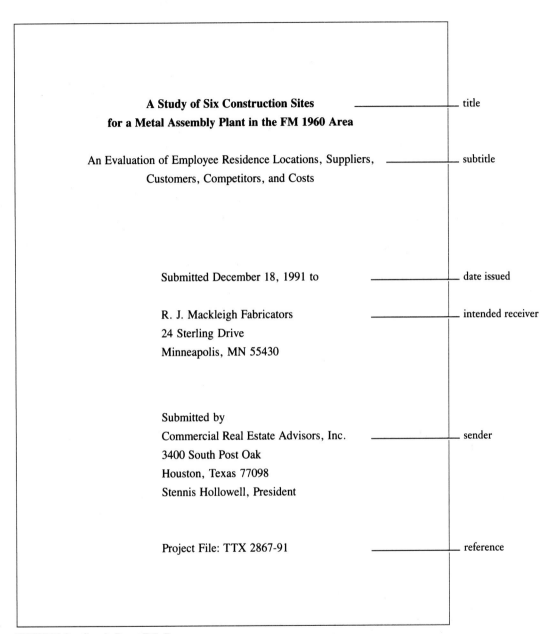

FIGURE 13-2. Sample Report Title Page

strict word limits, so edit the abstract carefully and delete unnecessary words. Corporate records stored in company data bases, as well as published reports, need abstracts for efficient retrieval in an era of electronic storage. Sentences or phrases copied from the report need not be footnoted or placed in quotation marks. Key words used in an unusual sense may be italicized. (See Figures 13-5 and 13-6.)

Table of Contents

FIGURE 13-3. Sample Table of Contents

Introductory Summaries or Executive Summaries

Introductory and executive summaries do not differ in content or organization, but they are given different titles depending on whether the decision makers in the organization call themselves "executives." Academic reports have "introductory summaries"; most company reports have "executive summaries." As you might expect, an introductory or executive summary places the key information of the report in context. It offers the reader two parts: the foreword and the

Table of Illustrations

page

Aerial view of Simpkins Road site   8

Diagram of Simpkins Road site   9

Photograph of Simpkins Road site   9

Aerial view of Thomas Avenue site   11

Diagram of Thomas Avenue site   12

Photograph of Thomas Avenue site   12

FIGURE 13-4. Sample Table of Illustrations

summary of conclusions and recommendations. The *foreword* (not forward) means "that which must be spoken before," what the writer and reader should know before launching into communication. The foreword reviews (1) the situation (or problem); (2) issues, tasks, or questions that are involved in the problem; (3) the writer's responsibilities; and (4) the writer's primary communication purpose (to request, recommend, explain, or propose). The second part of the introductory summary presents a synopsis of conclusions and any recommendations.

L. V. Waerdt, "How to Maintain Your Integrity and Avoid Liability for Giving Honest References," *The Chronicle of Higher Education,* vol. 34, no. 4, Oct 87, section 2, pp. B2-B3.

Abstract

This article discusses the recently adopted practice of giving only job titles and dates of employment as references for former employees. The author suggests three ways that additional information can be provided without fear of liability proceedings.

FIGURE 13-5. **Descriptive Abstract**

L. V. Waerdt, "How to Maintain Your Integrity and Avoid Liability for Giving Honest References," *The Chronicle of Higher Education,* vol. 34, no. 4, Oct 87, section 2, pp. B2-B3.

Abstract

Many companies now give only job titles and employment dates as references for former employees. Employers may give additional information without incurring legal liability by making sure that the comments are factual and accurate, supported by written evidence in the firm's files, and free from personal animosity or prejudice.

FIGURE 13-6. **Informative Abstract**

Two report types whose traditional features strongly influence the organization of the discussion section are presented here: the proposal and the progress report.

Proposals

The discussion section of a proposal answers the following questions:

- *Why does work need to be done? What benefits will result?* This section presents information about the organization's problem or objectives and the benefits that may result.

- *What problem do you propose to solve or what objective will you accomplish?* Usually, companies write proposals because the client or funding agency has objectives it wants to accomplish or problems it wishes to solve. Make certain that you can demonstrate the existence of the problem or the value of the objective.

INTRODUCTORY SUMMARY

Foreword

Competition and Upcoming Labor Negotiations Require
Increased Efficiency and Productivity

Situation
Issues: competition,
contract expiration

Need for strategy
Responsibilities

Keen competition with the four national chains in Renton have lowered
our profits, partly because the chain stores enjoy greater economies of
scale and lower wholesale prices. We should expect pressure on our
costs in about five months, when our contract with the grocery checkers expires. The checkers will almost certainly expect a raise when
their contract is renegotiated, which would increase our total labor
costs. I was asked to investigate the computer scanning devices (CSD)
available and to develop projections for the effects of purchasing or
leasing this equipment over the period of the anticipated labor contract

Communication
Purpose

in our three stores. This report compares available devices and describes the flexibility each of the possible financing
arrangements would provide in the upcoming negotiations.

Summary of Conclusions

Information found

Conclusions

Studies of CSD use show that efficiency of an individual checker can
be increased an average of 9 to 13 percent. After evaluating the financing options available, I conclude that we could reduce the number of
checkers by nearly 10 percent and still offer the remaining checkers a
raise in their base salaries of 6 percent per year plus performance
bonuses.

FIGURE 13-7.   Introductory Summary with Conclusions but No Recommendations

- *How will you do what you propose and when will you do it?* Explain what methods
  will be used, who will use them, and when the work will be done. Sometimes a
  project schedule should be enclosed in this section of the discussion.

- *Why will you be successful?* Explain what distinctive competencies you or your
  team bring to this task. Tell what advantages your method or project schedule
  offers.

- *What will the work cost?* Attach a budget and a budget narrative. A budget is a
  list of expenses, classified by type and sometimes further divided by time peri-

ods. A budget narrative explains the entries in the budget, telling how they were calculated, what assumptions were made, and to what extent they might be expected to vary.

Proposals that consultants prepare for clients are discussed in Chapter 20, "Consultants' Communications." The Document Spotlight presents an internal proposal in which a training specialist proposes a new budget item to her director.

Progress Reports

Progress reports enable managers to monitor authorized work, detect problems, and make decisions about resource allocation. For political reasons, a writer should cause his or her accomplishments to be perceived in a positive way. On the other hand, a writer's ethical responsibilities require that reports present any problems, delays, or new developments honestly. In an optimal situation, the progress report format contains a flagging section on the first page where the writer can call managers' attention to any problem that needs special attention. A writer using this section should be rewarded, not penalized.

The traditional form of the progress report answers questions organized by time:

What project are you working on *now?*

What work has been done in *earlier periods?*

What work was done *this period?*

What work is planned for *the next period?*

Within the frame created by these questions, each section may be further subdivided by task or topic since a project may involve different people doing different types of work simultaneously. If the report begins with an introductory summary of about one paragraph, that may be the place to direct management's attention to specific pages or parts of the report. Progress reports sent to managers within a company are usually designed as memoranda; progress reports sent to clients are usually written as letters. Some progress reports may be very long, such as progress reports on huge research projects. These are presented as formal reports.

❑ FEATURES OF AN EXCELLENT REPORT

An opportunity to write a report can be valuable to your career. Good reports may be circulated widely, and having your name on such a document can build your reputation. A sloppy, unprofessional document, on the other hand, can become an albatross around your neck. Each time you have an opportunity, you should strive to write not just a mediocre report, but an excellent one. An excellent report tells something new, embodies a communication strategy, emphasizes its argument, distills recommendations, and subordinates its analytical machinery. Each of these features (and their opposites) will be discussed in turn.

DOCUMENT SPOTLIGHT

SHORT PROPOSAL

Richfield Industries, Inc.
2478 Industrial Park Highway
Pittsford, NY 14534

April 14, 1991

PROPOSAL FOR A COMPUTER WRITING LABORATORY

Submitted to R. J. Stevens, Director of Training

Prepared by Dr. W. J. Farish, Training Specialist

Summary

Explains why the facility is needed

Explains what problem will be solved

Nature of the Problem   Richfield Industries needs a computer writing laboratory for the use of employees in the professional writing workshop and business English classes. This laboratory would also benefit employees who are interested in improving their writing skills but are unable to attend regular training classes. Our line employees cannot learn skills necessary to advance in the workplace unless they have access to computers.

Explains what benefits will result

Benefits   The teaching of writing on all levels at Richfield Industries would be more effective if we installed a computer laboratory. Employees would be able to improve their communication skills, thus cutting the costs of miscommunications, especially in the troubleshooting reports written by shift workers. Furthermore, Richfield would be in a position to promote from within.

Total Cost

Plan I	Individual units	$38,300
Plan II	Networked system	$45,800

Explains project schedule

Time Schedule   Once funded, the lab could be in operation in less than a month. Research and testing of program effectiveness would start immediately, as would the possible development of software, and should be complete by the second year.

(Continues)

DOCUMENT SPOTLIGHT

SHORT PROPOSAL (*continued*)

Discussion

Explains what objective will be accomplished

Why Richfield Industries Needs a Computer Writing Laboratory Richfield Industries teaches 550 employees per quarter in its professional writing, technical writing, business English education, and remedial writing programs. These employees could acquire necessary skills more efficiently if Richfield Industries had a computer lab dedicated to writing. Our two existing computer labs are used to capacity for technical training. These two small labs, each equipped with 16 computers, are seldom available for writing classes, which must be worked into the remaining time slots. In the last three years, only one business English class and two sections of the professional writing seminar were offered in a computer lab. The technical writing program, in particular, will suffer in the future if the company cannot provide the employees access to the same computer hardware and software that they will use for writing on the job. Furthermore, communication skills are essential for promotion. The importance of the computer as an aid in writing is beyond question. Computers are being used in most major universities and many corporate training programs in business English and technical writing. Richfield Industries needs to establish a computer lab that is set up for all stages of writing—inventing, composing, revising, and editing.

Explains how equipment will be used

The Computer Writing Laboratory Program The computer writing laboratory will consist of twenty computer work stations with word processing software, as well as grammar, usage, and style programs for checking documents and for instruction. The laboratory should also have at least four units with desktop publishing capabilities.

Explains when the work will be done

The laboratory would be used for classes thirty hours per week and for independent work and tutoring ten hours per week. During the independent use period, assistants trained in helping writers and in using computers would be on duty.

Professional and Technical Writing Classes Professional and technical writing classes would be conducted daily in the lab. Our regular training classes would be scheduled to allow every participant at least one day in the lab.

Business English Classes The lab would also be used to provide remedial English programs for employees who need individual help. Programs such as *Comp-Lab Writing Modules* (Prentice-Hall), and similar programs that now accompany many remedial texts provide units on noun plural forms, subject-verb agreement, past-tense verb forms, and other problems.

DOCUMENT SPOTLIGHT

SHORT PROPOSAL (*continued*)

Independent Use and Tutorials Finally, the lab would be open to all employees over 60 hours a week so that employees concerned with correct and effective communication would use a text analysis program to improve their style.

A survey of former participants in the writing programs showed 85 percent would have liked to have received training on the computer.

Instructors Involved

Explains proposers' qualifications

Dr. Wanda J. Farish, Training Specialist. Formerly associate professor of English, Director of the Writing Specialists' Program and the Professional Writing Internship Program, Richfield Community College. *Education:* B.A. and M.A. Boston University. Ph.D. Johns Hopkins University. *Relevant experience:* Teacher of technical and professional writing since 1976.

Dr. Mark Camanelli, Director of the business English program at Richfield Industries since 1985. *Education:* B.A., M.A., and Ph.D. University of Oklahoma. *Relevant experience:* Has taught one class of remedial English in the present computer lab; conducts a writing laboratory each quarter, sending employees to the computer lab to work on grammar modules on a space available basis. Has attended numerous conferences on use of computers in training.

Presents costs (parenthetical remarks explain basis of costs)

System Recommendations and Estimated Costs The totals in both plans are based on prices quoted on personal computers and reflect the available discount.

Plan I

20 independent work stations (CPU and monitor)	$20,000
4 dot matrix printers	1,800
2 laser printers	4,000
Software (word processing, text analysis, etc.)	3,500
Personnel for first year	9,000
TOTAL	**$38,300**

Plan II

20 work stations set up for networking	$22,000
network server	6,000
4 printers	1,800
2 laser printers	4,000
Network cable and installation	1,000
Software	2,000
Personnel	9,000
TOTAL	**$45,800**

AN EXCELLENT REPORT

- tells something new
- embodies a communication strategy
- emphasizes the specific argument
- distills recommendations
- subordinates the analytic machinery

An Excellent Report Tells Something New

Readers need rewards. They want to believe they have learned something by reading your report. New understanding doesn't have to depend on new data; sometimes new interpretations or new perspectives are just as helpful. The following list of questions can help you find a new perspective.

1. *Is there an alternative definition of the company's problem that would provide a richer, more helpful understanding of the situation?* If you've been thinking of the problem as a marketing problem, how would your information look if you thought about the situation as a production problem, financing problem, staffing problem, management problem, or resource allocation problem? Nobel prize winner Herb Simon once remarked that people solve only the problems they define. Expanding your definition of the problem may provide a new perspective, identify unacknowledged causes, or point to alternative or more complex solutions.

2. *Is there a reasonable comparison that might shed new light on your information?* If you compared your results with those of other divisions, other companies, or industry-wide data, what would you see?

3. *If you changed your time frame, how would the results or data look? Is there a trend that can be detected with a longer time frame?* Looking at industry data from a longer period may help you develop a comparison, even if data for your company over a longer period are unavailable.

4. *If you partitioned the results, would you find any helpful insights?* Is there anything about your information that suggests an unusual distribution or frequency? Sometimes a significant factor is masked because it is lumped in with other kinds of data. The events at a single plant, store, or department may vary significantly from the average data and supply a critical clue.

5. *How do the present results look when viewed from the perspective of the company's goals or your department's objectives?* Are you on target, behind, or ahead?

6. *Are there any indications that there is an international or intercultural issue involved?* Chapter 17, "Communicating in International Contexts," may help you identify cultural differences that may affect your situation.

An Excellent Report Embodies a Communication Strategy

As explained earlier (Chapters 4 and 5), a communication strategy should include a comprehensive purpose, a persuasive approach, content organized into strategic issues, and criteria for judging the success of the communication. Every aspect of a report, from its organization of issues to its format and style, implements the communication strategy.

Comprehensive Purpose   By defining a comprehensive purpose, the writer can design the report efficiently, breaking the report as a whole into two sections, an introductory summary and a discussion section. Those purposes that involve the primary audience should be addressed with the executive summary, so that decision makers too busy to read the entire report will have the key information pertinent to the decision.

Persuasive Approach   Because a principal characteristic of all reports is information, writers may neglect the persuasive approach in a communication strategy. The writer may thoughtlessly open the report with a paragraph likely to offend the readers or make them defensive. The following highly negative paragraph would surely provoke a defensive reaction from the company president to whom it was addressed.

The Pronto campaign has been a disaster from start to finish. I have already identified ten things you did wrong. First, you didn't have a strong marketing plan for the new cereal. Second, you didn't do much market research; you just thought that if you put something new on the shelf somebody would buy it. Third, the sales representatives weren't trained to sell it, and they didn't get enough shelf space in enough stores. . . .

The writer probably doesn't mean that the president himself actually did all ten things, but by using the general "you" and by accumulating all the negative evaluations at the beginning, the writer makes the reader feel defensive. Furthermore, the tone is hostile and scolding (for example, "you just thought," "ten things you did wrong"). If the persuasive approach had been to make the president perceive ten ways the next campaign could succeed and if the writer had tried to create a sense of shared responsibility, the opening would have elicited a more favorable response:

Pronto can succeed the second time out if we follow new tactics. A short marketing study with test groups will help us define the advantages of the new cereal before we take it to the stores seeking shelf space. With a better understanding of our product, we can train the sales representatives more effectively. . . .

Organizing the Report   Common mistakes sometimes cause writers not to plan a communication strategy. They assume that readers already know the purpose of the report, the problem that was assigned, and the situation or problem that will be discussed. As a result, writers sometimes "jump in" and start presenting facts for which readers are unprepared. At other times, writers assume that readers have lots of time and will read the report straight through from beginning to end. Instead, busy readers read selectively, seeking parts that pertain to them. A long report, especially one that has no headings, frustrates readers. A communication strategy should help writers avoid such mistakes by organizing information appropriately for readers.

A poor communication strategy focuses on what the writer has done, rather than on what the reader needs to know about what the writer has done. When the writer sits down to tell the reader "what I did," the result is often a chronological record of the writer's attempt to solve the problem. Part of the communication strategy should be to emphasize the argument, so that the reader can easily remember the writer's claims and reasoning. The criteria in the communication strategy enable the writer to evaluate drafts of the report to control the report's quality.

An Excellent Report Emphasizes the Argument

Emphasize the Argument by Organizing

The communication strategy chosen for a report should include a structure for the argument: an organization pattern intended to address readers' uncertainties. Some of the most common organization patterns in reports are problem-solution, need-satisfaction, benefits for the reader, and logical course. The names of the first three patterns suggest the way the organization of the report will reduce the reader's uncertainties. The last pattern, logical course, is designed for the rational reader who is committed to the most logical decision or outcome possible, regardless of benefits or satisfactions.

In many cases, the issue tree or coding scheme used in planning the report's organization will enable you to arrange the material effectively. A convincing argument enables the reader to perceive and remember the key points and their logical relationship by controlling the order and pace of information.

Emphasize the Argument with Headings

A writer can also foreground the argument with headings and with the introductory phrases of paragraphs. Compare the two sets of headings below. Which one helps you understand the argument immediately?

SET A	**SET B**
Introduction	Jetrex Has Lost Market Share
Product Market Mix	Market Niche Strategy Offers New Opportunity
Porter Analysis	
BCG Analysis	Jetrex Can Lead in Microtype Applications
Marketing Strategy	Jetrex Can Sell Microtype Services to Present Customers
Summary	
	Five-Year Projections Show Early Break-Even

The graphic hierarchy in report headings should reflect a hierarchy of thought. Graphic hierarchies combine position on the page, the height of the letters, boldfacing, underlining, numbering, and other optional features. Word processing allows many more format choices, including boxes, drop shadows, and changes in fonts (letter shapes), than typewriters. Possibly because of these new options, numbering report sections has declined in popularity. The examples in Figure 13-8 and Figure 13-9 illustrate two graphic hierarchies, one of which uses centered main headings.

A NEW MARKETING STRATEGY FOR JETREX

Jetrex Has Lost Market Share

Market Share 1985–1988
    Typesetting for financial printing
    Typesetting for retail customers
    City government contract
Market Share 1989–1991
    Typesetting for financial printing
    Typesetting for retail customers
    City government contract

Market Niche Strategy Offers New Opportunity

The General Typesetting Market
The Microtype Market

Jetrex Can Lead in Microtype Applications

Type and Graphics from Software for PC-based Products
Type and Graphics from Software for Apple Products
Graphics and Slides from Custom Software

Jetrex Can Sell Microtype Services to Present Customers

Working with Software Vendors
Direct Sales to Companies
Geographic Service Areas

Five-Year Projections Show Early Break-Even

Growth of Demand
Sales Projections

FIGURE 13-8.   Graphic Hierarchy

A NEW MARKETING STRATEGY FOR JETREX

Jetrex Has Lost Market Share

Market share 1985–1988
    Typesetting for financial printing
    Typesetting for retail customers
    City government contract
Market share 1989–1991
    Typesetting for financial printing
    Typesetting for retail customers
    City government contract

Market Niche Strategy Offers New Opportunity

The general typesetting market
The microtype market

Jetrex Can Lead in Microtype Applications

Type and graphics from software for PC-based products
Type and graphics from software for Apple products
Graphics and slides from custom software

Jetrex Can Sell Microtype Services to Present Customers

Working with software vendors
Direct sales to companies
Geographic service areas

Five-Year Projections Show Early Break-Even

Growth of demand
Sales projections

FIGURE 13-9.   Graphic Hierarchy Using Centered Main Headings

The characteristic that seems most likely to capture the greatest attention should have the highest rank in the hierarchy, but experts no longer agree whether position on the page, letter height, or boldfacing should have greatest rank. A centered heading commands attention at the top of the page, but attracts less notice in the middle of the page. Letter height is quite noticeable, especially when combined with boldfacing. A long heading in all capital letters is harder to read than initial caps only on each word or initial caps on the first word of the sentence or phrase. The headings in either example could have been numbered.

```
1.0
   1.1
               1.1.1
               1.1.2
               1.1.3

   1.2
               1.2.1
               1.2.2
               1.2.3
2.0
   2.1
   2.2
                          (and so forth)
```

Emphasize the Argument with Paragraph Leads

Many executive readers skim the first sentences of paragraphs to get the gist of a report. If the key ideas are tucked in the middle of paragraphs, the readers may miss them. Notice that in the following example, the introductory phrases of the paragraphs do not suggest the subjects of the paragraph or the logic of the argument. Of thirty paragraphs in this writer's report, eighteen began with phrases about the writer. The first twenty paragraphs begin with the following phrases:

Para. #	Para. Begins	Para. #	Para. Begins
1	**I feel that**	11	The development team
2	One problem with	12	**I recommend**
3	If after careful market research	13	**I also believe**
4	**I recommend**	14	The sales force pursued
5	**In the long run, I believe**	15	**I feel that**
6	The company's marketing mix	16	**I think that**
7	**I agree that**	17	**I see**
8	The company has historically	18	**I also think that**
9	**I view the**	19	**I feel this**
10	**I also criticize**	20	Insufficient incentives

Foreground the Argument with Style

People say actions speak louder than words. In printed language, independent clauses speak louder than any other structure. If the writer puts low-content words in the independent clause, such as "there is" or "it is" or "I think," the important topic is shifted to less prominent parts of the sentence. For example, in the opening paragraph below, the writer's actions occupy center stage and the ideas about the course of action she recommends are shifted to obscure parts of the sentences. The independent clauses have been boldfaced.

It is my belief that the model C12 pizza dough mixer holds great sales potential for the company. **It is unfortunate that** the company has not yet found the key to unlock this profitable door. **I would like to present my opinion** on the actions that Restaurant Products Manufacturing has taken trying to promote the C12 **and submit my recommendations** on ways to achieve the goal of market acceptance. Before I do so, however, **I will give** a brief analysis of the market environment and a picture of the company as I see it.

Look at what remains when these boldfaced terms and other "I" Phrases are stripped away:

the model C12 pizza dough mixer holds great sales potential for the company.

the company has not yet found the key to unlock this profitable door.

the actions that Restaurant Products Manufacturing has taken trying to promote the C12

ways to achieve the goal of market acceptance.

a brief analysis of the market environment and a picture of the company.

By recombining these important ideas and inserting details, a much·more compelling set of claims emerges:

The model C12 pizza dough mixer holds great sales potential for Restaurant Products Manufacturing, but the company has not yet found the key to unlock this profitable door. The company's marketing program has overlooked the chains and franchises that offer high volume sales. A brief analysis of Restaurant Products Manufacturing's market environment will show why a dual strategy can achieve rapid market acceptance. I recommend two approaches to securing higher volumes: (1) qualifying prospects among present customers more effectively, and (2) approaching the large chains such as Pizza Inn, Pizza Hut, and Mr. Gatti's with volume discounts.

A static "equation" style also makes the reader's work more difficult. A static style depends on linking verbs, such as forms of "to be," "seems," and "becomes." On either side of the linking verb are noun phrases or clauses that the linking verb presents in a kind of equation: $X = Y$. The eighty-four-word passage below demonstrates this style.

This market **is** still in its infancy, yet sales are projected to reach $100 million in 1991 and $600 million by 1995. This **is** an attractive, yet risky market. The potential for rapid growth **is** tremendous.

Due to the tremendous profit potential, competition **is** sure to be tough. **It is** certain that IBM will be entering this market soon with its own product. Additionally, **there are** an undetermined number of additional competitors developing similar products. The barriers to entry and exit **are** relatively low.

The important ideas here are the projected high sales and the competition this potential will attract. By removing the linking verbs and focusing on "who does what," the tension between these ideas (sales potential and competition) can be emphasized in the two paragraphs:

Sales in this infant market will reach $100 million in 1991 and $600 million by 1995. This attractive yet risky market offers Conwell rapid growth.

The tremendous profit potential will spur tough competition. IBM will soon enter the market with its own model, and additional competitors who face relatively low entry barriers are already developing similar products.

The fifty-five-word revision has about 35 percent less "verbal fat." The style emphasizes key elements in the argument, placing them in the controlling independent clauses of sentences and at high-visibility points in the paragraphs (the beginning and end). You can review sentence structure with Chapter 7.

An Excellent Report Distills Recommendations

Concise recommendations belong in the introductory summary; more complete recommendations belong in the body of the report.

Business readers are action-oriented. They want to know and remember what you recommend and why. Because readers read selectively, you should plan the placement of recommendations carefully. A useful report may be passed around to groups of people who will implement your recommendations and to others who may be affected by the consequences. These people may not need to read the entire report, but they will need to read selectively for information. If your recommendations are scattered throughout the report, readers may not be able to remember them. Boxes, lists, and bullets or numbers help emphasize recommendations. Put the recommendations together in places readers can find. Use headings to help readers locate these sections.

Usually both the introductory summary and the final section of the discussion should contain your recommendations. The version of the recommendations you place in the summary should be concise, so that readers can remember them. Make the sentences very easy to read. The version in the concluding section of the report may be more lengthy, explaining details of implementation.

Short form of recommendations for the executive summary:

- replace or repair motors in the "people movers"
- renovate skate-rental area and redecorate ice rink
- let contract for construction of Irish wagons.

Longer form of recommendations in the discussion:

Replace or repair motors in the "people movers." The "people movers" in the east wing of the complex leading to the ice rink have experienced many breakdowns. The motors should be rebuilt or replaced before the holiday shopping season begins in November. David Schmidt should send one of his staff to meet with the consultants to determine whether the motors should be shipped to Italy for rebuilding or be replaced with a domestic product.

Renovate the skate rental area and redecorate the ice rink. The small structure where skates are rented should be torn down and replaced with a new chrome and glass rental booth with neon lighting, as shown in the diagram. All trim should be repainted and the carpeting in the observation area at the west end of the rink should be replaced.

Let the contract for construction of Irish wagons. Custom designed Irish peddler's wagons will be leased as retail space in the west wing's botanical garden. The designs for these wagons are attached in Appendix C. These wagons will be featured in promotion plans for the west wing.

An Excellent Report Subordinates Analytical Machinery

Make your message, not your method, stand out.

Readers want to know what you think and, to a limited extent, why. They do not necessarily want to become a specialist in your field. To inspire confidence, you should reduce jargon because the additional attention the reader must pay to new definitions, procedures, and models often will reduce comprehension. *Your report should showcase specifics that indicate the implications of your work in the particular situation.* Use appendices to document the process of analysis. If the reader is interested, he or she can study the appendices later or pass them on to a staff member for expert consideration.

Paragraph leads, just discussed, can either conceal or emphasize the analytical approach you have used. The first sentence below emphasizes the analytical machinery and introduces only the topic of the analysis; it does not present the conclusion or point uncovered by the analysis. The second sentence shows the point of the analysis.

1. Here is a list of the company's strengths produced with the SWOT model.
2. Todd Company surpasses competitors in production facilities as well as research and development capability.

Headings also can emphasize or conceal the technical aspects of the analysis. In the two lists of headings shown on page 304, Set A emphasizes the analytical models (the Porter analysis and the BCG model), whereas Set B emphasizes the results of the analysis. A reader who does not know that a Porter analysis describes competition in an industry might not know what kind of information the section contains. A heading such as "First-Mover Strategy" will bewilder a reader who does not know that "first-mover" is marketing jargon for a company that introduces a product never before offered in a particular market.

REPORT PREPARATION PROCESSES

Develop a Report Preparation Scenario

Many situations and circumstances require the preparation of a report. If the situation is routine, no doubt many such reports have been prepared before, and there may be a fixed scenario for preparing the report. If the situation is unusual, you may have to plan a scenario for properly completing the report. Use your organizing skills to create a plan that will enable everyone who should participate to contribute in appropriate ways.

Preparing Routine Reports

The very name "routine report" means that many similar reports have been prepared in the past. The scenario for the situation should disclose where information should be obtained, who should review the report, and other preparation steps. Check the format of these reports, their organization, and their style. Their content arrangement usually follows typical patterns. Your company may also expect employees to follow a particular style sheet or report preparation guide; ask a coworker whether one exists. In addition, the methods used by a particular discipline (such as accounting or industrial psychology) may guide the organization, arguments, and style of a routine report. Figure 24-1 of the Financial Accounting Communications chapter presents an operating report prepared by an apartment management company. This monthly operating statement illustrates a short, routine report.

Analyzing Old Reports with Descriptive Outlines

Once you have found old reports in the files, you can learn fairly quickly how they are organized by using a descriptive technique. On your computer screen or on a legal pad, draw a vertical line down the center. Write "What" in the left-hand column and "How" in the right-hand column. For each paragraph of the report, write in the left-hand column a one-sentence summary that captures the primary point. Immediately across in the right-hand column, jot down what the paragraph "does" to express this message. In the right-hand column you will write phrases such as "introduces the problem," "defines the problem," "explains two examples," "quotes from last year's report," "compares data with industry averages," "presents and explains a table about drilling depths," etc. When you look over the outline, you will be able to see how the writer constructed the argument. This method, which is especially valuable for understanding the ways that specialists build arguments, can also be used to analyze the articles assigned in courses.

Be alert to weaknesses in the old reports you analyze. Ask others, including your supervisor, for examples of effective reports you might imitate. You probably can't afford to drop completely a section that appears in all earlier reports, but you may be able to rearrange the order of sections or change the headings to improve the report forms you inherit. You may certainly improve the style and selection of evidence.

Preparing Nonroutine Reports

When a new type of report must be written or when a new kind of problem or opportunity arises, writers cannot rely on routine report preparation procedures. In some of these situations, writers must gather information directly by means of surveys, interviews, or other tests, using the methods of social science or marketing research.

Especially in nonroutine situations, writers must combine information developed within the company with information about the industry or competitors. Fortunately, information about industries and companies is much easier to acquire than it was a decade ago. Chapter 12, "Research Strategies for Business Reports," explains many resources now available electronically and in print.

Planning the Process

A report is part of the overall scenario for dealing with a situation, so its preparation should be part of the scenario plan. In many companies the adage "Better late than never" has been replaced with "Better never than late." An employee who can't make deadlines may cause the entire company to lose an opportunity. Find out when your report is due, then set your target forty-eight hours before the deadline. If something does go wrong, there will be time to respond.

Make a list of all the people who must contribute information or ideas to the report. Make a separate list of all those who will review and comment on the report before it is produced. Work back from your deadline and set milestones for your project. Include target dates for obtaining information, processing data, having figures or illustrations prepared, drafting time, reviewing time, revision, production, and distribution. There are several software packages for personal computers that assist with project scheduling. A writing project, like any other project, deserves to be well managed.

Make a list of the names and phone numbers of those people who will retrieve information, prepare illustrations, distribute your report, and perform other vital support tasks. Treat these people as the valuable associates they are; people in the mail or photocopying rooms sometimes determine whether you succeed or fail. Waiting until an emergency comes up is no way to build the kind of relationship that will ensure cooperation. Stop by and get to know these people early in the project.

Getting Started

You don't have to wait until the project is complete to begin writing your report. You may have a substantial portion of the report finished before you even begin the first task on the project. Information assembled during the proposal stage of a project must usually be incorporated into the final report. Before you begin the project, you should have written a definition of the problem, the scope of the work to be done, an explanation of the assumptions underlying your analysis, a description of methods, a justification of criteria, definitions for key aspects of the project, and a bibliography of references or works consulted. These sections may have been part of your original proposal, or they may be documents in progress on your computer.

DOCUMENT SPOTLIGHT

SAMPLE REPORTS

In the following examples, the writers have explained their situation, emphasized the new information (that a new venture is feasible for Medic Quik Clinics; that enormous cost savings can be obtained by constructing an alternative cap on a waste site), embodied a communication strategy, put the claims of their argument in the foreground, and subordinated the detailed analysis by placing the information in later parts of the report. The communication strategy of the feasibility study is to make the action appear easy by defining the opportunity in detail and showing that long-term risks are minimal. The strategy of the letter report is to emphasize the logic of the claims and the benefits to Emerson Legal Services' client, Amalgamated Chemical, and to encourage Amalgamated Chemical to hire Wilson-Walker Engineering for additional consulting work. After all, wouldn't you want to hire someone who had just saved you $6,000,000?

MEMO REPORT

MEMORANDUM

DATE: 11 October 1990

TO: Carol Clark

FROM: Chip Stofer

SUBJECT: Feasibility Study for "House Call" Service

Why Medic Quik Clinics Should Enter the House Call Business

Several market indicators point to an emerging market for a visiting physician or "house call" service. Over the next decade the over-sixty age group will become the largest ever and will also have the highest average disposable income on record. Marketers have begun to call this group "the super seniors." Able to afford medical care and disinclined to go to physicians' offices, the super seniors will pay for the convenience and emotional comfort of being treated in their own homes. At present, two sixty-square-block areas of the city with a high proportion of super seniors are underserved by our own walk-in clinics and by hospitals.

House calls are a logical extension of Medic Quik Clinics' existing business. The present reception staff in the clinics could handle the inquiries and scheduling expected in the first six months, and the clinics could provide the home base and support for a physician hired to make house calls. A leased van, supplies, and promotional expenses for six months

(*Continues*)

SAMPLE REPORTS (*continued*)

would enable us to test this market for less than $85,000. Even if the service is discontinued in the future, the supplies can be used in the clinics and the promotion will have a residual benefit for the walk-in clinics. I recommend that we plan a promotional campaign for this service to begin in February 1991.

[the rest of the report contains sections with the following headings]

The Super Seniors

Local Opportunities

Impact on Present Clinics

Costs

Proposed Implementation

Appendices: Demographic Studies, Map, Articles

LETTER REPORT

The case presented next is disguised. The place names, company names, and certain amounts have been altered to conceal the actual companies and agencies involved, except for the Environmental Protection Agency (EPA). The following report was presented in the form of a letter to Emerson Legal Services, which represented Amalgamated Chemical, a firm affected by changes in the Environmental Protection Agency's regulations. The letter was written by Wilson-Walker Engineering Consultants, a consulting company which had been asked to evaluate the specifications for a waste disposal site that the state agency had instructed the Amalgamated Chemical Company to follow. The diagram shows the entities involved in the situation. Amalgamated Chemical, the "firm" in the center of the diagram, is influenced by several companies, agencies, and other groups mentioned in the letter.

As you will see in reading the letter report, the entities communicate not only with Amalgamated Chemical, they communicate among themselves, and they review and evaluate one another's documents. Circle the names of the various "players" in this situation as you read the letter. For example, the lawyer to whom the letter is addressed represents Amalgamated Chemical, and the consulting engineering firm sends its report to the lawyer instead of to Amalgamated Chemical. The letter refers to another engineering consulting firm that has made recommendations to a state agency. *The solid lines among the boxes show entities that interact directly. Dotted lines link entities that interact indirectly* (for example, the EPA approves the report that Neville Consulting Company recommended).

DOCUMENT SPOTLIGHT

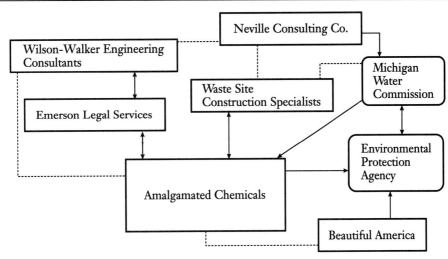

Diagram of Amalgamated Chemical Company's Environment

Wilson-Walker Engineering Consultants
143 North Pickering Ave.
Winona, Michigan 58766
December 14, 1990

Mr. Charles Schwartz
Emerson Legal Services
3400 West Loop Towers
Detroit, Michigan 58109

Dear Mr. Schwartz:

As you requested, we have conducted a brief review of the waste disposal sites owned by your client, Amalgamated Chemical, and specifications dated September 11, 1989 prepared by Neville Consulting Company (NCC) for the Michigan Water Commission (MWC). These contract documents and specifications were to be used for the construction of an RCRA vault of sixty thousand cubic yards. The vault would hold all waste and affected soil now present at Amalgamated Chemical's Decatur site. The total costs currently estimated by NCC are $6,540,000. Our review suggests that costs on this project can be reduced by nearly $6 million, or 85 percent.

The MWC and the EPA should carefully consider the following items to reduce costs, minimize damage to the environment, and provide protection for public health.

(Continues)

SAMPLE REPORTS (*continued*)

1. The Record of Decision selected by the EPA, alternative 6, increased implementation costs by 270 percent because incorrect volume specifications were considered at that time. Corrections will reduce costs by $4,640,000.

2. The unnecessary two feet of clay added to the bottom liner should be deleted, saving $360,000. This design feature is not required by either federal or state regulations.

3. To take full advantage of the site features, alternative 6A should be substituted for alternative 6, saving approximately $1,000,000 more.

Present landfill cap design not necessary

The current landfill cap design that NCC prepared for the MWC far exceeds MWC guidelines as outlined in Technical Guideline #3, Topic "Landfills." The cap should be redesigned to meet the MWC standard of four feet of clay and one foot of topsoil or a multi-layer equivalent. Neither the state nor the federal regulations require a design of the thickness that the state's consultant has recommended. The environmental activists from "Beautiful America" who testified at the hearing supported the consultant's alternative, but without any technical justification for their choice.

Revised alternative 6A offers cost savings

Wilson-Walker Engineering Consultants has used its proprietary computer model to evaluate the hydrogeologic performance of both the Record of Decision (Alternative 6) and the revised alternative 6A. We concluded the design for 6A should maintain its integrity under all anticipated conditions. In light of the significant cost savings and other errors that were overlooked in the original hearing, we believe that you should petition the EPA's Washington office for a review.

Budget constraints did not permit us to undertake a complete review of the contract documents between Amalgamated Chemical and Waste Site Construction Specialists, Inc.; therefore, the ten-page technical discussion attached to this letter should not be construed to represent a complete review. We would be pleased to conduct a more detailed review for Amalgamated Chemical. Please contact me if you have any questions.

Sincerely,

Sandra DeBraemaker, P.E.
Vice President

Attachments

Introductory headings (or title page, if the report is formal)

Do the introductory headings include the

_____ Source

_____ Receiver

_____ Date submitted

_____ Addresses and telephone numbers

_____ Name of contact if not the person named as source

_____ Project number or other references

_____ Title of the report or subject line

    _____ Can this report be distinguished from others in the file?

    _____ Is the purpose or nature of the report clear, not just the topic?

_____ Does the layout of the page direct attention?

_____ Do the introductory headings embody a graphic hierarchy?

_____ Is the page aesthetically pleasing?

Letter of Transmittal

_____ Does the letter present the report directly?

_____ Do the contents help the reader understand the purpose or situation?

_____ Do the contents reveal the importance or relevance of the report?

_____ Does the writer express appropriate professional enthusiasm for the opportunity to have completed this project?

_____ Is the style of the letter formal but warm?

Abstract

_____ Has the writer chosen either an informative or descriptive abstract and followed its conventions?

_____ Does the abstract contain any words that cannot be understood in context? Is the abstract complete?

_____ Does the abstract meet the length limit (if any)?

Table of Contents, Table of Illustrations, or List of Figures

_____ Are the lists complete?

_____ Are the page numbers correct?

Introductory Summary or Executive Summary

Does the foreword review

_____ the situation (or problem)

_____ issues, tasks, or questions that are involved in the problem

_____ the writer's responsibilities

_____ the writer's primary communication purpose (to request, recommend, explain, or propose).

_____ Does the summary of conclusions show a clear relation to the problem and issues?

_____ Are the recommendations clear and precise?

Appendices

_____ Are the appendices titled in such a way that their relevance to the report is clear?

_____ Are the appendices arranged in the approximate order that a reader might need them?

_____ Are the pages of the appendices clearly numbered?

For Proposals Only

_____ Explains why the work needs to be done

_____ Explains what benefits will result

_____ Explains what problem will be solved or what objective will be accomplished

_____ Explains methods and project schedule

    _____ Explains what methods will be used

    _____ Explains who will use them

    _____ Explains when the work will be done

    _____ Includes a project schedule

_____ Explains proposer's qualifications

_____ Presents costs

_____ Explains costs

(Continues)

☐ CHECKLIST FOR REPORTS *(continued)*

For Progress Reports Only

____ Describes project succinctly but with sufficient detail for identification

____ Stresses accomplishments

____ Presents progress in a positive way

____ Contains a problem-flagging section on the first page

If organized by time:

____ Explains what work has been done in earlier periods

____ Explains what work was done this period

____ Explains what work is planned for the next period

____ Contains sufficient information to enable management to make timely decisions

Report Evaluation

____ Does the report present something new?

____ Does the report emphasize its argument?

 ____ Does the organization make the logic clear?

 ____ Do the headings answer questions?

 ____ Do the lead sentences forecast the message of each paragraph?

 ____ Does the style of the writing make the main points highly visible?

____ Does the report subordinate analytical machinery and emphasize results instead?

____ Does the report distill recommendations? Is the phrasing clear and memorable?

As you can see, writing a preliminary draft of the foreword section will almost certainly clarify your project objectives and lead you to the next step: planning the work you must do to explore issues, answer questions, perform the tasks, or run the tests. When you draft the foreword, you may have no idea of what conclusions you will reach. Any of the idea-generating techniques (such as mind-mapping or freewriting) recommended in Chapter 5, "Developing Communication Strategies: Generating and Organizing Ideas," can be used to help you identify topics relevant to the situation. Once you have completed your work or obtained the necessary information, you must analyze your audience and plan a communication strategy as explained in Chapter 4, combining the persuasive strategy with the report format features.

Organizing New Reports

As discussed in Chapter 5, you should fill out a strategy planner when you face a new situation or when you must write a new kind of document. To organize your ideas, you may prepare an issue tree or code your freewriting with symbols. What questions are you answering for your readers? Which questions are most important? Which audience needs the answers to these questions? Which must be answered before others? Avoid using chronological order that reflects your own intellectual or professional process. Readers want *their* questions, not yours, answered. Transform writer-based prose into reader-based prose. Put your technical analysis in an appendix; explain only those key technical terms that are absolutely irreplaceable in the summary and discussion. Most reports have multiple readers, and unless the primary decision makers have extensive knowledge of your specialty, avoid jargon such as "BCG models" (for Boston Consulting Group models).

❏ COMMUNICATION CHALLENGES

PRELIMINARY EXERCISE 1 Obtain a copy of your college's annual report or announcements for students. Describe the organization of the document, its parts, and the graphic hierarchy used in its headings.

PRELIMINARY EXERCISE 2 Select some project in which a club or other group you belong to is engaged. *Write a one-page progress report*, noting the goals of the project and the progress you have made so far in accomplishing your objectives. Conclude with a summary of steps that remain to be taken, who will take them, and when. Prepare this report in a memorandum format and address it to the highest ranking officer in the organization. For this assignment assume that you are the person in charge of the project.

EXERCISE 1

Visit your campus placement or career planning service. Talk with the director about four companies that usually hire several students from your college each year. Ask how many times they visit the campus and what procedures they use in recruiting students (follow-up interviews, plant trips, get-acquainted parties, receptions). Obtain copies of their recruiting information. *Write a report to be kept in the placement office for students who might want to seek employment with these companies next year.* Use a copy of the strategy planner, Figure 13-10, to prepare a communication strategy for your report.

EXERCISE 2

Read an article from a business publication about some aspect of the field in which you are concentrating (for example, you might be majoring in business but concentrating your upper level courses in accounting or marketing or personnel management). *Write a hundred-word informative or summary abstract* that could have appeared at the beginning of the article.

EXERCISE 3

As your instructor directs, work alone or in a group to investigate traffic and parking problems at your campus. If there are many problems, limit your investigation to one problem that seems to cause serious dissatisfaction: too few spaces, lots located far from buildings in which classes are held, too few spaces for important visitors to campus, lack of covered parking, lots that flood during seasonal storms, poorly lit parking lots that cause security problems, etc. Your campus police station may be helpful in providing information about the number of crimes reported in parking lots, the number of parking tickets issued, times of the year in which problems occur, and other information.

Write a formal report, using diagrams and tables to illustrate and define the problem. If your instructor so directs, consider ways this problem could be solved and present your recommendations in the report as well. Address the report to the people on your campus who could take action on this problem. At some campuses, the campus safety committee, the traffic committee, the head of buildings and grounds, the vice president for operations, or the campus business manager might have such responsibilities. You will have to discover the right person or persons who would be the audience for your report. Use a copy of the strategy planner (Figure 13-10) to prepare a communication strategy for your report for this audience.

EXERCISE 4

Underwood Engineering, a company that employs about 400 people at its headquarters, has decided to move its national office from Albany, New York, to your city. Choose a site where its new offices might be built in your city and assume that the construction of this facility has already occurred. *Then prepare a guide for employees moving to the city. Explain parts of the city where they might look for residences; list several real estate firms that might help in locating residential properties or*

Event		Date Time
		Audience Issues: Uncertainties
Location		
Contact:		
Primary Audiences		
Secondary Audiences		Comprehensive Purpose
Transmitting Audiences		
Preferred Response		Lowest Acceptable Response
Persuasive Strategy		
Organizing pattern: Fulfill purpose, answer questions, create emphasis		
Media and Channels		
Visual Aids		
Criteria for Evaluation		

FIGURE 13-10.   Strategy Planner

apartments; describe the primary shopping areas in the town, the entertainment attractions, educational institutions and medical centers. Include important traffic patterns, and any other valuable information for prospective residents.

EXERCISE 5

Suppose that you're about to write a routine monthly report to the plant manager. The plant manager is very cost-conscious and scrutinizes reports for evidence of cost overruns. You see that the expenses for your department's office supplies are just under budget for the quarter; perhaps 91 percent of the budget forecast. You decide to look at the time frame. For the last two quarters the numbers were 98 and 96 percent respectively, but you were slightly over budget in office supplies for last year as a whole. What else has been under budget? Telephone costs, it turns out, have dropped by a slightly greater margin: 91, 85, and 82 percent in the first three quarters of the year. Are you just not very good at estimating your expenses? Did you budget for price increases that never occurred? You run some quick checks and find that the new price sheet for office supplies is up just about what you expected. Telephone rates have been the same this year as last year. What happened in the first quarter? The new electronic mail system was installed and people began going to classes on how to use E-mail. You've met all your performance targets; there have been fewer absences than usual in the department; clearly it hasn't been a case of doing less and therefore using less. Use a copy of the strategy planner (Figure 13-10) to prepare a communication strategy for your report. *Write an introductory paragraph for your report that will bring your monthly record to the plant manager's attention in a positive way without setting up unreasonable expectations for the future. What exactly might your news be?*

EXERCISE 6

Outback Alligators, a fast food chain that entered the market following the very popular "Crocodile Dundee" films in the late 1980s, has 400 "stations" with drive-through windows and an "outback deck" for informal dining. The company plans to open one of its stations near your campus. The company's specialties include a flaky pastry sandwich called "the Waddie," containing spicy beef, chicken, or lamb; a salad bar; and Australian soft drinks and beers. The company would like to find a place that students are likely to pass going to and from the campus on a major traffic route. *Your job is to select a site and write a letter report of two to three pages justifying your choice.*

Survey the area around your campus for an appropriate spot for Outback Alligators. You may need to take a traffic count during peak and slack periods to develop an estimate of the pass-by traffic from which customers might be drawn. You may consider sites on which present construction would have to be demolished (but don't tear down a hospital or ten-story high rise). Your city ordinance No. 44822 states that "driveways may not be cut within less than 20 feet of an intersection."

Use the strategy planner to prepare a communication strategy for your report. Design a report to meet the company's criteria. Describe the location and how it meets the needs of Outback Alligator. Draw a diagram of the location and the position of the restaurant. If you select a corner location near an intersection you should note where driveways will have to be positioned to comply with the ordinance. Include information about the size of the student population and any characteristics of the situation that would influence their behavior as potential customers. Send your report to Vern Whiteley, Corporate Real Estate Manager, Outback Alligators, 1129 Bayview Drive, Portland, Oregon 97233.

IF YOU WOULD LIKE TO READ MORE

Varner, I. I. (1987). *Contemporary business report writing.* New York: Dryden Press. This book explains the report preparation process and describes different types of reports in detail; it also covers issues such as ethics and international reports.

Lesikar, R. V., & Lyons, M. (1986). *Report writing for business* (7th ed.). Homewood, IL: Irwin. This book approaches report preparation as a process of information gathering, structuring, and editing. An appendix contains nearly seventy pages of report problems for practicing report writing.

Mathes, J. C., & Stevenson, D. W. (1991). *Designing technical reports: Writing for audiences in organizations* (2nd ed.). New York: Bobbs-Merrill. Although focused on technical reports, this book presents an excellent discussion of the function of reports in organizations. Many aspects of audience analysis, report structure, and report functions accepted as commonplace today originated in this book.

NOTES

1. Occasionally, in job searches or business planning, individuals prepare reports for their own use. A job seeker may accumulate specific types of information about the companies he or she is interested in contacting, as explained in Chapter 19, "Job Search Communications." A person who is considering starting a business may prepare a report on the industry or business opportunity, primarily as a way of defining possible courses of action. Parts of such a report might become appendices in a financing proposal for a new venture, as described in Chapter 28, "New Venture Communications."

2. J. C. Mathes & D. W. Stevenson, *Designing technical reports: Writing for audiences in organizations* (2nd ed.). Indianapolis, IN: Bobbs-Merrill (1991). Mathes and Stevenson were the first to link report design and the function reports play in solving organizational problems. This discussion depends on their analysis of the two-part structure of reports.

DESIGNING DOCUMENTS

OBJECTIVES

This chapter will help you

- translate your communication strategy into a document design

- plan the overall use of space

- create a professional image with typefaces

- compose a graphic hierarchy to direct the reader's attention

- strategically choose other graphic elements

PREVIEW

Changes in computer software have given writers greater control over the final form of their documents. Most future business professionals will not make a career of managing publications, but everyone will need to know how to translate communication strategies into effective letters and reports.

As you design letters, reports, and other documents, you should convert your communication strategy into a document design. In this process you should allocate page space, select appropriate typefaces, emphasize ideas with white space, develop a graphic hierarchy, and strategically use headings, color, and other graphic treatments.

❏ NEW TECHNOLOGY: NEW POWER FOR WRITERS

Changes in computer software have enabled business people to create documents such as letters, reports, newsletters, and spreadsheets with relative ease. Sophisticated word processing and page layout programs, such as Xerox Ventura Publisher® and Aldus PageMaker®, have made graphic design an art for everyone. In the early 1990s we talk about designing printed documents, but soon hypertext, a system of linking different levels of electronic text, will provide more complex opportunities.

One person can now do all the tasks previously performed by several people.

A decade ago, the graphic design and layout of publications such as newsletters required a number of people using a variety of different machines. The process began when a writer composed text, or "copy," with a pencil and paper. The writer was uncertain how the copy would be transformed during the design and layout stages of production. A secretary typed this copy, and the typewritten document was sent to a designer, who created a rough design or "pencil layout." The designer marked up the typewritten copy accordingly, showing different print sizes and type treatments (boldface, point size, and so forth) and sent the copy to a "type house." There, a diligent typesetter retyped all the copy and sent it through a processor. The designer cut the strips of type and pasted them onto layout boards. Any illustrations were prepared by an artist or the designer and pasted on the boards. Photographs were prepared by the printer and inserted into the "plates" that would be run on the press.

Writers must learn additional skills.

This complex process now can be accomplished by one person using one computer that sits on a desk—hence the name "desktop publishing." One person has to synthesize the functions that earlier were performed by several different individuals. Desktop publishing and word processing have given writers new power.

Now Writers Can Design Documents

However, document *design* is more than the process of formatting text to make it visually appealing. Karen Schriver, a professor of rhetoric and document design, notes that document design is more adequately represented as "information design" or as "communication design," because it includes everything from creating the communication strategy (which you have learned about in earlier chapters) through translating that strategy into an electronic or hard-copy representation.[1]

You will produce some documents yourself; you will interact with professionals to produce others.

Most future business professionals are now expected to have keyboard skills; some manage their own publications, but everyone will at least need to know how to translate communication strategies into effective letters and reports. Furthermore, most people will interact with publication specialists of various kinds at some time.

For example, you may find yourself as a "one-person show," such as an executive director of a nonprofit organization. Along with your multitude of other duties, you might handle the complete desktop publishing process for promotional materials, from writing copy to designing the product on a computer.

In contrast, as an entrepreneur you may work with an advertising agency to obtain promotional materials for your company or service. You must understand what makes a promotional piece effective in order to work with your designer or agency. What will succeed? What pulls the reader in? In this chapter, we explain what you will need to do as you design letters and reports. We will also explain some of the aspects of design that you should consider when you work with professionals.

Document Design Affects Customer and Employee Satisfaction

Superior document design has won Chubb & Sons, Inc. and Shearson Lehman Hutton the attention of scholars and the loyalty of customers. Kenneth Morris, president of the firm that worked with these companies, attributes their success to their analysis of how laser print technology could be used in the primary processes of their businesses: issuing insurance (Chubb & Sons, Inc.) and handling financial transactions for customers (Shearson Lehman Hutton).[2] Chubb's new policies, consisting of component coverages, are printed on demand by the 9700 electronic printer, reducing vast amounts of paperwork and simplifying the issuing process. From the viewpoint of customers and agents, the policies are completely customized; from the company's viewpoint, the process is totally mechanized and economical. In addition, the simplified design makes it easy for agents and customers to find the most frequently needed information, now located in prominent places on the page. Compare Figure 14-1, the old Chubb policy, with the redesigned policy in Figure 14-2.

Good design places the information readers need most in the places where it is easiest to find.

Morris and his staff achieved a similar result for Shearson Lehman Hutton. The redesign of the Shearson documents turned complicated brokerage account reports that customers could use only with difficulty into powerful marketing tools for the company. The new Shearson reports present the most frequently requested information in unambiguous language. The three most important pieces of information—the value of investments in the account, the earnings for the period, and a summary of gains and losses—head the report. This simultaneous consideration of content and format are what Shriver means by "communication design" or "information design," not just graphic design.

Morris explains the challenge as follows:

> *Access to information*—our ability to locate what we want when we want it—is becoming an ever more important issue. . . . The traditional focus on easy words, short sentences, readable type, and functional color is now subsumed by broader, often more fundamental concerns: What information should be presented? How can it be displayed most effectively for the customer and most economically for the company producing it? What technological and systems changes are necessary?[3]

As you communicate through documents and printed materials, you will go through a similar process. You must decide what your audiences need and which ideas are most important to them. You must place that information in an appropriate place. You must ensure that all your readers can understand the language you use. You must help the reader anticipate the overall organization of your document, and you must lead the reader through the text with graphic devices.

Issued by the Stock Insurance Company Herein called The Company | Policy Number | Agent Number | Sub-Agent Number
FEDERAL INSURANCE COMPANY | 01-234-6789 | 1-63603 | 000
INCORPORATED UNDER THE LAWS OF NEW JERSEY

AUTOMOBILE INSURANCE

CHUBB GROUP of Insurance Companies

AMENDED DECLARATIONS EFF 04/19/89

100 William Street, New York, N.Y. 10038 | 3200 Wilshire Boulevard, Los Angeles, Calif. 90010

** THIS IS NOT A BILL **

Item 1. Named Insured & Mailing Address–Number, Street, Town, County, State, Zip.

John A & Jane B Doe
456 Main Street
Hometown, USA 12345

Item 2. Policy Period 06
Renewable To | Inception Date 04 01 89 | Expiration D 10 01

At 12:01 A.M. Standard Time and is continuab[le] subject to our consent, for successive periods provided in General Provision 1.

Item 3. Coverage is provided where a limit of liability or a premium is shown

	A. Liability each accident	Auto No	B. Medical Payments each person	C. Uninsured Motorists UNDERINSURED MOTORISTS each accident	D. Damage To Your Auto (ACV means Actual Cash Value): Amount or ACV for Other Than Collision and/or Collision	Other Than Collision less deduct. of	Collision less deduct. of	Towing Labor per disablement
COVERAGES LIMITS	$ 300000	1	$ 10000	300000	ACV	200	200	2
	Limit of Liability against Coverage A is the same for all auto(s) insured by this policy.	2	10000	300000	ACV	200	200	2:
		3	10000	300000	18464	200	200	2:
		4						
PREMIUMS TERM	$ 232.50	1	$ 1.50	23.50	73.50		182.00	2.0
	220.50	2	1.50	23.50	155.50		260.00	2.0
	232.00	3	1.50	23.50	84.50		237.50	2.0
		4						
AP	161.50						169.00	
RP								

Forms attached to the policy, if any:
01-02-152*01-02-202*14371*01-02-213*A1070*
01-02-249*25101*A1247*01-10-974*01-02-246*01-02-271*01-02-273*01-02-293*

Total Premium Adjustment: ADD$ 356.50 | Term End. Premium $ 178.5[0] | Total Term Premium $ 1937.5[0]

INSTALLMENT PAYMENTS | Liability | Auto Damage | TOTAL | Due Date | Liability | Auto Damage | TOTAL | Due Date
YOU WILL BE BILLED SEPARATELY BY THE COMPANY FOR ANY PREMIUM DUE

Item 4. DESCRIPTIONS OF AUTO(S) OR TRAILER(S)

Auto No	Year	Trade Name	Body Type	Spec. Auto Type	Vehicle Identification Number (VIN) or Serial Number	Chubb Vehicle Code	Act. Pur. Cst. or Ave. Ret. Price	Anti-Theft Device	Pass. Restr.	Emp. Disc.	State Registered	Sym	Rate Class	Te
1	85	VOLVO	4 WAGN		ZYX012A345B678			2	2	N	Y	8	20PF20	6
2	82	BMW	4 SED		BCH9876F654B12		22000	2	2	N	Y	15	49PO24	6
3	89	VOLVO	4 SED		JHY56C78H2321A		18464*	2	2	N	Y	8	20PF24	6
4														

Item 5. GARAGE LOCATION The auto(s) or trailer(s) described in this policy is principally garaged at the mailing address unless otherwise stated.
AUTO NO 1 / 2 / 3 / 4

Item 6. DRIVER INFORMATION

Dr. No.	Married	Sex	Birth Date Mo.	Day	Yr.	Licensed Since Mo.	Yr.	Driver Training Credit	Student at School 100 Mi. From Home	Good Student Credit	Princ. Oper. Auto Used
1	YES	M	03	28	45	03	65	N/A	N/A	N/A	12
2	YES	F	03	28	42	03	62	N/A	N/A	N/A	
3	NO	F	01	10	73	04	89	NO	NO	YES	3
4	NO	F	01	11	73	04	89	NO	NO	YES	
5											
6											

Item 7. LOSS PAYEE
AUTO NO
1 ABC Financial Corporation
2
3 Car Dealer of America
4

Item 8. AUTOMOBILE USE
1 PLEASURE
2 PLEASURE
3 PLEASURE
4

Item 9. CHARGEABLE DATES

ISSUE DATE 04/25/89 | ISO CODES

ADD DRIVER NO. 3,4--CHANGE DRIVER NO. 2

Producer & Address 0 41

Ourtown Insurance
5 Oak Road
Hometown, USA 12345

This page, together with policy jacket provisions completes the above numbered policy

035 40
035 40
035 40

BY ____________________
AUTHORIZED REPRESENTATIVE
INSURED

FIGURE 14-1. Old Chubb Policy

Why Design Matters

Ordinary readers expect extraordinary design quality.

Businesspeople today expect very high quality work in promotional materials and everyday documents. Just as viewers are dissatisfied with video productions that are less than broadcast quality, people also reject poorly designed memos, reports, and promotional materials. The standards and expectations of your readers have risen.

$\mathcal{M}$*asterpiece.*   ***Premium Summary***

CHUBB

WILLIAM AND MARIE HARRISON
23 WHITNEY LANE
MADISON, ANYSTATE 12345

Page 1
Effective Date 4/30/87
Policy no. 10026411-01
Policy period 4/30/87 to 4/30/88
Producer name MASTERPIECE AGENCY

We are pleased to enclose your Chubb Masterpiece Policy, customized to provide the coverage you requested.

This chart shows at a glance what coverages you have and the related premiums.

	Property covered	**Coverage**	**Premium**
Home and Contents	HOUSE AT 23 WHITNEY LANE MADISON, ANYSTATE	HOME,CONTENTS, LIABILITY	$ 2,364.00
Valuable Articles	SILVERWARE	VALUABLE ARTICLE	$ 166.00
Vehicles	1984 MERCEDES	COMPREHENSIVE & COLLISION, LIABILITY	$ 1,366.00
	1986 MERCURY	COMPREHENSIVE & COLLISION, LIABILITY	$ 481.00
Total Premium			**$ 4,377.00**

Your policy includes a Coverage Summary and policy provisions that explain your coverage in more detail.

We've also enclosed a statement and bill. If you choose one of our convenient installment plans, your payments will be slightly higher than the premium shown above because of the small service charge.

You now own one of the most highly regarded insurance policies. We stand behind each of our policies with the same personal service that is the hallmark of the Chubb Group of Insurance Companies.

FIGURE 14-2. Redesigned Chubb Policy

Furthermore, busy readers and less skillful readers depend on features of document design to increase the efficiency of their reading. Less skillful readers are less able to think about their own understanding as they read. They need more explicit guidance. Less able readers are not aware that they need to be strategic, plan ahead, and check their own understanding.[4]

☐ CONVERT YOUR COMMUNICATION STRATEGY INTO A DOCUMENT DESIGN

Design signposts that show what a good reader would remember about your text.

The document design, therefore, should make prominent the signposts that an excellent reader with plenty of time would construct mentally during reading: What information is most important? What are the main components of this message? Where is this information located, in case I need to look for it again?

How are the ideas related? Why does this message matter to me? The communication strategy created as you plan the document enables you to answer these questions. Its analysis of the audience's uncertainties, its statement of comprehensive purpose, its persuasive appeal, and its organized pattern of ideas (see Chapters 4 and 5) help you design the document by translating this strategy into visible text.

Designing before Drafting

In some situations, you can plan the design of the document before you actually draft text. The advantage is that you can avoid writing more copy than you can use. Sometimes the length of your document will be limited by other people's requirements. Requests for proposals may specify maximum length. Indeed, when business managers specify a length for a document, they usually mean the maximum length; in contrast, professors usually specify a minimum length. By planning the overall design of the document before you draft, you can estimate the length of various sections and write with those targets in mind. If you intend to take this route, you should complete your strategy planner (see Chapter 5) before you consider document design.

Designing from Drafted Copy

Sometimes you will have a draft complete before you begin the design process. For example, if you are composing a summary report that combines the progress reports, budgets, or plans of several people in your department or task force, you may have text to work with before you begin planning how the document will look. If you work in a publications department, you may be given draft copy for editing a publication and you may do none of the drafting yourself.

Before desktop publishing was possible, the separation of duties explained earlier meant that writing and design occurred in separate steps. This is no longer absolutely necessary. We will explain the differences between designing before drafting and designing from a completed draft as we go through the steps of document design.

Plan the Pages of the Document

Define the Communication Area of the Page

Plan the pages by setting the margins for your pages. Your document's pages will have boundaries or margins that define what Paul Anderson has called the "communication area" in the center of the page.[5] In this communication area you can plan the arrangement of your text, both single pages and series of pages. You probably already use a basic page design for your college papers, although you may not have given much attention to this design (see Figure 14-3).[6] Be

(a) The communication area of a page

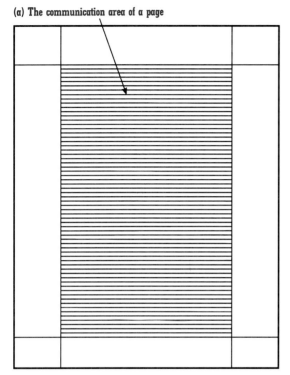

(b) Basic layout for a student paper

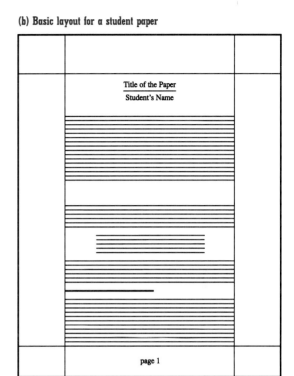

FIGURE 14-3.   Page Layout

consistent in your use of outside margins throughout the pages of the document (unless you have an excellent reason to change them) because the basic communication area should provide a coherent, continuous physical context for your message.

If you already have drafted the text, you can work with the draft copy to estimate length. If you have not yet drafted text, you can turn your mind map or other planning tool into an outline with the outline function of your word processing program.[7] You can write the number of paragraphs or pages beside each heading in the outline and sum them to estimate document length.

If you are preparing a type of document that has an established company format (such as a report), you should consider whether that format can achieve your comprehensive purpose. Companies should challenge themselves to re-evaluate their report designs, as Chubb & Sons, Inc. did. Sometimes you may want to change formats just to overcome the inertia of your readers' old habits.

Page design should reflect the content divisions of your outline or issue tree.

Plan the Number of Columns in the Communication Area

The number of columns chosen for the page may reflect a number of considerations. The size and number of the illustrations you have chosen will suggest how the rest of the copy should be divided and positioned. Artists who lay out pages

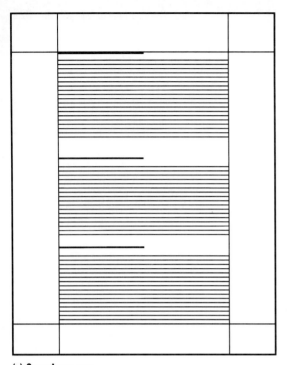

(a) One-column page

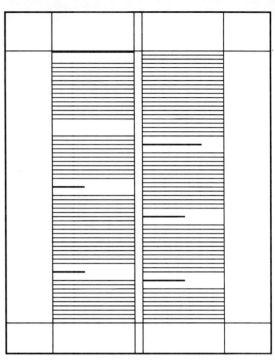

(b) Two-column page

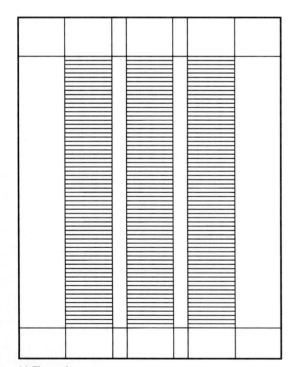

(c) Three-column page

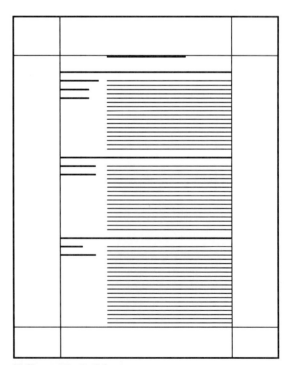

(d) Horizontally-divided page

FIGURE 14-4.   Dividing the Page

are interested in the overall pattern of the page, and they must take into consideration the size and shape of any illustrations planned for the text. Also, when an explanation can be paired with an illustration, the reader can jump from one column to another to make comparisons. The number of columns may depend partly on what your audience is used to seeing. For example, people expect letters to have one column. It's hard to imagine how a two-column letter would look. Figure 14-4 shows layouts with different column divisions.

Longer Layouts

Avoid long stretches of unbroken text by planning two-page spreads of your paper or report.

Business documents may be produced on only one side of the page or on both sides of the page. Whenever the document is printed on both sides of the page and pages are bound by staples, clips, or other means along the left-hand margin, the two pages the reader can see simultaneously are called a two-page spread. Think in terms of spreads; do not design one page at a time. Whenever the document will be printed on both sides or copied double-sided, draw a series of two-page spreads that will help you visualize your entire report. Looking at a series of spreads will enable you to see where the illustrations or visuals fall, where the text is unbroken or visually dense, and what visual rhythm the document has. *If you have never considered the design of the reports or papers you prepare for classes, take advantage of these situations to practice document design skills.*

When pages are printed on both sides and bound so they appear side by side, this layout becomes a horizontal spread. Designers refer to a horizontal "magic line" for horizontal spreads—an invisible demarcation on which the copy is "hung." Think of the design of the spread as a horizontal communication area that makes a whole, not just as two separate pages that happen to be aligned together. Imagine how you are going to lead the reader through all the ideas on the two-page spread, and create a path for the reader's eye. The illustrations in Figures 14-5 and 14-6 show two-page spreads that use different column widths. In Figure 14-5 the layouts utilize a one-column format, in which type stretches from the left to the right margin. These examples demonstrate that a one-column format can be anything but static, as text is "wrapped around" charts, illustrations, and photographs of varying sizes. Figure 14-6 exhibits a two-column format, which enables illustrations to be sized in one- or two-column widths. To further demonstrate the flow of a two-page spread, large illustrations may stretch over the two facing pages. In all these examples, the text and graphics are arranged to consider the overall effect of the two-page spread.

FIGURE 14-5. Layout of One-Column Spreads for a Three-Page Report

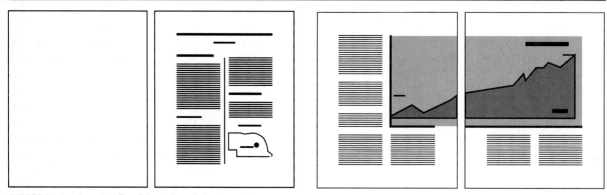

FIGURE 14-6. Layout of Two-Column Spreads for a Report

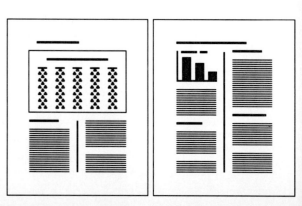

Case: Designing a Brochure for an Executive Development Seminar

Jesses H. Jones Graduate School of Administration
Rice University
Office of Executive Development

Designers: Kathryn McAllister and Corinne Zeutzius

The writer and artist worked together to create a document design that appropriately matched the needs of the client, the Jones Graduate School's Office of Executive Development, which offers continuing studies programs to managers, executives, and professionals.

The communication strategy identified these readers and the kinds of information they needed to decide whether to attend. Their document design had to reflect the image of the Jones Graduate School and Rice University and call attention to participants' evaluations. Their strategy, therefore, had to reflect the university's high standards and tradition of excellence. They wanted a classic and traditional image that was subtle and not overwhelming. Yet, the design still had to draw the reader into the written communication.

The designers' first step was selecting a typeface that adequately fit this communication strategy. Times Roman was chosen for its traditional appeal, although a typeface such as Goudy Oldstyle would have worked as well to create a "classic" feel. You will notice in the illustration that the typeface is used conservatively with few changes in the size of the type. For example, there are size variations only in the body text, subheads, and major headline. Boldface and italic type are used sparingly and strategically, making those blocks treated with bold or italic more noticeable and important.

The designers were faced with another challenge—they did not have illustrations or photographs to supplement the design. They needed some graphic elements or treatments that would break up the "sea of grayness" that can occur with an all-text, no-graphics design.

The first graphic element selected was the outside border that runs the perimeter of the margin. The second choice was a two-column layout, which lends itself to the creation of attractive lists and allows more graphic flexibility if boxes are included in the design. In this particular instance, it was decided that a box would be ideal. Not only would the box serve as an essential graphic element, but it also would encapsulate the quotations from previous participants in the executive programs. This separation of the box from the rest of the text tells the reader instantly that the boxed copy is different and important. While the box could have been kept within the border, a design decision was made to allow it to extend outside of the border—creating almost a three-dimensional effect and adding an interesting tilt to the total balance of the page.

Monday and Tuesday, October 2–3
Monday: 1 to 4:30 p.m.
Tuesday: 9 a.m. to 4:30 p.m.
Tuition: $495
(Two or more registrations, $445 each)

How to Manage the Sales Force

How do the strongest and most successful companies build and maintain a high-performance sales organization? By applying today's proven managerial tools and concepts to a changing environment.

The successful sales manager is a great planner, trainer, problem solver, counselor, and evaluator. Your challenge is to build a high-performance sales team capable of working together, sharing ideas, and supporting one another in a way that enables the company to achieve its goals.

This seminar is structured to provide you with the tools you need to manage, motivate, and succeed as a sales manager.

Who should attend ■

"How to Manage the Sales Force" will provide national or regional sales managers and marketing executives with the ability to improve the performance of their groups and companies. In addition, CEOs and managers who support sales and marketing will find this seminar helpful in better understanding the sales force and in uncovering ways to improve their companies' overall performance.

You will learn to ■

- Recruit high-performance sales personnel
- Determine your sales markets
- Use effective sales leadership strategies to build high-performance sales teams
- Train your sales personnel to be able to sell successfully in any business climate
- Motivate everyone on the sales force—old hand or newcomer

Outline ■

Contrasting the skills required to succeed in sales with the skills required to succeed in sales management

Developing the necessary leadership skills— setting goals, gaining commitments, motivating the sales team effectively, etc.

Defining the role, key job functions, and responsibilities of a professional sales manager

Interviewing and hiring high-performance sales personnel

Setting sales goals

Developing your sales leadership style

Coaching and counseling and appraising sales performance

Instructor ■

Don James is a professional speaker, trainer, author and management consultant. He is president of Human Dimensions, Inc., a Dallas-based sales training and management consulting firm. Mr. James has trained thousands of managers and sales professionals in the United States and Europe in new ways to meet the business challenges faced in today's business climate.

Mr. James' business background includes more than 26 years in executive management, operations management, sales and marketing, and human resources management and development. He is an active member of the National Speakers Association, presenting more than 250 seminars, workshops, and keynote addresses each year. Mr. James is a dynamic speaker with a unique ability to educate and motivate participants with practical insights and techniques for increasing their effectiveness in a rapidly changing world.

"I gained a tremendous amount of knowledge that I previously had no idea existed—or let's say, it was there. I just didn't know where to find it or how to identify it."

Byron Weaver, Vice-President
Industrial Industries, Inc.

"As a new sales manager, the greatest concern I had was the transition. This course has given me the tools necessary to achieve personal and corporate goals and objectives in a very systematic way. I strongly recommend this course to any individual who is a new sales manager. Well done."

Peter S. Batura, Direct Line Sales Manager
Summus Computer Systems

Color was another graphic treatment strategically applied to this layout. The color should not overwhelm a layout but should be used to highlight important elements in the design or break the monotony of black ink. Color—like any graphic treatment—can lose its effectiveness if overused. Therefore, the box, which graphically serves as an illustration or photo replacement, worked well with the spot of color. Also, tiny color blocks were used as highlights beside each subhead in the layout. And finally, the dates and other course information were printed in color to demonstrate their difference and importance. This color treatment also keeps the information from clashing with the major headline.

Now hold this page at arm's length and pretend you are a prospective participant. Notice how your eye travels. While the colored box may first attract your attention, you quickly are drawn to the main headline, "How to Manage the Sales Force." Then your eye jumps from subhead to subhead. You instantly can decide whether this course holds anything of interest to you; and based on that, you may choose to read the rest of the text on the page or go on to another page in the booklet. Did the document fulfill its overall communication strategy?

❑ CREATE A PROFESSIONAL IMAGE FOR THE DOCUMENT

"Image" is the combined effect of all your design choices.

The graphic elements not only capture and direct attention, they create an image for the page that may correspond to the company producing the document, its audience, and the subject matter, as demonstrated in the case. The image is the product of all the elements, but some of the basic tools are typeface or font, lines or "rules," point size, and special effects.

The image should be professional, but the professional images of different industries and companies vary. The documents of a manufacturing firm usually look different from those of a financial services firm, or a firm directed toward a specific market segment. For example, the materials from John Deere Tractor, American Express, and TOYS-R-US are quite different. Becoming sensitive to your own reaction to various designs and layouts is the best way of recognizing the appropriate look for your materials.

Typefaces affect the aesthetic "character" of the image.

Typefaces are the visual symbols or characters that represent the alphabet, numerals, and punctuation marks. Each typeface has its own particular design and appearance. Today most computer users are acquainted with a whole array of typefaces or "fonts," with Times Roman and Helvetica being two of the most popular.

Times Roman 12 point. A well-known "serif" font.

Helvetica 12 point. A well-known "sans serif" font.

Serif versus Sans Serif

As you can see from the samples on the preceding page, fonts differ from each other. Times Roman letters have a finishing "tail" or serif, and it is known as a serif typeface; Helvetica is "sans serif" or without tails. Serif typefaces generally are considered a more traditional and conservative style, and sans serif faces are viewed as more contemporary. For instance, a financial institution that is trying to preserve its established, traditional image may choose a serif type. However, a financial institution that is looking for a more contemporary image may use sans serif in its promotional materials.

This is not a hard and fast rule. Every font creates its own mood, and the choice of type can be vital to the impact of a promotional piece. Examine some of the fonts in the sample shown in Figure 14-7 and consider the effects they have. Are they strong? Modern? Impressive? Unobtrusive? Squatty? Elaborate? The text describes a residential real estate broker's solution to a promotion problem in a real estate newsletter. Which font would be most appropriate for such a newsletter?

Some designers choose to mix typefaces. A common mix is Times Roman as the body text and Helvetica for the headlines. Keep in mind that serif type generally is used for body text, because sans serif type may be more difficult to read at smaller point sizes. However, when used in headlines, sans serif can make a strong statement.

In this example, the headline is Helvetica and the body text is Times Roman. The body text illustrates the use of "greeking," nonsense words that form body copy to show a type style for design purposes. When the design is executed, the body copy will be the actual text.

BIC to merge with Kraftco

Lorem ipsum dolor sit amet, consectetuer adipiscing elit, sed diam nonummy nibh euismod tincidunt ut laoreet dolore magna aliquam erat volutpat. Ut wisi enim ad minim veniam, quis nostrud exerci tation ullamcorper suscipit lobortis nisl ut aliquip ex ea commodo consequat.

❑ COMPOSE A GRAPHIC HIERARCHY

Margins Are the Basis of the Hierarchy

Principle of design hierarchies: Big = Important.

Most cultures use graphic hierarchies in which the larger items are the most important. The eye sees the difference in height, width, darkness, or shape and interprets it. The size of areas, letters, and margins directs the eye to important items in the document. The left margin is usually wider, and the larger white area on the left side of the page therefore anchors the text, drawing the eye to the left as an orienting vertical element in the design. Compare the appearance of the two letters shown in Figure 14-8. Which looks more stable and professional? The sentences in the second example have been grouped into logical paragraphs around the four principal points of the letter.

Palatino (Serif)

How could I get my flyers to the buyers driving through neighborhoods looking at homes? Walking through a hardware store, I found my answer—a 4-foot clear plastic tube with orange caps intended for storing and shipping maps and blueprints. I cut mine into 1-foot lengths that could be attached with a bracket to yard signs. I soon had flyer dispensers on four of my listings, and my calls and showings increased. I approached Sandy Williams of Goodwill Industries with the product idea, and soon handicapped men and women were manufacturing the items.

Goudy (Serif)

How could I get my flyers to the buyers driving through neighborhoods looking at homes? Walking through a hardware store, I found my answer—a 4-foot clear plastic tube with orange caps intended for storing and shipping maps and blueprints. I cut mine into 1-foot lengths that could be attached with a bracket to yard signs. I soon had flyer dispensers on four of my listings, and my calls and showings increased. I approached Sandy Williams of Goodwill Industries with the product idea, and soon handicapped men and women were manufacturing the items.

Optima (Sans Serif)

How could I get my flyers to the buyers driving through neighborhoods looking at homes? Walking through a hardware store, I found my answer—a 4-foot clear plastic tube with orange caps intended for storing and shipping maps and blueprints. I cut mine into 1-foot lengths that could be attached with a bracket to yard signs. I soon had flyer dispensers on four of my listings, and my calls and showings increased. I approached Sandy Williams of Goodwill Industries with the product idea, and soon handicapped men and women were manufacturing the items.

Avant Garde (Sans Serif)

How could I get my flyers to the buyers driving through neighborhoods looking at homes? Walking through a hardware store, I found my answer—a 4-foot clear plastic tube with orange caps intended for storing and shipping maps and blueprints. I cut mine into 1-foot lengths that could be attached with a bracket to yard signs. I soon had flyer dispensers on four of my listings, and my calls and showings increased. I approached Sandy Williams of Goodwill Industries with the product idea, and soon handicapped men and women were manufacturing the items.

FIGURE 14-7. **Examples of Serif and Sans Serif Fonts**

Northwest Library Association
Central Office: 984 Sweeny Road, Suite 108
Darvanell, OR 97206

September 27, 1990

Dr. Helen P. Mitchell, Director
Office of Continuing Studies
Castlewick Community College
P.O. Box 1899
Verde Vista, OR 97211

Dear Dr. Mitchell:

Congratulations on receiving funding from the Northwest Committee for the
Humanities for your touring photo exhibition of Northwest Indian life.

I appreciate the need for you to move ahead quickly with contacting the
libraries in the geographic areas of the state.

I communicated your request to the NLA Executive Board at the July meeting. It was understood that it was then too late to arrange for an exhibit in
the fall of 1990.

Accordingly, the Board agreed that if the project was funded, Castlewick
Community College would have permission of the Northwest Library Association to approach the districts with regard to showing the exhibit in the fall
of 1990.

The first of the district meetings will be held this Saturday with the remainder following closely. All districts have, I believe, completed the mailings to their members. I am attaching a calendar of the ten meetings.

Copy for the Fall issue of the *Northwest Library Journal* is due October 1
with a publication date of October 31. All the member libraries will receive
the *Journal* even if you do not succeed in contacting them at their district
meetings.

By copy of this letter I am informing the president of your situation in the
hope that she may have some suggestion for us or for you.

Meanwhile, my very best luck to you with the project, which sounds most
interesting.

Yours truly,

Jerre Harmon

Jerre Harmon
Administrative Coordinator

cc: President Dianah Belle

(a) Narrow Margins; Too Many Paragraphs

FIGURE 14-8. *Comparing Margins and Paragraph Blocks*

Northwest Library Association
Central Office: 984 Sweeny Road, Suite 108
Darvanell, OR 97206

September 27, 1990

Dr. Helen P. Mitchell, Director
Office of Continuing Studies
Castlewick Community College
P.O. Box 1899
Verde Vista, OR 97211

Dear Dr. Mitchell:

Congratulations on receiving funding from the Northwest Committee for the Humanities for your touring photo exhibition of Northwest Indian life. I appreciate the need for you to move ahead quickly with contacting the libraries in the geographic areas of the state.

I communicated your request to the NLA Executive Board at the July meeting. It was understood that it was then too late to arrange for an exhibit in the fall of 1990. Accordingly, the Board agreed that if the project was funded, Castlewick Community College would have permission of the Northwest Library Association to approach the districts with regard to showing the exhibit in the fall of 1990.

The first of the district meetings will be held this Saturday with the remainder following closely. All districts have, I believe, completed the mailings to their members. I am attaching a calendar of the ten meetings. Copy for the Fall issue of the *Northwest Library Journal* is due October 1 with a publication date of October 31. All the member libraries will receive the *Journal* even if you do not succeed in contacting them at their district meetings.

By copy of this letter I am informing the president of your situation in the hope that she may have some suggestion for us or for you. Meanwhile, my very best luck to you with the project, which sounds most interesting.

Yours truly,

Jerre Harmon

Jerre Harmon
Administrative Coordinator

cc: President Dianah Belle

(b) **Larger Left Margin Anchors Four Paragraphs**

Type Styles Organize the Hierarchy

You should organize the type styles of the characters into type "treatments," sets of type styles that organize a graphic hierarchy. In creating a type treatment, you may work with the point size of the characters, all caps or initial caps and lower case letters in combination, boldfacing, underlining, italics, and shadowed or outlined letters.

Bold	Initial Caps Only
Italic	Outline
ALL CAPITAL LETTERS	Shadow
SMALL CAPS	plain text

These features can be combined with indenting and your plan for allocating page space to create a graphic hierarchy. Your reader will take letter height into consideration as the highest-ranking characteristic, because letter height creates the most attention. Centering draws more attention when the item occurs at the top of the page than when a centered item occurs elsewhere.

The following example is a simple four-level graphic hierarchy:

14-POINT TITLE CENTERED
12-POINT ALL CAPS BOLD LEFT
12-point Bold Initial Caps Indented
12-point plain text indented

You must be consistent with your type treatment. For example, if the subhead on page one is 18-point bold, it should be 18-point bold on page four; if you use an 11-point italic caption underneath the photograph on page six, be sure to use an 11-point italic caption under the photo on page fourteen.

The most widely used type styles are bold and italic. Outline, shadow, and small caps are novelty treatments that should be reserved for special occasions only. Keep in mind that any graphic treatment (such as type styles) can be overused. When you implement such elements too often in your design, the reader finds it difficult to determine what really is important in your message. Choosing the appropriate point sizes and type styles is part of effective visual persuasion. The example in Figure 14-9 is from an IRS form given to a design team for revision. It has a cluttered, hard-to-read appearance because too many type styles are crowded together.

2. Your marital and filing status situation is any one of the following:

- You file as a qualifying widow(er) with dependent child. (See the special rule on page 10 under **Box 2, Married** filing a joint return.)
- You were a nonresident alien during any part of 1987 and you do not file a joint return. *(Note: You may have to file Form 1040NR.)*
- At the end of 1987 you were married to a nonresident alien or dual-status alien who had U.S. source income and who has not elected to be treated as a resident alien. *(Note: You may use Form 1040A if you are considered unmarried under the rules explained on page 11 for Married persons who live apart.)*

FIGURE 14-9. *Too Many Type Styles*

Use All-Caps (Uppercase) Sparingly

All-caps hides the shape of words.

All-uppercase letters can be used in design, but use them sparingly for headlines or subheads. USED TOO OFTEN IN A DOCUMENT, ALL UPPERCASE CAN MAKE THE COPY DIFFICULT TO READ. PLACE THIS BOOK AT ARM'S LENGTH AND SEE HOW DIFFICULT IT IS TO DECIPHER THIS MESSAGE. Readers cannot see the shapes of the words when all the letters are capitalized; avoid all caps when there are more than five words.

Avoid underlining in desktop publishing; choose bold or italic as alternatives. The underline may run through the tails of your letters, distorting the words and decreasing readability. The use of the underlines for emphasis is a holdover from the days of typewriters, when bold and italic were not readily available.

Type Sizes Indicate Level of Importance

1 inch = 6 picas = 72 points (12 points in a pica).

Most word processing programs offer a variety of point sizes. When dealing with the size of type, we use a measurement system that is based on picas and points. To understand this measurement system, remember this simple math: There are 6 picas to an inch. The pica is further divided into points. There are 12 points per pica, or 72 points to an inch. Figure 14-10 illustrates this system.

As you can see, 72 points would be appropriate for a major headline in promotional materials, but not for regular body text, which should be 9 to 12 points.

1 inch
6 picas
72 points

Ascenders ↑

x-height

Descenders↓

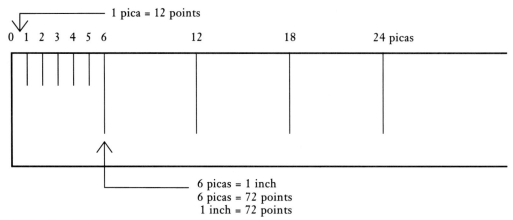

1 pica = 12 points

0 1 2 3 4 5 6   12   18   24 picas

6 picas = 1 inch
6 picas = 72 points
1 inch = 72 points

FIGURE 14-10. **Measuring in Picas**

Body text, Times Roman, 8 point

Body text, Times Roman, 9 point

Body text, Times Roman, 10 point

Body text, Times Roman, 11 point

Body text, Times Roman, 12 point

Body text, Times Roman, 13 point

Body text, Times Roman, 14 point

X-height = height of a letter without an ascender or descender (for example, an x).

The point size of type is determined by its height and depth, which includes the ascenders (the top portion of letters, such as "h" or "b"), the x-height (the center portion of the letter, based on "x"), and the descenders (the lower part of letters, such as "g" or "y"). Helvetica gives an illusion of being bigger than Times Roman because its x-height is greater than the x-height of Times Roman. In truth, although they do have different widths, Helvetica and Times Roman measure the same overall height from line to line.

Helvetica 24 point

Times Roman 24 point

Another aspect of type size involves the "set width," which is the horizontal measurement of type. Below are two sentences, again offering a comparison of Helvetica and Times Roman.

Careful planning reduces costs.　　(Helvetica)

Careful planning reduces costs.　　(Times Roman)

Although both are 14 point, the first example, in a Helvetica typeface, is wider than the Times Roman example below it. Again, the total depth of 14 points for the two typefaces is equal; but the set width is larger for Helvetica than Times Roman. This fact should be considered when selecting typefaces for your documents. While Times Roman 12 point would be appropriate for a company report, Helvetica 12 point would appear too large.

Major newspaper headlines can range in size from 36 to 120 points. Report headlines and subheads may range from 14 to 24 points. Simply changing the point sizes of your type can turn a boring layout into one with impact, as is demonstrated in Figure 14-11.

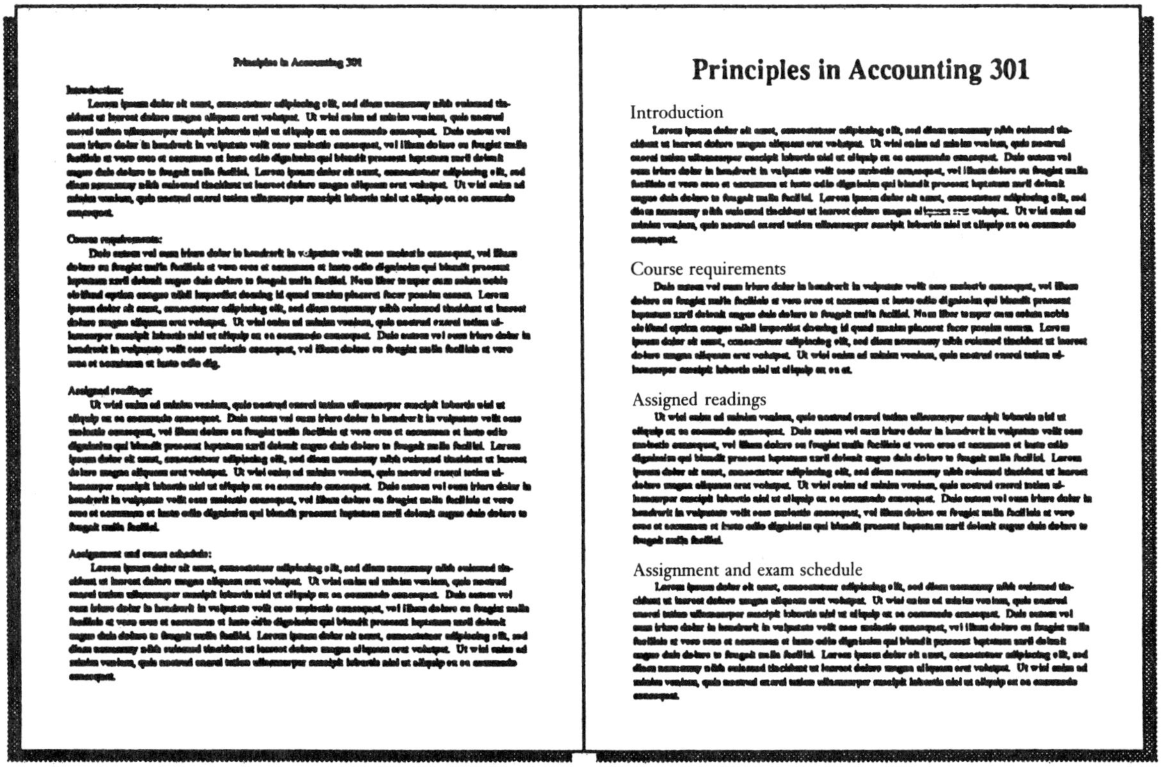

FIGURE 14-11.　Impact of Type Size

Choose the right point size for the column width.

In addition, you also should consider the number of columns when you choose point size. The most recent versions of professional word processing programs allow multiple columns. The combination of column width and point size will affect the ease of reading. Narrower column widths invite the reader's eye to pick up shorter groups of words conveniently. The 8 1/2″ × 11″ page is too wide for a reader's eye to grasp an entire line of text at once, especially if the type is quite small. Most one-column documents such as letters therefore use larger type sizes (10 to 12 points). However, if you choose a narrow column width, you should also choose a smaller type size (such as 9 to 10 points) to avoid creating columns with too few words, large gaps, and many hyphenated words. The consequences of combining a narrow column with a large point size are shown in Example 6 of the section on text alignment.

Prefer variations in one font to several contrasting fonts; make all contrasts meaningful. Three typefaces is the absolute maximum on a single page.

Text Alignment

From the previous examples in the chapter, you also will have noticed a difference in alignment of the text. For instance, most body text will be "flush left," where the left-hand side of text aligns with the edge of the column:

EXAMPLE 1, FLUSH LEFT

Last summer, the company set up a task force to evaluate
new products for the next wave of computer expansion.
Two-thirds of the machines the task force chose are used
primarily for word processing, and half of the units are
equipped with database programs with graphics capabilities.

Occasionally in desktop publishing, graphic designers choose to implement "flush right" alignment, such as this example.

EXAMPLE 2, FLUSH RIGHT

Last summer, the company set up a task force to
evaluate new products for the next wave of computer
expansion. Two-thirds of the machines the task force chose
are used primarily for word processing, and half of the units are
equipped with database programs with graphics capabilities.

"Centering" is popular for headlines.

EXAMPLE 3, CENTERED

Sales Force Completes Mission

Most word processors also offer a choice of either "ragged right" or "justified" lines. The copy in the paragraph below is ragged right, which leaves uneven measurements on the right side of the copy.

EXAMPLE 4, RAGGED RIGHT

Last summer, the company set up a task force to evaluate new products for the next wave of computer expansion. Two-thirds of the machines the task force chose are used primarily for word processing, and half of the units are equipped with data base programs with graphics capabilities.

In justified text the right and left sides are even, or "justified."

EXAMPLE 5, JUSTIFIED MARGINS

Last summer, the company set up a task force to evaluate new products for the next wave of computer expansion. Two-thirds of the machines the task force chose are used primarily for word processing, and half of the units are equipped with data base programs with graphics capabilities.

The advantages of justified text include its polished appearance and very defined blocks of copy. However, uneven spacing can occur between words in documents using justified type, which can appear unnatural to the eye. This usually occurs when the column widths are relatively small and the type is slightly large. More hyphenation occurs in justified text as well.

EXAMPLE 6, JUSTIFIED NARROW COLUMN WITH LARGE TYPE

Last summer, the company set up a task force to evaluate new products for the next wave of computer expansion. Two-thirds of the machines the task force chose are used primarily for word processing, and half of the units are equipped with data base programs.

Ragged right copy sometimes is easier for the eye to discern and presents a more contemporary look.

❏ STRATEGICALLY CHOOSE GRAPHIC ELEMENTS

Graphics and Photos

Illustrate assertions that the reader must accept in order to understand or agree with you.

Before you complete your initial design for any of the pages, decide which ideas in your argument need illustrations. Ask yourself whether you need to illustrate the points of your discussion. The table below suggests types of illustrations appropriate to different kinds of points.

How to Choose Illustrations

POINT TO BE ILLUSTRATED	PHOTO	LINE DRAWING	DIA-GRAM	FLOW CHART	BAR CHART	LINE GRAPH	COLUMN CHART	PIE CHART	PICTO-GRAM	DOT CHART	COMPONENT DIAGRAM
Nature of the topic	•	•	•						•		
Frequency of occurrence						•	•			•	
Change over time	•			•	•	•	•				
Causes of the topic	•			•		•					
Consequences of the topic	•		•	•		•					•
Rank of the topic					•						
Comparison with others	•				•	•		•			•
Correlation with others										•	
Subject in a field	•	•									•
Attribute or interpretation of the topic	•	•							•		
Parts of the topic	•	•	•					•			•

The preparation of illustrations is explained in Chapter 15. The placement of these illustrations on the page directs the reader's attention, expands and reinforces the reader's understanding of the topic, and increases the efficiency of the communication.

Place Photographs and Line Art to Achieve Balance and Stability

Photographs—whether black and white or color—become integral parts of a document design. They are one of the most common graphic elements because they quickly can add balance to a page by providing a nice mix between body copy and graphics. Photos assist the designer in creating a graphic hierarchy in the document because they create immediate visual impact and usually command the reader's attention. Additionally, you can create a hierarchy with photos by making the most important photo the largest on a page and other less important photos a smaller size. This size difference contributes to the overall balance of the page.

Placement of illustrations creates balance, motion.

Figures 14-12 and 14-13 demonstrate the importance of photos in the overall balance and effectiveness of a layout, which can affect the reader's perception of the story. In Figure 14-12, the photos seem to be haphazardly placed on the page and the copy is hard to follow. However, Figure 14-13 demonstrates a well-balanced page, one that suggests the smaller photos are related to the more important, larger photo. This example also uses white space in an effective manner by creating a sense of openness around the graphic elements. The tighter, internal white space acts as glue to keep the elements together in a packaged appearance. Ironically, in Figure 14-14 the headline says that the rodeo gives prisoners a day of freedom but the rigidly organized photo layout puts each photo in a cell. The layout shows no freedom at all.

White space directs the eye, controls the flow of the design.

Create a Path for the Eye

You should lead the reader's eye from the upper left to the lower right of the page in most single-page documents, as the design in Figure 14-15 does. You may create this pattern with vertical columns or with horizontal rectangles, but the overall design should have stability and balance and create a clear path through the page. Look at the designs in Figures 14-15 through 14-17 and notice how your eye moves through the design. Where do you look first in each case? Where does your eye move next? Where does it stop? A page such as that shown in Figure 14-16 stimulates tension because of its opposing elements, but it doesn't facilitate reading or comprehension.

A glance at the layout for the *ASCT News* cover shown in Figure 14-15 shows the horizontal rectangle as the identifying title of the whole design. Within the horizontal area, called a "banner" headline, are two levels of information: the big title and the small explanation, "Official publication of the American Society for Cytotechnology." Your eyes also tell you instantly that there are two types of information in two vertical columns, divided with a vertical line or "rule," and that the wider one contains the more important information. A centered headline, "Health Research Stamp Issued," catches your attention next, introduced by the small italicized subhead, "New US Stamp." The large blow-up of the stamp pulls your eye through the copy to the bottom of the page. In the slender column to the left are the titles of the articles in the newsletter, introduced by the boldfaced all-caps heading, "IN THIS ISSUE." The ASCT logo anchors the bottom of the narrow column.

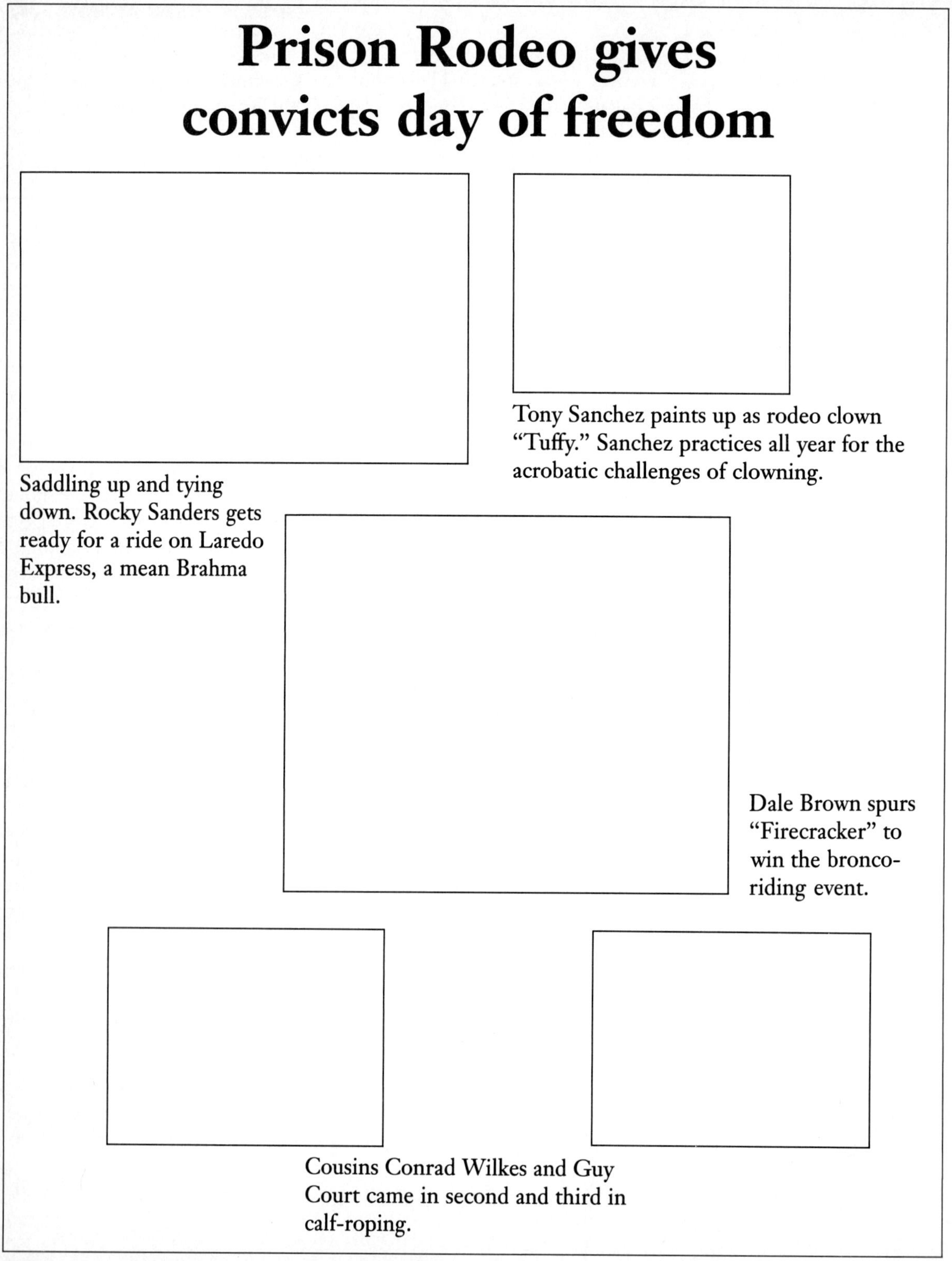

Prison Rodeo gives
convicts day of freedom

Saddling up and tying down. Rocky Sanders gets ready for a ride on Laredo Express, a mean Brahma bull.

Tony Sanchez paints up as rodeo clown "Tuffy." Sanchez practices all year for the acrobatic challenges of clowning.

Dale Brown spurs "Firecracker" to win the bronco-riding event.

Cousins Conrad Wilkes and Guy Court came in second and third in calf-roping.

FIGURE 14-12.   Unbalanced Layout, Photos Placed Haphazardly

Prison Rodeo
gives convicts day of freedom

Grand parade features Rodeo Marshals Ted Klinger and Gordon Vasey with guest star Candace Bergen.

Winners (above): Cousins Conrad Wilkes and Guy Court came in second and third in calf-roping behind "Duster" Coggan (below), who earned the highest score in the rodeo's history.

Dale Brown's "Firecracker" leaps for the sky. Ride 'em, Dale!

FIGURE 14-13.   Balanced Layout, Photos Help Create Hierarchy

Prison Rodeo gives
convicts day of freedom

FIGURE 14-14.   Rigid Layout

ASCT News

OFFICIAL PUBLICATION OF THE AMERICAN SOCIETY FOR CYTOTECHNOLOGY

VOLUME V
NUMBER 11
1984

IN THIS ISSUE

New US Stamp

Health Research Stamp Issued

A 20-cent commemorative stamp recognizing the achievements made possible by health research was issued May 17 in New York City, the U.S. Postal Service has announced.

Health research is a matter of teamwork between chemists, psychologists, endocrinologists, physiologists and even mathematicians and engineers, among others. Together, these health professionals have made dramatic strides in the development of technical and medical innovations which prevent disease and prolong life.

Today, because of the important work done by dedicated health researchers, diseases such as polio, small pox and yellow fever are no longer incurable, and people around the world now lead more productive, happier and healthier lives.

The horizontally oriented stamp was designed by Tyler Smith of Tiverton, Rhode Island, under the direction of Richard Sheaff, a design coordinator for the Citizens' Stamp Advisory Committee. Mr. Sheaff also was the typographer of the stamp.

The design features a variety of laboratory paraphernalia used by health research professionals in performing their work. Above the design in a single line of white type is "Health Research USA 20¢."

© 1984 U.S. POSTAL SERVICE ALL RIGHTS RESERVED

FIGURE 14-15.   Layout That Leads the Eye Upper Left to Lower Right

Source: *ASCT News*, Volume 5, Numbers 7 and 11. Reprinted by permission of the American Society for Cytotechnology.

The cover of the theater newsletter in Figure 14-16 signals a different organization. It also has a banner headline, set off with a thick bar, but the rest of the page is divided in three columns that all pertain to the same story. No rules separate the columns. Instead of leading your eye to the end of the text at the lower right-hand column, this design creates a problem for your eye, inviting it

ALLEY THEATRE

ENCORE

"WE'RE WORKING VERY HARD HERE"

Claude Purdy Building Fences

In a phone conversation from Milwaukee, director Claude Purdy spoke enthusiastically of FENCES, by August Wilson, and the co-production process which Milwaukee Repertory Theatre and The Alley have embarked on. It is this season's first production in the Neuhaus Arena stage.

"We can't help but mine the play." Purdy declared. The generous amount of time allowed for both him and the actors to explore their characters, to live the parts, can only lead to what Purdy describes as a deepening. "The action deepens because of the play's density, the actors will grow...the deeper you go, the more you find."

The play, a 1987 Pulitzer Prize winner, and Purdy have come together before. He has directed it twice before: at the GeVa, and at the Pittsburgh Public Theatre. Nevertheless, he constantly discovers new aspects and angles. "Although it has no stamp of history, it is nonetheless a classic [in the literal sense of the word], it is a poetic examination of the Black experience in America."

Set in the late 50's somewhere in urban America, the play tells the story of Troy Maxson, the son of a sharecropper, and at one time a Negro League baseball star, with potential frustrated by the racial barriers of his time, now struggles as a garbage worker to forge a life of dignity and worth.

"FENCES," says Purdy, "forces a re-examination of the history of the Afro-American culture and its place in present-day America." The Alley/Milwaukee co-production, will ensure that as many people as possible have a chance to do just that. A third theatre will also be presenting this production: the Arizona Theatre Company in Tucson and Phoenix.

Each theatre has a different type of performance space—Milwaukee has a thrust, the Alley has an arena, and Arizona has a proscenium—Purdy feels that this variety provides an interesting challenge for him, the actors, and the designers. "Co-production offers all kinds of benefits," he observed "and I am more than happy to be involved in this process."

Coming to Houston for Purdy is almost like coming home. He was born in Lake Charles, Louisiana and expects to see "all kinds" of friends and family among the Alley audiences.

FENCES opens on January 25, with previews beginning January 20.

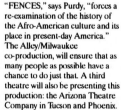

Claude Purdy

August Wilson

FIGURE 14-16. **Layout with Opposing Photo Elements**

Source: Reprinted by permission of the Alley Theater, Houston, Texas.

simultaneously to go to the photos in the lower right and the lower left corners.

In contrast, the layout in Figure 14-17 from the same newsletter draws your eye to the center of the bottom. The three columns end in a horizontal rectangle with playwright Edward Albee's face in the center. The three columns contain a preface and introduction to the interview with Albee, which begins at

ALLEY TALKS WITH ALBEE:

Impressions of the Playwright for the 1990's
from a conversation with Alley Artistic Associate Michael Wilson

"You take the trouble to construct a civilization...you make government and art, and realize they are, must be, both the same...you bring things to the saddest of all points...to the point where there is something to lose...then all at once, through all the music, through all the sensible sounds`of men building, attempting, comes the Dies Irae. And what is it? What does the trumpet sound? 'Up yours.' I suppose there's justice to it, after all the years...'Up yours.'"
—George, Act II, **Edward Albee's** **WHO'S AFRAID OF VIRGINIA WOOLF?**

On October 13, 1962, Edward Albee's WHO'S AFRAID OF VIRGINIA WOOLF? shattered the American drama. Overnight, it made obsolete the naturalistic mode of writing, turning some of our most time-honored plays into fossils.

The Alley is pleased to have Mr. Albee with us to direct his landmark play as the theatre's first offering for our 1990 Winter/Sping Season. During his recent visit to Houston, I spoke with Mr. Albee over a casual lunch at the River Cafe. With candid intelligence and often a spontaneous ire, he addressed an expansive number of topics including art, criticism, government and society. Throughout the conversation, however, a consistent theme emerged—that of civilization as an endangered species. Following, are selecions from our talk:

On Art and Government

MW: Theatres have such a lack of funding from the government, and what little they do have, is being significantly threatened at this time.

EA: It sure is being threatened by the reactionary know-nothings in this country. The aesthetic education of our people is an integral part of their formal education guaranteed by Congress. It must not be censored. How can you make an informative decision about anything until you know everything about it? It's the Jesse Helms of this world that are trying to limit our access to choice. What a cluck he is. He's dangerous. Most clucks aren't dangerous. He's very dangerous.

continued on page 6

Edward Albee

FIGURE 14-17.   Layout with a Single, Unifying "Anchor" Photo

Source: Reprinted by permission of the Alley Theater, Houston, Texas.

the top of the third column with a subhead in contrasting red. The centered primary headline and subheading are dominated by a wide bar or "rule" across all three columns and the headlines. A small italicized phrase, "continued on page 6," extends into the right-hand margin above the photo, leading the reader to turn the page and read more.

Introduce Photos and Figures

Photos may be introduced simply through their captions, but if they are closely related to the discussion they should be introduced in the text as well.

Figures (graphics, diagrams, and so forth) should be introduced before they appear. Then the text should comment on the figures. Do not restate the contents of the figure, but show how its information relates to your argument. Answer the question, "So what?" Point out the range of the numbers; the average, or other significant pieces of information that relate to the points you are making in the argument. After all, the figure is supposed to show something that can't be stated as well in words. Let the words direct the reader to the important visual point of the figure.

Emphasize Ideas with Lists

Use lists to make components and series memorable.

Use lists to make the components of a whole stand out. Because human beings have a very hard time remembering more than seven items (can you name all seven of the dwarfs?), short lists are better than long lists. A list of three or four items is ideal—easily remembered. Use numbers for lists whose items have a rank or priority associated with them or for lists that present a sequence of steps or items that must follow one another in a particular order.

Use bullets or asterisks (such as • or *) for equivalent items that do not have a rank or a sequence. Position lists within a sentence when the items are so simple and easy to remember that they need no visual emphasis. Put items in a vertical list when the items are unfamiliar or complex. *Punctuate lists consistently.*

Introduce lists with a clause, not a phrase. For example, introduce a list of regions with "We analyzed four regions:" instead of "Analyzing the following:"

Lists may be placed on the page in one of four ways, ranging from the slightly noticeable to the strongly contrasting placement in space. Which you choose is up to you, but be consistent about the placement of lists throughout the document.[8]

The first placement, only slightly different from ordinary paragraph treatment, is flush left with item contents wrapping around to the left margin. The second placement indents both the left and right margins with the item contents wrapping around to the left margin. The third option indents the entire item and the item contents wrap directly under the bullet. The fourth option makes the bullet or number very prominent with the item contents indented behind the bullet by two or more spaces.

Four Options for Bulleted Lists

• Wentworth and Associates' proposal recommended six specific consultations with our representatives.

   • Wentworth and Associates' proposal recommended six specific consultations with our representatives.

   • Wentworth and Associates' proposal recommended six specific consultations with our representatives.

   • Wentworth and Associates' proposal recommended six specific consultations with our representatives.

Direct Attention with Titles, Headings, Rules, Screens, and Boxes

Titles and headings help the reader scan the document. A dense page offers few cues. Other graphic elements that you can use in your design include rules, boxes, screens, and color.

Rules

Lines of any thickness used in your layout are known as "rules." They can be used graphically to spice up a page or add graphic consistency throughout a document.

Rules can be used both horizontally and vertically. Those used vertically commonly are known as "column rules," because they are used to visibly split the columns in your layout. Figure 14-19(a) shows such a column rule, which is a hairline thickness, used to split two columns.

FIGURE 14-18.   Rule Types

(a) Border and Column Rule

FIGURE 14-19. The Graphic Hierarchy of a Brochure Page

Monday and Tuesday, October 2–3
Monday: 1 to 4:30 p.m.
Tuesday: 9 a.m. to 4:30 p.m.
Tuition: $495
(Two or more registrations, $445 each)

How to Manage the Sales Force

How do the strongest and most successful companies build and maintain a high-performance sales organization? By applying today's proven managerial tools and concepts to a changing environment.
The successful sales manager is a great planner, trainer, problem solver, counselor, and evaluator.
Your challenge is to build a high-performance sales team capable of working together, sharing ideas, and supporting one another in a way that enables the company to achieve its goals.
This seminar is structured to provide you with the tools you need to manage, motivate, and succeed as a sales manager.

Who should attend
"How to Manage the Sales Force" will provide national or regional sales managers and marketing executives with the ability to improve the performance of their groups and companies. In addition, CEOs and managers who support sales and marketing will find this seminar helpful in better understanding the sales force and in uncovering ways to improve their companies' overall performance.

You will learn to
Recruit high-performance sales personnel
Determine your sales markets
Use effective sales leadership strategies to build high-performance sales teams
Train your sales personnel to be able to sell successfully in any business climate
Motivate everyone on the sales force—old hand or newcomer

Outline
Contrasting the skills required to succeed in sales with the skills required to succeed in sales management
Developing the necessary leadership skills—setting goals, gaining commitments, motivating the sales team effectively, etc.

Defining the role, key job functions, and responsibilities of a professional sales manager
Interviewing and hiring high-performance sales personnel
Setting sales goals
Developing your sales leadership style
Coaching and counseling and appraising sales performance

Instructor
Don James is a professional speaker, trainer, author, and management consultant. He is president of Human Dimensions, Inc., a Dallas-based sales training and management consulting firm. Mr. James has trained thousands of managers and sales professionals in the United States and Europe in new ways to meet the business challenges faced in today's business climate.
Mr. James' business background includes more than 26 years in executive management, operations management, sales and marketing, and human resources management and development. He is an active member of the National Speakers Association, presenting more than 250 seminars, workshops, and keynote addresses each year. Mr. James is a dynamic speaker with a unique ability to educate and motivate participants with practical insights and techniques for increasing their effectiveness in a rapidly changing world.

"I gained a tremendous amount of knowledge that I previously had no idea existed—or let's say, it was there. I just didn't know where to find it or how to identify it."

Byron Weaver, Vice-President
Industrial Industries, Inc.

"As a new sales manager, the greatest concern I had was the transition. This course has given me the tools necessary to achieve personal and corporate goals and objectives in a very systematic way. I strongly recommend this course to any individual who is a new sales manager. Well done."

Peter S. Batura, Direct Line Sales Manager
Summus Computer Systems

(b) Plain Text Added

(continued)

Monday and Tuesday, October 2–3
Monday: 1 to 4:30 p.m.
Tuesday: 9 a.m. to 4:30 p.m.
Tuition: $495
(Two or more registrations, $445 each)

How to Manage the Sales Force

How do the strongest and most successful companies build and maintain a high-performance sales organization? By applying today's proven managerial tools and concepts to a changing environment.

The successful sales manager is a great planner, trainer, problem solver, counselor, and evaluator. Your challenge is to build a high-performance sales team capable of working together, sharing ideas, and supporting one another in a way that enables the company to achieve its goals.

This seminar is structured to provide you with the tools you need to manage, motivate, and succeed as a sales manager.

Who should attend

"How to Manage the Sales Force" will provide national or regional sales managers and marketing executives with the ability to improve the performance of their groups and companies. In addition, CEOs and managers who support sales and marketing will find this seminar helpful in better understanding the sales force and in uncovering ways to improve their companies' overall performance.

You will learn to

- Recruit high-performance sales personnel
- Determine your sales markets
- Use effective sales leadership strategies to build high-performance sales teams
- Train your sales personnel to be able to sell successfully in any business climate
- Motivate everyone on the sales force—old hand or newcomer

Outline

Contrasting the skills required to succeed in sales with the skills required to succeed in sales management

Developing the necessary leadership skills—setting goals, gaining commitments, motivating the sales team effectively, etc.

Defining the role, key job functions, and responsibilities of a professional sales manager

Interviewing and hiring high-performance sales personnel

Setting sales goals

Developing your sales leadership style

Coaching and counseling and appraising sales performance

Instructor

Don James is a professional speaker, trainer, author, and management consultant. He is president of Human Dimensions, Inc., a Dallas-based sales training and management consulting firm. Mr. James has trained thousands of managers and sales professionals in the United States and Europe in new ways to meet the business challenges faced in today's business climate.

Mr. James' business background includes more than 26 years in executive management, operations management, sales and marketing, and human resources management and development. He is an active member of the National Speakers Association, presenting more than 250 seminars, workshops, and keynote addresses each year. Mr. James is a dynamic speaker with a unique ability to educate and motivate participants with practical insights and techniques for increasing their effectiveness in a rapidly changing world.

"I gained a tremendous amount of knowledge that I previously had no idea existed—or let's say, it was there. I just didn't know where to find it or how to identify it."

Byron Weaver, Vice-President
Industrial Industries, Inc.

"As a new sales manager, the greatest concern I had was the transition. This course has given me the tools necessary to achieve personal and corporate goals and objectives in a very systematic way. I strongly recommend this course to any individual who is a new sales manager. Well done."

Peter S. Batura, Direct Line Sales Manager
Summus Computer Systems

Monday and Tuesday, October 2–3
Monday: 1 to 4:30 p.m.
Tuesday: 9 a.m. to 4:30 p.m.
Tuition: $495
(Two or more registrations, $445 each)

How to Manage the Sales Force

How do the strongest and most successful companies build and maintain a high-performance sales organization? By applying today's proven managerial tools and concepts to a changing environment.

The successful sales manager is a great planner, trainer, problem solver, counselor, and evaluator. Your challenge is to build a high-performance sales team capable of working together, sharing ideas, and supporting one another in a way that enables the company to achieve its goals.

This seminar is structured to provide you with the tools you need to manage, motivate, and succeed as a sales manager.

Who should attend ■

"How to Manage the Sales Force" will provide national or regional sales managers and marketing executives with the ability to improve the performance of their groups and companies. In addition, CEOs and managers who support sales and marketing will find this seminar helpful in better understanding the sales force and in uncovering ways to improve their companies' overall performance.

You will learn to ■

- Recruit high-performance sales personnel
- Determine your sales markets
- Use effective sales leadership strategies to build high-performance sales teams
- Train your sales personnel to be able to sell successfully in any business climate
- Motivate everyone on the sales force—old hand or newcomer

Outline ■

Contrasting the skills required to succeed in sales with the skills required to succeed in sales management

Developing the necessary leadership skills— setting goals, gaining commitments, motivating the sales team effectively, etc.

Defining the role, key job functions, and responsibilities of a professional sales manager

Interviewing and hiring high-performance sales personnel

Setting sales goals

Developing your sales leadership style

Coaching and counseling and appraising sales performance

Instructor ■

Don James is a professional speaker, trainer, author, and management consultant. He is president of Human Dimensions, Inc., a Dallas-based sales training and management consulting firm. Mr. James has trained thousands of managers and sales professionals in the United States and Europe in new ways to meet the business challenges faced in today's business climate.

Mr. James' business background includes more than 26 years in executive management, operations management, sales and marketing, and human resources management and development. He is an active member of the National Speakers Association, presenting more than 250 seminars, workshops, and keynote addresses each year. Mr. James is a dynamic speaker with a unique ability to educate and motivate participants with practical insights and techniques for increasing their effectiveness in a rapidly changing world.

> *"I gained a tremendous amount of knowledge that I previously had no idea existed—or let's say, it was there. I just didn't know where to find it or how to identify it."*
>
> Byron Weaver, Vice-President
> Industrial Industries, Inc.

> *"As a new sales manager, the greatest concern I had was the transition. This course has given me the tools necessary to achieve personal and corporate goals and objectives in a very systematic way. I strongly recommend this course to any individual who is a new sales manager. Well done."*
>
> Peter S. Batura, Direct Line Sales Manager
> Summus Computer Systems

Borders

Rules and borders define areas.

Borders are lines around the edge of the page, usually following your page margins. In Figure 14-19(a), you see the column rule and also the border, which runs around the perimeter of the margin. Your text will fall within the border. You may recognize this initial layout of the brochure for the executive development seminar highlighted earlier in this chapter. It was the first step the desktop publicist took when preparing the Jones Graduate School's Office of Executive Development document design, which was explained in the case study earlier in this chapter.

After the column rule, border, and page numbers are placed on the page, the text is added to the layout as shown in Figure 14-19(b). In the next example, Figure 14-19(c), you will notice how the desktop publicist develops a graphic hierarchy. The major headline has the largest point size, followed by the subheads, and then the body text. Further treatments are applied to the type, including italic in selected spots and lists. One list uses bullets to draw attention to key points, while the other list uses hanging indents (the second line is indented under the first line).

Boxes

Boxes are constructed around a block of text, graph, or a photograph. You also may use boxes if you wish to separate an article from the main text. This treatment, sometimes called a "sidebar," draws the reader's attention to something on the page that you consider important. This was the idea in Figure 14-19(d), where a box now encloses the quotations from the past participants of the program.

Screens

Boxes and screens say, "This content is different."

Sometimes boxes of copy or other graphic elements are "screened" with a percentage of black or colored ink. Usually—but not always—screens are additions to boxes. Again, the screen of color can emphasize an item in your layout. Therefore, use screens sparingly—their overuse can confuse the reader as to what is important on the page. Many word processing programs and graphics programs, as well as desktop publishing packages, allow you to "fill" areas with different types of patterns, creating effects with laser printers that are quite similar to the screens produced by professional printing.

Screens generally are 10 to 50 percent of the original color. So, if you are using black ink and screen it back to 10 percent, a light gray will result. Similarly, if you screen back royal blue by 20 percent, you will have light blue. Therefore, the text still is quite legible through the screen. (A word of warning: Certain colors do not lend themselves to screens. If you screen back a shade of red, often you end up with pink.)

Screening also can turn an ordinary text block into an attractive graphic element. For example, with many promotional pieces, you may not use photographs or illustrations. For this reason, a colored screen was added to the box in the completed brochure shown in the case and in Figure 14-19(d).

Color

Color conveys emotion, attracts attention.

You may wish to use "spot" color and "full" color in your promotional materials. Spot color uses one or two colors strictly as a highlight. The tiny colored squares after each subhead in the executive development brochure are an example of spot color. Also, text may be colored to create emphasis. Note the dates/tuition text block on the brochure—the text is in color ink to draw attention to the information. The color screened box also is considered spot color. This process can be cost-effective and visually persuasive. Gerald Murch, a color specialist, recommends that warm colors (those with long wavelengths, such as red, orange, and yellow) should be used to signify a need for action or response. Cool colors are generally used to indicate status or background information. Most people experience warm colors as advancing toward them and cool colors as receding or distant.[9] Color is discussed further in Chapter 15.

Full color, on the other hand, can be an expensive process. Color photos would be used in the layout, and colors would be used selectively as graphic elements throughout the product. Generally, full color is used in publications of magazine quality, such as a year-end, thirty-two-page annual report to stockholders. The publication should have a quality appearance; it should use color, paper, texture, and design carefully. Writers, editors, artists, and photographers would be needed on a project of this magnitude.

Using black ink with no additional colors also is an option. For in-house products on a low budget, black and white may be the only option. However, by wisely using type styles, fonts, screens, and white space, you should not lose any impact from your message. Remember, a 20-percent screen of black ink equals gray, which can create essential contrast in your design.

❑ SUMMARY

As you produce documents, you must translate your communication strategy into a document design. Relying on your plans for organizing the document, you should allocate page space, create a professional image through selection of typefaces, compose a graphic hierarchy, and strategically choose graphic elements. You should select visuals for the document that will reinforce key points in your argument. To accomplish these tasks in preparing your letters and reports, you must have a basic grasp of document design principles.

CHECKLIST FOR DOCUMENT DESIGN

OVERALL DESIGN

____ Have you designed the information, not just the page? Is the most valuable information in a prominent place?

____ Does the design relate to the organization of information in your communication strategy planner?

____ Does the design reflect your persuasive approach? How?

____ Do the design and typefaces create a personality or image for the document?

____ Do the rules call attention to groupings or organization without overwhelming the page or looking busy?

____ Does the color direct attention without distracting?

____ Is there sufficient white space?

LEADING THE READER'S EYE

____ Does unnecessary white space interrupt the flow of the design?

____ Does the design lead the reader's eye from the upper left hand corner to the lower right hand corner?

____ Are there illustrations for all the concepts the reader may not know or may need to visualize in order to understand your points?

DIRECTING ATTENTION

____ Are the point sizes large enough to read?

____ Are phrases longer than five words placed in upper- and lowercase letters?

____ Are there any places where the page looks cluttered?

____ Do the highlighting features direct attention without distracting?

____ Do boxes, screens, and other special elements achieve specific purposes?

Working with design professionals may require an even greater understanding of the technology and theory of design. This chapter—while only scratching the surface of graphic design and desktop publishing—provides a framework for understanding the subject from a business professional's perspective. If you are moving into a profession that will require more graphic design knowledge, you should consider taking a design, desktop publishing, or publications course in a continuing study program, technical art school, communication department, or computer center.

❑ COMMUNICATION CHALLENGES

PRELIMINARY EXERCISE 1 Analyze three company logos consisting only of letters (not other designs or emblems) that you encounter on a day-to-day basis, such as the logos of the Coca-Cola Company, IBM, Levi Strauss, McDonald's, Neiman Marcus, and so on. Why is the design of the letters appropriate for the company? Are the typefaces serif or sans serif? Would you change anything about the logo? Is it easy to understand, or does the design interfere with perception of the meaning?

PRELIMINARY EXERCISE 2 Pick up a copy of a locally produced newsletter, one-page promotional flyer, or brochure, such as a publication produced by your church, school, or apartment complex. Analyze the graphic design and consider what you would do differently if you were the designer. Items to evaluate include use of white space, type hierarchy, type style, typeface, and overall graphic effectiveness. *Write up your evaluation (one to two pages, double spaced) and be prepared to discuss your analysis in class.*

EXERCISE 1

Get copies of *USA Today* and *The Wall Street Journal*. Compare the two of them by considering:

Typefaces

Type styles (such as italic or bold)

Size and use of headlines, subheads

Use or lack of color

Size and use of photographs and line art

Inclusion of sidebars

Incorporation of graphic elements, such as boxes, screens, rules, etc.

The length of articles

Use of white space

Based on these items, discuss the appropriateness of the graphic design. What do you think the markets of each newspaper are? How is the design appropriate for these markets? Would you do anything differently?[10]

EXERCISE 2

Work on your own or break into teams of four to five. Your assignment is to develop an image for your company. Decide what kind of business your company is—an accounting firm, financial institution, a law practice, a service company, beverage manufacturer, car dealership, a stereo store, etc. Come up with a company name. Discuss promotional pieces that you think may assist in the marketing of your company—brochures, annual reports, advertisements, flyers, etc. *Choose one of the promotional pieces your company wishes to pursue and discuss:*

What typeface(s) you might use and why (refer to examples from this chapter)

Whether you would use color

If a logo or publication name is needed

Whether you would have photographs and/or line art

What graphic elements to use, such as type styles, borders, rules, and screened boxes

What would be the overall appearance and effect of your publication

Always keep your market in mind: What image would your audience consider appropriate for your business? Who is the audience?

EXERCISE 3

Compare the two newsletter covers (Figures 14-20 and 14-21). Which is more successful in creating a path for your eye? Why do you think so?

EXERCISE 4

Write an analysis of the page shown in Figure 14-22, from the Blue Cross of Washington and Alaska brochure titled, "Bluechip: We've combined our extensive health-care experience with today's most advanced technology to bring you more accurate claims payment, faster turnaround, and more value for your benefit dollar." *What design changes would you recommend to represent the ideas of the copy more effectively on the page? What changes in typeface or type treatment would you recommend?*

ASCT News

OFFICIAL PUBLICATION OF THE AMERICAN SOCIETY FOR CYTOTECHNOLOGY

VOLUME V
NUMBER 7
1984

Comments from the President

Whither Cytotechnology?

On April 6-7, 1984, the National Council on Health Laboratory Services (NCHLS) sponsored a symposium entitled "The Clinical Laboratory — Changing Directions in the 1980's". The ASCT's representatives at this meeting were Patricia Ashton, Karen Biernat and Shirley Greening.

The NCHLS is composed of approximately two dozen member organizations representing professional societies and government agencies concerned with health laboratory practice and regulation. The ASCT, ASC, CAP and ASCP are included in this membership. The NCHLS serves as a forum for input into personnel and laboratory quality assurance, curriculum development, professional certification and laboratory accreditation standards.

The April Symposium centered on ways in which the health care industry would be effected by the federal government's prospective payment system (PPS) and diagnosis-related groups (DRG's), and provided a forum to discuss methods of responding to these changes. Your ASCT representatives felt this meeting was the most comprehensive discussionwe had heard to date because representatives from private industry and independent labs, small and large hospitals and private physician groups expressed both their special interests and specific problems in dealing with these new regulations. Topics covered such diversified areas as the role of the laboratory from the perspective of the practitioner and the consumer, the social and economic impact of the new health care delivery system, the role of specialty labs and how they will cope with DRG's, the changing roles for laboratory personnel, and changes in technology for the future. (See also *ASCT News* Vol. V, No. 6, pp. 43-44.)

We left this symposium with mixed feelings. On one hand we sensed, as many cytotechnologists have already expressed, a certain level of misgiving, if not fear, that prospective payment would so drastically change the way we practice that the laboratory and its personnel would evolve within the next ten years into a totally mechanized commercial industrial complex, manned by rows of robotic technicians pushing buttons. Indeed, there were those that felt this was already the case in some of the clinical laboratories! An undercurrent that there was or is a perceived manipulation of our roles and our professions by "outside forces" beyond our control was unexpected but felt. Conversely, we were very impressed with the ideas and plans that these people are developing: ways of improving tests and technology to adapt to the economic changes, creating new tests, streamlining operations, and a sense of challenge to come up with a "better mouse-trap".

How will Cytotechnology respond to these changes? And what types of adjustments will be made to accommodate the changing directions of laboratory services? Do we see any changes taking place at the present time? Continued on next page

FIGURE 14-20. Newsletter Cover No. 1

A publication of the Press Club of Houston and the Houston Chapter, Society of Professional Journalists

the journalist

Volume 1, No. 2   October 1989

SPJ counts down to national convention, Oct. 19

by Susan Bischoff

More than 1,200 journalists are expected to attend the 80th Society of Professional Journalists convention Oct. 19-22 at Houston's Westin Galleria.

The convention opens Thursday, Oct. 19, at 1 p.m. with a welcome from Mayor Kathy Whitmire. The keynote speaker Frank Bennack Jr., chairman of the Hearst Corp., will announce the results of a Hearst study, "The American Public's Hopes and Fears for the Decade of the 1990s."

An orientation session for first-time SPJ conventioneers will be held at 5 p.m. Thursday.

The opening night reception starts at 6 p.m., Oct. 19, in the NCNB Center. Taste of Texas foods, wine and beer will be served (see story, this page).

The USS Iowa Gunner's Mate Kendall Truitt will appear on a media ethics panel at 7:30 a.m., Friday, Oct. 20. SPJ's First Amendment Counsel Bruce W. Sanford and Ellus Rubin, Truitt's attorney, also will be on the panel exploring the press' performance in covering the Navy's investigation of the USS Iowa explosion.

The professional development sessions get under way after Friday morning's early bird session with Truitt. For a complete list of pro

development sessions, call Susan Bischoff at the Chronicle.

Friday's luncheon speakers are syndicated columnist Jack Germond and former NBC correspondent Richard Valerani. They will discuss the role of the free press in a democracy.

Helen Thomas, UPI's White House bureau chief, gets roasted Saturday at lunch. John Seigenthaler, editor and publisher of Nashville's The Tennessean and Jacqueline Adams, White House correspondent for CBS, are confirmed roasters.

Al Neuharth, founder of USA Today and chairman of the Gannett Foundation, will speak at Saturday evening's banquet. He also will sign copies of his new book, "Confessions of an S.O.B.," at 5 p.m. Saturday.

The exhibition hall will be open all day Wednesday through 2 p.m. Saturday.

A chapter leadership conference will be conducted Sunday at the hotel from 8 a.m. to noon. For more information on the leadership conference, contact Ira Perry at the Post.

A job fair for minorities will be held Oct. 18-19, followed by an open job fair on Oct. 20. For information, contact Walter Johns at the Chronicle or Major Garrett at the Post.

Tickets for opening night, Bennack's speech, the USS Iowa panel and all pro development sessions are available for $10 each at the door, as long as space is available. Tickets for all meal events are available for $25 at the door.

Susan Bischoff, assistant managing editor of the Chronicle, is chairman of the convention heads up the SPJ scholarship committee.

Tasty Texas fare to feed conventioneers

by Randall A. Shields

A gala reception featuring Texas produced food and drink and an evening of comedy at Houston's Alley Theater will kick off the Society of Professional Journalists national convention Oct. 19.

Local members of SPJ are invited to help welcome national convention guests at a "Taste of Texas" reception from 6 to 8 p.m. in the lobby of NCNB Center, 700 Louisiana.

Food and drink for the evening will be coordinated by the Texas Department of Agriculture's Taste of Texas group. Spirited music will be provided by the award-winning Jazz Quartet from Houston's High School for the Performing and Visual Arts.

The fun will continue as the cur-

tain rises on the Alley Theater's update production of "Measure for Measure," the Shakespeare classic with a new twist.

Alley Director Gregory Boyd said the production takes a wild new look at this fascinating comedy/drama of sexual revenge and sexual justice, showing it to be as much a play of the 1990s as anything now being written. The play contains provocative language and situations and is recommended for mature audiences.

SPJ members (and their guests) not registered for the convention may attend the reception for $10. Tickets to the Alley's "Measure for Measure" also are $10.

Randy Shields, public relations manager for AT&T, is organizaer of the opening night reception.

1

FIGURE 14-21.   Newsletter Cover No. 2

*A CLAIMS-PROCESSING
NUCLEUS SUPPORTED BY
FOUR KEY SUBSYSTEMS*

CLAIMS-PROCESSING SYSTEM

BLUECHIP offers fully automated claims processing. Once the claims examiner has entered patient data, provider data, and claim line-item information into the system, BLUECHIP takes over. Its functions include:

- Verifying patient and provider eligibility
- Determining whether the specific procedures or items listed in the claim are covered for that patient
- Determining whether the charges are reasonable
- Coordinating benefits among primary and secondary carriers
- Calculating deductibles and co-insurance amounts
- Collecting detailed utilization data from each claim processed

If the claim contains discrepancies that BLUECHIP cannot resolve, it will suspend the claim for review by a claims examiner. In a few cases—for example, those where the situation is medically complex—our staff stays involved throughout the processing of the claim, to provide the necessary special attention. But for the vast majority of our claims, BLUECHIP handles the bulk of the processing activity.

To carry out its claims-processing functions, BLUECHIP works in an on-line mode with several integrated data bases. These data bases contain all the information needed to process a claim.

SUBSCRIBER SUBSYSTEM

The Subscriber Subsystem contains the history for all of our subscribers—as well as for the dependents of each subscriber. For each individual listed, it provides the following data:

- Age
- Sex
- Relationship to subscriber
- Other health insurance coverage
- Limitations on coverage unique to that individual

BLUECHIP uses this information to determine patient eligibility.

PROVIDER SUBSYSTEM

The Provider Subsystem lists key information for all eligible providers. These "provider profiles" can be accessed either by provider name or by type of provider (doctor, hospital, dentist, etc.). Information listed for each provider includes:

- Type of provider
- Location (important for cost-comparison information)
- Other identifying information (e.g., license number)
- Who should receive the check (patient or provider)

BLUECHIP uses this information to determine whether the provider listed on the claim is eligible, and to whom the payment should be made.

REFERENCE SUBSYSTEM

The Reference Subsystem contains three types of medical definitions:

- Procedures (e.g., tonsillectomy)
- Diagnoses (e.g., pregnancy)
- Application rules (e.g., corporate policy regarding coverage for certain types of services)

BLUECHIP uses the Reference Subsystem to determine if a particular service is eligible for coverage. For each medical term listed, the Reference Subsystem specifies the code used by BLUECHIP, any applicable age or sex restrictions, and a complete definition of the term.

BENEFITS SUBSYSTEM

The Benefits Subsystem is one of BLUECHIP's most critical elements. It contains all the benefit and coverage details specific to each contract, including:

- Deductibles—how much, for which family members, and for which services
- Co-insurance levels—how much the patient pays
- Stop loss points—at which point 100 percent of the cost is reimbursed
- Benefit limitations—exclusions and lifetime maximums on particular services

This subsystem answers two types of questions for BLUECHIP: whether a specific service is covered under a group's contract, and how much of the charge Blue Cross will reimburse.

FULLY AUTOMATED CLAIMS PROCESSING

Taken together, the four subsystems provide BLUECHIP's claims-processing nucleus with all the data needed to process routine claims automatically, without human intervention. This automation results in not only increased efficiency and lower turnaround times, but also fewer errors. And these factors, in turn, mean better service for our members—as well as lower health-care costs for employers.

This automation results in not only increased efficiency and lower turnaround times, but also fewer errors.

FIGURE 14-22.   Brochure Page Design

Southeast Regional Conference on Child Abuse and Neglect

Opryland Hotel • Nashville, Tennessee • November 14–16, 1983

FIGURE 14-23. Cover Design

EXERCISE 5

Imagine that you work for an advertising agency as an account representative. You are preparing to meet with the chairperson of the collection of groups organizing the Southeast Regional Conference on Child Abuse in Nashville. Your designer has just handed you the design for the cover of the conference brochure, shown in Figure 14-23. What strengths can you explain to the chair? How do the layout, logo, and typeface create an image that suits the theme and the atmosphere of the conference? *Make notes for your discussion with the chair.*

EXERCISE 6

Imagine that you are the marketing department manager for Sykes Datatronics, Inc. of Rochester, New York. Your designer has recommended the layout shown in Figure 14-24 for pages in your document catalog, which offers products and current documentation for products to Sykes customers. What do you think of the layout? What do you think of the typefaces? *Explain your reaction to the way this layout suits the audience and uses of the document.*

EXERCISE 7

How many levels does the graphic hierarchy in the résumé have? (See Figure 14-25.) Does it need more levels? What changes would you recommend? Are the present levels consistently used?

GĒNUS-PT™ SYSTEM

The GĒNUS-PT is a compact smart terminal. Engineered to accompany the GĒNUS-GC/3 group computer in a system configuration, the GĒNUS-PT system includes, among its many features, a 14" diagonal, non-glare display screen, a 128 ASCII character set, a graphic character set, and a detachable keyboard. The terminal also has transmit and receive speeds up to 19,200 baud programmable tabs, and bidirectional smooth scrolling.
$75.00

CDA100004 1984
GĒNUS-PT TERMINAL FIELD SERVICE MANUAL

This manual is the hardware manual for the GĒNUS personal terminal. It provides the service technician with removal, replacement, and troubleshooting procedures. It also provides preventive maintenance instructions.
$50.00

9980A5013 1984
GĒNUS-PT OPERATOR'S DOCUMENTATION KIT

This manual provides the terminal operator with site preparation and installation instructions, and instructions on the general operation of the terminal. A section of this document describes the characteristics of the terminal from a programmer's viewpoint for users who wish to program their computer to control terminal functions. The following documents are included in this kit:

- GĒNUS-PT Personal Terminal Quick Reference Card
- GĒNUS-PT Operator's Guide

$55.00

CDA100002 1984
GĒNUS-GC/3 MAINTENANCE MANUAL

Written for the service technician, this manual provides detailed hardware and board circuitry information about the major assemblies of the GĒNUS-GC/3 system. This manual provides a description of assembly and subassembly interaction and operation.
$75.00

CDA100003 1984
GĒNUS-GC/3 PERIPHERAL FIELD SERVICE MANUAL

This manual provides the troubleshooting and preventive maintenance procedures necessary to service the GC/3-HDE and GC/3-MTU peripheral upgrades.
$50.00

CDA100005 1984
GĒNUS-GC/3 SYSTEM REFERENCE MANUAL

This manual is written for the GĒNUS-GC/3 system user who is familiar with programming. It provides an in-depth description of system hardware and software. The system's functional specifications are also covered in this manual.
$75.00

FIGURE 14-24. Catalog Layout

Source: 1984 Catalog, pages 24 and 25. Reprinted by permission of Sykes Datatronics.

Lee DeSoto

80 West Center Street, Suite 603
Akron, Ohio 44308
(216) 376-8755

Objective   A career in Marketing/Sales in a company serving international markets, leading to broader management responsibilities.

Education   Kent State University, Kent, Ohio
Bachelor of Arts, June, 1986
Master of Business Administration, June 1990

Experience   IBM Corporation, Cleveland, Ohio, June 1989 to present
Marketing Sales Assistant
Assist marketing representatives in meeting proposal requirements for commercial and government accounts. Conduct copier demonstrations for prospective customers. Generate sales leads through prospecting, thereby reducing the number of cold calls normally made by marketing representatives.

Akrosil, Division of International Paper Corporation, Menasha, Wisconsin, June 1986 to May 1989
Market Research Assistant
Participated in Kent State University sponsored business seminar in Beijing, China. Conducted market assessment of the Chinese pressure-sensitive adhesive industry. Submitted formal report to Akrosil detailing the status of the pressure sensitive adhesive industry, and the potential for penetrating the Chinese market.

Kent State University, Kent, Ohio, September 1986 to present
Academic advisor
Provided academic counseling for undergraduates in the School of Business as an alumni associate. Organized mock interviews, panel presentations, and career planning workshops.

Other Activities   Member, Alumni Management Association; Chairperson, Professional Development Committee, 1987. Olympics of the Minds coach; awarded first place regional competition, second place state competition, 1986. Junior Achievement Advisor; awarded runner-up company of the year, 1985. Intramural fencing team captain, 1985–1986.

FIGURE 14-25.   Résumé

IF YOU WOULD LIKE TO READ MORE

Erickson, B. (1987). The revolution's on your desk. *Currents, 13,* 14–17.

Figgins, R. (1988). The Gutenberg 2001: What desktop publishing could mean to business communicators. *The Bulletin of the Association for Business Communication, 51*(2), 1–4.

Kramer, D., & Parker, R. C. *Using Aldus PageMaker® 3.0* (2nd ed.).

McCarthy, R. (1988). Stop the presses! An update on desktop publishing. *Electronic Learning, 7,* 24–30.

Murch, G. M. (1985). Using color effectively: Designing to human specifications. *Journal of the Society for Technical Communication, 32,* 14–20.

Nace, T., & Felici, J. (1987). Desktop publishing skills: A primer for typesetting with computers and laser printers. Reading, MA: Addison-Wesley.

Parker, R. C. (1988). *Looking good in print: Basic design for desktop publishing.* Santa Barbara, CA: Ventura Publications.

White, J. V. (1982). *Editing by design* (2nd ed.). New York: R. R. Bowker.

Shriver, K. (1989). Document design from 1980 to 1990: Challenges that remain. *Technical Communication, 36,* 316–331.

NOTES

1. K. Shriver, "Document design from 1980 to 1990: Challenges that remain." *Technical Communication, 36* (1989), 316–331.

2. K. M. Morris, "Electronic publishing: A broader role for simplification." *Technical Communication, 36* (1989), 356–361. Morris's firm is Seigal & Gale Communications, headquartered in Pittsburgh.

3. Morris, 357.

4. A. L. Brown, "Metacognition: The development of selective attention strategies for learning from texts." In H. Singer & R. B. Ruddell (Eds.), *Theoretical models and processes of reading* (3rd ed.), 501–526. Newark, DE: International Reading Association and Erlbaum (1985).

5. P. Anderson, *Technical writing: A reader-centered approach.* San Diego, CA: Harcourt Brace Jovanovich (1987), 454.

6. Paul Anderson pointed out students' perceptions of page designs in their papers during a conversation at a Conference on College Composition and Communication meeting in 1987.

7. Not all word processors have an outlining function. Microsoft Word® offers this option.

8. A summary of the rules of widely used style guides can be found in G. A. Plunka, "The editor's nightmare: Formatting lists within the text." *Technical Communication, 35* (1988), 37–44.

9. G. M. Murch, "Using color effectively: Designing to human specifications." *Technical Communication, 32* (1985), 14–20.

10. This exercise was adapted from P. Moore, "Using the front page of *The Wall Street Journal* to teach document design and audience analysis." *The Bulletin of the Association for Business Communication, 52* (1989)1, 25–26.

GRAPHICS: VISUAL PERSUASION

OBJECTIVES

This chapter will help you

- select ideas that need visual representation

- choose graphics that make your points clear and persuasive

- create graphics for oral presentations and reports

PREVIEW

A graphic is a photo, line drawing, diagram, chart, or other visual that is produced for use in a presentation or printed or electronic document. A graphic gives communicators and their audiences a common reference point that helps them understand one another more quickly and completely than they might through words alone. As you plan your communication, look for opportunities to show visually the nature of your topic, its parts or attributes, frequency of occurrence, change over time, the influences of causes, the rank or priority of one topic over another, and other comparisons.

Graphics not only inform but interpret, and they therefore are an important part of your persuasive strategy. When an audience perceives information visually in a pattern, the pattern establishes the way that each piece is related to the whole. For example, a rising trend line on a graph causes the viewer to see each item or point in the context of that trend. Different types of graphics can make these relationships vivid, or they can obscure them. An effective communicator must learn which types of graphs direct the viewer's attention to the type of comparison or relationship he or she wants to emphasize.

Human perceptual abilities and cultural differences influence how well people read graphics. Some types of displays are more difficult to understand than others; knowing the strengths and weaknesses of different graphic techniques will enable you to create effective graphics for your audiences. You must also, however, take into account the cultural differences that affect how viewers understand graphic aids. For example, "pies" in the United States are round and are cut in wedges, so "pie charts" are easy for U.S. audiences to understand as a representation of a part-to-whole relationship. In countries where pies are baked in squares or rectangles, however, viewers may have had less practice in perceiving wedges as a third, fourth, or fifth of a circle. Thus, you should make your graphics easy to understand and appropriate for the culture of your viewers.

In preparing your graphics, you should create a graphic hierarchy and labels that help your viewers understand the main point immediately. Each graphic should have only one point; graphics shouldn't do "double duty." Message headings or titles, complete labeling, balanced composition or design, data that relate only to the main point, and a unified design will help your viewer get the message quickly. When your presentation or document contains several graphics, the set should be consistent in design and sufficiently varied to stimulate interest. Many technical advances in computer graphics programs allow business communicators to prepare graphics easily.

❑ NEW TECHNOLOGIES FOR GRAPHICS

New technological advances in film, video, photography, photocopying, facsimile transmission, digital scanning, and computers have supplemented or replaced many familiar manual and mechanical processes. These tools, especially computers, have enabled people to express their ideas with visual designs called "graphics." This term once referred either to techniques of print-making or to representations of numerical data, such as charts. Today the term "graphics" not only expresses both of these earlier meanings but also refers to the many products of new electronic processes. Overhead transparencies, 35mm slides, bar charts, line drawings, flip charts, and handouts based on projected computer images are all called "graphics."

Graphics can enable business communicators to analyze relationships or trends. Other courses, such as quantitative methods, psychology, and statistics, will instruct you in the use of analytical graphics.

❑ GRAPHICS PERSUADE

Graphics, whether pictorial or statistical, persuade partly because they convey culturally prescribed meanings. In U.S. culture, a rising diagonal is traditionally "good"; downward verticals or diagonals are "bad," suggesting losses, deficits, or declines. Such lines are read from left to right. "Mountain charts," as they are called in financial marketing departments, are assumed to have a strongly motivating effect on investors (see Figure 15-1). Different sizes in similar items suggest differences in power, value, or importance. A mere glance activates an attitude toward the information in the figure. Well-known brand logos also stimulate automatic responses. Parents everywhere know the power of McDonald's "Golden Arches." You will draw on these cultural expectations as you implement your persuasive appeal with graphics.

Persuasive Appeals and Graphic Strategies

What's Your Persuasive Strategy?

By the time you are ready to choose graphics, you will have already analyzed your audiences and developed a communication strategy. Part of your communication strategy is your persuasive appeal (discussed in Chapter 4). Imagine a situation in which you must convince a manager she should adopt a different cost accounting system. To succeed, you must persuade her the old one is insufficient and that the new one will yield important benefits. Your graphics should support each of these key persuasive functions: illustrate the problem, identify its cause, and demonstrate the benefits of the solution you propose.

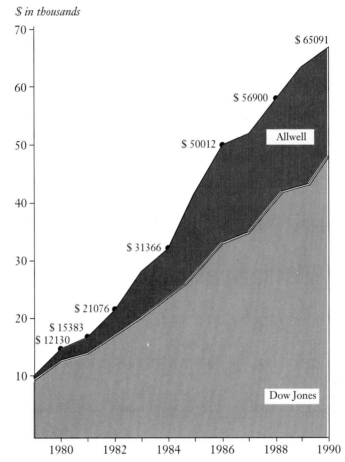

Allwell Fund Total Return Performance

$10,000 Invested in Allwell Fund vs. Dow Jones Industrials Average Reinvested

$ in thousands

$ 65091

$ 56900

Allwell

$ 50012

$ 31366

$ 21076

$ 15383

$ 12130

Dow Jones

1980   1982   1984   1986   1988   1990

This chart illustrates the growth of $10,000 invested in the Allwell Fund on January 1, 1979 to $65,091 on March 31, 1990 and the growth of $10,000 invested in the Dow Jones Industrial Average on January 1, 1979 to $48,232 on March 31, 1990.

FIGURE 15-1.   *"Mountain Chart" Showing Long-Term Positive Trend*

GUIDELINES FOR PERSUASIVE GRAPHICS

Implementing a Persuasive Appeal with Graphics

If you can create a feeling of discrepancy or dissonance that suggests an important uncertainty and a need for action, then the audience will be more motivated to reduce the dissonance through the action you request. A photo of the problem, perhaps a person standing at a photocopier that isn't working properly or a column chart showing decreasing revenues compared with anticipated revenues, can make the reader believe the problem is worth addressing.

If you can associate your request or proposal with something the reader already values or feels strongly about, you can use that association to encourage the same attitude toward your request. A photograph of a prior event or an image associated with that event (such as a trophy, logo, or tool used in the event) can recall shared experiences and values.

How would the reader or listener finish a statement beginning, "Yes, but . . ."? What is the hinge or crux of the situation? A graphic that can directly address the crucial concern may help. If you believe the audience's main resistance will be "Where will the money come from?" a graphic that deals with that question should be prepared. Place this graphic early in the presentation or report. For example, if your department wants new software and if you have two VAX computers that you intend to sell and replace with two less expensive machines, you might use a graphic titled "Margin from VAX sale will fund software purchase" early in your presentation.

Is the audience predisposed to do what you request? A graphic that recalls a historic declaration of purpose or that illustrates a value the audience is known to rank high can associate this predisposition with your proposal or idea.

Is your relationship with this audience strong? Images of groups or symbols of groups can call up images of solidarity. The repetition of a logo on slides and reports can remind audiences of motivating relationships.

❏ SELECT IDEAS THAT NEED VISUAL REPRESENTATION

Some ideas need representation more than others. If the audience (meaning either listeners or readers) is unfamiliar with the subject, you should choose graphics that illustrate the subject. A photo, line drawing, diagram, or word slide may be used for this purpose. As suggested, some ideas must be accepted (such as "funds are available") before the audience will be persuaded of your conclusion. Such ideas and their support should be reinforced by visuals if possible. The following table, a repetition of the table in Chapter 14 (see page 346), shows the many types of graphics that you might use in your storyboard to support these points.

The placement of these illustrations on the page, described in Chapter 14, directs the reader's attention, expands and reinforces the reader's understanding of the topic, and increases the efficiency of the communication. This chapter explains how to plan and prepare graphics for oral presentations and reports, including graphics based on data.

Illustrations Suited to Different Types of Argument Points

POINT TO BE ILLUSTRATED	PHOTO	LINE DRAWING	DIA-GRAM	FLOW CHART	BAR CHART	LINE GRAPH	COLUMN CHART	PIE CHART	PICTO-GRAM	DOT CHART	COMPONENT DIAGRAM
Nature of the topic	•	•	•						•		
Frequency of occurrence						•	•			•	
Change over time	•			•	•	•	•				
Causes of the topic	•			•		•					
Consequences of the topic	•		•	•		•					•
Rank of the topic					•						
Comparison with others	•				•	•		•			•
Correlation with others										•	
Subject in a field	•	•									•
Attribute or interpretation of the topic	•	•							•		
Parts of the topic	•	•	•					•			•

Planning Graphics

Use Storyboards to Plan the Series

In preparing your communication strategy and organizing your ideas, you will already have created a structure for your presentation or document (as explained in Chapter 5). If you are preparing an oral presentation, your next step is to prepare your storyboards. If you are preparing a report or other written document, you may already have completed a preliminary draft, or you can prepare a special version of storyboards as the basis of both your writing and your graphics preparation.

Storyboards display both your main points and your graphics, so that you can see the logic of the whole presentation or document and the figures or overheads it will contain. The column on the left of the page allows for a main point and supporting points to be displayed, as shown in Figure 15-2. If you have used an issue tree to organize your ideas, its branches will fit horizontally on the storyboard, rather like an outline, as shown in Figure 15-3. The column on the right will enable you to sketch miniature graphics that correspond to your argument points. Some of your visuals will be word slides; others may be photos, diagrams, line drawings of products or equipment, maps, organization charts and such. Still others will present interpretations of data you have analyzed.

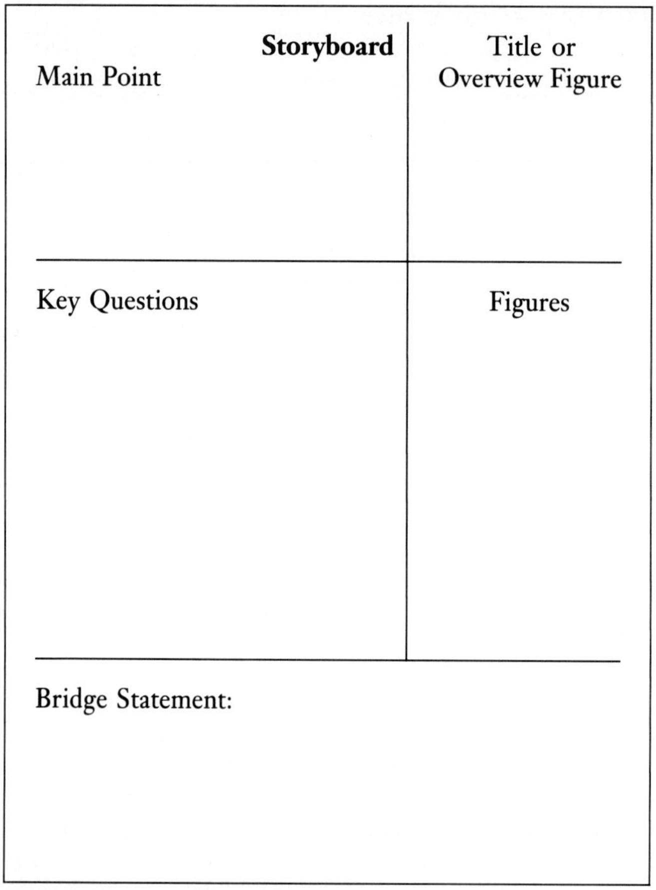

Storyboard	
Main Point	Title or Overview Figure
Key Questions	Figures

Bridge Statement:

FIGURE 15-2.   Sample Storyboard Form

Don't expect one graphic to support several points. Professional consultants and designers recommend that each graphic, whether a slide, overhead, or flip chart, answer only one question (or make one point). Furthermore, they recommend that the answer or point be made part of the title of the slide or overhead. Where a series of points must be logically linked, separate overheads can present each point and a summary overhead can illustrate the relationships among them.

Place the storyboard sheets side by side, or overlap them, showing the right-hand columns, to see the visual structure of the presentation. If too many visuals are words only or if you have too many graphs without a word slide to summarize points, you will be able to detect these problems and introduce more variety or more help for your listeners and readers. In the series of storyboards for presentation of a new smoking policy (shown in Figure 15-4), the sketches for the conclusion of the talk are all word slides, a boring finish. A picture of healthy employees competing in a softball game and wearing T-shirts with the company logo might convincingly depict the health benefits of nonsmoking for company employees.

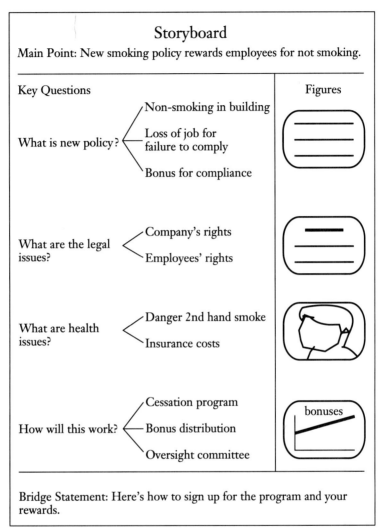

Storyboard

Main Point: New smoking policy rewards employees for not smoking.

Key Questions

What is new policy?
- Non-smoking in building
- Loss of job for failure to comply
- Bonus for compliance

What are the legal issues?
- Company's rights
- Employees' rights

What are health issues?
- Danger 2nd hand smoke
- Insurance costs

How will this work?
- Cessation program
- Bonus distribution
- Oversight committee

Figures

bonuses

Bridge Statement: Here's how to sign up for the program and your rewards.

FIGURE 15-3.   Completed Storyboard

Plan Presentation Graphics That Reveal Your Organization and Overall Plan

If you are planning an oral presentation, make sure your storyboards include graphics that preview the overall structure and that remind the audience of where you are in the presentation. Unlike readers, listeners cannot reread earlier statements to remind themselves of the speaker's purpose and organization. Therefore, presenters should use graphics that announce the structure of the presentation in advance and that periodically remind the listener where the speaker is in the overall presentation. These graphics serve much the same purpose as headings in a report.

The New Nonsmoking Policy Rewards Employees

- What is the new policy?

- How will the program work?

- How will employees receive bonuses?

Knowing the structure helps listeners place each piece of information in a larger pattern. You can keep the larger pattern in view with several techniques:

- Use a separate, stationary image to display the outline of the presentation, such as a flip chart, poster, overhead on a separate projector, outline on a blackboard, or handout.

- When you come to a new section of the presentation, show the headings for earlier and later sections in a subdued tone on overheads or slides. Put the point now to be discussed in a bright color or in boldfaced letters.

- Choose an icon that represents the pattern of ideas in your presentation, such as a series of arrows, a path, or other images.

Effective Word Graphics

The most important thing you can do to make an effective word graphic is to write "answer titles" that express an answer to a question about the topic. Instead of "First Quarter Sales," say "First Quarter Sales Increased" (the answer to "What happened to first quarter sales?" Instead of "Expansion Risks," say "Expansion Risks Can Be Managed." This technique allows you to focus on your results and to subordinate the analytical machinery behind the results (as explained in Chapter 13, "Writing Reports").

Word graphics need a coherent hierarchy to tell the viewer which ideas are most important (see Chapter 14). Use larger letters or letters with a different type treatment (such as bold) in the title. Help the audience recognize the meaning of the words by using initial caps only, not all caps. A single capitalized word followed by words all in lowercase helps the viewer grasp the meaning of the whole heading.

This: **Expansion risks can be managed**
Or this: **Expansion Risks Can Be Managed**
Not this: **EXPANSION RISKS CAN BE MANAGED**

As a rule of thumb, titles of more than five words usually should not be set in all capital letters.

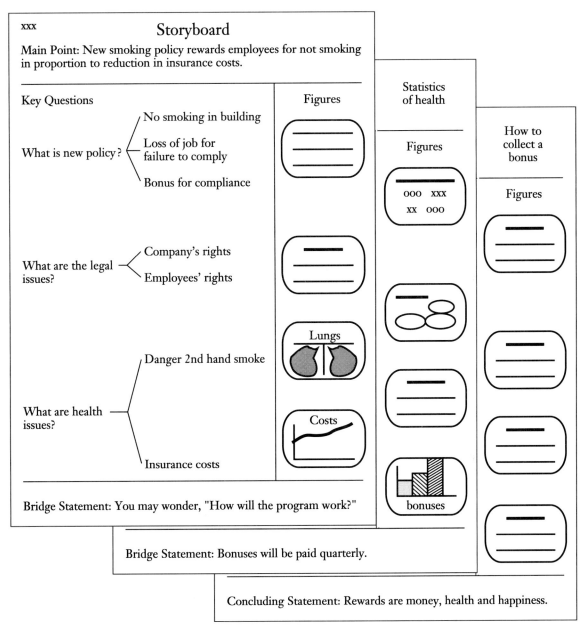

FIGURE 15-4. Storyboards Arranged to Show Series of Graphics

Don't use too many words in your title; strive for precision and conciseness. Agent/action/result clauses are easy to remember, whereas cluttered word graphics are hard to remember. If you are using color in word graphics, choose combinations of colors that do not compete for the reader's attention, and use color sparingly (see page 388 in this chapter).

❑ PREPARING GRAPHICS

Steps in Implementing Your Plan

Your storyboards probably contain many sorts of graphics. Since everything from photos to flow charts can now be incorporated in computer-processed documents and presentations, people use more types of illustrations than they did when multiple mechanical processes were required. The nine steps that follow describe the overall preparation process for computer and mechanical graphics. The next section gives more specific instructions for dealing with those graphics that require traditional charts based on analyzed data, such as bar charts, column charts, line graphs, and dot charts.

Design Background Frames

Your first step is to create the backgrounds for different types of overheads and slides shown on your storyboard. Your computer graphics program may contain templates or preset design choices, such as those shown in Figure 15-5. The overall design should frame the graphic and present a coherent and consistent framework for all the overheads in the series. If you choose different templates for different kinds of messages or graphics, these should be coordinated in color, typeface, and general design to create coherence for the presentation as a whole. Try to use either a horizontal or a vertical format without mixing the two. Follow a policy about where you position the company logo. Choose an overall "look" that suits the company and the topic. Don't use an "old fashioned" fancy border for an industrial company or childlike drawings for a bank.

If you are working without a computer, design a background frame and make several good photocopies on which you can press down letters and prepare charts. An art supply store can provide you with tapes that are lines of various widths. These can be applied to the paper on which the design is developed. Special overhead transparencies can be fed through a photocopier. You can also obtain transparent tapes that will adhere directly to the transparency and colored pens (both permanent and temporary) for writing on transparencies.

The frame should not compete with the message. The border should not be so wide that the viewer's eyes jump back and forth from the message to the frame. Position the information, figure, or chart to lead the reader's eye. Notice that in Figure 15-6(a), the centered design tends to maintain attention on the title as well as the three points, whereas the left-to-right design in Figure 15-6(b) tends to lead the eye to the three points only. The left-to-right diagonal is not appropriate for this overhead, since the information does not stand alone and is really a subset of the claim about the review of activities in 1991.

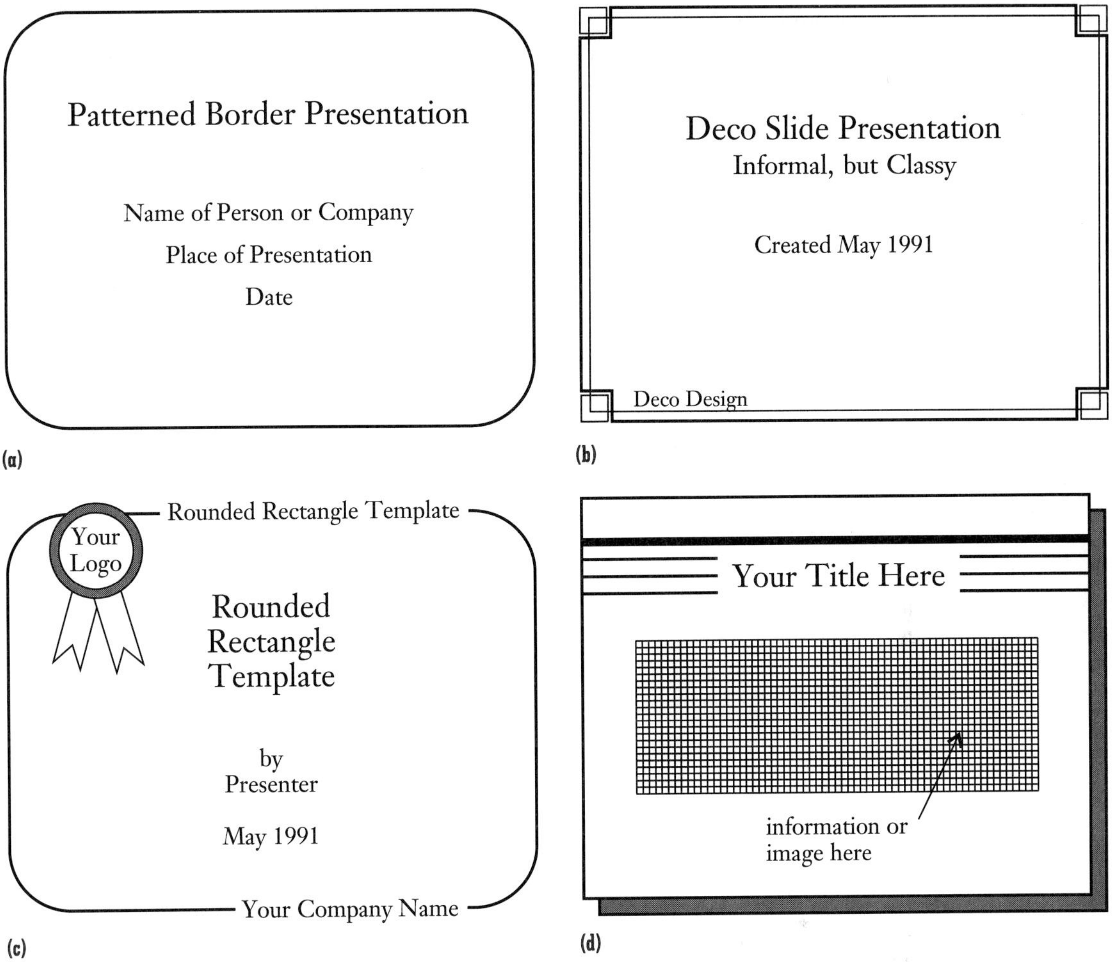

(a)

(b)

(c)

(d)

FIGURE 15-5. **Templates for Overheads**

Source: *Using PowerPoint Templates,* © 1988 Microsoft Corporation. Reprinted by permission of Microsoft Corporation.

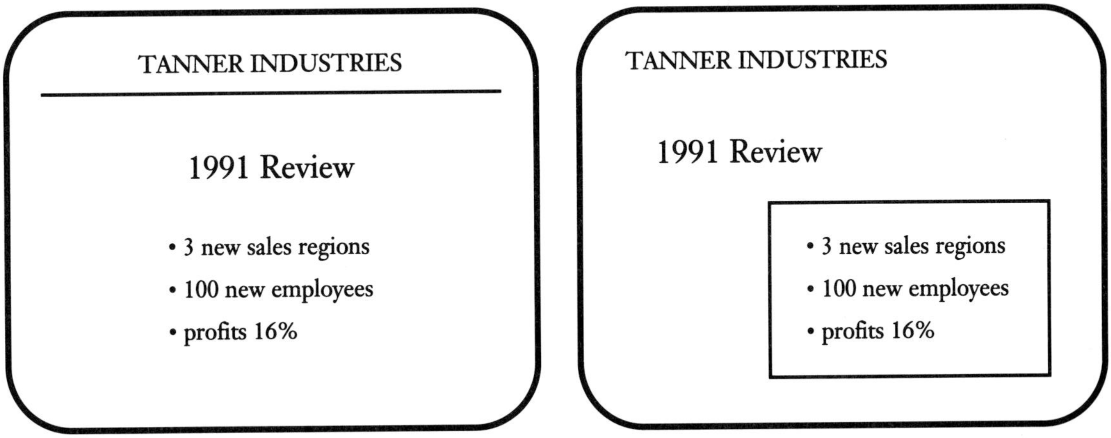

(a) Centered design

(b) Left-to-right design

FIGURE 15-6. Overhead Design

Create a Graphic Hierarchy in Type Styles and Line Widths

- The title should go at the top and should be approximately twice as high in point size as the rest of the type in the overhead.
- Use different type treatments (bold, italics, underlined, and so forth) and different point sizes of the same font, instead of mixing fonts.
- If you do change fonts, use fonts that are compatible: fonts that have similar letter shapes, x-heights, and so forth (see Chapter 14).
- Use a heading that reinforces the spoken message; don't substitute a technical term in the overhead for a more general term to be used in the talk.

Choose lines or rules of different widths, representing the most important element with the widest line. For example, in a graph the following items would have different widths that reflect their differing importance.

The chart line	wide
The axes for the chart	medium width
The grid or tick marks	narrow

The Display Should Dominate the Overhead and Coordinate Well with the Title

Compare the two designs in Figures 15-7(a) and 15-7(b).

Present Only Essential Data Needed to Support the Point You Are Making, and Group Data Not Pertinent to the Main Point under a General Heading

Information that is not pertinent to the point you are making will distract the audience. Don't include information in a graphic that you are not going to discuss or that you don't want the audience to consider. Group the data that do not pertain to your point under a general heading, such as "other expenses."

Leave Enough Room within Areas or Boxes

When you enclose text within a box or place it in an area, leave some room around the text. This is important for technical reasons if you are making slides with a computer, because when film recorders process your computer-generated slide they reproduce it slightly differently than the laser printer does. The characters will expand during the processing. Leaving space around the text will prevent the text from overflowing the box during the transformation from computer disk to film.

In a Bar Chart or Column Chart, Juxtapose Bars/Columns or Make the Bars Wider than the Spaces between Them

When bars or columns are the same width as the spaces between them, an optical illusion occurs that makes it hard to distinguish the bar and the space. Figure 15-8 presents RMI's total sales revenue. Compare the difference in effect when the bar size is the same as the space between bars.

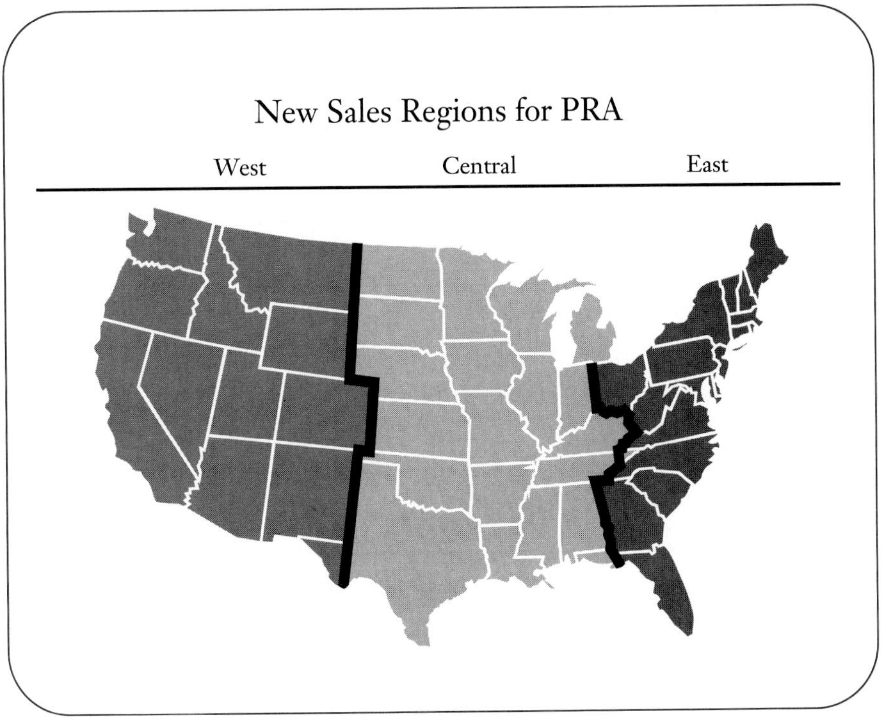

New Sales Regions for PRA

West Central East

(a) Display dominates space

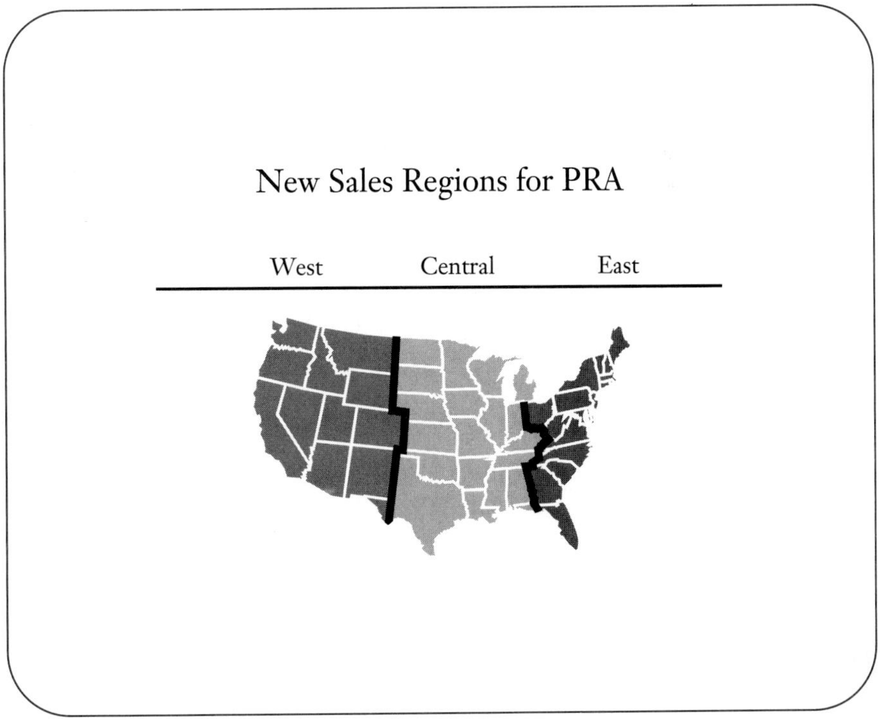

New Sales Regions for PRA

West Central East

(b) Display is lost in background

FIGURE 15-7. Fitting the Display Properly

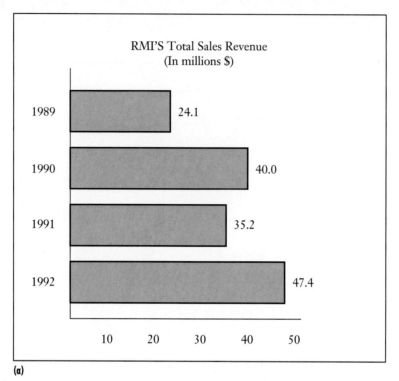

(a)

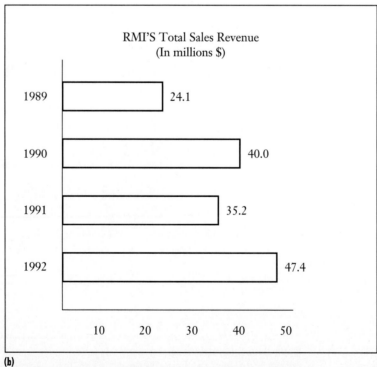

(b)

FIGURE 15-8.   Effects of Bar Width

Eliminate Data Points to Emphasize the Shape of the Trend

Unless readers will be interested in specific data points, eliminate them and use a line to show the shape of the trend. Dot charts with a great many data points can be confusing.

Emphasize Answers to Questions with Color, Arrows, Boldfacing

Direct the reader's attention to key information with color, arrows, and other devices that make the graphic easier to read. For slide presentations in a darkened room, use bright type on a darker background. For colored overhead presentations in a normal room light, use dark type on light backgrounds. We have used an arrow on the deviation column chart in Figure 15-13(d) to pinpoint key information.

Accommodating Human Perceptual Abilities

Researchers have been studying human perceptual skills to determine which kinds of graphics are easiest for human beings to interpret. Naturally, the audience's familiarity with a particular type of graphic will influence the ease or difficulty of the task for any particular person, but all audiences tend to find some tasks easier than others. The research findings shown here can provide a framework for planning and evaluating graphic designs. One guide, "make the data stand out," is sometimes expressed as "maximize the data/ink ratio." To a professional designer, this phrase means that one should spend ink on representing the data, not on decorating the graphic area with distracting grids, lines, and so forth. Since many factors (including color and pattern) contribute to distraction, we have settled on "make the data stand out." Unnecessary and distracting decoration or background is called "chartjunk."[1]

How Audiences Interpret Graphics

AUDIENCES' VISUAL SCANNING	ELEMENTARY PERCEPTUAL TASKS
1. Varies with complexity of display	Ordered tasks from most to least accurate:
2. Varies with distinguishability of items in the display	1. Position along a common scale
3. Increases linearly with information load	2. Position on identical nonaligned scales
	3. Length, direction, angle
	4. Area
	5. Volume, curvature
	6. Shading, color saturation

> ## GUIDELINES FOR EVALUATING GRAPHICAL DISPLAYS
>
> 1. Is a graph the best way to present the data?
> 2. Is the search task as simple as possible?
>
>   - label clearly
>   - make data stand out
>   - reduce clutter
>
> 3. Are the elementary perceptual tasks required of the viewer easy (high in the ordered list of tasks)?
>
> ---
>
> Source: Cochran, J. K., Albrecht, S. A., & Green, Y. A. (1989). Guidelines for evaluating graphical designs: A framework based on human perception skills. *Technical Communication: Journal of the Society for Technical Communication, 36,* 27.

Figure 15-9, a graph from Société Nationale Elf Aquitaine's 1988 Annual Report, illustrates the difficulties volume, curvature, and shading can create for viewers. The design attracts attention, but is hard to use and interpret.

Don't display one-dimensional information in a two-dimensional form (such as area). Pictographs are notoriously misleading for exactly this reason. Such distortion misleads readers and viewers. The design of the student-produced overhead in Figure 15-10 is supposed to indicate a change in one dimension, amounts sold. The area of the largest pictograph is deceptively greater than the vertical multiple.

❑ TRADITIONAL GRAPHICS: PRESENTING ANALYZED DATA

As we said earlier, one meaning of "graphics" in earlier periods was "displays of numerical data." Many business graphics still are devoted to presenting numerical data, and learning how to choose and execute different types of charts is still useful.

Plan Your Message

Clarify the Question and Select Appropriate Data

Good graphics must rest on good data. To choose data wisely, you must define exactly the question you are trying to answer for your audience. Poor graphics are likely to be the result of vague definitions and poor information choices. Sometimes the data at hand do not fit the needs of the decision maker or the situation. Once the definitions and assumptions have been clarified, it may be easier to find useful data. When graphics are asked to serve the wrong purposes, no amount of design sophistication can compensate for the inadequacy. *The single most important piece of advice in this chapter is to title your graphic with more*

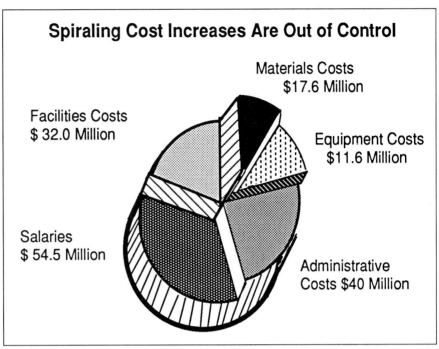

FIGURE 15-9. Graph That Does Not Accommodate Human Perceptual Abilities

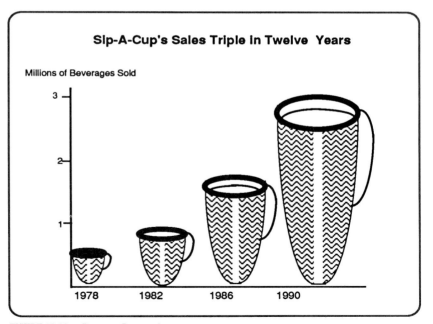

FIGURE 15-10. Deceptive Pictograph

FOCUS ON CHOOSING COLORS

Because color is a physical sensation, color choices should be made on the basis of human perceptual sensitivities and interpretive processes. Human beings react strongly to hue and saturation. Hue is the sensation of discernable color; humans can perceive colors across a spectrum ranging from violet (short wavelength, 400 nm) to red (long wavelength, 700 nm). Saturation is related to the number of wavelengths contributing to a color sensation. As the band of wavelengths narrows, the resulting color sensation becomes more saturated—the wider the band, the less saturated the color. Gerald Murch offers the following guidelines for choosing colors.

Use Color to Accommodate Human Perception

1. *Avoid the simultaneous display of highly saturated, spectrally extreme colors.* Reds, oranges, yellows, and greens can be viewed together without refocusing, but blues cannot be easily viewed simultaneously with red. Avoid using extreme color pairs such as red and blue or yellow and purple, which require frequent refocusing and cause visual fatigue.

2. *Avoid pure blue for text, thin lines, and small shapes.* Our visual system is just not set up for detailed, sharp, short-wavelength stimuli. However, blue makes a good background color.

3. *Avoid adjacent colors that differ only in the amount of blue.* Edges that differ only in the amount of blue will appear indistinct.

4. *Older viewers need higher brightness levels to distinguish colors.*

5. *Colors change appearance as ambient light level changes.* Displays change color under different kinds of ambient light—fluorescent, incandescent, or daylight.

6. *The magnitude of a detectable change in color varies across the spectrum.* Small changes in extreme reds and purples are more difficult to detect than small changes in other colors. Also, our visual system does not readily perceive changes in green.

7. *Difficulty in focusing results from edges created by color alone.* Our visual system depends on a brightness difference at an edge to effect clear focusing.

8. *Avoid red and green in the periphery of large-scale displays.* Avoid red and green especially for small symbols and shapes. Yellow and blue are good peripheral colors.

9. *Opponent colors go well together.* Red and green or yellow and blue are good combinations for simple displays.

10. *For observers with color vision difficulties, avoid single-color distinctions.* Colors that differ only in the amount of red or green added or subtracted from the two other primaries may prove difficult to distinguish.

Use Color to Make Interpretation Easy

1. *Do not overuse color.* The benefits of color as an attention-getter, information-grouper, and value-assigner are lost if too many colors are used.

2. *Group related elements by using a common background color.* You can prepare the user for related events by using a common color code. A successive set of images can be shown to be related by using the same background color.

3. *Similar colors connote similar meanings.* Elements related in some way can convey that message through the degree in similarity of hue.

4. *Use brightness and saturation to draw attention.* The brightest and most highly saturated area of a color display immediately draws the viewer's attention.

5. *Link the degree of color change to event magnitude.* Make the degree of change in profits and losses, for example, distinct through color change.

6. *Order colors by the spectral position.* To increase the number of colors on a display requires imposing a meaningful order to the colors. The most obvious order is that provided by the spectrum. Use the mnemonic ROY G. BIV (red, orange, yellow, green, blue, indigo, violet) to remember the order of the colors.

7. *Warm and cold colors should indicate action levels.* Traditionally, the warm (long-wavelength) colors are used to signify action or the requirement for a response. Cool colors, on the other hand, indicate status or background information. Most people also experience warm colors advancing toward them—hence, forcing attention—and cool colors receding or drawing away.

Adapted with permission from G. M. Murch. (1985). Using color effectively: Designing to human specifications. *Technical Communication: Journal of the Society for Technical Communication, 32,* 14–20.

than the topic; tell the reader the point you are making or the question you are answering. Then, the viewer can make a better determination of whether the data fit the question.

Is There a Comparison in Your Message?

Gene Zelazny of McKinsey & Company has pointed out that most of the messages based on data analysis involve *comparisons:* component comparisons, item ranking comparisons, time series comparisons, frequency distribution comparisons, or correlation comparisons.[2] If you enter a career that will require you to create graphics frequently, you would do well to study Zelazny's book, *Say It with Charts.* Once you have identified the type of comparison involved, you can choose the graphic that will most effectively illustrate that comparison. First, we will review the definitions of these five comparisons and suggest how to recognize them.

Component Comparisons Component comparisons are also called "part-to-whole" comparisons. When a part is divided by the whole, the result is a percentage. Zelazny suggests that you look for phrases in your message that suggest percentages of the whole.[3] Such phrases include "share," "percentage of the total," or "X percentage of *New Woman*'s readers graduated from college."

Item Ranking Comparisons When you focus on the comparative rank of items, you want to know whether one is larger, smaller, or about the same as another item. The ranking may be determined by relative cost, size, value, newness, or some other feature. Look for phrases in your message such as "equal to," "bigger than," "less than," or "first, second, third," as in "Honda ranks first in sales in Nevada."

Time Series Comparisons Familiar phrases that indicate trends or change over time signal time series comparisons.[4] Look for phrases such as "have increased in the third quarter," "have fallen in the last month," or "steady growth" as signals of a time series comparison. "Abbot Laboratories' dividends increased annually for eight years."

Frequency Distribution Comparisons Frequency distributions are one of the most basic of all analytical comparisons. They show how many items fall within the boundaries of succeeding numerical ranges. Knowing how the values of a variable are distributed can be very useful. If your message contains phrases such as "distribution of," "the majority of X," or "fall equally in Y categories," probably you are dealing with a frequency distribution comparison. A sample is "The majority of April catalogue purchases were in the $150–$200 range."

Correlation Comparisons Correlations attempt to confirm a relationship between two variables. The trigger words for such comparisons include "relationship between," "varies with," "increases with," or "fluctuates with," as in "purchase satisfaction increases with customer education level."

This would be a good time to test your understanding of these five types of comparisons by analyzing some messages in preliminary exercise 1 in the Communication Challenges.

Choose Charts That Suit Your Message

Once you have identified the comparison implicit in the message, you must choose the best kind of chart to present that message. Designers for annual reports and special marketing materials may offer you innovative special effects that we will not discuss in this chapter, which sticks to the basic rules. However, be wary of choosing an elaborate artistic representation unless it satisfies basic criteria of legibility, simplicity, and consistency in the graphic hierarchy. This chapter sticks to the basic chart forms: the pie chart; bar chart, column chart, line graph, and correlation chart. Use the table below to identify the charts suited to your message.

TYPES OF CHARTS USED TO SHOW COMPARISONS

Type of Comparison	Type of Chart
Component comparison	Pie chart, component bar chart
Unit comparison	Bar chart
Time series comparison	Column chart, line graph
Frequency distribution comparison	Column chart, line graph
Correlation comparison	Dot graph, deviation bar chart

Component Comparisons: Pie Charts

People are familiar with cutting pies into servings, so the circular "pie chart" has long served as an easy method of representing parts of the whole. Remember that people have trouble visualizing more pieces than one would ordinarily cut from a pie: six to eight are the maximum and three to four are better. If you have more than eight components, try to combine components or lump those that are of little individual importance into a category called "other."

Furthermore, you should only represent those items that you actually intend to discuss in your argument. For example, if you wish to show that Instant Quaker Oatmeal has a 46 percent share of the instant hot cereals market, you will do well to lump all the other instant hot cereals together as "other cereals," unless you want to prompt a discussion of why each of the competitors has the particular share it has. If your point is to show that Instant Quaker Oatmeal has a bigger share of the market than last year or that the share has grown steadily over the last five years, you should go directly to the item comparison (this year versus last year) or to the time series comparison that would express those ideas.

If you choose a pie chart, begin the division of the pie with a vertical line that runs from the center of the pie to the top. People are accustomed to measuring proportions from a visual anchor, and this vertical line is the visual anchor for a pie chart. Arrange the parts from smallest to largest, beginning with the visual anchor, as shown in Figure 15-11. If you need your audience to recog-

Instant Quaker Oatmeal has 46%
of the Instant Hot Cereal Market

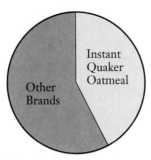

FIGURE 15-11.   Pie Chart Showing Component Comparison

nize small differences, choose a bar chart instead, because human beings can compare line lengths against a scale more accurately than they can compare areas, especially those bound by curves and angles in combination (see the table "How Audiences Interpret Graphics," on page 385).[5] Avoid using many contrasting textures or patterns for the components. If only one component is the point of the comparison, draw attention to that component with shading or by "exploding" the pie wedge. Many computer programs automatically fill the component wedges with contrasting patterns that actually make the comparison harder to evaluate. If you have to use such a program, it may well be worth the time to recreate the chart in a program that gives you more control over the shading, color, line widths, and other techniques, such as Cricket Draw® or Harvard™ Graphics.

Unit Comparisons: Bar Charts

Unit comparisons rank the items according to some criterion. Horizontal bar charts and vertical column charts are usually used for this purpose. On a horizontal bar chart, a scale may be presented on the horizontal axis; the vertical axis is simply the line on which the various items being compared are placed. If there is no horizontal scale, place numbers at the ends of the bars. Make the spaces between the bars narrower than the bars themselves. Label each bar. Because bars are shown horizontally, it is easier to label the bars than it is to label vertical columns.

As you begin to transform your message into a graphic, remember the situation and the questions you need to answer. Suppose that your firm sold its chief product in Canada as well as in the United States. Your management might want answers to the following questions:

Are our total sales increasing or declining?

Are there different trends in our sales in the two countries, or are the sales trends the same?

What is the relationship between the sales in the U.S. and the sales in Canada?

You have the opportunity to make two different types of comparisons simultaneously: comparisons over time and comparisons between countries.

In this situation, divided bar charts can be helpful. If the divided bars are arranged along a vertical axis, the components may be distinguished by shading or with letters. You may show the total annual sales for the two countries on separate bars, dividing each bar into the U.S. and Canadian sales components, as shown in Figure 15-12(a). This version makes it more obvious to the viewer that total sales in 1991 and 1992 have been less than the total in 1990, because it is easy for viewers to contrast the totals with the single scale of the bottom axis.

A second option, shown in Figure 15-12(b), is to align the components of each divided bar along a central vertical axis, creating a deviation bar chart. In this version the shift in the source of sales from Canada to the U.S. is more obvious, but the decline in the total sales since 1990, which was easily seen in Figure 15-12(a), is not as visually obvious.

A third type of bar chart, the grouped bar chart, is shown in Figure 15-12(c). The grouped bar chart will help your viewers or readers compare the differences between U.S. and Canadian sales for each year as they look at each pair, but this chart does not invite the viewer to look at all the bars of a single color quite as much, and so in this version neither the trend in total sales nor the proportional shift from Canada to the U.S. is quite as obvious.

Time Series Comparisons: Column Charts and Line Graphs

Time series comparisons may be illustrated either with column charts or with line graphs, depending on the type of data. Time is always plotted along the horizontal axis or "baseline." Choose between a column chart and a line graph as follows:

- If you have only a few points of data, such as the total annual sales figures for four consecutive years, represent each sales total with a vertical column.
- If you have many data points, use a line graph. For example, if you are plotting the weekly average price per share of a mutual fund for a four-year period, you will have over 200 data points, which are best represented by a line, not by 208 columns (see Figure 15-1).

Column Charts   Vertical column charts should be labeled, and the space between columns should be narrower than the columns themselves. Since it is hard for people to estimate the exact amount represented on most vertical scales, most people appreciate having the columns labeled with exact amounts (rounded off to whole numbers, of course). Column charts, like bar charts, may be stepped, grouped, divided, or shown as a deviation along one axis to facilitate comparison, as shown in Figure 15-13(a–d). A special form of vertical column chart used in business is the range column chart, which shows the spread between low

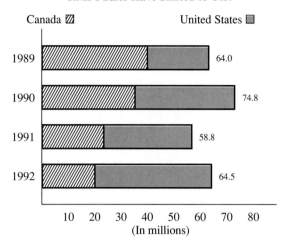

(In this version it is more obvious that total sales have declined since 1990)

(a) Divided bar chart

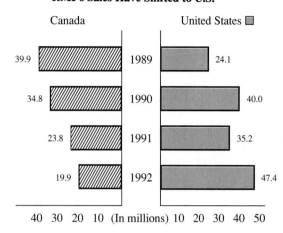

(In this version the shift in source of sales is obvious, the decline is not)

(b) Deviation bar chart

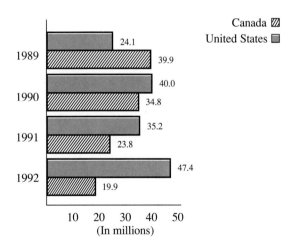

(In this version neither the trend nor the decline is especially obvious)

(c) Grouped bar chart

FIGURE 15-12. Variations on the Bar Chart

Most Telephone Orders Are Between $100 and $150

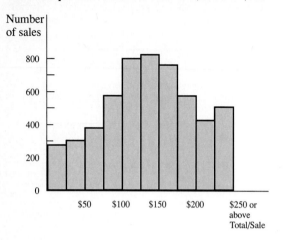

(a) **Stepped column chart**

Larger Telephone Orders Include Women's Clothing

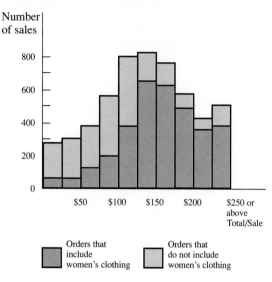

(b) **Divided column chart**

Franconia Sales Exceed Oreton Sales

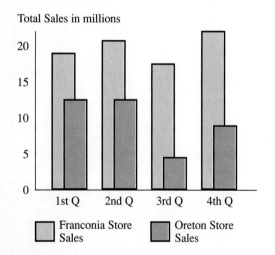

(c) **Grouped column chart**

FIGURE 15-13.   **Variations of the Column Chart**

Telephone Sales Have Revived Profits

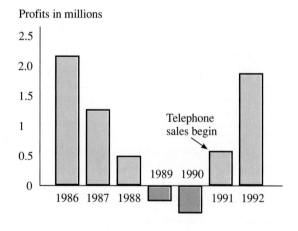

(d) **Deviation column chart**

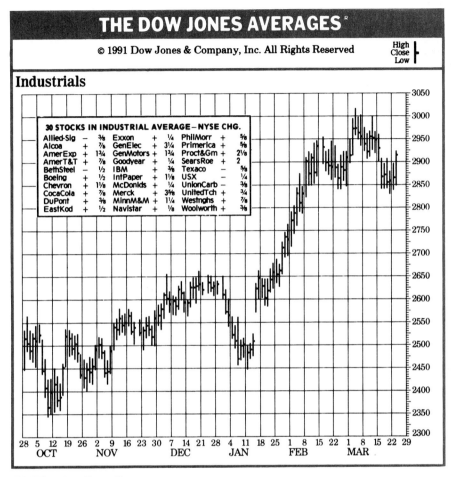

FIGURE 15-14.   Range Chart

Source: Reprinted by permission of *The Wall Street Journal*, November 18, 1989, © Dow Jones and Company, 1989. All rights reserved worldwide.

and high amounts, such as the low and the high price of a stock on a particular day or for a particular period. In range charts, such as the one shown in Figure 15-14, the average may be shown with a line or dot across the column or bar.

Line Graphs   Line graphs show change over time or compare trends, and therefore the line that represents the data points should stand out more than the base line (which shows the time scale) or the vertical line (which shows the amounts on the vertical axis). Any grid needed to help audiences judge amounts of change should be light (faint) in comparison to the width of the trend line. This is shown in Figure 15-15(a) and (b).

Since an audience cannot easily follow many trends at once, especially if the data points overlap, you should limit the number of trends shown on any one chart. Two are much easier for an audience to relate to than three; three are

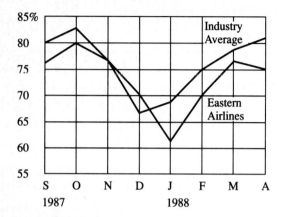

**Eastern Airlines' On-time Performance
Lagged Industry Averages in Early 1988**

Percentage of flights arriving within 15 minutes of
scheduled arrival time

Source: Department of Transportation

(a) Line graph without hierarchy of line widths

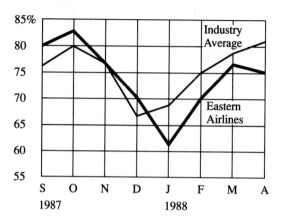

**Eastern Airlines' On-time Performance
Lagged Industry Averages in Early 1988**

Percentage of flights arriving within 15 minutes of
scheduled arrival time

Source: Department of Transportation

(b) Line graph with hierarchy of line widths

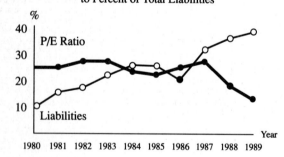

Increasing Risk at ArtCo
ArtCo's Price/Earnings Ratio Declines Relative
to Percent of Total Liabilities

(c) Cluttered line graph

FIGURE 15-15.   Line Graph Types

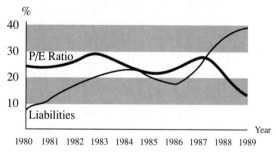

Increasing Risk at ArtCo
ArtCo's Price/Earnings Ratio Declines Relative
to Percent of Total Liabilities

(d) Smoothed line graph

easier than four; and more than four trend lines begin to look like earthworms
covering a grate. A series of graphs that pair one trend with each of several other
trends is usually much more illuminating than the earthworm pile. The key
trend line should dominate. Too many data point representations on the line
make the line look like a lost necklace and interrupt the viewer's perception of
the line as a whole, as happens in Figure 15-15(c).

When a trend can be subdivided or when the trends in the comparisons do
not cross one another, a silhouette comparison can be created by filling in the

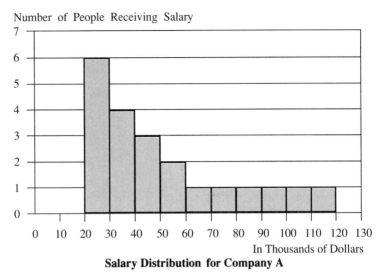

FIGURE 15-16.   Frequency Distribution Column Chart

area under the lower chart line with a design or color different from the one used for the area under the higher line chart (as shown in the "mountain chart" in Figure 15-1).

Frequency Distribution Comparisons: Column Charts and Line Graphs

Frequency distributions are used to demonstrate important variables (Figure 15-16). An airline might want to know what proportion of flights are on time, what proportion of flights are within ten minutes of scheduled arrival, and so on, because surveys have shown that passengers' satisfaction decreases sharply when flights are not on time. In presenting such information, the grouping or size of the ranges across the horizontal axis can be extremely important. For example, if all flights that arrived within the first twenty minutes were classed as "on time," the vast majority of all flights might be described as "on time." However, if "on time" were defined as arriving within five minutes of the scheduled time, only a small proportion might fall in that category.

Correlation Comparisons: Dot Charts

Correlations show whether types of information are related; that is, whether an increase in one will produce an identifiable change in the other. Usually, such comparisons are made to determine whether the actual results or data follow the pattern of relationship that we expect. If you have many items of data, a dot chart will show whether values cluster in an expected pattern, as shown in Figure 15-17. Sometimes deviation bar charts (see Figure 15-12) show correlations well when one is looking for related patterns of change in each of the components.

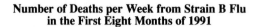

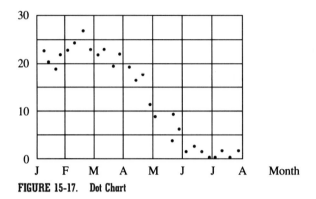

FIGURE 15-17.   Dot Chart

❏ OTHER GRAPHICS

Flip Charts, Slides, and Computer Projection

Flip Charts   Flip charts have several advantages, but they have been superseded in many firms by newer technologies. They are, however, made from inexpensive materials and if your time is not needed for other projects, you can make them by hand. Some computers can print on pin plotters capable of printing pages large enough for a flip chart easel. It is important to check out the room for flip chart use, just as it is to check out the projectors for overheads or slides.

Determine the maximum distance between your flip chart and the viewers. Be sure you make the flip chart content legible. Letters should be at least one and one-half inches high if they are to be read from twenty to twenty-five feet away. Prepare one flip chart and view it from the distance you think the most remotely seated person will view it. Test the legibility. Remember that the older the viewer, the more likely he or she is to have some difficulty in reading small letters, and many decision makers are past the age of forty-two, the magic boundary according to eye specialists. Can the decision maker read the sample page easily and quickly? Design flip charts with the same rules as overheads and consider how the sequence of word pages, chart or table pages, and symbolic images will stimulate or bore the viewer. Be sure to sum up ideas with a word page periodically. Staple together two blank pages between each flip chart page. The blank pages prevent the ink from bleeding through and makes only one design visible at a time.

Slides The presentation packages available for the front-running personal computers, such as Cricket® Presents, Microsoft® Power Point, and Harvard™ Graphics have made slide production enormously more affordable than it was when all the artwork for slides was produced manually. These software packages were designed for creating professional-quality visuals, primarily overhead transparencies and 35mm slides. By typing text onto the screen, selecting background and text colors, inserting graphics, and arranging the slides in order, these programs enable the user to print the slides on a digital film recorder that can be processed by a service bureau.

To create effective slides, limit the amount of information on any one slide. Each slide should have *only one point*. Too often, executives try to save money on slide presentations by using a table or chart that presents several points. Computer graphics have so drastically reduced the cost per slide that such tactics are unwarranted. Overloaded tables defeat the presenter's purpose because all of the audience will not be focusing on the same point simultaneously. Create a design that leads the viewer's eye to the point. Make the data display large enough that the display dominates the frame.

Make special effects special. Don't overuse color, borders, icons, and other elements on your slides. Many of the presentation package companies at first recommended cluttered, garish slides that demonstrated every feature in the package. Don't be misled by the manual or the promotional materials for your software program. Some were developed by computer specialists with no knowledge of graphic design.

Computer Projection The images that usually are shown on the computer monitor can be projected with a small device placed on an ordinary overhead projector. Furthermore, some of the graphics programs can be automatically timed so that the image changes dynamically on the screen, making the chart bars grow, imitating change over time in the data set. Miniature versions of the overheads, along with additional text, can be printed as handouts for people attending your presentation.

Remember to check the size of the room in which you will be operating the equipment to ensure that the size of lettering you have chosen will be legible. Many students have been astonished when the point size that seemed very large to them as they sat at their computer screens was virtually illegible when projected. Don't even think about using a font smaller than 24 points for computer projection in a room of 20 people, and 48 points is even better. *It doesn't matter how fancy the technology is if the people who need the information can't see it.*

This is 24 points

CHECKLIST FOR GRAPHICS

FOR A SERIES OF GRAPHICS:

_____ **1.** Does the series have variety?

_____ **2.** Are there graphics that give the audience an overview of the organization of the communication?

_____ **3.** Are there periodic reminders of the progress in the talk or document?

_____ **4.** Are the word graphics effective? Do they tell the answer to an audience question?

_____ **5.** Are the word graphics concise? Are there any unnecessary words?

_____ **6.** Do the graphics have a consistent shape, frame, and type style?

_____ **7.** Is the font or typeface suitable for the subject and the company?

_____ **8.** If you use overheads, have they been numbered?

FOR INDIVIDUAL GRAPHICS:

_____ **1.** Is the display (chart or figure) positioned to dominate the space and coordinate well with the title?

_____ **2.** Is the graphic appropriately titled? (not just a topic)

_____ **3.** Is the graphic limited to one point?

_____ **4.** Is everything on the graphic related to that point only?

_____ **5.** Has "chartjunk" (unnecessary decoration and detail) been removed?

_____ **6.** Is there a coherent graphic hierarchy in letter sizes and line widths?

_____ **7.** Is there sufficient white space around text?

_____ **8.** Has special emphasis been created with boldfacing, arrows, or other means of directing the audience's attention?

_____ **9.** Is the search task as simple as possible?

     _____ Is the graphic labeled clearly?

     _____ Is clutter reduced to a minimum?

     _____ Do the data dominate the design?

_____ **10.** Does the graphic require easy tasks (those that are high on the ordered list)? (the easiest tasks of visual discrimination have the lowest numbers)

     1. position along a common scale
     2. position on identical, nonaligned scales
     3. length, direction, angle
     4. area
     5. volume, curvature
     6. shading, color saturation

◻ CHECKLIST FOR GRAPHICS

TO DETECT PROBLEMS IN COLOR DISPLAYS:

_____ 1. Does the graphic use highly saturated, spectrally extreme colors side by side?

_____ 2. Does the graphic use pure blue for text, thin lines, or small shapes?

_____ 3. Are there any adjacent colors that differ only in the amount of blue?

_____ 4. Are the colors sufficiently bright for older viewers?

_____ 5. Are the colors suited to the light in which they will be seen?

_____ 6. Are differences in hue sufficient to make differences clear?

_____ 7. Are lines as well as colors used to differentiate important edges?

_____ 8. Have green and red been eliminated from the periphery of large-scale displays?

_____ 9. Have the contrasts been used well? Are opponent colors paired to emphasize differences?

_____ 10. Are there single-color distinctions that observers with color vision difficulties could not detect?

_____ 11. Has color been used sparingly?

_____ 12. Are related elements grouped by color?

_____ 13. Have similar colors been assigned to items of similar meaning?

_____ 14. Are the degrees of color change linked to degrees of difference in meaning?

_____ 15. Are the colors ordered by spectral position (ROY G. BIV)?

_____ 16. Are warm colors used to indicate items that need action or response?

FOR CHARTS DISPLAYING ANALYZED DATA:

_____ 1. Are the data appropriate to the question under investigation?

_____ 2. Can the audience tell from the title what the message is?

_____ 3. Does the chart display the kind of comparison inherent in the message?

_____ 4. Are the bars easy to see (wider than spaces between them)?

_____ 5. Are the patterns used on bars or areas simple (not distracting)?

_____ 6. Have unnecessary parts been grouped into an "other" category in the pie chart?

_____ 7. Can the comparison be seen easily?

_____ 8. Have trends been displayed clearly (with a heavy chart line, silhouette pattern, or other means)?

_____ 9. Have unnecessary decorations (distorted second or third dimensions, and so on) been eliminated?

_____ 10. Are the axes labeled so that all can be read without turning the graph sideways?

Integrating Text and Graphics

Figures, whether graphs, tables, photos, or drawings, should be integrated with the words of the text. Integration does not mean that every item of data in the graphical display has to be described in words as well as in the figure. Instead, the text should direct the reader's attention to the ways in which the graphic answers the questions of interest in the situation. Often, this means that the words of the sentences point out the means or other summary calculations, the largest and smallest items in the array, trends and patterns in the data, and the most important or salient terms.

Don't merely dump the figure into the text, hoping the reader will figure out the relationship. Similarly, place figures where they will benefit readers most. Position figures close to the discussion, so that the reader can benefit by contemplating both simultaneously. There is little more irritating than reading instructions or discussions on an unfamiliar topic when the illustration is several pages away or tucked in the back of an appendix. If the primary graphic display must be very large (such as a stratigraphic figure in a geologic report), extract a small detail from the figure and place it in the text, or from a large table, construct a small "two by two" table to display the key numbers.

ADOPT STANDARDS OF EXCELLENCE

Predictable problems may occur when someone with little design training begins to design graphics. Many people don't want to put much time into preparing graphics, and they try to cut corners by putting enough information on one slide to support three or four points. Or, they dump their lab notebook, table of data, or other information onto an overhead transparency through the photocopier. Cluttered slides are hard to read. Listeners may direct their attention to deciphering the information and analyzing it with their own questions and assumptions, tuning out the voice of the presenter. Letters that are too small to read, too many words, and inconsistent graphic hierarchies make the overhead or slide fail as a reinforcing tool.

COMMUNICATION CHALLENGES

PRELIMINARY EXERCISE 1 *Write the type of comparison involved in each of the messages below.*

a. The productivity of welders correlates with their level of training.

b. The workover rates of the three production lines in the plant were about the same.

c. The largest group of customers purchases luncheon meals in the $5.25 to $8.95 range.

d. TechnoPartners' earnings per share has been increasing over the last five years.

e. Two sales representatives sold many more homes than the other fourteen sales representatives.

f. The United Way spends only 9 percent of its funds on administrative expenses.

g. Surprisingly, the largest number of new hires last year was in the forty-to-forty-five age group.

h. The largest share of the computing budget is allocated to the engineering department this year.

i. Profitability is directly associated with sales volume.

j. Oil prices are projected to rise over the next eight years.

k. The task force concluded that the size of raises was not related to gender.

PRELIMINARY EXERCISE 2 *Sketch the general outline of a graphic you could use in your storyboards for each of the points shown in the list in preliminary exercise 1.* The table below summarizes your choices.

TYPE COMPARISON	TYPE OF CHART
Component comparison	Pie chart or component bar chart
Unit comparison	Bar chart
Time series comparison	Column chart or line graph
Frequency distribution comparison	Column chart or line graph
Correlation comparison	Dot or line graph or bar chart

EXERCISE 1

On a cold January morning, your officemate in the marketing division of Dunstan Pharmaceutical Products hurries into your office and closes the door. "Marty," he says, "I've found it. If this new drug testing law goes into effect, governments will have to buy test kits for every last employee!" You reply, "*Every* government worker? How many people is that?" He pulls John Wright's *The American Almanac of Jobs and Salaries* off the shelf and looks up the chapter "On the Public Rayroll." "Write these down for me, Marty. At the last census, 2.9 million civilians worked for the federal government; 2 million in the military; 3.7 million were state government workers; 2.6 million worked for municipalities; 1.8 million worked for counties; and 5 million worked for towns, villages, and school districts." You agree to help by preparing an overhead to show the proportion of the market that will open up at the state and local level, even if Dunstan Products doesn't go after the federal contracts.

EXERCISE 2

One of the summer interns, Harmon Farb, turned in an overhead for your use in a presentation the following day about Tasty-Lite, a new "fake fat" food product R&D has come up with. "Harmon," you remark, "I know you spent some time preparing this overhead, but I would like some changes made. For starters, there's too much information on this overhead. I think we need more than one overhead. Furthermore, there are

Lite 'n' Tasty

Genneco's low-calorie international desserts

- both single and family packs
- four different European desserts to try
- French pastries, German Strudel, English scones
- also Mexican flan

Weight conscious

- low calorie

Health conscious

- international sophistication
- new tastes and new foods

Price/Value

- highest quality will give value for money

some basic things wrong with it. I can't tell what points you're making. It isn't clear that you can appeal to special market segments with these products and at the same time address all those people who want to eat less fat. I don't think this will convince the new products committee to take any action." Look again at Harmon's overhead and explain the kinds of changes that need to be made. Either *write these changes out or annotate a photocopy, noting BOTH the problems you identify and the kinds of changes you would make.* Suggest also the kinds of numbers or illustrations that Harmon might use to make these overheads more persuasive.

EXERCISE 3

At Mountain Cedar General Hospital, the net income from service to patients is the revenue from patients minus the cost of care. The total net income is what the hospital earns, including revenues from such things as television service, video sales, and coffee shops. Mountain Cedar General Hospital serves a large metropolitan area in the northern part of the United States. For the past four years the hospital has been struggling

	1985–86	1986–87	1987–88	1988–89
Total patient revenues	$199	$215	$240	$265
Income from service to patients	$4	0.6	($5.2) loss	($5.6) loss
Total net income	$16.1	$7.6	$2.3	($0.6) loss

as the government reduced and more strictly controlled its Medicare payments. *Your job is to prepare three overheads for use at the board of directors meeting.* The overheads should show the total patient revenues, income from service to patients, and the total net income over the last four years. The information you have received from the controller is expressed in millions of dollars.

Consider carefully the title as well as the proper design for these charts.

EXERCISE 4

Review the following graphics, using photocopies of the evaluation checklist, and identify their weaknesses and strengths. Be prepared to discuss them in class.

Evaluation Checklist

1. Data on graphic limited to "need to know," not "nice to know"

   Low   High

   1   2   3   4   5

2. Appropriate headings: noun, verb, and important point

   Low   High

   1   2   3   4   5

If visual is a chart or graph:

3. Appropriate labels for better understanding

   Low   High

   1   2   3   4   5

4. Readability of type size (appropriate for audience size of 25)

   Low   High

   1   2   3   4   5

5. Appropriate use of chart form (line, bar, pie, diagram)

   Low   High

   1   2   3   4   5

6. Appropriate emphasis of main point

   Low   High

   1   2   3   4   5

If visual is a text visual: (Check yes or no)   YES   NO

  7. No more than 4 to 6 lines of text   _____   _____

  8. Uses phrases   _____   _____

  9. Upper- and lowercase type   _____   _____

10. Readability (for audience of 25 in size)   _____   _____

11. Technique used for emphasis of main point   _____   _____

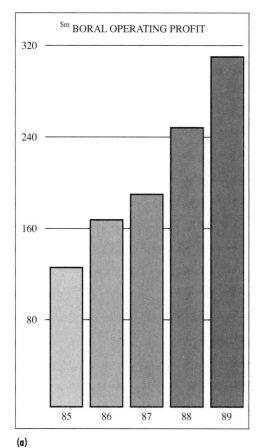

$m BORAL OPERATING PROFIT

320

240

160

80

85 86 87 88 89

(a)

Source: Ad for Boral, Ltd. *Wall Street Journal,* Nov. 1989

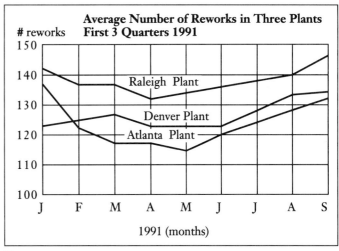

Average Number of Reworks in Three Plants First 3 Quarters 1991

reworks

150

140 — Raleigh Plant

130

Denver Plant

120 — Atlanta Plant

110

100

J F M A M J J A S

1991 (months)

(b)

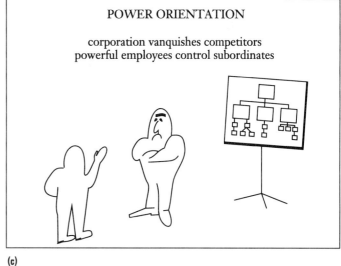

POWER ORIENTATION

corporation vanquishes competitors
powerful employees control subordinates

(c)

WORLD TRADE MARKET SHARE (FY 1490)

18.00%

34.00%

23.00%

25.00%

Spain
Portugal
England
All Other

(d)

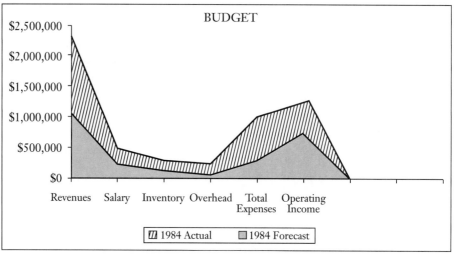

(e)

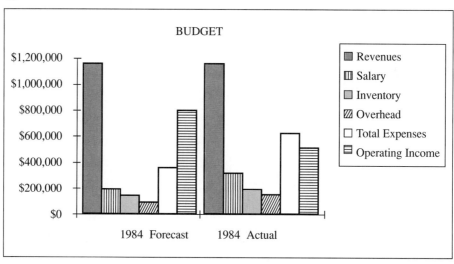

(f)

EXERCISE 5

The decade of the 1980s was disastrous for the savings and loan industry. Aggregate earnings of federally chartered savings and loan institutions fluctuated wildly and the assets of its insurance fund, the Federal Savings and Loan Insurance Corporation, plunged. Looking back, 1986 was the year when the Federal Home Loan Bank Board should have seen the "writing on the wall." *Draw two line graphs that tell the story vividly.* Alert the executives of the Board to the dramatic change in aggregate income and to the enormous "draw down" on reserves. The figures shown here are in BILLIONS of dollars.

AGGREGATE EARNINGS OF FEDERALLY-CHARTED S&Ls	FS&LIC RESERVES
1982 ($4.2) loss	$6.3
1983 $1.7	$6.4
1984 $0.9	$5.2
1985 $3.8	$4.7
1986 $0.2	$1.9

EXERCISE 6

You've been working on your report for the career planning workshop, and you've uncovered some interesting information. One survey by Heidrich & Struggles showed that the average chief executive officer spends about 17 hours each week in meetings. Twenty percent spent 0 to 9 hours in meetings; 37 percent spend 10 to 19 hours; 25 percent spend 20 to 29 hours; and 18 percent spend 30 or more hours in meetings each week.

In a separate survey, the Wharton Center for Applied Research found that senior executives spend an average of 23 hours a week in meetings, while middle managers reported 11 hours of board meetings. Furthermore, meetings take preparation. Senior managers said that if they had to lead the meeting, they needed an average of 45 minutes to prepare; if they were to make a presentation, preparation time jumped to 147 minutes. If they simply needed to participate in the meeting, they spent an average of 17 minutes preparing.

In contrast, middle managers need an average of 75 minutes to prepare for leading meetings, 104 minutes to prepare a presentation, and 21 minutes to prepare for participating. Senior managers felt that about 58 percent of their meetings were productive; middle managers estimated that 54 percent were productive. Senior managers concluded that 22 percent of the meetings they attended could have been handled with a memo or over the phone. Middle managers felt that 29 percent of their meetings could have been handled in these ways.

Prepare the storyboards and graphics for a three-minute presentation to a workshop of students in a career-planning class using information that you select from these notes.

EXERCISE 7

This summer you are working as an intern for Dan Bladwin, the assistant director of development at Cody College, a medium-sized private college. "Say, we've got bad news, here, I think," Dan tells you, pointing to a study prepared by the National Institute of Independent Colleges and Universities. "This looks really bad. I don't think private colleges like Cody are getting their share of corporate support any more. I'd like to talk about these numbers with President Thompson next week. *Why don't you do something with these numbers to show private colleges' position in relation to public colleges' with respect to corporate funding. We need to compare where private colleges were back in the early 50s with their position today.* Then later, I'll pull together an analysis of our own corporate support for comparison. Get a graphic ready for me by Monday, won't you?" *Determine the message, identify the comparison, choose the chart form, and prepare one or more graphics as Dan has requested.*

	TOTAL SUPPORT		PRIVATE INSTITUTIONS			PUBLIC INSTITUTIONS		
	All Insti-tutions	Amount	Num-ber	Amount	Share Total	Num-ber	Amount	Share Total
1956–57	772	76,300,000	654	65,800,000	86.2%	118	10,500,000	13.8%
1960–61	915	127,600,000	741	92,400,000	72.4%	174	35,200,000	27.6%
1962–63	887	145,000,000	716	103,200,000	71.1%	171	41,900,000	28.9%
1968–69	856	218,400,000	671	156,100,000	71.5%	185	62,300,000	28.5%
1973–74	880	273,700,000	674	170,700,000	65.7%	206	94,000,000	34.3%
1978–79	882	436,200,000	668	260,800,000	59.8%	214	175,400,000	40.2%
1983–84	982	1,052,600,000	707	557,100,000	52.9%	275	495,500,000	47.1%
1984–85	979	1,307,500,000	709	677,700,000	51.8%	270	629,800,000	48.2%
1985–86	1004	1,436,900,000	717	722,700,000	50.3%	287	714,200,000	49.7%
1986–87	1008	1,547,700,000	718	832,200,000	53.8%	290	715,500,000	46.2%
1987–88	992	1,570,200,000	697	783,200,000	49.9%	295	785,900,000	50.1%

Source: Council for Aid to Education

EXERCISE 8

In class, discuss the kinds of human perceptual tasks required for a viewer to make sense of the graphic about membership in a business organization. What do you think the designer wanted to show?

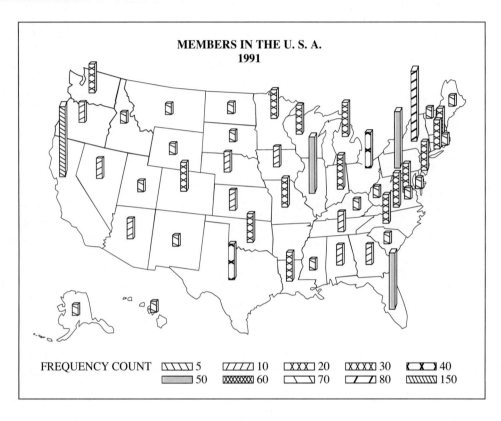

CASE: SUPPORTING THE HERITAGE FESTIVAL

The following case is intended to provide the basis for class discussion. Read the case and be prepared to discuss the answers to the questions at the end. Prepare the graphic in the exercise if your instructor so directs.

When a civic committee was planning a multi-ethnic festival to celebrate the 150th anniversary of a town's founding, it asked local corporations to sponsor some of the events. On his way to a management meeting, the president of one such company, DDR, asked the head of Human Resources, "Do we have enough Asian workers to help with the Asian festival too, or should we just support the Black, German, and Hispanic festivals? We're having a meeting tomorrow. Get that data for me and fix up a graphic, OK?" The Human Resources director checked the computer and found the following information on the employees:

	NO. EMPLOYEES	PERCENT
Black	2500	28.4%
Hispanic	1900	21.6%
Asian	1200	13.6%
Anglo	3200	36.4%
Total	8800	100%

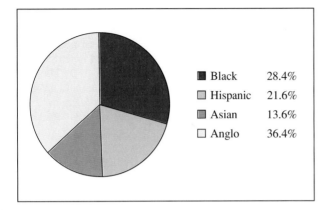

■ Black	28.4%
▨ Hispanic	21.6%
▨ Asian	13.6%
☐ Anglo	36.4%

With the flick of a finger, the director generated a pie chart, a form commonly used to show part-to-whole relationships, with the computer. Then the director tried to decide on a title for the graphic. The president's question had been: "Do we have enough Asian workers to help with the Asian festival too, or should we just support the Black, German, and Hispanic festivals?" The director fiddled with different titles that might pertain to the question: "Enough Asians for Festival Support," "Asians Only a Small Part of DDR," or "Too Few Asians for Festival Support." The director finally decided on a descriptive title that didn't answer the question at all: "Ethnic Backgrounds of DDR Employees."

■ Does the director have all the information necessary for answering the president's question? What is still missing?

■ What assumptions about the allocation of company support were involved in the question?

■ What other bases might be appropriate for determining which projects to support? What errors or problems are likely to be caused by the data categories drawn from the employment forms? Only four types are listed: Anglo, Hispanic, Black, and Asian.

■ Where do Australian and Canadian employees belong? Would the company's support of the German festival represent them as "Anglos" in any significant way?

Assignment Suppose that the purpose of the graphic were to illustrate that the number of Asian employees met the well-defined standard of 10 percent to justify corporate support. Apply the ideas in the discussion of designing for human perception abilities. How could you revise the graphic to make it easier to see that the Asians are eligible for support? *Prepare a new graphic.*

IF YOU WOULD LIKE TO READ MORE

Theory

Cochran, J. K., Albrecht, S. A., & Green, Y. A. (1989). Guidelines for evaluating graphical designs: A framework based on human perception skills. *Technical Communication, 36*(1), 25–32. The source article for the framework presented in this chapter.

Kostelnick, C. (Summer 1988). A systematic approach to visual language in business communication. *The Journal of Business Communication, 25*(3), 29–48. Argues that visual elements are not neutral, but rhetorical. Offers a twelve-cell schema for classifying modes and levels of visual elements and ranking business documents.

Tufte, E. R. (1983). *The visual display of quantitative information.* Cheshire, CT: Graphics Press. A classic work on graphics. Separate sections cover graphical practice and theory of data graphics.

Presentations

Holcombe, M. W., & Stein, J. K. (1983). *Presentations for decision makers: Strategies for structuring and delivering your ideas.* New York: Van Nostrand Reinhold. Practical and concise, with an excellent chapter on designing overheads for presentations.

Karten, N. (1988). How to use visuals in your presentation. *Performance & Instruction, 27*(2), 9–10. Identifies problems that occur when special features on computer programs are overused.

Simpson, R. S. (1987). *Effective audio-visual: A user's handbook.* Boston: Focal Press. Teaches how to choose media, how to prepare programs and materials, and how to implement decisions. Describes the use of audio-visual equipment in a variety of settings, from training and conferences to museums and exhibitions. Explains production systems as well as technical details such as lenses, screens, and computers in audio-visual presentations.

Layout

Donahue, B. (1978). *The language of layout.* Englewood Cliffs, NJ: Prentice-Hall. Primarily for layout artists, the explanations of the vocabulary of layout and the excellent examples help editors and managers who need to work with publications people grasp the concepts that will be discussed in marketing support sessions.

White, J. V. (1982). *Editing by design: A guide to effective word-and-picture communication for editors and designers* (2nd ed.). New York: R. R. Bowker. Primarily for people working with magazines, this text has many examples and helps would-be editors develop taste and sensitivity to visual elements.

NOTES

1. W. S. Cleveland & R. McGill, "Graphical perception and graphical methods for analyzing scientific data, *Science 229*, (1985) no. 4716, 828–833; also "Graphical perception: Theory, experiments, and application in the development of graphical methods," *Journal of the American Statistical Association*, *79*, (1984) 3 & 7, 531–553.

2. G. Zelazny, *Say it with charts: The executive's guide to successful presentations.* Homewood, IL: Dow-Jones Irwin (1985), 21–23.

3. Zelazny, 21.

4. Zelazny, 22.

5. J. K. Cochran, S. A. Albrecht, & Y. A. Greene, "Guidelines for evaluating graphical designs: A framework based on human perception skills." *Technical Communication*, *36* (1989) 1, 25–32. These authors draw heavily on the sources in Note 1.

ORAL PRESENTATIONS

OBJECTIVES

This chapter will help you

- maintain the attention of your audience

- use visual aids effectively

- deliver your presentation with confidence and poise

- use questions and answers to reinforce your message

- evaluate your own presentations and those of your colleagues

PREVIEW

The ability to make an effective oral presentation is crucial in virtually all areas of business. Competent speakers advance farther and more rapidly than those who are less verbally adept.

Successful presenters thoroughly analyze their audiences, prepare scripts and visual aids that match the requirements of the situation, and deliver their material with confidence and continuous attention to the reactions of their listeners. Speakers can rapidly improve through conscientious practice and evaluation of their speaking skills.

❑ ORAL PRESENTATIONS

This chapter is not a scholarly treatise on rhetoric or public speaking. It is a collection of practical information on how to prepare and deliver an effective, goal-oriented oral presentation. As a businessperson, you will be called upon to speak in various situations with varying degrees of formality. Yet in virtually all situations, speakers who adopt an extemporaneous style and remain in continuous interpersonal contact with their audiences are more effective than those who resort to lecturing or who erect slide presentations and video shows as barriers between themselves and their listeners. *Extemporaneous* and *impromptu* are not synonymous. *Impromptu* speeches are unrehearsed and given on the spur of the moment. *Extemporaneous* speeches are carefully prepared and thoroughly rehearsed, but delivered in a conversational style that establishes a dialogue between the speaker and the audience.

According to *Fortune* magazine, "The 30 minutes an executive spends on his feet formally presenting his latest project to corporate superiors are simply and absolutely the most important 30 minutes of that or any other managerial season."[1] The single most promotable quality in your portfolio of business assets is the ability to conduct an effective oral presentation—whether it is stand-up and formal, with a hundred or so people in the audience, or sit-down and informal with just the boss in her office. Without this ability, you may be viewed as an effective technician, but you will not be accepted as top management material.

Effective presentation skills prove your ability to influence others, to promote your goals and those of your company. Effective presentation skills demonstrate that you can handle pressure, maintain responsibilities, think clearly, and organize yourself. As you increase the effectiveness of your presentation skills, you increase your own self-confidence and self-esteem, and you increase your value to your firm.

The opportunities for oral presentations are many and growing. Within your company, you will certainly participate in one-on-one interviews, but you will also have the opportunity to make presentations at departmental meetings, staff or employee meetings, in training programs, in project reviews and other briefings. Outside your organization, you may make presentations to customers or clients; you may be a presenter at professional meetings, in civic organizations, and at stockholder meetings; or you may make goodwill speeches—perhaps as a member of a speaker's bureau.

Businesses are increasingly relying on the public relations exposure available through corporate video and through public radio and television. According to one corporate official, "The power of TV is very special, some say magical. . . . With more people depending on TV for both news and information, very few businesses can afford to ignore it. . . . There is always a demand for someone who can intelligently discuss what's going on. Companies should not expect TV and other journalists to make their arguments for them. It's not their job. You damn well better learn to do it yourself."[2]

BUSINESS COMMUNICATION TODAY

ADVANTAGES AND DISADVANTAGES OF ORAL PRESENTATIONS*

ADVANTAGES

- *A presentation is immediate.* Unlike a written message, which can be put aside until later, your spoken message must be listened to—or tuned out—immediately.

- *A presentation is personal.* You establish a face-to-face interaction with your audience. You can monitor your listeners' reactions and adjust your message accordingly.

- *A presentation can utilize a wide range of communication channels: verbal, auditory, and visual.* Our culture is becoming increasingly oral and visual. Many people dislike reading; they will, however, give their attention to concrete examples (a flesh-and-blood individual accompanied by appropriate visual aids), dynamically presented.

- *A presentation lets* you, *not just your paperwork, become the spokesperson.* As a speaker, you can quickly gain prestige by demonstrating leadership skills.

DISADVANTAGES

- *The spoken word leaves no record behind.* Compensate by preparing handouts that stress your key points. If you prepare an outline for your audience, you can distribute it at the beginning of the presentation so it can serve as a signposting aid and a note-taking device for your audience. Be warned, however, that reading material can present a powerful distraction to your listeners. Do what you can to keep attention focused on *you*.

- *Presentations can be expensive.* Presentation materials, including audiovisual aids, can cost thousands of dollars. Preparation time for the presenter and support staff, and time away from other work for the presenter and the audience, must be considered. Presentations may also involve travel expenses and the cost of rented conference facilities.

- *The presentation goes at the speaker's pace, not that of the audience.* Knowledge of any given topic, attention spans, and listening skills vary; your listeners cannot go back to reread a difficult passage or a paragraph when their attention wanders. Therefore, you must use eye contact to monitor your listeners' reactions and you must constantly adjust your presentation to meet their needs.

- *An unprepared speaker can turn the most promising of projects into rubbish.* If the speaker comes across as disorganized, insecure, or flippant, no amount of planning, research, or evidence will be able to win the audience. You need a clear sense of goals and a carefully planned organizational strategy to establish clear and viable meanings within your presentation. (See Chapter 5.) Shallow analysis produces a shallow presentation.

*For a more complete discussion, see Leonard F. Meuse, Jr. (1980), *Mastering the Business and Technical Presentation.* Boston, MA: CBI Publishing Co., 2–7.

The power of commercials and talk shows is already well known, but companies are employing video in other ways as a strong public relations tool. For example, some corporations now send their annual reports to stockholders as a VHS video in lieu of the traditional glossy pamphlet. The video, using audio and visual presentations from corporate personnel and customers, gives stockholders a more personal view of corporate officers and products. The financial statements, which formed the original basis for the genre of annual reports, are then inserted on a card or pamphlet inside the cassette jacket.

Video can be used internally to distribute corporate news programs, to communicate up, down, and laterally, and to provide training. Until recently, teleconferencing referred only to a phone call among three or more individuals,

COMMUNICATION STRATEGY CHECKLIST

Use this checklist to review your strategy's four major elements: comprehensive purpose, persuasive approach, relevant content organized into issues, and criteria for evaluating success.

COMPREHENSIVE PURPOSE

_____ Does the purpose include your intentions toward each of your audiences?

_____ Does the purpose address the most important uncertainties of each audience?

_____ Does the purpose reflect your personal objectives, the company's objectives, and your department's objectives?

PERSUASIVE APPROACH

Have you answered each of the following questions?

_____ How easy will it be to influence my audience?

_____ What should be the basis of the persuasive appeal?

_____ What social process will be most effective?

_____ What medium will be most effective?

_____ How can I maximize my personal effectiveness?

How Easy Will It Be to Influence My Audience?

_____ Do the audience and I share a mutual understanding of the scenario?

_____ Has the audience done this or felt this before?

_____ Is the audience predisposed to do what I request?

_____ Is my relationship with this audience strong?

What Should Be the Basis of the Persuasive Appeal?

_____ Power, coercion

_____ Policies or laws

_____ Corporate values

_____ Shared goals or mutual needs

_____ Mutual benefits

_____ Benefits for the audience

_____ Credibility of the speaker

_____ Expertise of the speaker

_____ Credibility of the medium

_____ History of the relationship

_____ Preferences of powerful people

_____ Desire to be part of the group

_____ Desire to lead the group

_____ Personal appreciation

_____ Cultural values

Did you consider the following options?

If you can recommend something that will alleviate an important uncertainty, emphasize how the action can effectively address the uncertainty.

If you can associate your request or proposal with something the subject already values or feels strongly about, you may be able to induce the audience to hold the same attitude toward your request.

If you can create a feeling of discrepancy or dissonance that suggests a need for action, then the audience will be more motivated to reduce the dissonance through the action you request.

What Social Process Will Be Most Effective?

Did you consider each of the sequence and media possibilities listed below?

_____ Document before discussion

_____ Discussion before document

_____ Group meeting

_____ Electronic conferencing

_____ Going through superiors

▢ COMMUNICATION STRATEGY CHECKLIST

How Can I Increase My Personal Effectiveness?

How have I planned to demonstrate each of the following?

_____ *Goodwill and fairness*—perceived concern for the audience

_____ *Expertise*—knowledge and intelligence

_____ *Prestige*—attributed power

_____ *Self-presentation*—the audience's perceptions of my personality and presentation skills

CONTENT AND ORGANIZATION

_____ Does the *content* address the audience's beliefs and feelings?

_____ Does it satisfy their need for information?

_____ Is it organized into strategic issues?

CRITERIA FOR JUDGING SUCCESS

_____ Are the criteria for judging the success of the communication specific and operational, so that I can measure the results?

---

but with the increasing sophistication of video equipment, video teleconferences are becoming more frequent. They save the time and expense of travel, establish a more personalized forum than a phone call, and provide a more immediate response than a letter. Because each speaker can participate from his or her own location, no one is placed at the potential disadvantage of visiting the other person's "territory."

Planning Your Presentation

Begin by Planning a Communication Strategy

You recall from Chapters 4 and 5 that any successful communicator begins by analyzing the situation, analyzing the audience, and developing a communication strategy. This section reviews the points made in earlier chapters as they pertain to oral presentations. The following form can be used in planning your presentation.

Audience Analysis Is Essential

If you haven't already read Chapter 3, take time to look at the sections titled "Understanding Your Audience" and "Analyzing Audience Needs with the Concept of Uncertainty." Our analysis of others is generally shallow, stereotypical, and less informed than it could or should be. If you study the audience's needs thoroughly, asking and listening to discover their perspective, you will make few mistakes. Above all, you will not assume their needs are identical to your own.

In addition to analyzing audience uncertainties with the forms in Chapter 3, you may analyze a number of specific demographic issues. Size is an important consideration: a group of ten will require a more intimate speaking space, less grandiose gestures, and more subtle vocal inflections than will a group of fifty. Gender is another vital characteristic; if you are speaking for an all-male or all-female audience, you might need to adjust your choice of materials and your speaking style.

Your Listeners Will Be There for Various Reasons

Although sometimes your audience chooses to attend because they want and need the information you are prepared to give them, you may often find yourself addressing a "captive audience" with mixed purposes and unequal expectations about how you will be spending their time. Your listeners may be there for the following reasons:

1. *Because their participation in the project gives them a stake in what you are saying.* Ideally, you should be able to treat these audience members as allies and encourage their participation in discussion segments of the presentation.
2. *Because their positions in the firm require their presence.* These listeners will have vested interests in various functional areas within the firm: marketing, strategic planning, accounting, and legal, to name a few.
3. *Because they want to protect their own areas of interest.* This is part of your *secondary audience.*
4. *Because they must act upon what you have to say.* These listeners (like those in group 3) may be skeptical of your area of expertise, your affiliations, and your expectations of them.

You can win even the most potentially hostile audiences if your prepare adequately to fulfill their needs, if you deal with them in an open manner that says, "I'm here to discuss the topic and the issues, not to lecture you," and if you work to highlight the qualities in yourself and in your topic that your listeners will most admire. What can you show them that will win them over? The qualities that audience members admire in a speaker, introduced in Chapter 4, are goodwill and fairness, expertise, prestige, and self-presentation skills. You must, however, develop skill in demonstrating these qualities with a light touch, using humor and evidence, not a heavy-handed, know-it-all attitude.

Goodwill and fairness. You can demonstrate your warmth and your perceived concern for the audience through the nonverbal communication techniques listed above. Add individual contact with audience members before and after the presentation. Call on them by name whenever you can. Integrity, loyalty, and ethics affect an audience's sense of your goodwill. Care enough about your listeners to set an example for them.

Expertise. The best defense against stage fright is a consummate knowledge of your material and the related subject matter. Base your knowledge upon experience and study. It's imperative that you stay up to date. Expertise also includes intellect and the ability to think on your feet. If you haven't yet developed this ability, you can make your listeners think you have it. This requires careful preparation and anticipation of the audience's questions. You need evidence: statistics, testimonials, war stories, guarantees to prove your success or that of your product. And you need tact: If you "toot your own horn," make it clear that you're doing so for the audience's benefit.

Prestige. Audiences like speakers who have talent and ability. You don't have to be a virtuoso, but it helps if you can make your audience aware of some of your past triumphs. A strategic introduction, preferably by someone other than yourself, can establish your credits. You can also demonstrate your talents as you speak.

Self-presentation. Energy is the easiest thing to demonstrate if you have it; the hardest thing to fake if you don't. If you don't have it, do whatever it takes to "psyche yourself up." You can demonstrate energy through facial expressions, eye contact, vocal inflection, gestures, movement, and attention to the needs of your audience.

After you inventory your own positive characteristics and all the pertinent organizational roles, obtain as much feedback as you reasonably can. In many corporations, drafts of even minor speeches are routinely channeled through numerous levels in an attempt to consider the entire organizational context as well as the speaker's goals and those of the audience.

Length Is a Vital Consideration

Before you can decide what to say, you must know how much time you have to deliver your message. Audiences will forgive many ills, but they will not forgive the two cardinal sins: *being unprepared* and *speaking for too long.* This is doubly true on television, where everything is split into segments and a protracted speech will simply be turned off.

The human attention span is limited, and though estimates vary, a good rule of thumb states that if you go past fifteen minutes, you need some very stimulating subject matter to keep the audience's attention centered on *you.* Another good rule of thumb is "Always leave 'em wanting more."

The average speaking rate is 125 words per minute. A five-minute talk, therefore, will require only 625 words. If you type your script, about two double-spaced pages will equal a five-minute talk. You will have to limit the number of key ideas to two or three, and you will have to limit the amount of detail accordingly. Include only the vital, the interesting, and the directly applicable. One well-made point is better than four barely-scratched surfaces.

Preparing Your Presentation

Organize, Then Trim Your Notes to a Key-Words Outline

In the realm of oral presentations, conventional wisdom works: Tell them what you are going to tell them; tell them; tell them what you told them. The presentation plan below shows a capsule of the standard presentation format.

PRESENTATION PLAN

Introduction: Win the audience

- Get attention — Be interesting and establish a sense of relationship with the audience.
- State your purpose — Present inducements and makes goals and benefits explicit.
- Preview the context — Provide oral and visual signposts to establish an explicit forecast of how the presentation will be organized.
- Present good news — Introduce the most important aspects of who, what, when, where, why, and how, while the audience is most attentive.

Body: Establish main points and present evidence

- Provide cues — Continue to provide verbal and visual signposts: enumerated points, summary sentences, transitions, and strategic visual aids.
- Balance general and specific information — Include concrete evidence for understanding and "bits of spice" for interest.

Conclusion: Make the point (your news) unforgettable

- Summarize — Stress important points.
- Close — Give your audience a "sense of an ending."
- Stress action — Let your listeners know what will happen next and who is responsible.

To give your presentation cohesiveness and power, begin planning your content with the tip of the pyramid—the news. At the center of your strategy lies your *conclusion—make all roads lead in that direction.* If you are planning a sales presentation, you will call it your *close.* What action should your listeners take as a result of hearing your presentation? What new knowledge or perspective should they attain? If you write your close first, you will find it easier to make all the other elements—the specifics in the body and the attention-getters in the introduction—build toward that conclusion. A picture of the basic presentation structure would look like Figure 16-1.

The body of your presentation should enumerate and support key points that build upon the introduction and build toward the conclusion. Be sure, after you've decided upon the key content elements, that you go back into the body of your talk and add some spice to what you say. David Peoples, a professional speaker and seminar leader for IBM, observes that our job as speaker is to keep our audience's minds away from the beach. "To do this we need to structure our presentation so that we add a touch of Hot Spice every six to eight minutes."[3] When you build in attention-getting devices at fairly short intervals, you add life to the presentation and keep the audience in a lively and attentive frame of mind.

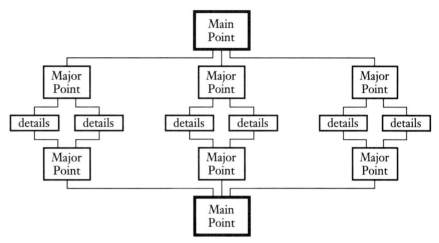

FIGURE 16-1.   **Basic Presentation Structure**

Your spice can take many forms: a human-interest story, a war story from personal experience, a joke, a distinctive visual aid, a cartoon, a role-play, perhaps even a pop quiz. The pop quiz technique can be presented as a true-false or fill-in-the-blanks questionnaire on a visual aid, to give the audience an idea of what they should have learned up to this point. The quiz should be used as a mnemonic device, not to embarrass or penalize audience members in any way.

The questionnaire also can be a good introductory device to prepare your audience for the presentation and to increase their interest in specific aspects of the talk. It lets them know what to look for. Consider handing out the "quiz" as people enter the meeting room, then working through the answers together as you move to your conclusion.

The close must tell your audience how they should use your presentation; the body must convince them to act upon your conclusion, but when you deliver your presentation, nothing is more important than the introduction. Your audience members will quickly decide whether you have anything interesting to say, and they will immediately adjust their listening skills accordingly. You must know your introduction cold; while you may refer to your prompts during the body of the presentation and even after the first minute or so of the introduction, you should be able to maintain constant eye contact as you deliver the first sixty seconds of your presentation. And you must be flexible enough to adjust your introduction at the last minute to fit the day's headlines or coffee break story, to compensate for unexpected turns of events as your host introduces you, or to incorporate the views of the speakers immediately preceding you.

Very often in public speaking situations, but less often with business presentations, someone will be introducing you to your audience. Too many speakers underestimate the importance of this formal introduction by their host. If someone will be introducing you, provide him or her with a biographical sketch or a brief script. Not only does writing your own introduction save your host the trouble, it can help to ensure that your presentation begins on the right note. If you write your own introduction, you can keep it brief while ensuring that it establishes your credibility with your audience and arouses their interest in the topic.

Your introductions—the one in which your host introduces you and the one in which you introduce your topic—must accomplish two things: motivate your audience members to pay attention to what you have to say, and support your close.

Use Techniques to Get Your Audience's Attention

Some attention-getting techniques relate to content, some to delivery style. Remember that you must *know your introduction cold*, and you must deliver it with an enthusiastic voice, confident posture, and direct and sustained eye contact. The content of your introduction might incorporate any number of the following attention-getting techniques, but it is essential that it include the first one: empathy.

Create attention with empathy. You might pay the audience a compliment by referring to the surroundings or to the occasion itself; noting your audience's recent accomplishments creates goodwill and can only increase your credibility. You might mention topics of current interest to the group, especially if those topics are positive. You might highlight elements of your own background that are similar to those of your audience. A review of the audience checklist should suggest several points of common ground.

Create attention with an anecdote. Some speakers are proficient at telling prepared jokes, but you may be more comfortable with your material if you develop a human-interest narrative appropriate to the occasion. You might refer to something you've read or to some event in your own life. Make the story simple, direct, and relevant. Unless you have a great deal of time and you can make every element of the story integral to your point, keep it short. Practice your anecdote several times until you are comfortable with the story, confident that you've added the appropriate embellishments and can tell it in a relaxed manner. If it is supposed to be funny, try it out on a few friends in advance. Humor is a risky business. If you take the risk and your joke doesn't fly, move on to the business at hand. Never be the first to laugh at your own comedy.

Create attention with a startling fact or opinion. This approach requires careful audience analysis, but it can also carry the message that "this person means business." Statistics can be used to advantage in this situation: "While you are listening to me speak this afternoon, three people will die, and at least fifteen people will be hospitalized because of automobile accidents. Ten of those people could have walked away with only minor injuries if their automobiles had been equipped with air bags."

Create attention by getting your audience involved. If you are truly an expert on your subject, and you know more about it than about your audience, you can ask why audience members are there, ask for their opinions on the topic, or ask what aspects of the topic they would like you to discuss. Listeners will be impressed with your self-confidence, but you must then follow through and address their concerns.

With all of these attention-getting approaches, preparation is the key. You must know your audience, know your stories, know your facts, and know your subject matter. Preparation puts you in control, and being in control does wonders for your nerves.

The Right Way to Prepare Is the Way That Works for You

Just as we learn and think in different ways and take different approaches to different scenarios, we can choose among several alternative modes for preparing a presentation's content. Some people write a complete script, others prepare only an outline or a mind map, while others prepare a storyboard like the one in the chapter on formats and media aids. The key is to adopt an organizational strategy that incorporates adequate general information plus memorable and convincing details.

You must also include adequate signposting to let your audience know where you are in the overall scheme of things and where you are headed. Add a signpost at the end of your introduction by telling your audience (and showing them with a visual aid) what major points you will be discussing. Use signposts at transition points, verbally (and perhaps visually) telling your audience what territory you have just covered and where you are now leading them. Introduce a signpost in the conclusion by restating your major points and telling your listeners what will happen next.

The best business presentations are neither memorized nor read, but delivered in an extemporaneous style using unobtrusive prompting devices. An extemporaneous presentation adopts a conversational tone—something you cannot achieve if you put pages of notes between yourself and your listeners. As you organize your presentation, give careful thought to what types of prompting devices you will use.

Situations when you will be reading from a script are, fortunately, limited and specialized. A highly technical presentation might, under extreme circumstances, require such specific wording that reading from a full paragraph of script would be required. In virtually every other situation, however, you simply must not let yourself fall into the trap of standing before your audience holding pages of script. It's fine to generate a verbatim script as you plan your presentation, but during the rehearsal stage whittle your prompts down to a set of key words only. Figure 16-2 is an example of a key words prompting device. These key words can be used as one of the visuals for a talk about effective delivery techniques. They even form an acronym, VEGA, which helps the audience remember the key points. The speaker can then embellish the key words, giving them meaning and telling the listeners how to apply the VEGA concept to their speaking style.

The script shown in Figure 16-3 is not an example of key words. Although the content is good, it would not serve well as a prompting device because it would require too much of the speaker's attention.

FIGURE 16-2.   Key Words Visual

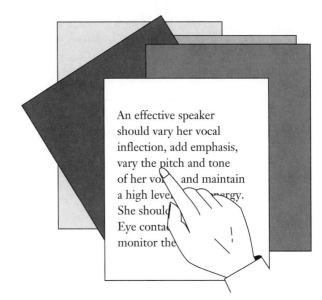

FIGURE 16-3.   Ineffective Cues

You can write your cues on pieces of paper or on index cards, but you will look much more professional (and appear better prepared and more organized) if you write your cues on your visual aids. Often—as shown in Figure 16-2—the visual aid itself will be all the cue you need. If it serves as a signpost for your listeners, who do not know your presentation, it should provide more than adequate information for you, who have analyzed the situation, prepared the script, and rehearsed the presentation. As you rehearse, you will find that the visual aid will quickly jog your memory, putting your mind on track for the next portion of the presentation even if audience questions have led the discussion slightly astray. To recall especially difficult points, technical information, or statistical details that are not included in your visuals, you can add notes to yourself by lightly writing them on your flip chart, on the back of the previous flip chart, on the frames of your transparencies, on the slip-page between transparencies, or on your personal copy of the handout. Situations requiring such measures will be rare and will diminish as you become a more practiced speaker.

In addition to creating prompting devices for the technical or statistical details, you should also write a note to yourself in the following instances:

■ If you plan to tell a joke, write its key point and punch line.

■ If you plan to insert a human-interest story, write a key word to remind yourself.

■ If you need to pass out a handout, write "handout" in the margin of your notes.

■ If you plan to ask a question, remind yourself with a key word or just a question mark.

- If you plan to include a freehand graph or schematic, draw it in miniature on your notes.

- Depending upon your particular delivery needs, include periodic reminders to smile, to make eye contact, to stand still, or to move.

- Write the specific times when strategic visuals should go up. This is the best way to keep yourself on schedule and to avoid committing one of the two deadly sins—speaking for too long.

As you practice speaking from your visual aids, concentrate on making them a signposting aid for your audience, not a crutch for yourself. We have all suffered through so-called presentations given by "experts" who stood, as if glued, beside an overhead projector, reading their transparency slides like a script. This is not the proper way to use an overhead projector, or any other form of visual aid.

Use Visual Aids to Increase Interest and Retention

Appropriate visual aids can help your listeners clarify their thinking; visuals can make you more persuasive and they can add the spice that keeps your audience tuned in. An increasing variety of visual aids is available to you, from the chalkboard to the computer projection screen, but one visual aid you can always count on is yourself. In reality, your presentation never ends and neither does your role as chief visual aid. You must continue to sell your ideas (and yourself) during the question-and-answer period, during lunch or cocktails, even around the water cooler or coffee-maker at break time. Since listeners will tie you and your subject closely together, you should work to maintain your enthusiasm, energy, and engagement, and make sure your audience can see these qualities in you.

During the "center-stage" portion of your presentation, you should also make the best possible use of the other visual media available to you. Some general pointers on using visual aids:

- As a rule of thumb, plan to use no more than one visual aid per minute: a fifteen-minute presentation will require no more than fifteen slides. Don't overload your audience with specifics they will never remember.

- Give your audience one to two seconds to absorb each new visual aid before you start to talk. If you talk while they read, they won't listen. If you give them a chance to review the material, they will see that you are in control—and comfortable with silence.

- State the news for each visual: what it means, why you included it, why it's important to the audience.

- Don't read each visual verbatim. Your audience members can read, at their own pace, when it's convenient to them. Make your role as presenter indispensable: explain, embellish, add spice of your own. Give each visual added meaning and personality.

- Mix visual media in your presentations: alternate flip charts with transparencies or 35mm slides. Alternate transparencies with video and handouts. Use colorful banners to highlight your key points. Be creative and give your audience some variety.

- If you are traveling, keep the vital presentation elements safely with you. Murphy's cliché, "anything that can go wrong will go wrong" applies doubly to presentations and particularly to visual aids.

- Always get there early and make sure all the equipment is present, working, and suited to the site.

- Always bring your backup kit: spare bulb, markers, adhesive, push pins, screwdriver, scissors, staples, paper clips, and a white sheet or some pieces of easel paper (in case you have to make yourself a screen).

Handouts

These are among the easiest visual aids to make. They can also be a valuable tool for keeping your listeners on track during the presentation, ensuring that they go away with accurate information, and providing them with some permanent reference material.

Should you distribute handouts before, during, or after the presentation? It depends. You should time the distribution of your handouts to coincide with the presentation's purpose. If your purpose is to inform your audience, you will distribute exercises and workbook materials before the presentation, but an article, traditional formal report, or other reference information probably should be distributed at the end. This keeps your listeners from becoming readers until *after* the presentation. Sometimes you can coordinate handouts with other visual aids; for example, a procedures manual or a list of features and benefits might be distributed as a model when introduced.

As with every form of visual aid, the most effective handouts are those that are actively incorporated into the presentation. Introduce the purpose of your handouts, tell your audience how to use them, and consider using a "fill-in-the-blanks" approach: get your listeners actively involved by making them complete the handouts themselves, as you speak.

A Model or the Object Itself

The object (or a model of it) provides an excellent visual aid when you are discussing something concrete—the new model XYZ portable cellular telephone, for example—particularly if your audience is able to see it in operation. Before you decide to use a model (or the real thing) as a visual aid, answer these questions:

- Can you make it work, and work right, the first time? (Practice.)
- How much will it cost?
- Will it be large enough for everyone to see? If not, would it be practical to provide a sample for each audience member?

- How durable is the product or model? Will it stand up under transportation and handling?
- Would a cross-section or cutaway of the product add to the audience's perception of its features and benefits?

If you are not satisfied with the answers to these questions, perhaps you can use slides, video, or other photographic media to give the audience a concrete idea of what the product looks like and how it will perform.

Video

When used correctly, a videotape can enliven your presentation; it adds color and music; it can demonstrate your product, your service, or a specific aspect of your topic; and it can take some of the pressure off you, particularly if the presentation you are making must be a lengthy one. Video should be used with care, however, and never abused. Here are suggestions for using videotape or a movie in your presentation:

- Make certain the medium is suited to the audience. Computer projection doesn't always match the clarity and color of television's nightly news. Will your audience be forgiving or resentful?
- Make certain the content is suited to the audience. The information must be right on target, and so must the style and tone.
- Make certain the tape and equipment are in perfect working order. Get there early and run a preview to be sure.
- Incorporate the video into your presentation; do not let it become the presentation and do not expect it to stand alone. Always introduce the video and tell why you are using it.
- Set some goals for the viewers. What should they learn?
- Challenge the audience in some way. Ask them to get some specific pieces of information from the film.
- Make certain everyone can see and hear comfortably.
- Discuss the film after the showing. Be sure to include the specific pieces of information you asked the audience to look for.
- Ask your listeners if they can see themselves applying the concepts presented in the video.

Projection Slides

Slides are the medium of choice when the audience is large (200 or more), when you will be repeating the same presentation for different audiences, when the subject matter lends itself to photographs or graphic display, and when the environment is formal. Projection slides are colorful, permit artistic creativity, and are not necessarily expensive to produce. Shots of people and sites can be obtained for a modest investment; computer-generated charts, tables, graphs, and key words can be reproduced in brilliant colors, even when the computer only works in black and white. The cost of these computer-generated slides is about $5.00 each, not including the cost of your time to generate the graphics or the cost of the computer program (approximately $200.00) that interacts with the production company's equipment.

The suggestions for using projection slides are similar to those for using video, but there is one additional drawback: Projection slides require low lights, which can place you—the star—in the shadows.

- Keep yourself, not the slides, at the forefront by interacting with the audience and the visuals during the entire presentation.
- Use a remote control to give you flexibility.
- Use a laser-pointer to incorporate significant aspects of your slides into your spoken presentation.
- Keep the lights as bright as you can, and encourage audience participation with open-ended questions (see "After the Presentation" later in this chapter).

Flip Charts, Easel Pads, and Posters

These props are suited to informal presentations and small groups. They encourage the use of color and creativity, and the raw materials they require—poster board or flip chart paper and colored markers—are inexpensive and readily available. Another advantage is that they require a well-lit room. On the down side, flip charts, easels, and posters are cumbersome to use and time-consuming to produce, and they tend to get dog-eared and torn when they travel. If you do prepare your flip charts in advance, with easel paper, remember to use only every other sheet, leaving a blank sheet between visuals. This keeps your audience from being distracted by seeing a shadow of the upcoming visual while you're discussing the current one. Staple the blank page securely to the visual page, so you'll flip them both at the same time. Use posters, easel paper, or flip charts in the following circumstances:

- When you need to keep a series of visuals before the audience, you can place posters around the room or tack up individual sheets of easel paper.
- When you want to encourage group discussion and at the same time create a record, easel paper is the perfect medium. At the beginning of a training session, I will frequently ask the group to name their goals for the course. As I jot down the responses, individuals in the group can see the similarity of their goals and our group commitment to achieving them. During the training session, the group goals are there for all to see, and I can check with my audience periodically to see whether I'm on track. At the end of the day, I can roll up the easel paper and take it back to my own office; I have a record of what my customers want my product to do for them, and I can adjust future brochures and course work accordingly.

Banners

These items can be expensive and require a relatively long lead time to produce. You can, however, create paper banners for an informal presentation in less than five minutes, using a personal computer and a $35.00 program. Banners can repeat your key points, while adding color and graphic appeal to your presentation. You do have to make sure that you have some way of attaching them to the walls.

Chalkboards and Writing Boards

These props, and other media that allow you to create your visuals as you go, serve very well during discussion periods and as supplementary media when used in concert with other visual aids. Remember that you are using your audience's time to prepare your visual aids, so be as swift about it as you can. While you write, concentrate on facing your audience as much as possible. Do not speak toward the board.

Overhead Transparencies

These are the visual aids most business presenters choose today. They are inexpensive, quick and simple to make, and they can be produced in a variety of ways: with a copier, a transparency maker, a laser printer, or a color plotter. You can use an overhead projector in a lighted room, thereby maintaining eye contact with your listeners. You can also pace the presentation to fit your needs and those of your listeners. You can write on the transparency, reveal parts of a slide in increments, build your message using the overlay technique (placing transparencies with more information on top of more simple transparencies as your talk progresses), and you can reuse them. Overhead transparencies give you *control.*

Why, then, do so many people complain after attending presentations made with an overhead projector? Part of the problem lies in the machine's versatility. It allows the speaker to take control, but too often the speaker abdicates, expecting the projector to do all the work of projecting meaning and personality as well as words and graphics. Audiences, however, find nothing stimulating about watching a stationary object (the speaker) reading to them from slides they could easily have read themselves. To encourage accolades, not complaints, follow these pointers.

BEFORE THE PRESENTATION

- Prepare clear, colorful, uncluttered transparency slides.
- Frame your slides or use the preframed variety.
- Number your slides in case they get jumbled.
- Clean your slides carefully before each use.

IMMEDIATELY BEFORE THE PRESENTATION

- Place the screen in a corner, if possible, so you won't be standing in front of what your audience needs to see.
- Arrange the reflector (on the projector head) to project the image high on the screen (above your head). When you use the screen for pointing, you can lower the image temporarily.
- Make sure none of the light or projected image spills over, off the screen. That's a distraction no one needs.
- Position the first slide on the projector. Check for focus and clarity. Make necessary adjustments.
- Turn off any lights directed toward the screen.

HANDLING VISUALS DURING THE PRESENTATION

- Move around. Point out specific information directly on the slide, at times. At other times, move away from the projector and point to the screen.
- Write on your slides using a colorful vu-graph marker.
- Use the revelation technique, where appropriate, to pace your audience's reading with your speaking. The best way to use this technique is to place a blank piece of paper *under* the transparency, then pull it out slowly as you discuss each element on the slide. The weight of the slide will hold the paper in place and keep it from sliding off the projector, revealing your secrets prematurely.
- Do not talk to the screen or the projector. Talk to the *audience*.
- Do not read from your slides.

Proper use of overhead projectors (and all other forms of visual aids) requires practice with the visual medium, rehearsal with your script, and site preparation. Remember that the most important visual aid is you; the other visuals are only your tools. It's up to you to make them perform as they should.

Prepare Yourself

According to Jack Hilton, who has represented more than half of the *Fortune* 500 companies as a television consultant, here is what you can expect from the average audience: very few will remember your name, virtually all will remember your affiliation, few will remember a single point you make, and all will decide promptly whether they like you or not.[4] Your goal is to make yourself, your presentation, and your key points unforgettable—in a positive way.

Preparation is the key. You have prepared your content so that the number of key points are limited, so they are presented in a dynamic and convincing way, and so they are repeated strategically. The other essential ingredient is to prepare *yourself*.

REHEARSE!

The two deadly sins are being unprepared and speaking for too long. These sins go hand-in-hand. If you are prepared, you will have rehearsed, and if you rehearse, it is easy to time your presentation. In a training session I recently ran for six executives, one of the assignments was to prepare an eight-minute presentation. They were given two weeks to prepare and rehearse. On the day of the presentations, I asked two group members to help me time the speakers. One spoke for seven minutes; one spoke for eight minutes; one spoke for eleven minutes; and three spoke for over fifteen minutes! When I told them how long their eight-minute speeches had taken, all four of those who had gone over the time limit were amazed that they had spoken for so long. All three of those who had taken more than fifteen minutes *admitted that they had not rehearsed.* You cannot omit this essential element in preparing your presentation.

If you've written a complete script, practice several times from the script. This will give you greater control later, when you are presenting from your keyword prompts. Stand before a mirror with the tape recorder on (or, better yet, stand before a videocamera and microphone). *Time the presentation to make certain it isn't too long.*

Watch and listen to yourself. Play and replay the tape recording while you get dressed, while you commute, while you eat dinner. The repetition will help you incorporate the specifics and the rhythms into your subconscious so that the actual presentation will be second nature to you. *Ask yourself whether the main points are clear and receive adequate emphasis.*

Try to rehearse on location at least once. An on-site rehearsal will give you a feel for the room: its size, the acoustics, the external noises, the location of your support systems (microphone, lectern, water glass) and visual aids. How close can you get to your audience? Can you dispense with a lectern (the ideal situation) or does the staging require a podium and microphone? If you can't rehearse on-site, at least visit the site to help you diminish the possibility of unpleasant surprises.

Delivering the Presentation

Wear Clothes That Fit the Situation

Obviously, your analysis of the audience and the situation will provide you with information about the appropriate costume for your presentation. You should plan to dress as formally as the most formal member of your audience. Wear a suit that is comfortably broken-in, but don't let it be so comfortable that it doesn't look crisp anymore. Make sure you've had a recent haircut, that your hair is out of your face, and limit jewelry to the most elegant and essential. In short, make sure nothing detracts from your image or distracts from your message.

If you are being videotaped, avoid choosing black and white as your wardrobe for the day. Medium blues and charcoal grays are best for suits, and solids project better than pinstripes. Don't choose strongly patterned or shiny fabrics.

They don't photograph well, and they tend to overwhelm the surroundings: the audience will watch your suit instead of you. A little color near the face will accentuate the complexion and make you look more robust on camera.[5]

Let Your Stance and Posture Send a Message of Confidence and Openness

Keep shoulders straight and relaxed, not tight or drawn up near your neck. Arms should be away from your sides, giving you room to breathe and providing an image of relaxation and openness. Lean slightly forward from the waist. If you are sitting, don't let your back touch the chair back; keep hands on or above the table, not in your lap.

Vary Your Voice

Nothing is worse than listening to a speaker drone on and on in the same tone of voice, using the same pitch, at the same speed, with no pauses or volume changes. If you're interested in what you're saying this probably won't happen to you, but if you know that being nervous affects your voice, make a conscious effort to add variety to your pitch, volume, and tone. Vary your rate of speaking. Pause in the appropriate places, for emphasis.

Fear can do strange things to people's voices. It can make you speak from your throat, which makes the pitch go up (you'll sound unsure of yourself) and weakens your ability to speak with adequate volume and strength. Sometimes your voice might even crack. Become conscious of what it feels like to speak from your diaphragm: You might try placing your voice in your head, then your nose, then your throat, then lowering it to project from your rib cage. This is the power position for your voice.

As you practice, place your fingers below your rib cage and use your diaphragm muscles to push your hand outward as you speak. This means you are supporting your voice with the strength of your diaphragm. Try using your lungs to force your breastbone up and out. This gives you additional breath support.

If you do have problems with your voice or throat, avoid drinks with caffeine, which acts as a diuretic and dries your mouth. Drink plenty of water instead.

Tailor Your Gestures to the Situation

Large, even grandiose gestures have been used effectively by such famous speakers as Winston Churchill, John Kennedy, and Jesse Jackson, but grandiose gestures will not work in a small group setting or when you are participating in a videoconference. Begin speaking with your hands relaxed at your sides or resting lightly on the table or lectern. Then incorporate gestures as a natural part of the conversation with your audience. Make your gestures fit the topic and the situation.

If you have a very hard time incorporating movement into your presentations, you might note specific gestures in the margins of your notes or prompt. Do so with caution, however, since your gestures should reinforce your message. If they appear staged and unnatural, they will only draw attention to themselves and away from the point you are making.

Make the Most of Eye Contact

Use eye contact to monitor your audience, to establish a sense of dialogue, and to stress your sincerity.

If your audience contains fewer than thirty people and you are speaking for three minutes or more, you can spend at least six seconds looking into the eyes of each individual listener. Eye contact tells the audience member he or she is important to you and that will make an impression! Avoid the trap of concentrating your eye contact on the smiling faces. This is fine for the first minute or so, while you're building confidence; but challenge yourself to devote an equal amount of eye contact to each person in your audience. Sustain each gaze for about four seconds—or you can make a practice of moving to a different audience member each time you complete a phrase. One word of caution: If you concentrate your eye contact on any single individual, you will make that person, and many others in the audience, uncomfortable.

You can win the most begrudging audience members if you give them eye contact, smile at them, and call them by name.

Get Control of Your Nerves

Most experts agree that your acceptance as a presenter will depend in large measure upon whether your audience likes you. Unfortunately, the fear of being disliked makes many speakers nervous, which makes them defensive, which alters their personality from open and friendly to closed and tense, which does nothing to make the audience like them. The advice that you should lose yourself to find yourself definitely applies to public speakers. Put your audience's needs first. If you address the needs of your audience, monitor their reactions, and forget about yourself, you will win in two ways. First, you'll be a more effective speaker; second, you'll forget about your nerves.

Regard Yourself as the Expert

I recently spoke at an insurance convention where I followed Terry Bradshaw, former quarterback for the Pittsburgh Steelers. There was I, English teacher ordinaire, about to follow a legendary leader of men in the speakers' lineup. Imagine my surprise when he shook hands with me and confessed that he felt a little insecure speaking before an English teacher.

Mr. Bradshaw mentioned that when he first began appearing as a public speaker, he kept comparing his own efforts to those of the noted orators who spoke with him. This made him extremely nervous—until he realized that he could offer the audience a gift that none of the other speakers had. He had a unique set of experiences, a personal expertise that the audience wanted him to share with them.

Most good speakers get nervous when they encounter a new audience, but they use that nervous energy to add vitality to their presentation style.

If you have prepared adequately, you have a wealth of information to offer your audience. This puts you in a position of power and it should provide a strong incentive for self-confidence.

Get to the Site Early

If you arrive early, you can become comfortable with the surroundings, try out your visual aids, meet some of your listeners, and relax for a few minutes.

Do Not Create a Need to Apologize

You should not need to apologize for inadequate preparation, for unclear visual aids, for a "technical" topic, or for anything else. If some difficulty arises on the day of the presentation (you have a flat tire and arrive at the meeting five minutes late, for example) review the situation carefully before you apologize. Chances are no one noticed that you were late, so why tell them so? If, on the other hand, you are 30 minutes late because someone rear-ended you on the freeway, apologize profusely for ten seconds, then go on with the program. Make the most of the opportunity for yourself and your audience, without calling unnecessary attention to negatives.

Imagine the Worst Thing That Could Happen

No matter what you fear, it probably cannot be worse than something that actually happened to a man who was destined to become a regular guest on the Mike Douglas Show. One Christmas, one of the show's producers, Roger Ailes, decided to invite a complaint manager from a local department store to tell about the unusual gifts people had returned. During the live performance, Mike Douglas, the complaint manager, and three other guests were seated on a platform. The complaint manager kept rocking his chair back and forth, and one of its legs kept inching toward the edge of the platform; eventually he fell backwards off the stage. As Roger Ailes describes it:

> Well, this guy was so comfortable with himself that he just picked himself up, picked up the chair, walked around in front, put down the chair, sat down, and without ever missing a beat he continued the story he was telling. The audience and the whole television crew gave him a spontaneous standing ovation for coolness under fire. He was so comfortable throughout the whole episode that the audience just loved him. . . . I learned a lesson from that complaint manager 20 years ago and it has always stuck in my mind. We are all human. Accidents can happen. We are not perfect. We may even make fools of ourselves. But if we can smile and keep on going, we can win the audience.[6]

Imagining a worst-case scenario helps put you in control. You can work to diminish the possibility that the worst will actually happen; if some difficulty arises, you will already have a prepared response. If some unimagined *faux pas* should occur, follow the complaint manager's example: Instead of calling attention to the glitch, go on with the program as if you are in control of yourself and the situation. After imagining the worst, visualize yourself at your best.

What If Somebody Asks You to Speak When You Haven't Prepared?

When you give an impromptu presentation, remember the advice of Ralph Waldo Emerson: "A few strong instincts and a few plain rules suffice us." Go with your feelings about the subject and the audience. You will want to keep your talk short, and your audience will not be expecting anything elaborate. A quick mind map can give you insight into your knowledge and opinions, providing ample material for a brief speech.

Your two primary concerns will be content and delivery. Here are the "few plain rules":

- Organize around your conclusion.
- Include facts, anecdotes, and verbal illustrations.
- Stress logical connections.

For delivery style, simply remember to establish a conversation with your audience. Enthusiasm is the key. Maintain and demonstrate an enthusiastic attitude toward your audience and topic, and you will find it impossible to dwell upon your own feelings of nervousness.

Make the Most of Your Setting

The more control you have in a given situation, the less likely you are to feel insecure. Although a speaker rarely has complete control of the physical setting for his or her presentation, some degree of latitude always exists. Insofar as is possible, plan and arrange the following elements of your presentation site.

- Seating and physical layout are sometimes permanently arranged. When you can make adjustments, however, do so with the following goals in mind: Keep the speaker as close as possible to as many audience members as possible, and give every audience member the best view possible—of the speaker, the visuals, and each other. These criteria usually mean that angled rows are better than straight ones, and a U-shaped arrangement of three short tables is better than a long, oval conference table. As we have already seen, it can also mean that your screen should be positioned at an angle instead of directly behind the speaker.

- Lighting should be bright enough for your audience members to take notes and read your handouts, but not bright enough to fade the image on your screen. Dimmers and separate light switches for speaker, screen area, and audience area are a help.

■ Distractions can occur in almost any setting. Do what you can to anticipate them and to compensate. Do you have to contend with noise from hallways or other meeting rooms? Are the doors at the front, inviting an interruption with each latecomer? Is the room long and narrow, forcing you into a lecture format?

■ Your visual aids and other props will need adequate support. Make sure you have a blank wall or a screen, supports for your posters, pointers, markers, and spare parts. If the unexpected does occur and, for example, your projection bulb burns out, be prepared with a replacement.

■ Constraints on your physical movement should be evaluated and diminished as much as possible. If you must speak from a platform, can it be made larger? Can a stair be added to the front for easier access to your audience? If you need to amplify your voice, perhaps a lapel microphone is available, so you won't be tied to the lectern.

After the Presentation

Prepare to Handle Questions and Answers

The best way to get your audience involved in your presentation is to ask questions. Not only is this a valuable technique for sparking discussions, it also gets even the quiet audience members—those who might not give you a verbal response—intellectually committed to the discussion. You might not get instant participation from everyone, but chances are good that they will all be thinking about the answers to your questions. You have probably known teachers who carried this one step further: You can increase the likelihood that your listeners will begin formulating mental answers to your questions if you call on them occasionally, by name. Unlike your teacher, you, as a business presenter, should choose only those audience members whom you can reasonably expect to have a defensible opinion on the topic. For example, if you know you have an accountant in the group, you can ask his opinion of the balance sheet on Chart X. You can ask an engineer how Detail 2 compares with Detail 3. Your questions can fall flat, however, if you choose such simple ones that the answers are obvious, if you choose such difficult ones that no one feels secure in answering, or if you choose the wrong people to call on by name.

You can use questions to introduce a new topic or a new aspect of your current topic, to conclude or summarize a portion of your presentation, and to check your audience's level of comprehension. Here are some pointers for an effective questioning technique:

■ *Plan your questions and note them on your prompting device.* Your questions should be designed to provide an orderly, focused discussion.

■ *Ask open-ended questions.* Queries that begin with "how," "why," or "what" invite more open responses than those than begin with "does," "is," and "do."

Questions that ask for opinions, and that cannot be answered in a single word, are more likely to invite discussion. They are also more likely to enable you to incorporate the next pointer:

- *Always give positive feedback to answers.* Let respondents know what is good about their answers. If certain aspects of an answer are weak, or wrong, keep the issue open for discussion. Assume the role of facilitator, not judge and jury. You can pose leading follow-up questions such as, "where . . ." and "what if . . ." to encourage your listeners to reach the conclusion you desire.

- *Encourage participation.* Make your first few questions thought-provoking, but simple enough to ensure ready responses and correct answers.

- *Pause for a few seconds after you ask a question.* Give your listeners time to think.

- *If answers to your questions indicate that listeners lack a firm grasp of the topic, try approaching the concept from a different, more concrete and basic perspective.* If you anticipate difficulty, bring additional handouts and visual aids and pull them out if necessary.

Encourage Questions from the Audience

You don't really know how well you are addressing your audience's needs, how clearly you are speaking, or how persuasive you are being until you find out what the questions are. Knowing your listeners' needs, affiliations, expectations, and prejudices will help you anticipate the questions they may ask, and you should certainly prepare for the most likely ones. We become so adept in our areas of expertise, however, that we can easily lose sight of the perspectives of our listeners. It is also difficult to tell at what points your listeners may have become distracted, where you might have used a word or acronym that was unfamiliar, or where you might have raised an issue that needs further explanation. Encourage questions from the audience in the following ways:

- *During your introduction, invite your listeners to ask questions.* Unless you have a logical reason for deferring questions, tell your listeners to stop you whenever there is a question. One logical reason for deferring questions is a controversial topic. Such an issue may require some quiet listening and careful evaluation on the part of your audience before you allow a potentially heated discussion to begin.

- *Answer in a positive manner.* Never allow sarcasm or even the smallest amount of ridicule to appear in your voice. Ask for elaboration only if you honestly don't understand or you need some extra time to think; never to embarrass a person who has asked about something that seems obvious to you.

- *Listen carefully to the questioner.* Don't interrupt. Otherwise you are very likely to answer the wrong question. Don't assume that this question will be identical to the one you heard last Tuesday, and even if it is, don't say so. Active listening can be fairly difficult if you have been presenting on the same subject for a long time, and you have heard all the questions 100 times or more. Don't let yourself get lazy.

- *Make direct eye contact as the question is asked, and during the first three seconds of your response.* To avoid establishing an exclusive dialogue, include all your audience in your answer.

- *Unless you are speaking to a very small group and the question is very simple, rephrase it in your own words.* Do this to make certain you understand the questioner's intent and to give yourself some time to organize an answer.

- *Keep your answer short and specific.*

Speakers sometimes fear the audience's power to ask questions; that fear becomes fairly obvious to the audience. A speaker who fails to make direct eye contact, who asks for questions while staring at her notes, and who prepares a full thirty minutes of content for a thirty-minute presentation is obviously unwilling to entertain questions. Don't let yourself fall into that trap. If someone asks a question that is particularly difficult, and for which you have not prepared, chances are—if you've done your homework—that the question will also be off-track. This inappropriateness will be fairly obvious to your audience, which is a point in your favor. Problem questions can be handled with a variety of strategies:

- *Rephrase the question.* Bend it slightly to make it fit your issues. Try to find some point of agreement: Mr. Lambert might say, "This idea about instituting a no-smoking policy is absolute nonsense. How can you expect to force something like that on workers who value their personal freedom?" If you are dedicated to seeing the policy implemented, you might begin your response as follows: "Mr. Lambert, I agree that we need to protect the personal freedoms of our employees. One of those freedoms is the right to breathe clean air in a healthy working environment. . . ."

- *Ask the questioner to elaborate.* If the questioner is attempting to cause trouble, the need to elaborate forces her to choose between further exposing her pettiness or steering her question toward the issues, which can provide you with an avenue of response. Most people will say too much, when given the chance—providing you with valuable clues to a proper response. At the very least, this approach will give you a little more time to think.

- *Offer to speak with the person individually after the meeting.* If a questioner is both hostile and persistent, mention that "we are taking too much of the audience's time with this issue." After offering to meet with the individual later, move on to something else.

- *Never, never bluff, and never apologize if you don't know the answer.* If you bluff, you may be wrong, which means you are not giving your listeners an honest exchange for their time. In addition, it probably will be obvious that you are bluffing. If you apologize, you imply that you didn't prepare enough. Both approaches weaken your credibility and your own self-esteem. If the question relates to your topic, promise to find the answer and follow up on your promise.

PRESENTATION GUIDELINES

____ Understand the Goals of the Presentation

____ Analyze the Situation

____ Analyze the Audience

____ Adapt the Message to the Needs and Expectations of the Audience

  ____ Base your reasoning on their level of knowledge and experience.

____ Use their terminology and language.

____ Address their sense of appropriateness and need for information.

____ Prepare Yourself

____ Prepare Productive Visual Aids

____ Prepare for Possible Questions and Objections

- *Give hypothetical questions hypothetical answers.* Vice President Dan Quayle was criticized for his response to the debate question, "What would you do if the president were killed?" This criticism was focused in two areas. First, he seemed unprepared for a question that he should certainly have anticipated and rehearsed. Second, his answer (that he would first pray and then consult the cabinet) was too literal. A hypothetical response would have gone along these lines: "That would, of course, depend upon the circumstances of his death and the state of national security at the time . . ."

- *Use nonverbal power techniques.* Before you respond, sustain a long pause coupled with unwaveringly direct eye contact. The nonverbal message is, "I know what you are up to." If he is seated and you are standing, give yourself the advantage of height by walking over and standing beside him. This must be done in a friendly, nonthreatening way, but the movement will underscore your control.

Seek Feedback

You should take the trouble to distinguish between hostile questions and questions posed by fair-minded but independent thinkers who are raising valid issues. The independent thinkers can give you valuable insights and new perspectives. Using a feedback sheet at the end of a presentation can help you gain opinions from those who did not choose to reveal their responses during the question-and-answer session. Planning and preparing a sheet for distribution in advance shows that you do indeed care about their ideas. If there is no one providing support services, ask one or two members of the audience before the presentation whether they would pass out these forms at the end.

Many of the exercises below are designed to provide you with insights from your peers and colleagues. You will also find opportunities to practice your presentation skills as you explore the applications chapters in the second half of this textbook. Use the guidelines and evaluation form below to prepare and rehearse your own presentations and to evaluate presentations given by yourself and your colleagues.

▢ PRESENTATION EVALUATION FORM

Scale: 1 = superior, 2 = good, 3 = fair, 4 = needs work, 5 = deficient

WAS THE PRESENTATION EFFECTIVE?

What were the most effective elements?

_____
_____
_____
_____
_____
_____

What were the least effective elements?

_____
_____
_____
_____
_____
_____

DELIVERY

____ Was movement appropriate to ideas?

____ Was body language open and relaxed?

____ Was the voice loud enough, clear, varied, and free of distractions (such as "ah" and "um")?

____ Was eye contact well-maintained and distributed to all audience members?

____ Was the face appropriately animated?

____ Was the pace effective, with appropriate pauses and timing?

____ Was the speaker poised, confident, and aware of the audience's reactions?

ORGANIZATION

____ Did the introduction establish credibility, get attention, and give a clear sense of direction?

____ Was the central discussion easy to follow (signposting)?

____ Did the conclusion establish the necessary action?

____ What was the main point?

VISUAL AIDS

____ Were the visuals easy to grasp?

____ Were they easy to read (large, clear lines, uncluttered)?

____ Were they integrated into the presentation?

____ Did the speaker rely on them too much?

LANGUAGE

____ Was the language concise, clear, and vivid?

____ Was it adapted to the audience?

Additional comments:

▢ COMMUNICATION CHALLENGES

EXERCISE 1

Evaluating Presentations   The best way to improve the style and content of your oral presentation is to establish a support group skilled in evaluating and critiquing the presentations made by its members. Useful evaluations provide feedback that is both specific and supportive. When you evaluate a colleague's presentation, you should use a checklist like the one provided and you should describe content and behaviors (delivery style), not personality. Provide both positive and critical comments. The positive comments help us see our strengths, the things we do not need to change. The criticism helps us to see where we can improve. Word your comments objectively: "I didn't like the body language" sounds subjective, and it fails to tell the speaker what specific changes he should make. It would be more helpful to say, "Instead of putting your hands behind your back, use them for natural gestures."

Evaluate the comments below. What makes them valuable (or worthless)? How can each of them be improved?

1. Your discussion of time management was extremely useful, but you should be more specific about establishing objectives.
2. I personally enjoyed your humor and wit, and look forward to hearing you again.
3. There were some problems with your voice.
4. Your delivery is well-timed; the content was fine-tuned to the needs of advertising managers. The information about affect positioning was especially helpful.
5. This speaker is a real wimp.
6. All that drivel about affect positioning made absolutely no sense.
7. The speech was good, but it wasn't what I was expecting.

EXERCISE 2

Illustrative Visual Aids   In conjunction with a presentation you are preparing for one of the cases in this textbook, *prepare a series of flip charts or transparencies:*

a. Write out the key point of your presentation.
b. Write the three key supporting points.
c. Draw pictures to illustrate each of those points.
d. Add "spice" by developing an even more imaginative visual.

 Example: You need to convince your boss, Mrs. Strohmeyer, that current production techniques are cumbersome and inefficient.

 Key point: Unless our manufacturing process receives needed upgrades, Strohmeyer Manufacturing may be surpassed by our new competitors.

 Hint: Helpful tools for producing pictorial visuals include the following: Computer graphics programs and clip art files, an optical scanner, clip art books available at art supply stores, and a photocopier that enlarges.

Strohmeyer Mfg. Holland Mfg.
Projected Revenues Projected Revenues
1990–1998 1990–1998

Illustration

This system succeeded until its environment changed.

Imaginative Illustration

EXERCISE 3

Thinking on Your Feet   This exercise will give you practice in impromptu speaking, or thinking "on your feet." You will need a hat (or a plastic or cardboard container) to gather topics.

a. Each member of your class writes two impromptu topics on a scrap of paper, then puts them into the hat.
b. Each speaker draws a topic from the hat.
c. After three minutes of preparation, each speaker gives a three-minute presentation on that topic.

VARIATIONS:

1. Speakers are not allowed the three-minute preparation time. They must draw their topics as they come to the front of the class.
2. After giving their impromptu presentations, speakers must develop a script or storyboard and a series of visual aids to accompany a ten-minute presentation on the same topic.

COMMUNICATING IN INTERNATIONAL CONTEXTS

OBJECTIVES

Studying this chapter will enable you to

- understand the skills—awareness, open-mindedness, empathy, and adaptability—needed to become an effective communicator in a different culture

- use a checklist of questions for researching another culture

- understand important aspects of the Japanese and Mexican cultures

- plan communication strategies for an international scenario

PREVIEW

As companies become more globally interconnected, more employees conduct business with people from other cultures. Because the meanings of both words and actions are specific to a given culture, miscommunications can often occur unless those who communicate share common understandings. Miscommunications can be extremely costly; they can get in the way of doing business, lower sales, delay funding, or create difficulties among fellow employees from different cultures.

Obviously, having a basic knowledge of any culture with which you are dealing is crucial. To develop such knowledge, you will need to research that culture through reading or talking with knowledgeable people. You should seek information about such topics as attitudes toward keeping appointments, expectations about negotiations, and views about socializing with coworkers. The checklist of research questions in this chapter provides you with an organized method for learning about another culture. Reading the answers given about the Japanese and Mexican cultures gives you factual information and illuminates the differences that occur among cultures.

To be an effective communicator in another culture, you will need to develop four skills: awareness, open-mindedness, empathy, and adaptability. You will need to resist natural tendencies to assume that your way is the only way and that members of other cultures are strange or wrong in their actions and perceptions. Empathy can provide understanding, which can help you to adapt communications to fit the scenario within a specific culture.

❏ THE INTERNATIONAL CONTEXT

When in Rome, Do as Romans Do

New communications technologies, exporting, foreign investment, and joint ventures have created a global economy.

This adage was never more relevant than in today's business world. Companies from different cultures are becoming more and more interconnected. The business world has not only shrunk because of telephones, fax machines, satellite communications, videotaping, and other technology, but because businesses seek global markets. United States investors substantially increased investments abroad during the 1980s, while foreign investors significantly increased their share in U.S. assets and companies.

For example, a U.S. parent company sold most of its worldwide telecommunications affiliates, including those in the United States, to a Netherlands holding company controlled by a French telecommunications company. The U.S. parent then purchased a minority interest in the same Netherlands holding company. As business arrangements involving multiple international partners become more and more common, businesspeople from companies of all sizes will be dealing with foreign colleagues, foreign banks, foreign suppliers, and foreign consumers.

Your career will include working with people from other countries and cultures.

The odds are high that you will form business relationships with people from other cultures, and you may very well at some point in your career work or receive training in a foreign country. To deal effectively with international business contacts, you must recognize cultural differences and you must acquire the skills to overcome these differences. If you don't possess such skills, you may lose an important sale, fail to get funding for an expansion, or be unable to develop the team spirit required to complete a proposed project. You will also find that trying to establish a business relationship with those from another culture can produce anxiety if you lack a strategy for overcoming cultural barriers.

The Importance of Understanding Cultural Differences

Learning a new culture is like learning a dance.

Miscommunications often occur between individuals from different cultures because meanings are specific to given cultures. Businesspeople must plan their communications to fit the attitudes and viewpoints of the audience within a specific culture. William Condon compares learning a culture to learning a dance.[1] He suggests that in the beginning new dancers step on toes until they understand the movements. The more they dance, the better they become at moving in harmony with the other dancers. They become aware of the use of space, rhythm, and time—the ways in which to interact with the other dancers.

People learn a culture through socialization, a largely *unconscious* process of observing, imitating, questioning, and experimenting. In contrast, when working with another culture, people must *consciously* attempt to learn about that culture to avoid miscommunications. Within a culture people share concepts and strategies that give a sense of order to society. For example, the use of the first name in American business circles is usually seen as an appropriate form of address when conversing in person or over the telephone. The French share a different concept. French business associates invariably use the surname. To use the first name is considered to be too familiar and can cause offense.

In the United States a man steps aside in the elevator to let a woman exit first. The Japanese have a different custom when exiting elevators. Japanese men exit first from the elevator, and the younger man or the one with the lesser status allows the older man or the man with greater status to go first. When an American goes to Japan or a Japanese comes to the United States, differences in such simple strategies as these may lead to momentary feelings of confusion. When people step outside their own society, they often feel confusion because they are unsure of the rules of the game. Eventually, if they stay long enough in the new society and if they are sensitive to differences between cultures, they learn; order seems to return. The Business Communication Today example illustrates problems that can be caused if a business person does not understand the culture of an international audience.

Skills Needed for Effective Communications in Other Cultures

Words, logic, and actions must reflect cultural understanding gained by awareness, open-mindedness, empathy, and adaptability.

In the communications model used throughout this text, culture is one element that provides context for communications. Understanding the context of any communication enables the writer to choose better communication strategies— words, logic, and actions—thereby reducing misunderstandings. Analyzing another culture will reveal aspects of the culture that affect business scenarios. To understand a culture, you must develop four essential skills: awareness, open-mindedness, empathy, and adaptability.

Awareness

You must first become aware that different cultures interpret actions differently and respond differently. For example, Americans often use legal processes to settle disputes, such as suing other companies when rights of trade seem to have been violated. If a U.S. company being sued feels that it has not violated any laws, it will most certainly defend itself in court. If a company chose not to defend itself and did not speak out publicly against accusers, Americans would view this lack of defense as an admission of guilt. Because beliefs are deeply entrenched, it is sometimes difficult to believe that another culture would behave differently. Kenichi Ohmae, a Japanese business authority and director of McKinsey & Company's Tokyo office, argues that Japanese businesses may indeed act differently under these circumstances and should not be presumed guilty.

Ohmae has discussed the U.S. Commerce Department's 1986 semiconductor pact with Japan in light of the cultural differences between these countries.[2] The U.S. government accused the Japanese semiconductor industry of unfair competition through selling large quantities of low-priced chips in the U.S. market, a practice known as "dumping." In an effort to help the U.S. semiconductor businesses, the Commerce Department established prices for chips,

INEFFECTIVE INTERNATIONAL COMMUNICATIONS

Members of the economic development council of a major U.S. city embarked on a mission to attract a Japanese car manufacturer to their city. They spent a week in the company headquarters in Japan, giving carefully planned presentations to various groups within the company. Japanese company officials wined and dined the visitors every night, and the promoters used these opportunities to explain in even more detail the advantages their city offered. The Americans believed that these dinner invitations were signs of the interest generated. After returning to their city, the Americans sent letters asking the Japanese to visit their city to continue negotiations. The Japanese answered, thanking them for the invitation and saying that they would enjoy a visit; however, no visit and no negotiations were forthcoming. The weeks turned into months as the Americans wondered what had gone wrong.

Cultural assumptions caused the delegation to misinterpret actions and words.

If the American business ambassadors had been more in tune with the Japanese culture, they would have understood the junctures at which differences started to create misunderstandings and planned a different communication strategy. The Americans had offered an aggressive marketing approach complete with presentations, video tapes, and transparencies—all showing what a wonderful place for manufacturing their city would be. The primary difficulty lay in the Japanese attitude toward boasting. The Japanese judge boasting by the principal parties to be in poor taste, and the reaction is often one of embarrassment. To fit the Japanese culture more appropriately, the American businesspeople might have engaged an intermediary to boast for them.

Another misunderstanding resulted from the Americans' interpreting the dinner invitations as strong signs of interest in their proposal; during these dinners, they continued to press their proposal. Japanese customarily entertain visitors out of a sense of politeness. They wish to know visitors better and to discern their character through observing them and discussing subjects unrelated to business interests.

Japanese value a relationship and protecting guests' feelings most. Formality takes precedence over real intention.

The Japanese feel they must first spend time building a relationship and a core of trust before business issues can be decided. The Americans in the example should not have hoped to negotiate a deal after only a week's visit. The Japanese prefer an indirect style when engaged in business transactions. The American promoters, on the other hand, felt that each meeting provided an opportunity to sell directly. The Americans should have allowed the Japanese to direct the conversation during dinner and resisted the inclination to discuss business. The Japanese insinuation that they might visit the American city was another means of showing politeness, not a statement of their intentions. In this example, the Japanese ways of showing politeness and their indirect manner of communicating were misunderstood. As this example demonstrates, understanding the meaning of actions in another culture is necessary for planning communication strategies tailored to that audience.

set tariffs for Japanese products, and established fines for any Japanese price-cutting on semiconductor chips sold in the United States. These actions were taken against all Japanese companies, regardless of whether they were involved in the dumping episodes. The Japanese companies did not choose to answer the dumping accusations. Ohmae contends that Americans assumed the Japanese semiconductor industry as a whole was guilty, although that may not have been the case. To the Japanese, keeping silent is not an admission of guilt. This action, Ohmae says, points to a cultural difference in style:

> The Japanese way of coping with a problem is not necessarily to solve the problem but to make the problem less painful. Very few companies in Japan will say "We are right," when a fellow company is suffering from being accused by someone else. Companies, even if they are innocent, take the attitude of being quiet for fear that when they are in a similar situation, nobody else will help them.[3]

As Ohmae explains, different attitudes and reasons for actions exist. You must be aware that attitudes and actions are culture-specific.

Open-Mindedness

Resisting cultural prejudice is difficult but necessary.

Too often people refuse to believe that there is a basis for acting differently in other cultures. It is easy for Americans to say to Mr. Ohmae, "Why wouldn't anyone fight against accusers? 'Silence gives consent.'" Instead, communicators must hold prejudices at bay and avoid jumping to unwarranted conclusions.

For example, the fact that in Mexico a person is often late for an appointment does not mean that such lateness is an insult or that Mexicans are unreliable in relationships. Mexicans view interpersonal relationships as more important than sticking to schedules; therefore, they view the constant monitoring of time as an impolite gesture. A Mexican businessman may be late because he has spent extra time at a previous appointment. Understanding the concept that underlies the behavior can prevent unjustified conclusions.

Empathy

Empathy depends on imagining the implications of common human feelings.

The ability to put oneself in another's place is important to any kind of communication, but it is even more important in cross-cultural communication. Until people have gained experience within a different culture, they have to rely on reading about the culture, on information gained from asking questions about attitudes and feelings, or on nonverbal signals. At times empathy may be the only avenue through which people can understand the needs and feelings of others and change their own behavior, as the next example shows.

Imagine that you are talking with a Japanese business associate, someone you've met only recently. You have just returned from lunch and as you turn to go to your desk, you reach out and touch him on the shoulder in a friendly gesture as you say, "Enjoyed lunch. I'll see you later." He laughs, although nothing funny has occurred. If you have read about typical Japanese reactions, you may know that the Japanese often laugh when they are embarrassed. Recognizing that an uncomfortable situation has occurred can lead you to empathize with his feelings of embarrassment. Empathy makes it possible for you to role-play mentally another person's possible feelings and reactions. You might conclude that he expects more formality and feels more comfortable when greater physical distance is maintained. This type of experience can cause you to change your future behavior in accordance with others' cultural expectations, leading to better communications. Empathy can help you think of ways to elicit a wanted response or avoid an unwanted one.

Adaptability

Adaptable people adjust their actions because they appreciate cultural differences.

To respond effectively in another culture, you may have to act in new ways. For example, the different time orientations found in other cultures present many frustrating experiences for Americans traveling abroad. All cultures have ways of dealing with the passage of time. Americans tend to see time as a linear progression, and they break that progression into segments: time to eat, time to sleep, time to work, etc. Americans are time-driven, but perhaps not as time-driven as the Swiss. Other cultures, such as Italy's or Mexico's, see time as much more fluid.

People from these cultures have difficulty dealing with Americans' seeming preoccupation with time. In fact, Mexicans have become so aware of this difference that they will often ask when scheduling an appointment with a Norteamericano, "Mi hora o su hora?" (My time or your time?) Awareness of differences allows people to adapt to another culture. It makes excellent sense to address such potential differences explicitly. Assume a Mexican businessperson wished to go to lunch at 2 P.M. and invited an American for lunch at 2 P.M. because he expected the American to arrive punctually. If the American came at 3 P.M. because he believed that the Mexican businessperson expected guests to arrive an hour late, both people might be seriously inconvenienced. The first time you are invited to a social event, it is useful to acknowledge potential misunderstandings directly and ask, "I understand people don't always express time in the same way. Does your invitation mean that it would be most convenient for me to arrive around (the hour for which you were invited)?"

When persons from two different cultures are involved in a business relationship, who should be expected to adapt? In business the answer depends on who is buying and who is selling. Adapting to another culture certainly will help a businessperson to sell a product. As an example, the advertisement in Figure 17-1 implies that the National Bank of Kuwait's people understand and are willing to adapt to Western customs, as portrayed in the offering to shake hands. (The custom in Kuwait is to greet by embracing and kissing on the cheeks, not by shaking hands.)

Mutual goals should motivate cultural understanding.

Ideally, two employees of different cultures working for different companies would both try to understand and accept different attitudes. When people from different cultures work for the same company, the context provided by company style, policy, and goals takes precedence over national cultures and indicates the direction for adapting. If employees cannot adapt, they will have

FIGURE 17-1. Cross-Cultural Adaptability

From *The Economist* (1988, February 6). Reprinted by permission of the National Bank of Kuwait SAK.

difficulty in establishing effective communications and attaining mutually shared goals. If you find yourself in a situation involving fellow employees from another culture, consider the ultimate goal in the relationship and the benefits and/or costs involved in achieving that goal. Let that goal and the understanding of cultural differences serve as guides in determining whether and how to change your own behavior.

Analyzing Cultures to Plan International Communications

Four steps can lead you to the basic cultural knowledge needed for effective communication:

1. *Use the International Communications Checklist* in this chapter for questions that you should ask about another culture.

2. *Interview knowledgeable people or read to find specific answers.* See the list of resources and additional readings at the end of this chapter. Although natives of a culture can usually provide you with the information you seek, they may not readily anticipate the difficulties you might encounter. People who have lived and worked in another country for at least two years may provide much useful information because they know first-hand the difficulties that an outsider may have.

Cultural information can be obtained from many sources.

You may find other knowledgeable people within university departments, especially in foreign languages and international relations departments. Chambers of commerce often have lists of people familiar with different cultures, and within your city may be groups (such as the Japanese-American Society) whose members are interested in specific cultures. Look for a list of area associations in your public library. Consulates can also offer information on their countries and may be able to give you other resources. Chapter 12, Research Strategies for Reports, suggests ways of researching information on specific companies.

3. *Validate your answers through discussions with others and adjust your answers accordingly.*

4. *Apply your knowledge in planning communications.*

Checklist contains items likely to interfere with communication.

The International Communications Checklist is organized by culturally specific areas, such as orientation toward time, that might cause misunderstandings. All of these questions are important, but the degree of importance will depend on a particular communication situation. Your answers to the checklist questions will give you commonly acceptable standards for behavior, even though acceptable behavior may cover a range of possibilities. As you become more knowledgeable about a culture, you may discover additional issues. Some answers to the checklist questions for Japanese and Mexican cultures are given later in the chapter. Naturally, many other countries are also very important in international business, and this chapter gives you a method for learning about the cultural differences in other countries.

INTERNATIONAL COMMUNICATIONS CHECKLIST

GENERAL BELIEFS AND ATTITUDES

——What are the predominant religious influences?

——What are the holidays?

——What is the attitude toward age?

——What is the attitude toward individualism?

ORIENTATION TOWARD TIME

——How important is tradition?

——What are the working hours?

——How are appointments viewed?

GOALS AND STATUS

——What is the attitude toward status?

——How is status displayed?

——What are goals considered to be worth working for?

——What is the attitude toward work?

BUSINESS RELATIONSHIPS

——What is the attitude toward socializing with business associates?

——What is the attitude toward women in business?

——What is the attitude toward gift-giving?

——What is the attitude toward privacy?

NEGOTIATIONS

——What is the attitude toward agreements?

——How are negotiations conducted?

——How long might negotiations take?

SOCIAL CUSTOMS

——What are some customs related to lunch and dinner invitations?

——Should a guest bring a gift?

——What are appropriate greetings?

——What may be properly discussed?

——What is the attitude toward talking about or showing feelings?

——What are proper physical distances?

——What gestures are to be avoided?

USING THE CHECKLIST: LEARNING ABOUT JAPANESE AND MEXICAN CULTURES

General Beliefs and Attitudes

Beliefs and attitudes underpin culture. Actions often unconsciously depend upon beliefs and attitudes that are instilled at an early age. For example, in America the belief that persons should be judged on their merits without regard to sex, age, marital status (and other conditions) accounts for laws, social programs, and even business practices. In deciding to hire someone to perform a service, most Americans, especially those in large urban environments, do not ask or care about family background as would many Mexicans or Japanese. Believing in the concept of self-reliance, Americans do not commonly turn to family connections to find help in solving a business problem. In other cultures, getting jobs and promotions may be strongly influenced by family connections. As more Japanese companies seek to use merit as a basis for employment and promotion, conflicts with tradition may occur.

What Are the Predominant Religious Influences?

Predominant religious influences account for many of the beliefs, attitudes, and values within a culture. For example, in Northwestern Europe, where the Industrial Revolution occurred, Christian Protestant groups dominated. These groups emphasized the importance of work and the individual's duty, values sometimes cited as cultural elements. Realizing the major values inherent in religions and the place held by that religion in the society will provide a background for understanding many behaviors.

In Japan, the predominant religious influences are Shinto, known as the "way of the Gods," and Buddhism; Confucianism exerts a strong influence on ethics. Shinto's mythological influence emphasizes natural phenomena and mythological ancestors. Buddhism, in contrast to Shinto, shows the way to individual salvation. Buddhism, which originated in China, influences architecture, the arts, and literature. Within the last three centuries, Confucianism, more of a doctrine of ethics than a religion, has come to be the prevailing ethical influence with its emphasis on etiquette, education, and hard work. In *The Japanese Mind*, Robert Christopher concludes the Japanese are not a strongly religious people; he contends that they are more committed to their own ethnic group than they are to any one religion.[4] This lack of strong religious and ideological influences may encourage flexibility and the ready acceptance of innovative ideas.[5]

In Mexico, the predominant religious influence is Catholicism, which, while it permeates the culture, does not extend its influence much to the government or to business practices. Religion and society are kept further apart in Mexico than in the United States. For example, in Mexico churches are not allowed to own property as they are in the United States.

What Is the Attitude toward Age?

In most technologically advanced societies, youth is often more respected than age. The place of the older members of society seems to be eroding, even in Asian cultures that have a strong tradition of revering the wisdom that comes with age. For example, in the past a Japanese grandmother expected to spend her later years living with one of her sons (usually the elder) and dominating her daughter-in-law's house. Now the Japanese home often contains only the nuclear family. Although respect for age is still publicly acknowledged, in actuality the status of older members may be declining.

In Mexico, age is noticed and often commented upon. Young people's respect for the older members of society, such as parents, is assumed to be part of the homage paid to family. John Condon says that the respect of the son for the father is viewed not merely as the father's due, but that "for Mexicans *respect* was found to be an emotionally charged word involving pressures of power, possible threat and often a love-hate relationship."[6] The implication is that while much tribute is paid to authority, and authority is to be clearly recognized, the *appearance* of respect may be more important than the commitment.

Jack Seward, who spent several years working in Japan, illustrates how authority in the form of status or age often takes precedence over consensus in Japan.[7] Seward recalls an incident when he was asked to poll the workers in his department of a camera company to see where they would like to go for a company retreat. He diligently surveyed each one and found that the majority in his department preferred the city of Ito. When he and other pollsters met to determine the outcome of the votes in the different departments, they found that no clear consensus existed. During the course of the meeting the president's assistant stated that the president preferred Suwa. Another vote was taken, and Suwa prevailed as the choice. Mr. Seward was asked if he would like to change his vote so that consensus would reign. He refused because he felt that as a representative of the others in his group, he could not change his vote. Several times over the course of the next few days, he was asked to change his vote. He later found that buses had been scheduled for Suwa before any of the polling meetings had been held by the departments. In this case, consensus followed authority.

In Japan, the publicly held view is that older people serve as representatives and symbols of respect. For that reason young American managers may have more difficulty in negotiating with older Japanese managers. Americans who wish to influence Japanese decision makers should try to minimize age differences by selecting people for work in Japan who may be close to the age of their Japanese counterparts.

What Is the Attitude toward Individualism?

In Mexico every person is seen as part of a larger family group, not as an isolated individual. Of all groups, the family reigns supreme; one is known by one's family, as evidenced in the son's keeping his mother's family name and the married daughter's keeping of her own maiden name. For example, a son named Juan whose mother's family name was Guerria and whose father's family name was Andres will have the name of Juan Andres Guerria. His mother's married name would be Helena Guerria de Andres. In this way both the mother's and the father's families are made known.

In Japan the individual is viewed as much less important than the group, whether the family group or the work group. One of society's lessons is conformity, expressed in the proverb, "the nail that sticks up must be hammered down." This means that in Japan people are expected to act, behave, and dress in an inconspicuous manner.

Orientation toward Time

How Important Is Tradition?

Both Mexicans and Japanese view tradition as important. Even though Mexico celebrates its freedom from Spain, Mexicans are proud of European ties and influences such as the influence of Spanish law on Mexican law. Family tradition also influences Mexican law enforcement. Mexican law itself is often strictly interpreted, but once the machinery is set in motion, participants seek ways to circumvent the law. Often one's family or employer is able to mediate.

Japanese traditionalism perpetuates cultural values and avoids Western influence. The Japanese do not fear technological changes. Instead, they fear Western influence will disrupt the family's authority and erode dedication to work and achievement.

What Are the Working Hours?

Working hours in Mexico tend to run from 9:00 or 10:00 A.M. until 2:00 P.M., when banks, many shops, and governmental offices close. These places reopen at 4:00 P.M. and stay open until 8:00 P.M. or later.

In Japan businesses are open longer hours than in the U.S. and the standard work week in the past has consisted of at least two Saturdays a month. In September 1987 the Japanese Parliament made the forty-hour work week the standard for laborers; however, it is expected that it will take several years before the work week actually is reduced to forty hours.

How Are Appointments Viewed?

In Japan appointments are strictly kept and the Japanese tend to be punctual. To arrive five minutes early shows respect. Formal meetings often do not last long, because much actual business is done through informal preliminary discussions to gain consensus.

In Mexico punctuality is not considered important. If one is an hour late, he or she apologizes. If less than an hour late, there is no need to apologize. Meetings tend to last longer than they do in the U.S., with very little concern for time.

Goals and Status

What Is the Attitude toward Status?

In both Japan and Mexico, differences in status are to be recognized. Status is displayed through the obsession with titles in both countries and, especially in Japan, through the insistence on going through proper channels. In Japan the recognition of status extends even to social invitations. Persons rarely invite those above them in their work organizations.

In both Latin America and Japan the family's status largely determines the individual's status, reducing social mobility. In Japan getting into the right school gives one a chance for upward mobility. The race for the right school starts with kindergarten and continues through high school. To hope for a good position in a company, a person must have gone to one of the dozen or so recognized universities.

What Are the Goals Considered to Be Worth Working toward?

In Mexico a group of managers for different companies named prestige, expertise, and leadership (in that order) as life goals.[8] Another extremely important goal is protecting feelings of dignity, both individual dignity and family dignity. An affront to one's dignity is a severe provocation, not to be easily forgotten or overlooked.

In Japan material wealth and happiness are seen as acceptable goals. When wealth is achieved, however, a sense of decorum should pervade its display. The typical Japanese seeks respect that comes with status or by achieving a collective goal (such as having a successful business or successful children).

What Is the Attitude toward Work?

Mexicans view work as a necessity and often obtain jobs though contacts, especially relatives. In Mexico work is seen as a means to enjoying life through leisure. Their view of scheduling tasks differs from U.S. views. They assume that several things can be done at once and resist prioritizing tasks; this is sometimes called a "mañana" attitude, which Americans find frustrating. In a typical Mexican office, people wander in and out, interrupting the discussion as each is greeted and offered coffee. U.S. businesspeople are used to completing high-priority tasks immediately and to receiving undivided attention when they make a business call. Business and social activities are not so clearly divided in Mexican culture as they are in our own culture.

Japanese expect to join a company for life and perform many different tasks during their careers. The company offers life-long security and promotion based on seniority more than merit. Japanese seek to develop generalists in their businesses, and some of one's jobs might be totally unrelated to previous jobs. The Japanese compulsion for success motivates the employee to learn new skills. In Japan both employer and employee feel a deep sense of obligation toward one another. Vacations are not taken as readily in Japan as in the United States. Few Japanese workers take all of their allotted vacation time.

Business Relationships

What Is the Attitude toward Socializing with Business Associates?

In Mexico social and work groups overlap. Friends and coworkers share parties and fiestas. Interpersonal relations are established after work through socializing. Mexicans expect to become friends with coworkers, customers, and clients, inviting them out for drinks or to their homes to meet their families. On these social occasions business may not even be discussed—the family, sports events, and other topics will be used as vehicles for becoming friends.

Like Mexicans, the Japanese also see a strong need for getting to know prospective associates. They go to bars and restaurants after work instead of at lunch. The business lunch does not provide the time needed to develop a relationship. Japanese believe that knowing a person's character, to be read in manners and attitudes, takes much time.

Although the Japanese are masters of politeness, it is extremely difficult for an outsider to be admitted into their circles. Prevailing attitudes divide groups into "they" and "we." Introductions are very important in Japan. For this reason, Americans should make efforts to arrange for introductions before visiting a company. These can often be arranged through professional associations, alumni connections, or through American companies that have Japanese on their staffs. The family group, school group, and work group compose the Japanese people's world. Very little horizontal mixing occurs between groups. A word of warning: women, including wives, are not included in invitations to go to dinner with a work group.

What Is the Attitude toward Women in Business?

An American woman can be successful in Mexico if she is exceptionally good at her job, because expertise is highly valued. American women can usually accomplish more in a Mexican business environment than their Mexican counterparts, because the American businesswoman has a certain amount of prestige. The Mexican attitude toward women in general is that women are frail creatures who need to be protected by society's prohibitions.

A corollary is the Mexican belief that men are incapable of resisting their sexual impulses, so rigid social structure and prohibitions are required. For such reasons, women are advised to wear dresses or suits for all activities except sports. A Mexican man may serve as mentor to an American businesswoman and satisfy the image of needed protector. An American woman in Mexico will most likely have to avail herself of escorts among her male business associates. For example, she will probably not be allowed to go home unescorted following an after-dark meeting. She will also be attended to with chivalry—men will open doors and pay the luncheon check. Nevertheless, on the job she can attain independence through her professional demeanor and expertise.

In Japan, it is still very difficult for women to attain status in the business world, but they do exert influence on the family's financial affairs. Christopher points out in his book, *The Japanese Mind*, that Japanese women serve as the family's financial managers and the managers of the home and children.[9] He suggests that these influences may lead to changes in the status of women in the future. One problem with attaining status in the Japanese business world relates to education. Women rarely go to the best schools where many career contacts are established for use throughout life. Women usually work until they marry or until a child is born. Because women are excluded from the dinners and after-work entertainment of the working group (which are so important in establishing relationships), it would be difficult at this time for an American woman to conduct business effectively in Japan.

What Is the Attitude toward Privacy?

In Mexico business is not viewed as a private affair, but a public one. Few Mexican businesses have private offices. In general, within the Mexican business or social world, privacy does not tend to be highly valued. Japanese businesses, for a different reason, also have few private offices. Because business in Japan is seen as a team activity, private offices would undermine the team spirit.

Although Japanese businesses lack private offices, the Japanese believe strongly in privacy. That is one reason Japanese rarely invite Americans to their homes. Another reason is that the Japanese home differs greatly from the American home in space and luxury. Japanese who have visited American homes may feel self-conscious about inviting Americans to their own homes. They have a sense that their home lives and those of their wives and children should be kept separate from their work lives.

To the Japanese, privacy is more of a mental state than a spatial reality. The Japanese believe that life is composed of "cells" that allow room for everything. This concept compartmentalizes activities. There is the "cell of office" and the "cell of home." Japanese believe one can be alone among crowds when a person is in the "alone" cell. On trains, a Japanese person may withdraw into this alone cell. The careful observer will learn to recognize the alone cell and accommodate it.

What Is the Attitude toward Gift Giving?

While the United States government has strict rules against officials' giving or accepting gifts that might be construed as bribes, other countries have different customs and attitudes. In Mexico many in bureaucracies and lower-level governmental jobs (such as customs officials or petty magistrates) expect some money in exchange for a service, much as U.S. waiters expect a tip. To avoid problems that may ensue from frequently bringing in items through customs, businesspeople are well-advised to get a local person such as an attorney to handle these affairs. To avoid problems with traffic officials, it is best not to rent or bring a car to Mexico, where taxis are plentiful and cheap.

The Japanese, who tend to be shy in the presence of strangers, see gifts as a bridge to overcoming social distance. A gift symbolizes respect and acknowledgment. Before giving a personal gift, however, you should be careful to decide if you want to establish a gift-giving relationship with another, because this sets up an obligation that is unending in its reciprocity. You should also be careful not to give a more expensive gift than the recipient might be able to reciprocate in kind. Chocolates and liquor are especially liked. If giving liquor, you should try to give a well-known brand; much respect is paid to brand names.

In Japan gifts are sent to customers on three special occasions: O-chugen (in midsummer), O-seibo (end of the year), and after the giver has returned from a trip abroad. When traveling, one Japanese custom is to take a list of gift recipients to a department store clerk, along with a budget, and let the clerk select gifts and have them delivered.

Negotiations

What Is the Attitude toward Agreements?

Americans tend to see agreements in absolute terms: once promises have been made, Americans consider them unalterable. Of course they can be altered, but not easily and not without unusual circumstances. Some cultures see a wider range of circumstances under which promises may be altered. In both Mexico and Japan, harmony in interpersonal relations is seen as a primary objective. As a social lubricant in some situations, promises are made to make the other party feel good. In Mexico there are five different ways of promising, with these different meanings:

Me comprometo = I commit myself.

Yo le aseguro = I assure you.

Sí, como no, lo hago = Yes, sure, I will do it.

Tal vez lo hago = Maybe I will do it.

Tal vez lo haga = Maybe I might do it.

These meanings are arranged in a hierarchy starting with the most committed intention and ending with the least committed.

Samovar, Porter, and Jain point out in *Understanding Intercultural Communication* that "this agreement concept ranges from a durable agreement that everyone recognizes to agreement being unlikely. The problem, of course, is to understand the differences . . . in their cultural sense so that a correct version can be rendered in another language."[10]

In some cultures, such as Mexico, refusing a request is judged to be extremely impolite; as a result, a person may be evasive. Americans, who believe in being direct and assertive, may be extremely frustrated when they have been told, "Yes, I will come in to work on Saturday," but the person does not show up. In this case, the employee may have been saying yes without feeling obligated to fulfill the promise, because in Mexican culture it is difficult to say no.

Americans view agreements in terms of contracts, an attitude conveyed through legalities and the use of lawyers. Consumer protection has many advocates in the United States, but in Mexico, the attitude is very much one of *caveat emptor* (buyer, beware). In Japan, Jack Seward points out, the people believe in agreements through relationships, not contracts, and that the best relationship involves "flexibility based on trust."[11] In Japan the force of public opinion is used more often than legal action.

Americans expect an agreement to hold once it has been established. The Japanese see change, including change in agreements, as continually occurring. It is difficult for Americans to understand why the Japanese change their minds after agreement has been reached. Americans may rewrite a contract to make changes, but the Japanese see any change as a reason to start negotiations and contract writing all over again. Jack Seward discusses the Naniwa-bushi style of reopening negotiations, which is played out in three parts: setting the stage, relating the tragic event that befell the characters, and finally, lamenting the misfortunes.[12]

How Are Negotiations Conducted?

In Mexico negotiations are conducted much as they are in the United States. Each party has a hidden high and low point beyond which they will not waiver. The negotiations proceed as a series of tradeoffs, getting closer and closer to the hidden points.

In Japan negotiations are viewed as disagreements, which the Japanese do not like to confront directly. For that reason, intermediaries are almost always used in negotiations. The Japanese tend to take much more time for negotiations than the Americans, preferring to sit and drink tea, talking of unrelated subjects while at the negotiation table. The characters of the participants, revealed in these informal remarks, may affect the final outcome.

Because of the often maddening (to Americans) negotiation pace, the Americans will sometimes concede more, simply to end the process. American businesspersons wish to conclude negotiations so that they can get on with their jobs; intermediaries have the advantage in that negotiating *is* their job.

In preparation for business decisions within a company, the Japanese have a method known as *nemawashi*, which means "spadework." Those that might oppose a decision are sought out so that any disagreements can be smoothed over and consensus can reign. Informal meetings are held to assess attitudes and change proposals. The formal meeting is simply a matter of "rubber-stamping."

Negotiations in both Mexico and Japan invariably take longer than Americans expect. In both Mexican and Japanese cultures, people believe that a relationship must be developed before business can be accomplished. A relationship cannot be established long-distance. In both cultures, doing business face-to-face is necessary. In Mexico even brochures sent by mail usually go unread. The Japanese will read the brochures, but they serve as only an introduction. The Japanese take the long-term view of doing business, not a short-term one devoted to balance sheets for the current year. If they decide to do business, they expect the relationship to continue into the future.

Social Customs

What Are Some Customs Relating to Lunch and Dinner Invitations?

Although the custom is changing because of American influence, lunch in Mexico is the main meal of the day, often lasting from 1:30 P.M. until 3:30 P.M. or 4:00 P.M. Lunch can be used as a time for getting acquainted. At times a business associate may even be asked to a family's home for lunch. An employee may very well bring his associates along when invited to lunch at a restaurant. Socialization is viewed as a group endeavor. As in the United States, the one who offers the invitation is expected to pay, unless a woman has invited a man. If a woman wishes to pay, she will have to make arrangements ahead of time with the restaurant to have the bill sent to her. This arrangement will avoid the presentation of the check after the meal.

Some Mexican customs concerning dinner also differ from those found in the United States. When visitors are invited to dinner at someone's home, they should not arrive at the exact time of the invitation, but should allow at least thirty to forty-five minutes before arriving. They should not expect to eat immediately. Dinner will probably not be served before 10:00 P.M. and will last until midnight. In Mexico spouses would be invited and guests should expect to meet the family. As explained earlier, these conventions can create serious inconvenience if both the host and the guest do not make clear which customs they are following. By being explicit the first time two parties meet for dinner about the expected time of arrival and by affirming the exact time that guests should arrive, both parties can gain a common understanding and be at ease.

At a business dinner in either Mexico or Japan, business would probably not be discussed. Both cultures believe that before doing business, a relationship must be established. In Mexico visitors will invariably be asked about their families, because Mexicans view getting to know about one's family as a way of getting to know a person. The Japanese will also be inclined to ask about family. The Japanese try to avoid personal opinions and do not want to talk about controversial issues (for example, Japanese-American trade relations). The Japanese use entertainment extensively as a way of getting to know a person and building trust.

In Japan it is improper to invite someone of a higher status to dinner except at the end-of-the-year celebration, when bosses are often invited. The person who extended the invitation is expected to pay; however, in Japan, calling attention to money is considered bad form. The bill should be paid without taking any notice of the amount.

Some ceremony attends the Japanese dinner. The host often toasts guests and is very conscious of filling their glasses. In Japan drinking alcohol makes almost anything allowable. When persons are under the influence of alcohol, they are forgiven even for insulting the boss. In a society with such rigid forms of behavior, drinking is viewed as a safety valve.

Even though wives are not invited to business dinners in Japan, social groups exist in which wives are included. These groups tend to be international in composition with Japanese who have lived and studied abroad often involved.

Should a Guest Bring a Gift?

If invited to a host's house in Mexico, a person is not obligated to bring a gift. However, flowers or candy are often brought. In Japan, gifts are customary when invited as a guest to someone's home. Cakes and fruit are often given to the host.

How Can a Person Get an Introduction?

In Mexico, people are introduced just as they are in the United States, through mutual acquaintances or through self-introduction. Self-introduction in Japan is difficult and undesirable, because a proper introduction requires a sponsor, a custom that helps to place people in their proper groups. The sponsor, in fact, is held responsible to some extent for the welfare of any friendship that may ensue. If a disagreement should arise, the sponsor of the introduction is often drawn into the relationship to solve the dispute. At any introduction, the calling card is expected and is used as a vehicle to make other inquiries about one's school and acquaintances. The importance of the calling card (*meishi*) is attributed to the fact that it identifies one's name (family), one's title, and one's company.

What Are Appropriate Greetings?

Mexicans greet each other in the same fashion as Americans and all persons in a group are introduced, except servants, who are not to be noticed. In Mexico men and women will embrace those they have not seen for some time.

Japanese greetings are much more complicated. In greeting each other Japanese tend to take a humble posture and may begin by apologizing, saying, "I am sorry that I was rude when last we met," which probably bears no resemblance to reality. They may thank the other person for dinner when, in fact, it was the greeter who bought dinner. When Japanese greet Americans, they want to shake hands instead of bowing.

What May Be Properly Discussed?

In Mexico and Japan the purpose of conversation is to learn about one another. Japanese do not like to discuss personal opinions and they will not speak for the group. If a controversial subject is introduced, the Japanese will try to avoid answering directly until they have discerned the opinions of others, which is accomplished in an indirect manner—often through reading the facial expression or posture of another. The Japanese are skillful at indirect, diffuse discussion, thinking that they can learn more about the true feelings of a person through nonverbal means. They are more at ease with silence than Americans. In conversations with subordinates, the Japanese in the position of superiority takes the initiative in leading the conversation. In conversations among peers, the same Japanese may be more passive.

What Is the Attitude toward Talking about or Showing Feelings?

In Mexico inner qualities that represent the uniqueness and dignity of the individual are valued. This unique quality, known as the soul or spirit (*alma* or *espíritu*), and the emotions, are talked about more often than among North Americans. Emotions such as anger and sadness are displayed and accepted more openly than in the U.S.

Orientals are careful not to show their emotions on their faces because they do not want to impose their private feelings on others. The Japanese read emotions through gestures, facial expressions of others, and even breathing patterns. The Japanese try through the act of apology to avoid confrontation and displays of anger. Even when they feel that they are not to blame, they will apologize because establishing blame is less important to them than securing harmony in a group. Because of the wish for harmony, the Japanese give bad news in an indirect way, sometimes skirting the issue or burying the message in a letter. The Japanese are known for smiling often and for laughing incongruously to show amusement or embarrassment or distaste for a subject that they do not want to discuss.

Because the Japanese tend to refrain from displaying emotions on their faces, Americans think that they are aloof and unemotional. Paradoxically, the Japanese feel that the Americans are unemotional and that their business demeanor is "dry." The Japanese feel that emotion is often a driving force in business matters.

What Is the Attitude toward Formalities?

In Mexico, in general, being comfortable in a social situation is stressed over formalities. Mexicans may very well flatter persons or offer to give them valuable personal items (which should properly be refused) to make them feel good.

The Japanese rely on rituals and formalities in relationships. Hierarchies in terms of age and status are to be noticed and given proper reverence. Filling the cup of a host, holding the door for a superior, and similar formalities are all noted in Japan. (These formalities are also followed in Mexico.) One Japanese formality involves silence. Some subjects are thought to be too disgraceful to even comment on. Ohmae touched on this aspect when he said that some Japanese companies remain silent in the face of accusations.

What Are the Feelings toward Touch?

In Mexico touch is commonplace. Mexicans tend to stand much closer to the person they are talking with than do Americans. In fact, this physical closeness makes some Americans so uncomfortable that they try to find ways to barricade themselves behind their desks, often to no avail.

The Japanese tend to keep the same distance as Americans, but they are so used to the crush of humanity in their crowded cities that rarely do they say, "Excuse me." This response is partially due to the idea that you do not owe a stranger the courtesy that is due a member of your group.

REVISITING THE INEFFECTIVE COMMUNICATION EXAMPLE

The differences between languages are often blamed for miscommunications between cultures. If parties speak the same languages, we might expect miscommunications to be virtually eliminated. Of course this is not the case. Even within the same culture, miscommunications occur when actions or words are interpreted differently from the communicator's intentions.

A checklist can help business people develop communication strategies appropriate to different cultures.

There is much more to communications than correct syntax. We must also understand the nuances of language, the situation in which communication occurs, and the unspoken aspects of communication. Included in the unspoken aspects are logic systems, appropriate models of behavior, and attitudes toward concepts such as time and space. To receive intended meaning from a message, whether that message be verbal or nonverbal, the listener has to understand the cultural context.

In the example at the beginning of the chapter, promoters representing an American city were unable to attract a Japanese car manufacturer. They had not developed a specific communication strategy that would be appropriate to the Japanese culture. After practicing the skills of awareness, open-mindedness, and empathy, the American businesspeople should have adapted their usual marketing strategy in several ways. They should have sent brochures about their city ahead of time so that they might be used for promotion. When the promoters arrived in Japan, their primary purposes should have been making a favorable impression and establishing a relationship. They should have planned several communication episodes as part of their strategy. Having a representative in Japan to promote their cause would have made their own relationship with their audience nonconfrontational. After making several visits to Japan, the Americans should then have invited the Japanese to their city as negotiations through the representative prospered. Such culturally specific communication strategies can help businesspeople succeed in increasingly prevalent international and intercultural situations.

This would be an appropriate time to do the preliminary exercises at the end of the chapter, to consolidate your knowledge about learning about other cultures and developing awareness, open-mindedness, empathy, and adaptability.

COMMUNICATION CHALLENGES

Exercise 1 is to be completed by groups; exercises 2, 3, and 4 are to be completed individually.

PRELIMINARY EXERCISE 1   Identify students in your class who have lived abroad or who come from another culture. *During class, divide into groups and let groups interview students about their cultures, using the checklist for learning about a foreign culture.* This activity may be used as practice for the interview to be held as part of Exercise 1.

PRELIMINARY EXERCISE 2   As an alternative to preliminary exercise 1, a group of foreign students from your school could present a panel discussion about their native cultures for the class and a question-and-answer session could follow the panel's presentation.

PRELIMINARY EXERCISE 3   Call the local chamber of commerce to obtain the name of an international company or foreign-owned business that has offices in your town or city. Send a letter requesting an interview with an executive who would be willing to talk about the culture of the country in which the company is located. Using the checklist, interview the executive. *Write a one- to two-page memorandum about the interview, describing the most significant cultural differences you discovered.*

EXERCISE 1

In a group of four or five students, plan a report on the cultural differences that a company might face entering markets in another country (not Japan or Mexico). Your task is to prepare a report for company executives on issues about which they need to be informed. Make a list of foreign students in your college, division, or class, or obtain such a list from a foreign students' organization on your campus. *Write to two of the foreign students, telling them about the project and asking them to discuss the customs of their country with your group.*

Use the International Communication Checklist and references at the end of the chapter plus other resources in your library to find additional information in preparation for your interview. Make a list of questions you have not been able to answer through your library search that you would like to discuss with the students. Meet with the students, following standards of courtesy appropriate to the culture of your informants during the meeting. *Write a letter of appreciation to your informants.*

Prepare the report, which should be approximately five to ten pages long. Present your report in class, following guidelines for time and other matters that your instructor recommends.

EXERCISE 2

List business functions and business decisions that may be affected by attitudes toward the following:

Time

Agreements

Work relationships

Examples:
Function: Attitude toward time affects promptness of deliveries.
Decision: Attitude toward time affects scheduling decision.

EXERCISE 3

Choose a country and imagine that you have just been told that you are going to that foreign country as a marketing manager for a gear manufacturing company.

a. From the questions in this chapter, choose ten questions that you would most like to ask about your chosen country.

b. List some possible resources for answering these questions.

c. Using these resources, answer your ten questions.

EXERCISE 4

Imagine that your group is in the marketing department for Quality Adhesives Products, a manufacturing and distributing company for adhesive products used in electronic and medical applications. Your department has been asked by the vice president of marketing to plan a strategy to expand to both Tokyo and Mexico City. What are the most important issues in international communication to keep in mind in designing and implementing this strategy? You plan to hire locals for sales positions. *Using the information in the chapter on Japanese and Mexican cultures, collaborate to write the following:*

A plan for acquainting the sales force, composed of locals, with differences between their cultures and the U.S. culture. You know that members of the sales force will sometimes come to the U.S. and will be working with others from the U.S. You want to anticipate areas in which they will find differences. *To accomplish this, for each country make up a list of five crucial differences and the problems that might occur because of these differences. Then devise communication strategies for presenting these differences to each of your audiences.*

CASE: COMPUTER SYSTEMS EXPERTS (CSE)

You are a manager with Computer Systems Experts (CSE), a large United States corporation that assists companies in developing information systems. You and another staff member, Bill Rymer, are working together in Mexico City to develop an information system for the accounting department of Seguros Internationales, a large insurance company. The job is just beginning. You have been in Mexico for only a few weeks but you plan to stay until the job is completed, which may be two years.

Part A. Selling More Work

Your company wants to sell more services to Seguros, and one of your jobs is to accomplish that. A key potential client is Sr. Martinez, a senior manager in another Seguros office. You have made an appointment with Sr. Martinez for 10:00 A.M. this morning.

You and Bill arrive at 9:45 A.M., and the secretary and Sr. Martinez both come forward to greet you. The secretary offers coffee, while Sr. Martinez asks about your family and Bill's family. You talk with him briefly and tell him you're ready to talk with him about information systems.

He apologetically explains that he has to finish a report before he can talk with you further. You wait forty-five minutes; then you tell the secretary that you and Bill must leave and that you will return another day. Sr. Martinez comes forward to tell you goodbye, agreeing that another day might be better. On the way out, you tell Bill that you think Sr. Martinez was trying to get rid of you.

You decide that you need to plan a strategy to interest Sr. Martinez in your product. You read about cultural differences.

Assignment   Analyze your first meeting with Sr. Martinez in light of your new knowledge of cultural differences. Plan a strategy that will lead to the opportunity to present your product to Sr. Martinez. *Write an explanation of your strategy.*

Part B. Problems for the Female Manager

You have just found out that another manager, Mary Wright, is being sent to Mexico to work with you and Bill. Bill suggests to you that Mary may have problems because she will have to deal more directly with the Seguros staff, who are all male. He thinks you should write Mary and inform her of some problems that she may encounter. You are not as pessimistic as Bill because you know Mary is very capable. You think it would be

good for Mary to begin to prepare herself for this cultural difference, however.

Assignments

a. Write Mary an appropriate memo explaining some of the difficulties that she might encounter.
b. Assume that you are Mary and that you have received Jim's memo and have researched the difficulties. *Write him a memo telling him how you are going to overcome the difficulties he has pointed out.*

Part C. Broken Promises on the Job

You often feel that trying to handle a problem at work is difficult for several reasons. It takes a long time to find out about the problem; while people will promise to solve the problem or say that it has been solved, the problem persists.

For example, it took half a day for you to find out that a Seguros team leader in charge of a team of programmers was having difficulty getting programs finished on time. The team leader didn't come directly to you. He went first to your secretary, then to your assistant, and finally to you. When you heard of the problem, you went directly to the programmers and asked if some of them could work over the weekend. They all promised to work on Saturday. On Monday, you discovered that none of them had worked. You went directly to the programmers and angrily complained. Since then the programmers, the team leader, and even the team leader's secretary have been cool to you. You suspect that even fewer programs will be finished this week; this is an ongoing problem.

Assignments

a. Analyze the communication problems and the cultural differences that are contributing to these problems.
b. Plan a strategy to overcome the problems so that you are again on target with your programs and you are no longer treated coolly.

IF YOU WOULD LIKE TO READ MORE

Cross-Cultural Communications and International Business
Brislin, R. W., Cushner, K., Cheerie, C., & Cheerie, M. (1986). *Intercultural interactions: A practical guide.* Beverly Hills, CA: Sage. Presents critical incidents and broad coverage of main problem areas.

Condon, J. C., & Yousef, F. (1975). *An introduction to intercultural communication.* New York: Bobbs-Merrill. A useful introduction to cross-cultural communication, this book offers information on communication elements such as values, languages, nonverbal behaviors, and social organization.

Hall, E. T. (1973). *The silent language.* New York: Doubleday/Anchor Press. This classic on complex nonverbal behavior describes the "elaborate patterning of behavior which prescribes the handling of time, spacial relationships, attitudes towards work, play, and learning."

Hofstede, G. (1980). *Culture's consequences: International differences in work-related values.* Beverly Hills, CA: Sage Publications. The author analyzes organizational theory and behavior in light of the cultures of various countries, including Germany, Japan, France, and India.

International Labour Office, Editorial and Document Services Department. (1977 March). *Terminology guidance to make your work easier: English, French, Spanish, German, Russian.* Geneva: International Labour Office (U.S. Educational Resources Information Center, ERIC Document ED 145 669, 32 pp.). This pamphlet contains the names of official titles of personnel, offices, bureaus, branches, departments and other organizational units of the International Labour Office. You may order other pamphlets in this series, which is designed to help editors, translators, and other businesspeople.

Jenkins, S., & Hines, J. (1987). Business letter writing: English, French, and Japanese. *Teaching English to Speakers of Other Languages, 20*(2), 327–349.

Ricks, D. A. (1983). *Big business blunders.* Homewood, IL: Dow Jones-Irvin. Discusses problems businesses have had in international markets.

Ruch, W. F. (1984). *Corporate communications: A comparison of Japanese and American practices.* Westport, CT: Quorum.

Samovar, L. A., Porter, R. E., & Jain, N. C. (1981). *Understanding intercultural communication.* Belmont, CA: Wadsworth. This book discusses culture, communication theory, and the obstacles to effective communications across cultures.

Yun Kim, Y., & Gudykunst, W. B. (Eds.). (1988). *Theories in intercultural communication.* Beverly Hills, CA: Sage. The authors cover coordinated management theory, adaptation in intercultural relationships, and especially intercultural and interpersonal communications.

Japanese Culture
Christopher, R. C. (1983). *The Japanese mind.* New York: Fawcett Columbine. This book on modern Japanese society covers such topics as the role of Japanese women, the Japanese's relationships with foreigners, educational competition, and other fascinating aspects of Japanese life.

Haneda, S., & Shima, H. (1982). Japanese communication behavior as reflected in letter writing. *The Journal of Business Communication, 19*(1), 19–32. This article is useful for understanding the format and organization of letters received from Japanese companies. Japanese will not expect you to use these forms when you write them in English.

Johnston, J. (1976). Business communication in Japan. *The Journal of Business Communication, 13*(2), 65–70. Comments on the intercultural difficulties of business communication.

Lu, D. (1987). *Inside corporate Japan: The art of fumble-free management.* Cambridge, MA: Productivity Press. Discusses three Japanese management styles rooted in local history and economic conditions, provides insight into American companies that have done well in Japan, and includes a guide to Japanese etiquette for doing business in Japan.

McCormack, G., & Sugimoto, Y. (Eds.). (1989). *The Japanese trajectory: Modernization and beyond.* New York: Cambridge University Press. Provides a perspective on the effect of official policies and predictions for the future. Includes index and useful bibliographies.

Mitsubishi Corporation. (1988). *Tatemae and honne: Distinguishing between good form and real intention in Japanese business culture.* New York: Free Press. Contains 500 key entries of crucial business expressions that are traced back to cultural roots.

Nakane, C. (1970). *Japanese society*. Berkeley, CA: Center for Japanese and Korean Studies. The author discusses Japanese society in terms of the corporate group.

Powers, R. G., & Kato, H. (Eds.). (1989). *Handbook of Japanese popular culture*. New York: Greenwood Press. Covers communication in informal social situations.

Reischauer, E. O. (1972). *The Japanese*. Cambridge, MA: Harvard University Press. The values, political system, social organization, traditions, background, and international relationships of the Japanese are discussed in this well-known book.

Seward, J. (1968). *Japanese in action*. New York and Tokyo: John Weatherhill. The author discusses the Japanese language and offers many anecdotes that illustrate Japanese customs and values.

Mexican Culture

Condon, J. C. (1985). *Good neighbors: Communicating with the Mexicans*. Yarmouth, MA: Intercultural Press. Discusses many aspects of cultural differences between Mexico and the United States.

Diaz-Guerrero, R. (1967). *The psychology of the Mexican culture and personality*. Austin, TX: University of Texas Press. The author discusses Mexican society and the Mexican personality as influenced by family structure, relationships, values, status, ideas about respect, and other cultural phenomena.

Paz, O. (1961). *The labyrinth of solitude*. (L. Kemp, Trans.). New York: Grove Press.

Ross, S. R. (Ed.). (1978). *Views across the border: The U.S. and Mexico*. Albuquerque, NM: University of New Mexico Press.

Obtaining Additional Information

Information on many cultures may take time and considerable research to obtain. Below is a list of databases and specific organizations that provide information on publications and on international business and communications.

DATA BANKS

Lockheed Dialog
Bibliographic Retrieval Services
New York Times Information Bank
Dun and Bradstreet Database

REFERENCES

Gale's *Encyclopaedia of Associations* gives information on trade associations and other nonprofit organizations; Volume 4, *International Organizations*, gives information on nonprofit organizations headquartered outside the United States. These organizations can offer information on international businesses.

Interaction Directory lists interest groups and institutions involved in intercultural relations. For "Culturgrams" on specific cultures, write to Kennedy Center for International Studies, Publication Services, Brigham Young University, Box 61 FOB, Provo, UT 84602.

Moody's International Manual and *Moody's International News Reports* give information on international businesses.

Worldwide Chambers of Commerce Directory lists foreign chambers of commerce.

Business Intelligence Program
SRI International
333 Ravenswood Avenue
Menlo Park, CA 94025

Society for Intercultural Education, Training, and Research
1414 Twenty-Second Street, N.W.
Washington, D.C. 20037

International Communication Association
P.O. Box 9589
Austin, Texas 78766

Intercultural Relations Institute
Stanford University
Stanford, CA 94305

Intercultural Press, Inc.
70 West Hubbard St.
Chicago, Illinois 60610
Has a series of UPDATES and INTERACTS on specific cultures.

NOTES

1. W. S. Condon, "Communication and order, the micro 'rhythm hierarchy' of speaker behavior." In J. T. Harris & E. Nickerson (Eds.), *Play therapy in theory and practice* (1974).

2. K. Ohmae, "The U.S.-Japan chip pact: What went wrong." *Electronic Business* (1987, August 1), 37, 40.

3. Ohmae, 37.

4. R. Christopher, *The Japanese mind.* New York: Fawcett Columbine (1983).

5. Christopher, 55.

6. J. Condon, "So near the United States: Notes on communication between Mexicans and North Americans." In L. A. Samovar and R. E. Porter (Eds.), *Intercultural communications: A reader* (6th ed.). Belmont, CA: Wadsworth (1990), 108–113.

7. J. Seward, *Japanese in action.* New York and Tokyo: Weatherhill, (1968), 37–38.

8. B. Bass, & P. Burger, *Assessment of managers: An international comparison.* New York: Macmillan (1979).

9. Christopher, 102.

10. L. Samovar, R. Porter, & N. C. Jain, *Understanding intercultural communication.* Belmont, CA: Wadsworth (1981), 141.

11. J. Seward, *Japanese and American business practices.* Tokyo, Japan: New Currents International (1985), 82.

12. Seward, *Japanese and American Business Practices,* 77–78.

INTERNATIONAL CORRESPONDENCE

OBJECTIVES

This chapter will help you prepare international correspondence

- by reducing possible misinterpretation

- by making international correspondence easy to read

- by using conventions of international postal services

PREVIEW

In addition to understanding other cultures, you should follow conventions or organization and style that suit your readers' culture. To prevent misunderstanding, you should make international correspondence easy to read. You should organize the document to accommodate national preferences, use the "one paragraph / one idea" formula, and reinforce verbal messages with visual aids. To avoid misinterpretation, you should use experts in important situations, consider the foreign legal context of the communication, and avoid cultural metaphors. The foreign legal context will influence the expectations that foreign readers might have in reading and interpreting your communication. Addressing communications properly will enable the postal services to process your communication with maximum efficiency.

❏ WRITING IN INTERNATIONAL CONTEXTS

When you write to people from other cultures, you should respect their values and take action to avoid miscommunication. If you write in English, which is acceptable particularly in Japan, the Netherlands, and the Scandinavian countries, you should not try to imitate slavishly their style. However, you can modify some habits, such as conventions of expressing dates and times, to avoid offense or confusion. Check the table of conventions to make sure that you have not misled your readers.

Dates

U.S. CONVENTION	EUROPEAN CONVENTION	INTERNATIONAL STANDARD
month/day/year	day.month.year	year, month, day
9/1/1991	1.9.1991	1991, 9,1
September 1, 1991	1 September 1991	1991 September 1

To avoid confusion, spell out the name of the month. Also remember that the international date line occurs in the middle of the Pacific Ocean, so that when it is September 1st in Chicago, your oriental business colleagues will say that it is September 2nd. Such differences can create great confusion when companies are planning an international teleconference or when business travelers make hotel or airline reservations.

Times

Times can also be confused. U.S. companies observe two twelve-hour periods and indicate time as A.M. and P.M. Europeans, on the other hand, simply divide the day into twenty-four hours, as the American military does. For Europeans, 7 o'clock is always in the morning. Two o'clock P.M. would be 1400 hours. Expect bus, train, and airline schedules to use the twenty-four-hour convention.

Prevent Misunderstandings

Review your document drafts for possible ambiguities that may arise because of cultural differences and conventions.

Make Documents Easy for a Non-English Speaker to Read

Organize the document to accommodate national preferences. Americans believe in getting to the point, but other cultures sometimes prefer other patterns of information. The Japanese prefer a narrative or chronological organization leading up to the main ideas. (See Business Communication Today: Features of Japanese Discourse, later in this chapter.) The French prefer data before conclusions; the Germans, like Americans, state the point first. In spite of these preferences, American businesspeople should provide an American-style executive summary, because if the reader must translate the English document and does not read

English easily, it will surely be easier to translate a summary than to translate the entire document.

Use the "one paragraph/one idea" plan. Breaking your argument into easily remembered points will help the reader who is having to devote considerable attention to the decoding of the language.

Use visual aids to reinforce verbal messages. The ability of visual aids such as graphs and figures to sum up information and interpret it reduces the stress of processing information written in a foreign language. Furthermore some cultures, such as the Chinese and the Korean, value statistics and technical information.

Avoid Misinterpretations

Use translators, consultants, advisors, and native speakers of a language from your own company in important situations. If the transaction will have great impact, seek the help of experts. The money you spend will surely be less than what you might lose through a serious blunder. One writer who was preparing a brochure for simultaneous use in the Japanese and American markets learned from a Japanese consultant that the text of the brochure would damage her company's credibility if distributed in Japan. She had emphasized the diverse backgrounds of the company's executives, many of whom had worked at three or more different prestigious U.S. companies. The Japanese consultant advised her that these career changes would cause Japanese readers to wonder why the company had chosen to hire such disloyal and untrustworthy people, for that was how they would view professionals who had worked with several companies. What a U.S. audience would count as proof of broad experience would be interpreted negatively in Japan.

Consider the foreign legal context of your communication. In many matters you may need a lawyer experienced in international business to review your document. The laws of other countries are sometimes quite different than U.S. laws. For example, in some countries an employer must pay a fired worker up to three years' salary. Arrangements with dealerships, franchises, and marketing companies are likely to be subject to widely varying international laws. Furthermore, both France and Germany prohibit advertisements that claim a firm offers better products than its competitors. Americans, who are used to comparison advertising, are sometimes surprised at these restrictions. Audiences from another culture may interpret business documents in light of the legal systems with which they are familiar. To protect your firm and to ensure good relationships, you should know the legal context in which your document will be interpreted.

Avoid cultural metaphors in international communication. Culture provides the basis for many business metaphors, especially terms from sports, hunting, and military life (for example, "He struck out with that idea," "Don't propose that; that dog won't hunt," or "Recommend it and see if he salutes."). Your readers may not understand your meaning, even if they can translate all the individual words. Metaphors are powerful, but relying on unfamiliar metaphors can mean your audience misses the major point you intended to make.

BUSINESS COMMUNICATION TODAY

FEATURES OF JAPANESE DISCOURSE

According to Koreo Kinosita, professor emeritus at Gakushuin University in Japan, Japanese have several language habits that influence both spoken and written discourse, especially oral language. The following list is derived from Professor Kinosita's work.

1. *Respect for others' positions.* To avoid hurting the other's feelings, it is polite to deny one's own wants and to avoid causing a host any inconvenience. If asked whether Monday or Tuesday would be better for a meeting, it is considered polite to say, "Whichever you prefer." Americans would tend to state their preferences and requests directly.
2. *Indirect expressions.* These statements enable one to respect another's position. Generalizations accomplish indirection. If asked if one is hungry, the reply, "I always have a late supper" would avoid putting pressure on the host to supply dinner. Giving a narrative account instead of making a judgment is another form of indirection. For example, instead of answering a question yes or no, a Japanese speaker may simply recite the sequence of events to avoid making the judgment, especially if it seems the audience favors one answer or another.

3. *Frequent, even excessive use of polite language.*
4. *A review of the data or experience always placed before the point or conclusion.*
5. *Lengthy greetings and other preliminaries that preface the discussion of practical matters.*
6. *Solicitous comments* that seem meddlesome to Westerners.
7. *Details left unspecified.*
8. *Dislike of direct, logical debate.* Japanese expect others to agree because of an ongoing relationship, not because of the strength of the argument.

Professor Kinosita concludes that since international business must be efficient, Japanese people should choose different standards for business and personal situations. In a business situation, the Japanese person should be direct and pay less attention to courtesy so that workers can perform their jobs. On the other hand, he believes the quality of personal life would suffer if respect and courtesy were abandoned there.

Koreo Kinosita. (1988). Language habits of the Japanese. *The Bulletin of the Association for Business Communication, 51,* 35–40.

Based on my past experience as a communication specialist at McKinsey & Co., which has offices worldwide, I recommend that you adapt, not adopt, foreign letter conventions. No U.S. writer would feel comfortable writing an opening such as the one Haneda and Shima offer as an example of a Japanese letter:

Allow us to open with all reverence to you:

The season for cherry blossoms is here with us and everybody is beginning to feel refreshed. We sincerely congratulate you on becoming more prosperous in your business.[1]

Nonetheless, a U.S. writer opening a letter to a colleague in Japan could say:

Dear Mr. Kajiwara:

On U.S. television we have recently seen pictures of the maples turning red and gold at Denboim Garden in Asakusa. I hope you are enjoying this beautiful season in Tokyo.

Our company has begun production of an improved version of the valves you purchased last year, and I wanted to tell you that when you need replacements we can offer an even better product. . . .

DOCUMENT SPOTLIGHT

BUSINESS LETTER CONVENTIONS FOR MEXICO AND LATIN AMERICA

The following table explains the conventions for preparing the conventional parts of a business letter in Spanish.

COMPONENTS	CONSIDERATIONS	INSTRUCTIONS	EXAMPLES
Subject Line	What is my subject?	Name the product or service.	*Asunto:* Presentación del embrague seco #CL-310 para uso en bombas de turbina (Subject: Introduction of dry clutch #CL-310 for use in turbine pump)
Salutation	Do I know the person who would make the decision to buy?	If yes, use his name and title. Titles are very important. If no, address to the company. Abbreviations are often used.	Estimado Ing. González, Jefe de Ventas (Dear Engineer González, Sales Manager) Señores: (or) Srs:
Body: Introduction (1 paragraph)	Do I know the reader well?	If yes, use a familiar, personal opening.	Apròvecho la presente ocasión para enviarle un afectuoso saludo e informare de nuestro nuevo y revolucionario producto. (I am using this opportunity to send you an affectionate greeting and to tell you about our new, revolutionary product.)
		If the reader is known slightly, use a more formal but friendly opening.	Me dirijo a Ud. con el propósito de informarle acerca de nuestra compañía CLUTCH INTENATA. (I'm writing to inform you of our company CLUTCH INTENATA. . . .)
	What is my purpose?	Explain	
	What products or services does my company provide?	Explain	

(Continues)

COMPONENTS	CONSIDERATIONS	INSTRUCTIONS	EXAMPLES
	What response do I want from the reader?	Tell the reader what response you expect.	
		Write a longer opening paragraph than is typical in English. Use the words "you," "I," and "we."	
Body: The Pitch (2 or more paragraphs)	*What are the advantages for the reader?* Profits? Growth potential? Improve sales of related products? Marketability? Low-maintenance features? Firm, early delivery?	Use details and explanations. Feature/function/benefit Address the reader's needs and uncertainties.	
	What services can I provide the buyer? Credit? Sales presentations? Installation? Training? Demonstrations? Guarantees? Test results?	Organize points from most important to least important.	
Body: The Product	What are the most important features of the product? Design? Materials used? Installation needed?	Provide a brief overview.	
Closing (1 paragraph)	*The best approach.* Can I pin him down to an appointment?	Translate into Spanish	I will be in your city from April 1 through 8. It would give great pleasure to see you and discuss my proposition in detail. I will call you soon so that we can arrange a meeting.

BUSINESS LETTER CONVENTIONS FOR MEXICO AND LATIN AMERICA (*cont.*)

COMPONENTS	CONSIDERATIONS	INSTRUCTIONS	EXAMPLES
	Second best approach. Can I get him to call me to discuss the product?		Please call me at (713) 775-5221 so that we can discuss the product in more detail and arrange a meeting.
	Third best approach. Can I get him to write for more information?		Si requiere más información acerca de las especificaciones tecnicas y estudios detallados realizados acerca del embrague estamos a su disposición. (If you need more information about the technical specifications and detailed studies about our clutch, we are at your service . . .)
(1 sentence)	What courteous closing can I leave him with?	If the reader is *well known*, be extremely personable.	Sin más por el momento, quedamos sus atentos y seguros servidores. (Until later, we remain your respectful and obedient servants.)
			Si les interesa este proposición les agradecería su pronta respuesta. (If this proposition interests you, we would be happy to receive your prompt response.)
Signature		More traditional signature, but always acceptable. Write the name of your company, followed by your signature. More Americanized	Compañía CLUTCH INTENATA Por _____ Ing. Ralph Peterson Jefe de Ventas Atentamente,
		In either case, include title: Ing. or Sr.	_____ Sr. George P. Jones Jefe De Ventes

While this version is less florid and solicitous, it displays the same generosity of spirit that the Japanese opening displays, and it is based on the kind of genuine experience that a businessperson who follows events in Japan and notices local news references to Japan would have. It is good Yankee business sense to pay attention to the things that matter to your customer. Iris Varner has commented that the warm personal Japanese touch is out of place in an American context, but when you are writing to the Japanese, not to Americans, it shows cultural sensitivity to bend in that direction without trying to imitate the exact

---

(letterhead with address)

(date)

Mr. José González
TECHNICO Inc.
245 Villa Real
Monterrey, Mexico

Dear Mr. González:

REPUBLICO will soon introduce its new dry clutch to be used as standard equipment on turbine pumps. The excellent engineering design results in less maintenance and lower costs than other models.

We hope you will become a distributor for the REPUBLICO Clutch CL-310. We think that this product will prove to be a money-maker for you.

Our sales brochures are being sent to you under separate cover. After reviewing the brochure, please contact us if you need additional information.

We hope to hear from you soon.

Sincerely,

Ralph Peterson
Sales Manager

Typical Export Sales Letter

style of their expression.[2] You can take on a more formal air with the French, and be more direct with the Germans.[3] Adapt to their way of doing things; don't merely adopt their way of doing things. People everywhere are becoming more used to U.S. ways, and lavish sentiment would seem out of place if your letter were compared to other U.S. letters.

In the examples that show many of the business conventions of Mexican letters, we recommend that if you write in English, you use greater courtesy and more personal expressions. That does not mean that you match the florid style of some Spanish prose.

(letterhead with address)

(date)

Sr. José González
TECHNICOS Inc.
245 Villa Real
Monterrey, Mexico

impersonal, no courteous language emphasizes company product, not relationship

Estimado Sr. González:

REPUBLICO introducirá muy pronto su nuevo embrague seco para uso como equipo normal en bombas de turbina. El excelente diseño de ingeniería hace posible dar poco mantenimiento a bajo costo.

Esperamos que Ud. sea distribuidor del nuevo embrague seco de REPUBLICO CL-310. Creemos que este producto eventualmente traerá muchos beneficios económicos para Ud. Le estamos enviando por separado nuestros catálogos de ventas. Después de recibirlos, le agradecemos ponerse en conacto con nosotros si necesita información adicional. Esperamos su pronta contestación con respecto a este asunto.

Sinceramente,

U. S. style close

not enough details provided about the product

Ralph Peterson
Jefe de Ventas

A Negative Example of Literal Translation from English to Spanish

(letterhead with address)

(date)

Ing. José González
COMPAÑÍA TECHNICOS Inc.
245 Villa Real
Monterrey, Mexico

Asunto: Presentación del embrague seco #CL-310 para uso en bombas de turbina

Estimado Ing. González:

Me dirijo a Ud. con el propósito de informarle de nuestro nuevo y revolucionario producto, el embrague seco de la serie CL-310; el cual ha probado ser un producto bien acogido para el uso con bombas de turbina. Creemos que este producto puede ser muy productivo para ustedes; ya que según estudios realizados por nosotros, el producto aumentará sus ventas debido a su aceptación ya que proporcionará mayor vida a las turbinas que ustedes venden. Esperamos que ustedes lleguen a ser distribuidores del nuevo embrague seco de la COMPAÑÍA REPUBLICO.

[insert specific details about marketability, services, product]*

Si requiere más información acerca de las especificaciones técnicas y estudios detallados de nuestro embrague, estamos a su disposición para enviarlos nuestros folletos y para presentaciones detalladas con cualquiera de nuestros agentes autorizados. [insert details about methods of contact]*

Sin más por el momento quedamos sus atentos y seguros servidores.

COMPAÑÍA REPUBLICO

Por_____
Ing. Ralph Peterson
Gerente General de Ventas

*[notes to writer]

Good Export Sales Letter to Reader the Writer Does Not Know Well

Letter 2

(date)

Engineer José González
COMPAÑÍA TECHNICOS Inc.
245 Villa Real
Monterrey, Mexico

use subject line

Re: Introduction of dry clutch #CL-310 for use in turbine pumps

use title

use last name of person who has not yet asked you to use the familiar term

emphasize relationship; "I," "you," "we."

Dear Engineer González:

I wish to inform you about our new, revolutionary product, the dry clutch CL-310; this clutch will prove to be a well-acclaimed product for use with turbine pumps. We believe that this product will be very profitable for you; clearly, according to our actual studies, the product will augment your sales because of its acceptance and the longer life which it will give to the turbines that you sell. We hope that you will be a distributor of the new dry clutch from REPUBLIC COMPANY.

[insert specific details about marketability, service, product]*

If you require more information about the technical specifications and actual detailed studies of the clutch, we are at your disposal to give you our brochures and a detailed presentation from one of our authorized agents. [insert details about method of contact]*

Until later, we remain your respectful and obedient servants.

REPUBLIC COMPANY

Courteous and gracious ending, formal but personal

BY_____

Ralph Peterson
General Sales Manager

*[notes to writer]

Translation of Good Export Sales Letter

DOCUMENT SPOTLIGHT

INVITATION TO FOREIGN CLIENTS

A medium-sized software firm had enjoyed considerable success with order and inventory control software it sold to retailers in the auto parts business. Because of various changes in the Internal Revenue Service regulations, it had modified its programs and at the same time improved them. It decided to invite all its customers to a users' conference to be held in the Southwestern city where its main offices were located. Among the firms that used the company's software was a Japanese company in northern California and four companies in northern Mexico. The product manager, Konrad Phelps, wrote the following draft announcing the users' conference. The letter was to be sent with the vice president's signature, because she would be the host for the conference. When the vice president reviewed the draft, she made several comments and noted that the Japanese firm should receive a revised version and that the letters to the Mexican firms should be translated into Spanish. The comments she made in the margins of this draft apply the principles discussed in this chapter. Phelps used the checklist on page 481 to plan his revisions.

After Phelps looked at the comments, he realized that some of the firm's very good customers might have had trouble with the language he had used to make the event sound exciting and dramatically Southwestern. Several phrases and clauses would make sense only to people familiar with ranch life and cowboy talk, like "tie up your horses in our corral," "new and temporary hands," "ride the mechanical bull and do the Cotton-eyed Joe," "ride the range," "throw a rope on that dogie and put him in the pasture," and "passel." Some executives might

take offense at being called "pardners," a word that might not even be listed with that spelling in the Japanese-English dictionary.

U.S. preoccupation with times and scheduling was obvious in the first draft. Phelps had not offered the Japanese client choices or respected the client's right to make decisions. Phelps also had presented immediately the purpose of his communication. The organization of the letter was intended to highlight the dramatic, most beneficial events, but did not accommodate the foreign readers' preferences for chronological topic order. He had overlooked the fact that some foreign companies would not be affected by the U.S. tax regulation changes.

Furthermore, the guests could benefit from visual aids, such as a brochure of the conference facility to see how to dress, what the rooms and facilities looked like, and an idea of how western dancing is done. Some casual terms, such as "putting everybody up," might simply be ambiguous.

Phelps prepared the two revisions shown on pages 485–488. One is for the president of the Japanese company, and Phelps worked with a translator to prepare the other, a more suitable letter for the Mexican executives. (An English translation of this letter is included.) English letters are acceptable when written by U.S. firms to Japanese firms. The Latin American countries, however, are extremely pleased when a U.S. company writes in Spanish. Writing in Spanish does not mean simply translating a U.S.-style letter literally, but using the Spanish conventions for letter writing, which are formal, elaborate, and above all, courteous.

CHECKLIST FOR INTERNATIONAL CORRESPONDENCE

Did I practice awareness?

_____ Open-mindedness?

_____ Empathy?

_____ Adaptability?

Did I make documents easy for a non-English speaker to read?

_____ Organize the document to accommodate national preferences?

_____ Use the "one paragraph/one idea" formula?

_____ Use visual aids to reinforce verbal messages?

Did I avoid confusion?

_____ Consider the foreign legal context of my communication?

_____ Avoid cultural metaphors?

_____ Express dates and times as this audience will expect and understand?

FOR LETTERS TO JAPANESE FIRMS

_____ Did I offer lengthy greetings before discussing practical matters?

_____ Did I maintain respect for the other's position?

_____ Did I answer indirectly so that I put no pressure on the other person?

_____ Did I use narrative accounts to avoid expressing a judgment immediately?

_____ Did I review the data or experience before expressing my conclusion?

_____ Did I offer solicitous comments?

FOR LETTERS TO READERS OF SPANISH

_____ Did I use a subject line?

_____ Did I use the title as well as the name of the reader?

_____ Was my opening paragraph longer and more courteous than the typical business letter for U.S. readers?

_____ Did I begin my signature with the name of my company?

_____ Did I include my professional title or courtesy title (Mr. or Ms.) before my name?

_____ Did I show my position in the company after my name?

D O C U M E N T   S P O T L I G H T

INVITATION TO FOREIGN CLIENTS (*continued*)

spell out month

7/8/91   DRAFT

[inside address]

Too informal

Howdy Pardners! *— may not recognize*

might be read literally

spell out date Southwestern Express Software wants you to tie up your horses in our corral *may be seen as boasting*

on Friday, 9/6/91, for three days of good news about the improvements in the

QuikControl Program you have been using. These improvements will help you *should emphasize our relationship to these people*

efficiency may not seem important to them keep tax records automatically and calculate your income tax more easily than

ever before.

culturally limited *stereotype of Indians, may be taken literally, mixed metaphor*

So throw a rope on that dogie and put him in the pasture while you and two of

sentence is long, negative, complex

your staff make big medicine with us to keep the tax man away from the door.

may be misunderstood if read literally

Having not only taken care of the government's changes, but having added

change the order to chronological sequence several new features, we're ready to roll 'em out, and our own wrangler, Kent *use one idea per paragraph*

Kerry, will introduce our new training tutorial that will allow you to teach new

and temporary hands how to use the order terminals in less than thirty

Phelps's Draft with Vice-President's Comments

DOCUMENT SPOTLIGHT

INVITATION TO FOREIGN CLIENTS (*continued*)

4

who will make money? not clear

minutes. When we're not showing you how to make more money with this

?

program, we'll ride the range to a whole passel of action-packed adventures.

could be taken literally

We've included late afternoon swimming and tennis on Friday. We've lined up a

barbeque and rodeo for you Saturday at the Rancho Grande's arena in Lever

Canyon—the bus leaves at 6 p.m. sharp, so get a move on; afterward you can

don't emphasize punctuality to Mexican guests

ride the mechanical bull and do the Cotton-eyed Joe at the Rancho Grande's

possible to misread this

Silver Dollar dance hall. Plus, for those of you who can stay over Sunday

afternoon, we have tickets to the football game at our new sports arena.

make clear it is not soccer

We're putting everybody up at the Rancho Grande on the Southwest Highway.

have Mexican guests send response to me personally

Please call H. J. Johnson to confirm your attendance. We'll get back to you

add president's title

soon with more details.

Too informal

Sincerely,

Judith Kerner

Vice President

Phelps's Draft with Vice-President's Comments (*continued*)

▢ PHELPS'S CHECKLIST FOR INTERNATIONAL CORRESPONDENCE

Did I practice awareness?   *I read several articles on Mexican and Japanese cultures.*

✓ Open-mindedness?   *I let Japanese priorities determine my organization of the letter.*

✓ Empathy?   *I tried to imagine how they might feel about the invitation*

✓ Adaptability?   *I modified my sense of rigid scheduling.*

Did I make documents easy for a non-English
speaker to read?

✓ Organize the document to accommodate
national preferences?   *Yes.*

✓ Use the "one paragraph/one idea" formula?   *Yes, I used more paragraphs.*

✓ Use visual aids to reinforce verbal messages?   *Yes, I added a brochure and a map.*

Did I avoid confusion?

✓ Consider the foreign legal context of my   *Noted differences in tax laws for*
communication?   *foreign companies. Japanese company is joint venture; pays U.S. taxes.*

✓ Avoid cultural metaphors?   *Yes. Changed many of the "Western" terms.*

DOCUMENT SPOTLIGHT

INVITATION TO FOREIGN CLIENTS (*continued*)

July 8, 1989

[inside address]

be humble and appreciative

Dear Mr. Iyama:

We appreciate very much the opportunity you have given us to provide software to Hisaka Company. We hope that this product has contributed to your success. Your company was the first in Northern California to adopt our products, and many other companies have followed your example. We hope to justify your confidence in the QuikControl Program by improving it whenever possible, so that your company will enjoy the benefits of the best technological support possible.

These improvements will help you comply with Internal Revenue Service regulations, keep tax records automatically, and calculate your income tax for your locations in the United States more easily than ever before. Several other changes have been made that should enable your workers to cooperate very effectively. Our manager of employee training materials, Kent Kerry, has developed a new training tutorial. It will help your in-house staff teach new and temporary employees to use the order terminals.

explain benefits; emphasize cooperation

We would be honored if you would allow us to explain these recent improvements to you. I invite you and two of your associates to attend a three-day conference. It will be held at the Rancho Grande on the Southwest Highway beginning Friday, September 6th, 1991. We also have planned several entertainment and social events that we hope you will enjoy.

We hope that your visit will be entertaining and relaxing. We have planned late afternoon swimming and tennis on Friday. A barbeque and rodeo are planned for Saturday at the Rancho Grande's arena in Lever Canyon; afterward we will have dancing and entertainment at the Rancho Grande's Silver Dollar dance hall. The weather will be warm, so please wear casual

explain weather and attire

Revision for Japanese Customer

INVITATION TO FOREIGN CLIENTS (*continued*)

have him call some-one of his own rank

clothes to stay cool. In addition, if you enjoy U.S. football, we have tickets for you to the Sunday football game to be held at our new sports arena. I have enclosed brochures showing the Rancho Grande (where the conference will be held) and a map of our city.   *use visual aids and graphics*

Please call our president, Mr. H. J. Johnson, collect to say whether you and your associates can be our guests. You could arrive Thursday afternoon or Thursday evening, whichever you prefer. I will make reservations for you at the Rancho Grande and arrange for a limousine to take you directly from the airport to the hotel when you arrive.

Sincerely,

Ms. Judith Kerner
Vice President

Revision for Japanese Customer (*continued*)

D O C U M E N T   S P O T L I G H T

INVITATION TO FOREIGN CLIENTS (*continued*)

July 8, 1991

Engineer Thomas Garcia
[inside address]

RE: Invitation to attend conference on recent software improvements

Dear Thomas:

/ use first name because you have established a business friendship

friendly and gracious opening

Please permit me this opportunity to tell you I enjoyed visiting your offices very much last month. I would also like to send greetings to your family. My husband and I were so glad that all of us were able to have dinner together.

invite spouses where possible

My company appreciates very much the opportunity you have given us to provide software to your company in Monterrey. We hope to justify your confidence in our products. I would like to invite you and your wife Alicia and two of your associates and their spouses to attend a conference at the Rancho Grande Resort for three days beginning Friday, September 6, 1991 to hear about recent improvements in our software.

one idea per paragraph

Several changes have been made that should enable your workers to cooperate very effectively. At our conference, our manager of employee training materials, Kent Kerry, will introduce a new training tutorial. It will help your in-house staff teach new and temporary employees to use the order terminals.

emphasize cooperation

emphasize entertainment

We have planned several entertainment and social events that we hope you will enjoy. We hope that your visit will be entertaining and relaxing. We have included late afternoon swimming and tennis on Friday. A barbeque and rodeo are planned for Saturday at the Rancho Grande's

Revision for Spanish Customer

INVITATION TO FOREIGN CLIENTS (*continued*)

explain dress and weather

arena in Lever Canyon; afterward we will have dancing and entertainment at the Rancho Grande's Silver Dollar dance hall. The weather will be warm, so please dress in casual clothes. On Sunday, if you enjoy U.S. football, we have tickets for you to the football game to be held at our new sports arena. I have enclosed brochures showing the Rancho Grande (where the conference will be held) and a map of our city.

use first names if he has told you to

I hope you and Alicia and your associates and their spouses can be our guests. We will make reservations for you at the Rancho Grande and arrange for a limousine to take you directly from the airport to the hotel. Please call me collect by August 1 so that I can select the best accommodations for you.

explain deadline

no need to call someone higher up. You have established a friendship

Southwestern Express Software Company

BY: _____

Ms. Judith Kerner
Vice President   — *Mexican-style closing*

Revision for Spanish Customer (*continued*)

International Correspondence

There are three types of international mail:

LC mail, an abbreviation for the French words *lettres* and *cartes* (letters and cards), consists of letters, letter packages, aerogrammes, and postal cards.

AO mail, an abbreviation for the French words *autres objets* (other objects), consists of regular printed matter, books and sheet music, matter for the blind, publishers' periodicals (second class), and small packets.

CP mail, an abbreviation for the French words *colis postaux* (parcel post), resembles U.S. domestic fourth-class mail, which includes packages of merchandise or any other articles that are not required to be mailed at letter-postage rates. Current personal correspondence cannot be included in this class.

The U.S. Postal Service also offers Express Mail International Service (EMS), International Priority Airmail (IPA), International Surface Air Lift (ISAL), International Electronic Post (INTELPOST), International Postal Money Orders, and several optional special services described in U.S. Postal Service Publication 51, available free at local post offices.

To prepare letters for international mail, follow the instructions in the most recent edition of U.S. Postal Service Publication 51, addressing envelopes and packages as shown below. Seal all registered letters and registered letter packages. Send other letters and packages as follows:

Ordinary letters and small packets may be sealed

Printed matter may be sealed if postage is paid by permit imprint, postage-meter stamps, or second-class indication

Any matter for the blind should be left unsealed

☐ CHECKLIST FOR ENVELOPES TO FOREIGN COUNTRIES

____ Did you use Roman letters and Arabic numerals?

____ Did you place address lengthwise on only one side of the article?

____ Did you show country of destination in capital letters?

____ Did you put foreign postal codes on the line *above* the name of the country of destination?

____ Did you write the name of the country of destination last in the address and without abbreviating the country's name?

____ Did you use the English words for the names of the post office, province, and country? (earlier parts of the address may be in the foreign language, provided that you represented them in Roman characters)

____ Did you give your name and address, including the ZIP code, in the upper left corner of the address side?

____ Did you mark the class of mail on the front of the envelope or package, either in English or in the foreign language equivalent?

____ Did you mark airmail articles "Air Mail" or "Par Avion"?

Affix the green customs label Form 2976 to small packets, letters, and letter packages containing merchandise and material on which duty may be due, indicating the value of the item on the form. If the sender prefers not to declare the value on the outside, or if the contents exceed $120 in value, complete and enclose Form 2967-A, Customs Declaration (only the upper portion of the green label should be affixed to the cover of the package).

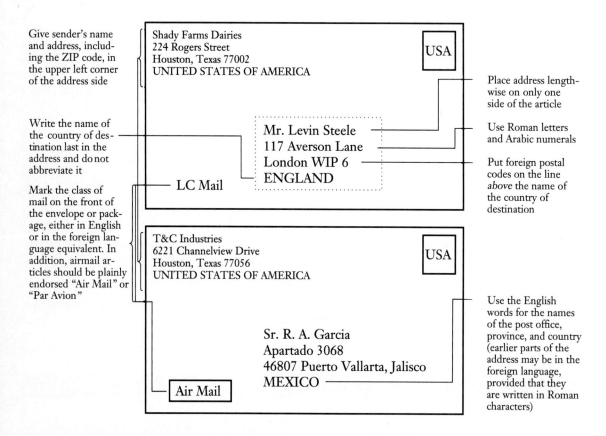

Give sender's name and address, including the ZIP code, in the upper left corner of the address side

Place address lengthwise on only one side of the article

Write the name of the country of destination last in the address and do not abbreviate it

Use Roman letters and Arabic numerals

Put foreign postal codes on the line *above* the name of the country of destination

Mark the class of mail on the front of the envelope or package, either in English or in the foreign language equivalent. In addition, airmail articles should be plainly endorsed "Air Mail" or "Par Avion"

Use the English words for the names of the post office, province, and country (earlier parts of the address may be in the foreign language, provided that they are written in Roman characters)

Shady Farms Dairies
224 Rogers Street
Houston, Texas 77002
UNITED STATES OF AMERICA

USA

Mr. Levin Steele
117 Averson Lane
London WIP 6
ENGLAND

LC Mail

T&C Industries
6221 Channelview Drive
Houston, Texas 77056
UNITED STATES OF AMERICA

USA

Sr. R. A. Garcia
Apartado 3068
46807 Puerto Vallarta, Jalisco
MEXICO

Air Mail

☐ COMMUNICATION CHALLENGES

PRELIMINARY EXERCISE 1   *Write, call, or visit a company in your city that interacts with foreign suppliers, owners, or customers.* Ask whether you may receive a copy of a letter so that you can see its conventions of page layout, headings, and style. Explain that you do not want to see any proprietary information and that you would be happy for them to conceal any sensitive information with a marking pen or label. Assurance that you only wish to become familiar with foreign correspondence will make your request more acceptable in most circumstances. Bring the correspondence you obtain to class and compare the conventions of the documents you collect. Sometimes even when a foreign business person writes in English, differences in cultures are evident in the placement of information, the topics chosen, and the formality of the phrases.

PRELIMINARY EXERCISE 2   Rephrase the following sentences to avoid cultural metaphors:

1. You can make a first down with this strategy, every time.

2. This presentation will satisfy the brass, even if they believe in spit and polish.
3. Everything goes so smoothly with this software that no one will holler, "foul ball!"
4. This waterbed heater keeps you snug as a bug in a rug.
5. You can't get to first base unless you're well prepared.

PRELIMINARY EXERCISE 3 *Choose one of the following three activities and bring the results to class.*

a. Ask members of your class from foreign countries or other foreign students you know to give you an example of a phrase that confused them when they first came to the United States. Collect and write down at least one example. Compare examples in class.

b. Alternatively, if you have visited a foreign country, explain a phrase that you misunderstood at first.

c. Go to your library and obtain a copy of Mitsubishi Corporation's *Tatemae and Honne: Distinguishing Between Good Form and Real Intention in Japanese Business Culture* (New York: The Free Press, 1988). It traces 500 crucial business expressions back to their cultural roots. For example, a "water business" in Japan is a business for which there is a shifting demand; it may be in vogue for a time, but the demand may dry up or move away. Restaurants, entertainment clubs, and other faddish ventures are "water businesses." The expression rests on the phenomenon of spring water that may not flow constantly or a brook that may alter its course. *Copy the entry for an expression that interests you and be prepared to discuss it in class.*

EXERCISE 1

You work for your university bookstore as an order clerk. Dr. Charles Preventer, Professor of Biology, is going to lead a two-week walking tour in England for your university alumni group. The tour is scheduled for July, and it is now January. Professor Preventer says that special maps for exploring the Romney Marsh area around Rye (about 60 miles south of London) have been prepared by a local group called the Rye Ramblers. These maps are part of a series called "Country Walks Around Rye," and he says he saw them in the Martello Bookshop in Rye last summer. Your usual wholesalers don't carry these local publications. This set of circumstances means a new problem must be solved; your usual method of obtaining books won't work. You must write to initiate a new transaction.

Professor Preventer says that he is particularly interested in the map for the walk to Winchelsea, following Henry James's footsteps, and for the walk along the shoreline in the Rye Harbour Nature Reserve, which is excellent for birdwatching. Unfortunately, he did not bring back either of these maps, so you're not quite certain of their proper titles. *Write to Mr. Dominic Martello at the Martello Bookshop, 26 High Street, Rye, East Sussex, TN31 7AN and ask whether he can sell you copies of these maps.* Professor Preventer expects twenty people in his group, and you'll probably need a couple of extra copies just in case. You need to have these maps by June 1. Use your campus bookstore's address for the letter.

EXERCISE 2

Your company, Essex Instructional Materials, has a joint venture with a small Japanese film company, Nagata Video and Film Company, to produce educational materials about Japan for use in U.S. social studies classes in kindergarten through grade 6. These materials will include videotapes, workbooks, readers, and a computer simulation game. The materials will be created in Japan but mass-produced in the U.S. Four of your staff will go to Tokyo for a year to collaborate on this project. Your staff includes professional educators who are specialists in educational methods in U.S. grade-school social studies. The Japanese production company has arranged for housing for the Essex people.

Your boss, Steve Andrews, has asked that you check into the question of medical care for your people while they are in Japan. You have checked with the insurance agent for your group insurance policy, and she told you that the company will cover expenses of your four employees, but that major medical costs, such as surgery, will require a second opinion from the physicians at either Tokyo Sanitarium Hospital or Saint Luke's Hospital in Tokyo, the company's agents in Tokyo. She also said that both of these hospitals have English-speaking doctors, and that Tokyo Sanitarium Hospital is closer to the offices of the production company where your employees will work.

Andrews suggested that you write a letter to Tokyo Sanitarium Hospital to inquire whether the hospital offers services on a contract basis. If so, you would like to make arrangements for your people to go there for any medical treatment that may be necessary during their stay. You need to know whether they offer contract services (so that they would bill Essex directly) and how your employees should contact the hospital for care if they become ill. You have no reason to expect extra hazards in Japan; it is considered as safe for Americans as Canada or Western Europe, but one of the specialists in your group is diabetic and will feel safer if he has access to care. The hospital's address, given to you by your insurance agent, is Dr. Akira Nagai, Chief Administrator, Tokyo Sanitarium Hospital (Tokyo Eisei Byoin), 17-3, Amanuma, 3-chome, Suginami-ku, Tokyo, Japan. *Write a letter to Dr. Nagai; prepare an envelope as well.* Your address is Essex Instructional Materials, 120 Harcross Lane, Suite 4000, Urbana, IL 61801.

EXERCISE 3

Revise the draft of the letter below to a Japanese company that has recently opened local offices.

Scott Printing
2427 Wellhausen Street
1410 East Beach
Galveston, TX 77550

October 1, 1991

Mr. Tomoko Otsuka
Manager
Nakamura Interests, Inc.
1240 Bay Boulevard
Galveston, TX 77550

Dear Mr. Otsuka:

Welcome to Galveston. We noticed your new office and are glad to have you in the business neighborhood. You won't lack high quality printing for your business here, because we're as close as first base. We have substantial experience, so if your company needs letterhead stationery, business cards, envelopes, invitations, or brochures prepared for use in Galveston, we can handle it for you. And at a good price that won't put a hole in your pocketbook.

We think we can beat any estimate and match any quality in printing services. I would like to come by on Friday to show you our samples. Would 10 a.m. be convenient? Please call my secretary, Fran Jacobs, and let her know if you can make it.

Again, welcome!

Sincerely,

Buck Carpenter

Manager

IF YOU WOULD LIKE TO READ MORE

The preceding chapter has a long bibliography on intercultural and international communication; many of the items listed there include comments or sections on correspondence and reports.

Haneda, S., & Shima, H. (1982). Japanese communication behavior as reflected in letter writing. *The Journal of Business Communication, 19*(1), 19–23.

Hildebrandt, H. (1973). Communication barriers between German subsidiaries and parent American companies. *Michigan Business Review.*

Varner, I. I. (1987). Internationalizing Business Communication Courses. *The Bulletin of the Association for Business Communication, 50*(4), 7–11. Contains a comparison of letter openings and closings for French, Japanese, and German letters. Based on analyses of business communication texts from other countries. Aimed at teachers, but contains good examples.

Varner, I. I. (1988). A comparison of American and French business correspondence. *The Journal of Business Communication, 25*(4), 55–65. Gives many examples.

NOTES

1. S. Haneda & H. Shima, "Japanese communication behavior as reflected in letter writing." *Journal of Business Communication, 19* (1982)1, 29.

2. I. I. Varner, "Internationalizing business communication courses." *The Bulletin of the Association for Business Communication, 50* (1987)4, 10.

3. I. I. Varner offers good examples of French conventions in "A comparison of American and French business correspondence," *Journal of Business Communication, 25* (1988)(4), 55–65.

JOB SEARCH COMMUNICATIONS

OBJECTIVES

This chapter will help you

- analyze your values, aptitudes, needs, and goals

- apply your knowledge and experience to your job search communications

- use interpersonal communication skills to develop employment leads

- prepare a strategic résumé

- write a convincing job application letter

- participate effectively in an employment interview

- negotiate the terms of your employment

PREVIEW

In Mark Twain's words, "The happiest and most successful person works all year long at what he would otherwise choose to do on his summer vacation." If this description surpasses your expectations for your own career, it should do so only slightly. The first step in finding the right job is finding out what you enjoy; thus you have probably been exploring potential career choices throughout your life. The second step in finding the right job is formulating objectives based upon what you like to do and what you do well.

Like any other communications scenario, marketing yourself for employment requires that you also give careful consideration to the needs and perspectives of your audience—the job market and companies that might hire you.

A well-organized job search requires four steps:

1. Decide what types of scenarios you would like to play as you earn a living and build your career.
2. Determine which industries, companies, and positions will offer you these scenarios.
3. Communicate in writing, by telephone, and in person.
4. Negotiate an employment agreement.

❏ FINDING THE RIGHT JOB

Writing a résumé and cover letter and interviewing for a job are very similar to preparing a proposal for a client, a topic that receives extensive coverage in Chapter 22. You must define and analyze the true needs within the situation; you must decide whether the company's needs fit your aptitudes and abilities. If they do, you must write a convincing résumé, promote it with a custom-tailored cover letter, and close the deal with a winning presentation and strong negotiating skills.

As Lawrence Peter once observed, "If you do not know where you are going, you will probably end up somewhere else." The job search is often compared to an experience in sales and marketing, but the commodity you are promoting is yourself. Good salespeople establish empathy with potential customers. They study the market, determine what the needs are, and how their product can fulfill those needs. If they don't have the right product, they may even work to develop a new one. If, however, you focus your job search on audience needs to the exclusion of your own preferences, you will end up slighting yourself and, ultimately, your employer as well.

First You Must Consider Yourself

Too many job seekers fail to consider their own needs first. They find out what positions are open, what occupations seem to promise the most potential for growth and future income, and what experience they have from past jobs or course work that might translate to positions currently available. This approach may serve for obtaining a temporary source of income, but it is no way to plan for a satisfying and rewarding future. In the words of Richard Nelson Bolles,

> As you set about your job-hunt, you have got to know what it is you want—or else someone is going to sell you a bill of goods somewhere along the line that can do irreparable damage to your self-esteem, your sense of worth, and your stewardship of the talents that God gave you.[1]

What Are Your Values?   In *Go Hire Yourself an Employer*, Richard K. Irish asserts, "Big business buys young people by the boxcar the same way it buys raw materials: a lot goes on the 'scrap heap.' And younger graduates themselves, innocent of what they want, become disillusioned."[2] Speaking less metaphorically, Betty N. Michelozzi in *Coming Alive From Nine to Five* asks, "Can you work 60 hours a week moving up the corporate ladder, nurture loving relationships . . . grow your own vegetables, recycle your cans on Saturday, jog daily, be a Scout leader, meditate, play golf at the country club and do yoga?"[3] You must determine what in your life will receive top priority, what comes second, and so on—and make your career choices based on that decision. If you choose to become an auditor for a large accounting firm, you may not have much time to devote to long-term relationships or organic gardening. If, on the other hand, you decide to teach philosophy, you will have to make different sacrifices—a lower income or, possibly, no income at all.

What Do You Do Well?   Decide what you want by focusing on what you both do well *and* enjoy doing. If the philosophy-teaching scenario seems attractive to you, why? Do you perform well as a mentor for others, are you a strong public speaker, do you like working with ideas, do you relish probing questions or a heated debate, do you enjoy contributing to the intellectual development and creative thinking abilities of others? If so, your challenge in creative thinking is to determine how you can channel these abilities into job market commodities that employers are eager to buy.

The Dictionary of Occupational Titles divides these job commodities into three major categories: the ability to deal with *people, data,* and *things* (primarily mechanical).[4] These skills can be further segmented into a hierarchy of increasing complexity. You can visualize this hierarchy as a pyramid: The least complex skills—skills available to larger portions of the population—are at the base of the pyramid. The most complex skills are at the pinnacle.

For instance, in dealing with *people,* most individuals can follow someone else's guidelines; fewer people can instruct others; and only a few people make good counselors, priests, and consultants. In working with *data,* most people can collect data and compare data, but fewer people know how to process data statistically or design computer programs for interpreting data, and an even smaller group of people knows how to optimize processes on the basis of analyzed data. In working with *things,* most people can load and unload objects; fewer people can perform operations on things, such as carpentry or car repair; and only a very few can create surgical tools, cut crystal with diamond saws, or set up a drill string for an offshore well.

What Do You Like to Do?   Bolles suggests that, as you analyze the skills you most enjoy using, you imagine yourself at a party where people are gathered in six corners of a room.[5] The corner they choose depends upon their favorite skills and interests. The six skill orientations are represented in Figure 19-1. Dean C. Dauw classifies these skill orientations, or "competencies," somewhat differently, as "realistic, investigative, artistic, social, conventional, or enterprising."[6]

What Are Your Limitations?   Another aspect of self-assessment is knowledge of your weaknesses and of weaknesses that others might perceive, even if they do not exist in reality. What are your limitations in knowledge, experience, and ability? Does your temperament disqualify you from certain types of work—are you easily bored or discouraged? Do you prefer to work alone? Do you fear a loss of security? Does your soft-spoken manner mislead people into thinking you lack leadership qualities? Does your quick laugh make others wonder whether you take anything seriously?

Knowing your liabilities—both real and apparent—allows you either to choose an occupation that minimizes them or to choose a course of action that overcomes them. If, for example, you enjoy working with people but fear public speaking, you might enroll in a speech course, join Toastmasters, and volunteer to make announcements for a group you belong to at school, at the office, or in another organization. If you lack experience in some crucial area, determine what similar experiences you may have had and concentrate on transferring that experience into the new environment.

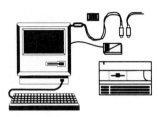

1. Athletic/Mechanical:
   prefer to work with objects,
   machines, plants, or animals

2. Observing/Analytical:
   prefer to investigate, analyze,
   evaluate, solve problems

SKILLS ORIENTATION

6. Clerical/Numerical:
   prefer working with data and
   details, following through on
   others' instructions

3. Artistic/Creative:
   prefer unstructured situations,
   using intuition, imagination,
   creativity

5. Managerial/Administrative:
   prefer working with people —
   influencing, persuading, or
   managing for organizational
   goals or economic gain

4. Healing/Training:
   prefer working with
   people to enlighten,
   help, develop, or
   cure them

FIGURE 19-1. **Skills Orientation**

In Your Past Lie the Keys to Your Future

One graduating student, for example, had spent his summers working as a lifeguard and swimming instructor. To plan his résumé strategy, Ted constructed a
mind map around the following areas: people skills, data skills, and mechanical
skills. He demonstrated *people skills* because he had coached both male and
female swim classes and achieved several measures of success: His students
learned to use all the major swim strokes. They performed well as a team and
got along well with each other. Ted also used his people skills to establish a supportive working relationship with the parents of his students. He used his *data
skills* as he collected fees, kept student records, and maintained accounts of his
coaching income for the club managers. He demonstrated *mechanical skills*
through his swimming ability and his ongoing maintenance of the pool.

Ted decided that the most rewarding aspects of his summer jobs had been the administrative responsibilities and interpersonal contacts. He knew he could also draw upon the technical knowledge and mechanical skills he had developed, and he decided that he could best combine these factors through an administrative position in a country club or fitness center. Ted outlined a three-pronged strategy for finding a job:

1. *Research:* Using the telephone, library, and personal contacts to learn the names and addresses of suitable country clubs and fitness centers within a twenty-mile radius of his target city in North Carolina
2. *Writing:* Sending a résumé and an individualized job letter to each of the targeted organizations
3. *Follow-up:* Calling the recipients of his résumés and job letters a week after they were mailed

Potential employers were impressed with the experience reflected in his résumé, the focus and personal attention indicated in his job letters, and the initiative demonstrated in his follow-up phone calls. During interviews, they were impressed with Ted's knowledge of his own goals and his ability to show that his goals and abilities fit their needs. Ted was able to choose a position that met his requirements for a job.

Virtually every library, placement office, and career counseling center has a section dedicated to career research. The people and publications in these centers will help you perform the self-assessment phase of analyzing your preferred skills and aptitudes, and they can help you determine which career areas will allow you to use those skills. Do not expect anyone or anything else to find your job for you, however: not your placement director, nor flooding the market with résumés and letters, probably not even interviewing with the small percentage of companies that send recruiters for on-campus interviews. You, operating in person and making strong use of your interpersonal communication skills, are the best candidate for presenting yourself as a prospective employee.

❏ DEVELOP LEADS THROUGH INTERPERSONAL COMMUNICATION

Placement offices, employment agencies, and the classified section of the newspaper are logical sources of leads, but many of your most valuable job search leads are the ones you develop yourself through networking: goal-oriented communications with your friends; people you associate with in clubs, churches and civic organizations; and people you know from past jobs or committee work. Join a professional association and become an active, contributing member. When you evaluate your past employment, even summer jobs, remember your customers and vendors—not just your immediate employer, but everyone else you dealt with on the job. Write a note on back of each business card you collect: where and when you met, whether any commitments were made, and any other pertinent information.

Like other effective communications strategies, your networking should have specific goals. Keep your contacts informed: Tell them you are conducting a job search. Tell them what kind of job you are looking for, where you want to work, and what your background is. Providing contacts with a copy of your résumé is a great way of giving them a specific picture of your background while simultaneously convincing them that you are serious about finding the right job. As you begin to call on your contacts, keep a complete record, including name, title and company, phone number, dates contacted, referrals received, and follow-up information. Your contacts may not be able to offer you a job or even give you a concrete lead, but they will often be able to give you the name of an individual who specializes in your career area and who may even be in a position to hire. You can then call that individual, using your contact's name as a reference, and request an *information interview*.

Seek Information Interviews

When you call to request an information interview, be knowledgeable about the company you are calling and about your own self-evaluation. Instead of presenting yourself as a person seeking an employment interview, indicate that you are doing research on your field of interest. "Mr. Jones, Travis Smith suggested that I call you. I am completing my degree, and Travis said that you would be a good source of information about the current job market and career path in human resources." At the very least, the information interview will give you added insight into your field of interest and provide interviewing experience in a non-threatening environment. But because many openings are never advertised and because some employers will even *create* an opening for the right person, one of your best strategies for finding the right job is to initiate these interviews on your own.

Although the goal of such interviews will be primarily to gain information about your area of interest, columnist Sheryl Silver reports that this approach often produces job offers, even for persons who have not received job offers as the result of more conventional search methods.[7] She suggests that networking in this manner produces more referrals, added insights into a variety of fields, and a less threatening interview environment in which a nervous job candidate can relax and present himself as a researcher instead of a job searcher. A key to this approach is to make it clear to your contacts that you have no expectations they will have a job for you; you merely want their thoughts and advice.

After you conduct an information interview, be sure to follow up with a thank-you letter. Keep all your networking contacts informed about how your job search is progressing, and do something nice for them in return for their help. For example, you might copy a recent article in their field of interest and mail it with your letter of thanks.

Organize Your Résumé around Skills and Achievements

Your résumé will probably establish your potential employers' first impression of your work. The résumé is a personal document, and you may want to express your personality by taking some creative license. Be careful, however, because the résumé is also an extremely formal document. While its primary purpose is to help you get an interview with the right company, another of its purposes is to prevent your being screened out. Accordingly, you should know what a professional résumé looks like and what your potential employers will prefer to see.

A survey of the chief personnel officers at Fortune 500 corporations, conducted in 1985, revealed that 96 percent preferred the initial contact by a job applicant to be in writing.[8] Seventy-seven percent of the personnel officers welcomed inquiries even when they had no current openings. Most respondents preferred both a résumé and a job letter. They wanted short résumés of one to two pages. These respondents gave special preference to résumés that included a list of three references, and they also wanted information about why those references were qualified to give recommendations. The résumé's most important pieces of information include college and postgraduate education, work experience, special aptitudes, and other qualifications. In contrast to much contemporary advice that personal information should be omitted from résumés, the majority of respondents to this survey wanted personal information, probably because it indicates an openness on the part of applicants to disclose information about themselves that the potential employer cannot legally request. Thus, reporting information about birthdate, gender, height, religious affiliation, marital status, and the number of children might give an applicant an edge—if the information is construed positively by the person reading the résumé. If your birthdate, religion, or marital status might be construed as a liability, omit it.

Personnel officers preferred to see proof of specific skills rather than mere experiences. Thus "managed the night shift on weekends" would be less appealing than "supervised three employees, maintained the ledger, closed out the daily books, and handled customer complaints." In fact, one of the problems cited by respondents was that applicants tended to be vague instead of specific about how their qualifications fit job requirements. Other problems with applicants included their failure to list a career objective and a specific job objective, their lack of knowledge regarding the company receiving the application, and their tendency to "oversell" themselves.[9] The appearance of overselling can be avoided by giving specific evidence that demonstrates levels of skill and specific accomplishments: "Controlled $20,000 in transactions each weekend" sounds much more objective than "skilled in monetary transactions and extremely honest."

Résumé writing requires the following skills:

Creativity—the ability to apply past experience and achievements to your current job search

Organization—the ability to present information in the most persuasive and effective order

Artistry—the ability to present information in an attractive and strategic format

Sometimes the résumé is called a data sheet or a vita, but in the business world, résumé is the most commonly-used term. In your job search research, you may find references to several types of résumés:

Chronological résumé, in which your education, employment, and other experiences are listed in reverse chronological order (see the sample résumés in this chapter)

Functional résumé, in which you describe specific types of experience, skills, and achievements according to a strategic hierarchy instead of a strict chronology

Combination résumé, which begins with a statement of functional skills and then presents job and education history in a chronological format

Fact sheet, which consists of an informal listing of past experiences and is not generally accepted for a professional job search

Letter résumé, which presents an executive summary of aptitudes, skills, and experiences in letter format

The final hiring decision is usually made not by the personnel or human resources officer, but by the executive or manager who will supervise your department at work. Therefore, it will often be to your advantage to direct your job search communications to that individual. A 1987 study of such hiring executives in the Memphis area indicates that 56 percent preferred the chronological résumé, 31 percent preferred the combination format, and only eight percent chose the functional format.[10] Résumé 1, for Theodore G. Brittain, is an example of the combination format that highlights the applicant's skills but also presents his specific work and educational experience. The other sample résumés, which appear at the end of this chapter, are in chronological style. The overwhelming majority preferred a two-column format with headings occupying the left column and information being presented in the right. (All the sample résumés use this format.) Only 8 percent of the respondents preferred that headings be centered.

Like the personnel directors, the hiring executives strongly preferred to see short résumés (two pages or less) and a stated job objective. A little surprisingly, however, the objective does not need to be particularly specific or even concise. The most preferred version (chosen by 50 percent) was "Seeking entry-level accounting position in progressive firm with opportunity to utilize my educational background in accounting and data processing"; the second-favorite version (preferred by 30 percent) was "Entry-level accounting position."

In accordance with their counterparts in personnel, and in contrast with much current advice on résumé writing, these executives strongly preferred (by 71 percent) a listing of specific references on the résumé. If you are sending your résumé to several target organizations and you do not want to have your acquaintances inundated with phone calls, you can include references in your job letter instead. This strategy also allows you to choose specific references for specific positions.

Highlight Your Ability to Learn and Adapt

Research conducted jointly by the United States Department of Labor and the American Society for Training and Development during the late 1980s indicates that employers seek workers who are prepared to grow and to acquire new skills quickly. They should adapt readily to change, and demonstrate "strong interpersonal skills." According to this recent research, "Business strategies—such as collaboration, exemplary customer service, and emphasis on quality—require workers capable of teamwork, listening, creativity, goal-setting, and problem-solving." The "standard academic skills" are not enough. Employers now seek other "key basics as a foundation for building broader, more sophisticated job-related skills." [11]

A strong résumé will demonstrate that you can do the following:

- Continue learning and acquiring new knowledge and skills, no matter what the learning situation
- Listen and respond to customers, suppliers and coworkers
- Think on your feet and address problems quickly
- Derive innovative solutions
- Believe in yourself and your potential for success
- Set and reach specific goals
- Get along with customers, suppliers, and coworkers
- Work with others to achieve goals
- Negotiate a consensus
- Understand the organization's goals and how you can contribute
- Assume responsibility and motivate coworkers

As you can see from this list, potential employers strongly emphasize communication skills. In the words of the researchers,

> Central to competitiveness, communication skills help employees get and keep customers, inspire innovation, contribute to quality circles, resolve conflict, and give meaningful feedback. Poor communication skills, resulting in lost productivity and errors, can cost companies heavily. [12]

Your strategy for demonstrating these abilities will require specific evidence, particularly the use of examples and statistics. If you have achieved on-time production, set new precedents, or exceeded quotas in your past work or volunteer experience, you can use these accomplishments as examples of your ability to set and meet specific goals. Your evidence must also be targeted to the industry and the position you have chosen for your job search.

RESUME CHECKLIST

____ Does the heading include your name, address, and phone number?

____ Is your career objective clearly stated?

____ Does the education section highlight your degrees and any special projects or coursework related to your career objective?

____ Does the experience section highlight achievements and provide specific evidence?

____ Is additional information specific and relevant?

____ Is the logical arrangement clear and consistent?

____ Do you maintain a professional tone?

____ Does the style stress action and results?

____ Is the overall document effective and persuasive?

Volunteer and community involvement, special projects in college, and seemingly unrelated job experiences can sometimes be used as examples of how well you fit the requirements for your chosen career. If, for example, you want a career in financial management but your work experience was limited to summer employment as a physician's receptionist, you would certainly highlight any experience you gained with the doctor's ledger sheet and banking transactions. You would, however, need to focus your résumé on additional types of experience. As business manager for a college magazine, one student secured $3,200 in advertising revenue, halved the magazine's debt to the university, and introduced effective accounting procedures to minimize future costs. This type of experience, though not strictly related to outside employment, should receive prominence in the résumé of a future financier.

Evidence of specific results and transferrable skills will greatly strengthen your résumé. Include dollar amounts and percentages as you highlight the types of information outlined below.

PROVIDE SPECIFIC INFORMATION ABOUT THESE TYPES OF EXPERIENCE:

- Examples of anything you've done that increased profits, decreased costs, or streamlined operations
- Examples of effectiveness as an independent worker
- Examples of effectiveness in a team environment working toward group goals
- Examples of situations where you acquired new skills on your own
- Examples of leadership, management, communication, or training skills
- Examples of problem-solving skills
- Examples of transactions you conducted with customers, clients, and co-workers

- Projects or procedures you designed or implemented that decreased turnover or absenteeism or improved productivity
- Leadership roles in professional associations
- Publications
- Courses taught or public speaking experience
- Professional seminars attended; special projects at school
- Volunteer and community involvement
- Goals you reached or exceeded

Tailor Your Job Letter to the Specific Company and Position

If we established an analogy between finding a job and choosing a spouse, we could equate the following stages:

JOB SEARCH	SPOUSE SEARCH
Self-evaluation	Growing up
Market evaluation	Playing the field
Résumé writing	Deciding on what "type" you want and presenting yourself as the corresponding "type"
Job letter writing	Persuading a single individual, who seems to fit the desired "type," to go out with you
Interviewing	Determining whether the two of you are a good match

When you reach the job letter stage, you should have a clear idea of where you are going and what it will take to get there. You should also have a good idea of what the other side is looking for, and you should tailor your letter to match those specific needs. You may have read that there are two kinds of job letters: "prospecting" letters that indicate your interest in any suitable position at the company, and "invited" applications that respond to an advertisement. Both situations require a similar strategy, however. When people are ready to get serious about marriage, they don't want to date someone who is just playing the field. You should demonstrate your interest in the specific company, show that you have done research into the company's needs and that you know the requirements of the position, show that your background fits the reader's needs, and demonstrate that you are serious about working and a career. Incidentally, it also helps if you (and your document) look your best.

Among personnel directors in a study of Fortune 500 companies, 99 percent agreed that good grammar and spelling are essential, and 91 percent agreed that letters and résumés should be neatly typed. Ninety percent of the personnel officers agreed that tone was important, and they indicated that the job letter's content should state why the applicant is interested in the particular company, how the applicant's qualifications fit the job requirements, and then should request an interview.[13] Thus the job letter requires persuasion and applies a simple and standard approach to organizing a business letter: an introduction, body,

---

JOB LETTER CHECKLIST

_____ Does the heading include your name and address?

_____ Does the inside address name the specific recipient and use a courtesy title (Mr., Ms., Dr.)?

_____ Does the first paragraph motivate the reader?

    _____ Do you demonstrate interest in the specific company?

    _____ Do you introduce yourself?

    _____ Do you name a specific position or work area?

    _____ Do you cite an outstanding qualification?

_____ Does the body highlight specific achievements and demonstrate that you fit the position in question?

    _____ Does your experience show you can do this job?

    _____ Do you show that you have prepared for this line of work?

    _____ Do you demonstrate that you are motivated to perform the work required for this position?

_____ Does the close establish momentum and provide contact information?

_____ Is information job-specific and relevant?

_____ Is the logical arrangement clear and the style professional?

_____ Is it easy to find your phone number? Your references' phone numbers?

---

and conclusion. You will find it helpful to review Chapters 4 and 5 for strategies and Chapters 6 and 9 for word choice and professional style.

Your job letter should incorporate the information shown in the Job Letter Outline in Figure 19-2. Tailoring that information to your own experience and your potential employer's needs should provide an adequate challenge and a certain degree of creative stimulation. If it doesn't, perhaps you are applying for the wrong job. Your job letter should not present a rehash of your résumé but, instead, demonstrate that you are a custom-tailored fit for the reader's needs.

You will notice that, although the sample letters at the end of this chapter vary slightly in their organization, they still incorporate all the persuasive elements suggested in the outline.

The Interview

In the research and writing stages of your job search, you are the person in control. You determine the criteria, the order, and the content. When you enter a job interview, however, you will relinquish much of the control you enjoyed during the earlier stages in the process. Obviously, it will be in your best interests to plan for and manage those aspects of the interview process that legitimately _do_ fall under your control.

Your Name
Street or Box Address
City, State Zip

(area code) phone number

Date

Recipient's Name
Title
Company Name
Street or Box Address
City, State Zip

Dear Ms. _____:

First Paragraph: Motivate the reader.

    a. Why you are interested in the company (use names of sources)
    b. Who you are
    c. Why you are writing (name a specific job)
    d. What is outstanding about your qualifications

Second and Third Paragraphs: Provide specific evidence and tie it explicitly to the reader's needs.

    a. Work experience that applies to reader's needs (what did you accomplish that shows you can do *this* job?)
    b. School experience that applies to reader's needs (what special projects did you complete that helped you to prepare for *this* position?)
    c. Other experience that applies to reader's needs (what leadership, management, or technical skills have you demonstrated in other organizations that you can apply on *this* job?)

Closing Paragraph: Establish momentum.

    A. Include references' names and phone numbers (if they are not in your résumé)
    B. Request a meeting
    C. Provide contact information:
        When can you be reached?
        Will you be in the area soon?
        Will you call the reader?

Sincerely,

Your Name

Enclosure: Resume

FIGURE 19-2. Job Letter Outline

Remember that first impressions are lasting. They will establish expectations in the mind of your interviewer, and they will likely set the tone for the rest of the interview. Because the first impressions you give and receive will be primarily nonverbal, packaging is everything. You can create an image of self-confidence, dependability, proper preparation, even business savvy with your appearance (clothing, hairstyle, nails, shoes, hosiery, grooming), your greeting, eye contact, handshake, and facial expressions. Although this information seems obvious, persons who are otherwise intelligent and well-educated arrive for interviews every day wearing inappropriate clothes, a crumpled suit, or the wrong color shoes. Interviewers notice these details—they give priceless information about your motivation, preparation, and sense of appropriateness.

As the verbal exchange progresses during the interview, you will be able to rely on the steps you undertook to research your strengths, weaknesses, likes, dislikes, and aptitudes; to research suitable jobs and career paths; and to research the company and position for which you are interviewing. Be prepared to do the following with a sense of modest conviction.

- Highlight your technical and personal assets.
- Give examples of success with difficult situations.
- Relay compliments you've received.
- Compliment former superiors and how you learned from them (do not criticize *any* former coworker).
- Show that you understand the interviewing company's mission and goals and how you can further those goals.
- Demonstrate enthusiasm for and commitment to the position in question; highlight skills and experience that emphasize your good fit.
- Ask intelligent questions about the company, position, and the individual interviewer, based on your research and the information you gain during the interview.
- Handle illegal or discriminatory questions, if they are asked (see the following list).
- Be ready to field questions regarding your shortcomings by demonstrating that you are aware of your weaknesses and have learned to compensate for them.

You generally should not mention weaknesses unless the interviewer asks about them; however, if your background has some obvious shortcoming you should consider broaching the subject yourself. If, for example, the job posting asked for an experienced lab technician but you have no directly related work experience, you might mention your college experience in chemistry, biology, and physics lab. You could bring samples of your lab notebooks as evidence of your ability to perform rigorous, organized laboratory procedures. If you have also spent your summers working as a medical assistant, you should be able to demonstrate important similarities between the two positions.

The following questions may violate state or federal nondiscrimination guidelines, but some interviewers ask them anyway.

DISCRIMINATORY QUESTIONS

Have you changed your name? What was your original name? ("What was your maiden name?" is an acceptable inquiry.)

Where were you (or your parents) born?

What church do you belong to? Who is your pastor or priest?

What race (or ethnic group) do you belong to?

What is your birthdate? (unless this information is needed to maintain apprenticeship requirements, satisfy legal minimum-age requirements, or prevent interference with benefit programs)

What is your native language? What language do you commonly use when you are at home?

What is your marital status? How many dependents do you have?

What does your spouse do?

Have you ever been arrested? ("Have you been convicted of a felony?" is an acceptable inquiry.)

Do you own your home?

What is your height and weight? Do you have a handicap? (unless there is a bona fide job-related reason for possessing particular physical abilities)

What is your military status?

What political party do you belong to?

What kind of child-care arrangements have you made?

Do you plan to have children?

The employment interview is a structured communications situation where accurate audience and situation analysis are vital. You should decide now how you will respond to illegal or discriminatory questions, and practice that response. If you answer the question, the employer will continue to ask such questions of others, perpetuating the discrimination. Practice a response that conveys your own high ethical standards to the employer; for example, "Mr. Smith, although I know that XYZ is trying to find the most valuable employee for this position, I also know that this question is illegal and it would be fostering discrimination if I were to answer it."

To give you a better understanding of how the interview scenario might be structured, we have included a model followed by campus interviewers (Figure 19-3). Although the exhibit presents a general model, interview scenarios vary among interviewers, companies, and situations. Even the same interviewer will vary her interviewing style and responses, depending upon internal and external influences upon her own needs and goals. Is she pressed for time? Has she already interviewed four other people today? Did she argue with her spouse at breakfast? Did she skip breakfast and lunch?

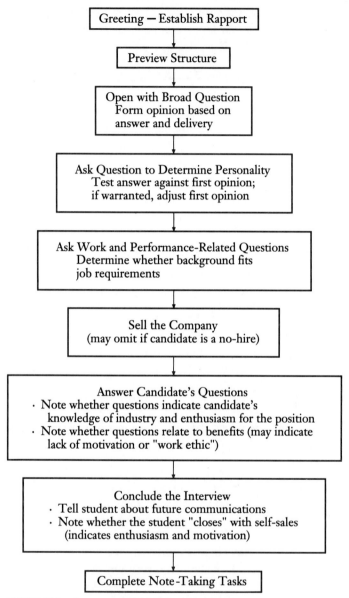

FIGURE 19-3.   Interviewer's Model for Campus Interviews

    The better prepared your interviewer is, the more structured the situation
is likely to be and the more consistent you can expect the interviewer to be in the
approach she takes and the types of impressions she forms. Research shows,
however, that both experienced and inexperienced interviewers are likely to
make the following mistakes:

1. Talking too much
2. Using poor listening techniques (in particular, jumping to conclusions)
3. Failing to analyze the facts gleaned from the interview and correlate them to the position at hand
4. Giving the applicant verbal and nonverbal cues regarding the "correct" answers to questions (often these cues are given in advance or as the question is asked, giving astute interviewees an opportunity to make the most of their communication skills; they can simply mirror the interviewer's positive expectations)

Clearly, you should make the most of your own interpersonal skills to monitor the situation, to ensure that the interviewer hears the information that makes your strongest case, and to demonstrate how your abilities fit the position. You must also monitor the interviewer's communication style, and consider whether you wish to adjust your own style to mirror her expectations.

Every Interview Requires Written Follow-Up   After each interview, write a short thank-you letter to your interviewer. Mention the position for which you interviewed and one or two key topics you discussed. If the interviewer was away from his office, you should also mention the date and place. Confirm your interest in the position and the organization. Briefly highlight your "fit" by mentioning specific points the interviewer considered important. If travel, relocation, or

Do's	Don'ts
Remember that you do have a chance—otherwise, you wouldn't have gotten the interview.	*Don't* get discouraged if the interviewer seems cool or noncommital. Many experienced interviewers purposefully avoid a warm communication style.
Use direct eye contact and a firm handshake.	
Be honest. If you exaggerate your past salary or responsibilities, you undermine your credibility and seriously damage your chances.	*Don't* talk for too long. Every good salesperson knows that elaborating too much will kill the sale.
	Don't submit to the *power of the pause*. If the interviewer allows a long silence after you answer a question, don't be intimidated into elaborating.
Learn all you can about the company and prepare questions that demonstrate that knowledge.	
Plan a strategy and stick to it. Find ways to bring your strongest, concrete selling points into the conversation.	*Don't* light a cigarette.
	Don't give the impression that you are just "shopping around."
Bring a copy of your résumé.	*Don't* forget to close. Try the WIN strategy: *What* has the interviewer said she needs? How can you fill those needs to *improve* her situation? *Now*, what do you want? Why not ask for the job?
Make your body language speak assertively. Sit forward and make direct eye contact.	

FIGURE 19-4.   Interview Do's and Don'ts

⌐ I N T E R V I E W   C H E C K L I S T

___ Did you use the available sources for research?

   ___ Annual reports and 10K reports

   ___ Computerized search for articles in newspapers and journals

   ___ Dun & Bradstreet Million Dollar Directory

   ___ Standard & Poor's Register of Corporations

   ___ College Placement Annual

   ___ MBA Employment Guide

___ Do you know the industry?

___ Did you research the company? Your interviewer?

___ Do you know the company's competitors?

___ Do you know the position?

   ___ Vital skills

   ___ Procedures and methods

   ___ Significance within the corporate hierarchy

   ___ Current status in the job market

___ Have you practiced asking and answering strategic questions?

___ Do you have an extra copy of your résumé and work samples with you?

___ Is your "interview suit" freshly pressed?

long hours are at issue, confirm your willingness to comply with these conditions. Mention anything you have done since the interview that demonstrates your interest or increased ability.

Even if you have decided the position is not for you, express your gratitude toward the person who gave you an hour or so of his day and toward the company that sponsored him. This is simple good manners, but the old adage that "it's a small world" is particularly true in business. You will be gratified at how often a small courtesy will be remembered in the future. Although the particular position may not seem attractive, you may someday find yourself doing business with that company or with that individual at another company. There are three sample follow-up letters at the end of this chapter.

After You Have Successfully Negotiated the Search, You Are Ready to Negotiate the Terms of Your Employment

Being prepared will build your confidence and improve your communication skills. Exercise 8 at the end of this chapter presents a list of interview questions for you to practice answering, but one question that you will almost certainly have to deal with is, "How much are you worth?" If this question comes up early in the interview situation, you will probably want to defer it by requesting additional information about the position itself, what it requires, and where it fits in the organizational structure.

Either through advance research or direct questioning, you should learn how much the people immediately above and below you are making. You should know the range of pay within your targeted position and you should aim for the top of that range. Remember that your future raises will be based upon the salary you negotiate when you are hired. Richard Lathrop, in *Who's Hiring Who?*, suggests that you request a salary 5 percent above the top of the range. This indicates that you must have reasons for placing such a high value on the quality of your work. Lathrop presents the following guidelines:

> State your pay requirements in a range, while indicating that where you settle depends upon several factors.
>
> Put your minimum at 10 percent higher than the absolute minimum you will accept.
>
> Do not hesitate to ask what pay range the company has in mind.
>
> Remember that it's easier to get a raise before you start than after.[14]

Thomas C. Keiser in "Negotiating with a Customer You Can't Afford to Lose" notes that the most effective salespeople have difficulty negotiating the best price because they focus so strongly on their customers' needs. They begin to take on a customer perspective which allows them to convey an "uncanny understanding" of and empathy for the customer.[15] Like effective salespeople, the most successful job hunters may be the least successful in negotiating a fair salary. As you move into salary negotiations, you should begin acting as a partner with your future employer. This partnership requires a problem-solving role that seeks a creative way to meet the needs of both parties.

As Roger Fischer and William Ury observe in *Getting to Yes*, "Few things facilitate a decision so much as precedent. Search for it."[16] What are the industry standards? If the company has presented itself as growth-oriented, innovative, and responsive, it should want to exceed mere averages. If you are an effective salesperson—effective at selling *yourself*—here is where you can make your empathy with the company's perspective pay off. What is the employer's point of view in this negotiation? If you were in the decision makers' position, what would you most want to happen? What would you want to avoid? Your strategy is to show that providing you with the salary and benefits you require will improve the consequences of the company's decision—from its point of view. As you seek different options, look for those that give you common ground, shared interests, and mutual benefits. These options will make their decision easy. Fischer and Ury stress that you should prepare ahead, first by being creative (brainstorming or mindmapping is an excellent option here), then by deciding what strategy will make their decision easy for them and beneficial for you. They offer the following advice:

> To evaluate an option from the other side's point of view, consider how they might be criticized if they adopted it. Write out a sentence or two illustrating what the other side's most powerful critic might say about the decision you are thinking of asking for. Then write out a couple of sentences with which the other side might reply in defense. . . . A final test of an option is to write it out in the form of a "YESable proposition." Try to draft a proposal to which their responding with the single word "yes" would be sufficient, realistic, and operational.[17]

If, for example, the salary range for the position you want at ABC is $29,000–$32,000, which is relatively high for comparable positions in the industry, you should consider all the arguments against increasing the range. A few examples appear below.

"It would set a precedent with current and future employees, who would expect to receive comparable pay."

"ABC simply can't afford to meet the industry standard, but makes up for low pay with an outstanding training program."

"If I agree to bring you in at $32,000, my manager will criticize me for going against company policy."

Your counters to these statements must be tailored to the specific scenario in question, but you have many tools at your disposal.

Silence. The power of the pause is mentioned in Figure 19-4. Silence is a valuable tool when you are negotiating and you know that you have a position of strength. The other person may fear you have reached an impasse and may volunteer a concession.

Supposition. "Suppose, for example, that I could show your manager that I'm worth the extra $3,000?"

Reversal. "What would you do if you were in my situation?"

Openness. "What additional concerns am I overlooking with this salary proposal?"

Most likely, salary is not the only thing open to negotiation. If you are applying for a position within a fixed salary range, you may be able to negotiate for a longer vacation, dental insurance or insurance paid wholly by the company, an office (or a larger office), a personal computer with a printer, and other tools that will make your work both more pleasant and more productive. The greater your range of options and the larger the number of negotiable elements, the stronger your position will be. In Keiser's words, "The more variables you have to work with, the more options you have to offer; the greater your options, the better your chances of closing the deal." [18] Knowing the company, its employment policies, and its culture will give you the power of knowing what factors can be negotiated.

Negotiating the terms for your employment requires expert use of all your communication skills: verbal, nonverbal, and written. If you prepare adequately to apply those skills, however, you should be able to establish a suitable career pathway for yourself—and a partnership with your new employer.

34521 West Oak
Fayetteville, Arkansas 72543
(501) 235-0421

March 2, 1992

Mr. Clarence G. Greene, President
Echo Beach Spas
4565 Petal Rose
Raleigh, North Carolina 27476

Dear Mr. Greene:

The article on Echo Beach Spas in the "Today Section" of Sunday's
Raleigh Herald stressed the positive attitudes and the energy of your
employees. It also mentioned that you will be adding a new spa location in June. My background, attitude, and abilities match the profile for
your organization, and I would like to contribute to the administration of
your new spa.

I will obtain my degree in business administration from the University of
Arkansas this May, and I am seeking a career that will combine my
business knowledge with my experience as a trainer and team leader.
As my résumé indicates, my primary area of experience has been in a
sports and fitness-related environment during the summers at River
Road Country Club in St. Louis, and during the school year in athletic
activities at the University. My academic work included courses in accounting, business law, economics, and marketing. For my marketing
project, I evaluated the feasibility of opening an upscale sporting goods
store in Springdale, Arkansas. I believe this project will give me some
insights into the start-up operations for your new Echo Beach Spa.

My parents recently moved to Raleigh, which gives me added incentive to locate in your area. I will be visiting them during spring break
(March 16 through 24). Would it be possible to meet with you at that
time? I will call early next week to arrange an appointment.

Sincerely,

Theodore G. Brittain

Theodore G. Brittain

Enclosure: Résumé

Job Letter 1

QUESTIONS

1. Is Ted too vague about the position he wants?
2. Why does he name the four areas of course work?
   Could he make the sentence describing his course work more meaningful?
3. Is the last sentence in the letter too pushy?

THEODORE G. BRITTAIN

SCHOOL ADDRESS
34521 West Oak
Fayetteville, AR 72543
(501) 235-0421

HOME ADDRESS
34287 Partridge
St. Louis, MO 75443
(743) 334-9876

OBJECTIVE
Administrative position in a fitness or sports-oriented environment.

EDUCATION
University of Arkansas, Fayetteville
Bachelor of Business Administration, May 1992. Activities: swim team, intramural football and soccer.

ADMINISTRATIVE SKILLS
Organized and directed a weekly exercise class at the University. Maintained a productive learning environment for nine teams of young swimmers, fostering an atmosphere of group communication and commitment. Maintained accounts of coaching income, recorded class and team memberships, and logged competition results. Collected fees. Swim teams and individual team members won a total of 49 awards (24 first-place) during three summers.

INTERPERSONAL SKILLS
Led teams and motivated individuals to give their best efforts. Dealt with parents who sometimes felt their children were being asked to spend too many hours at practice; helped parents understand the benefits of swim team activities. Trained individuals with varying degrees of aptitude and experience to enjoy the water and improve their swimming ability. Each year, over 80% of students re-enrolled for the following year.

EXPERIENCE
Summers,
1989-1992
River Road Country Club, St. Louis, Missouri.
Swimming Instructor and Lifeguard. Taught swim classes, coached swim team. Collected fees, maintained records and accounts. Supervised pool maintenance.

REFERENCES
Coach R. D. Nelson
Athletic Department
University of Arkansas
Fayetteville, AR 72543
(501) 237-6785

Mr. George Lemans, director
River Road Country Club
St. Louis, MO 75442
(743) 534-8876

Mr. and Mrs. P. G. Scott
Parents of swim students
33245 Pinedale
St. Louis, MO 75442
(743) 324-9043

Ms. Grace Stevens
Exercise class member
4356 Richmond
Richardson, Texas 75081
(214) 255-9832

Résumé 1   (Combination Style)

34521 West Oak
Fayetteville, Arkansas 72543
(501) 235-0421

March 30, 1992

Mr. Clarence G. Greene, President
Echo Beach Spas
4565 Petal Rose
Raleigh, North Carolina 27476

Dear Mr. Greene:

Thank you for spending so much time with me last Thursday. I am excited about the possibility of joining Echo Beach Spas as a training specialist.

I also enjoyed meeting Cindy Carter and Janell Newmann. They were able to provide me with a great deal of information about what my position might entail. I found them and the spa itself to be everything the <u>Raleigh Herald</u> had described.

As you requested, I have enclosed a copy of the report for my marketing project. You will probably be most interested in pages 3-8. I look forward to hearing from you and learning your decision early in April.

Sincerely,

Theodore G. Brittain

Theodore G. Brittain

Enclosure

Follow-up Letter 1

331 Baker Street
Houston, Texas 77002

22 March 1992

Ms. Elizabeth W. Prine
Tyler, Rodweey, and Prine
1543 Smith Street, Suite 3100
Houston, Texas 77002

Dear Ms. Prine:

During a recent conversation with Craig Drury, an accountant with your firm, I learned that you have an internship available for this summer. I believe that I have excellent qualifications for this position, including practical experience in general ledger bookkeeping and three years of college business courses with a concentration in accounting.

According to Mr. Drury, your internship position involves data collection and computer modeling in your international department. My work under Professor Margaret Richards has given me a great deal of exposure to computer modeling. In addition, my education has provided me with experience in computer applied solutions to international investment hedging strategies. My knowledge of Spanish and French should enhance my ability to contribute in your international department.

Professor Richards (234-5678) and Dr. John Peterson (234-5689), the department chairman, would welcome your request for further information about my qualifications. I am confident that my experience would allow a smooth adjustment to this position, with a minimum of training and effort on your part. Since I am just a few miles away from you in downtown Houston, I am available to discuss your requirements at your convenience and will call you on March 29 to request an appointment.

Sincerely,

James R. Showell

James R. Showell
(713) 456-2345

Enclosure: Résumé

Job Letter 2

QUESTIONS

1. How would you describe the tone of this letter? Does it sound enthusiastic, businesslike, and persuasive; or is it cocky? Justify your answer by listing three pieces of supporting evidence.

2. Does Jim's letter simply repeat the information in his résumé, or does he make the information in his résumé apply directly to Ms. Prine's potential needs? Provide three quotes from Jim's letter and résumé to prove your point.
3. Does the last line sound helpful or pushy?

JAMES R. SHOWELL

331 Baker Street
Houston, Texas 77002
(713) 456-2345

OBJECTIVE   Summer internship with an accounting firm.

EDUCATION   RICE UNIVERSITY, Houston, Texas.
Jesse H. Jones Graduate School of Administration
Master of Accounting, May 1992.

Floor Representative, Dormitory Council, 1986-1989. Voted on allocations from $2500 yearly social budget. Organized activities.

EXPERIENCE   SHOWELL CONSTRUCTION COMPANY, Houston, Texas.
Payroll/Accounting Assistant, September - May 1992, part time. Process weekly payroll for 25-30 employees. Reconcile bank accounts. Prepare monthly statements to principals and employees and prepare monthly analysis of accounts receivable. Analyze various accounts and allocate costs among jobs in progress. Translated field office manual to Spanish.

SOUTHERN EQUIPMENT COMPANY, Houston, Texas.
Office Assistant, Summers 1988-1991.
Prepared monthly equipment rental billings.
Maintained equipment records.

ACTIVITIES   Campus Chorale, intramural sports, lived and studied in Spain during junior year in college.

SPECIAL   Working knowledge of PASCAL, SPSS, and LOTUS. Fluent in
SKILLS   Spanish, reading ability in French.

Résumé 2   **(Chronological Style)**

331 Baker Street
Houston, Texas 77002

5 April 1992

Ms. Elizabeth W. Prine
Tyler, Rodweey, and Prine
1543 Smith Street, Suite 3100
Houston, Texas 77002

Dear Ms. Prine:

Thank you for inviting me to your offices and for introducing me to Irma Gladwell. She provided me with excellent and enthusiastic information about your firm and the goals in the International Accounting Department. Now, I am even more interested in joining your firm.

Meanwhile, I am working on an accounting project, under Professor John Randall, that deals with public accounting principles in Guatemala. Irma mentioned that one of your clients is strongly interested in investments in Central America, so I hope my research will be useful at Tyler, Rodweey and Prine.

Sincerely,

James R. Showell

James R. Showell
(713) 456-2345

Follow-up Letter 2A

QUESTIONS

1. What evidence do you see that the writer focuses on the *reader's* perspective in this letter?
2. Business writers are often instructed to avoid subjective terms like "hope," "feel," "think," and "believe," and to substitute objective terms like "demonstrate," "show," "know," and "prove." Do you think Jim should omit the word "hope" from his last sentence?
3. Is this letter long enough? Why, or why not?

331 Baker Street
Houston, Texas 77002

5 April 1992

Ms. Irma Gladwell
International Department
Tyler, Rodweey, and Prine
1543 Smith Street, Suite 3100
Houston, Texas 77002

Dear Irma:

Thank you for making my visit to Tyler, Rodweey, and Prine so pleasant and informative. I mentioned your interest in Central America to my accounting professor, John Randall, and he was able to assign me to a term project that deals with public accounting principles in Guatemala. Perhaps the project report will be helpful to you.

If I can supply you with any additional information, please call. I will be very happy to hear from you.

Sincerely,

James R. Showell

James R. Showell
(713) 456-2345

Follow-up Letter 2B

QUESTIONS

1. Should Jim have written "Dear Ms. Gladwell" instead of "Dear Irma"?
2. Should Jim provide more information about the nature of his term project?
3. Would you say that Jim's letter ends in a cliché? (Clichés are discussed in Chapter 6.) Can you suggest a stronger close?

Sara Ann Crawford
2475 Oakwood, #270
Columbia, Missouri 64000

March 2, 1991

Mr. John Schwartz
Environmental Management Department
Arthur and Thomas, Inc.
42 Pinedale
Cambridge, Mass. 02140

Dear Mr. Schwartz:

The article on Arthur and Thomas in the October issue of <u>Smithsonian</u> presented an impressive record of your company's environmental achievements. I believe my experience in product development and my training in biology and the health sciences provide a base from which I can make a significant contribution to your Environmental Management Department.

As my résumé indicates, I will soon be completing my Bachelor of Arts degree in biology at the University of Missouri-Columbia. My summer and part-time work for the last three years has been focused on research and development. Working in a local laboratory last summer, I tested a new type of diagnostic equipment. My testing produced results that led to the expansion of the product's market throughout the United States. The skills I acquired during this development project--both evaluating and reporting on the product--would help me meet the demands upon Arthur and Thomas for clear and concise information regarding your Impact and Access Services.

I will be in the Cambridge area during spring break, March 20 through 24. May we meet to discuss my qualifications? You can reach me between 6:00 and 8:30 A.M., Central Time, at (417) 667-7000. If it is more convenient to call at another time, and I am away from home, my answering machine will take your message.

Sincerely,

Sara Ann Crawford

Enclosure

Job Letter 3

QUESTIONS

1. Is Sara's purpose in writing to Mr. Schwartz made clear?
2. Does the second sentence seem too abrupt or pushy?
3. What types of specific information does Sara include to convince Mr. Schwartz that she can contribute to the Environmental Management Department?
4. Should Sara have typed her name under the signature line?

SARA ANN CRAWFORD

2475 Oakwood #270
Columbia, Missouri 64000
(417) 667-7000

OBJECTIVE   Research Associate in environmental or biomedical laboratory.

EDUCATION   UNIVERSITY OF MISSOURI-COLUMBIA.
Bachelor of Arts, Biology, May 1991.
Honors, Dean's List (7 semesters).

EXPERIENCE   VETERINARY MEDICAL DIAGNOSTIC LABORATORY, Columbia, Missouri.

April 1990-
May 1991

Research Technician, summer and part time.
Performed bacteriological research, testing new diagnostic equipment. Assisted in data compilation and manuscript preparation. Contributed data for manuscripts published in the Journal of Veterinary Medicine.

Summers 1988   MEMORIAL HOSPITAL, Columbia, Missouri.
and 1989   Laboratory Assistant.
Supervised and performed tissue culture experiments to study immunological regulatory mechanisms. Trained incoming technicians. Served as liaison for researchers and technicians. Maintained laboratory supplies.

May-August   USDA-SOIL CONSERVATION SERVICE. Columbia, Missouri.
1987   Cartographic Aid.
Organized research data. Adapted and reproduced maps, charts, and graphs. Prepared visual aids for presentations.

ACTIVITIES   Volunteer, Omega House, hospice for cancer patients. Secretary, Campus Investment Club.

REFERENCES   Professor Janice Collins
Department of Biology
University of Missouri-Columbia
Columbia, Missouri 76543
(756) 897-6852

Dr. Howard McGovern
Veterinary Medical Diagnostic Laboratory
Columbia, Missouri 76543
(756) 123-8765

Sara Ann Crawford
2475 Oakwood, #270
Columbia, Missouri 64000

April 3, 1992

Mr. John Schwartz
Environmental Management Department
Arthur and Thomas, Inc.
42 Pinedale
Cambridge, Mass. 02140

Dear Mr. Schwartz:

The highlight of my trip to Cambridge last week was my visit to Arthur and Thomas, Inc. The work you are doing in environmental management is vital, challenging, and extremely important to the future of our planet. I'm excited about the possibility of becoming a part of such a challenge.

Thank you for the tour of your operations and, particularly, for your friendly enthusiasm and encouragement. I look forward to hearing from you soon.

Sincerely,

Sara Ann Crawford

Follow-up Letter 3

QUESTIONS

1. Does Sara's first paragraph sound enthusiastic or gushy; genuine or put on?

2. What can Sara do to strengthen this letter?

COMMUNICATION CHALLENGES

EXERCISE 1

Review the Skills Orientation diagram (Figure 19-1). Write down the appropriate orientation areas to complete these sentences:

1. I feel most comfortable working in this area:

_____

2. I also feel very comfortable working in the following areas:

_____

3. I feel least comfortable working in this area:

_____

EXERCISE 2

Review the accomplishments listed in the résumés shown earlier in this chapter, then *write fifteen phrases that describe your own experiences and apply them to your career objective.* Begin each description with an active verb. Make each description as specific and convincing as possible and make each one applicable to your job search. Examples:

- Acted as liaison between students and faculty while serving on the University Honor Council
- Supervised ten clerks and set a departmental record for high productivity
- Implemented and administered new quality control policy, resulting in an 18 percent reduction in customer complaints
- Prepared visual aids for presentations
- Processed weekly payroll for fifteen employees
- Translated field office manual to Spanish
- Participated in the preparation of grant proposals, including planning, information-gathering, writing of the manuscript, and final editing

EXERCISE 3

1. Complete the following.

My next job should allow me to use the following skills:

_____

I would like to develop my skills in the following areas:

_____

My next job should provide the following structure (or freedom):

_____

My next job should offer the following salary:

_____

In five years I should be:

_____

2. List your objectives.
  a. My goal for immediate employment
  b. My goal in five years
  c. My goal in life
3. List occupations you will consider
  a. For my next job
  b. As a career

EXERCISE 4

Write, or revise, your résumé based on exercises 1 through 3. If you will not be graduating this year, either write a résumé you can use in your search for summer or part-time employment or write as if you were graduating, presenting yourself as a degreed applicant.

EXERCISE 5

Conduct an information-gathering interview, as suggested in the section entitled "Develop Leads through Interpersonal Communication."

EXERCISE 6

Understand your audience's perspective.[19]

1. Do some reading on at least three target companies. Chapter 12 offers some specific guidelines for finding sources and conducting research into specific companies. How large are your target companies? What are their missions? What are their products? Who has the power within these organizations? What are the key aspects of corporate culture?
2. Choose one company to receive your custom-tailored job letter and résumé. First answer the questions in (1) above, and at least nine of the following.

When was the company founded?

Where is headquarters? Where are the branches located?

Is it privately owned, a partnership, or a public corporation?

How many employees does it have?

What are its recent and long-term trends in financial status?

What are its current trends in sales and service?

Do employees belong to unions?

What is the number and status of women and minority employees?

What are the company's goals?

What should be the company's goals?

How can you help further those goals?

Why do you want to work for this company?

Why should they want to hire you?

Who would be your potential manager(s)?

3. Assume the role of campus recruiting officer for that company. Write a recruiting brochure based upon your research and targeted to students at your school.

4. After your instructor has approved the brochure copy, design an appropriate layout, including charts, photographs, and white space. Refer to Chapter 14 for help with formats.

EXERCISE 7

Write a job letter (attach your résumé) to a *named individual* at the company of your choice. Apply for a specific position and include at least two statements that indicate you have researched the organization. For your

instructor's benefit, underline those two statements (of course, you will not underline them in the letter you actually mail). If your letter responds to a newspaper ad or job posting, bring a copy of the advertisement to your instructor.

EXERCISE 8

How would you answer these questions if they were asked in an interview for the position specified in exercise 7?

Tell me about yourself.

What can you offer us?

What have you accomplished?

What are your weaknesses?

If you could choose any job anywhere, what and where would it be?

What are your plans for the future?

Why do you want to work for us?

How would you describe the position you are seeking? What duties do you expect to perform?

What important trends do you see for our industry?

Tell me about your last employer.

Would you rather work with numbers or words?

How do you feel about drug testing of employees?

What are your hobbies?

What do you like to read?

How creative are you?

Are you continuing your education?

How much should we pay you?

Do you have any questions? (List six.)

☐ INTERNATIONAL BUSINESS COMMUNICATION: THE JOB SEARCH IN FOREIGN COUNTRIES *

Introduction

As more and more businesses have international connections and as students are looking for jobs not just in the United States but also in other countries, it becomes important that both students and instructors are familiar with job placement practices in other countries. In addition, it becomes necessary for man-

*This section is written by Iris I. Varner, Professor of Business Communication, Illinois State University.

agers and recruiters to understand that the application materials must be seen in the cultural context of the applicant. For example, a Japanese applicant usually appears more timid and shy than an American applicant. However, that does not necessarily mean he will not be an effective salesperson; he may simply be acting as is expected of a Japanese job applicant. Similarly, a French applicant who submits a handwritten cover letter does not indicate that he is careless and unprofessional; he acts according to French practices.

Methodology

The information presented in this study is based on a survey of international members of the Association for Business Communication (ABC) and on personal experience. International members of ABC were asked to respond to a questionnaire on job placement procedures in their respective countries. They were also asked to comment on a résumé and cover letter written by an American student who was looking for an entry-level job after graduation. In addition, sample résumés and cover letters from the various countries were requested. The 1988 directory for ABC members was used for the listings and addresses. A summary of the survey responses is presented in Table 19-1.

Since there were no ABC members from France and Germany, personal experience and interviews with exchange students were used to gain information on the job search in these two countries. I have worked in both Germany and France. For several years I have helped exchange students from Germany and France with résumés and applications for internships and entry-level positions.

The respondents from a particular country did not always agree on the acceptability of certain practices; sometimes they contradicted each other. For example, one respondent from Nigeria said that résumés are always typed; the other said they are always handwritten. Contradictory responses were interpreted to mean that both practices are acceptable.

TABLE 19-1   Summary of Survey Responses

COUNTRY	NUMBER OF RESPONSES	USABLE RESPONSES	QUESTION-NAIRE ONLY	COMMENTS	SAMPLES
Japan	8	8	2	6	2
Canada	4	4	1	3	0
Australia	4	3	1	2	0
Belgium[1]	2	2	0	2	2
Nigeria	2	2	1	1	0
Great Britain	1	1	1	0	1[2]
Israel	1	1	1	0	0
Mexico	1	0	0	0	0
Singapore	1	1	1	0	0

1. Both the Belgian respondents were from the Flemish-speaking part of Belgium.

2. The respondent from Great Britain sent an entire résumé book.

Findings

The findings show that practices vary widely. For example, a good U.S. résumé is not necessarily a good résumé in Australia, and usually not acceptable in Japan.

The study of the career placement procedures examined résumés and cover letters.

Résumés

Résumés are used in all the countries surveyed, but their form and organization can be quite different as Table 14-2 shows. Sample résumés are shown at the end of this section.

Except in Australia, Israel, Nigeria, and Japan, résumés are always typed or typeset. In Australia, Nigeria, and Israel both handwritten and typed résumés are acceptable.

In Japan résumés are traditionally handwritten. Handwriting is easier than typing because a functional typewriter must have at least 2,000 characters. Computers, on the other hand, allow the writer to enter the information in *Hiragana*, a syllabary, and convert it to *Kanji*, the traditional script. During the past few years these computers have started to change business communication practices, including the preparation of résumés. Students buy a printed résumé form, and they fill in the information by hand. As a result, all Japanese résumés have the same format and are organized in the same way.

In all countries résumés tend to be organized in outline form with headings. The essay form for the résumé is disappearing, but it is still acceptable in Australia, Israel, Nigeria, and Germany. In Germany, companies traditionally have requested a handwritten *Lebenslauf* (vita) which gives information on parents, siblings, and date and place of birth. A typical first sentence would read as

TABLE 19-2 Format and Appearance of Résumés

Country	TYPED			OUTLINE		
	always	sometimes	never	always	sometimes	never
Australia		●			●	
Belgium	●			●		
Canada	●			●		
France	●			●		
Germany	●				●	
Great Britain	●			●		
Israel		●			●	
Japan		●		●		
Nigeria		●			●	
Singapore	●			●		

TABLE 19-3   Personal Information on Résumés

Country	NAME			ADDRESS			PHONE NUMBER			PARENTS			CLUBS, HOBBIES			HEALTH			MARITAL STATUS			PHOTO-GRAPH			REFER-ENCES		
	always	sometimes	never	always	sometimes	never	always	sometimes	never	always	sometimes	never	always	sometimes	never	always	sometimes	never	always	sometimes	never	always	sometimes	never	always	sometimes	never
Australia	•			•			•				•		•					•		•				•		•	
Belgium	•			•			•				•		•				•		•				•			•	
Canada	•			•			•					•	•				•			•			•			•	
France	•			•			•					•	•				•		•				•			•	
Germany	•			•			•				•		•				•		•				•				•
Great Britain	•					•			•			•	•					•	•			•					•
Israel	•			•			•					•	•				•		•				•			•	
Japan	•			•			•				•		•				•		•			•				•	
Nigeria	•			•				•			•		•				•		•			•				•	
Singapore	•			•			•					•	•				•			•			•			•	

follows: "I, Christina Boehmer, was born on June 9, 1967, in Soest, Westfalia, as the second child of the pharmacist Alfred Boehmer and his wife Ute Boehmer nee Zerbe." Today most of this information is still presented in most résumés, but it is given in outline rather than essay form.

In all countries examined, the résumé gives the name of the applicant. The rest of the information that U.S. students typically provide varies from country to country (see Table 19-3).

U.S. résumés never provide the name of the parents. Applicants look for a job based on their qualifications, not on family connections and social standing. In Australia, Belgium, Japan, Nigeria, and Germany it is acceptable to provide the name of the parents. In Japan applicants sometimes also provide information on the jobs that parents or brothers hold. If this information is not provided on the résumé, the company may ask for it in the interview.

During the past decade, U.S. résumés have concentrated much more on skills and experiences directly related to career goals. Very seldom do applicants give information on marital status or health. The argument is that these topics have nothing to do with how qualified an applicant is for a particular position. Many companies do not want that kind of information because they are concerned about lawsuits based on discrimination against applicants based on marital status, age, and health (King 1981; Harcourt and Krizan 1989).

From the survey, however, it is obvious that other countries do not share this concern. In Belgium, France, Germany, Great Britain, Israel, Japan, and Nigeria, the résumé always indicates the marital status of the applicant. In the remaining countries marital status is sometimes listed.

TABLE 19-4 Information on Education Presented in Résumé

Country	CAREER OBJECT.			DATE OF GRAD.			GPA			PERCENT OF EXPENSES EARNED		
	always	some-times	never	always	some-times	never	always	some-times	never	always	some-times	never
Australia		●		●				●				●
Belgium		●		●				●				●
Canada		●		●				●			●	
France			●	●					●			●
Germany			●	●					●			●
Great Britain			●	●					●			●
Israel		●			●				●			●
Japan		●		●				●				●
Nigeria		●		●				●				●
Singapore		●		●				●				●

In many other countries a photo is acceptable (or even required). Because photographs provide information about race and ethnic background, it is not acceptable in the United States to provide a photograph with the résumé.

Information on educational background is important for entry-level positions in all countries, but the specific presentation varies (see Table 19-4).

In the United States many students list their grade point average on the résumé and state that they are willing to relocate. Harcourt and Krizan (1989) recommend that these two items should be emphasized on résumés. Others (King 1981; Rich 1987) suggest that the grade point average is particularly important for new college graduates.

U.S. students and recruiters are used to considering GPA in determining a student's achievements and future potential. In many countries, GPAs are not calculated. For example, at German universities, students do not have American-style transcripts. There is no measure for credit hours, and there is no GPA. Students take a minimum number of required classes and many electives. Depending on the course of study, students take some qualifying examination to be allowed to enroll in upper-level courses. What ultimately counts is whether the students pass the final examinations, both oral and written. The grades students receive during their studies are not relevant for the final examination. French students also do not have a U.S.-style transcript and calculated GPA. Clearly, a U.S. firm wanting to recruit German or French students must be aware of these different practices.

In the United States it has become very acceptable for students to state what percentage of their college expenses they have earned. The only other country where this seems to be acceptable is Canada. The Japanese respondents pointed out that in Japan this would be unacceptable and would be considered

TABLE 19-5   Work Experience Presented in Résumé

Country	WORK EXPERIENCE		
	always	sometimes	never
Australia		●	
Belgium	●		
Canada	●		
France	●		
Germany		●	
Great Britain	●		
Israel	●		
Japan		●	
Nigeria	●		
Singapore	●		

boastful. Furthermore, the student might come across as too independent, a trait Japanese companies do not consider positively.

American graduates looking for entry-level positions tend to list summer jobs they have held to show that they are responsible and did not just rely on their parents to pay for their education. Work experience, no matter in what area, is considered positive. This is different in other countries (see Table 19-5). Germans feel that students should study; working interferes with studying and is, therefore, not necessarily an asset. If Germans list work experience, the experience is related to the career the student is seeking. A job at McDonald's is not an asset for a finance major who is interested in a banking career.

As pointed out earlier, Japanese firms do not value U.S.-style independence and drive. Work experience during school might indicate that the student is too independent and may have trouble fitting into the group and adapting to the company culture.

Cover Letters

In the U.S. a cover letter always accompanies the résumé. It should be positive, assertive, adapted to the particular company, and typed. A handwritten letter would indicate that the applicant is not very serious and has little business orientation.

In Australia an assertive cover letter may be considered to be pushy, and it would be unacceptable to call the company for follow-up information after sending a letter. In Nigeria cover letters are typically handwritten. The Nigerians believe the personal effort of writing the letter by hand is positive. In Israel and Canada cover letters can be assertive, and the applicant can call the company for follow-up information.

Belgian letters can by typed or handwritten, and it is acceptable to call the company for follow-up information. The two respondents did not agree on assertiveness. One felt the letter should be assertive; the other one felt it should not be.

A Japanese student trying to get a job with a Japanese firm never writes a cover letter. Cover letters are used only for applications with foreign firms. Traditionally, cover letters are handwritten, but increasingly they are written on a word processor.

In Great Britain cover letters are only written and submitted if the company specifically requests one. In France, cover letters are often handwritten because companies submit letters for handwriting analysis to determine the true character of the potential employee.

Foreign Reactions to an American Résumé and Letter

The Australians found the American examples too assertive and boastful. They also felt that listing the work experience was too strong. The Australians model their résumés and cover letters more after the understated British style, but the American approach is gaining acceptance.

The Israeli respondent indicated that experience should come before education even in entry-level positions because a degree does not necessarily help. The respondent liked the American assertiveness, and commented that in Israel "chutzpah" seems to work very well.

The Canadians wanted the "sales approach" of the letter toned down. They also commented that the résumé listed too much information. One respondent commented that nobody would seriously believe that the applicant had a job, was active on campus, earned a big part of his college expenses, and had a good GPA. This simply was too much.

In the United States it is acceptable to present education and experience in either chronological order or reverse chronological order; the latter method has become more prominent. In Belgium experience and education are always listed in chronological order. The Belgian respondents found the American organization of reverse order confusing.

The Japanese felt the letter was too assertive and direct for Japanese business. They emphasized that in Japan letters must be very polite and euphemistic. They also must conform to the traditional style of business letters in which the writer typically opens with a comment on the weather or the season and a reference to the prosperity and health of the reader. As explained in Chapters 17 and 18, Japanese letters are more indirect; they imply more than what they actually say (Haneda and Shima 1982; Johnston 1980).

☐ CONCLUSION

The survey shows that conventions on résumés and cover letters in other countries vary from U.S. practices. The U.S. approach is considered very direct, assertive, impersonal, and, in many cases, too pushy for the cultural and business environment in other countries.

☐ RECOMMENDATIONS

Foreign students who study at American universities and are applying for jobs in the United States after graduation should be made aware that the job search in the United States may differ considerably from the procedure in their native countries. If they are too timid in the letter and if the résumé does not follow American practices, these students may be at a disadvantage and never be asked for an interview.

American students should be made aware that résumés and cover letters are different in other countries. If, for example, they apply for a job with a Japanese firm in the United States, that firm will probably use American résumés and cover letters. However, the knowledge that Japanese firms in Japan follow different procedures may give the applicant an advantage. The students would be well-advised to be somewhat less assertive in the cover letter and to be more subdued in the interview. The students would also gain if they came across as group-oriented and willing to fit in, rather than being interested in fast advancement and promotion.

An American graduate seeking employment with a German firm should evaluate the appropriateness and importance of any work experience. If the job does not relate to career goals, it is best to omit any reference to it on the résumé. Anyone looking for a job with a French firm should consider submitting a handwritten cover letter.

American students preparing for the job search know that most personal questions are illegal in the United States. They should realize that questions on marital status, age, health, and family connections are common practice in many foreign countries.

REFERENCES

Haneda, S., and H. Shima. 1982. Japanese communication behavior as reflected in letter writing. *Journal of Business Communication*, 19.1:19–32.

Harcourt, J., and A. C. "Buddy" Krizan. 1989. A comparison of resume content preferences of Fortune 500 personnel administrators and business communication instructors. *Journal of Business Communication*, 26.2:177–90.

Johnston, J. 1980. Business communication in Japan. *Journal of Business Communication*, 17.3:65–70.

King, L. 1981. Playing the recruitment game to win. *Industrial Engineering*, 13.1:66–74.

Rich, G. E. 1987. Careful! Resumes speak louder than words. *Business Education Forum*, 41.6:12–14.

JERRY W. HARPER JR.

CAREER OBJECTIVE

To obtain an entry-level position as a financial analyst with continued opportunities for growth and advancement. Long-term goals include career advancement and completion of an M.B.A.

EDUCATION

Illinois State University, Normal, Illinois. 8/87 - 5/89
Bachelor of Science Degree. **Finance** major. **Business Administration** minor. Accumulative GPA 3.24 on 4.00 scale.

Danville Area Community College, Danville, Illinois. 6/85 - 7/87
Associates of Science Degree. Business Concentration.

Eastern Illinois University, Charleston, Illinois. 8/84 - 5/85
General Studies.

INTERNSHIP

Citizens Savings and Loan, Normal, Illinois 9/85 - present
Responsibilities will include tax and insurance escrows, loan collection procedures, loan payoffs, loan closures, loan file maintenance, and various loan services.
Supervisor: Ron Pacha, (309) 452-1102.

WORK EXPERIENCE

Provided 85% of College Expenses

Big R, Warehouse Supervisor, Danville, Illinois. 9/85 - present
Supervised shipping and receiving activities and organized and assigned daily warehouse duties.
Supervisor: Glen Natschke, (217) 442-5800.

Watterson Cafeteria, Normal, Illinois. 8/87 - present.
Promoted to Level II supervisor. Examine student identification.
Supervisor: Diane Sawyer, (309) 438-3976.

Recording & Statistical Printing, Danville, Illinois. 6/85 - 9/85
Assisted in relocating plant facilities to new location.

Arby's Restaurant, Danville, Illinois. 6/82 - 6/85
Prepared sandwiches, provided customer service, and maintained building and lawn.

ACTIVITIES AND INTERESTS

Financial Management Association, Volunteer work for political candidate, Red Cross blood donor, and intramural sports.

REFERENCES

Miss Dorothy Dean
Lecturer
Business Education Department
Illinois State University
Normal, Illinois 61761
(309) 438-3369

Dr. Benjamin W. K. To
Assistant Professor
Management Department
Illinois State University
Normal, Illinois 61761
(309) 438-5306

Mr. Glen Natschke
Store Manager
Big R
Danville, Illinois 61832
(217) 442-5800

CONTACT INFORMATION

Current: (until December 13, 1988) 315 Smith, Normal, IL 61761
(309) 436-1340.

Permanent: R. R. #6 Box 441, Danville, IL 61832.
(217) 443-4358.

U.S. Résumé Sent to Foreign Specialists

315 Smith
Watterson Towers
Normal, IL 61761

September 14, 1988

Mr. Stephen Perry
Director of Personnel
Palmer American National Bank
2 West Main Street
Danville, IL 61832

Dear Mr. Perry:

A college education in finance and my work experience as a
finance intern have given me a solid background in finance.
This background will enable me to perform quality work in the
loan servicing department at Palmer American National Bank.
Dr. Benjamin To informed me of the opening that you currently
have for a position in the loan servicing department.

In obtaining a bachelor's degree with a major in finance from
Illinois State University, I was able to secure an excellent
financial information base. I gained valuable technical and
practical knowledge about the finance field through core
finance courses. I was able to utilize this knowledge in a
hands on manner through the application of case analysis and
computer simulations. I can successfully apply the knowledge
acquired from these courses to do the best possible job in
the loan servicing department at Palmer American National
Bank.

Working as a finance intern provided valuable practical
experience in a financial atmosphere. The internship gave me
the opportunity to apply financial knowledge to business
problems and to communicate results which could be used to
make financial decisions. Involvement in a professional
financial association has given me invaluable insights into
the financial community and has strengthened **my** interest in
the dynamic field of finance.

Mr. Perry, may I have an opportunity to interview with you
regarding a position in the loan servicing department? You
may reach me at 309 436-1340 between 10:00 a.m. and 5:00 p.m.

Sincerely,

Jerry Harper

Jerry W. Harper, Jr.

Enclosure: Résumé

履歴書

中田 信秀

学歴・職歴

学歴

昭和37	3	練馬区立開進小学校 卒業
40	3	練馬区立開進中学校 卒業
40	4	東京都立平和台高等学校 入学
43	3	東京都立平和台高等学校 卒業
43	4	T大学理工学部 入学
47	3	T大学理工学部 卒業

職歴

昭和47	4	A製作所株式会社 入社
49	4	同社 名古屋支店 勤務
54	3	B技術開発株式会社に出向
57	3	A製作所東京支社に復帰
60	4	都合により退社

以上

身上書

昭和40	10	日本商工会議所主催 珠算検定 3級合格
47	4	普通自動車 第一種免許 取得
50	1	情報処理技術者 第2種 取得

趣味・特技
　囲碁、音楽鑑賞
　サッカー・野球

健康状態　良好

志望の動機
1. 貴社の将来性
2. 貴社の業務に私の技術や研究
　 経験を生かして取組

職種　システム設計関係
勤務地　東京

Japanese Résumé

Arnaud MARCHAIS
Né le 13/12/64 (25 ans)

Adresse universitaire
901 W. Market, Apt. 4
Normal, IL 61761
U.S.A.
(309) 452-6975

Adresse permanente
8 rue Maurice Ravel
94440 Santeny
FRANCE
(1) 43-86-02-69

FORMATION

Mai 1990   M.B.A. (Master of Business Administration) option marketing, Illinois State University, U.S.A.
* Nommé "1989-1990 Outstanding M.B.A. Student".
* Au plan national, nominé par "l'American Marketing Association" pour le titre de "1990 Marketing Scholar of the Year".

Juin 1988   Diplômé de l'ESSCA (Ecole Superieure des Sciences Commerciales d'Angers), option commerce international.

Juin 1983   Baccalauréat serie C, Paris

LANGUES

Anglais : Lu-écrit-parlé couramment.
2 ans et demi aux U.S.A

Espagnol : Lu-écrit-parlé couramment.
"Diploma de la Camara Oficial de Comercio de Espana".
2 ans à Caracas, Vénézuéla.

EXPERIENCE PROFESSIONNELLE

Août 88/Mai 90   Illinois State University.
"Graduate Assistant" au le département de marketing.
* Chargé de l'enseignement d'un cours de management.
* Chargé de recherche.
* Publication d'un cas, "Which International Market and What Product Strategy?", dans le "Student Learning Guide to Accompany Marketing", 3ème édition (1989), par Jim Grimm, éditions John Wiley and Sons, New York.

Juil./Août 87   Treficable Pirelli.
Assistant Commercial, agence commerciale de Paris.
Vente et participation à la réorganisation de l'agence.

Oct.85/Sept.86   Service National.
Chef de cabine sur Nord 262 et Mystère 20 au sein de la 65ème Escadre de Transport de l'Armée de l'Air.
Chargé de la formation commerciale des stewards.

Juil./Sept.85   Air France.
Juil./Sept.84   Steward, division des vols long-courriers.

Sept.83   Carrefour, magasin de Pontault-Combault (77)
Assistant chef de rayon "surgelés".

ACTIVITES COMPLEMENTAIRES

Août 89/Mai 90   Illinois State University.
Vice-President de l'association des élèves de M.B.A.
Organisateur d'une campagne de télémarketing.
Août 88/Mai 89   Représentant des élèves au "College of Business Executive Council".
Trésorier de l'association des élèves de M.B.A.

Oct.86/Juin 87   ESSCA.
Oct.84/Juin 85   Attaché de presse du bureau des élèves.
Oct.83/Juin 84   Délégué de promotion.
Responsable du financement du baptème de la promotion 1983/1987.

CENTRES D'INTERET

Voyages : Séjours en Inde, Japon, Hong-Kong, Amériques du Sud et du Nord, Afrique...

Sports : Tennis, ski, football (10 années de club, 7 ans capitaine d'équipe).

French Résumé

<u>Lebenslauf</u>

<u>Angaben zur Person</u>

Name	:	Christina Boehmer
Addresse am Studienort	:	401 Walker Hall
		Normal, Illinois 61761
		USA
		(309) 436-4870
Heimataddresse	:	Luetgenbusch 10
		4772 Bad Sassendorf-Ostinghausen
		West Germany
		02945/2476
Geburtstag	:	9. Juni 1967
Geburtsort	:	Soest
Familienstand	:	ledig
Vater	:	Alfred Boehmer
		(verstorben im Februar 1982)
Mutter	:	Ute Boehmer, geb. Zerbe

<u>Ausbildung</u>

1977-1983	:	Hansa Realschule Soest
1983-1986	:	Archigymnasium Soest
August-Dezember 1986	:	Intensive English Institute an der
University of		Illinois in Urbana/Illinois
seit Januar 1987-		
Dezember 1989	:	Illinois State University in
		Normal/Illinois
		Studienfach: Marketing (Hauptfach)
		Business Administration
		(Nebenfach)

<u>Berufserfahrung</u>

Juni-Juli 1986 und		
Juni-Juli 1987	:	Stationshilfe in der
		Westfaelischen Klinik fuer
		Psychiatrie Lippstadt
August 1987-Mai 1989	:	Kuechenhilfe an der Illinois State
		University
seit August 1989	:	Bueroangestellte im department of
		Marketing, Illinois State University

<u>Ausserschulische</u> <u>Aktivitaeten</u>

seit April 1988	:	Mitglied in der Studentenverbindung
		Delta Sigma Pi (Studentenverbindung
fuer		Studenten der Betriebswirtschaft)
August 1988-Mai 1989	:	Praesident der European Student
Association		

<u>Besondere</u> <u>Kenntnisse</u>:		fliessend in Englisch
		Kenntnisse in Textverarbeitung

German Résumé

IF YOU WOULD LIKE
TO READ MORE

Bolles, R. N. *What color is your parachute? A practical manual for job hunters & career changers*, Berkeley, CA: Ten Speed Press, revised annually.

Holland, J. L. (1985). *Making vocational choices.* Englewood Cliffs, NJ: Prentice-Hall. Contains the "self-directed search" instrument, which provides a basis for determining suitable occupations to target for personal research.

Holland, J. L. (1986). *The alphabetical occupations finder.* Psychological Assessment Resources, Inc. (1-800-331-TEST; in Florida, 1-813-968-3003). Used with the "self-directed search," this resource will help you determine specific occupations that fit your personality, goals, and job requirements.

Lathrop, R. (1977). *Who's hiring who?* Berkeley, CA: Ten Speed Press. A series of search scenarios and interview conversations; information on scouting the job market, evaluating your qualifications, preparing job search documents, interviewing, and negotiating.

Michelozzi, B. N. (1988). *Coming alive from nine to five: The career search handbook* (3rd ed.). Mountain View, CA: Mayfield. Combination handbook and workbook; a lively step-by-step approach to self-evaluation, the job market and its trends, and the job hunt.

Occupational outlook handbook. Bureau of Labor Statistics, U.S. Department of Labor. Describes occupations by the nature of the work, locations, necessary training, and other qualifications. Published annually.

NOTES

1. R. N. Bolles, *What color is your parachute? A practical manual for job hunters & career changers.* Berkeley, CA: Ten Speed Press (1987), 66.

2. R. K. Irish, *Go hire yourself an employer.* Garden City, NY: Anchor Books (1978), 13–14.

3. B. N. Michelozzi, *Coming alive from nine to five* (3rd ed.). Mountain View, CA: Mayfield (1988), 1.

4. *The dictionary of occupational job titles.* Washington, DC: U.S. Government Printing Office (1977).

5. Bolles, 73.

6. D. C. Dauw, *Up your career.* Prospect Heights, IL: Waveland Press (1980).

7. S. Silver, "Informal approach may help land job." *The Houston Post*, August 14, 1988, L-1, 14.

8. N. Spinks & B. Wells, "Letters of application and résumés: A comparison of corporate views." *The Bulletin of the Association for Business Communication* 50(1987, September)3, 9–16.

9. Spinks & Wells, 9–16.

10. G. E. Morse, "A study of the preferences of executives for the style, format, and content of résumés." In S. J. Bruno (Ed.), *Proceedings of the Association for Business Communication* (1987), 97.

11. A. P. Carnevale, L. J. Gainer, A. S. Meltzer, & S. L. Holland, "Workplace basics: The skills employers want." *Training & Development Journal* (October, 1988), 25.

12. Carnevale and others, 25.

13. Spinks & Wells, 9–16.

14. R. Lathrop, *Who's hiring who?* Berkeley, CA: Ten Speed Press (1977), 192–196.

15. T. C. Keiser, "Negotiating with a customer you can't afford to lose." *Harvard Business Review*, 66(1988, November-December), 6.

16. R. Fisher and W. Ury, *Getting to yes: Negotiating agreement without giving in.* New York: Penguin Books (1981), 8.

17. Fisher and Ury, 82.

18. Keiser, 5.

19. Parts of this assignment are adapted from E. A. Goodrich, "Researching the organization—The career library and the application letter," and E. O. Yu, "Developing persuasive strategies: A different approach to the job application assignment," *The Bulletin of the Association for Business Communication*, 51(1988, June)2, 22–25.

PART FIVE

SPECIALISTS' PERSPECTIVES

MARKETING COMMUNICATIONS

OBJECTIVES

By studying this chapter and participating in the case study project, you will

- practice analyzing the needs of audiences whose priorities and interests differ from yours

- plan scenarios for introducing a new program

- plan communication strategies

- write documents included in a marketing campaign

- develop a sales presentation using slide show storyboards

PREVIEW

With or without the aid of consultants and advertising agencies, a marketing department must analyze customers' needs and purchasing decisions, the company's competitive position, and the feasibility of different solutions to the company's marketing problems. The marketing department must effectively communicate the results of its analyses to numerous other departments within the company and to other audiences in the external environment. Differences between the priorities of different departments make these communication tasks especially sensitive.

More often than not in these contexts, communicating means *selling*, or more accurately, creating the condition under which listeners, viewers, or readers become convinced that they are wise to *buy*. Marketing people thus are always busy persuading others. They must persuade colleagues in manufacturing to make products that research says will move; those in finance to fund research, new products, and marketing promotions; and so on. Volumes of research notwithstanding, the marketer's "practice" is rarely mistaken for science, wherein a + b = c at all times. The practitioner's most powerful tool, then, is the ability to communicate persuasively.

In the Natco case that follows, the vice president of marketing must use information gathered through marketing research and other experience to seize a critical opportunity. As the case progresses, the interaction of forces in the external environment with characteristics of this particular company creates urgent problems that you will be invited to solve.

❑ MARKETERS MUST COMMUNICATE

Marketing may be defined narrowly or broadly. Narrowly defined, marketing's purpose is to increase customers' knowledge of a company's products and services, with the goal of making those customers more inclined to make purchases. More broadly (and accurately) defined, marketing means the whole process of analyzing market opportunities and customer preferences, coordinating the development and testing of new products and services, and planning for the distribution, promotion, and sale of all products. Regardless of the scope of their responsibilities, marketing people must spend a high proportion of their time communicating.

Even under the narrower definition, the marketing department must communicate effectively with many other departments within the company and many companies outside. For its own planning purposes, the marketing department may do any or all of the following:

Obtain information about new products from the research and development (R&D) department, the new product department, or from product managers

Conduct market research or work with outside specialists to obtain information

Communicate with the production or inventory management departments to know when products will be available for shipment

Prepare promotional and educational materials for sales personnel

Coordinate advertising, public relations, and promotions for products

Arrange for product testing and consumer feedback sessions about new products

Oversee the preparation of packages, labels, manuals, warranty booklets, installation and operation manuals, and follow-up documents

Virtually no situations occur in a marketing department that do not entail speaking, writing, and other media considerations. Furthermore, these communications are invariably subject to legal scrutiny. The advertising the marketing department approves; the manuals, labels, and tags that accompany the product; and the warranties it attaches to products may be the basis of product liability suits. Communication failures can therefore have serious financial implications. Thus, communication is crucial to the marketing department's success and to the company's success.

Some of the functions in which marketing departments are heavily involved, such as advertising, public relations, publications, and product testing, may be carried out by other departments or by companies the firm hires to do this work on its behalf. Therefore, marketing people often have to become expert in interdepartmental and external communication. They must learn to obtain information from a variety of sources inside and outside the company. Because their audiences are not usually members of their own departments, marketing people must be scrupulous about defining terms and making references clear. Furthermore, because these audiences often have different values and different priorities, marketing communicators must usually rely on persuasive techniques. Marketing documents must be unusually complete, so that when used in a variety of contexts all the necessary information will be available to the readers or listeners. These requirements challenge the professional's organizing and stylistic abilities.

Philip Kotler has prepared a chart summarizing possible conflicts and differences in perspective between marketing and other departments, shown in Figure 20-1.

DEPARTMENT	EMPHASIS	MARKETING EMPHASIS
Research and Development	Basic research Intrinsic quality Functional features	Applied research Perceived quality Sales features
Engineering	Long design lead time Few models Standard components	Short design lead time Many models Custom components
Purchasing	Narrow product line Standard parts Price of material Economical lot sizes Purchasing at infrequent intervals	Broad product line Nonstandard parts Quality of material Large lots to avoid stockouts Immediate purchase for customer needs
Manufacturing	Long production lead time Long runs with few models No model changes Standard orders Ease of fabrication Average quality control	Short production lead time Short runs with many models Frequent model changes Custom orders Aesthetic appearance Tight quality control
Finance	Strict rationales for spending Hard and fast budgets Pricing to cover costs	Intuitive arguments for spending Flexible budgets to meet changing needs Pricing to further market development
Accounting	Standard transactions Few reports	Special terms and discounts Many reports
Credit	Full financial disclosures by customers Low credit risks Tough credit terms Tough collection procedures	Minimum credit examination of customers Medium credit risks Easy credit terms Easy collection procedures

FIGURE 20-1.   Conflicts between Marketing and Other Departments

From Kotler, P. (1984). *Marketing Management* (5th ed.), p. 731. Englewood Cliffs, NJ: Prentice-Hall, Inc. Reprinted by permission of Prentice-Hall, Inc.

Both large and small companies may choose to use consultants and outside firms to conduct market research and prepare advertising and promotion. Unless the work volume is exceptionally high, most companies cannot afford to pay top-flight market researchers and advertisers to work for them as full-time employees. As a result, many marketing managers must work with outside market research companies and advertising agencies. The marketing managers must then explain (or justify) the results obtained and propose projects to other managers and executives, who have power of review.

Often a marketing manager's most formidable tasks are reducible to almost pure communication problems. On a regular basis, for example, the marketer tries to persuade colleagues in other departments to spend (the manager will use the word "invest") money on activities characterized by a relatively high level of risk. A commercial's selling power often cannot be measured with great confidence until the commercial is produced and run for an extended time—meaning that a considerable amount of money has been spent! The same holds true for a new product.

Marketing is, ultimately, equal parts science and art; a business discipline to be practiced but rarely mastered. Is this to say that market research has little value? Absolutely not; the value of research has been well proven. But you are wise to read your research reports knowing that human beings defy you whenever you treat them as mere statistics. If the weather is tough to predict, people are much tougher. Prominent names populate the community of companies that have paid huge prices in the course of mistaking research reports for crystal balls. Evidence of their errors appears in the form of closed stores, discontinued products, and last year's model in this year's new-car showroom.

Understandably then, in the marketer's universe, people are skeptical about "facts"—which underscores the vital importance of the marketing manager's communication skills. Like the attorney, the successful marketer rarely has the evidence to guarantee a favorable decision. Skills of persuasion play an enormously important role.

This chapter features a case that will introduce you to a few of the legal, interdepartmental, and external communication problems that can occur in marketing management. You will participate in this case as a marketing manager of National Oil Company (Natco). You will use information generated by market research consultants, an architecture firm, and an advertising agency to persuade your senior executives and the owners of your retail outlets to undertake a major marketing project.

As you read this case, you should read with a detective's eye. Look for the important groups in the external environment that affect the case. Note in the margin the key individuals, other involved departments, and information about the corporate culture of Natco. As you picture the marketing vice president's situation, you will develop insights and strategies to cope with the problems of persuasive communication that arise.

As you respond to these challenges, apply ideas from the core chapters. Analyze the situation with the clues you have noted and merge your own creative processes with those of the organization to develop strategies. Use the concept of uncertainty to discover your audiences' information needs, beliefs, and feelings. Link these three aspects with the creative techniques described in the earlier chapters on communication roles and communication strategies.

Try to find a surprising connection that will capture your audiences' fancy. "Fancy" may seem a frivolous term, but few of us become excited and committed to the dull and ordinary. ("Fancy" originally meant "imaginative.") In many companies, marketers must absorb other employees' fear of looking silly so that these same employees can feel free to join in projects.

Whenever you need to communicate, imagine a variety of scenarios that could involve different people, different media, and different logical communication strategies. Play these scenarios in your head to imagine "what if" scenes and their outcomes. Visualize key individuals as they hear your ideas. If you concentrate, you can often imagine their gestures or words of response. Always imagine a "Yes, but" for each audience. These are statements that express a listener's objections or reservations about an idea and begin, "Yes, but. . . ." These help you prepare for questions and attitudes you must address.

❏ INTRODUCTION TO THE COMMUNICATION PROCESS

Good packaging plays a surprisingly integral part in successful marketing—it forms a central issue in the following study—and that makes the topic worth considering even before tackling the Natco case.

The term "package" encompasses many meanings for a marketer. Most of the time it carries the meaning for which you know it best: a label, sleeve, box, bottle, can, or other product container. Frequently, however, it will mean the combining of various products or services to form a distinct, multifaceted offering. For example, your bank considers your checking account (which might be linked with credit or debit card privileges, an automatic teller machine card, overdraft protection, and a special "preferred customer" fee structure) to form a product "package."

A retailer's storefront is an aspect of its packaging. (The same is true for banks; just glance at any major city's skyline for confirmation.) So is the retailer's signage, interior decor, uniforms, and so on. You perhaps never consider yourself to be *paying* for such items. However, all of these elements—architecture, paint colors, furnishings, and more—are part and parcel of what you are *buying*. These elements blend to form an image—part concrete, part ethereal—that the marketer uses as one asset in persuading you to do business with one retailer instead of another.

Naturally, good marketers try to package their products to win your favor. Accordingly, differences in packaging can provide insights into marketing strategy. At this time, turn to preliminary exercises 1 and 2 at the end of the chapter.

Case: National Oil Company (Natco)

The Situation Today   It must have been easier the last time someone suggested a change in service station appearance. At least that is what you imagine, as you ready yourself to type word one of your presentation. How simple it was before 1973: 12,000 stations and every one owned by National Oil Company. If they had known what you do now, they would never have recommended that retail distribution of Natco products be changed. But that is muddy water under the bridge. The fact remains, you have the research concluding that big changes must occur now, if Natco is to have a shot at regaining trust and prominence so that it can once again compete head-to-head with the big guys such as Exxon, Mobil, Shell, and Chevron.

Reflecting on today's Natco stations, you are reminded of how Charles Smith explained the selling of Natco's revolutionary Wholesale Marketing "Jobber" Program in 1973: "As America took to the automobile in ever-increasing numbers, so too did the independent business people who foresaw a rich new marketplace along Roadside America," Chuck had said. "And soon it seemed that no matter where the motorist might roam, some all-American entrepreneur was sure to be ready and waiting to satisfy some need." Natco's problems today derive from the decision to place distribution of Natco's products in the hands of those entrepreneurs.

A Historical Perspective   One of the most innovative of the early producers and distributors of petroleum products was National Oil Company of Austin. "Hey, we were the first to have a filling station with a gas pump where you could see that gasoline inside," Chuck recalled for you. "We used to be a company able to step out, with courage, and be different—you know, without fear of criticism or risk."

The trouble started with the oil shortage of 1972. Until then, Natco retail marketing had a structure made up principally of company-owned service stations operated by franchise dealers. Suddenly it found itself surrounded by an industry in flux, with its future in question. Self-serve stations came out of nowhere to grab public attention and steal market share with gas at a discount. National Oil executives decided that they did not want to be stuck with several thousand company-owned service stations when *service* was out of fashion. Consequently, they decided to change the retail distribution channels of Natco from coast to coast.

In groups of six or less, all 10,000 of Natco's company-owned stations were sold to independent wholesale distributors, or jobbers. Today, as director of marketing for Natco, you have 1000 such entrepreneurs (owners of 5500 outlets) to make happy. Of course you also have John "Paul Jones" Taylor, your vice president (a retired Navy admiral), and 3.7 million Natco customers and credit card holders. Unfortunately, the message you have for Taylor now is certain to wrinkle his brows.

Presumably, having a network of these independent distributors, doing business in turn with independent dealers who operated and sometimes owned their outlets, would be fine. According to plan, "Natco would relieve itself of worry about the complex retailing of the gasoline and oil products. Attention could then be turned entirely to the products themselves and to the channels of wholesale distribution to business and industry." At least that is how Mr. Taylor explains it today.

Unfortunately, Natco did not count on the operators of Natco stations wanting ownership for reasons *other* than the retailing of Natco products. In fact, the wholesalers saw opportunities and seized them. They bought weaker locations in the secondary Natco markets at depressed prices and, in general, kept the Natco identity at those weaker stations. They also bought the better locations, however, and these they often (all *too* often) parlayed into cash by reselling them to real estate developers. Worse, they sometimes kept the stations intact but changed their identities. Natco stations in some prime spots of major markets suddenly put on new faces: the faces of Natco competitors! As a result of these three actions, the Natco name became associated with secondary locations, lost its prime locations, and experienced a deteriorating image as multiple variations on the Natco logo and station design began to appear.

As a result of the jobbers' decisions, Natco has essentially lost control over the retailing of its products. Demand for Natco products has fallen, and market share over the past five years has declined. Such a trend must be stopped, and company executives have turned to marketing for a solution. You believe that two steps must be taken, preferably at the same time. You want to investigate consumer perceptions of Natco in order to pinpoint the factors affecting lowered demand. Such a study should be conducted by market research professionals. In addition, you need an in-house audit of your jobbers (wholesale distributors) in order to learn more about the reasons why sales of Natco products have declined. Ultimately, you hope that the low average sales volumes of Natco products can be raised. Until you know more about the jobbers and about the customers' preferences, you won't be able to recommend a solution to the problem.

While the study by the market research consultants, Greenwood Marketing Research, will cost about $175,000, you think that your own staff can conduct an audit of your 1000 distributors with funds already in the budget. Now, turn to exercise 1 at the end of the chapter.

You Talk to the Distributors   The six-month audit of your wholesale distributors (jobbers) revealed plenty. Your goal was to uncover the reason the company's distributors were allowing the erosion to occur. Indeed, could something be done?

The findings were interesting, if somewhat predictable. Jobbers no longer perceived value-added benefits in the Natco name, so they had begun using Natco as a swing supplier. They were buying from other oil companies when pricing was comparable. Only when Natco's prices fell well below those of its competitors did the distributors purchase from Natco.

The same image perception (or lack of it) apparently explained why the distributors had sold newly purchased Natco stations, notably those in great retail locations, or had retrofitted Natco's architecture and begun selling a major competitive brand. Simply put, the distributors wanted to leverage a great location to the maximum in order to get every possible dollar of sales out of it. As Natco's public profile diminished, so did the value of its name on that great piece of dirt. Other nomenclature, more heavily advertised, was available and, unfortunately for Natco, proved more desirable.

One memorable case uncovered in the research has painted a clear picture. A distributor in Nashville owns ten stations, three of which carry the Natco brand. The seven non-Natco stations are selling an average of 65,000 gallons of gasoline monthly. The three Natco outlets pump less than 30,000 each.

The distributors say that your brand just is not strong enough any longer. They are holding on, distributing Natco products, for a couple of reasons. According to the interviews your task force conducted, about half of the jobbers huddle up close to Natco because they believe in the products, the people, and, most importantly, that some day the company will awaken and become a force again. Many of these distributors are second- or even third-generation Natco families. They are driven by loyalty. Virtually all of them do business in markets of 25,000 population or less.

The other 50 percent of Natco jobbers are with you because the company lets them run their businesses the way they want to, with minimal company interference. They value their freedom so much that they willingly sacrifice income potential to secure it. Fully 40 percent of these also make their homes in small cities and towns, most often in the heartland states of Middle America.

Knowing all this, you now understand why in the past few years the wholesale distributor system has begun to grow. There were just over 700 full-line distributors in the Natco network in 1984. That number increased to about 850 in 1985 and topped 1000 in 1987. These distributors (jobbers) serve Natco dealers, whose number has also been growing—from fewer than 3560 to 5500 in four years. This growth has occurred at a time when the number of oil industry jobbers and dealers in the United States is declining—so powerful is the pull of freedom to operate as one pleases.

Differences aside, all the jobbers realize that a consistent, attractive look given to the Natco brand could mean money in their pockets. They just do not know how to get it done, and certainly do not want a change to begin at their expense. The research makes this clear.

A Look at the Consumer Marketing Research   The research tells you that in the markets where it is known, Natco has an image problem that is worsening.

Even you, with your fifteen years in the oil business, have learned a lot in the last eighteen months. Consumers have told you, in the 224-page document on your desk, that 53 percent of their purchasing decisions are made within a half-block of service stations. They carry both cash and credit cards, so that when they see their gauges on empty, they start shopping. Here, in that roadside marketplace that Chuck told you about, Natco is getting killed. You have 1000 owners and the stations *look* like it. Nothing is consistent but Natco's inconsistency, you reflect to yourself. Heck, some of the stations are places where you would not stop to use a phone, let alone pump gas into your tank, pour oil in your crankcase, or ask for advice.

The irony in all that, of course, is that Natco motor oils and gasolines, category to category, rank with the finest made anywhere in the world. Tests prove this on a regular basis. In your own industry, it is common knowledge.

The time-honored slogan, "You know the difference. It's Natco" has taken on new meaning altogether. While its product quality has remained the same, Natco has become a different company! In ten years its average volume of light oils (gasoline) has plummeted and its presence in the larger, prestigious, high-volume markets has nearly disappeared.

Time to Go to Work   You are now growing familiar with Natco's real-life strengths and weaknesses. Under any circumstances, solving its image problem will take time. And while you are applying a remedy, the company's marketing and advertising must go on. So here lies your dilemma: Retired Admiral Taylor has seen the irony in the "You know the difference. It's Natco" slogan. He has asked you to suggest a replacement slogan to serve as a tag line for Natco's advertising. Your primary audience comprises your current Natco customers and your prospective customers. But your distributors and dealers need to like the slogan, as well.

"Find the good in all this muck," Taylor says. "Give us something we can hang our hat on—a mark of punctuation at the end of a Natco commercial. You can do it."

Surprisingly, perhaps, one of the qualities to look for in a marketing slogan is its *truthfulness*. This does not mean that a slogan cannot exaggerate a little. A slogan must, after all, advance your cause. But if a phrase does not ring true with your customers, then they will dismiss it as being so much advertising hype. Moreover, they are apt to dismiss your other product and service claims, too.

Your slogan should have more to offer than truth alone, of course. You derive benefit from its success at communicating a unique claim ("The Real Thing"), a distinctive market niche ("The Heartbeat of America"), a call to action ("Reach Out and Touch Someone") and more—while being brief, easy to understand, and eminently memorable! Now, turn to exercise 2 at the end of the chapter.

Beauty's Only Skin Deep after All   The research presentation (resulting from your $175,000 investment) is something you will never forget. Douglas Morton of Greenwood Marketing Research said, "You gentlemen have a gargantuan dilemma here. The architecture of your branded outlets from place to place varies substantially, which is what I had expected in a system whose outlets are owned by hundreds of independent businessmen. I'm sure this is not all bad," Morton added, "but I can't right off tell you what's good about it. And it's especially terrible now that you've got more gas and oil than you know what to do with!"

Morton knew what he was talking about, because Natco was the third oil company for which he had recently conducted a customer audit. The feedback stayed consistent, if the name on the title page did not.

Customers told Mr. Morton that the four key influences affecting their selection of a service station are:

1. the appearance and overall cleanliness of the station
2. the station's location, or convenience (including accessibility to the driveways)
3. the station's brand or the signage
4. the station's reputation for quality and service.

"Why no mention of products?" you asked.

"The product quality is what we call a 'gotta have,'" Morton told you. "If you don't have it, you don't play with the big guys. If in the public's mind you are one of the major oil companies, then they assume you have a top-quality line of products. At least you have parity. It's that simple. You gotta have it, but you don't get a lot of credit for it."

Unfortunately, a coat of paint and a shiny new sign count for almost as much as a hundred-year tradition of innovation in engine fuels and lubricants. After your conversation with Morton, you sit down to define the company's problems, combining the market research with what you've learned from the jobbers. Simply put, you now know that once again Natco has to make the package as attractive as the products inside. Indeed, your job is to convince a host of entrepreneurs, 60 percent of whom live and work in markets of fewer than 25,000, and 50 percent of whom view you through the eyes of convenience store or "C-store" owners. For them, Natco is merely oil on the shelf, gas at the pump, and a dozen other auto supplies (all of them high-profit-margin products) within a universe of 2000 products handled at each C-store location.

These independent business people have been doing all kinds of identity-building on their own, too. Sure, they have kept the Natco "Globe" logotype pretty much as the company had approved it in 1965. But, alongside it, they have built distinctive identities not always complementary to the Natco signage. "Henry's Pack 'n' Sack" used one color scheme and Mel's "Natco Toot 'n' Tell 'Em" used another. Your research tells you that in nationwide marketing, such variety kills. The more consistent and attractive the look, the better. The public comes for service, not surprises.

As a group, Natco dealers *do* merchandise products and services. Unfortunately, various types of merchandising are carried out in the street, the pole sign, the pump island, and inside the building. Methods include rented curb signs, handwritten pump toppers, various window posters, and more. These methods are generally prohibited in your competition's company-owned outlets, because the communication devices are known to be considered tacky by the driving public. But then, for your competitors, law and order in the realm is enforced by executive fiat. You do not have that luxury.

Your Solution: A New Image for Natco To make this work, you have to find a way to capture the imagination of the independent jobbers and to persuade them that they cannot do without reconstructive surgery on their image. Your points of leverage are few. You have the loyalty of some jobbers. You have the research showing that consumers choose stations by appearance. You have the jobbers' innate fear of your competitors, who are currently upgrading their appearance. And you have the annual supply contracts—the jobbers' tickets to do business—with Natco, that is.

According to your best estimates, figured by Third Dimension Architects of New York City, a facelift for Natco's stations would in total cost about $12 million, or the equivalent of your entire annual advertising budget. Third Dimension, at your request, has done some exploratory drawings to illustrate the potential of a new image for Natco. Their station designs, constant in their beige, yellow, and blue colors, and their clean, "layered" style make an unforgettable presentation when juxtaposed with Natco's patchwork quilt of current outlets.

FIGURE 20-2.
Proposed Signage Design for NATCO

You cannot help but think that, if the independent wholesalers could see this idea, they would approve it. But you know full well that they would never fund the facelift to the tune of $12 million. Nor will National Oil, of course, because the margins on dwindling gasoline and oil sales remain slim. The answer to the question, "Where is the money to come from?" came from Third Dimension: "Why not try some type of incentive program?"

The Image Improvement Program To start distributors on the right road, Natco has to lend a hand in a way that will buy a lot of new image without straining slim margins.

That is where the "New Image Improvement Program" comes in. The brainchild of Third Dimension, the program creates a way for incremental sales to help pay for image improvements. In short, Natco jobbers will be able to accrue funds for image improvements based on Natco gasoline purchases.

To kick the program off, Natco jobbers who purchased 85 percent or more of their 1989 contract volume will have 3/10 cents per gallon put into an accrual fund, effective January 1990. They will have until December 31, 1990 to use the accruals for image improvements.

After January 1, 1991, Natco wholesale distributors who have lifted (sold) 85 percent of their contract volume each month during a calendar

EXERCISE 3

Use the mind-mapping technique shown in the chapter on communication strategies to capture the viewpoint of the jobbers by representing their concerns about this program. The map on page 557 indicates just a few of the jobbers' concerns and is intended as a suggestion of how to begin this map. It is not complete. (See Chapter 5.)

Next, *analyze the differences in emphasis or priorities among the stakeholders, creating a table similar to the one in Figure 20-1.*

EXERCISE 4

As you think back over the past weeks, you feel Mr. Taylor's lack of confidence and remember your concern about Mr. Hawes's hawkish views. You recall the anxiety you felt about the possibility that jobbers might abandon ship once the slightest word leaks out about "another doggone paint and plaster program." Then your own confidence returns. You might be able to establish good communications with the jobbers through the several years of building the new image and marketing it to the U.S. public. This whole change won't have to take place overnight. You can use this opportunity to build a long-term relationship. It is time to think about how to sell this program.

The starting point for this effort is the same for marketing any other idea, product, or service. Use the Marketing Planning Outline on page 554 for ordering your thoughts as you work your way toward a change destined to be considered a milestone in Natco history. Remember, your job now is selling to the distributors first, secondarily to consumers.

EXERCISE 5

Develop a scenario for presenting your program to the 1000 jobbers. There are many ways to go. You should plan how to unveil the new image, but you must also consider how to follow up on the initial announcement. Consider employing the following techniques and media. Be prepared to discuss in class why you elected to use or not to use each one.

Videotape

Memoranda

Printed brochures

A full-scale station mockup

A television spokesperson

A two-day national jobbers' convention

Small-group discussions with jobbers

The architects' audiovisual presentation

Letters

A television commercial

A "new image" newsletter

A theme for the new image effort

Questionnaires to jobbers

A press conference

Choose one of the techniques you intend to include in your scenario and prepare a communication strategy sheet for the event or document.

EXERCISE 6

Whatever techniques you choose to convince the jobbers to buy the new image program, you will find that some jobbers need someone to visit them with a sales/marketing pitch. To equip your salesperson, you must translate the essence of your arguments into a portable presentation. You may choose slides with an audio tape, or use a videotape format. *Select one or the other, tell why, and then develop a compelling script using storyboards.* Important: You will not be there when these presentations are made, so be comprehensive in your audio/visual message. However, please keep the show to less than ten minutes (you may refer to Chapter 16, Preparing Oral Presentations). In preparing for your presentation, employ the following Creative Worksheet.

CREATIVE WORKSHEET

1. What are you actually selling in this new image plan?
2. What medium (slides or video) are you using? What are the strengths and weaknesses of this medium?

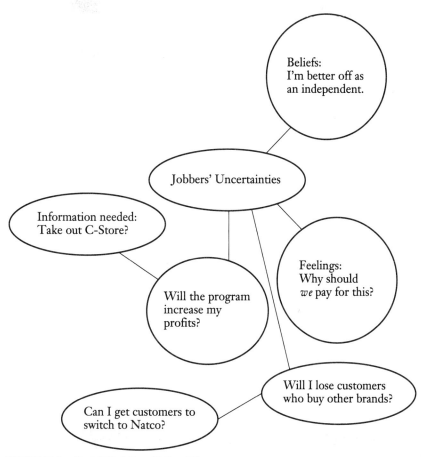

FIGURE 20-4. Partial Mind-Map of Jobbers' Uncertainties

3. What is the most important point you wish to make in this sales presentation?

4. Who is your audience? Consider culture, age, gender, education, and any other key personality-shaping factors. What makes these people tick?

5. From what you know, what do you think is the single most important (persuasive) benefit you can offer this audience as an inducement in selling the new image program? What can you promise them?

6. Why should they believe you can deliver on your promises?

7. Are there other benefits to be realized from the new. image program? Can you prove them?

8. Describe the personality of Natco that you want to emerge in this sales presentation. Be specific in selecting your adjectives. What implications does this have for your creative work?

EXERCISE 7

Create the following communications:

a. A memo to the Distributors Council that compels them to come to a meeting with you. *Sell* them on the meeting without revealing the new-image agenda. By announcing the plan when everyone is present, you have a better chance of dealing with objections, persuading a higher proportion of the group, and building enthusiasm in a group setting.

b. Create an agenda for the meeting of the council.

c. Assume that you gather the majority of the Natco jobbers together at one place for a new-image presentation. Decide what materials (brochures, guidelines, etc.) you will give them to *take away* from that gathering. Then, write a cover letter for the handout package that introduces the material.

d. Write a summary document, in whatever form you deem most appropriate, to Mr. Taylor. Explain what you are going to do during the campaign to persuade the distributors and why. This report will be sent to him about a week before the meeting of the Council. Your objective is that he read your document and observe, "This modest young person will receive our gratitude and a *solid* expression of it. If the program doesn't bear fruit, it's surely someone else's fault." (After all, you did not do this merely for Natco.)

COMMUNICATING ABOUT REAL ESTATE

OBJECTIVES

By studying this chapter, you will learn to

- prepare letters to prospective clients

- describe a property using the "feature/function/benefit" method

- evaluate advertisements and documents according to pertinent legal considerations

PREVIEW

This chapter explains the communication responsibilities and processes of real estate professionals and people who hire them. This knowledge will be valuable to you either as a businessperson involved in a real estate transaction or as a real estate professional. If you have not had any real estate courses, you will learn how to apply basic communication strategies to real estate communication situations. If you have studied real estate, you will learn how to apply your knowledge to situations through types of marketing letters, property descriptions, advertisements, and file documents.

Writing is a vital part of all interactions involving real estate, because real estate professionals must document all their oral communication as well as prepare many documents during the process of negotiating agreements. In essence, real estate professionals manage the communication process among sellers, buyers/tenants, and a variety of other professionals. Real estate professionals must verify what was understood or intended, obtain written replies, make written notes on all telephone conversations, confirm that counteroffers have been made, and document the presentation to owners of all the prospective buyers' or tenants' offers. Almost all states require that real estate agreements must be in written form to be binding. In many states licensed real estate practitioners are required to maintain comprehensive files on all interactions, regardless of whether sales or leases result.

A variety of business conditions cause companies to communicate about real estate. A typical transaction involves six stages, requiring a variety of documents and presentations. These stages are:

1. Analysis of user's needs
2. Negotiations
3. Contract development
4. Contract execution
5. Follow-up for contract compliance
6. Adjustments

The signing of the contracts marks the beginning, not the end, of a long-term relationship and ongoing communication between tenant and owner or buyer and seller. All real estate communication occurs in a complex legal context that requires professionals to monitor their communication for potential promissory claims that might create legal liabilities.

The actual names and addresses of companies, individuals, and properties mentioned in this chapter have been disguised, although the examples are drawn from actual cases. However, the names of companies and organizations in the advertisements are genuine.

---

*Certified Property Manager

☐ COMMUNICATION: THE CENTRAL PROCESS IN REAL ESTATE TRANSACTIONS

Real estate and space considerations are part of most business functions. Businesses may own or lease manufacturing, office, warehouse, or retail space. They use buildings, fixtures, mineral resources, underlying land, surface and subsurface rights, and improvements to generate wealth. As a result, almost all business people must communicate from time to time about real estate and its impact on their businesses.

People Communicate about Real Estate for Many Reasons

Changes in the external environment may change companies' space requirements.

Changes in the external environment of a business may cause real estate activity, and business environments change constantly. Customers move; suppliers relocate; transportation costs increase; new regulations and land restrictions limit land use; taxes increase; and the labor supply may shrink or relocate. The value of the land on which a company operates may increase in value to the point that an unexpected profit may be gained by its sale. On the other hand, increases in rents may drive a company to seek more economical facilities (see Figure 21-1).

Changes in a company's industry may cause the company to seek new uses of property it has leased or purchased. The major downturns in the oil and steel industries are good examples of how powerful forces motivate real estate action. When the business base dissipates, real estate activities of all types are almost certain to follow. Major conglomerates may sell or shut down unprofitable divisions. Corporate real estate offices or surviving management personnel may put the surplus facilities into the real estate market. Facilities may be sold or subleased, and the employees may find it necessary to sell their homes.

Economic booms will also affect real estate. The government's decision to enter the space race created new clusters of companies and communities in Huntsville, Alabama; Cape Kennedy, Florida; and Houston, Texas. Several states benefited simultaneously when expanded government contracts necessitated the hiring of additional employees and the expansion of manufacturing facilities and office space.

Through political incentives, states such as Massachusetts converted their depressed industrial manufacturing economies into high-tech successes. Real estate activities included redevelopment of existing commercial areas as well as development of previously raw land. Silicon Valley emerged in California when the orange groves near San Francisco were transformed to computer companies' manufacturing sites (see Figure 21-2). Furthermore, the development of a new industry has residual effects on local economies and real estate: new homes, shopping centers, medical facilities, and other support services are needed for an expanding population. All of these activities result in real estate transactions of various types and communication between companies and real estate professionals.

Internal changes in a company may create real estate activity.

Internal changes in the company may also create real estate activity. When a company decides to open new branches in the same city or in new markets, it must usually seek new or expanded facilities for operations, distribution, and re-

Western Commercial Company
Real Estate Specialists

October 21, 1991

Mr. Ben Barnes
Bayright Advertising Company
6383 Richmond Concourse
Chicago, IL 60616

Dear Ben:

Given the present extreme competitiveness of the Chicago advertising business, I realize you may wish to reduce operating expenses. A new office lease could give you that opportunity. Some properties are available that are leasing for rates well under what you are now paying at your Richmond location.

Consider these possible locations:

Wichita Tower at
Central Circle Mall   17-40,000 sq ft   4+ yrs
$13.00/sq ft   (Nicely improved; wall coverings; conventional office, etc.)

Willow Central   18-100,000 sq ft   6 yrs
$14.00/sq ft   (Conventional office, high grade finish areas, wet bars, etc.)

City Castle Area   25-130,000 sq ft   4 yrs
Negotiable

Northwest Crossing   19,000+ sq ft   5 yrs
$13.15/sq ft   ($5/sq ft over standard allowance)

This sample is only a fraction of the properties that we might discuss. I have some data on interesting properties we could review, so that you could meet the economics and space profile that both you and your New York headquarters are seeking.

Best regards,

Wes Taylor
WESTERN COMMERCIAL COMPANY

WJT/nmd

FIGURE 21-1. A Transaction Resulting from a Business Downturn

PALMS REALTY SPECIALISTS
135 San Pedro Boulevard
Menlo Park, CA 94026

November 25, 1990

Mr. E. Douglas Brown
President
THE QUAD GROUP
1601 Blackpoint Park Drive
Menlo Park, CA 94026

Dear Doug:

I enjoyed visiting with you by phone yesterday and regret that it has
been so long since we have had any contact. The booming economy
has everyone unusually busy. I was glad to hear of the Quad Group's
expansion plans and wanted to let you know that we are here to assist
you in any way possible.

The Quad Group will undoubtedly need additional facilities soon because of your new long-term contract. Perhaps we could review some
of the alternatives that might be available to you. Please call us soon to
plan for the company's space needs. We will set a time to accommodate your hectic schedule.

Best regards,

R. J. Davidson

RJD/cw

FIGURE 21-2. **A Transaction Resulting from a Business Boom**

tailing. Companies may diversify their product line through direct expansion of
their own facilities, or by acquiring other companies and their facilities through
mergers, acquisitions, and takeovers (see Figure 21-3). These business transactions in and of themselves may generate substantial real estate activities. These
changes lead to situations in which people communicate about real estate. You
can practice analyzing how real estate marketing letters address readers' needs
by turning now to the preliminary exercise in the communication challenges at
the end of the chapter.

Crowne
Commercial
Real Estate Services, Inc.
Real Estate Consultants

January 9, 1991

Mr. Wallace Rogers
Controller
The Aztec Corporation
2000 S. Oak Avenue
Tulsa, OK 73166

Dear Mr. Rogers:

A recent *Wall Street Journal* article confirmed that The Aztec Corporation will enter a new period of growth as an affiliate of Central Allied Technologies Corporation. Mr. Ron Miller of Aztec's Operations Group suggested that I send you an outline of my company's business philosophy, services, and a résumé of my experience, since you will be assuming responsibility for Aztec's long-range office planning. I am extremely interested in assisting you and your firm with any changes in facilities that may occur as a result of this acquisition. I believe that my varied experience as an office leasing specialist representing tenants, as a Certified Property Manager, and as a Developer Operations/Construction/Leasing representative can be useful to you during the upcoming months.

Over the past fifteen years I have had the opportunity to represent the office and industrial space requirements of a number of Tulsa companies such as Central Pipeline, OST Production, International Trading, and U.S.F. & G., to name a few. I believe that the present office building market situation offers your company many opportunities for favorable transactions either as a Purchaser or Tenant.

I can well imagine that your schedule is extremely crowded because of the acquisition. To accommodate your schedule and avoid requesting any of your regular business time, I would like to offer to take you to lunch, dinner, or drinks at your earliest convenience. Please look over the enclosed materials. I will call Thursday to see if we can arrange a mutually convenient time to meet.

Sincerely,

R. L. Johnson
President

RLJ/djb

2800 Prairie Drive — Suite 482 — Tulsa, Oklahoma 73166
(405)439-3387

FIGURE 21-3.   A Transaction Resulting from an Acquisition

Who Communicates about Real Estate?

Many people are involved in a real estate transaction.

A variety of people may become involved when a company seeks to change its space. Real estate transactions have often been called the largest multiple-party deals in business (see Figure 21-4).

People in the Company

Communication will involve people at many levels of the company.

Don't underestimate the number of people within a company who will become involved in a real estate transaction. The people who are officially involved in the decision process are essential, of course. Many others who are not within the decision process will want to make their voices heard as well. The number of people involved directly and indirectly depends on the structure of the company, the size of the project, and the economic impact of the transaction itself. When major resources must be committed, high-level executives, financial consultants, legal eagles, and "peasants" of all types will be involved. These people all perceive themselves as having a stake in the transaction, and therefore communicators must not overlook their concerns.

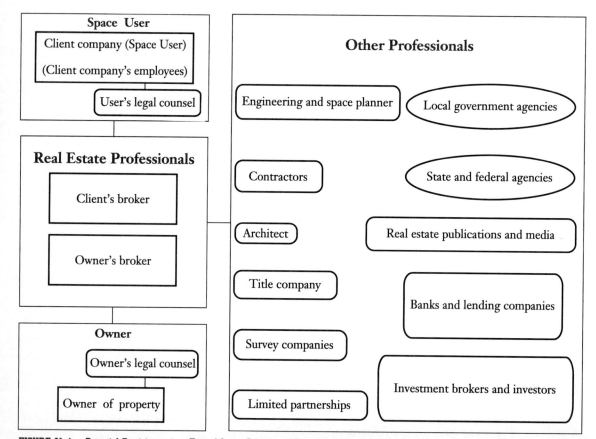

FIGURE 21-4. **Potential Participants in a Typical Large Commercial Real Estate Transaction**

Eventually, someone in the company's local office will be made the "contact person." This individual may be an operations manager, office services manager, or financial manager. This person must submit his or her plans to the local manager for approval. In large companies, the local manager then submits plans, leases, and other documents to the regional or district manager, who in turn sends these to a vice president (or other person) at the corporate level. Once corporate headquarters receives the paperwork, the matter is turned over to the corporate real estate officer, who may involve other corporate staff, such as corporate lawyers and corporate finance officers, in the review of the project. The corporate real estate officer might also seek the services of professionals outside the corporation.

The local contact person will probably approach a broker to represent the company in its search for new space or other services. The contact person may request applications from several brokers or brokerage companies and review all of them before selecting one, in a manner similar to the way advertising agencies and other professional services companies are selected.

Real Estate Professionals

Both owners and prospective tenants are usually represented by real estate professionals.

The second group likely to be involved when a company changes space consists of *real estate professionals*. These include the broker who represents the company or client seeking space, as well as the broker who represents the developer, owner, or seller. Some transactions may involve both *commercial brokers*, who typically deal with the business-related activities such as manufacturing, distribution, warehousing, office and retail facilities, and land use; and *residential brokers*, who provide services related to employee housing.

FOCUS ON BUSINESS COMMUNICATION

WHO IS A REALTOR?

Some, indeed most, real estate professionals are likely to be Realtors®. The term *Realtor* is a registered trade name that may be used only by members of the state and local real estate boards affiliated with the National Association of Realtors® (about 1,850 local boards). This term designates a professional who subscribes to the strict code of ethics of the National Association of Realtors® that governs the real estate practices of its members. Individual states license brokers and salespersons, who are then eligible to apply for membership in the National Association of Realtors®. The use of the name "Realtor" and the distinctive seal in advertising is strictly governed by the rules and regulations of the national association.

Other Professionals

Many other professionals in other fields (finance, construction, etc.) may be involved.

As mentioned before, very large real estate transactions, illustrated in Figure 21-4, may include the representatives of many other professional disciplines. These include accountants, tax advisors, developers, architects, space planners, building contractors, public utilities, lawyers, title companies, mortgage companies, banks and other lenders, engineering survey companies, inspection companies, pest control firms, urban planners and governmental authorities (such as fire marshals, zoning officials, and building inspectors). In the more complex transactions, one may also find news media, real estate publications, investors, stock brokers, limited partnerships, advertising agencies, the investment arms for brokerage companies, and financial services groups.

Real Estate Transactions Begin with Communication

Real estate transactions may begin with any of four communication situations:

1. A property owner's representative or broker calls or sends letters to prospective tenants/buyers.
2. A prospective tenant/buyer directly approaches an owner's representative or broker.
3. A broker calls or sends letters to a prospective tenant/buyer, wanting to represent the company in its search for space.
4. A prospective tenant/buyer approaches a broker to represent the company.

Each of these situations will be discussed in turn.

Many marketing communications are used in the initial phase of a transaction.

Many marketing activities are involved in this early stage of real estate transactions. The developer's company needs to make the real estate community and prospective tenants aware of its building. The brokers seeking to represent developers or owners and prospective tenants need to promote their services. Advertising, marketing letters to prospective tenants and buyers, letters describing available properties (often accompanied by a brochure for a specific building), marketing letters to developers, and letters of introduction are used in these marketing efforts. During periods when there is excess supply of office space, competition on all professional levels increases. Marketing activities also increase, because nothing happens until someone knows about an available service or product.

Situation 1: Owner's Representative or Broker Contacts Prospective Tenant/Buyer

Property owners' representatives write many types of documents to promote the property.

Property owners or developers usually hire a real estate broker, sometimes called "the listing broker" or "the broker of record," to oversee the lease or sale of their properties. In the case that follows, Redtree Realty has been hired to represent the developers, Elwith Services Company, which owns an eleven-story office building, the Wichita Tower. Lynn Redtree, the president of Redtree Realty, is the listing broker. Lynn has been a licensed Realtor® for ten years and formed her own company three years ago.

Brokers describe properties by the feature/function/benefit method.

Brokers such as Lynn write many types of documents to present their properties to other brokers and prospective tenants or buyers. Some of these documents include information about the property: articles about the property, press releases, letters to other brokers, letters to architects and city planners, letters to arrange construction of interior features (called "buildouts") required by the company that will lease or buy the space, applications for building permits, etc. Brokers may write advertisements for a property, or they may work within an advertising agency. They often prepare comparative analyses of properties, and they write letters that will be sent out as direct mailings.

Situation 2: Prospective Tenant/Buyer Directly Approaches the Owner's Representative

A manager, driving down the freeway, could see an interesting property such as the Wichita Tower and send a letter of inquiry to the listing broker, Redtree Realty, whose sign would be posted in front of the property. In this letter, the manager would include vital information about his company's needs and perhaps specific requirements about the price his company was interested in paying. Redtree Realty would respond with a "fill-in-the-blanks" strategy (described in Chapter 5) providing the kind of information just described in a comparative analysis, and would offer to meet with the manager to discuss the transaction.

Situation 3: Broker Offers to Represent Prospective Tenant/Buyer

Brokers seeking to represent clients must create a perceived need for their services.

This scenario presents the writer with a challenging problem. The real estate company has to create a need for its service, telling the prospective client what it can do. Like the listing broker, the client representative must link the features of its service with the benefits the client will receive. In some situations, the writer will want to make the reader uncomfortable with proceeding alone by describing the complexities of real estate decisions and the economic consequences of poor decisions, a communication strategy used also in the Merrill Lynch ad shown later in this chapter. At the same time, it is essential that the tone and approach be ethical and professional.

In the case that follows, Wes Taylor is a licensed representative of Western Commercial Company. Bayright Advertising Associates, a New York firm, has a local Chicago office that has not been particularly successful recently. Since Bayright is trying to reduce its costs, it might be a candidate for less expensive space, as Taylor proposes in the letter shown in Figure 21-1.

Brokers such as Taylor, who wish to represent clients, prepare marketing/solicitation letters, reports to clients, comparative analyses of available properties, descriptions of meetings and phone calls, legal document reviews, cover letters, requests for information, negotiations, and oral presentations. Some of these will be described in a later section of the chapter.

THE PROCESS OF "WRITING UP A PROPERTY"

In writing the marketing documents, brokers often employ a principle of sales writing called "feature/function/benefit." They select those features most likely to be valued by prospective tenants and buyers, describe each feature, tell how it functions or works, and note the feature's benefits to the tenant or buyer. The following sentences from the Wichita Tower letter use this principle:

> The Wichita Tower is located at the corner of Broad Avenue and the Central Expressway at the entry to Central Circle Mall (*feature*). Excellent access from these major thoroughfares make this location easy for employees and clients to reach; retail stores, hotels, restaurants, and other professional offices are only one to two minutes away (*function* of location). Both clients and employees will prefer the convenience of this address (*benefit*).

Benefits are sometimes the long-term financial implications of a construction feature. A broker might show the client the long-term financial implications of having high-grade hallway and lobby appointments that will not need replacement, giving lower operating costs over a ten-year lease. In the sample marketing letter, the design of the Wichita Tower, its location in the city, and its construction are presented in this way.

In addition to marketing letters, listing brokers usually write marketing literature that compares the features of the properties they represent to those of their competitors' properties. As the listing broker, Lynn Redtree must prove to prospects and to other brokers that the Wichita Tower offers advantages, so she would develop an analysis of competitors' properties, showing the economics of their properties, add-on factors, and design efficiencies. Often these comparisons are presented as tables or charts.

In the letters that accompany a comparative analysis, brokers must reveal the benefits or advantages of a property for its price range. Buildings are rated according to a classification system as A, B, and C quality properties. A broker who represented a class B building might downplay its relatively inaccessible location, but emphasize that it has all the other benefits (such as luxurious construction) that are usually available only in a class A building.

The comparison must present a concise, convincing argument whose key points the reader will remember. In the comparison, the writer should detail the pluses and minuses; that is how a property or a lease is sold. The writer should mitigate the bad points, cost-justify the decision, and emphasize the benefits for the client.

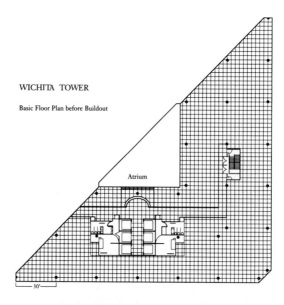

WICHITA TOWER

Basic Floor Plan before Buildout

Atrium

30'

THE PROCESS OF "WRITING UP A PROPERTY" (*continued*)

Redtree Realty
P. O. Box 5759
Chicago, IL 60617

April 11, 1991

Dear Broker:

Many of your clients seek a location whose address itself says "Success." Wichita Tower, designed by internationally famous K. R. Tonugi, can provide exactly such a prestigious address. I invite you to bring your clients to Wichita Tower, where a dramatic interplay of shapes and spaces awaits them.

They will find a lush greeting year-round in the eleven-story atrium, even on Chicago's coldest snowy days. Meticulous construction and elegant interiors will speak comfort to each individual entering the building. Your clients will know you appreciate their taste for quality when you show them this building.

The Wichita Tower is located at the corner of Broad Avenue and the Central Expressway at the entry to Central Circle Mall. Excellent access from these major thoroughfares makes this location easy for employees and clients to reach; retail stores, hotels, restaurants, and other professional offices are only one to two minutes away. Both clients and employees will prefer the convenience of this address.

Rates as attractive as the architecture distinguish the Wichita Tower. State-of-the-art computer technology controls mechanical systems and minimizes operating expenses. I look forward to giving you a personal tour through these excellent facilities. Please call soon to arrange a showing.

Sincerely,

Lynn Redtree
President

Attachments: Specification sheet and diagram

ELWITH SERVICES COMPANY
P.O. Box 5542
7896 Cherryhill Ave.
Chicago, IL 60617

Richard Raider
Contracts Administrator

January 3, 1991

Redtree Realty
ATTN: Ms. Lynn Redtree
P.O. Box 5759
Chicago, IL 60617

<u>OFFICE SPACE FOR LEASE</u>
CONTR-L-2800/2036

Dear Ms. Redtree:

We have determined that an exclusive brokerage arrangement would be suitable for leasing our property, the Wichita Tower. The successful broker would serve as Elwith Services Company's (ESC) primary point of contact with other real estate brokers and would be listed as ESC's broker in real estate industry publications. In addition, we are seeking a broker who can assist ESC in preparing and executing marketing efforts for our facility. If you wish to submit your qualifications to represent ESC, you are requested to do so by the close of business on Monday, January 21, 1991.

The following is a list of items of information that should be included in your response:

1.   A list showing individual blocks of commercial space in excess of 50,000 square feet that were leased during the past year in which your firm was the procuring broker.

2.   An explanation of the marketing strategy your firm would propose for leasing the available space, together with an estimate of what you would consider to be reasonable monthly marketing expenses.

3.   A resume of the individual who would be assigned to handle the ESC account.

4.   A copy of your pro forma brokerage agreement for commercial office space.

The requested information should be addressed to ESC as follows:

<u>BY U.S. MAIL</u>	<u>BY COURIER</u>
Jerry D. Short	Jerry D. Short
Contracting Unit	Contracting Unit
Elwith Services Company	Elwith Services Company
P.O. Box 5542	7896 Cherryhill Avenue
Chicago, IL 60617	Chicago, IL 60617

After reviewing the information requested above, ESC plans to conduct a tour of the facilities for interested brokers. In addition, a presentation and discussion of the economics of the space to be leased, the pro forma lease document, the type of tenant desired, general building rules and regulations, and guidelines concerning buildout, rent abatement and lease duration will precede the tour. The tour and presentation is scheduled to begin at 10 a.m. on Friday, February 1, 1991, and will be followed by a luncheon at 12 noon. Please indicate in your response to this letter the number of representatives from your firm who will be attending the tour, discussion, and luncheon.

Any questions concerning this inquiry should be directed to Roy Keller at 432-2077.

Sincerely,

J. D. Short, Manager
Contracting Unit

JDS-fm

FIGURE 21-5.   An Owner Seeks a Broker

Situation 4: Prospective Tenant/Buyer or Seller
Approaches Broker to Represent the Company

Companies may write requests for proposals to prospective representatives.

When a company intends to build or lease a facility in a new city or location, or when a company has a building for lease, it may approach a broker to act as its representative. It will then usually send out a letter that sets out the terms for services and describes the process by which the broker will be selected. In some cases, the letter will also describe the criteria by which the brokers who apply will be evaluated. Elwith Services Company's letter, shown in Figure 21-5, is a sample of this kind of solicitation. Brokers may offer other services by letters. These consulting services might include lease analyses, market evaluations, and other applications of professional knowledge.

The Communication Processes of a Typical Transaction

After a company has decided that it needs to change its space, a typical six-step sequence occurs, reflected in the Merrill Lynch Realty ad in Figure 21-6 and outlined in Figure 21-7. Bayright Advertising, working with Western Commercial Company, follows this sequence in the example that follows. We will illustrate this sequence by describing what happens after Bayright Advertising and Elwith Services select their respective representatives, Redtree Realty and Western Commercial Company.

1. Analysis of User's Needs

When the client needs to change its space, the broker usually assists by analyzing the company's needs. Wanting to get by with the smallest possible quarters because of his company's financial distress, Mr. Barnes of Bayright worked with Wes Taylor of Western Commercial. This needs analysis led to a request for proposals. Taylor had on file many letters from other brokers, such as the one he had received from Lynn Redtree about Wichita Tower (see Document Spotlight). Taylor's letter on behalf of Bayright Advertising was sent to Redtree Realty, among several other brokers. Taylor used Bayright's name in his letter, primarily because he felt that the prospect of having the local branch of a New York advertising firm in a building might induce owners to offer more favorable terms than they would offer to an unknown small space user. At other times, a broker might request proposals without naming the client firm, as happens in the letter shown in Figure 21-8.

Taylor's request described the area needed, the possibility of future expansion, the conditions of future renewals, the desired right to cancel, the right to mitigate damages, needed improvements and other needs, translated into the customary terminology of real estate proposals. For example, Bayright wanted to house several types of employees in a small space, and therefore needed a large number of small offices plus a conference room and one larger office for meeting with clients. The request for proposal, accordingly, expressed this in-

When you lease
office space,
you don't just
live with
your mistakes.

You live in them.

Every time you step off the elevator, you'll be reminded of your decision.

If you leased the right space, you'll have an office that's comfortable for everyone—one that meets your needs in a cost-effective manner, yet has room for future growth.

If you leased the wrong space, you'll have headaches. Every day.

Merrill Lynch can spare you the headaches. We have a nationwide network of commercial real estate experts who can walk you through the entire decision-making process.

First, we'll work up a *Pre-plan*, a document that identifies, very specifically, the business needs that your new space must satisfy.

Next, we'll perform a detailed *Space Requirement Analysis* based on these needs, taking into account projected growth in staff levels, alternative workstation and layout concepts, special utility needs, location preferences, and any other relevant requirements.

Then, we'll do an *Economic Comparison* of several alternative spaces, identifying the positives and negatives of each choice. This will give you a meaningful basis for comparison, expressed in terms of your total cost-of-occupancy.

Finally, we'll negotiate the lease.

As you can see, we're not just brokers. We're professional advisors, as valuable to your company as your attorneys and your accountants. We can oversee your entire search, or provide specific assistance to your own real estate department.

Leasing office space is a heavy responsibility. Let Merrill Lynch help you work it through. Because ultimately, nobody will remember how tough the decisions were.

Only how right.

Merrill Lynch Commercial Real Estate

Merrill Lynch

© Merrill Lynch Realty Commercial Services, Inc. 1984

Atlanta • Baltimore • Chicago • Dallas • Los Angeles • Miami • New Orleans • Newport Beach • New York City • Orlando
Phoenix • San Diego • San Francisco • Stamford • Tampa • Washington, D.C.

FIGURE 21-6. The Sequence of Property Leasing

1. **Analysis of User's Needs**
   Examine company's operations and needs
     (Optional: Consultant prepares space analysis)
   User's review and approval
   Establish selection criteria
   Survey market alternatives
   Compare criteria and alternatives
   Select primary candidates
2. **Solicit Proposals**
   Financial analysis of initial proposals
3. **Negotiation with Other Professionals**
   Negotiate with other specialists
   Update proposal request
   Solicit final proposals from candidate buildings
   Review of finalists' proposals

4. **Contract Development and Execution**
   Negotiate lease provisions
   Joint legal analysis
   Participate in final round of negotiations
   Arrange for leases to be signed
5. **Followup for Contract Compliance**
   Check for contractual and construction compliance
   Peripheral services (subleasing, etc.)
6. **Adjustments**
   Request and obtain adjustments

FIGURE 21-7.   Steps in a Typical Real Estate Transaction

tensive use of space in the number of doors wanted per hundred square feet of space. Parking spaces, visitors' spaces, and various rates were also included in the request for proposal.

Lynn Redtree, representing Elwith Services Company, the owner, responded to this request with a proposal that compared Wichita Tower favorably with other Chicago competitors.

2. Negotiation with Other Professionals

Once the client has received the owner's proposal, the client's broker prepares an analysis of the proposals received. Upon the client's approval of one of the proposals, the client's broker then begins the negotiation with the owner's broker and with architects, space planners, and people who will provide related services in making the space ready for occupancy. These transactions must be carefully documented in memoranda and letters so that all agreements will be fully traceable.

Bayright found the central atrium of Wichita Tower very attractive. The conference room overlooking the atrium would impress clients, and the shape of the remaining undefined space would provide easy communication for the designers, writers, layout people, and other specialists working on projects. Nevertheless, some changes had to be made to the space so that a small darkroom would be available for the photographer and a workstation could be set up for the computer graphics specialist. The computers required "clean lines," dedicated electrical circuits to supply power for that equipment only. Western Commercial sent letters to the building manager, general contractor, and electrical contractor, with copies to Bayright Advertising Associates and to Redtree Realty, which represented the owner of Wichita Tower.

Colony West Realty
35600 West Loop South
Houston, Texas 77047

September 17, 1991

Ms. Lynn Redtree
President, Redtree Realty
P.O. Box 5759
Chicago, IL 60617

Dear Ms. Redtree:

A tenant prospect of Colony West Realty intends to establish a branch office in the Chicago central business district. I have outlined briefly the tenant's space requirements. Please address these points in a proposal to be delivered to our office in Houston no later than Friday noon, October 11.

AREA	Central business district
OCCUPANCY	December 28, 1991
FLOOR PREFERENCE	3rd floor or higher
SQUARE FOOTAGE	4100 square feet (Net Rentable Area)
LEASE RATE (annual)	
ESCALATIONS BASE STOP/YEAR	1991 base year
"ADD-ON" FACTOR	_____
TERM	60 months
BUILDOUT REQUIREMENTS	See space program
PARKING	3.5 spaces/1000 sq. feet NRA covered parking preferred
RENEWAL OPTIONS	One (1) five-year renewal
EXPANSION OPTION	Two thousand (2000) sq. ft. Net Rentable Area ($+/-$ 20%), contiguous to the lease premises after 24 months.
LEASE INDUCEMENTS	Rent abatement _____ months. Turnkey improvements Yes ___ No ___
ATTACHMENTS	Building Brochure Floor Plan Lease Agreement

Colony West Realty on behalf of our tenant prospect appreciates your interest and response to this request for proposals. Should you have any questions, please contact us at (713) 428-9999.

Sincerely,

Tim Satterwhite, Representative
Colony West Realty

attachments: Client's Space Program

FIGURE 21-8.   Sample Request for Proposal Letter

3. Contract Development

Leases must be legally correct and easy to understand, because many people without legal training must read and use them.

When the negotiations with contractors and other professionals are complete, these are incorporated into the real estate contract for sale or lease of the property. These contracts are almost always written and reviewed by lawyers. The brokers have a responsibility to their clients to make sure that the lawyers have written these documents clearly so that their clients can understand the provisions. Otherwise, misunderstandings damaging to the relationship between the owner and the tenant could develop over time.

Real estate contracts, including leases, easements, and water and mineral rights contracts, are not just one-time events. They are "living documents," as the Bayright/Wichita Tower case shows. As a result, they must be drafted so that numerous readers can clearly understand the original intent of the parties over long periods of time. A lease may cover use of a property for only a few hours (lease of a hotel ballroom for a trade show) or for over a hundred years (ground lease for an office building). The lease document governs the relationship between landlord and tenant and dictates the daily use of the leased property.

Real estate professionals ensure all parties understand the transaction.

Some of the parties who are affected by the lease from time to time may have extensive training in reading legal contracts, but others may have little or no knowledge of such instruments. The lawyer who draws the lease may spend most of her time on contracts; the building supervisor or property manager who must administer the lease on a daily basis may read such documents only occasionally. As a result, it is important to draft leases so they may be understood by the broad group of people who may have reasons to read them. An office lease, for instance, may be reviewed by a secretary, office services manager, bookkeeper, maintenance supervisor, property manager, legal counsel, comptroller, architect, senior corporate officer, etc. In the Wichita Tower transaction, Wes Taylor and Lynn Redtree both met with the lawyers who drew the lease to make sure that all the provisions represented the owner's and the tenant's expectations correctly. Then the two brokers delivered these leases to their respective clients.

Real estate professionals are responsible for the clarity of communication.

4. Contract Execution

Contract execution simply means the signing and notarizing of the leases or contracts. Wes Taylor took the leases to New York, where they were signed at Bayright Advertising Associates' corporate headquarters. He then brought them back to Chicago, where Lynn Redtree presented them to Otis Elwith, the president of Elwith Services Company, Inc., for signature.

5. Follow-up for Contract Compliance

Real estate representatives often continue to serve clients by ensuring that provisions in a contract are strictly followed. Just before Bayright moved into its new offices in Wichita Tower, Wes Taylor inspected the buildout. He found that while the electrical circuits had been installed correctly for the computers, the dimmer switches needed in the conference room to adjust the room for slide presentations had been omitted. Taylor wrote a letter on behalf of Bayright Advertising Company to Redtree Realty and another to the Wichita Tower building manager with copies to the appropriate contractors. These parallel letters ensured compliance with the contract. The switches were quickly installed before the advertising agency actually moved into the offices.

6. Adjustments

Over time, new requirements arise and adjustments may be needed. Bayright was fortunate in that one of its retail clients, KIDDI-TOYS, decided to embark on an aggressive television promotion of its new suburban stores. Bayright decided to expand its space and add offices for two people who would buy air time on television stations in the area and oversee the production of the television ads, even though these would be filmed in a commercial studio. Taylor represented Bayright to Redtree and Elwith Services Company to lease additional space and arranged the contract for regular use of the commercial studio at Pro-Vision Production Company.

With the passage of time, lease documents may be amended to reflect changes in relationships between the parties, such as changes in ownership, expansion and contraction of space leased, time extensions, additions or deletions of services to be performed, changes in construction, signage, parking, security, and other services. Like personal relationships, real estate relationships are not constant or fixed, but mirror the lives of the principals.

Communicating in a Complex Legal Environment

Most people think they have some knowledge of real estate, but their experience is mostly limited to residential transactions. Therefore, the professional real estate practitioner has to communicate new information about something people think they know already. Typically, the client is actually a novice in real estate. He or she may know little of changes in the law and of precedents that have legal consequences. In order to protect the customer, the professional has to exercise extreme care so that the client can make informed decisions. New trends in consumer protection have sharply reinforced real estate professionals' recognition of their obligations to help users/clients deal with these complexities. Professionals themselves face conflicting forces. On the one hand, the client's lack of understanding creates a need for the professional's service; on the other, the professional has a legal obligation to ensure the client's comprehension. On a daily basis, the real estate professional has to address the problem of how to market his or her knowledge, to protect its value without misleading clients. Figure 21-9 shows a letter bringing the implications of certain lease terms to a prospective client's attention.

The licensed real estate practitioner has both a legal and professional responsibility to protect the communication process. He or she must ensure that all principal and peripheral parties to a transaction understand the transaction. Misinterpreted written documents or undocumented verbal conversations might cause serious problems; perhaps even lawsuits. The broker must be able to convey precisely and accurately the client's intent, concerns, or wishes in daily communications with the various interested parties.

Meredith Leasing Advisors, Inc.
3837 Tennyson Drive
Houston, Texas 77005

June 12, 1991

Jim Fisk
Nelson Microsystems Company
3187 Turnbull Avenue
Houston, Texas 77019

Dear Mr. Fisk:

Thank you for your phone call today regarding the meaning of net rentable area (NRA) in the proposals that were submitted for your review. This term affects the economics of your office space lease and refers to one of the main reasons we have recommended that you choose the office suite in Smith Tower.

The net rentable area in a lease includes both the area within your lease premise walls (the net usable area) and a portion of the corridors, lobbies, restrooms, and other public areas called "the common area allocation." Common areas are truly not usable space in which you can conduct business. Therefore, you must consider both the price per square foot for the NRA as well as the percentage that is allocated to common areas.

The amount allocated to common areas varies considerably from building to building, ranging from as little as 6 percent to as much as 30 percent. Therefore, the higher the allocation, the more expensive your usable lease space becomes. For instance, Smith Tower has a 10% common area allocation compared to Weldon Plaza's 15%. All pricing and square footage measurements reflect the individual building's common area allocations. In your present proposal, this difference would cost you $0.50 more per usable square foot if you were to occupy space in Weldon Plaza.

Both Smith Tower and Weldon Plaza are similar in quality and location, your primary concerns. While the NRA prices are similar, the common area allocations differ. Therefore, Smith Tower's greater economic value lies in the lower cost per usable square foot and the lower overhead cost for your firm. Smith Tower becomes the obvious choice, all other things being equal. Should you have any additional questions, please call us.

Sincerely,

Conrad Phelps
President

FIGURE 21-9.   Explaining the Significance of Industry Terms

THE LEGAL CONTEXT AND THE NEED FOR PROFESSIONALS

To the ordinary person, real estate transactions appear simple, perhaps as simple as telling the owner that a company would like to have its offices in part of his large building. What appears simple is actually complex because properties have a history, and their present and future use is governed by all the legal documents that have developed over time concerning that property and by all the present laws, ordinances, and regulations of the various legal entities in whose jurisdiction the property exists.

Much of the property now in the United States was once owned by other countries whose real estate laws differ. A property that was originally part of a Spanish land grant given by the King of Spain to one of his nobles, according to the provisions of Spanish law, may give the property owner title to the land underneath an adjacent river out to the river's center. A property originally governed by English common law may reserve the ownership of the river for the government, making the river and the land under it public property. The property's legal history may determine how a company can now use the land: whether it can drill a water well, how high new buildings may be, where roads or drives can be located, or whether residential and commercial structures can be placed on the land.

Different states have different laws that affect a property's history. In Colorado, separate contracts must be prepared for the water rights to land involved in a real estate contract. Under Colorado law, water rights are assumed to be reserved to the original owner unless transferred in a separate contract. The real estate contracts alone will not reveal the potential water use for a particular property.

In the last fifty years, people have become much more concerned about the safety of the environment and how land use affects the quality of life. They have demanded that governments control land use, ensuring parks, green spaces, and more open land to allow for infiltration of rainwater. All of these concerns have increased the complexity of real estate transactions.

In addition, the complexity of real estate transactions has increased as new financing and investment vehicles have been introduced. Necessary but complex tasks, such as evaluation of the economic effect of a lease or purchase on a company's profitability and cash flow, require the specialized knowledge of tax advisors, financing specialists, and lawyers. Most businesspeople, who deal with real estate only occasionally, are unaware of the full complexity of transactions and this rapidly changing legal environment.

Because of the legal history of the language of real estate, what appears to be obvious really is not. For example, most people think they know the meaning of the phrase "square foot." Most people would think the phrase meant an area measuring twelve inches on each side. Unfortunately, there are many different kinds of square feet in real estate:

Gross square feet	The total floor area of a building as measured from its exterior walls
Net rentable square feet	The interior area measured from the interior facing of outside walls, not counting corridors; may or may not include common public areas such as restrooms, lobbies, and corridors
Usable square feet	Excludes common areas, restrooms, lobbies; includes what is confined, and allows the best comparison of spaces in different buildings

A person mistaking net rentable square feet for usable square feet might believe he had leased sufficient square feet for six offices of twelve feet by fifteen feet, only to find the space would provide offices of only ten feet by fourteen feet. One popular "rule of thumb" regarding real estate is: "Whatever appears to be fact is probably not. Check the definition with a professional."

Civil litigation creates precedents that affect communication about real estate. Terms that seem to have a common-sense meaning sometimes have developed legal histories that give them a special limited meaning in a particular legal jurisdiction. For example, in the state of Nebraska, the phrase "more or less" following a description of the size of a piece of property means that the parties writing the contract agree to the specified price without regard to the actual area of the property.

Case: River Land in Nebraska

A company was selling undeveloped river land that could not be conveniently surveyed until after the leaves fell from the trees in the fall. When the president of the out-of-state company selling the land signed an agreement for sale in the late summer, he thought the phrase "seven and one-half acres, more or less" simply reflected the fact that the land had not yet been surveyed, so that the precise area could not be expressed. When the actual survey was completed, the land proved to contain over thirteen acres, but the price of the property could not be adjusted. The buyer therefore was able to purchase the land for his business at about half the price per acre the seller had originally believed his company would receive.

Technical Vocabulary Creates Need for Professionals

The technical language used in real estate communications is confusing to the layperson and confusing to the inexperienced employee or manager in the company that seeks to improve its space. This vocabulary puts the layperson at a disadvantage. Its technical implications are hard to understand but they translate to financial and legal consequences, just as in the example above. If the seller had requested that a Nebraska lawyer review the agreement for sale, the lawyer could have advised him that the price would not be changed regardless of what acreage the survey later established, and the agreement could have been worded differently. The specialized vocabulary also impinges on the legal use of a facility. Confusion about the precise meanings of common terms causes conflict and forces an elaborate definition of terms throughout letters, proposals, and contracts. A system of certification has been established by professional groups to ensure that brokers keep abreast of the complex legal situation, as noted in the following advertisement. The sophistication of the industry in relation to the user has become a problem in real estate communication.

IN REAL ESTATE
IT'S THE FINE PRINT
THAT COUNTS

How successful you are at buying or selling your home depends on how professional and experienced your real estate agent is. It's important to work with an agent who can help you get the best price or interest rate, find the right home or buyer and help you understand those vital fine points at the closing.

Be sure you are getting one of the best real estate agents in the business. Select a REALTOR® who has earned the CRS (Certified Residential Specialist) designation. A CRS has completed hours of advanced study in listing, selling, law, investment, taxes and much more. A CRS is a proven performer with years of experience and professionalism.

So insist on the best for your real estate transactions...demand a CRS.

To receive the name of the CRS nearest you, call: **800/621-7035**

Certified Residential Specialist

Most states' laws concerning the practice and conveyance of real estate assign the real estate practitioner multiple responsibilities in overseeing all the various aspects of the transaction. Before the contracts are written, numerous letters and conversations link service contractors such as surveyors, engineers, architects, contractors, attorneys, title and insurance companies, and other professionals. The real estate practitioner has the responsibility of clearly understanding the various issues affecting his client and ensuring that everyone involved understands these issues, too. All oral communications of the various negotiations or offers must be documented so that any differences may be resolved easily. In addition, it is the responsibility of the real estate practitioner to see that all offers made between the principal parties are documented and delivered.

Almost all states require that real estate agreements must be in written form to be binding. These must be publicly recorded for the principals' as well as the public's interest and protection. As a result, most states require or recommend that an attorney draft the contracts. The real estate broker collaborates with the attorney to make sure the language of the contracts is clear and that the contracts are understood by the parties.

Comprehensive files are necessary even if no sale or lease results.

In many states licensed real estate practitioners are required to maintain comprehensive files on various transactions regardless of whether sales or leases result. Should any question arise to the competence, ethics, or actions of the broker or the client, the broker must be able to provide evidence that he or she acted competently and impeccably. Undocumented recollections may become hazy or confused with the passage of time; however, a complete and accurate file of clear, well-written documentation delivered in a timely manner to the principal parties is the real estate broker's best defense.

All promotional literature, including letters and advertising, exists in a legal context. When a client relies on a description of a property as being safe or suited to some specific type of business, the client's reliance on that description is now seen as creating legal responsibility. Lawsuits against both brokers and owners are becoming increasingly common. If a broker promotes a location for a specific type of use, such as a restaurant, he or she should ascertain how well similar businesses have fared in that location. Tenants or buyers may have the right to rescind the lease or contract and sue for up to triple damages if the advertising misrepresented the property. Words such as "safe" may lead tenants or buyers to expect protection from hazards (such as robberies) that are difficult for the owner to control.

In summary, when writing as a real estate professional, remember that you must document all communication: Verify what was understood or intended, obtain written replies, make written notes on all telephone conversations, confirm counteroffers, and document your presentation of all offers. Always expect that someone will be missing from meetings and that written explanations may be necessary for those who are missing. Although individual documents have specific readers with specific interests and needs, your communications may be subject to scrutiny by multiple readers over a long period of time, and these audiences must also be kept in mind.

☐ REAL ESTATE COMMUNICATION CHECKLIST

1. If you are uncertain about whether a fact should be disclosed, ask yourself the following questions:

____ Considered from the standpoint of fairness, is this something I would want to know regarding this acquisition or use of this property?

____ Would I be able to defend successfully my actions and ethics as a knowledgeable, licensed professional if called upon in a court of law?

____ Is the economic risk that might be created by t! failure to disclose justifiable?

2. Consider whether the public communication (advertising or promotional literature) is inaccurate or misleading:

____ Would a consumer (buyer or tenant) tend to rely on the benefits extolled as a result of this advertising or written communication?

____ Could these expectations lead to legal action if they were not met?

You must review your work with a cautious, perhaps even skeptical, eye when analyzing the potential reader's expectations that depend on the accuracy and veracity of the claims or implied warranties of the text.

☐ COMMUNICATION CHALLENGES

PRELIMINARY EXERCISE Imagine yourself as the reader of each of the letters in Figures 21-1, 21-2, and 21-3 and answer the following questions about each letter:

a. What kinds of changes have occurred in the business environment of the reader's company?

b. What seems to be happening inside the reader's company?

c. What are the most pressing features of the reader's business situation?

d. How is the reader likely to define his or her problem?

e. What are the reader's feelings about this situation likely to be?

f. What does the reader believe that might affect his or her response to the situation?

g. What knowledge does he or she lack that might influence his or her actions?

h. What communication strategy is the writer using to address the reader's uncertainties?

i. What other communication strategies might be appropriate for pleasing this reader and addressing his or her uncertainties?

In a few sentences, compare the differences between the readers of these letters. How similar are the communication strategies of the three letters?

EXERCISE 1

You have been hired by Redtree Realty as a summer intern and you recently gave Gladys Brown, the president of a small freight forwarding company, Canada Expediters, Inc., a tour of Wichita Tower. Everything went smoothly until she turned to leave through the front door. "This is a very nice building, and it would indeed impress our clients," she remarked, "but I feel I would be paying for features that aren't essential to my business, like those fancy ceiling light fixtures you showed me." She smiled, "Architects just get carried away—artistic temperament, I suppose." You are left facing the revolving door, unable to answer. Karl Sweet, the broker assisting Ms. Brown, had already exited.

The building has state-of-the-art parabolic lighting fixtures that produce significant energy savings. You're concerned that if Ms. Brown believes that these fixtures are frivolous, she may choose offices elsewhere.

Lynn Redtree remarked to you earlier how electrical costs have spiraled. Sophisticated parabolic lighting fixtures may save 10 percent to 15 percent of a building's operating electrical budget, or 10 to 15 cents per square foot per year. Since Gladys Brown is thinking of a 6000 sq. ft. lease, these fixtures can save her $600 to $800 per year, or $3000 to $4000 over the five years of the lease she has discussed.

You decide to write a letter for immediate courier delivery explaining to Ms. Brown that what she perceives as an architect's artistic whim can save her money. Your regular city courier will be by in about an hour to pick up deliveries. *Write a short letter to Ms. Brown right now and send a copy to Karl.*

EXERCISE 2

In this assignment you are an employee of Western Commercial Company. Your boss, Wes Taylor, just returned from inspecting Bayright Advertising's new suite of offices in Wichita Tower. Unfortunately, the dimmer switches in the conference room have not been installed as ordered. "Look here," he says, opening the Bayright file, "we specified dimmer switches at both the front and back of the room for both banks of lights in our letters of November 20th to Redtree Realty and Electroservice Contractors."

You look down at the letter he is holding and read the following provision:

> Conference Room changes: Replace conventional rocker lighting switches with rheostat dimmer switches according to the blueprint drawings dated November 15, 1991, page 3, electrical schematics, detail number 15.

Wes continues, "Write two letters for my signature. One goes to Redtree Realty to tell them everything wasn't completed according to the contract specifications. The other goes to Bill Hand, the building manager of Wichita Tower, and we'll send a copy to Electroservice Contractors. Explain that these rheostats (dimmer switches) have to be installed before Bayright takes possession of the space on December 20th. Stress the urgency of this situation, because it is already December 11 and Bayright has a new client presentation on December 28. Then call Central Express Couriers to pick up the letters at 4 P.M."

You note from the letter of November 20th that Electroservice Contractors has its offices at 1212 Lakefront Avenue, Chicago, IL 60618, and that Mike O'Flannery is the manager. Wichita Tower, of course, is located at Broad Avenue and Central Expressway, Chicago, IL 60616. *Write the letters for Wes Taylor's signature.*

EXERCISE 3

Redtree Realty also represents a central business district office building, Main Plaza, owned by a large insurance company. The insurance company does not require the entire building, and the sixth floor, which is a multitenant floor, has a suite of offices available for lease.

Lynn Redtree gives you the diagram of the space and a letter from this morning's mail. She tells you, "Please write a letter to this Houston broker who sent us a request for proposal. I've filled out the proposal form that will go with your letter. I've also attached a copy of the Main Plaza diagram and description. Let's make this letter very specific. You need to show how the space in Main Plaza could be built out to meet the tenant's needs and to benefit the small law firm he's representing."

The letter that Redtree received from Houston is shown in Figure 21-8 of this chapter. The space program mentioned in the letter is shown here. Review the letter before proceeding.

Colony West Realty

Client's Space Program: Legal Firm

Number	Type	Size	Total (sq. ft.)
3	Attorney offices	15 × 15	775
1	Senior Partner office	15 × 20	300
2	Specialists workstations	12 × 12	288
2	Secretarial Areas	10 × 12	240
1	Paralegal	10 × 15	150
1	Conference Room	20 × 22	440
1	Library	20 × 15	300
1	Coffee Bar	10 × 6	60
1	Open Concept Area		450

Defined Area	3003
Undefined Area (circulation factor 20%)	600
Total usable square feet	3600
NRA (est. 15%)	540
TOTAL RENTABLE FEET (estimate)	4140

Additional Specifications:

Wall coverings: Two walls for reception, attorney offices, and coffee bar; three walls for senior partner office. Dedicated circuits: (5) 110/15 amp. Electric Outlets: (2) duplex per office, (1) quad per office.

This is the proposal form that Lynn Redtree had filled out:

PROPOSAL TO COLONY WEST REALTY Date: September 24, 1991	
Prepared by: Redtree Realty Address: P.O. Box 5759, Chicago, IL 60617	
AREA	Central business district
OCCUPANCY	December 28, 1991
FLOOR	Sixth floor
SQUARE FOOTAGE	4140 square feet (Net Rentable Area)
LEASE RATE (annual)	$16.00
ESCALATIONS BASE STOP/YEAR	1991 Base Year $6.00
"ADD-ON" FACTOR	15%
TERM	60 months
BUILDOUT REQUIREMENTS	See space program
PARKING	3.5 spaces/1000 sq. ft. NRA covered parking $35.00 per month
RENEWAL OPTIONS	One (1) and five (5) year renewals
EXPANSION OPTION	Two thousand (2000) sq. ft. Net Rentable Area (+/− 20%), contiguous to the lease premises after 24 months.
LEASE INDUCEMENTS	Rent abatement _6_ months. Turnkey improvements Yes _X_ No ___
ATTACHMENTS	Building Brochure Floor Plan Lease Agreement

EXERCISE 4

This morning Kent Leonard, the industrial park specialist in Redtree Realty who is supervising your work during your apprenticeship at Redtree, tells you: "We've got a real problem on our hands and I need some ideas. We've been listing this small industrial park on Forrest Boulevard for over six months now and we've only found two tenants. There's no explanation for why it's been so slow."

Forrest Industrial Park has 435 feet of frontage on a major freeway with direct access off Kelly Drive exit ramp, which has a daily traffic count of 150,000. What's more, utilities have been laid and all boundary and access streets are in place. The shell for the first 85,000 feet has been built. It is outside the city limits and therefore has lower tax rates, and would be a great place for light manufacturing companies.

Leonard continues, "Luckily, there's an Illinois Manufacturing Association convention next month, and I want to take a half-page ad in the convention newspaper. We'll use a picture of the property, of course. Draft some leads that will get some of those convention goers out to see the property before they leave Chicago. If they see how easy it is to get there, they'll realize what a convenient location it will be for customers. Give me a couple of approaches. Keep your copy for each ad down to 150 to 175 words, plus a headline." *Use a feature/function/benefit approach in preparing the ad copy.*

EXERCISE 5

As an assistant to Lynn Redtree, write a marketing letter promoting Wichita Towers as an office site to brokers representing computer companies or companies with substantial computing or data processing departments. The eleventh floor of Wichita Towers (15,600 sq.ft.) has 8000 sq. ft. of fully-equipped data processing space. This area has a raised floor, a backup power supply, heavy duty electrical cables, and special HVAC (heating, ventilation, and air conditioning). Since this space is already fully equipped, no additional buildout costs are necessary save those additional partitions or partial partitions to shield desk space for workers. This windowed area, with double reflecting glass shield to reduce heat transfer, overlooks the park toward the lakeshore, making this computing space uncommonly attractive to data processing employees, who often must work in windowless rooms. *Use a feature/function/benefit approach in preparing the letter.*

EXERCISE 6

As an assistant to Wes Taylor, write a letter to Lynn Redtree at Redtree Realty (using addresses shown in the examples), explaining the need for two additional offices for Bayright Advertising. Bayright's lease with Wichita Tower included an expansion option of 2000 square feet after twenty-four months at the same rate. Since the lease is only six months old, Bayright is not entitled to exercise this option but you know that contiguous space is in fact available next door to Bayright's offices. Ask for the same lease rate that Bayright now has and request 300 square feet for the two offices, including two interior doors, but no special wall coverings. Send a copy to Bayright and to the Wichita Tower building manager.

MAIN PLAZA
Floor Six

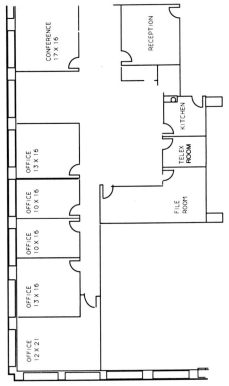

OFFICE 12 X 21	OFFICE 13 X 16	OFFICE 10 X 16	OFFICE 10 X 16	OFFICE 13 X 16	CONFERENCE 17 X 16

FILE ROOM

TELEX ROOM

KITCHEN

RECEPTION

Size: Approximately 4,714 Net Rentable Area
Condition: Very good—Will consider some reasonable modifications
Possession: Within 15 days of lease execution
Term: October 31, 1996
Rental Rate: Will compete below comparable sublease market.
Parking: Six spaces in the building included in the term.
Expenses: Base year 1991

ALL BROKERS PROTECTED
REDTREE REALTY
P. O. BOX 5759
CHICAGO, IL 60617
(317) 524-8282

FOR INFORMATION CONTACT
LYNN REDTREE

The information contained herein has, we believe, been obtained from reasonably reliable sources and we have no reason to doubt the accuracy of such information; however, no warranty or guarantee, either express or implied, is made with respect to the accuracy thereof. All such information is submitted subject to errors, omissions, or changes in conditions, prior to sale, lease, or withdrawal without notice. All information contained herein should be verified to the satisfaction of the person relying thereon.

DIAGRAM FOR EXERCISE 3

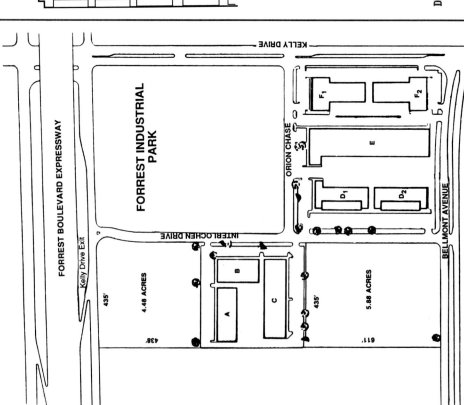

FORREST BOULEVARD EXPRESSWAY

Kelly Drive Exit

FORREST INDUSTRIAL PARK

KELLY DRIVE

INTERLOCHEN DRIVE

ORION CHASE

BELLMONT AVENUE

435'

4.48 ACRES

438'

A

B

C

435'

5.88 ACRES

611'

F_1

F_2

E

D_1

D_2

DIAGRAM FOR EXERCISE 4

EXERCISE 7

As a longer project, choose either option A or option B.

Option A. Prepare a report for classmates on a real estate issue of current interest to business people in your area of the country. To find issues, you might talk with a real estate professor, interview a Realtor® in your city, read some of the trade publications on real estate in the list below, or look for articles on real estate in your local newspaper or regional business journal. Some issues that you might consider include environmental issues, disclosure to prospective buyers or tenants of hazards associated with properties (such as fiberglass and asbestos), the financial situation of municipal utility districts, contaminated waste sites, or the nature of the "agency relationship" (the obligations of a real estate professional to a client). Your report should explain the conflicting positions or conditions that cause the topic to be an issue, the history of this issue, and possible outcomes pending legislation or trends.

You can find the national real estate trade journals listed below at your local Board of Realtors® office. In addition, most states have their own publications, such as the *Texas Realtor*, which are published by the state real estate boards of the National Association of Realtors®. Write the national association at the address shown for *Real Estate Today* to request the addresses of state and local boards near you.

Real Estate Today

National Association of Realtors®
430 North Michigan Avenue
Chicago, Illinois 60611
Contains articles on sales, finance, management, and commercial real estate investments, plus columns on special topics, such as real estate law and pending legislation.

Real Estate Forum

12 West 37th Street
New York, NY 10018
A basic national news publication on commercial properties, developers, financing, and recent developments in real estate financing, marketing, and legal issues.

Journal of Property Management

430 North Michigan Avenue
P. O. Box 109025
Chicago, IL 60610-9025
A publication of the Institute of Real Estate Management

Option B. Select a commercial office building or shopping mall and interview the leasing agent for the building about the history of the project, its tenant list, the way the building is marketed, the features that make the property distinctive, and problems that the developer faces in the long-term management of the project. If possible, collect copies of marketing materials and advertisements used to promote the property. Tour the property and observe the spaces. What features that are not emphasized in the marketing literature might be described as providing benefits? What evidence of problems can you see? What business trends in the area might affect this property in the future (such as competing properties, changes in the types of business operating in the area or changes in land use, new regulations or increases in taxes or utilities)? Prepare a report for your classmates, analyzing the property and its history. List its current or potential problems and recommend any strategies that you think might be appropriate for keeping this property attractive. Attach the materials you have collected as appendices to your report.

EXERCISE 8

Evaluate the assignments you prepared earlier in this chapter for misleading statements, or commitments that might create liabilities (words such as *safe*, for example). In addition, you may wish to look at real estate advertisements in your local newspaper or check issues of the *Wall Street Journal* (usually the Friday issue contains real estate ads) in your library. Can you spot any problems with rosy language that prospective tenants or buyers might take as an implied warranty?

IF YOU WOULD LIKE TO READ MORE

Ring, A. A., & Dasso, J. (1981). *Real estate principles and practices* (9th ed.). Englewood Cliffs, NJ: Prentice-Hall. Basic text covering fundamentals of the real estate industry: basic vocabulary and practices.

Semenow, R. W. (1979). *Questions and answers on real estate* (9th ed.). Englewood Cliffs, NJ: Prentice-Hall. Organized to answer specific questions. Good for clarifications. Explains situations, language, and legal concepts of documents.

Reilly, J. W. (1982). *The language of real estate* (2nd ed.). Chicago: Real Estate Education Company. Organized to answer hundreds of questions; defines terminology; cites precedents.

Janik, C., & Rejnis, R. (1986). *All America's real estate book: Everyone's guide to buying, selling, renting, and investing*. New York: Penguin Press. Contains basic explanations in laypersons' vocabulary.

Senn, M. A. (1985). *Commercial real estate leases: Preparation and negotiation*. New York: Wiley. For professionals. Explains how to deal with specific leasing situations and document preparation.

CONSULTANTS' COMMUNICATIONS

OBJECTIVES

By studying this chapter, you will learn to

■ approach consulting as a unified process

■ perform the communication roles of a consultant

■ use the varied communication skills needed in different stages of consulting

■ write effective project proposals and reports

PREVIEW

A consultant proposes, conducts, and reports the results of individual client assignments or projects. Virtually all consulting work begins with a proposal to a client and culminates in a written report at the assignment's end. In consulting, the proposal, assignment, and report are so strongly linked that their development actually becomes one process, called the consulting process. Indeed, the success or failure of a consulting assignment usually hinges on the relationship between the initial proposal and the final report. Communication with clients is a continuous activity, and consulting activities require clear, concise, and accurate communication. Thus the quality of that communication establishes the quality of each consulting assignment and ultimately the quality of the consultant.

This chapter explains the communication skills necessary to the consulting process: the types of writing, speaking, listening, negotiating, and presenting that consultants do. A consultant's communications need to be effective: effective proposals obtain assignments for the consultant, and effective reports communicate the consultant's findings and recommendations clearly and accurately.

❏ A FUTURE IN CONSULTING

Would you like to use your skill in conducting market surveys to assist companies in deciding whether to introduce their product in new markets? Would you like to use your talents for developing computer applications by helping companies install customized systems? Could you succeed in the competitive world of management consulting, helping large companies restructure, set goals, or increase productivity? Perhaps you should consider a career in consulting, the profession of independent experts who provide specialized advice and services.

A career in consulting offers many challenges. Work assignments tend to be varied, and your talents and creative abilities are employed to the fullest. Salaries and bonuses are generally in line with many other professions. Visibility in the consulting profession is high, and you may be tempted with lucrative offers to work for client firms after successfully completing a consulting assignment. Drawbacks of a consulting career relate primarily to the lack of a well-defined career path, a higher-than-average number of career-related risks, erratic hours and cash flow, and perhaps a great deal of travel.

If, however, you have a high capacity for reasoning, possess strong analytic skills, are empathetic, well-educated, and moderately ambitious, these drawbacks need not represent insurmountable obstacles to joining the ranks of practicing consultants. In addition, all consultants need integrity, objectivity, good judgment, and psychological maturity. They must be able to understand and relate to people from a wide range of backgrounds and communicate well.

❏ WHO IS A CONSULTANT?

The Institute of Management Consultants, Inc. defines consulting as follows:

> Consulting is an independent and objective advisory service provided by qualified persons to clients in order to help them identify and analyze problems or opportunities. Consultants recommend solutions or suggest actions with respect to these issues, and when requested, assist in their implementation. In essence, consultants help to effect constructive change in private or public sector organizations through the sound application of substantive and process skills.[1]

Consultants use their knowledge and experience to help businesses.

Consultants give professional advice or services regarding matters in their field of special knowledge or training. Many professions are essentially consulting positions; examples include the activities of physicians, engineers, architects, psychologists, or lawyers. The practicing consultant shares many common traits with these highly regarded professions. Like a physician, a consultant diagnoses the needs of the client and proposes a remedy. Like a psychologist, a consultant may be called upon to give the client an increased awareness of the client's role in society or in business. Alternatively, the consultant's job may be to provide expert knowledge in a particular field, such as engineering, architecture, marketing, finance, or accounting.

In providing these services, a consultant becomes a resource upon which the organization can draw periodically, a professional advisor and counselor, and a catalyst for improvement and change. A consultant's recommendations often prescribe change, and this allows the consultant to influence the organization. Consultants maintain many close relationships with a variety of parties. They communicate with the managers who hired them, the client's employees, external auditors, lawyers and other professionals working for the client, as well as the community at large. As professionals, consultants must act ethically and reasonably toward all of these people. A consultant's work is always highly visible and is judged by a large number of people.

Consultants must possess a variety of skills and talents that often require extensive training, education, or experience. A consultant should adopt a code of ethics and maintain professional standards in delivering services to clients and in dealing with the general public. The consultant generally should establish fixed fees that are not contingent upon other outcomes or events; for example, a legal suit or business venture. Additionally, many consultants are expected to hold professional certificates issued by a government agency and to abide by regulations. Examples include the American Institute of Certified Public Accountants (the AICPA), the Institute of Management Consultants (the IMC), and engineering certification agencies.

> Consultants may be specialists in a particular field or they may apply general management principles.

Consultants have long been lumped into two major categories: specialists and generalists. Because of the business world's increasing complexity, many consulting firms have chosen to specialize in areas where it is feasible to guarantee competence and remain current in the field. Consulting firms can specialize in technical fields, industries, or geographic areas. The consulting field has grown rapidly. Public accounting firms have expanded into the consulting arena and now comprise the largest and fastest-growing category of consultants.[2] Individual practitioners and internal consulting groups (consultants working within a particular firm) constitute another large contingent. Generalists, on the other hand, take a different approach. The generalist approach relies upon and applies the basic principles of business management to specific problems or situations. Generalists are of the opinion that the consulting process, when carefully applied to the individual needs of the client, will achieve the results desired. They believe it is not necessarily important that the consultant be an expert in the area.

> Consultants provide expertise without creating the long-term costs of hiring additional permanent employees.

But why should anyone use a consultant? Consultants are generally more expensive than full-time professional staff, and are less knowledgeable about the organization than employees. However, consultants provide an independent viewpoint, and can be sufficiently detached from the organization to remain objective. An experienced consultant possesses specialized knowledge and skills. This may ensure that the project has the highest possible chance for success. Consultants can also provide ready-made solutions to short-term problems or can provide temporary assistance in a critical area, which can actually be less expensive than hiring more staff.

A consultant must be aware of the external and internal factors that shape the client's communication paths. Frequently, the consultant must help to

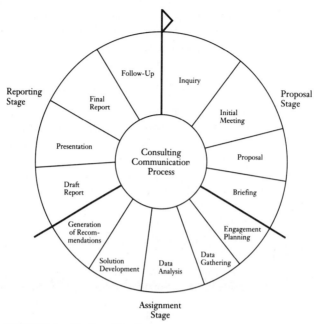

FIGURE 22-1. The Consulting Process

bridge the gap between the client and those outside the company. The consultant can help the client interact with external bodies such as government, media, labor unions, regulatory agencies, product markets, or even competitors. In addition, the consultant has to understand and make allowances for those aspects distinctive to the client firm: its structure, technologies, and culture. In short, the consultant must be aware of all the factors identified in Figure 22-1. Communication is thus a primary skill required for a consultant's professional success.

WHY CONSULTING IS A PROCESS

The consulting process stages: proposal development, assignment, and reporting.

The *consulting process* consists of generating consulting opportunities, proposing consulting projects to prospective clients, planning the individual tasks associated with the project, gathering facts, examining findings, generating conclusions, and communicating recommendations to the client. Additionally, it may be the consultant's responsibility to implement the changes recommended. At any given time, a successful consultant may have several projects underway. Some projects will be in the early stages; others will be nearly complete. As shown in Figure 22-1, each consulting project has three major stages: the proposal development stage, the assignment stage, and the reporting stage.

In practice, these three major consulting stages are subdivided into several components. The proposal development stage can be logically subdivided into four components: the inquiry/request for proposal (initiated by the client), the initial meeting, the preparation of the proposal, and the proposal briefing. The assignment stage can be divided into engagement planning, the client assignment, and the development of solution alternatives. The presentation-of-results stage can be divided into four substages: the draft report, the presentation, the final report, and the follow-up.

The steps are not simply a linear progression, however. Although it would probably be acceptable to skip or merge some of the substages on smaller assignments, for larger assignments several others may be added. For example, many consultants (such as architects and engineers) actually perform the work they recommend. Alternatively, the entire consulting assignment might focus on defining the problem. Problem analysis continues throughout the life of the assignment.

❑ COMMUNICATION IN THE CONSULTING ENVIRONMENT

Because communication is involved in all phases of the consulting process, ineffective communication during the consulting engagement will mar the final result. The techniques for analyzing communication situations, managing relationships, creating communication roles, and using an appropriate style as described in earlier chapters are applicable to a consultant's communications. Figure 22-2 shows the communication skills commonly applied at various stages in the consulting process.

Understanding the audience is the first step in writing effectively. Use words and concepts familiar to the audience, including technical jargon appropriate to that audience. The consultant must be able to present all the information that is relevant to that audience without boring them with unnecessary details. For example, consultants often communicate with top management at a too-detailed, basic level (perhaps because the consultant wants to assure management that he or she understands the problem). Usually, over-communication quickly bores members of this particular audience, making them unreceptive to the more significant aspects of the consultant's message.

Understand the information needs of your audience.

Everything that a consultant writes should have a purpose. An excellent way of exploring purposes is to analyze the audience's uncertainties—the differences between what the audiences already know, believe, and feel about the situation and what they need to know, believe, and feel in order to take appropriate action. Analyzing these uncertainties focuses the consultant's attention on the issues that matter most to the audiences. With these issues in mind develop a comprehensive purpose, or reason for assisting the firm, that links the objectives of the client's organization (the particular individuals who will be involved as audiences in the communication) with your own purposes. The comprehensive purpose is the first element in your communication strategy.

Develop a comprehensive purpose.

By organizing the message to address audience issues, information can be presented in a way that makes its pertinence clear, and shows the relation between the client's objectives and the work performed. In addition to writing reports, consultants often prepare presentations as well. Consultants should strive to transform lengthy written documents into concise and visually appealing oral

Organize to address audience issues.

STAGES	COMMUNICATION SKILLS
PROPOSAL DEVELOPMENT	
Inquiry/request	Specific expertise
Initial meeting	Listening skills
Proposal development	Interviewing skills
Proposal briefing	Writing skills
	Summarizing
	Analyzing
	Persuading
ASSIGNMENT STAGE	
Engagement planning	Information gathering
Data gathering	Analytical techniques
Data analysis	Direct observation skills
Solution development	Ongoing dialogue skills
Recommendation generation	
REPORTING STAGE	
Draft report	Report preparation skills
Presentation	Presentation skills
Final report	Follow-up skills
Follow-up	

FIGURE 22-2. Components of the Consulting Process

presentations that complement their written reports. Both proposals and reports must show that the consultant understands the client's needs. The report should present all the data relevant to reaching the consultant's conclusions and recommendations and should outline the actual steps taken during the consulting process. The body of the report need not (and usually should not) imitate the sequence of the consultant's work.

Write with a lively style.

Proposals and reports should be written in a lively style. Many otherwise good consultants suffer from "Consultantese," an obscure and complex writing style that hides the real message (or lack thereof) from the reader. A proper writing style balances completeness and conciseness, presenting sufficient information to justify the conclusions in the minimum number of words. Short, simple words and sentences, logical paragraphs, and hierarchical graphic headings help readers understand the proposal or report more quickly. Ineffective reports are not just hard to read, they're hard to write, and increasingly hard to sell, as the consulting field becomes more competitive.

THE PROPOSAL DEVELOPMENT STAGE: USING LISTENING, SUMMARIZING, ANALYSIS, AND PERSUASION SKILLS

The first stage in the consulting process is the proposal development stage. The first phase in this stage is the inquiry. Consultants receive inquiries from prospective clients in many different ways. They may telephone the consultant informally or send a formal request for proposal, depending upon the type of consulting practice. Prospective clients usually approach a consultant because of

1. an ongoing relationship (repeat business)
2. recommendations from other clients
3. the consultant's general reputation.

Advertising is not one of the more common reasons. Professional skills are notoriously difficult to market. Except for the very largest firms, ordinary advertising is not very effective. While a certain amount of self-promotion is to be expected from the best consultants (the largest firms resort to image advertising), advertising does not help very much. To use a medical analogy, it is difficult for a doctor to attract patients before some discomfort is felt. In business, the potential client should recognize a need for the consultant's services. A common pattern for consultant's communications during the proposal development stage is shown in Figure 22-3.

The Inquiry and Initial Meeting: Listening

When you respond to the client's inquiry, you and the potential client need to meet to determine whether your services might be useful. This is the second phase of the proposal development stage. This meeting serves as an information-gathering opportunity for both of you, and sets the stage for your reply or proposal. On large contracts, or if the client is a public agency, a common practice is a bidding conference where all hopeful consultants are present.

Listen actively and take notes.

In the initial meeting, you must rely heavily on communication and interpersonal skills. You must be a good listener, absorbing all information about the client's needs and wishes. You must be able to empathize with the client. Prospective clients are offended by condescending, arrogant consultants.

Obtain feedback to ensure accuracy.

During an initial meeting, your client may be prepared to discuss the company's needs in detail, and it would be imprudent not to be ready to absorb and retain this information. You should be prepared to take notes at this meeting. Even though this approach may appear studious, clients would rather have you take notes than call later about the same information. Since you have not yet been retained, taking notes also gives the impression that you are attentive to detail and well-organized. Restating the client's explanation ("Let me see whether I understand you . . .") allows your client to clarify any initial misunderstanding and demonstrates your concern and ability to appreciate the problem.

Before writing the proposal, you should do enough background research to prepare a quality proposal. You should know as much as is economically possible about both the problem to be solved and the client firm (see Chapter 12 on company research). For example, you may visit the firm, conduct interviews of those close to the problem, and discuss their preliminary opinions informally with others. An analysis of the decision makers' uncertainties will also help you present a more effective proposal (see Chapter 3).

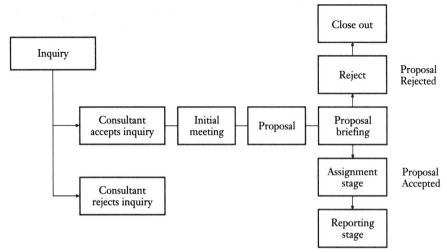

FIGURE 22-3. Steps in Handling a Consulting Inquiry

Write a letter of thanks regardless of whether you submit a proposal.

If, after the initial meeting, background research, and bidder's conference you decide not to offer a proposal, it is good form to send a letter to the prospect explaining the circumstances or the reasons behind the decision. For example, you may lack expertise or available time. The proposal stage of the consulting process holds much risk. Significant time and effort can be spent preparing proposals. A consultant must seriously evaluate every assignment that is offered and judge whether the proposal is worth writing. If the prospects for acceptance are low, you may decline to write a proposal.

Writing a Proposal: Summarizing, Analyzing, and Persuading

Proposals can be as brief or detailed as the situation requires; however, something in writing is considered to be necessary. There are two basic types of proposals: *the engagement letter*, which is an abbreviated, letter-style proposal; and *the formal proposal*, which is a much longer, more formal document used for longer and more complicated assignments. The tone of the engagement letter is more relaxed and conversational than the formal proposal, and is usually all that is required for shorter engagements. While the engagement letter can be briefer, it contains all the aspects of a longer proposal. For example, one sentence regarding the fee may take the place of a budget and contract submitted as part of a formal proposal.

Writing the proposal is a useful exercise. The proposal focuses the consultant's thinking on the assignment, communicating the consultant's understanding of the problem to the client. It serves as an outline for both parties and helps to sell the consultant's services. The proposal is usually the primary document detailing the work to be undertaken and as such, it establishes the contractual framework for the consultant's work.

The proposal is the central document of the project.

Generally, the proposal explains the client's current situation, the desired situation, the client's objectives, the consultant's approach to the problem, and the expected benefits if the client accepts the proposal. The proposal sets out what the client can expect from the consultant and what the consultant expects from the client. It defines the scope of the engagement and stipulates the cost of the consultant's services. The proposal also presents many of the administrative details: information regarding the cost of the consultant's services, the timing of the consultant's duties, staffing responsibilities, and specific assignment output. It is, after all, a contractual agreement between the client and consultant. Figure 22-4 shows the major elements of a proposal.

Cover Letter (if Formal Proposal)

Proposal Table of Contents (if Formal Proposal)

Proposal

    Introduction
        Purpose of proposal
        Background of the firm

    The Situation
        The present situation
        The desired situation

    Client Objectives
        The primary client question/client problem
        Other questions or problems
        Project constraints and/or options

    The Consultant's Approach
        Scope
        Methodology
        Specific study output

    Anticipated Benefits
        Expected results
        Impact of expected results
        Justification of costs

    Staffing, Timing, and Costs
        Team members
        Qualifications
        Support staff
        Research schedule
        Budget

    Closing
        Acknowledgement
        Anticipated response from client

Signature Line for Client's Execution or Formal Contract

FIGURE 22-4. Major Elements of a Proposal

The proposal is also a sales pitch. By definition, a proposal is an offer that is to be either accepted or rejected. As with other types of sales pitches, a certain amount of enthusiasm is needed. If the consultant is able to inject enthusiasm into the proposal, the prospective client will be more receptive. The proposal should also be results-oriented. That is, it should accurately present the specific benefits that the client will receive. A complete list of items to be delivered to the client, called "deliverables," should be included, as should the total cost to the client.

Changes will inevitably occur in the engagement, even after the proposal is written. Most consultants will admit that the scope or nature of a particular project is as likely to change *after* the proposal is accepted as *before*. Others freely admit that the proposal is merely an estimate, and the project will only fully take shape as the work proceeds. Good consultants reread their proposals frequently in order to stay on track and to confirm that their endeavors are for the benefit of the client. To the extent possible, the proposal should anticipate the necessary work steps involved and outline these steps for the benefit of both parties. Changes may require modifying the proposal or sending memos confirming project changes. Major changes may necessitate the mutual, signed consent of both parties, as an amendment to the prior agreement. In some states, certain professionals are legally required to keep a complete file of all project changes as well as records of work done.

The formal proposal is the best approach when submitting a proposal for a significant or complicated engagement. Usually a cover letter or letter of transmittal is used to present the proposal. The proposal typically includes exhibits, a table of contents, a firm vita, résumés of the professional staff, a schedule of accomplishments, plans for progress reports, and the planned paths of communication between consultant and client.

An oral presentation as well as a written proposal may be required.

Depending on the practices of the prospective client, the consultant may be requested to present the proposal verbally in addition to submitting a written document. A proposal briefing, whether delivered formally or informally over the telephone, confirms the consultant's understanding of the problem and answers any questions the client might have. For example, the consultant and the client may discuss the consultant's approach to the problem, the specific project output, expected client benefits, or the fee structure.

When dealing with U.S. audiences, the proposal should be direct, logical, and persuasive. Other cultures may resist American "hard sell" approaches, however. The chapter on international communication recommends ways of analyzing international audiences that can be applied to consulting proposals and reports. Each proposal should be uniquely suited to the situation. When responding to an RFP (request for proposal), the consultant will follow the structure dictated by the client's request (see the "fill-in-the-blanks" approach in Chapter 5).

It is very important not to short-change the proposal development stage of the consulting process. An effective proposal will win the engagement for the consultant, and must present all items on which the two parties must formally agree. An ineffective proposal will nevertheless remain in the hands of your prospect for some time and will be a lasting example of the quality of your work.

For this reason, all proposals (whether they prove to be successful or not) should be carefully written.

The proposal process concludes when the client, after reviewing the proposal, either accepts the services proposed, rejects the services outright, or requests further information.

An Actual Consulting Engagement: The "Fame" Case

One of my favorite consulting assignments, an interesting situation at my high school alma mater, involved an urban public high school of talented young people similar to the school popularized in the movie and television series "Fame!" I have disguised the names of the individuals and some of the details of the case.

Students at the school attend classes for a longer period each day than do their counterparts in regular high schools and take substantially more classes. For each student's art area, the school district records only one grade per semester. This is the average of all the student's grades in his or her art area, usually five or more classes. For example, a student enrolled in five courses each week is taught by five different instructors. The student would have only one grade recorded at the district level, the average of the five classes. Because the situation was unique to the school district, the district was unable to respond to the school's special information reporting needs.

The school was faced with an internal information management problem. Administrators had to keep school records current, provide students with art area report cards (in addition to the academic report cards issued by the school district), track the numerous art area classes offered to students within the school, and support the information needs of the instructors who teach there (such as supplying them with class rosters and grade reporting forms). The school could scarcely keep track of the classes that were being offered, when they were offered, which students were enrolled in what classes, and which instructors were teaching each class.

With 200 students, each enrolled in five of fifty different classes, two dozen different instructors (many of whom were working part-time), and grades due at the district level every six weeks, the manual information processing capabilities of the administrators were being stretched to the limit. School records were kept in a series of bins located in a school office. When it was time to process student grades, papers were literally moved from bin to bin as the information was processed and grades were recorded.

The school administrators contacted me personally, as a consultant with a background in computers and information management who also had a special interest in the welfare of the school. I knew that I could help the school, but first I had to gather more information in order to determine the staff's information needs. Also, I needed to ensure that I had the necessary skills for the project.

At the initial meeting, I talked with three people: a teacher, an administrator at the high school, and the principal. The administrator explained the current situation, and showed the manual method for keeping track of student activities. The principal expressed concern that the current method was sometimes risky and inaccurate, and was concerned that the current system was "a lawsuit waiting to happen."

I listened to what was said. Before proposing a solution, I paraphrased the problem for the others and asked if that was an accurate description of the problem. I then described a database management system (DBMS), a computer program that stores and retrieves data in meaningful ways. I asked whether the description sounded as if it would solve the information problems at the school. When they answered yes, I agreed to write a proposal. The document that resulted, a letter proposal, is presented in Figure 22-5.

THE ASSIGNMENT STAGE: USING PLANNING, OUTLINING, NOTE TAKING, AND PARAPHRASE

After the client accepts the consultant's proposal, the assignment stage, which has five parts, begins:[3]

- Problem definition and engagement planning
- Gathering data and fact finding
- Analyzing data
- Generating solutions and recommendations
- Implementing change and achieving benefits for the client

Ongoing communication during the assignment keeps the client abreast of your progress.

In the assignment stage, the consultant's talent in gathering information, analyzing problems, and generating solutions affects the quality of the assignment. Fact finding and analysis techniques, such as interviews, questionnaires, direct observation, and data gathering, require effective communication skills. The consultant usually has the highest degree of contact with the client during this stage, so the flow of information is at a maximum. Throughout the consulting process it is very important to provide the client with feedback regarding the progress of the consulting assignment.[4] Communication with the client through progress reports keeps the client informed during the assignment and ensures that the engagement is a collaborative effort. Good consultants call this "bringing the client along." The ongoing dialogue prevents surprises during the presentation of progress reports and the final report. In this stage, you will use communication skills continuously.

During the course of the project, you will prepare many types of communication for the client: the proposal, interim reports or letters, and working notes, data, and other engagement documentation. On smaller projects, progress reports may consist of an informal, spontaneous meeting or phone call. On larger projects, you may write progress reports regularly. On major projects, a progress report may itself be a major undertaking, depending on the audience and situation. During the project, meetings with diverse small groups will occur at different times. In some other cases, a large group meeting with a formal presentation might be necessary. The goal of the meeting, the size of the audience, the corporate culture, and the audience's attitudes will all be prime considerations in your development of a communication strategy.

The assignment stage consists of the agreed-upon tasks. If the primary work product of the assignment is a report, then the assignment stage consists of all the steps necessary to prepare the report. Or if the assignment involves the writing of a computer application, then development of the application occurs during the assignment stage. Two tasks will confront you at this stage:

1. Identifying issues: Problems to be solved, tasks or tests to be performed, and questions to be answered.
2. Creating outputs: Product-oriented results of the consulting project, including specific deliverables and client benefits.

Problem Definition and Engagement Planning

The assignment involves a problem-solving process.

During the problem definition stage you will fully define and describe the underlying problem. Planning the engagement involves the development of hypotheses, the preparation of key questions, the identification of data sources, and the specifying of research tasks. During the problem definition phase, you are not trying to find answers yet—only the right questions. Deciding on the right questions usually requires determining the issues and the hypotheses. It can be a real temptation to jump to conclusions regarding the reasons for the client's problems. With some discipline, you must restrict this stage to merely describing the problem or situation, without guessing as to the root causes (see Chapter 1 on problem solving for more discussion).

What is the problem? This should be the first question asked and the last one answered during the problem definition stage.[5] There are several potential pitfalls in identifying a problem:

- confusing symptoms with the root of the problem,
- accepting opinions of others without question,
- assuming that the client's problem is a person, or
- accepting one cause when multiple causes are involved.

"Plan the work, work the plan" is a maxim of engagement planning quoted in business management circles.[6] Before getting on with the work, map the steps necessary for the successful completion of the assignment. A consulting team will usually hold a kickoff meeting, during which the proposal is reviewed to define engagement milestones or checkpoints, and responsibility is assigned among the team. A work plan is then developed and all major work tasks are defined. A careful review of the proposal and an understanding of the client's objectives will allow the development of preliminary conclusions (or hypotheses) about the problems or questions confronting the client (see Figure 22–6). Hypotheses set the stage for collecting the facts by focusing the project and organizing the data collection. For example, early in the "Fame" case my firm hypothesized that our client did not fully understand the ways in which the in-

C & S Consulting Company
2439 Terrace View
Martin City, CA 94087

April 12, 1988

Mr. Frank Louder, Principal
The High School for the Arts
Suite 26, Margaret Shanks Administration Building
2416 Devon Street
Martin City, CA 94087

Dear Mr. Louder:

I enjoyed meeting with you yesterday to discuss the school's computing needs, and the role our firm can play in helping you achieve your goal of installing an information management system at the school. This letter is our proposal to analyze the school's computing needs, evaluate the current software and hardware options available to meet those needs, and implement the new system.

My understanding is that until now you have performed all information management activities manually. As we discussed, several aspects of a school's management readily accept computer automation, including:

- Student and teacher information,

- Course and classroom schedules,

- Class rosters, and

- Student report cards and transcripts.

You also need to be able to accomplish other tasks on your system besides word processing, including maintaining the school's journal and ledger, staff employment data, and information regarding the school's patrons. You are concerned that the new system be flexible, and that the system be inexpensive to maintain and operate.

Our Firm's Approach to the Problem

We feel that it would be more cost effective to replace your current system with a new system rather than to upgrade to these capabilities. The current system has been heavily and well used as a word processor, and has been of great benefit to the school. However, the additional cost of upgrading as opposed to replacing your system makes the cost of the new system more attractive. We propose that the following steps be taken on your behalf:

1. We will first collect additional information regarding the school's information needs and uses.

FIGURE 22-5.   Sample Letter Proposal

2. We will review information on computer hardware and software systems used in schools today, and develop specific recommendations regarding the optimal hardware/software solution.

3. We will negotiate with computer vendors, software vendors, and installation experts in acquiring and installing the system, develop the proper database design for the school, and train your people in the proper use of the system once it is installed.

Benefits to This Approach

This approach will enable you to direct your attention to managing the school, and you will not need to be concerned with the upgrade until the new system is installed and the changeover is made. You will have a new system that is functional, thoughtfully designed, and professionally implemented.

Once the system is implemented, you will be able to store and retrieve information regarding each student, the school's teachers and staff, the classes, the grades assigned to each student, and other information. As long as the information in the system is current, at the touch of a button you will be able to print a student directory, a list of classes offered, class rosters for the teachers, report cards and transcripts for the students, budget reports, and school calendars for planning purposes.

Timing, Staffing, and Costs

As you know, our firm has four individuals who specialize in computer applications design. I will have overall responsibility for your project and Janet Henderson will assist me. Each of our team members will bring his or her expertise to your application. This broad-based approach will ensure that your system will be well-designed, as it will represent the sum of our respective talents.

Based on the attached project schedule, we expect that the project will take from ten weeks to three months to accomplish. We anticipate that the professional fees for the project, as described above, will range from $9,000 to $12,000, exclusive of hardware and software expense and reasonable out-of-pocket expenses. In accordance with our customary practice, our fee will be based on actual hours expended at our standard hourly rate.

Thank you for allowing us to submit this proposal. We look forward to assisting you on this important project. If you have any questions regarding our proposed work, please give me a call. If, however, our proposal is acceptable to you in its current form, please sign in the space below and return one executed copy to our office. We will commence work as soon as we have received authorization to do so.

Sincerely,

Donald D. Clayton
President

Proposal Accepted By:

_____   Date: _____

FIGURE 22-5. Sample Letter Proposal (*continued*)

```
Review . . .               To Define . . .
    Proposal                   Client Objectives
    Meeting Notes              Assignment Objectives
    Interviews                 Issues
    Other Sources              Outputs
```

FIGURE 22-6.   Properly Planning the Engagement

formation system would be used to support the school. Further discussions with key staff members supported this hypotheses. Understanding this problem allowed us to focus on training at a conceptual level prior to implementation, in order to streamline the transition process.

Key questions organize analysis.

Key questions are an important analytical tool in consulting. Key questions are used to support, reject, or modify a consultant's hypotheses and preliminary conclusions. Key questions also steer the consulting project in some major way. Key questions are questions which, when answered, will allow the preliminary hypotheses to be tested and the assignment to proceed effectively. Key questions focus the project design and data collection phases about the hypotheses or major objectives of the project, and should be worded to maximize the consultant's understanding of the problem and minimize the irrelevant data gathered. Figure 22-7 displays some of the key questions used in the "Fame" project analysis.

The client's objectives, the project objectives, the consultant's hypotheses, key questions, and the issues at hand lead to the development of a planning tool called an *issue diagram*. An issue diagram (see Figure 22-7) is a type of flow chart used to map the objectives of the consulting assignment into the tasks necessary for the completion of the assignment. Every major issue for the client should have its own issue diagram. Although for simple projects the formal use of issue diagrams may be counterproductive, using a diagram increases the chance that you will remember the necessary steps to accept, reject, or modify each hypothesis and that you will carry out the data gathering as planned.

The issues, key questions, and eventually, the data necessary to answer the key questions, are placed on the issue diagrams. There are many ways to construct issue diagrams. As this tool is used, gaps in the hypotheses and key questions begin to stand out as the development of the planning stage nears completion. These gaps should be used to refine the hypotheses and key questions and guide the modification of the issue diagrams. The issue diagrams allow the consulting project to be "reverse engineered" by taking the objectives of the project and using those objectives to plan the intricate work steps necessary to achieve the objectives.

While this approach may sound elementary, issue diagrams form a road map for handling complex, multiple-issue problems for the completion of the assignment and may be the only way to fully understand all the issues. Issue diagrams are necessary in highly technical work, such as the analysis of airplane crashes, equipment failures, plant relocations, and other complex studies.

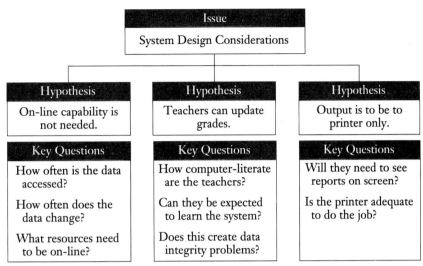

FIGURE 22-7.   A Sample Issue Diagram

Data Gathering or Fact Finding

Data gathering or fact finding is the second phase of the assignment stage. As the information necessary to solve the problem is collected, appropriate changes are made to the issue diagrams to refine, add, or eliminate preliminary conclusions, or to add key questions or data sources. Getting all the facts is not necessarily the most efficient thing to do. Getting all the *relevant* facts is the crucial part. If the assignment involves the creation of a physical product, then it is designed at this stage. In the "Fame" case example, after the needs of the school had been mapped on the issue diagram, the design stage involved the development of a computer system prototype that performs the necessary functions.

There are two types of data gathering: primary, or "self-generated" data gathering; and secondary data gathering, in which data originated by others are used in the analysis to answer the key questions. Primary data-gathering techniques are necessary to obtain the answer to many key questions, and secondary sources and methods can be used to check answers to key questions or to correlate the results of the primary data. Examples of primary data-gathering techniques include interviewing, using questionnaires, conducting opinion or business activity surveys, investigating the current producers in a potential market, or measuring the size of a market using direct observation. Examples of secondary data gathering include library research, collecting published reports, census data, newspapers, or any other use of data that has been prepared by someone else. Chapter 12 explains how to tap these secondary sources.

Generally, facts are available to consultants in three forms: records, events or conditions, and memories. Grouping data meaningfully is one of the most important ways that consultants can turn data into information for the benefit of the client. Data are organized to help the consultant use them easily in the analysis. You may group data in several categories: [7]

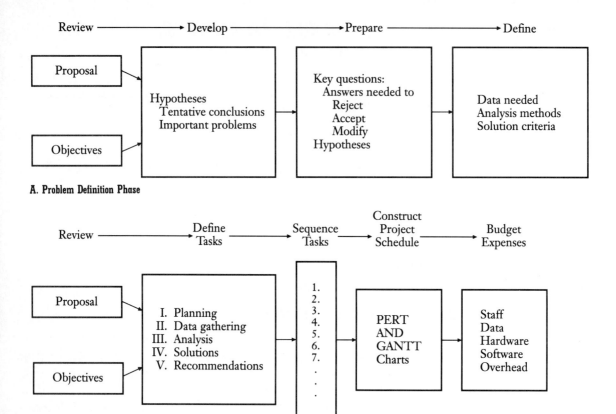

A. Problem Definition Phase

B. Task Coordination Phase

FIGURE 22-8. *Two Phases of Engagement Planning: Problem Definition and Task Coordination*

Events—timing, frequency, trends, cause, effect

People—age, sex, nationality, family status, qualifications, occupation, income, preferences

Products and materials—size, value, physical characteristics, source

Resources, processes, or procedures—production, location, distribution

Interviewing is probably one of the most powerful data collection skills you can master, and is yet another important communication skill. Interviews of one kind or another comprise a crucial part of almost all data gathering. Interviews are superior to questionnaires because every answer can be tested and elaborated. It is important to be fully prepared for every interview, so that you can obtain the needed information efficiently. You must also be a good listener. Preparation includes reviewing appropriate background data as well as preparing an outline agenda of the interview itself.

Direct observation is another fact-gathering technique available to the consultant. For example, Frederick Taylor, the famous time and motion efficiency specialist, observed employees on their job, how they did their work, how long each step took, and how much work was done. He studied their jobs and suggested ways in which these workers could perform their jobs more efficiently, sometimes resulting in dramatic increases in productivity.

Although hard data are always preferable, sometimes data are just not available for one reason or another. When important data are missing or unobtainable, the consultant can often make do with estimates. Estimates are makeshift; they can't really replace established data. Always identify estimates as such when you use them in your analysis. Estimates should be made by people who have first-hand knowledge of the situation. Estimates should be used judiciously, and not in the analysis of delicate situations. Sometimes, without even a rough estimate regarding a factor, the data analysis cannot be performed, so estimates must be used.

Summarize data to keep track of your research progress.

After gathering data from each source, the consultant should summarize relevant information to keep track of the information obtained. It is important to learn when to stop gathering data as well. A balance must be struck between accumulating all the relevant information and staying within the time and budget constraints of the project. You must follow the specifications developed in the planning stage, but expand them if necessary to include other newly recognized relevant information.

Because it is not uncommon to collect a large amount of data during this stage, a filing system should be used to organize the information you gather. The filing system should be able to handle all facts and data gathered during the assignment. It is also a good idea to keep a journal of facts and findings as part of the filing system. Such a system is crucial for information retrieval, as well as answering your client's questions efficiently during the assignment. If the recommendations outlined here are followed, then writing the consulting report itself will not be such a challenge.

Analyzing Data

Superior data analysis is the distinguishing feature of a good consulting project. The data-gathering stage is intended to produce a volume of facts or data without attempting to interpret the data. Up to now, the steps involved in the assignment have been fairly straightforward. When the analysis of data is performed, the intuitive leap that separates a consulting assignment from mundane reporting occurs. The data are transformed into information. Information is data that have been arranged, summarized, or synthesized to provide meaning to the client. If the data gathering was well-planned, then most, if not all, of the data gathered will be germane to the issues on the issue diagrams. Facts are then classified by issue and analyzed individually and collectively to determine their impact (see Figure 22-9).

There are four major approaches to factual analysis: decision-level analysis, input/output analysis, structured analysis, and unstructured analysis.[8] These techniques are taught in other management courses. Other data-analysis techniques favored by different specialties, such as marketing, operations research, finance, real estate, human resource management, and strategic planning may also be used in this stage of the project.

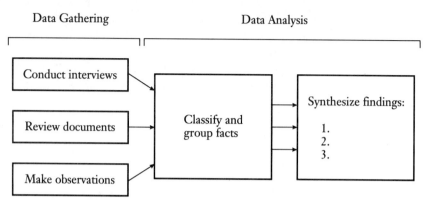

FIGURE 22-9. Data Gathering and Analysis

Findings tell what is significant about the facts.

The results of these data-analysis exercises are generally reported as findings. Findings make the intuitive leap from fact to issue. Findings go beyond the scope of the information gathered and attempt to discover the specific implications for the client. Findings are most often used to answer the question, "So what?"

An example of the difference between fact and finding can be expressed as follows:

Fact: The market we have researched is growing at 5 percent per year.

Finding: The market is growing too slowly to meet the client's market development criteria.

Findings may result from the synthesis of many facts, or from analysis of a single fact. Findings are generally divided into three categories: major, minor, and supporting findings. Major findings are relevant, accurate, and relate directly to the issues in the issue diagram. Minor findings impact major findings, and supporting findings do not impact the issues directly, but are still relevant and informative.

Generating Solutions and Recommendations

Conclusions relate findings to the key questions.

Although the client expects that you will find and recommend the best solution to the problem, it is seldom possible to point to an immediate and obvious solution. Most business and management problems that require a consultant are complex and have more than one possible solution. Developing recommendations involves identifying all possible solutions and evaluating the alternatives. Unless a thorough search is conducted, you cannot be confident that the best solution has been identified and recommended. For example, in the "Fame" case, the school administrators were interested in maintaining their information on a series of computer spreadsheets, perhaps using Lotus 123. Once the situation had been analyzed, however, it was determined that the database design was too complicated for a spreadsheet. A database thus became the solution to this problem.

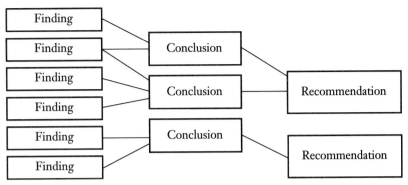

FIGURE 22-10.   Sample Logic Diagram

Generating solutions is similar to generating new ideas. The three most important ingredients are experience, research, and creativity. Solution alternatives can be researched and evaluated by whatever means are appropriate. Whenever possible, the analysis should employ a decision model that quantifies the significant factors in the problem. Each possible solution should be evaluated using established criteria, then compared against the other solution alternatives. Possible solution criteria include economic feasibility, operational feasibility, technical feasibility, scheduling feasibility, and legal feasibility.

Recommendations describe the actions necessary to achieve the client's objectives. In the reporting stage, recommendations should focus on the solution alternatives and the practical steps that will lead to the desired benefits. Clearly, in order to arrive at the optimum recommendation, all possible alternatives must be outlined and the ethical consultant will present each of these alternatives in the document (most likely in an appendix to the final report).

Usually, conclusions and recommendations are grouped together in the final report. They occur together so often that it must be remembered that conclusions and recommendations are each critical links in the intellectual chain; they must not be merged or confused.

An example of the difference between conclusions and recommendations could be expressed this way:

> *Conclusion:* The structure of the school's data is too complicated for a spreadsheet.
>
> *Recommendation:* The use of a database manager is recommended.

Recommendations show the implications of these conclusions for the client's problem.

Implementing Change and Achieving Benefits for the Client

The client's decision regarding the consultant's recommendations is subject to the same influences to which all other management decisions are subject. The number of important management decisions made on the basis of emotions is surprisingly high in business. It is essential that the consultant be aware of the client's personal preferences and of cultural, political, and other factors affecting decision making within the client organization. This will keep the consultant from putting forward solutions that may be technically ideal, yet doomed to be ignored. In many instances, the generation of the consulting report is the final step for the consultant, and the decision taken on the consultant's recommendations may be the final contact with the client. In other projects, the consultant may be responsible for installation of equipment, supervision of changes, or training employees to use a new system.

The Assignment Stage of the "Fame" Case

The administrators at the school liked my ideas and proposal, and were comfortable with me personally. Following some telephone conversations and discussions among themselves, the administrators returned the signed proposal. When I received the proposal, I met with my professional staff to discuss the assignment. At the meeting, we reviewed the proposal, developed specific project objectives and milestones, and subdivided the assignment into work steps to be accomplished by team members.

Based on the proposal, we logically divided the assignment into several parts: understanding the needs of the school, identifying software solutions, identifying hardware solutions, acquiring the necessary software and hardware, programming, system installation, documentation and training, project closure, and continuing support. The team felt that each logical step could be further divided into separate activities; these activities were listed and completion dates were estimated.

Each identifiable work step was entered into a project management software system, which allowed us to compute the minimum time required to complete the project. When each work step had been completed, the status of that work step was updated on the project management system. If a step took longer than anticipated or cost more than was budgeted, the client was informed of this, and the impact of the change on the total project schedule and budget was made known to the school staff.

During the assignment stage, I held weekly meetings at the school to discuss the progress of the project. As the project evolved, small changes were made to the overall project design and output specifications were tightened. Prototypes of the application were tested by the school staff, and improvements and modifications were made. The application was developed in approximately the minimum time that the work could be accomplished. Because we had done a good job of keeping the clients informed of the progress of the project, there were no surprises at the end of the assignment stage. Also, because the staff had been given hands-on training early in the project, training time at the end of the assignment stage was minimal.

The result of the conscientious application of sound consulting methodology was that the application was effectively implemented in a minimal amount of time. Management at the school was particularly pleased with the outcome. This rapid completion, combined with the increased power and flexibility of the new data base, proved to management that the system was extremely beneficial to the school.

❏ REPORTING OF RESULTS STAGE

Reporting the results is the final stage in the consulting process. The previous two sections involved winning the proposal and performing the assignment. This section concerns the challenge of communicating the results obtained from the steps completed. When a consulting assignment is completed, the results are usually presented both orally and in writing to the client. A wrap-up session is scheduled where the consultant makes a presentation on the assignment, the conclusions reached, and the recommendations generated.

The final report must stand alone and also must support the oral presentation at the final meeting.

The written report needs to be prepared to support the consultant in the final meeting and to document the assignment for the client. The structure of both the meeting and the report will depend on the type of work conducted and on the audience's needs. The complexity, thoroughness, and scope of the assignment all influence the nature of both the final meeting and the final report.

The classical approach to presenting the results of the consulting assignment is the written report. Regardless of the information submitted up to this point, the final report is a comprehensive document that presents the consultant's activities and important findings. For a relatively short assignment, the final report may be the only written record of the consultant's endeavors besides the proposal. The final report ties up all the loose ends in the consulting engagement, points out the benefits that would be achieved through implementation of the consultant's solutions, and presents any final recommendations to the client. An evaluation of client benefits is also included, if the consultant has been involved in the implementation of recommendations.

The issue trees that organized the analysis may be useful in designing the final report.

If the consultant has been working methodically, he or she would have gathered data based upon the steps outlined in the design stage and organized the results hierarchically and topically on issue diagrams (see Chapter 5). Using the key questions, hypotheses, facts, and findings from the assignment stage, the consultant has reached conclusions regarding the optimal solution for the client and generated recommendations based upon these conclusions. The consulting process is designed so that each step logically follows the previous step, and as such, the report should be the logical extension of the results uncovered in the preparation stage. The report is the instrument used by the consultant to communicate the findings of the study to the client. It should be written to benefit the client, with the client's long-term information needs in mind.

Appendices can present technical analyses that the primary decision makers do not need to read.

The language of the report is persuasive. Even if the client is ready for a change, the logical foundation of the consultant's recommendations should be apparent. It is the ethical obligation of the consultant to justify fully all recommendations and to document for clients and other interested parties the basis for the recommendations.

Document Spotlight: Sample Letter Report, pp. 314–316, shows a letter report from an engineering consulting firm to a client's lawyer. The letter reports on an assignment where the consulting firm has analyzed another consulting firm's study and has found the other consultant's conclusions to be unjustified. The consultant may choose to place the discussion of the data analysis in an appendix if the client is unable or unlikely to be interested to follow the data analysis, but the discussion must be included somewhere in the report.

Types of Reports

Once the consulting assignment has been completed, the consultant needs to determine the report format that will successfully convey the results of the assignment to the client. Some written documentation is almost always needed. The format of the report can substantially affect the cost and effectiveness of the assignment. Five types of reporting methods are commonly used: letters or in-house memos, discussion outlines, graphic summaries with charts and diagrams, operation manuals, and formal reports.

Informal letters and memos are used with clients who require a written report, but because of budget constraints, time constraints, or corporate culture are unwilling to invest in formal reports. When written well, letters and memos can effectively communicate the consultant's status, findings, and recommendations. By avoiding the bulk and flourishes of a formal report, informal letters and memos encourage an economical flow of information between the client and the consultant.

Discussion outlines consist of brief, skeletal statements arranged in outline form to assist in conveying the important issues and conclusions to the client. They are usually used in meetings or presentations to keep the presentation and discussion on track. A discussion outline provides a written record of the engagement, yet is simple to prepare and allows for great flexibility during the oral presentation. A discussion outline can be reproduced for the audience with generous space between points, allowing for note taking during the presentation. A number of commercial computer programs will prepare an integrated oral presentation and audience handout of this type.

Graphic summaries are an enhanced form of the discussion outline that combines sentences or phrases with graphics and charts to convey information quickly. Graphics can be used to bring otherwise boring numbers to life and to convey complex relationships that would be lost in a written description or table of numbers (see the chapter on graphics). This form of written report is especially useful for management organization reviews, marketing reports, and strategy reports. For some engagements, charts and diagrams constitute the entire written presentation. Flow charts, organizational charts, facility layouts, and matrix arrays are commonly used as well.

Formal reports, the most common type of consulting report, consist of several major parts which, when combined, become a powerful communication package. Formal reports are explained in Chapter 13. Attention should be paid not just to the body of the report, but to the context of the written (and possibly oral) presentation as well. Most reports are formatted in much the same way that books are formatted. Most reports have an introductory summary, major analytic blocks of information grouped into chapters, and one or more concluding sections or chapters. In fact, it is common to develop a chapter for each issue. The report explains the client's situation; issues, tasks, or topics pertinent to the situation; the consultant's assignment; the work done; conclusions reached; and major recommendations of the study. It should be designed to communicate the central findings of the engagement and stand alone as a complete document.

Reporting the Results of the "Fame" Case

The "Fame" case illustrates effective consulting methodology for a number of reasons. The assignment was both challenging to the consultants who performed the assignment and rewarding to the school administrators who placed their faith in the consulting team.

In reporting the results of the assignment to the school administrators, the consulting team used several methods. We passed out a discussion outline at a wrap-up meeting with administrators to discuss the completion of the project and to demonstrate that all the work steps in the project had been accomplished. Flow charts were projected in the meeting to show how the system worked and to give management an increased conceptual understanding of how the system operated. A user's manual and a programmer's reference manual were written and given to the school to document the system's operation.

Eventually, word of the system's successful implementation filtered up to the central administration office, which contacted my firm and requested an explanatory document that would describe the system to the superintendent in charge of arts programs. We responded by preparing an executive summary that fully described at an executive level the system's operation. Based on the executive summary and positive reviews from users at the high school, we were contacted to design and implement another system for the school district, resulting in another important engagement for the firm.

❑ COMMUNICATION CHALLENGES

EXERCISE 1

Each member of the class should choose a partner for this assignment. Have a fellow class member describe a business problem he or she has encountered. *Write a memorandum outlining your understanding of the problem.* Switch roles; present a situation you are familiar with to the other student and let the other class member write a memorandum. Schedule a follow-up session (or sessions) where you point out to one another the issues that the other person has correctly identified and mention those issues that may have been overlooked.

EXERCISE 2

Select an organization, local institution, or company with which you are very familiar. You might choose a club to which you belong or a department of your college or university. Arrange an appointment with the club president or with an administrator or manager in the college or company. Explain that you are working on an assignment for your communication course, and that you need to prepare a consulting proposal for a cli-

ent. The proposal you prepare can be used to hire an actual consultant later on, if the executive is interested. Using your listening skills, draw out the person's ideas about some of the problems the organization is currently experiencing. Some examples might include insufficient student assistants for the library, campus security problems, meal plan difficulties, newsletter design problems, parking assignments, public relations for a fundraising event, or other important aspects of student life.

As a first step, prepare a letter for the person you interviewed, thanking him or her for the interview and restating the principal aspects of the problem you think would be most suitable for a project. You may suggest a project that you or a group of students might conduct or one that would require the expertise of a professional consultant. After the person has confirmed that a project would be of interest, *request another interview if necessary and proceed to organize and draft the proposal or request for proposal.* Use a letter proposal unless the project is conducted by a group of students or is of sufficient magnitude to require a formal report.

EXERCISE 3

This exercise requires some thought, and perhaps some background research to prepare. Consulting divisions of the "Big 8" firms have been described as the fastest growing segments of their companies. *In a one-page memorandum, explain why this might be true and how the consulting divisions are able to capitalize on the opportunities provided by their audit and tax divisions and vice versa.* Your purpose is to expand your own understanding of the interactions among departments of consulting and accounting companies by accumulating ideas about different firms and their approach to consulting.

EXERCISE 4

A potential client has just left your office. After meeting with him, you realize that his problem is similar to an engagement you recently completed. You have the op-

tion of telling him what you already know, or going through the steps of the consulting process. Would you give him the benefit of your recently acquired knowledge at a reduced rate? Are you obligated to reimburse your original client for a portion of your fee? What if your knowledge consisted of information that is proprietary to your former client? Jot down your answers to these questions and be prepared to discuss them as a member of a consulting panel in your class.

EXERCISE 5

As a class, choose three business areas in which the class is interested. Try to invite several consultants to give a panel discussion on consulting and the types of communications they prepare in these areas. *The class should prepare thank-you letters and memos reviewing their findings afterward.*

IF YOU WOULD LIKE TO READ MORE

Barcus, S. W. (Ed.). (1986). *Handbook of management consulting services.* New York: McGraw-Hill. One of the best books on consulting published in the U.S.

Bloch, P. (1981). *Flawless consulting: A guide to getting your experience used.* Austin, TX.: Learning Concepts. Contains lots of practical advice on dealing with clients.

Burch, J. G., Jr., Strater, F. R., & Grudnitski, G. (1983). *Information systems: Theory and practice* (3d ed.). New York: Wiley. A work that distinguishes between ideal consulting theories and their practical application in information systems.

Kubr, M. (1986). *Management consulting: A guide to the profession.* Geneva: International Labour Office. A thorough and thoughtful book on consulting.

NOTES

1. This definition was developed by the directors of several management consulting associations with the assistance of their members and other scholars at a conference for University Education and Management Consulting, Salt Lake City, February 21–22, 1985.

2. An overview of rapid changes in consulting is found in "Management consultancy: The new witch doctors," *The Economist* (February 13, 1988).

3. At least two noted consulting references propose the five-part process scheme, including M. Kubr, "The consulting process," *Management consulting: A guide to the profession,* Geneva: International Labour Office (1986), 109–195; and M. E. Davis, "Problem definition," In S. W. Barcus (Ed.), *Handbook of management consulting services,* New York: McGraw-Hill (1986), 101–139.

4. A useful discussion on the finer points of client relations appears in P. Bloch, *Flawless consulting: A guide to getting your experience used.* Austin, TX: Learning Concepts (1981), 175–190.

5. One of the best U.S. texts on consulting is the *Handbook of management consulting services.* Several important concepts presented in this chapter are more fully explained there. See also M. E. Davis in note 3.

6. J. Graham, "Engagement planning." In S. W. Barcus (Ed.), *Handbook of management consulting services.* New York: McGraw-Hill (1986), 199–214.

7. Probably the most exhaustive and complete text on the consulting process. M. Kubr, "Diagnosis," *Management consulting: A guide to the profession.* Geneva, Switzerland: International Labour Office (1986), 133–166.

8. A work that distinguishes between ideal consulting theories and their practical application in information systems is J. G. Burch, Jr., F. R. Strater, & G. Grudnitski, *Information systems: Theory and practice* (3d ed.), New York: Wiley (1983).

❏ PERFORMANCE EVALUATION COMMUNICATIONS

OBJECTIVES

This chapter will help you

- analyze differences in performance appraisal situations

- separate evaluation from process feedback

- listen to and restate employee concerns

- choose feedback techniques suited to the company culture

- write defensible performance evaluations

- adapt different appraisal techniques to specific communication situations

PREVIEW

Performance appraisals affect employees' morale and productivity. Companies evaluate employees' performance in order to make important personnel decisions such as promotion and termination, to judge the results of the company's selection and training procedures, and to help individuals improve their performance. Inevitably, performance appraisals also affect workers' motivation and attitudes. Performance appraisals may involve both interpretations of outcomes and process feedback. Comments on outcomes do little to promote learning, but process feedback can strongly improve performance.

Once the purpose of the appraisal is determined, several aspects of the communication context become crucial. The legal, economic, and social pressures of the external environment limit the choice of appraisal systems. The culture and

structure of the organization create the climate in which appraisals are conducted. The type of working relationship between the employee and the supervisor will affect how each interprets meaning in the discussion. Whatever is said, the employee will amplify the importance of the communication, because each person is vitally interested in what others think about him or her.

The total performance evaluation system may include a variety of formal and informal written and verbal communications, all concerned with evaluating performance and providing feedback or guidance. Principal components consist of day-to-day interactions, evaluation procedures, formal appraisal sessions, written appraisals, and overall appraisal policy.

To adapt appraisal systems and techniques to a particular organization, a manager should consider the types of situations that govern the flow of information about the employee to the managers. Where situations limit the frequency of interaction or allow only partial views of employee behavior, formal mechanisms for observing and evaluating behavior and for providing feedback are necessary. Individuals' perceptual processes (availability bias, stereotyping, "halo" bias, and other tendencies) can interfere with fair appraisals. Evaluation techniques should be chosen to compensate for these biases. The most critical feature distinguishing the various procedures commonly used is the extent to which they focus on behavior as opposed to traits or tendencies.

Formal appraisal sessions should be conducted in a manner that is consistent with the company's legal environment, its culture and structure. Four approaches—"tell and sell," "tell and listen," "problem-solving discussion," and "mixed-model" participation—can reflect the level of formality, trust, and participation encouraged in the company. The essential point is that a manager should carry out whatever procedure has been selected in a manner that will accomplish the purpose it was intended to serve. The appraisal system and the manner of conducting performance appraisal reflect organizational policy.

The written appraisal, as well as the oral appraisal, has long-term consequences. To be legally defensible, a written appraisal must reflect the purpose of the appraisal, the conclusions or evaluation of performance during the period, and summarize the process feedback offered to improve performance in the future. The evaluation must be objective, expressed in neutral terms, and supported with descriptive evidence.

❑ PERFORMANCE EVALUATIONS

An Illustration: You Know How It Feels to Be Appraised

Imagine yourself in the office of one of your college instructors. It is near the end of the term and you are there to discuss your semester's work. The course is important to you: you need a C to graduate, and an A would greatly enhance your chances of landing a good job. It has been one of those courses in which class participation and ungraded written assignments contribute heavily to the final grade.

You know you have worked hard, and you feel that your comments were always rather insightful—considerably more so than those of your fellow students, if somewhat less numerous. You are certain your written work was good. Still, you can recall several occasions on which the instructor strongly challenged your position. And he also seemed much more attentive to a group of talkative, yet consistently uninformed, sophomores than he was to you. In fact, early in the semester he often called you by the wrong name; you had to correct him. Did he resent it? Could that or your tendency to disagree with his position have lowered his opinion of you? Does he really know how conscientious you've been? Does he care? The suspense has been building for some time now, and at last it is to be resolved.

How would you feel if during the ensuing conference the instructor went into great detail about the "sporadic" and often "misguided" nature of your class participation, barely mentioned your written work, and refused to reveal your grade for the course? Or if he told you that your grade would be a D, but refused to give any explanation beyond the statement that it "was all you deserved"? And suppose further that he volunteered "helpful advice" to make you a better student in the future?

Most of us, it's fair to say, would be quite upset, regardless of how this little scenario played out. We would resent being given what we perceived as an unfair evaluation, and even more would we resent the absence of any explanation (although it is doubtful we would have agreed with whatever explanation he might have offered). And having the grade withheld would have been devastating after so much anticipation. "Constructive criticism" would hardly have been well-received under any circumstances, given our understandable preoccupation with the final grade. We would probably have left the instructor's office with a very low opinion of the course, the instructor, and maybe even the school. Only if there were no alternative would we ever have considered taking another of this instructor's courses, and in that unhappy event, we would certainly not have been inclined to work as hard.

Improbable situation? Probably so, for the academic setting in which it was cast: colleges tend toward the compulsive in matters of grading and keeping students informed of their progress. In fact, behavior such as that depicted would be considered irresponsible in many schools—even grounds for disciplinary action against the instructor. By contrast, it is commonplace in work organizations. Employees can wait months or even years for some indication of how well they are doing, and when they are finally informed, the feedback is often vague, ambiguous, haphazard, subjective, and disappointing. Managers often emphasize negatives (where employees can improve) rather than positives (what they have done particularly well) in the misguided belief that only criticism can contribute to future performance. Emphasizing negatives fails to recognize the role of the listener in the communication episode. If one is not prepared to receive it in the right spirit, an instructor's (supervisor's) "constructive criticism" either fails to register or arouses negative feelings and counterproductive reactions.

Appraisal Communication Affects Morale and Productivity

As we shall see, the problem in evaluations of work performance generally reduces to a matter of poor communication, and the effect on the individual employee is much the same as you just experienced in the illustration. Extrapolated to an entire workforce, the consequences usually include low morale, high turnover, poor motivation, and a depressed level of overall competence. Done well, on the other hand, the evaluation process can actually improve workforce effectiveness through its impact on all these human reactions.

Performance evaluation includes both formal and informal oral and written communication.

The whole process of grading performance and providing feedback is referred to in the context of organizational management circles as *performance appraisal*. It can take a variety of forms ranging from informal, day-to-day coaching to elaborate, formal systems replete with rating scales and thick procedures manuals. Communication can be involved on several levels: ongoing verbal interactions between appraisee (usually the subordinate) and appraisor (usually the supervisor), written descriptions and explanations of the policies and procedures that are supposed to be followed in appraisals, formal appraisal interviews for the explicit purpose of reviewing the subordinate's performance, written materials for analyzing performance and documenting the session (often the focal point of the appraisal interview session), and general sessions during which managers discuss the individuals under their collective supervision (often comparatively). Distortion or failure of communication at any of these points can jeopardize the entire process.

The Context for Appraisal Communication

Of course, communication episodes do not occur in a vacuum. For appraisal in any form to have positive rather than negative consequences requires a context that is conducive to good communication. If employees do not trust management's motives or if they see the organization's reward-punishment system as basically unfair, for example, they will be predisposed to reject appraisal information out of hand regardless of how accurate it may be. Or if they perceive supervisors to be biased, it matters little what they have to say or how good the evidence is to back it up. (Would you not have been inclined to attribute your D to the instructor's bias rather than your infrequent and possibly flawed class comments?) Too, it goes without saying that some individuals are more receptive than others to constructive criticism, and further, that some combinations of individuals interact more comfortably with one another than do others. In short, individual and organizational personalities, coupled with the history of previous communications, color each communication episode—particularly when the message is as personal and consequential as the one involved in performance appraisal.

Most evaluation approaches can be made to work if they are adapted to the context and if communication is handled properly.

The remainder of this chapter focuses on the components of the appraisal process and the communication problems inherent in each. Techniques for addressing these problems are examined; however, the reader should recognize that formal procedures are mere tools. Their effectiveness depends on how wisely and conscientiously the manager implements them. And that, in turn, requires an understanding of how the technique is supposed to work and under what circumstances. One of the principal shortcomings of appraisal practices in today's organizations is over-reliance on *technique:* the belief that once one has the right rating form and procedures manual, all problems will evaporate. The truth is quite the reverse: if one understands the basic principles (and potential pitfalls) that underlie appraisal, almost any technique can be made to work. Therefore the emphasis in this chapter is on *understanding* rather than *technique.*

❏ HOW PERFORMANCE APPRAISAL AFFECTS A COMPANY'S SUCCESS

Objectives of Performance Appraisal

Performance appraisal may have multiple purposes: evaluation, development, or program analysis.

One of the chief difficulties in making appraisal a positive rather than a negative force in an organization lies in the fact that it serves multiple purposes. It is an *evaluation* scheme that figures into such important personnel decisions as salary administration (for example, merit pay increases), promotion, and termination; a *developmental* tool that provides individuals with the feedback they need to learn and improve their performance; and a *program evaluation* technique that enables the organization to gauge how well its personnel management systems (for example, selection, training, recruitment) are working.

Each of these objectives calls for a somewhat different kind of appraisal information used in a somewhat different way. Evaluation, for example, requires a summary index reflecting performance over a period of time (your grade in the course), whereas development requires explicit process information showing what you did to earn that grade (the professor in the opening vignette failed to provide this information until it was too late to help the student). As illustrated in this opening example, it is very difficult to accomplish both of these goals in the same appraisal episode: Preoccupation with the critically significant grading information interferes with assimilation of the "constructive criticism" information.

A related difficulty in successfully implementing an appraisal technique is that, intentionally or not, it will invariably serve two additional purposes: attitude and motivation control. People at work want to know how well they are performing (or how "important others" perceive them as performing), just as you did in your hypothetical course. And how well this information is communicated affects both how they feel about the work situation, and how strongly inclined they are to exert future effort on the organization's behalf. Recall your feelings and inclinations toward doing additional work under that instructor and you can easily appreciate this point. The manager who limits her appraisal activities to the annual "performance review"—the typical situation in work organizations—is likely to engender exactly the same reactions in her subordinates, particularly if the "final grade" is less than expected. Since it is typical for people to judge their own performance more favorably than others see it, the process is biased toward achieving negative results so long as appraisal is limited to a periodic (annual, biannual, semiannual) review.

How Outcome Feedback and Process Feedback Affect Employee Development

Outcome feedback grades performance; *process feedback* suggests how to improve.

Appraisal information generally falls into one of two categories: *end results* such as grades or accomplishments, and *processes* by which the results were obtained (for example, constructive criticism, behavioral analysis). The former, which tends to be more value-laden, provides an individual with *outcome feedback*, whereas the latter (*process feedback*) focuses on what one might do to improve. In the absence of process feedback, the person must draw his or her own conclusions on how any outcome was achieved, and those inferences can be extremely inaccurate. For example, we tend to take credit for favorable results and to blame others for unfavorable ones (hence your perception of the D as the result of bias rather than poor performance).

As we have just seen, it is important to evaluate performance in order to construct equitable reward systems and realistic expectations. But outcome feedback alone does little if anything to promote learning, development, or improvement. "Practice makes perfect" applies only if process feedback is provided; with outcome feedback alone the subordinate may improve very little, or worse, develop all the wrong habits. Bad habits, of course, affect future performance directly and indirectly through motivation and attitudes.

The basic message is that for performance appraisal to be most useful it should impart both outcome and process information. However, this is not easy to accomplish because outcome feedback tends to interfere with the perception of process feedback (i.e., the "final grade" tends to overshadow the "constructive criticism"). As we shall see later, one approach to resolving this conflict is to present the different kinds of feedback in widely separated review sessions.[1]

☐ THE INFLUENCE OF THE COMMUNICATION CONTEXT

Once purpose is determined, context becomes important.

One important consideration in deciding how to conduct performance appraisal, then, is *purpose*. Different strategies and emphases may be called for, depending on what we hope to accomplish through appraisal. Once that determination is made, a whole host of other factors becomes important. These factors comprise the context within which appraisal is carried out. To a large extent, context factors determine how well a particular technique or approach will work for the intended purpose. In some cases these factors limit the effectiveness of appraisal for any purpose. If, for example, a general atmosphere of distrust exists within an organization, people are unlikely to respond well to feedback no matter how accurate it is or what it is used for. While it is not possible in a part of one chapter to do justice to the full array of contextual variables, we shall try to illustrate representative kinds of factors that the manager should consider.

External Environment: Limits on the Choice of Appraisal Systems

State and federal regulations prohibit discrimination and affect the ways performance may be evaluated.

Prior to the Civil Rights Act of 1964, organizations were free to pursue virtually whatever policies they wished in matters of personnel management. They could hire, pay, promote, fire, or discipline people as they saw fit, subject only to constraints imposed by the labor market and labor organizations. Economic self-interest and social custom, which often included blatant race, sex, and age discrimination, were the principal considerations.

Today state and federal regulations prohibit discrimination. Moreover, employers are required to maintain records and submit periodic statistical reports detailing how their personnel practices are conforming to the "fair employment practices" laws. Grounds for seeking legal redress of inequitable treatment have generally expanded. For example, there is a current trend within U.S. organizations to increase efficiency and reduce labor costs in order to meet foreign price competition in world markets. This has commonly meant large-scale "reductions in force" (RIFs). Often the most expendable and costly employees are the older ones. However, if the organization's RIF policy shows "adverse impact" against older employees (a protected group), it may be called upon to justify the policy in court. An effective line of defense is afforded by performance appraisal. If it can be shown that the basis for layoffs is the relative contribution of the employee rather than age, chances for a favorable ruling are good even if the net effect is biased against older employees. A comprehensive, equitable appraisal system that tracks performance systematically over the years is strong evidence of an individual's contribution or lack thereof.

External factors such as legal, economic, and social pressures, therefore, argue against completely informal, verbal, undocumented, unsystematic appraisal. Furthermore, these considerations also favor appraisal products of a quantitative, objective nature. Dollar sales volume, days absent, or units produced are more easily defended than, say, an overall quality rating by one supervisor.

As we shall see later, however, informal, verbal, subjective techniques also have their place despite their weaknesses in providing legal evidence. It is through these less-structured communications that a manager conveys feelings, suggestions, impressions, and a host of subtle messages that are vital to the establishment of a good working relationship. By analogy, prenuptial agreements may be extremely useful in resolving subsequent marital disputes, but few marriages would survive without additional forms of communication!

Internal Environment: Structure and Culture

Organizations, like people, have personalities. These "organizational cultures" or "climates" as they are called, are pervasive, multifaceted characteristics that distinguish one organization from another and persist despite complete turnover of personnel, facilities, management, and other tangible features. In the aggregate, they define how the organization sees itself and to a great extent, how it is seen by others. Prominent among these distinguishing characteristics (or climate factors) are basic values, predominant managerial style, trustworthiness, openness, progressiveness, and similar traits. Like human personality, organizational climate/culture has been the subject of much research from which have evolved a variety of measurement instruments.[2]

While arguments persist on exactly how it should be defined and measured, everyone agrees that climate has an important bearing on everything else an organization does. For example, a large, conservative, bureaucratic firm operating in a fairly stable external environment (for example, a utility), would probably require a highly structured, formalized appraisal process. Managers would be encouraged to follow the letter of the procedures manual no matter where or whom they were supervising. The prescribed technique would likely have been adopted after careful study by the legal and personnel departments and only after a long list of approvals from line management. By contrast, a young, progressive organization that relies heavily on innovation for success in a rapidly changing environment (for example, a small computer software firm) might opt for a more flexible, informal, personal approach—one designed to promote individual growth and independent thinking.

Performance appraisal approaches must fit the culture of the organization.

Managers who fail to consider climate when implementing an appraisal technique are almost always doomed to failure regardless of the appraisal's intended purpose. For example, in an organization where trust is low, a system designed to improve employee motivation by clarifying expectations and equity perceptions would have little chance of doing so. People simply would not believe in the system. Where trust is high, almost any technique could be used effectively provided the manager understood how to use it and was conscientious.

One particularly noteworthy facet of the internal environment involves perceived values. Pervasive beliefs about what the organization's real priorities are, and hence what kind of behavior will be rewarded or punished, tend to shape everyone's performance. All too common is the belief that, despite official pronouncements to the contrary, the organization doesn't consider appraisal very important. What you really are expected to do is produce, not waste a lot of time "hand-holding" subordinates.

Exactly this situation exists today in a large oil company with which I am acquainted. This organization spent literally millions of dollars developing an elaborate appraisal system and tying it to compensation (i.e., the appraisal grades were a factor in raises, promotions, and terminations). Managers were provided with detailed manuals, charts, and instructions on how to use the system. But in the final analysis, none of the expected benefits have materialized. An investigation revealed a very simple explanation: Managers give appraisal short shrift in the (correct) belief that it figures far less in how they are evaluated and rewarded than does production. They conduct appraisals if and when they can spare the time, and usually in the most perfunctory manner! If the company really values appraisal and employee development as it professes, it has failed to convey that message to its managers. It makes them accountable for production but not for personnel evaluation and development. Formal pronouncements and procedures are thus not enough to ensure effective appraisal; a supportive climate is necessary as well.

Relationships Affect Evaluation

The appraisal process is an integral part of an ongoing relationship between supervisor and subordinate that focuses on performance of some set of activities. Naturally, therefore, the rapport between the individuals has a lot to do with how a manager should conduct the appraisal.

Kinds of relationships among workers determine which appraisal techniques will seem socially appropriate.

If the relationship is close and comfortable, as might be expected in a research team or construction crew where the supervisor works alongside the others, a highly formalized, rigidly structured approach would probably be considered artificial and stilted by all concerned. Whatever formal evaluations and feedback sessions the company might require would be recognized by both parties as mere confirmation of a common understanding built on their day-to-day interaction. The supervisor would not be likely to wait until the annual review to let someone know he had just done a great job or was gumming up the works!

On the other hand, many working relationships are more distant; what is expected of the subordinate and what he or she actually does are not so immediately obvious. Here it is essential that systematic procedures be implemented to ensure that the critical information is exchanged. Without such formalities, the risk is great that misunderstandings, misperceptions, misplaced blame and other serious distortions will develop.

Naturally, a host of factors determines what sort of working relationships evolve. Individual personalities, management styles, task structures, organizational structures, reward systems, and organizational climates are a few of the more prominent variables. We shall not even try to explain what impact each of these would have on the appraisal process. The point is, to communicate effectively in the appraisal setting, one cannot rely exclusively on a set of prescribed techniques. As in all communication, one must be aware of one's own tendencies and limitations, sensitive to the needs and expectations of the other person, and cognizant of the circumstances under which the communication is taking place.

People Amplify Evaluations, Whether Good or Bad

The one unique feature of the appraisal setting is that whatever message is conveyed, the receiver can be expected to amplify it tremendously, because there is nothing of much greater importance to us human beings than what others think of us. It never pays to underestimate this impact nor to forget that people amplify unintended or distorted messages just as much as they do intended and accurate ones. And because its human impact is so profound, appraisal has important ethical and social ramifications that extend well beyond the utilitarian concerns of organizational performance and success. We should never lose sight of the fact that cavalier disregard for the needs, aspirations, feelings, and values of individuals has immense social costs. Contributing to the destruction of a human ego or a promising career is not something to be taken lightly; failing to contribute positively to the development of another human being for whom we have formal responsibility is equally deplorable. When, as managers, we are charged with the appraisal function, failure to exercise that responsibility conscientiously, either through acts of commission or omission, is ethically questionable as well as practically ill-advised.

☐ USING APPRAISALS ON THE JOB

It is time at last to come to grips with the issue of how one actually *does* performance appraisals. What are the major components of a typical appraisal system, how does communication figure into each, and what techniques are there for implementing them effectively?

As I mentioned earlier, the total system may include a variety of formal and informal, written and verbal, objective and subjective elements, all concerned with evaluating performance and providing feedback or guidance. Principal components consist of *day-to-day interactions*, *evaluation procedures*, *formal appraisal sessions*, *written evaluations*, and overall *appraisal policy*. We shall now examine each in some depth.

A performance appraisal system may include day-to-day interaction, evaluation procedures, appraisal sessions, written evaluations, and policies.

Appraisals in Day-to-Day Interactions

Much of the information on which a manager bases his or her evaluation of subordinates is gleaned from day-to-day observation of what they do and say. The manager forms impressions of how reliable, conscientious, productive, ambitious, cooperative, and personable subordinates are just as we all do: through cumulative experience with their work habits, the quality and quantity of what they produce, the attitudes they express, the judgment they show, the ease with which they interact with their peers, and so on.

Assuming that the manager interacted with each subordinate on a regular basis over an extended period of time, we would expect his or her impressions to be reasonably accurate and the resulting appraisal reasonably fair. Similarly, we would expect the subordinate to get both process and outcome feedback on a more or less continuous basis. The manager would certainly be expected to point out mistakes and acknowledge appropriate (or especially meritorious) behavior as it occurred. Subordinates would thus have a good idea where they stand at all times.

Work Settings Affect the Opportunity for Appraisal

Unfortunately, we cannot count on any of this happening naturally. It can, in certain favorable situations; notably where there is good rapport between manager and subordinates, where the organizational climate is characterized by openness and trust, where employee development is an important objective of both organization and manager, and where the manager is close enough to the subordinates to see a truly representative sample of their behavior first-hand. A good example of such a situation would be a well-functioning research team in which manager and subordinates are all technical professionals who work closely together on joint projects. Communication tends to flow easily among all participants, since the "psychological distance" between organizational levels is mitigated by their "technical closeness," and there is a strong sense of group purpose.

Few companies are organized to permit easy, accurate, day-to-day feedback on performance.

Such situations are relatively rare in modern work organizations. More common are circumstances that present any of a host of barriers to communication. Consider the typical large, bureaucratic corporation in which direct contact between manager and subordinate is fairly limited; heavy emphasis is placed on formal procedures; both employee and manager are more concerned about their own careers than about vague, distant corporate goals; and the manager's impressions are vital to the subordinate's success. Informal interaction will provide a limited and probably distorted picture of the subordinate's behavior; feedback will likewise be minimal and of dubious quality. In this setting, formal mechanisms for observing and evaluating behavior, and for providing feedback, are a must.

Biases are most problematic when we fail to recognize them and the situation provides no structure or tools to help us combat them. Informal day-to-day interactions, particularly in the context of a typical bureaucracy, almost guarantee a high rate of inaccurate evaluations and distorted communications.

Biases tend to distort feedback and prevent accurate communication.

Furthermore, because of the social aspects of the situation, neither manager nor subordinate relishes communicating negative information. If the interpersonal relationship is reasonably good, why jeopardize it by telling people what they don't want to hear? Indeed, a good interpersonal relationship encourages the often false belief that each party *knows* what the other is thinking. Why make a point of telling someone what they already know? The result is that in-

BUSINESS COMMUNICATION TODAY

AFFECT YOUR EVALUATIONS OF OTHERS

Some well-established human tendencies interfere with one or another aspect of the appraisal process. There are biases in even the most conscientious, well-intentioned evaluator that tend to distort both the information gathered and conclusions drawn. A few of the more prominent are:

Availability bias—a tendency to judge a person's overall performance on the basis of a few easily recalled incidents that may not be at all representative.

Theory preservation bias—a tendency to seek evidence confirming our initial opinion of a person and to reject contrary evidence.

Halo bias—a tendency to over- or undervalue all aspects of a person's performance based on our positive or negative impression of one aspect (for

example, he's reliable, so we judge him high in creativity and productivity as well).

Stereotyping—a tendency to judge all people of a particular class (for example, women, Asians, older people, etc.) based on a consistent belief pattern that we hold about those classes.

Attribution biases—a tendency to attribute the causes of undesired outcomes to the subordinate and desired outcomes to our astute management or the subordinate's good fortune.

Rating scale biases—a tendency to judge everyone too favorably, unfavorably, or as average.

Comparative biases—a tendency to judge one person too favorably or too unfavorably based on comparison with an atypically good or poor performer.

formal day-to-day interactions often fail to address performance issues at all, or worse, convey distorted messages. For example, a subordinate reads the absence of criticism and the cordial relationship with the manager as an indication that all is well, only to learn, when an expected raise fails to materialize, that he was considered a below-average performer all along!

❑ EVALUATION TECHNIQUES

Keep systematic notes on employee performance to avoid biases.

Under optimal conditions, then, informal day-to-day interactions can yield accurate evaluations and effective feedback, but such conditions rarely exist. Thus, if this general approach is to be used effectively, it must be supplemented with techniques designed to compensate for its communication deficiencies. One such technique is to require managers to keep a diary or other systematic, written record of noteworthy (good and bad) instances of subordinates' behavior. This reduces the influence of nonrepresentative sampling, faulty memory, and judgment biases on managers' impressions and evaluations. It also serves to stimulate feedback: Managers can hardly ignore instances that they themselves have identified and documented as important—especially if they are repeated.

Other techniques are aimed primarily at the human frailties that bias perception and hamper feedback communication. All involve systematic training to overcome one or another of these counterproductive tendencies. Programs have been developed, for example, to improve one's coaching techniques, sensitivity to others and to the processes of social interaction, listening skills, and judgment accuracy (through so-called *debiasing techniques*). Common to all such programs is a heavy reliance on experiential exercises and process feedback. The trainee is exposed to illustrative situations, encouraged to analyze his or her own experiences and behaviors, provided feedback, and allowed to practice more appropriate behaviors. The hoped-for results are a deeper understanding of the processes involved and a more appropriate set of skills.

Active Listening

Listening skills are critical to accumulating accurate information and communicating about performance.

While space does not permit a full account of these techniques (most of which must be experienced to be appreciated, anyway), one illustration may prove useful: *active listening* techniques. As was established in Chapter 9, we humans are much better at talking than listening. From infancy on, it is our expression of what we feel, want, know, or believe that gets attention; not our ability to perceive accurately what others feel, want, know, or believe. Thus we develop some skill in sending messages, but very little in receiving them. Naturally, all senders and no receivers makes for a rather poor exchange, whether football or information is the medium of interest.

To deal with this problem requires conscious attention to—and development of—our neglected listening skills. The key principle is making listening an active rather than a passive process. This is accomplished by practicing rules such as:

- suppressing the urge to form a response while the sender is talking,
- recoding what the sender is saying into terms that are meaningful to us,
- recognizing our perceptual biases in the recoding process, and attempting to discount them,
- resisting the temptation to anticipate what the sender is sending before it is actually sent,
- obtaining verification (feedback) from the sender that the message received is the message sent (or, if it isn't, making the necessary corrections).

If you think these principles are too obvious to mention, try applying them to one of your own conversations sometime. You may be surprised at how passive your listening habits really are.

Evaluation Procedures

Whether or not informal interactions play a major role in the evaluation of performance, it is becoming increasingly common for organizations to require some kind of formal summary on a periodic (usually annual) basis. As noted earlier, these formal evaluations often coincide with annual personnel decisions, and constitute a justification for merit salary increases, promotions, and the like. They also become a part of the employee's permanent record.

Since this book is concerned primarily with communication rather than personnel management, we shall not discuss in any depth the multitude of structured techniques available for carrying out the formal evaluation. Typically they involve a rating, ranking, or descriptive procedure through which the supervisor summarizes a number of specified aspects of a subordinate's performance using a standard form. The most common is some type of graphic rating scale, as illustrated in Figure 23-1.

Whatever the format, the most critical feature distinguishing the various procedures is the extent to which they focus on behavior (actual or expected) as opposed to more abstract traits or tendencies. The more explicitly behavioral the orientation, the less opportunity there is for subjective biases to distort the evaluation. Conversely, the more trait-oriented the evaluation is, the more susceptible it becomes to the appraiser's interpretation. Figure 23-1, for example, is clearly aimed at traits (reliability, productivity, etc.). Were the points on the reliability scale expressed in terms such as "days unexcused absence," "days late,"

> Approaches that emphasize *traits* (what people are) invite greater subjectivity than approaches that emphasize *behavior* (what people do).

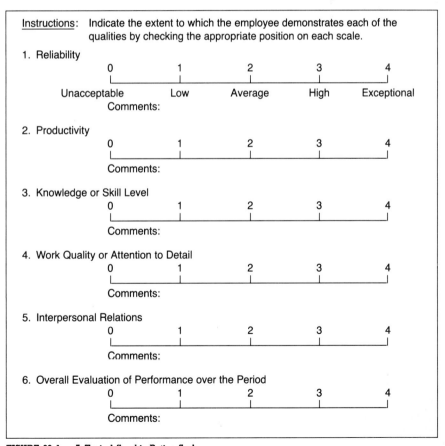

FIGURE 23-1.   A Typical Graphic Rating Scale

etc., and those on the productivity in "units produced," we would have a more behavioral procedure.

One other point worth noting is that structured summaries may vary considerably in the specificity and coverage of the performance described. One reason for having a number of fairly specific scales is to call the rater's attention to the multitude of important performance aspects (thus combating the "halo" bias). If some important aspect of a particular job were omitted from the list, the result would obviously be an unfair appraisal. Increasing the specificity, however, means that different jobs will be judged using different scales, and that, too, can appear unfair. Therefore, most systems reach some compromise between comprehensiveness and specificity. Often the compromise is a limited number of scales (as in Figure 23-1), with specific behavioral illustrations attached to the points on each one (as suggested above), known as the Behaviorally Anchored Rating Scale (BARS) technique (illustrated in Figure 23-2).

What you evaluate depends on why you are evaluating in the first place.

Obviously different purposes call for different emphases in an appraisal instrument (form). If, for example, the main objective is providing a uniform basis for merit pay increases, a comprehensive form that can apply to a wide range of positions is desirable. If developing personnel is the goal, uniformity is less important than specificity: You want to give feedback in enough detail and explicitness to enable the recipient to improve. It is difficult to do both effectively in the same instrument for the logical and psychological reasons discussed earlier. Increasingly, therefore, organizations are opting for multiple instruments: a structured, uniform "report card" such as Figure 23-1, plus one or more open-ended forms like that shown in Figure 23-3 on which the appraiser can provide narrative feedback tailored to the individual and his or her position. The separation can be extended beyond the forms themselves to the context in which the information is presented. As mentioned earlier, the technique of splitting the appraisal into two sessions would be a case in point: Development is discussed in one session using the customized form; personnel action is dealt with in another using the generic form.

In those work settings characterized by effective day-to-day interactions, feedback can be delivered in the informal mode as the behavior happens, leaving only the "report card" function for the formal evaluation. However, the key word here is "effective." As we saw in the last section and in our opening vignette, where day-to-day interaction is ineffective in conveying clear feedback messages, misunderstandings develop. These can escalate into real disasters when the "report card" is finally delivered. It is generally safer to provide some formal feedback mechanism, if only to verify the day-to-day understandings.

Formal Appraisal Sessions

Scenarios for appraisal interviews vary from company to company and department to department.

The principal setting for formally providing feedback is the appraisal interview. As in the opening illustration, it usually consists of a scheduled meeting between subordinate and supervisor called for the express purpose of reviewing the subordinate's work over the period just ending (for example, the previous year). Depending on the organization's overall appraisal policy (discussed later) and the

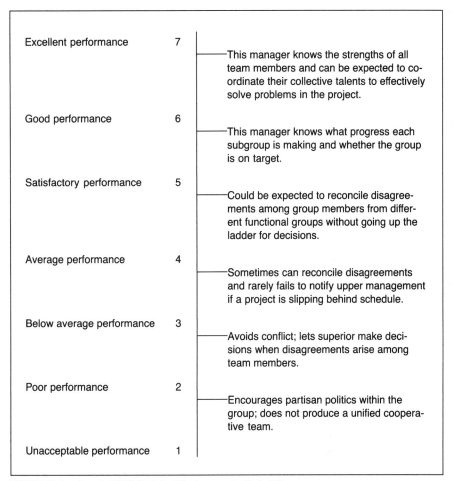

Excellent performance   7

This manager knows the strengths of all team members and can be expected to co-ordinate their collective talents to effectively solve problems in the project.

Good performance   6

This manager knows what progress each subgroup is making and whether the group is on target.

Satisfactory performance   5

Could be expected to reconcile disagree-ments among group members from differ-ent functional groups without going up the ladder for decisions.

Average performance   4

Sometimes can reconcile disagreements and rarely fails to notify upper management if a project is slipping behind schedule.

Below average performance   3

Avoids conflict; lets superior make deci-sions when disagreements arise among team members.

Poor performance   2

Encourages partisan politics within the group; does not produce a unified coopera-tive team.

Unacceptable performance   1

FIGURE 23-2.   Sample BARS Scale for Effectiveness of a Project Manager

manager's preferred style, the session may be more or less structured, focus more on the "report card" or development function, involve more or less active participation by the subordinate, and occur before or after the evaluation is final. Usually the meeting is documented by some written report, often simply the appraisal form signed by the participants.

Conducting the Interview

There is no universally effective approach for communicating in the appraisal interview any more than there is in any other context. As we have noted re-peatedly, success depends as much on the conscientiousness of the manager and the atmosphere of trust or distrust that exists as it does on the formalities. Nevertheless, several different feedback approaches have been identified, and research has provided some general guidance on how best to conduct appraisal interviews.

I. STRENGTHS—What strengths contributed to the employee's performance in the last year?

II. DEVELOPMENT NEEDS—What development needs should be addressed in order to enhance next year's performance?

III. DEVELOPMENT ACTIVITIES—Describe those activities to be undertaken to address development needs and enhance performance.

IV. RESULTS ON LAST YEAR'S DEVELOPMENT PLAN—What results were achieved on last year's development plan?

V. EMPLOYEE COMMENTS (Optional)

Career Discussion desired? _____ (check if yes)

FIGURE 23-3. *Personal Development—Present Position*

From the Monsanto Company. Copyright by the Monsanto Company. Reprinted by permission.

Beer, a researcher in organizational psychology, distinguishes four main ways to administer feedback: the tell and sell, tell and listen, problem-solving, and mixed-model approaches.[3] As the labels imply, they differ mainly in the extent to which the subordinate participates in the process.

- *Tell and sell* is a one-way, directive approach in which the manager tries to convince the subordinate to accept the former's conclusions.
- *Tell and listen* permits a response to the manager's message that may be incorporated, at his or her discretion, in the final judgment.
- *Problem solving* involves true discussion or two-way communication led by the manager, and an end result that reflects the exchange.
- The *mixed-model* approach is also a two-way, participative process, but one in which the subordinate leads the initial discussion, the manager follows, and then both work toward a joint conclusion.

Which approach should be followed, of course, depends on a host of personal and organizational considerations, including all those encountered so far in this chapter. For example, a manager whose preferred style is directive and who operates in a traditional bureaucratic organization would probably be better off using one of the "tell" options than trying to act participative. If she were convinced that her subordinate had not spent enough time contacting prospective new clients, she might say, "I've checked the log book and you're averaging only ten cold calls a week; that's simply not enough. Most of the other salespersons are averaging twenty." The subordinate would expect this sort of *tell and sell approach* and would be likely to respond appropriately to it even if he didn't particularly like it or agree with the conclusions. In fact, he would probably be highly skeptical of an uncharacteristic "participative" session in which she began by asking, "What's your view on the value of 'cold calls' compared to servicing our regular clients?" He'd think, "What does she have in mind, and why is she beating around the bush?" He would certainly not believe that she really cared what his view was!

Interview scenarios: tell and sell, tell and listen, problem solving, and mixed-model.

On the other hand, where the setting and the manager's style permit, the more participative *problem-solving* and *mixed-model* approaches clearly have more potential for motivating subordinates, improving their morale, and imparting process feedback. By involving the subordinate actively and playing down the dominance relationship, the discussion of weaknesses is more likely to be received in the right spirit than it is with the "tell" options. For example, were the above sales manager in the habit of soliciting subordinates' opinions and acting on them, asking his view on cold versus repeat calls would probably have produced a more thoughtful response, real discussion, and a shared conclusion that some number of cold calls (say, fifteen) was about right in this case. The subordinate would admit his deficiency and set about rectifying it. Similarly, positive feedback ("stroking," in the vernacular) is less likely to be masked by perceived criticism in the participative approach. Continuing the example, a comment by the manager that she is "really impressed by the way you've handled our most valued clients" would have given the subordinate a motivational boost undiminished by the mutual recognition that his new contact activity was a bit under par.

The essential point is that whatever approach you or your firm has adopted, you should carry it out in a manner that maximizes its intended purpose. If you are "telling and selling," you must be confident that you have done everything possible to maximize the fairness and accuracy of the message and to understand the perspective and probable reaction of the receiver. If you are "problem solving," you must enter into it with a sincere openness to the views of the subordinate and a conscious effort to avoid destructive blame-setting and dominance behaviors. You must also ensure that whatever conclusions are jointly achieved are mutually understood. Many a conference has concluded with both parties feeling good about the outcome, only to discover later that each had a somewhat different impression of what had transpired. There is no substitute for some form of written documentation to minimize such miscommunications.

Recently a large manufacturing company, concerned about the ineffectiveness of its appraisal interviews, conducted research to determine possible causes. Following each session, manager and subordinate were required independently to fill out an identical form indicating what specific topics were discussed and what messages were conveyed on each. Not only was there very low agreement on the precise message content, the two parties often identified entirely different lists of topics! Managers frequently reported emphasizing positive (or negative) messages that were completely omitted from the employee's list, or worse, were interpreted in exactly the opposite way! In many instances an evaluation intended to be laudatory and to suggest routes to even further growth was reported by the recipient as unfair criticism! Results from this study were subsequently used as the basis for an appraisal training program and a revised system in which a written and signed summary, including points of disagreement, was required at the conclusion of each session.

Recognizing the diversity of approaches and factors that contribute to the success of each, one can nonetheless specify a few general guidelines for conducting appraisal interviews. A recent summary, which is reproduced in Figure 23-4, therefore seems to be an appropriate conclusion for this section. To appreciate the significance of these suggestions, you need only apply them to the hypothetical interview in the opening illustration. How many would the instructor have satisfied? How much better would you have felt about it had he followed them more completely?

Written Performance Evaluations

The written appraisal as well as the oral appraisal has long-term consequences. To be legally defensible, a written appraisal must reflect

- the purpose of the appraisal
- the criteria explicit in the evaluation procedure
- the conclusions or evaluation of the performance during the period
- the evidence on which the conclusions are based
- the process feedback offered to improve performance in the future.

The evaluation must be objective, expressed in neutral terms, and supported with descriptive evidence.

1. Give the performance appraisal interview the symbolic attention it deserves. Conduct the interview in an official location (not during a coffee break or on the way to a client's office). Announce the meeting in writing well in advance, and encourage the employee to prepare. If you follow a specific form in the interview, make sure the employee has a copy so that he or she can review daily schedules and files and have important information available for discussion. Ask your secretary to hold your calls while you and the employee talk.

2. Make the scenario clear. For first performance evaluations, it is especially important to let the employee know in advance how long the interview will last and what topics will be covered.

3. Begin by listening. Ask open-ended questions that begin with "how" and "what." "How have things changed in your job since we talked last?" "What was your most satisfying project the past six months?" "What goals have you accomplished that we discussed last time?" Asked early in the interview, such questions will encourage the employee to participate throughout the interview.

   The interview is an opportunity for you to gather additional information that will enable you to evaluate the other information you already have accumulated. Restating what you have heard or asking questions that invite elaboration on an earlier comment will enable you to test the accuracy of your perceptions. For example:

   > Employee: Having the government people in my hair every month is really difficult.
   > Manager: Tell me about that. What kinds of problems do they create?

4. Be specific about the behaviors and traits you discuss. Avoid sweeping statements that include the words "always" or "never": "You're never on time to meetings." "You always seem about a week behind in your work." If you bring up actions without attributing motivations, you will have a chance to hear the employee's explanation and the causes for his or her work performance can be discussed mutually.

   Furthermore, whenever you must discuss negative behaviors, being specific enables the employee to see that you are dissatisfied with the action, not with the person. Someone who feels personally attacked will become defensive, but if you discuss the behavior as an action, not as a trait of character, both of you can discuss how that behavior can be changed.

5. Because employees tend to magnify whatever you say about them, you must make sure your body language and your spoken messages are consistent. If you frown or cross your arms across your chest while speaking praise for work well done, your nonverbal communication may sabotage your message. Videotaping a practice interview can help you know how you tend to behave.

FIGURE 23-4. **Ten Tips for Productive Performance Evaluation Interviews**

6. Although in some scenarios you will have to use a "tell-and-sell" strategy, most employees appreciate being able to suggest performance goals for themselves. You can always modify these goals during the interview. The opportunity to suggest goals helps the employee feel more in control and more committed to the course of action.

7. Avoid structuring the interview so that every word of praise is undermined by a word of criticism. Employees familiar with such an approach cringe during praise, waiting for the sentence that begins, "but. . . ."

8. Make sure that the purposes of the interview are emphasized during your conversation. If the purpose is employee development, be sure to review past improvements, present competence, and prospects for future growth. If the interview is used for evaluation of past achievements, make the goals, the criteria, and the evidence used clear. If the interview is also to be used as the basis for promotion, treat that topic separately. If the appraisal is to determine the success of training programs and other programs, let the employee comment on potential improvements to the programs.

9. Tie evaluative comments to process feedback that you have made during the period, so that the employee will see the link between the two kinds of appraisal information. Identifying this link will make you more aware of the two types of feedback you deliver as a manager, also.

10. Follow the appraisal interview with a copy of your written evaluation, either for the employee's comments and signature or for the employee's own file. A short meeting to discuss the written evaluation will make it much easier to identify and correct any misunderstandings about the content of your discussion.

FIGURE 23-4   (continued)

The Purpose of the Appraisal   The purpose of the appraisal powerfully governs the contents of the appraisal. As explained earlier, an evaluation system may be used as an evaluation scheme to determine promotions and other personnel decisions; it may be used as a developmental tool; and it may be used to evaluate the program of selection, training, and recruitment. Furthermore, the system used to achieve that purpose may emphasize either traits or behavior. These elements determine a great deal of what you will be expected to write.

For example, if an architectural firm's evaluation scheme emphasized outcomes and traits, then your report for one of your designers would connect outcomes and traits with evidence, as in the following excerpt.

outcomes	Henley has <u>met all of the project deadlines during</u> the past six months, and
traits: reliable,	<u>has beaten two of them.</u> His <u>reliability</u> and <u>productivity</u> have been high.
productive outcome	Furthermore, we have had <u>no complaints from clients</u> on any of the designs

<table>
<tr><td>trait</td><td rowspan="2"></td></tr>
</table>

	he produced, indicating a <u>high level of attention to detail.</u> He is still not fully
trait	familiar with the new graphics program now installed on the VAX, <u>so his skill</u>
outcome	<u>level is not quite as high as one would expect</u> for a candidate for a senior
	designer's position. However, the large number of projects he was assigned
trait	left little if any time for developing new skills. Henley <u>is amiable</u>, but his work
	does not require much interaction with others. His present job does not test
unknown trait	his <u>interpersonal orientation</u>. His overall evaluation during the period is
evaluation	therefore <u>a high "3."</u>

Had Henley been working in an organization that was interested in personal development and that emphasized behavior, his performance might have been described in this way:

	During the last six months Henley's strengths have been his <u>project</u>
existing proficiency	<u>completion and efficiency,</u> as well as his established <u>design skills.</u> He has
behavioral evidence	turned out <u>four major projects on deadline and two more</u> well <u>before</u>
change in work quality;	<u>deadline.</u> He <u>has become our most consistently reliable designer for</u>
new proficiency	<u>interiors.</u> He has an <u>excellent command of materials</u> and <u>can select</u>
behavioral evidence	<u>appropriate wall, floor, and window treatments</u> as rapidly and <u>successfully as</u>
comparative measure	<u>anyone we have employed.</u> His <u>experience in dealing with customers from</u>
of behavior proficiency	<u>the Middle East</u> has shown up in his "on target" choices, so that <u>we seldom</u>
results of experience	<u>have any alterations to make</u> in the plans.
	Henley needs more <u>experience in managing projects</u> now that he has
new target for development	become more familiar with our clients from those countries. I suggest that we
new opportunity for	<u>put him in charge of the next interiors project</u> we have in that area and <u>team</u>
development	<u>him with Ericson</u>, who is exceptionally good in client relations. Ericson can
	be a mentor for Henley.
evidence of past growth	As a <u>result of the courses on project planning and quality control</u> that
evidence of present	Henley attended last year, <u>his attention to detail and his productivity have</u>
development	<u>improved substantially.</u> He is <u>becoming more sensitive to client needs</u> and,
identified need for	with <u>a little help in interpersonal skills</u>, I think he can be promoted to a senior
development	design manager's position soon. Henley also <u>should be given a week to</u>
needed opportunity for	<u>work on the new graphics program</u> on the VAX. His schedule has been too
new development	full to allow any time for work on that program. He <u>accepts challenges</u>
evaluations of development	<u>readily and is eager to improve.</u> Henley is progressing nicely.

Whether you are working with a system that emphasizes traits or behavior, you must remember to choose words carefully so that the relationship between the trait or outcome and the evidence is clear. You must not attribute behavior or outcomes to causes that you are unqualified to diagnose. You must not attribute erratic behavior to drugs, alcohol, or mental illness. You must say that the person has not been reliable, and describe in neutral terms the ways this erratic behavior interrupted or complicated the work flow.

The Criteria Explicit in the Procedure   If the procedure calls for an evaluation of reliability, productivity, and such, your discussion should focus on these issues, although you may use the evaluation to bring other valuable qualities and potentials to the attention of management. Nonetheless, you should be careful about what new criteria you introduce, because if you are using different criteria to evaluate different employees, you may be guilty of discrimination.

You must be especially careful in describing types of behavior that might be evaluated by sexist, racist, or religious prejudice. You must not judge people by attributes that have nothing to do with their job performance. You must not evaluate an employee on personal attractiveness. You cannot describe a person's weight if there are no weight requirements for the job. You must constrain your prejudices. Just because a candidate is "well-connected" does not mean he or she is qualified for a position unless "connections" can be shown to be important for the job that must be done. Another employee may charge discrimination and unfair denial of promotion. If your description of the employee who did not get the promotion is equitably descriptive but the evaluation of the promoted employee is loaded with biased terms, your firm may lose the case.

Conclusions or Evaluation of the Performance during the Period   If your written evaluation does not make clear what your conclusions are, the employee, as well as other managers, may be misled by your discussion. If the purpose of the evaluation is development of the employee, it is especially important for the employee to be able to gain an accurate sense of his or her adequacy so that he or she can monitor progress.

The Evidence on Which the Conclusions Are Based   Describing the evidence on which conclusions are based grounds the employee's understanding of the conclusions on specific actions and provides a basis for legal defense of the firm's actions. Unless notes are kept in a systematic way, however, selective use of evidence may show bias or prejudice.

Process Feedback Offered to Improve Performance in the Future   A record of the advice given for future performance is essential for justifying future personnel decisions such as promotion, termination, or reassignment.

Written Evaluations Must Be Consistent with Other Documents and Records

Your performance evaluations and your recommendations to other employers must be consistent. If you terminate an employee on the basis of incompetence or poor performance, you had better not write a letter responding to the inquiry of a prospective employer stating he was a satisfactory employee. The former employee may come back and sue the company for termination without cause and use the recommendation letter to the other prospective employer as grounds. It is understandable to want to avoid saying bad things about anyone, but in this case, honesty or silence are the only acceptable policies. Many employers will only affirm that a person has worked for the firm during a specified period and describe the duties performed during that time.

Appraisal Systems and Organizational Policy

Formal appraisal systems are usually an integral part of an organization's overall policies for managing human resources. However they are actually implemented, which as we have seen can be a far cry from what the policymakers had in mind, such policies do have some bearing on the appraisal process. To illustrate this point, let us consider a few stereotypic examples.

Structural Policies of Traditional "Mechanistic" Bureaucracies

Giant organizations founded during the first few decades of this century tended to adopt a style of management that emphasized clear definition of work roles and their relationships (structure), heavy reliance on written procedures and rules, and most importantly, a centralized authority system that operated from the top down ("chain of command"). Despite some modernization, such organizations continue to stress formal written procedures, much documentation, and relatively "directive" supervision: an approach often referred to as "mechanistic" in the sense of being rigidly planned and inflexible.

In this context, appraisal procedures are generally spelled out in great detail using standard evaluation forms, mandated schedules and formats for appraisal sessions, supervisory review of appraisal results, and other controls. Consistent with the "chain-of-command" concept, supervisors rate subordinates and provide feedback in a tell-sell or at best a tell-listen fashion. Standardization is as complete as possible in design if not always in practice.

Participative Policies Characteristic of "Organic" Organizations

Many newer industries, together with a growing number of older ones, are adopting a different management concept. Prompted in part by a long-standing criticism of classical bureaucracy as overly "mechanistic" and in part by the dramatic success of the Japanese version of an alternative (the so-called "quality circles" concept), many organizations are involving their employees at all levels in functions traditionally reserved for management. Readers may have noticed, for example, TV ads for the Ford Motor Company that feature their "employee involvement program"—participation in decision making at the level of the shop floor in what was once the epitome of classical, mechanistic bureaucracies.

Participative management relies less heavily on formal rules, regulations, and authority systems, seeking instead to create an atmosphere of mutual trust and individual responsibility in pursuit of shared goals. This, of course, requires sharing of information. And standardization becomes less important than effective problem solving: The whole structure becomes more flexible, adaptive, or "organic." Naturally, participation is reflected in many aspects of the appraisal process. For example, the development objective takes precedence over the "report-card" function, less dependence is placed on highly structured forms and schedules, and feedback is more likely to be provided in a problem-solving or mixed-model fashion—often on a day-to-day, informal basis rather than during a formal appraisal interview.

A Synthesis of Policies: Management by Objectives (MBO)

How can an organization maintain some semblance of orderly structure and formal documentation while encouraging a participative philosophy? One strategy lies in a management system that is actually constructed around performance appraisal: MBO.

The essential idea is for participation to take place in the actual process of defining organizational goals and strategies. Manager and subordinate work together in developing a set of explicit objectives and action plans for the subordinate to pursue over specified time horizons (for example, six months, a year, five years). These goals and plans are written down, as illustrated in Figure 23-3, and used as a basis for subsequent appraisals. The appraisal session thus consists of a mutual review of progress toward the specified goals, discussion of any problems encountered, and consideration of possible changes—both in the plan and in the behavior of the subordinate. The result is an updated document, incorporating the agreed-upon revisions, which serves as the plan for the next period and the template for the next performance review.

Ideally, this process should be carried out for every subordinate-supervisor pair at every level in the organization. In this way, each supervisor is mindful of how the collective goals of his or her group fit into the larger objectives of the organization: It is spelled out in the planning document developed with the next-level supervisor. Part of the manager's responsibility is to ensure that the goals he or she negotiates with his or her subordinates are consistent with these next-higher-level goals.

Another intended feature of MBO is that the planning document will encourage more frequent communication between supervisors and subordinates (i.e., informal day-to-day interaction), thereby promoting greater accuracy and timeliness of information flow throughout the organization. Managers are supposed to monitor progress between formal review periods; subordinates are supposed to alert their managers to problems or necessary deviations from the plan as they occur.

Beyond these few guiding principles, MBO programs vary considerably in details of implementation. The approach can be adapted successfully to almost any kind of organization, provided it honors the spirit of mutual goal-setting, universal application, and explicitness in the written documentation. There have been many reported MBO failures, most of which can be traced to violations of one or another of these seemingly simple, yet fundamental requirements.[4]

A moment's reflection, however, reveals that the simplicity is an illusion. In actuality, meeting these conditions often requires what amounts to a complete overhaul in an organization's thought and behavior patterns. It is not an easy matter to get directive managers to accept the idea of mutually determined goals. They usually see it as an erosion of their authority, status, and cherished prerogatives, or as a sign of weakness. But unless they sincerely accept the philosophy, paying lip service to it can damage both their credibility and the effectiveness of the appraisal process. Neither is it easy to convince high-level managers and professionals that the process must apply to them as well as to other levels of the management hierarchy. But without their example, visible support, and contribution to the definition of overarching goals, the system is all but doomed.

Finally, defining appropriate goals and action plans and then committing them to writing in a clear, unambiguous form can be a difficult and time-consuming process. It generally requires explicit training and practice. Managers are often unwilling to devote the time and effort to what they perceive as unnecessary paperwork. But without adequate documentation, all the previously discussed problems inherent in informal face-to-face communication rear their ugly heads. Omissions, distortions, and misunderstandings can almost be guaranteed when appraisal time arrives. MBO can only produce the desired results to the extent that it clarifies expectations and minimizes manager-subordinate differences in the perception of both the appropriateness and nature of those expectations. That can only happen if the parties commit their understanding to writing, and if what is written is unambiguous.[5]

❑ REVISITING THE ILLUSTRATION

Imagine yourself back in your instructor's office for a replay of your appraisal session. How might the scenario have been altered to produce a more desirable outcome? Mindful of the considerations discussed, let's look at the scenario again.

Clarifying Objectives and Expectations

Presumably, the main purpose of college courses is development (learning); a secondary one is certification that development has occurred (i.e., a grade). Consistent with this priority, the instructor downplayed grading to the point of omitting it entirely throughout the course. In so doing, however, he neglected to consider the role of clear expectations and goals in motivation and attitudes, both of which can contribute to development. Had he communicated at the outset (via a written course syllabus) and on a day-to-day basis (verbally) exactly what aspects of performance he was attempting to cultivate and the relative importance he attached to each, the absence of grades would have been less detrimental. You would certainly have been aware that your written work was less critical than your in-class work, that you were expected to speak often, and that your own views were less important than your understanding of what he considered the "correct" views. You would have been far less surprised at the final outcome. Had he wanted to foster acceptance as well as understanding of course objectives, he might have succeeded with an adaptation of the MBO approach: contracting with each student for an explicit set of accomplishments.

Providing Process Feedback

Even had he failed to make his expectations explicit, development might have occurred had the instructor administered process feedback on a timely basis. While motivation and morale might still have suffered, your behavior would probably have come to approximate his expectations. Had he provided his "constructive criticism" verbally or in writing on each paper or comment—or even at frequent intervals—it would have been more salient to you and in all likelihood better received. By including it with the outcome feedback late in the course, it (and you) had no chance to improve.

Providing Outcome Feedback

If, in addition to day-to-day process feedback, the instructor had calculated and posted interim grades on a periodic basis, you might well have received a motivational boost. If nothing else, you would probably have been motivated to seek help when the results turned out to be less than you expected. And, of course, even if you had persisted in performing in inappropriate ways, you would have found the appraisal session less traumatic.

Planning the Appraisal Interview

Assuming that all else remained the same, could the instructor have handled the final review session better? Probably not. Regardless of how he presented the results or how helpful and considerate he tried to be, the damage had already been done. At this point, the listener (you), unable to do anything about past events, is attuned solely to one message: the final grade.

Had the process been explicit from the outset, your preoccupation with the result would have been attenuated somewhat. You might still have harbored serious doubts about equity had the grade been low, but the possibility of some constructive discussion with the instructor would not have been totally obliterated. Of course, a good grade—or one you considered equitable—would have turned the session into a real motivational opportunity.

The point is, course-end or year-end appraisals have limited potential in and of themselves to accomplish any useful communication purpose (although they may well serve other organizational purposes). Their effectiveness is conditional upon all the other elements of the appraisal system.

Managing the Communication Context

Similarly, the effectiveness of the system is conditional upon the context in which it occurs. Had explicit grading, structured courses, and other formalities been accepted as the norm at this college, the informal style adopted by the instructor would not have been well-received even if he had provided some semblance of feedback. On the other hand, had deemphasis of grading and structure been characteristic of the instruction at this institution, you might have been less disturbed by your appraisal even if it were low—but not entirely satisfied. Part of your concern, you will recall, was fueled by completely external considerations: the requirements of the job market you hoped to enter.

We do not know what the "organizational climate" was in this particular case. We can only surmise that this instructor was insensitive to it, just as he was to everything else outside his own narrow perception of the course. Had he viewed communication as a two-way process in which the perspective of the intended audience matters, he would undoubtedly have had better success in all aspects of managing his course—including the appraisal.

❑ COMMUNICATION CHALLENGES

PRELIMINARY EXERCISE 1   Evaluate the performance of one of your professors from the past semester, using the graphic rating scale shown in Figure 23-1. Do not tell the professor's name. Then *write a performance review using an evaluative approach explaining the ratings you gave.* The evaluation should be no more than one page.

PRELIMINARY EXERCISE 2   Evaluate your own performance as a member of a group, club, or work force. Apply a developmental approach and one other approach of your own choosing. *Write out your evaluations* (about one page each). Notice how the two different approaches cause different things about you to be recorded. Which evaluation would you be more inclined to accept?

PRELIMINARY EXERCISE 3   Practice active listening by working with a partner in your class. Describe to each other some accomplishment of which you are particularly proud. *Make a list of the personal traits you think the other person displayed in reaching that success.* Explain to one another why you associated the actions with those behaviors. You may be surprised by the traits that people infer from listening to a particular description.

EXERCISE 1

Using a performance appraisal approach that emphasizes development, *write a one-page summary performance evaluation of Ray Denton for the file, using information from Exercise 1, Chapter 1.*

EXERCISE 2

Review the information in Exercise 1 of the first chapter of this book, "Communication and Your Career." In this exercise, the manager of a small printing company had to decide what to do about Ray Denton, an employee. *Using a "Management by Objectives" approach, plan a performance evaluation interview with Ray to improve his performance.* Your objective is to help Ray develop the necessary skills, as explained in the exercise. Role-play this interview with another student playing Ray and a third student as an observer.

EXERCISE 3

Make a photocopy of the following performance evaluation. What are the purposes of this evaluation? Review the definitions of the biases that may interfere with accurate performance evaluation on page 623. These chief biases are: halo bias; stereotyping; attribution biases; rating scale biases; comparative biases; availability bias; and theory preservation bias. Read the evaluation to identify biases and other problems. *Circle or underline the phrases or sentences that reveal a bias or demonstrate some other inadequacy of the evaluation and note the type of problem in the margin.*

Monica Evans has worked for my colleague Roger Smith, who was transferred to the Jakarta office last month, as an administrative assistant for the past year. She's been holding the fort while we get someone in to replace Smith. She has several traits that seem to fit her for the job, but unfortunately, she isn't there for the handoff when the going gets tough. It's my theory that women just don't get the training in teamwork that they need. Monica's honest and detail oriented, but she doesn't seem to recognize what's important and lets things go that really need attention. Reports come in several days late without explanation, and I can't seem to get through to her. She put the Turner project together, and it was complete and professional. The slides for the presentation weren't ordered until four days before we had to go to Denver, so we had to pay 200% rush charges on them. Once you get her on a task, she goes for it, but she comes in late, and one time when we went out to celebrate the completion of a project she had three drinks at lunch. We can't afford to have an alcoholic keeping tabs on a project; there's too much responsibility and too much at stake. I think a shift to another position may be in order.

EXERCISE 4

The following evaluation was put in the file by Hayden Waters, who is a very busy and successful executive in the Laramie offices of a national car rental company. Read the evaluation Hayden wrote for one of the accountants, Del Carter, and speculate on the possible effect this evaluation may have on Carter's performance in the future, especially if he gets the kind of promotion Waters recommends. Waters didn't have much time to spend on this evaluation. *Write two or three paragraphs critiquing Waters' evaluation.*

In the past year, I can recall one major contribution that Del has made to our program, saving us thousands of dollars. He realized that one of our cost allocation techniques was causing us to underprice one class of cars, and he developed another method of tracking these costs. This alone will help ensure our profitability. Del works hard, and he's aggressive. He doesn't let the ordinary way of doing things stand in the way of coming up with better solutions. Since he's been busy with the budget, I have not had time to meet with him about his work recently, but I recommend that he be promoted to a position where he can supervise others and

have more authority, because we really need people like Del to have more force in our organization.

CASE: THE NATIONAL INSURANCE CORPORATION CASE

National Insurance Corporation, with offices across the country, is headquartered in Cleveland where the marketing, administrative, research, and actuarial staffs are located, as well as the operations department that processes electronically transmitted claims and applications from thousands of agents. Recently, management has determined that National needs to improve its evaluation of current employees so that personnel can be developed better in the firm's many specialized jobs and people can be channeled to positions where they can make the best contribution. Working toward that purpose, the Human Resources (HR) group has been asked to assess existing staff in greater depth and to become more involved in recommending staffing changes. Recently, your boss (the HR manager, Keith Kelley) took the first step, deciding to change performance evaluation procedures.

The old performance appraisal system was problematic in that it was standardized across the organization and used only a numerical rating system. The same fourteen job factors were used in all departments, regardless of the demands of the unit or specific positions in it. Under this system, people would apply for promotions or transfers, seeking higher posts, but the performance appraisal forms did not give enough information as to the person's suitability for the job he or she wanted.

Most significant, the standardization of job factors did not allow for assessing people in diverse positions and did not encourage the development of personnel. Most supervisors tended to think of the point rating system as simply a report card (90-100 = A, 80-89 = B, etc.), rather than a road map for better performance in the future. Another problem was that supervisors varied greatly in their use of the numerical instrument. Some rated all employees very highly, while others gave very low evaluations.

So the HR group decided to adopt a new appraisal system in two parts: the first, asking some generic, behavioral questions relevant across the board for determining merit pay on a uniform basis; the second, an open-ended, written assessment of each individual's strengths and weaknesses in a specific position.

The proposed new system, which is supposed to solve the standardization problem, is already causing some difficulties of its own, however. The manager of the Statistical Research department, John Jemmer, strongly objected to adopting the new system in a brief chat with your boss, Keith Kelley, yesterday and wanted to recite all his reasons. Because Kelley didn't have time to hear Jemmer out, he asks you "to go and see what Jemmer's problem is."

Kelley tells you to avoid defending the new system in your talk with Jemmer. "Give him a chance to get in his two cents about what's wrong with the new procedure," Kelley advises. "I want to make sure that everybody is with us on this thing. Jemmer should feel we're listening to him."

When you and Jemmer get together, you mention that Kelley was glad that Jemmer voiced his objections about the new performance appraisal system; finding out potential problems in advance should be valuable to Human Resources. Jemmer nods but launches into praise of the old system.

"Our people have a lot of confidence in the system we've been using. People know their ratings for the period and have developed a keen sense of what those ratings mean. You know, my actuarial assistant knows she has an 89 for the last quarter, and she's working to bring up her points. With this new 'qualitative' system, people won't really be able to tell much about their progress because it's nothing but a bunch of words." Jemmer holds up his hand, signaling you to hear him out. "Now, I realize that the new system will allow us to describe performance in terms of specific job objectives, but frankly, we trust numbers around here."

You start to explain about the numerical scale in the first section of the new system, but Jemmer has a head of steam up and on he goes. "You'd do us a big favor by just leaving the Statistical Research department out of this switch," he continues. "Since we're preparing the stats on entertainers and sports figures that the company will need when we start offering a new total dis-

ability insurance, we're especially busy right now. Lloyd's of London got burned with this type of product in the U.S. It's very important that we know what we're getting into—what kind of loss experience we're likely to have with all this going on. I simply won't have time to do this new appraisal system, and I don't think I can use it fairly. I know what I mean when I give Kim an 89, but I don't know what's what with this new form."

"Anyway, how can we compare people using words?" Suddenly Jemmer leans forward in his chair and looks you straight in the eye. "Why don't you look over our promotion record and see whether we can't just continue with what we've been doing?"

Reminding yourself that Kelley wants you to hold back with answers for Jemmer, you agree to take a look at what the data say. Back at your office, you begin looking up the records for the Statistical Research department. The number of transfers to other departments, the number of people terminated, the number of resignations, the number of people promoted, and the average number of months between promotions for the Statistical Research department are about the same as for all other departments in the company. In short, too many unsuccessful transfers and not enough individuals being groomed for future positions. It looks like Jemmer has confidence in the old procedure because it's familiar and because he believes in numbers. Also, the recent slow period in the industry has meant no growth in his department. Mostly he hasn't even had to replace the folks who've left. Only the old hands remain—the Kims who know what an 89 means, and probably a 91 or 92, too.

Because your boss highly values listening and consensus, you realize that Jemmer's complaints will have to be dealt with seriously. But you also believe that Kelley will insist that Jemmer's department use the new performance appraisal system like everyone else, although he might offer some training or even help to ease Jemmer's start-up problems. To move things along as expeditiously as possible, you decide to draft a memo to Jemmer for your boss's signature. That way, when you report back to Kelley you will have a tentative solution ready for him to review and sign, or if he wishes, to revise.

Write a memo to Jemmer for Kelley's signature.

IF YOU WOULD LIKE TO READ MORE

Beer, M. (1982, spring). Performance appraisal: Dilemmas and possibilities. *Organizational Dynamics*. Still one of the most concise, thoughtful, and constructive discussions of the appraisal process. A conceptual treatment with immense practical significance.

Bernardin, H. J., & Beatty, R. W. (1984). *Performance appraisal: Assessing human behavior at work*. Boston: Kent. An excellent discussion of modern practice and theory in performance appraisal. A comprehensive description of available techniques.

Carroll, S. J., & Tosi, H. L. (1973). *Management by objectives: Applications and research*. New York: Macmillan. A classic in the description and evaluation of management by objectives. Required reading for any potential user of this management tool.

Howell, W. C., & Dipboye, R. L. (1986). *Essentials of industrial and organizational psychology* (3rd ed.). Chicago: Dorsey. (See especially Chapter 6). The present author's attempt to capture both the essence and significance of various aspects of appraisal methodology. Expands upon some of the points introduced in the present chapter.

Latham, G. P., & Wexley, K. N. (1981). *Increasing productivity through performance appraisal*. Reading, MA: Addison-Wesley. Provides background and insightful critique of alternative approaches to performance appraisal, culminating in what the authors believe to be the most defensible method: Behavioral Observation Scales (BOS).

Locke, E. A., & Latham, G. P. (1984). *Goal setting: A motivational technique that works!* Englewood Cliffs, NJ.: Prentice-Hall. A theoretical and practical account of a technique, goal-setting, for which the co-authors are among the leading proponents. A "must" for anyone wishing really to understand how to implement this approach—and why it might be a good idea.

Schneider, B., & Schmitt, N. (1986). *Staffing organizations* (2nd ed.). Glenview, Ill: Scott, Foresman. An up-to-date overview of issues, techniques, and theory applicable to the full range of staffing functions. Performance appraisal is described as one of several strategies for achieving a good person-organization fit.

NOTES

1. H. H. Meyer, E. Kay, & R. P. French, Jr., "Split roles in performance appraisal." *Harvard Business Review*, *43* (1965, Jan/Feb), 123–129.

2. B. Schneider, "Organizational behavior." *Annual Review of Psychology*, *36* (1985), 573–611.

3. M. Beer, *Note on performance appraisal*. Boston: Intercollegiate Case Clearinghouse (1977).

4. B. D. Jamieson, "Behavioral problems with management by objectives." *Academy of Management Journal*, *16* (1973), 496–505.

5. E. A. Locke, K. N. Shaw, L. M. Saari, & G. P. Latham, "Goal setting and task performance: 1969–1980." *Psychological Bulletin*, *90* (1981), 125–152.

☐ FINANCIAL ACCOUNTING COMMUNICATIONS

OBJECTIVES

This chapter will help you

- become familiar with some of the legal and professional standards that affect financial accounting communications

- learn how annual reports are organized

- develop skills in organizing and writing notes to financial reports

- sequence information using pyramid structure, hierarchical arrangements, different logical arrangements, and strategic repetition

- understand the types of communications in which auditors are involved

PREVIEW

Accounting is the medium through which business organizations express their financial goals and record their achievements. Financial accounting is primarily concerned with score-keeping and reporting financial results to external audiences. This reporting is heavily regulated by laws and by professional standard-setting bodies. While some financial accounting reports may flow directly from the company to external audiences such as investors and creditors, others must be examined by Certified Public Accountants (CPAs).

Financial reports are organized to facilitate easy comparison with earlier reports. The organization or structure of most reports is consistent over time so that it is easy to compare results. Annual reports for public companies typically contain a letter to stockholders, a description of the company's business activities, and a financial section.

The primary financial statements (balance sheet, profit and loss statement, and statements of changes in financial position pertaining to equity and cash flows) are supported with notes and accompanied by management's narrative overview of the financial statements, a statement of management's responsibility for the contents of the report, and the auditor's opinion.

The annual report is usually a collaborative effort. The first two sections are often prepared by advertising agencies or by public relations officers; indeed, there are public relations firms that specialize in preparing the nonfinancial sections of annual reports. The financial statement section is prepared by management. Management of privately-owned companies may request that an auditor review statements. Public companies are legally required to have a CPA audit the financial section of their reports.

Notes, which enable readers to interpret the financial information, are organized and worded carefully to prevent misreading and to facilitate comparisons. Note writers often use a pyramid structure (starting with a general summary statement and expanding with detail) and strategic repetition. When they compare information from different time periods, they arrange similar types of information in similar sentence positions from one report to the next. They sequence information to explain causes and effects.

In addition to auditing annual reports, auditors prepare and present a wide range of documents and oral communications. Following the audit, the audit firm writes a letter to management to summarize the results of the audit and to offer advice. The wording of most of these communications is not as strictly controlled as the wording of annual reports, but complex problems of tone make them challenging to prepare. Richard Russler from Arthur Andersen & Company's Accounting and Audit Division stresses the importance of tone and organization, given the diverse audiences, which include partners and managers within the CPA firm as well as the executives and members of the board of directors of the client firm.[1]

The chapter ends with cases and exercises for communication practice. These prompts are designed to serve students with various levels of accounting experience. Even if you have not had a course in financial accounting, studying this chapter will teach you a great deal about the principal types of financial accounting reports. You will also learn to analyze, evaluate, and write the notes that explain the significant elements in financial accounting reports.

ACCOUNTING: COMMUNICATING THE GOALS AND RESULTS OF BUSINESS

Accounting information aids outsiders and management.

Accounting is the medium through which business organizations express their financial goals and record their success in achieving those goals. This medium provides valuable information to outsiders with financial interests in a firm, such as shareholders and creditors, and to regulators, such as the federal government. Internally, accounting information is needed for routine managerial decisions as well as strategic decisions such as restructuring an organization, considering a merger or acquisition, or developing a different marketing strategy. Accounting information is used as a standard for success and often establishes the basis for problem solving. Because of the many purposes that accounting information serves, effective communications are essential.

Three Types of Accounting

Accounting can be divided into three distinct types:

Financial reporting, which deals primarily with the publication of reports for external users (current and potential shareholders, creditors, and the government).

Managerial accounting, which focuses on providing management with the information needed to plan future projects and to control or oversee ongoing activities.

Tax accounting, which is intended to help the taxpayer determine the minimum tax that must be paid, and which reconciles taxable income to financial statement income.

The communications used in each of these fields differ, largely because the communications serve different audiences, have different purposes, and in some cases, conform to different types of regulations. In this chapter we deal with the kinds of reports and presentations used in financial accounting. Managerial accounting communications are the subject of the following chapter. Because a section on tax communication would require the reader to be familiar with tax regulations, we will not discuss tax communications. However, formats and types of communications used by tax accountants are very similar to those used in financial accounting communications.

Financial Accounting Communications

Securities and Exchange Commission regulations control reports.

Financial accounting communications may be divided into those that flow directly from the company to external audiences, and those that are audited by Certified Public Accountants.[2] Audited reports may be used by both external audiences and a company's management and directors. Privately held firms may choose to prepare their own financial accounting reports for creditors, investors, or other external audiences. Publicly held firms must follow the regulations of the Securities and Exchange Commission (SEC) in presenting financial accounting reports to stockholders and the public. Certain reports must be audited by CPAs. In this chapter we will first discuss financial reports that auditors prepare for their clients as well as for external audiences. The flow of these reports is shown in Figure 24-1.

One of the mainstays of all accounting communication is a summary of results. These results are often presented in the form of financial statements, but other forms of communication (such as oral presentations or a written narrative) accompany these reports to provide interpretation, explanation, or prediction. Financial accounting provides a form of score-keeping for internal and external audiences. The central reporting document for external audiences is the annual report. Writers must understand the legal context for these reports.

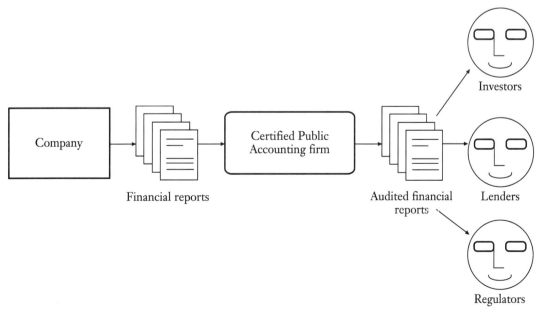

FIGURE 24-1.   Flow of Financial Accounting Reports

❑ THE LEGAL AND REGULATORY CONTEXT FOR FINANCIAL COMMUNICATIONS

Financial Accounting Reports

Financial accounting reports describe the economic results of previous activities to outsiders. They contain information about the recent profit-generating performance of a company as well as its future viability. Although the annual report is the primary vehicle used in reporting to the public, publicly held companies annually prepare other reports required by law for distribution to external audiences such as creditors, government agencies, and other interested parties. Unlike many other types of business communications, much of the information flow in these reports is formal and consists of required disclosures that conform to standardized reporting rules.

Some reports are required by law of all publicly held companies:

The annual report, which is the primary report used by current and potential investors and creditors, includes the primary financial statements and narrative information that explains the company's economic results of operations.

The form 10-K report, filed each year with the SEC, includes information similar to that of the annual report as well as additional disclosures about the nature of the business, the ownership structure, and the governance of the company. The format is prescribed in SEC Regulation S-X.

The form 10-Q report is a quarterly report required for some large companies.

Writers use different standard reporting rules in preparing these reports, depending on the type of report being issued. Government agencies establish the rules for reports that are to be submitted to them.

Rules for financial statements have a long tradition.

Financial statements for external use normally are prepared according to a set of rules called *generally accepted accounting principles* (GAAP). Generally accepted accounting principles have been established in a variety of ways, by a variety of standard-setting bodies. In the 1930s, Congress formally charged the Securities and Exchange Commission with, among other things, establishing a set of accounting principles for companies to use in preparing their annual reports. Although the SEC sets some accounting rules itself, the right to determine accounting principles was also delegated to the Committee on Accounting Procedures (CAP), an organization made up of practicing CPAs. The CAP was succeeded by the Accounting Principles Board (APB), which was eventually replaced with the current standard-setting body, the Financial Accounting Standards Board (FASB). Reporting rules established by the CAP are still in effect as part of generally accepted accounting principles, unless they have been specifically superseded by more recent APB or FASB pronouncements. In addition, for accounting issues with no specific authoritative pronouncements, accountants rely on precedents to determine appropriate accounting treatment. Taken together, all of these principles comprise generally accepted accounting principles, developed as shown in Figure 24-2.

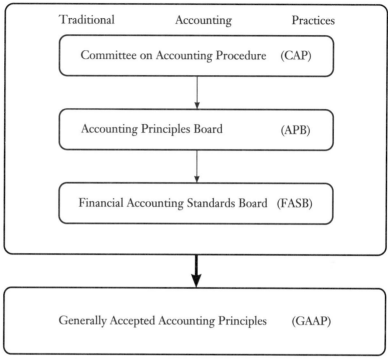

FIGURE 24-2.   Development of GAAP

The Annual Report

The annual report consists of several distinct sections that routinely follow a standard order: letter to stockholders; activities or business(es) of the firm; and financial reports. The first section, the letter to stockholders,[3] discusses the financial results of the company's ongoing activities and its expectations for the coming years. The second section usually outlines the types of activities or businesses in which the company is involved. The third section, the financial reports section, contains the principal financial statements, the notes, management's discussion and analysis of financial condition and results of operations, the management report, and the auditor's opinion or accountant's report.

Letter to Stockholders; Activities or Business(es) of the Firm

Management presents its view in the first two sections of an annual report.

These first two sections, which present management's view of the firm, may be written by different people in different firms. In smaller firms, an auditor may guide management's preparation of the letter to stockholders and the discussion of the firm's activities. In larger firms, the marketing department (in-house) or an advertising agency (outside) may prepare these sections, basing them on interviews with management about strategic plans and operations. These portions of the report endeavor to create an image of the company for a wide audience, including current and prospective stockholders/shareholders, customers, competitors, investors, analysts, and employees.

These initial sections contain the description and elaboration essential to creating images, whereas the financial sections are highly condensed, stressing facts in an objective manner. The management sections emphasize reasons and offer comments and opinions. Words are carefully chosen to convey credibility and responsibility on the part of management. Discussions of long-term benefits, positive results, and strategic decision making help to convey responsibility and optimism in the opening paragraphs from the *Federated Department Stores, Inc. 1986 Annual Report.* The following excerpt from that report conveys a strong sense of management-in-control through the frequent use of "we" and careful choice of words.

Dear Fellow Shareholders:

1986 was a year of vital decisions for Federated—a year in which we absorbed substantial short-term costs in order to position the company aggressively for long-term growth and to secure tax benefits prior to the tax rate changes in 1987.

We believe the strategic decisions made in 1986 will produce positive results, beginning in 1987. Certain of the actions taken, however, combined to exert negative influence on the year's earnings, masking performance improvement.

Net earnings for the fiscal year were $301.9 million, or $3.12 per share, excluding an extraordinary item. Including the extraordinary item, net income was $287.6 million, or $2.97 per share. For the fourth quarter, earnings were $171.2 million, or $1.82 per share. All per-share amounts are adjusted for the 2-for-1 common stock split on April 13, 1987.

We believe, however, that any thorough analysis of 1986 performance requires an evaluation of each strategic action in the context of its potential longer term benefit.

From *1986 Federated Department Stores, Inc. Annual Report* (p. 4). Copyright 1987 by Federated Department Stores, Inc. Reprinted by permission.

To facilitate easy reading, paragraphs are short, and simple sentences (only one subject and verb) predominate; variation and interest are added through phrases. The opening sentence contrasts with the others because of its length and the long clause introduced with a dash. The overall organization of this letter to shareholders begins with an initial summary followed by detailed sections about each strategic step that has been taken.

Financial Section

The financial statements of public companies are audited.

The financial section, which is examined by an independent CPA for publicly-held companies, comprises the last half of the report. This section begins with three primary financial statements:

1. Balance sheet (also known as the statement of financial position)
2. Statement of income (sometimes referred to as the profit and loss statement)
3. Statement of cash flows (also known as changes in financial position)

The balance sheet (the statement of financial position) describes the company's distribution of resources and claims on those resources at a specific moment in time, the date of the financial statements. The resources, called assets, are categorized by type, and the claims on those assets are divided into creditor claims (called liabilities) and owner claims (called shareholder equity). Specific rules are associated with the presentation of each of the assets, liabilities, and shareholder equity items on the balance sheet. Generally, the information in the statement is condensed, so notes to the financial statements are used to provide more detailed information about particular items such as inventories, debt, and employee benefit plans. In the annual report, companies normally provide balance sheets for the current year and the year immediately preceding it.

The statement of income presents the company's performance.

The statement of income measures the profit-making performance of the company over the past year. Expenses, which include the cost of providing goods and services as well as the cost of running the organization, are subtracted from sales revenue. Sales revenue reflects the total economic inflows from the sale of goods and services. The difference between sales revenue and expenses is operating income. Generally accepted accounting principles include specific rules for deciding when an inflow of cash or a promise of cash is revenue and when it is not. Generally accepted accounting principles also determine when an incurred cost is recognized as an expense. As was true for the balance sheet, the statement of income is sometimes condensed, so more information is provided in the notes to the financial statements.

The statement of cash flows measures changes in liquidity over the year.

The statement of cash flows measures the causes of changes in liquidity over the year. Companies report the changes in cash flow as a result of three different kinds of activities: cash from operations, cash flow from financing and shareholder equity activities, and cash flows from investments. Cash from operations reflects the inflow of cash as a result of the normal selling of goods and services, reduced by cash outflows for normal operations. Cash flows from financing and shareholder equity activities summarize the changes in cash from transactions such as issuing or redeeming long-term debt or issuing or repurchasing common or preferred stock. Cash flows from investments reflect the cash changes due to purchases or sales of land, equipment, acquisitions or dispositions of subsidiaries, or similar activities.

Generally accepted accounting principles allow companies to choose among several alternative accounting methods. It is widely believed that if there were only one method of accounting allowed for all companies, the selected method would accurately reflect the financial information of some companies very well, some less well, and some very badly. Thus, companies are expected to select accounting methods that best reflect the financial results being reported. For example, companies may select among different methods for depreciating their plant and equipment. Some methods provide for quickly recognizing the reduction in the cost of the plant and equipment, while other methods recognize the reduction more slowly. As another example, the company's selection of inventory flow assumptions (for example, FIFO—"First-in, first-out"—or LIFO—"Last-in, first-out") has a direct effect on reported income for both financial and tax accounting purposes. Given that choices among accounting methods available to companies can result in very different asset valuations and reported income, it is necessary that the user of financial statements be aware of the methods a given company is using. In response to this need, this information is provided in the notes to the financial section.

☐ STRUCTURING NOTES

Notes provide more information about the statements.

The first note is almost always the summary of significant accounting policies. In this note the company discloses the accounting methods selected, if there was a choice (see Figure 24-3). The note explains the impact of different methods if the choice makes a material difference or if disclosure is otherwise required. This statement of disclosures is usually organized by type of financial information, discussed in terms of the accounting method. The first topic is usually the broadest, with specific topics following in the order in which the items appear in the financial section.

Strategic Repetition

Begin a note with a summary sentence. Use strategic repetition and parallelism.

Strategic repetition of words directs the reader's attention and shows connections among statements in the notes. Figure 24-4 shows strategic repetition and the pyramid structure of each paragraph. Strategic repetition aids comparison of one year to the other. The most inclusive category in Figure 24-4, obviously, is "unusual items," which can be subdivided into "unusual items of 1986," "unusual items of 1985," and "unusual items of 1984." The items for each, in turn, may be divided into types of expenses or gains resulting from events that do not regularly occur. The most inclusive category is shown on the top; the items for each year occupy the next level of the hierarchy; the specific gains or expenses occupy the next lower level; their explanations follow on the lowest level. The diagram (Figure 24-5) points out the items that are of equal value (items on the same line are of equal value). This parallel structure helps the reader in making comparisons and gives signposts to follow, much as headings provide signposts. In planning a note, a writer will find it handy to use this kind of diagram to determine the order of items and to decide which items are alike and of equal stature.

If we compare the typed form with the placement of each topic in the hierarchical diagram below we can see the structure of the note more clearly.

1. SUMMARY OF SIGNIFICANT ACCOUNTING POLICIES

Consolidation   The consolidated financial statements include The Quaker Oats Company and all of its subsidiaries ("the Company"). All significant intercompany transactions have been eliminated.

Foreign Currency Translation   Assets and liabilities of the Company's foreign affiliates, other than those located in highly inflationary countries, are translated at current exchange rates, while income and expenses are translated at average rates for the period. For entities in highly inflationary countries, a combination of current and historical rates are used to determine currency gains and losses resulting from financial statement translation and those resulting from transactions. Translation gains and losses are reported as a component of shareholders' equity, except for those associated with highly inflationary countries which are reported directly in the income statement.

Marketable Securities   Marketable securities of $3.6 million, $38.1 million, and $6.3 million at June 30, 1988, 1987, and 1986, respectively, are included in the caption "Cash and short-term investments" on the balance sheet. Such marketable securities are stated at cost, which approximates market value.

Inventories   Inventories are valued at the lower of cost or market, using various cost methods, and include the cost of raw materials, labor and overhead. The percentage of year-end inventories valued using each of the methods is as follows:

JUNE 30	1988	1987	1986
Average quarterly cost	54%	52%	51%
Last-in, first-out (LIFO)	29%	31%	21%
First-in, first-out (FIFO)	17%	17%	28%

If the LIFO method of valuing certain inventories were not used, total inventories would have been $24.0 million, $14.6 million and $18.8 million higher than reported at June 30, 1988, 1987, and 1986, respectively.

During the fourth quarter of fiscal 1988 the Company refined its method of determining domestic grocery inventory value for financial reporting purposes including the capitalization of certain warehousing, transportation and other product-related costs. The change provides a better matching of production associated costs. The net effect of this change was to increase fiscal 1988 earnings $6.2 million (net of income taxes of $3.9 million). The cumulative after-tax effect of this change as of the beginning of the year is $5.1 million, or $.06 per share.

The Company takes positions in the commodity futures market as part of its overall raw materials purchasing strategy in order to reduce the risk associated with price fluctuations of commodities used in manufacturing. The gains and losses on futures contracts are included as a part of product cost. . . .

From: *The Quaker Oats Company 1988 Annual Report: Our plan is still turning brands into cash flow* (p. 54). Copyright 1989 by The Quaker Oats Company. Reprinted by permission of The Quaker Oats Company.

FIGURE 24-3.   Excerpt from Note 1, 1988 Quaker Oats Company Annual Report

2. UNUSUAL ITEMS

In 1986, the unusual items include a $31.7 million provision, before income taxes, for the expenses associated with the merger of two department store divisions and $18.6 million in gains from the sale by Federated Stores Realty, Inc., of its interest in two shopping centers. The equity in the gains on the shopping center is reported net, after reduction for federal, state and local income taxes, provision for profit-sharing expense and other expenses.

Unusual items in 1985 represent the gain of a $13.1 million before income taxes, on the sale of the Milwaukee-based Boston Store division and a provision for reorganization expense amounting to $48.2 million, before income taxes. The reorganization includes the merger of two department store divisions, the merger of two mass merchandising divisions and the reorganization or regionalization of selected corporate office and divisional functions.

The unusual items in 1984 represent the sale by Federated Stores Realty, Inc., of two shopping centers. The equity in the gains on these sales, amounting to $42.6 million, is reported net.

From *1986 Federated Department Stores, Inc. Annual Report* (p. 25). Copyright 1987 by Federated Department Stores, Inc. Reprinted by permission.

FIGURE 24-4. Note 2, 1986 Federated Department Stores Annual Report

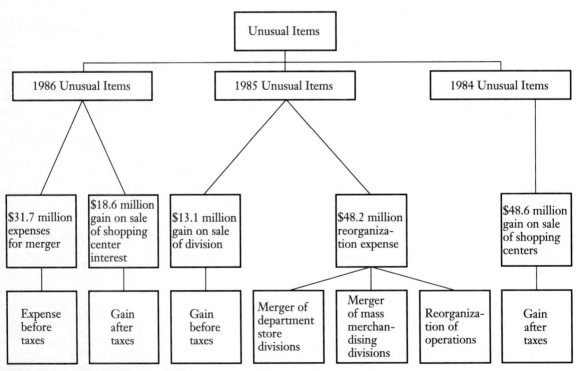

FIGURE 24-5. Hierarchical Diagram of Note 2

Logical Arrangement within Notes

Choose the best logical arrangement for your note.

As discussed above, the general framework of notes is often a pyramid structure, with the summary at the highest level, followed by levels of increasingly specific details. Within that general framework, however, different logical arrangements can be reflected in the words chosen and the sentence construction:

- *Topic/comment*, which offers an interpretation of an event or expense;
- *Classification*, which emphasizes similarities;
- *Comparison/contrast*, which usually emphasizes difference between time periods or differences in magnitude;
- *Cause-and-effect*, which emphasizes direct causality;
- *Antecedent (or situation) and consequence*, which emphasizes one action's following another.

Topic/Comment A topic/comment note usually begins with a descriptive statement of an event or amount, as shown in Figure 24-6. The following sentences comment about the first statement. "Topic/comment" is distinguished from classification, comparison, or cause-and-effect in that the interpretation does not analyze causes, but provides an explanation or an opinion about the significance or relevance of the event. In Figure 24-6, the first sentence presents the event—the renegotiation of two types of agreements; the second sentence describes its significance—what the company will be able to do because of these agreements. The next sentences in that paragraph describe how much the company did. The second paragraph describes the prior arrangement and details of that arrangement.

---

3. SALE OF ACCOUNTS RECEIVABLE

In December 1988, the Company renegotiated its revolving accounts receivable purchase and servicing agreements. The new five-year agreement permits the Company to sell a maximum of $62 million of accounts receivable on a revolving basis. At September 30, 1989, the sold accounts receivable totalled $55,500,000. The recourse provision was approximately $7,700,000 and is included in Accounts Receivable—Other at September 30, 1989.

    Prior to renegotiation, the agreement allowed the Company to sell $30 million of Receivables. The outstanding balances of sold receivables as of September 30, 1989 and 1988 were collected by the end of October 1989 and 1988, respectively.

From *Vista Chemical Company, Inc. 1989 Annual Report* (p. 26). Copyright 1990 by Vista Chemical Company, Inc. Reprinted by permission of Vista Chemical Company, Inc.

FIGURE 24-6. Note 3, 1989 Vista Chemical Company Annual Report

Classification   Much of the material in notes is arranged by classification, which reflects the organization of like elements such as expenditures and receivables. To emphasize like elements, present them in parallel structure (that is, use the same syntactic form, as explained in Chapter 7):

- Use the same part of speech (for example, nouns, infinitives, gerunds, etc.) to list all the items.
- Coordinate through conjunctions (for example, *and, or, but*).
- Introduce similar elements in the same positions in paragraphs.

A list has a parallel structure when all its items begin in the same way. In the example, "Unusual Items," Figure 24-4, coordination is used as the predominant sentence structure. With the exception of the last paragraph, like elements were introduced in the same sequence in each paragraph. In the last paragraph, the amount was introduced after the item.

Comparison/Contrast   Frequently, the primary function of a note will be to compare amounts in different years, as Note 5 (Figure 24-7) demonstrates.

Juxtaposition, like parallelism, also directs the reader's attention to contrasts. In the first part of this sentence from Note 5, the dollar amount follows the year, but in the second part the dollar amount precedes the year.

Merchandise inventories at the 1986 year end were $1,406.0 million, compared to $1,320.1 million at the end of the preceding year.

Parallel structure would have emphasized the difference this way:

Merchandise inventories were $1,406.0 million at the 1986 year end, compared to $1,320.1 million at the 1985 year end.

---

5. INVENTORIES

Merchandise inventories at the 1986 year end were $1,406.0 million, compared to $1,320.1 million at the end of the preceding year. At year end 1986, 1985 and 1984, inventories were $270.2 million, $261.3 million and $260.0 million lower than they would have been had the retail method been used without the application of the LIFO basis. This application resulted in after-tax charges of $4.4 million in 1986 and $3.8 million in 1985 and an after-tax credit of $5.8 million in 1984. Management believes that the LIFO method, which charges the most recent merchandise costs to the results of current operations, provides a better matching of current costs with current revenues in the determination of net income.

From *1986 Federated Department Stores, Inc. Annual Report.* Copyright 1987 by Federated Department Stores, Inc. Reprinted by permission.

FIGURE 24-7.   Note 5, 1986 Federated Department Stores Annual Report

This structure places the year after the amount in both descriptions and uses the same wording for the date. The version in the report places the contrasting elements close together, to force the reader's attention through juxtaposition. Juxtaposition works in a single statement, but parallel structure helps a reader who is dealing with more than one comparison, as in the "unusual items" note. Choose words that help the reader understand the comparison. Use words and phrases such as "unlike," "compared to," "however," "up from," "down from," "higher than," and "lower than" to emphasize comparison and contrast. Most of the comparisons will show change over time, such as in the sentences that follow the table from "Note 8: Common Stock and Redeemable Preference Stock" (Figure 24-8).

Cause-and-Effect and Situation/Consequence (or Antecedent/Consequence)   These are both used as the logical structures in Figure 24-9.

In the note the major content could be outlined as in this diagram:

(Situation)

Antecedent	Consequence	Cause	Effect
favorable interest rates	repurchasing debenture	repurchases	resulted in extraordinary loss

Cause	Effect
extraordinary loss	net of income tax benefit

As you follow this line of argument, notice that the effect or consequences may become the cause for the next result. *Writers should present elements in the order in which they happened when causality, not comparison, matters.*

☐ AUDITORS' COMMUNICATIONS

The annual report is the culmination of the auditor's involvement with the company. During the audit engagement, the CPA will communicate with the company and with outsiders in various ways. An audit is performed according to auditing principles and procedures collectively referred to as generally accepted auditing standards; they are determined largely by the American Institute of Certified Public Accountants' Auditing Standards Board.

In the first phase of the audit, the CPA will evaluate the accounting system. In this evaluation, the CPA attempts to verify that the accounting system functions according to design so all transactions are recorded accurately, no systematic errors or irregularities take place, and no employees circumvent the system. If the CPA is confident that the accounting system has worked properly throughout the year, then the second phase of the audit is made easier.

The second phase of the audit consists of determining whether reported account balances are reasonably stated (but not necessarily "correct"), making sure that the resulting financial statements are prepared according to generally accepted accounting principles, and issuing an audit opinion.

Changes in shares of common stock and redeemable preference stock are as follows:

	COMMON STOCK	TREASURY COMMON STOCK	REDEEMABLE PREFERENCE STOCK
Balance at June 30, 1985	41,994,698	1,672,958	375,541
Shares issued, primarily for option, stock purchase and profit sharing plans		(621,385)	
Shares acquired		1,908,700	(56,232)
Shares redeemed			(319,309)
Balance at June 30, 1986	41,994,698	2,960,273	—
Two-for-one stock split-up	41,994,698	2,960,273	
Shares issued, primarily for option, stock purchase and profit sharing plans		(853,684)	
Shares sold to benefit plans of acquired companies		(561,612)	
Balance at June 30, 1987	83,989,396	4,505,250	—
Shares issued, primarily for option, stock purchase and profit sharing plans		(1,127,886)	
Shares acquired		1,216,300	
Balance at June 30, 1988	83,989,396	4,593,664	—

In February 1988, the Company announced its intention to repurchase two million shares of its outstanding common stock on the open market. As of June 30, 1988, 770,300 shares have been repurchased. In January 1988, the Company completed the repurchase of two million shares (adjusted for the November, 1986 stock split-up) under a program announced in fiscal 1986, and in fiscal 1986 completed a two million (pre-split) share repurchase program announced in fiscal 1985.

Repurchased shares are used for general corporate purposes including stock option and incentive plans. . . .

From *The Quaker Oats Company 1988 Annual Report: Our plan is still turning brands into cash flow* (p. 58). Copyright 1989 by The Quaker Oats Company. Reprinted by permission of The Quaker Oats Company.

FIGURE 24-8.   Excerpt from Note 8, 1988 Quaker Oats Company Annual Report

---

3. EXTRAORDINARY ITEM

In 1986, the company took advantage of currently favorable interest rates by repurchasing $160.3 million of 10-1/4% Sinking Fund Debentures due 2010, $86.1 million of 10-5/8% Sinking Fund Debentures due 2013, $28.0 million of 11% Euronotes due 1990 and $22.6 million of 10-1/8% Euronotes due 1995. These repurchases resulted in an extraordinary loss of $14.3 million, net of income tax benefit of $14.5 million.

From *1986 Federated Department Stores, Inc., Annual Report* (p. 25). Copyright 1987 by Federated Department Stores, Inc. Reprinted by permission.

FIGURE 24-9.   Note 3, 1986 Federated Department Stores Annual Report

Audit communications are essential to the audit process.

The audit is accompanied by the necessary oral and written communications, both internal (to the audit firm) and external (to the client). These communications, shown in Figure 24-10, are essential in gathering and distributing information.

PHASE	COMMUNICATION	AUDIENCE	PURPOSE
Pre-engagement	Proposal	New prospect	Sales—targeted to prospect
	Engagement (job arrangement) letter	Client	Describe procedures, time and fees
	Engagement memo	Internal—team and partner(s)	Describe plans for audit
Engagement	Interviews with client	Self and client	Obtain information
	Notes	Internal	Document findings
	Work papers	Internal	Document findings
	Progress memos	Internal	Describe findings, problems, resolutions
	Oral presentations	Client	Describe issues, resolutions
	Audit opinion	Client/public	Describe conclusion as to fair presentation
	Notes	Client/public	Describe disclosures
	Oral presentation	Client	Describe results
	Management letter	Client	Detail potential problems; offer recommendations
	Engagement memo	Internal	Describe results and communications

FIGURE 24-10.   Audit Communications

An audit is a team process. The team consists of both client company employees and audit firm members. Members of the client company's audit committee and management meet with the auditors. Auditors must rely heavily on interviews with client personnel from various departments. The CPA firm's audit team typically consists of a partner, manager, and audit staff who are knowledgeable about auditing in a particular field (such as oil, technology, or manufacturing) and who are associated with this particular client. The partner has primary responsibility for the audit. The audit manager under the partner usually supervises the conduct of the audit. The audit manager may have several associates with varying levels of experience, from a few months to three or four years, working with him or her. Junior associates may be involved in vouching and writing memos and notes in workpapers. They may also be involved in preparing parts of presentations. In many cases the manager and partners are the ones who write the communications to clients. The internal engagement memos, notes, and the auditor's letter to management are usually written by the more senior associates, managers, and partners.

The Engagement Letter

Describe the job arrangements to the client.

The engagement letter details the audit process that will take place, including the degree to which the audit can be expected to uncover irregularities in the underlying accounting system. The letter points out management's obligation to cooperate and provide all relevant information to the auditor and states that the contents of the report are, in the final analysis, the responsibility of management.

The engagement letter typically has four parts that describe:

1. The work to be done
2. Procedures that will be performed on what entities during what time period
3. Evaluation of internal control
4. Fees

For the most part, this document's format is determined by individual CPA firms. For an example of an engagement letter, see Figure 24-11.

Audit Plan Memo

Describe your plans to your audit firm.

Although the memo describing plans for the engagement is an internal document, the writing style, focus, and level of writing skill are important. The document may go to various persons within the firm, including partners and managers. Because of the importance of the document within the firm, several drafts are usually written before a final document is produced.

Final Engagement Memo

Another internal document that provides a record of the engagement is the final engagement memo. This memo typically consists of three parts that describe

PSL
Certified Public Accountants
1299 South Loop Drive
Dallas, Texas 78505

September 22, 1990

Mr. Ben Smith
Abbot Grain Company
3 Clint Road
Fort Worth, Texas 78525

Dear Mr. Smith:

This letter confirms the arrangements made with Mr. Scott covering the examination that you wish us to make of the financial statements of Abbot Grain Company for the year ended December 31, 1990.

We will examine the balance sheet at December 31, 1990, and the related statements of income, shareholders' equity and changes in financial position for the year then ended in accordance with generally accepted auditing standards, including such tests of the accounting records and such other auditing procedures as we consider necessary to enable us to express our opinion on the consolidated financial statements.

Our examination will include a review of the Company's system of internal accounting control to the extent necessary to provide a basis for reliance thereon in determining the nature, timing, and extent of tests to be applied to selected recorded transactions and data. While our review will not encompass all control procedures and techniques, we will communicate to you any significant recommendations we have for improvement in the system, along with any comments and suggestions we have on other business matters.

An effective system of internal accounting control reduces the probability that errors or irregularities will occur and remain undetected; however, it does not eliminate that possibility. While we cannot guarantee that we will detect any such errors or irregularities, we will plan our examination to search for errors or irregularities that would have a material effect on the financial statements. We will bring any material errors or irregularities that we detect to the attention of the appropriate level of management and, if necessary, to the board of directors.

Our charges for the examination described above will be based upon the level of staff and time required to complete the assignment, plus out-of-pocket expenses. Billings will be submitted on a monthly basis. It is anticipated that our per diems for the examination of the financial statements will total approximately $60,000. We will, of course, endeavor to keep our charges as low as possible.

We are pleased to have this opportunity to be of continued service to you.

Very truly yours,

L. T. Baldwin
Partner

FIGURE 24-11. *Engagement Letter Example*

- procedures performed, specifically pointing out any deviations from original plan
- problems and resolutions
- results and audit opinion.

Auditor's Letter to Management

Following an audit, the audit firm writes a summary letter to the client company's management. The auditor's advisory letter presents some writing difficulties because of the importance of its tone. While the audit firm has a professional obligation to describe areas of actual or potential problems to the client, the tone must not offend that client. Analyzing the audience and fitting the communications to the client are extremely important in this communication. Unlike the notes or the audit opinion, the management letter is not derived from any set standard. The letter to management is confidential; therefore, it is not reproduced in the annual report. The letter in Figure 24-12, written by a partner, is an example of the kind of advice provided.

Case: An Auditor's Communication Strategy

Communication strategy requires careful planning.

Ms. Jackson conducted the audit of Abbot Grain Company and wrote the management letter in Fig. 24-12, even though it was signed by the partner in charge of the engagement. She planned her communication strategy by first determining her key message. This message was that Abbot Grain Company needed to strengthen internal controls through better separation of duties and better handling of cash receipts.

One of Ms. Jackson's primary objectives in the relationship with Mr. Smith was to build client goodwill. She wanted the client, Mr. Smith, to view her firm as a trusted business advisor. She believed that if Abbot Grain Company improved its internal control, she would be able to place greater reliance on the information she was given. Better information would enable her to reduce the number of substantive tests she had to perform, which in turn would reduce the costs of conducting the audit. Having Mr. Smith agree to the changes she recommended would benefit both the audit firm and the client.

Before writing the management letter (Figure 24-12), Ms. Jackson thought about the scenario for audit communications and decided two communication events were needed. In a scenario where no changes are recommended, only a letter might have been needed. In this case, however, she anticipated some resistance to the changes she believed necessary. To dispel resistance, she decided she would have a discussion with Mr. Smith before sending the letter. As she planned it, the first event would be an informal meeting with Mr. Baldwin, the partner in charge of the engagement, Mr. Smith (the grain company's president), and the grain company's controller. Ms. Jackson went through the strategy planner (Figure 24-13) to plan for the first meeting.

PSL

Certified Public Accountants

1299 South Loop Drive

Dallas, Texas 78505

March 21, 1991

Mr. Ben Smith, President

Abbot Grain Company

3 Clint Road

Fort Worth, Texas 77438

Dear Mr. Smith:

In examining the financial statements of Abbot Grain Company during our annual audit for the year ended December 31, 1990, we made several observations concerning internal control. Based upon these observations, we offer the following conclusions and recommendations. We emphasize that these comments are given as constructive suggestions that should enable you to establish better accounting controls and procedures in your organization.

Our recommendations involve the strengthening of internal controls through separation of duties. Although the small number of accounting personnel in your company makes separation of certain duties more difficult, we strongly recommend that the following procedures be followed.

Separation of Disbursement and Reconciliation

- A designated person in accounting should initiate and prepare checks. This person should not handle signed checks and uncanceled supporting documents.

- A designated person should prepare bank reconciliations. This person should not have other cash receipts and disbursement duties.

It is our understanding that the present procedures call for the second of dual check signers to review the documents supporting any disbursement before signing the checks. This internal control procedure is very important and should be maintained even though your recent change in office locations may make this difficult.

Cash Receipts

Internal control over cash receipts would be improved if the receptionist followed these steps:

1. Received all cash receipts,
2. Made an initial listing,
3. Placed a restrictive endorsement on all checks, and
4. Forwarded the checks to the accounting department personnel in charge of depositing and posting cash receipts.

Internal control is essential to the safeguarding of an organization. The American Institute of Certified Public Accountants has defined internal control as comprising "the plan of organization and all of the coordinate methods and measures adopted within a business to safeguard its assets, check the accuracy and reliability of its accounting data, promote operational efficiency, and encourage adherence to prescribed managerial policies."

Principles of good internal control require that responsibility for specific functions be fixed with specific individuals in the organization. In addition, the duties should be divided among employees so that the receiving, disbursing, and recording functions relating to any transaction are not placed in the control of one employee. Generally, complete separation of functions is not possible in smaller companies. However, such companies should segregate duties in such a way as to make internal control as effective as possible under the limitations imposed by the size of their staff.

We appreciate the cooperation extended to us during the course of our examination. Please call us when you would like to set up a meeting to discuss this report with your personnel.

Yours truly,

L. T. Baldwin

Partner

FIGURE 24-12.   Sample Auditor's Letter to Management

Event		Date Time
		Audience Issues: Uncertainties
Location		
Contact:		
Primary Audiences		
Secondary Audiences		Comprehensive Purpose
Transmitting Audiences		
Preferred Response		Lowest Acceptable Response

Persuasive Strategy
Organizing pattern: fulfill purpose, answer questions, create emphasis
Media and Channels
Visual Aids
Criteria for Evaluation

FIGURE 24-13. *Strategy Planner*

Because of her excellent performance in the past, the partner asked her to chair the meeting. She planned to set up the meeting in a conference room in her company. Having it in her offices might carry more psychological force and would get the client away from the interruptions that occurred at the grain store. The controller would be the secondary audience who could help Mr. Smith implement the suggestions; he might also play a watchdog role in the implementation.

Knowing issues and uncertainties helps you plan strategy.

Ms. Jackson thought of ways to emphasize the need for change because she not only had good professional reasons for recommending the change, she also knew the audience issues. For over twenty years, Mr. Smith had had Ruth Begley in his accounting department to handle all check writing and disbursement as well as bank reconciliations. This procedure had started when the company was small; Ruth had been Mr. Smith's trusted assistant. A few years before Ruth retired, Mr. Smith had hired someone to help Ruth, but the duties had never been clearly divided. At present two people worked in the accounting department, although three were really needed to handle the work and adequately separate the disbursement and reconciliation duties. To further complicate matters, Mr. Smith and the controller were in the company's main office, while the rest of the accounting staff was in another building some distance away. For this reason, supporting documents often had not been sent along with the checks that the controller signed as the dual signer.

Given the circumstances, Ms. Jackson believed the issues and uncertainties of the primary audience (Mr. Smith) were likely to be:

- A lack of appreciation for the professional reasons good internal control is needed (lack of information).

- An initial resistance to change based on the idea that "we've always done it a certain way" (feelings).

- A resistance to hiring a third person, even though the workload has expanded sufficiently to warrant it (belief/appraisal of past experience).

- A belief that having to send supporting documents along with disbursements is not that important because the controller knows about most of the large items. In addition, the feeling probably exists that documents might be lost if they were carried from one building to another (beliefs and feelings).

Relate criteria to your purpose.

In light of Mr. Smith's probable reasons for not changing procedures, Ms. Jackson felt that the purpose of the discussion was to gain agreement to the changes and move ahead on the discussion of options for handling the changes. Her evaluation criteria would be based on whether she achieved her purpose. If Mr. Smith agreed to consider the need for change and began to look at the options, she felt that her goal would have been achieved.

Media for the discussion would consist of an agenda sheet (Figure 24-14) that would provide structure for the meeting but also promote discussion.

MARCH 16, 1991

Overall Recommendation: To prevent potential problems, Abbot Grain Company needs to strengthen its internal control:

- Assets need to be safeguarded through good internal control.
- Good control procedures benefit both the client and the auditor.
- Abbot Grain Company needs to strengthen its control in the areas of separation of certain duties:
  - Disbursement
  - Reconciliation
  - Cash receipts

Several options are available for implementing recommendations.

FIGURE 24-14. Meeting Agenda

Organize issues to make the process of agreement easier.

To position the discussion and introduce her subject, Ms. Jackson would emphasize that good internal control would reduce audit costs and facilitate audit procedures, then point out specifically that growth in the business had caused a need for change (to counter the issue of "we've always done it this way") and finally assert that without change, risks were being taken. In her mind she saw a "problem/consequences-solution" organization to her discussion, with emphasis on the need for change. The agenda shows the essential argument she wanted to present as a way of organizing the discussion.

Because of the anticipated resistance, she felt that reasons needed to be given for change. Her argument is arranged according to the logic of cause and effect. When stated in a stripped-down version, the argument is that "Good internal control can help prevent employees from committing fraud." This statement lacked the tone needed to convey the message to the client, so she modified it to make it more appealing. For example, Ms. Jackson was careful to avoid the word *fraud*, instead emphasizing the safeguarding of assets. She placed the idea of safeguarding assets at the beginning of her sentence: "Assets can be safeguarded through better internal control." She used the passive voice construction (which places the object of a sentence first) to emphasize safeguarding of assets. In the initial phase of the discussion she planned to bring up the consequences that might arise if assets were not safeguarded.

The next logical step in the argument was that Abbot Grain Company did not have good internal control and therefore their assets were at risk. Ms. Jackson didn't want to overtly accuse the client of negligence, so she emphasized the need for change more than the cause of the problem with her statement: "Abbot Grains needs to strengthen its internal control. . . ."

The last statement on the agenda (about options available) leads to the next steps that should be taken. She felt that if the meeting could proceed to ideas about implementing the suggestions, then she had obtained her goal of having Mr. Smith become committed to her recommendations.

The agenda was written in complete sentences, which give more information than simple topics. Realizing that her audience would read the agenda as soon as she handed it to them, she did not want to be specific about the recommendations; so on the agenda she only wrote in the categories for which recommendations were being considered (i.e., disbursements, reconciliation, cash receipts). She had rejected the idea of a discussion outline with the recommendations fully written out because she did not want to have the recommendations rejected before they could be discussed.

To help prepare for the meeting, she thought of the "worst case" scenario, one in which Mr. Smith very strongly resisted the need for change. As backup she had three or four examples of small companies that had not separated accounting duties and what the consequences were. If she met resistance, her strategy then would be to emphasize possible financial loss.

The meeting went well and Mr. Smith did agree to separate duties. However, at this time, he was unwilling to hire an extra person. The controller (or Mr. Smith, in the controller's absence) would handle signed checks and noncancelled supporting materials until such time as Mr. Smith saw more need to hire another person. To facilitate the disbursement process (and as a compromise to hiring another person), Mr. Smith agreed to move the accounting department into the same building with him and the controller.

Because this meeting had achieved the purpose of gaining agreement to the need for change, Ms. Jackson's plan for the second communication episode had the purpose of providing a written record of the recommendations for both her own firm and Abbot Grain Company. The letter in Figure 24-12 is the result. In this particular case, Mr. Smith is not only the primary audience (the decision maker), but the secondary audience as well, because he will also implement the decision. He can distribute a copy of this letter to his employees to show them that this change has been strongly recommended by the auditors. Because it is a small, intimate company, he wants to dispel any feelings that he does not trust his employees.

This time the main audience issues are procrastination, and, as we just discussed, a need to cast the accounting firm as the impetus for the change. Given that the audience is now ready to act, Ms. Jackson does not repeat the organizational pattern of the agenda (concentrating on problems and consequences before mentioning solutions) in her letter. Instead, she gives the letter a "solutions-problem" organization with recommendations first.

In the letter, her recommendations are followed by a statement about the importance of internal controls. This structure is set up in the first paragraph to perform three functions: give background, introduce the subject, and stress the importance of the benefits. Within the body, recommendations are presented in two areas; within each area, recommendations are presented first and then commented upon: a "topic-comment" organization. The two paragraphs on internal control provide an incentive to act, even though they are placed after the recommendations. Since the secondary audience, the employees, would be less motivated by the prospects of reducing audit costs, these last two paragraphs emphasize principles and the actions of small businesses in general.

Audit firms may have long-term relationships with clients.

In addition to functioning on the audit team, the partner or manager may also function throughout the year as an external financial advisor to the company and is often called upon to discuss the company's affairs with interested outsiders. For example, it is quite common for the CPA to accompany management when the company is seeking to arrange outside financing. The CPA may be asked to indicate how a contemplated transaction should be recorded and disclosed in subsequent financial statements. The CPA may also be sought out by management in the event of an IRS audit. When a CPA provides management advice, the function of the communication is managerial, which is the subject of the next chapter.

❑ SUMMARY

Financial accounting reports are an essential element of the system of private investment on which the economy depends. For businesses to obtain capital, investors and financial markets must have accurate information about the results of business operations. Generally accepted accounting principles provide the language for recording and reporting business operations. By means of carefully structured documents, businesses maintain their legal and ethical obligations to their investors and creditors. By means of these same documents, investors and financial professionals obtain information that is crucial to financial decisions. Understanding the ways these documents are prepared and presented can enable businesspeople to read and use financial information with insight, even if they may not be involved in preparing financial accounting reports.

❑ COMMUNICATION CHALLENGES

PRELIMINARY EXERCISE 1 Obtain three annual reports from different companies for the same year. Read the letters to stockholders and the descriptions of the company's business(es). *Write a memorandum to your instructor explaining the principal image of the company that management wants to convey.* What corporate values does the report demonstrate? Do the three companies express the same view of the economy in the letter from management?

PRELIMINARY EXERCISE 2 Using the same annual reports that you obtained for exercise 1, analyze the way each letter to stockholders interprets the influence of the economy. *Write a paragraph comparing the way that these three management teams judged the economy's influence on their companies.*

EXERCISE 1

Obtain three annual reports for consecutive years from a public company. *Write a memo to your instructor describing one note such as "Extraordinary Items," "Pension Plans," or "Equity" from each.* Are these notes organized by comparison, contrast, change over time, cause-and-effect, situation and change, or topic and comment? Use a hierarchical diagram to depict the structure of notes in which comparison is the primary concern.

EXERCISE 2

Make a chart showing the relationship of the cause and effect or antecedent and consequence events shown in the following paragraphs. *Rewrite the following paragraphs as a Subsequent Event note*, making clear the relationships you have outlined. In the document shown below, Tixi-Bell Corporation is referred to as "The Company."

TIXI-BELL CORPORATION

Plan of Complete Liquidation: Agreement for Sale of Assets

On February 15, 1990, the Tixi-Bell Corporation and Mesotex Limited Partnership signed an agreement in connection with the liquidation.

The agreement was to acquire all of the Company's assets and assume its liabilities.

The transaction is subject to approval by the holders of two thirds of the Company's outstanding common stock and by holders of a majority of Mesotex Limited Partnership units voting thereon and on certain other conditions.

On December 21, 1990, the Company's Board of Directors unanimously approved a plan for complete liquidation of the Company providing for the conveyance of the Company's principal oil and gas properties to a master limited partnership.

For its assets, the Company would receive approximately 52,000,000 newly created Preference A units of Mesotex Limited Partnership.

Distributions on the Preference A units are subject to reductions of 75% of any federal income tax payable in connection with the liquidation of the Company if future tax law changes render existing tax-free liquidation provisions inapplicable to the transactions.

Pending legislation would generally repeal such existing provisions and could, if enacted, be applicable to the liquidation of the company.

Under the agreement the Company would distribute the units on the basis of 1.84 units per share to its shareholders pursuant to the liquidation plan.

The Preference A units would be entitled to receive cumulative preferential distributions in an annual amount of, and limited to, $1.25 per unit for five years, and thereafter the same distribution as on Mesotex's common units.

EXERCISE 3

Draft a well-structured Commitments and Contingencies note based on the following information. Commitments include long-term and short-term operating leases. Contingencies include any pending lawsuits and letters of credit. When reporting on lawsuits, the auditor must determine through the client's legal counsel whether an adverse result is probable, reasonably possible, or remote. In the following mini-case, an expected adverse result is remote; therefore, an estimated dollar amount of a loss does not need to be included in the note.

As you write your note, determine the best structure. Decide whether to use any charts or whether to explain your information only in sentences. You might want to look at a Commitment and Contingencies note in another annual report. Here's the scenario.

> The audit manager for which you have been working has been out of town conducting an audit for Sureen Corporation. He is in town today and has only ten minutes to prepare for a general weekly meeting of the audit managers. He explains, "I got a number of notes drafted on my laptop computer during the flight back from Duluth. However, I didn't draft the note for Sureen's Commitments and Contingencies. Here are my working notes. Draft a well-structured note. They don't expect any adverse results from the lawsuits, so we don't have to report any estimates of loss. On the operating leases, you'll need to total the

amounts for equipment, office space, and railcar for the years 1991 through 1993. Report the totals for each category as well as the amount and totals for each year."

Notes

Long-term and short-term operating leases yielded total leasing expense of $14,885,000 for 1990, $12,603,000 for 1989, and $11,175,000 for 1988.

Minimum lease commitments for noncancellable operating leases at September 30, 1990 are:

1991
Equipment = $576; Office Space = $2,059; Railcar = $3,958;

1992
Equipment = $443; Office Space = $2,245; Railcar = $4,055;

1993
Equipment = $185; Office Space = $2,445; Railcar = $3,225;

Company's various purchase commitments are for materials, supplies and services incident to the ordinary conduct of business. In aggregate, such commitments are not at prices in excess of current market. The Company is involved in various lawsuits and proceedings, including some involving environmental matters. It is not possible to determine the ultimate outcome. Management believes resolution will not have a material adverse effect upon operations or financial position.

At September 1989, Company was direct guarantor of $3,000,000 of bank loans made to one of Sureen's foreign affiliates. At September 1990, Company was direct guarantor of $220,000,000 for same.

CASE: GORRELL'S HANDYHOME CENTER MANAGEMENT LETTER

You are the junior auditor on an audit engagement with a lumber and hardware retail distributor, "Gorrell's HandyHome Center." During the engagement you have made the following notebook entries concerning inventory control. The audit manager has asked you to write up the inventory control portion of the auditor's letter to management. One of the difficulties with the communication is that the store manager, who is responsible for the inventory, is the owner's son. Using your imagination when necessary, fill out the communication strategy sheet for this communication. Then write this portion of the communication. Assume that the audit manager has drafted the letter headings and the introductory paragraph of the letter, plus other paragraphs on other topics. Begin your paragraphs with an underlined heading (in initial capital letters and lower case letters). Determine the organization and word choice based on your knowledge of the client and your purpose. Refer to the chapter section dealing with organization to prepare for this task.

NOTES: GORRELL'S HANDYHOME CENTER AUDIT ENGAGEMENT 11/04/1990

I experienced difficulty for the third year in a row in reconciling physical counts with records.

Receiving reports are required when material is delivered to a job or direct to inventory, but not when material is returned into inventory from a job. This documentation of items returned from job sites should be the responsibility of the store manager.

Unauthorized people are often allowed to pick up customers' orders. Recommendation: Store should require an approved purchase order from the customer before merchandise is delivered. If a purchase order is not obtained, make a telephone call to the customer and/or record driver's license number or license plate number of person doing pick-up. The person should sign for receipt of goods.

A copy of list of all returned items should be sent to purchasing. Receiving reports should be initialed when the items are placed in inventory. Appropriate entries should also be made to perpetual records and to the general ledger. Similar controls needed for items sent to job sites from inventory.

IF YOU WOULD LIKE TO READ MORE

Davidson, S., Stickney, C. P., & Weil, R. L. (1987). *Accounting: The language of business.* Sun Lakes, AZ: Thomas Horton & Daughters. A general introduction to accounting concepts.

Davidson, S., Stickney, C. P., & Weil, R. L. (1988). *Financial accounting: An introduction to concepts, methods, and uses* (5th ed.). Chicago: Dryden Press. An excellent introduction to financial accounting.

Fraser, L. M. (1988). *Understanding financial statements* (2nd ed.). Englewood Cliffs, NJ: Prentice-Hall. A concise guide to reading and analyzing financial statements.

Williams, J. R., Stanga, K. G., & Holder, W. W. (1989). *Intermediate accounting* (3rd ed.). San Diego, CA: Harcourt Brace Jovanovich. A comprehensive text for financial accounting.

NOTES

1. Richard Russler was very helpful in discussing accounting communications from an auditor's perspective.

2. CPAs, unless directly employed by a company, are presumed to be independent. Section 101 of the accounting code of ethics, *Professional Standards.*

3. "Letter to Shareholders" is also a common usage in the United States.

❏ MANAGERIAL ACCOUNTING COMMUNICATIONS

O B J E C T I V E S

This chapter will help you design managerial accounting communications as you

- analyze the needs of different members of your audience

- define your communication strategy

- use your planning process as a problem-solving tool

- manage tone

- organize an executive summary

- use graphics to direct attention

P R E V I E W

Managerial accounting techniques and information are used to direct attention to problems and solve them. Managerial accounting communications are especially important in problem-solving situations such as making capital investment deci-sions, adding or eliminating products, and deter-mining whether to make a component or buy it from an external source. Because managers, ac-countants, and consultants spend so much time in gathering and processing data, they seldom can devote much time to reflection and synthesis in the early part of a project. Planning reports and presentations, therefore, provides a valuable op-portunity for problem solving. Because their audi-ences are located throughout an organization and have diverse backgrounds, managerial accountants must write carefully to ensure their audiences can use their conclusions and recommendations.

Planning communications involves the steps de-scribed in the core chapters: analyzing the audi-ence, developing a communication strategy for the entire report or presentation, organizing the argument of subsections, and using an appropri-ate tone. In addition, accountants often need to develop suitable media aids to help audiences with little accounting background grasp the implica-tions of accounting information.

WHO COMMUNICATES ABOUT MANAGERIAL ACCOUNTING?

Various persons within a company and consultants or CPAs outside a company may use managerial accounting information to direct management's attention to problems and help solve them. Executives use managerial accounting in several ways: to define goals, highlight corporate strategies, evaluate results, and solve problems. Accounting results may be used to evaluate the performance of divisions or departments, which requires measuring actual results and comparing them with planned results. These results may be used to direct the attention of managers to those operations that were highly successful as well as those that need improvement.

Managerial accounting communications are used in planning, monitoring, evaluating, and solving problems.

Accounting information directs attention as an integral part of the organization's performance appraisal system (see Chapter 23, Performance Evaluation Communications). The individuals responsible for highly successful operations can be rewarded, while those who have not performed up to expectations can be called upon to explain their failure to achieve planned goals and their plans for improvement.

The planning and control cycle of the firm requires written and oral communications among individuals within a department or division as well as communications among levels in the firm. The planning and control cycle is the systematic process whereby the firm establishes short- and long-term goals, expresses those goals in the form of a budget, collects data on the actual results after implementing the plan, and compares the result with the plan to revise plans for the next cycle. In the formulation of plans to guide future operations of the firm, accountants are frequently called upon to evaluate proposed alternatives. Later, after plans are implemented, accountants are asked to collect and analyze data comparing actual results with planned results.

PROBLEM SOLVING AND MANAGERIAL ACCOUNTING

Scorekeeping and directing attention are the chief functions of many routine managerial accounting communications.

The internal scorekeeping and attention-directing functions of accounting processes in the planning and control cycle are ongoing activities associated with the routine operation of the firm. The comparison of budgets and actual expenses is a typical function that is recorded in operating reports, such as the one featured in the Document Spotlight. Managerial accountants also deal with nonroutine situations or opportunities that require accounting information. In these situations, accounting information provides data for special analyses and problem solving. Examples of these problem-solving situations include such decisions as capital investment expenditures, adding or dropping products, and determining whether to make a component or buy it from an external source. The transportation decision illustrated in the executive summary later in this chapter illustrates managerial accounting problem solving (see Figure 25-4).

The Routine Report

Routine communications usually have well-identified audiences.

In the routine situation of the operating report, Jeff, the controller, has mentally gone through the planning process. His purposes are to have senior management view the financial results for the year-to-date as favorable and accept the reasons for variances in March. He has thought of possible questions he might answer if the response is less favorable: how the unit is actively seeking to replace vacated students so that April net income will be positive, how vacancy time between Commercial Institute students may be reduced. As long as the situation continues to be routine (that is, variances are minor), Jeff will not have to spend much time thinking of his communication strategy for this report; however, if the situation changes or a new person writes the report, a strategy planner would prove valuable. If Jeff had filled out a strategy planner on this report, it would look like Figure 25-1.

The outline format in the operating report makes it easy for readers to compare similar items. The same items are reported beside the same letter each month (for example, II-A is always Cash Balances). Typically, operating reports begin with a description of how actual income and expenses differed from those anticipated in the budget (or a "statement of variances against budget" in accounting jargon) followed by comments on significant variances. Schedules are attached that show the monthly financial items on formal financial statements. The value of the narrative operating report lies in its readability and its power to highlight important issues that might not be as striking if communicated solely with the financial statements.

Another example of a routine memorandum is the one from Jessco Oil's vice president of finance (Figure 25-2). This document gives instructions to operating department accountants for completing the final budget forecasts. The critical requirements for this routine memorandum are that all necessary items be included and that instructions be clearly worded. This memorandum requires less audience analysis and planning than did the operating report, both of which were routine. A nonroutine report requires more planning.

The Nonroutine Report

Problem solving is the chief function of most nonroutine managerial accounting communications.

The nonroutine report provides much opportunity for problem solving in two areas: in the analysis required for finding a solution to the business problem and in the writing of the report, which calls for synthesis of data into conclusions and communication of those conclusions and/or recommendations. For example, the transportation report was the outgrowth of problem solving (the executive summary for this report is shown in Figure 25-4).

St. John's Hospital faced the problem of attracting more personnel for its expansion. Dan Campbell, a partner in a managerial consulting firm, was asked by St. John's to assist them in overcoming the problem of attracting additional personnel. In this capacity Dan and other members of his team were involved in

ROUTINE OPERATION REPORT

(Names and numbers in this report have been changed to conceal the identity of the company.)

In this example from Blossomtime Apartments, different people, either within the company or from an outside accounting firm, could have prepared the report. The controller of the company who manages the apartment unit could have prepared the document from various financial schedules, or the onsite manager of the apartment unit might have prepared all or part of the document based on financial schedules from the accounting office. Because the Blossomtime report is sent to senior management of the holding company owning the apartments to keep it abreast of the financial situation of the apartment unit, the writer in the example has emphasized a comparison of actual expenditures and budgeted amounts.

Blossomtime Apartments
A Project of Real Estate Enterprise, Inc.

TO: Senior Management of Real Estate Enterprise, Inc.

FROM: Jeff Smith, Controller of Blossomtime Apartments

DATE: April 30, 1989

NARRATIVE OPERATING REPORT

BLOSSOMTIME APARTMENTS

March 1989

This report summarizes operations for the Blossomtime Apartments for the month of March, 1989, and the year to date. We have attached our reporting package, which includes the Budget Analysis and Schedule of Accounts Payable and Disbursements, and the Schedule of Resident Accounts Receivable. We have also enclosed our newsletter, which previews coming events in the apartment complex.

I. FINANCIAL SUMMARY

The attached Budget Analysis shows that Blossomtime Apartments performed satisfactorily for March. Net income continued to be higher than the year-to-date budget target. Net income for the month was negative ($11,391) with year-to-date negative cash flow ($10,977), but the year-to-date net income stands at $78,590, which is $8000 above the budgeted amount of $70,590.

D O C U M E N T   S P O T L I G H T

ROUTINE OPERATION REPORT (*continued*)

Here are our comments on significant variances for the month, as reflected in the Budget Analysis.

A. Net income for the month decreased when the Commercial Institute students vacated eight apartments at the end of their lease term.

B. Operating expenses totaled $31,824, compared to the budgeted expenses of $32,783, and the year-to-date variance is $3723 under budget. The major March variance relates to Account #6885—Leasing Commissions. Actual commissions paid were $972, a variance of $828 under the budget of $1800. Much walk-in traffic and sales coming from word-of-mouth advertising contributed to the decrease in locator commissions.

C. Movement of Funds—No funds were received for operating deficits.

II. CASH POSITION

A. Cash Balances

The operating cash balance as of the end of March 1989 was negative ($3215). Rental delinquencies total $3100. Eight residents owe delin-
quent rents.

Security Deposit Cash Balance:	$24,785
Security Deposit Liability:	115
Replacement Reserve Deposit:	0

B. Payables

Vendor Payables:	$60,500
Other payables total: (itemized below)	30,000
Cable Service Charge: (due in 60 days)	500

C. Receivables

Resident receivables older than 30 days:	$ 0
Other receivables (due to unrecorded audit adjustment):	80

III. GENERAL INFORMATION

A. Occupancy—85% as of March 31, 1989.

Approximately 45% are one-year leases; 10% are three-month leases (to accommodate new home buyers).

B. Physical Plant—Roof repairs completed. Both swimming pools are being prepared to open in mid-May.

C. Maintenance—Staff began work on drainage areas.

D. Staffing—We are currently recruiting to replace the porter who left us. We no longer have an on-site security officer.

E. Recreation for residents—A volleyball game was organized and approximately 25 residents participated. Beer and soft drinks were provided.

Event	*Operating Report*	Date *April 30* Time *Not applicable*
		Audience Issues: Uncertainties
Location		*Can income be brought up quickly by replacing students who moved out?*
Contact:	*To be mailed*	
Primary Audiences *Chief financial officer*		
Secondary Audiences *Dept. of planning & budget*		**Comprehensive Purpose** *Inform management of results and show positive steps to deal with vacancies.*
Transmitting Audiences *None*		
Preferred Response *Note or phone call saying "all is well," "Keep on."*		**Lowest Acceptable Response** *acceptance of reasons and willingness to wait until May for higher income.*

Persuasive Strategy

Organizing pattern: fulfill purpose, answer questions, create emphasis
Summary followed by comparison that explains variances in cash balances, payables, receivables plus general information, especially what we are doing to keep present residents happy and to make property attractive to new renters. Emphasize good word of mouth referrals.

Media and Channels *Written memo to usual recipients attach newsletter*

Visual Aids *attached newsletter, schedules.*

Criteria for Evaluation *conform to usual format to make information easy to find; conciseness, directness.*

FIGURE 25-1. Strategy Planner for Operating Report

The officer responsible for budget preparation sends this quarterly memo to accountants in operating departments responsible for preparing estimates, which are later consolidated into a comprehensive firm budget. Estimate No. 4 is for the fourth quarter.

Administrative expenses are typically indirect costs; they cannot be traced to specific firm activities, and costs must therefore be allocated. The allocation instructions are contained on the Expense-by-Function schedule.

Net working capital is current assets less current liabilities.

Deep Drilling Company (affiliated company) drills on properties leased by Jessco Oil.

These two large projects involve limited partners. Expense and revenue estimates based upon Jessco's share of ownership are to be included in the budget.

Jessco Oil Corporation

MEMORANDUM

DATE: December 4, 1989

TO: Operations Accounting Staff

FROM: E. Jones, Vice President of Finance

SUBJECT: 1989 Forecast Estimate No. 4

Preliminary posting of the 1989 Forecast Estimate No. 4 worksheets has been completed. Please plan to return the finalized forecasts no later than December 21 and incorporate or note the following items while completing the forecasts:

To Be Noted in Completing Schedules 1 and 2

1. Administrative expense related to Jessco Oil's direct costs is based on the Expense-by-Function schedule as of June 16, 1989 (see attached schedule 1).

2. Jessco Oil's net working capital advance will remain unchanged from the 1988 actual amount, which results in no cash change for 1989. Interest income should be included at 9% (see attached schedule 2).

3. The one-month (1/12 of cash expenditure) working capital advance from Jessco's Wildcat Program will have no cash effect, assuming the 1990 investment level is consistent with 1989.

To Be Incorporated in the Final Forecasts

4. Administrative expense related to Deep Drilling Company is to be entered on Schedule 2.

5. The Burner Gas project and the Deep Well venture revenues and expenses need to be entered separately (schedules to follow).

FIGURE 25-2. Routine Managerial Accounting Memorandum   (*continues*)

The Integrated Planning System is a software package used to consolidate the budget. Accountants are to submit their estimates electronically.

All required Integrated Planning System control reports must be submitted on-line by each accountant. Please call if instructions for addressing batch job requests are required.

Attachments

FIGURE 25-2.   **Routine Managerial Accounting Memorandum** (*continued*)

both problem-solving and communication tasks. These tasks interface, as illustrated in Figure 25-3.

Problem solving often occurs during the preparation of communications.

Problem-solving tasks may be necessary either because of some need within the organization or because of changes in the external environment (as discussed in Chapter 2). Problem solving in managerial accounting includes contextual tasks: defining the management problem, applying managerial accounting methods and analytical techniques to develop a solution, determining who must approve and/or carry out the solution, developing an argument so that the audience will understand why this solution will work, and testing the solution to ensure its fitness, either before or after it is applied. (Typical steps in problem solving are presented in Chapter 1.) The communication tasks are interspersed with the problem-solving ones; they arise from the need to communicate expert knowledge. These communication tasks are concerned primarily with determining the message to be transmitted. Determining that message requires synthesis, which often leads to the insight needed to solve the business problem.

Forming logical and analytical claims requires the same cognitive processes used in creating statements.

As discussed in Chapter 1, the process of discovery often happens in the planning stage when the writer is analyzing the topic and determining the logic and content of the presentation or document. In fact, sketching out the essential points to be made and conclusions to be drawn can often serve as an aid to understanding. During the planning or the actual writing, a writer may come to see the problem in a different light and redefine the problem and its solutions. Business communicators frequently solve problems during the report writing or communication phase, because much of the data gathering and data processing go on under conditions that allow little time for reflection. The creative part of accounting work often begins when the person interprets the data in light of the management situation.

Primary Communications Tasks

The interfacing model of problem-solving and communications tasks (Figure 25-3) shows that the primary tasks are determining *what to say* and *how to say it.* Mike Harvey notes, "Care is needed in the way budget and performance in-

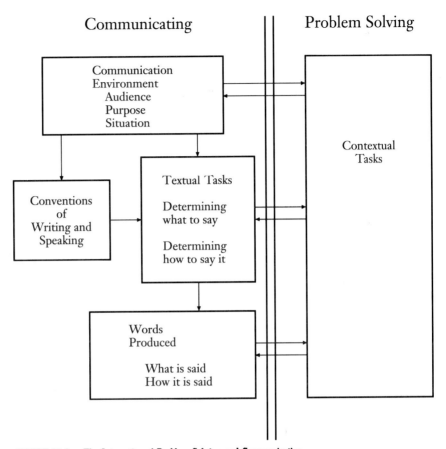

FIGURE 25-3.   The Interaction of Problem Solving and Communication

formation is presented, because this is likely to influence its reception."[1] What to say and how to say it are determined by the situation, the audience, the message, and the purpose. As a communicator you will analyze each of these.

Determining Communication Purposes

To formulate your comprehensive purpose, imagine what you want your audience to do.

As we have stressed, your communication purposes differ from your accounting purpose. Your main accounting purpose is defining the organization's problem and applying methods to develop information pertinent to its solution. Your communication purpose is not just to develop information, but to convince others to take action or to hold an opinion. In order to decide what elements of your technical accounting work must be explained, you need to decide exactly what this purpose is. In thinking through the purpose, you may find it less helpful to say, "My purpose is . . ." Instead, think of how you want the intended audience to act: "I want the board to agree that the pricing strategy we have used is inappropriate and that a gross margin pricing policy will help us meet our budget goals." In the transportation problem at St. John's, Dan wanted the Board to approve expenditures for van operations. His report should discuss the background of the problem and alternatives, and present arguments for the success of this method.

Determining the Message Content

Careful analysis of your purpose statement will guide you in identifying points of content. Your presentation or report must show the implications of your argument. In the case of van operations, Dan wished to show that this solution was better than the alternatives and that several reasons existed (employee interest, saving commuter time) for choosing this solution.

Determining Audience Needs to Develop Strategy

Identifying the audience helps determine what kinds of communication are needed and what persuasive appeal may be most convincing.

Once the audience has been analyzed, a communication strategy should be developed (discussed generally in Chapter 5; one in a financial accounting situation is discussed extensively in Chapter 24). The strategy will include the type of communication needed and even the organization of that communication. In the example we are discussing, the team decided upon a written communication because of the need to have various persons within the organization (i.e., the CEO and other executives, plus St. John's Board, composed of members of the community) understand the ideas and respond to them in different meetings. Tradition also played a part in determining the type of document needed: the board members preferred written documents that they could read prior to a meeting. The board members needed an overview, which was provided by the executive summary. Busy executives and community leaders appreciate a communication structured to answer their questions immediately.

Three primary elements of *how to say it* should be underscored as being especially important for managerial accounting communications to achieve their desired purposes: organization, tone, and the use of graphics to clarify and direct attention to essential ideas. In the remainder of this chapter, we discuss organizing the executive summary, achieving the appropriate tone, and using graphics.

How you say something is as important as what you say.

In these nonroutine situations (and sometimes in routine ones), your success may depend not only on the content of your communication but on the way that you present it. Some people assume that those who work with numbers don't have to pay attention to their relationships with audiences; indeed, some feel that showing concern with the audience's beliefs and feelings means being less objective. One way to balance these professional concerns is to separate them in your planning. Your accounting work and your insights into the problem will suggest "what to say" (the message or news of a communication). Your audience analysis and your purposes for the communication will help you evaluate "how to say" that message. You should create separate plans for each individual event in the scenario and prepare a communication strategy for each event, using the kind of communication strategy planning sheet shown in Figure 25-1 and discussed in Chapter 5.

Structuring an Executive Summary

An executive summary (Figure 25-4) condenses important information and places it at the beginning of a report. The executive summary is followed by sections that discuss the main issues in more detail. Because the executive summary is a synopsis of the more detailed sections of a report, the main ideas occur in both sections. If structured effectively, the summary will stand alone for audiences who do not need the details or who read the detailed sections selectively.

Structure your summary to answer questions.

After any study or project, an executive summary may be written to provide a record of results and recommendations. Although Dan Campbell and his consulting team wrote the executive summary in Figure 25-4 and the complete report primarily for the Board of St. John's Hospital, the CEO of St. John's was the first person to read them. Dan, the primary writer, was especially skilled in writing executive summaries. In writing this one, he decided that his two audiences (the CEO and the Board of St. John's) needed certain questions answered right away. He then wrote down a list of those questions and brief answers to help him pinpoint the content needed from the full report. Naturally, the first questions are about the report itself: to what situation does this report refer and what issues does it address? Dan summed these questions up as "What's the background?" In a natural sequence of events, he next discusses the problem, followed by the recommendations. Three primary sections present the benefits of the recommendation. These benefits are stated in section headings: "Private Vans Most Cost-Effective Option," "Van Service Reduces Commuting Time," and "Majority of Employees Prefer Vans."

QUESTION	ANSWER
"Introduction"	
What's the background?	St. John's needed to add staff; they set up task force to make recommendations
What's the problem?	Difficult to attract personnel because of transportation costs
What was done?	Task force investigated subsidy options
What's the recommendation?	Contract with a private van company to provide transportation
Why?	Benefits over other options
"Private Vans Most Cost-Effective Option"	
What were the options and their costs?	Bus, $16 a week; car, $30.80 a week; van, $8 a week
What is the most cost-effective option?	Van
Why does the van cost less?	Higher capacity utilization

QUESTION	ANSWER
"Van Service Reduces Commuting Time"	
On the passenger side, what makes the van attractive?	Reduced commuter time
What are the longest/shortest commuting times using a van?	95 min./50 min.
"Majority of Employees Prefer Vans"	
What percent would use them?	65% would switch to vans
Why do employees prefer vans?	Cleaner, quieter than buses
"Several Other Issues Need to Be Considered"	
What other issues need to be considered?	(See list in summary.)

Usually, you should write an executive summary after you have written your longer detailed report. In writing an executive summary, you should think of the questions for which your executive audience (such as a board or CEO) needs answers. Sometimes, all the principal questions are known in advance; you may have determined them as you planned the project in the first place. Or, you may have prepared such a list in developing an issue tree to organize the report. (Chapter 20, "Consultants' Communications," discusses the relationship between the planning and reporting stages of a project.)

Go through your longer document and find the answers or review your issue tree. Transform the questions into headings, provide transitions, and consider the tone that your strategy requires. Pay special attention to the beginning of the summary, making sure that you briefly identify the situation and the problem for which you have developed a recommendation/solution. Such a beginning provides a context for the document's readers.

You will notice that each section of the executive summary begins with "answer" headings that reply to the primary question of that section (e.g., "Private Vans the Most Cost-Effective Option" to answer the question, "What is the most cost-effective option?"). The "answer" heading communicates more information than a topic heading (for example, "Private Vans").

Achieving the Appropriate Tone

Choose words suited to the type of audience and the degree of familiarity appropriate in the situation.

Tone, achieved primarily through word choice, is one of the major concerns in managerial accounting communications. In managerial accounting, the tone may vary depending upon the type of audience and the degree of familiarity that seems appropriate to the relationship. In reports to audiences who use and prefer a formal style, such as investment bankers or boards of directors, the managerial accounting communication can be as formal as financial accounting communications (whose language often conforms exactly to the prescriptions of standards or laws). On the other hand, using stuffy, prescriptive, and staid language in all documents can make the managerial accountant appear to be sepa-

DETERMINING OPTIMAL EMPLOYEE TRANSPORTATION SUBSIDY

ST. JOHN'S HOSPITAL
December 15, 1988

EXECUTIVE SUMMARY

Following its physical expansion program begun last year, St. John's determined that it will need to add a minimum of 60 additional staff to handle nursing, building maintenance, and administrative functions. A personnel task force was set up to determine how we might attract the quantity and quality of personnel needed to fill those positions. Through surveying current employees, we determined that the major obstacles to attracting and retaining personnel at our downtown medical center location were the costs of parking, transportation, and commuting time. Consequently, the task force investigated subsidy options that would reduce those costs.

We found the most cost-effective option to be contracting with a van operations company to provide van service from four area locations. Compared to other options, van service was more cost-effective and reduced commuting time.

Private Vans Most Cost-Effective Option   We compared the costs of four commuting options on a cost per person per week basis:

COMMUTING OPTION	COST/WK	COMMENTS
Bus	$16	Used by 55% of current staff
Private car	$30.80	At average trip of 120 miles/week: Car expenses $.09/mi; parking $20.00/wk.
Van Service	$8.00	12 passengers/van

We considered subsidizing other options by an amount equal to the van service cost, $8.00 a week. This subsidy would reduce expenses associated with private cars by less than one-third and bus fares would be reduced by only 50%. Van service is substantially the most cost-effective method of transportation.

Van service is much more economical because vans carry 12 passengers, but the private car usually carries only one.

Van Service Reduces Commuting Time   Another attractive feature of van service is that commuting time would be reduced over local bus service or car because vans could use express lanes. During peak hours an average employee spends 100 minutes per day commuting in a private car or 130 minutes commuting by bus (based on a daily trip of 24 miles). The average van trip would cover 4.5 miles per day picking up people, taking approximately 35 minutes per day total for pick-up and delivery. Once on the

FIGURE 25-4.   Executive Summary from a Transportation Report

freeway, using express lanes, vans should reach their destination within 25 minutes. For the majority of riders, the van trip would take approximately 60 minutes commuting time per day. The longest time spent in commuting would be approximately 95 minutes per day, with the shortest time being around 50 minutes. The van trip would cost commuters less time than car or bus trips and offer door-to-door service.

Majority of Employees Prefer Vans   Surveying current employees, we found that 65% would prefer riding vans over cars or buses. When employees compared vans to buses, they gave the following reasons for preferring vans: Vans are cleaner, quieter, less crowded, have more comfortable seats, make fewer stops, and permit visiting with fellow employees. Of those who use cars, 70% of the employees would switch to using the vans; the remaining 30% would continue to use cars because they need the cars during the day.

Several Other Issues Need to Be Considered   Based on our findings, we recommend that St. John's consider contracting for vans to attract its needed personnel and to maintain existing personnel. Before making a final decision on van service, however, additional issues must be considered:

> What are the specific geographic neighborhoods to be given van service?
>
> How many vans would be needed?
>
> What percentage of van service should be subsidized by St. John's, 100% or less?

We suggest that the director designate persons to work with the personnel task force to investigate these issues.

The remainder of this memorandum discusses these topics in depth: cost of transportation, subsidy options available, subsidy options used by other agencies, employee interest in vans, and issues to be resolved.

FIGURE 25-4.   **Executive Summary from a Transportation Report** (*continued*)

rate from the company's team. A less formal style in communications to managers the accountant knows well, even a sense of humor, can win approval.

Tact maintains a good relationship and enables the audience to accept recommendations.

Because of the advisory function of many managerial accounting reports, tactfulness must always be considered. Although people often obey edicts from on high, they like to receive counsel from those who appear to be their friends and who think well of them. "All regional managers shall forthwith monitor closely all travel statements for amounts in excess of $2000" may be justifiable advice, but the tone of "shall forthwith monitor" is brusque, legalistic, and condescending. A clause pointing out the reason for the action as well as a substitution of phrases would make the request seem more reasonable: "To detect billing errors, regional managers should review all travel statements totaling more than $2000."

A collaborative tone should be used in many external communications as well as internal ones. An authoritarian tone says, "you must," "you need to," "you will," as in, "You must develop better systems management to compete." The authoritarian tone may be justified when you feel that such a tone will not cause resistance, but will, in fact, cause the client to act in a beneficial way. Such a tone may move the client to act quickly. In other situations, in which an audience has sought counsel but resists being told what to do, a collaborative tone might be more appropriate. A collaborative tone says, "Westcott can gain competitive advantage through developing better systems management." This statement emphasizes the advantages of the actions instead of emphasizing the imperatives.

An authoritarian tone often shows poor professional judgment. Joshua Grauer, who has taught hundreds of accountants in the "Effective Writing" courses at Touche Ross (Deloitte & Touche, as of 1989), insists accountants need to be scrupulously careful about absolute claims, regardless of the level of formality. He advises,

> Whether you write a letter to one client or an article thousands may read, you've got to be very careful with qualifying words: all-none, always-never, everything-nothing, will-may, and so on. Don't say "a Ruling *will* not apply" if you mean "it *may* not apply." Be careful not to say "more than 50 percent" if you mean "50 percent or more." Keep this need for precision in mind whenever you speak about anything in the absolute sense.[2]

Using Graphics to Direct Attention

Graphs interpret
information.

Graphics direct and focus attention. Accountants are extremely comfortable with tables and the tabular schedules that are used to organize numerical data, but many of the people who must read managerial accounting reports are much less familiar with these tables, and their lack of orientation to the table delays their reaction to the information. When designing documents and presentations, writers and speakers would do well to remember the maxim, "Tables present; graphs interpret." The regulations of *financial* accounting often prescribe rigidly the format of the report. However, *managerial* accounting is much more flexible. Sometimes accountants overlook important opportunities to use visual aids other than tables because they have become too familiar with the tables. As discussed in Chapter 15, Graphics: Visual Persuasion, most of the messages that businesspeople communicate with graphics are *comparisons*.

Graphs and table titles are a primary means of directing the audience's attention, one of the aims of using accounting information. Titles that convey a message are one way to direct attention. Unfortunately, as we pointed out in the discussion of executive summaries, writers often neglect this attention-directing method and instead of messages, write subjects. These subject titles can be rephrased to point out the interpretation of the subject, thereby creating a message:

SUBJECT	MESSAGE
Company sales trends	Sales in North Dakota Rising
Productivity by region	Highest Productivity in Northwest
Distribution of employees by age	Shortage of Experienced Workers Likely in 1995
Price versus catalyst sales	Higher Priced Catalysts Selling Well in South
Percentage of assets by division	Ohio Division Has One-Third Company Assets

> Many managerial accounting graphics will show component comparisons, item rankings, or changes over time.

Many of the comparisons in managerial accounting reports will be component comparisons, item rankings, or changes over time (explained in Chapter 15, Graphics: Visual Persuasion).[3] The bar graphs in Figure 25-5 compare the capital expenditures that a large company made in its department stores division and in its supermarkets division. The capital expenditures had been high for department stores in both 1990 and 1991. In a comparison of components, the graph shows each part as a percentage or proportion of the total. When you wish to rank items, the graph shows whether items are greater than or less than other items.

In a time comparison, the graph usually shows increases, decreases, or constant amounts. Occasionally, a managerial accounting report also requires a frequency distribution showing how many items fall into a series of progressive numerical ranges, such as, "In Milwaukee, most refrigerator sales were in the $600–$900 range." (Review Chapter 15, which indicates the most common graphic treatments of each of these types of comparisons.)

Department Store Capital Expenditures
Exceeded Supermarket Capital Expenditures
1990–1991

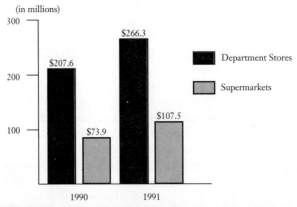

FIGURE 25-5. Column Chart Illustrating Comparison of Expenditures

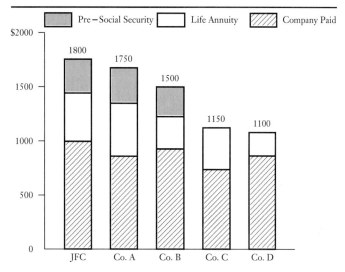

Retirement: 1/1/91 Age 60, 30 years service
Final Salary of $2700 per month.

FIGURE 25-6.   A Comparison of Total Employee Retirement Incomes

The bar graph in Figure 25-6 allows readers to compare the total retirement income for an employee of JFC Corporation with the retirement income of comparable employees who work for four other companies. The employee would be aged 60 with 30 years of service to the company with an average final pay of $2700 a month. The components of the bars enable readers to compare the sources of that income, which include a pre–Social Security annuity, an employee-paid life annuity, and a company-paid savings plan.

Tables present; graphs interpret.

You can contrast the interpretive power of a table with that of a graph by comparing Figures 25-7 and 25-8. The table in Figure 25-7 shows how much employees and companies contributed to the various companies' savings and investment plans. Figure 25-8 shows graphically how much companies and employees contribute to survivor protection. It is much harder to make a comparison quickly by reading the table.

Contributions to Savings Plan
Percent of Total

	BY EMPLOYEE	BY COMPANY
JFC	7%	7%
Co. A	6%	6%
Co. B	4%	5%
Co. C	3%	4%
Co. D	0%	4%

FIGURE 25-7.   Seeing Comparisons Difficult with Table

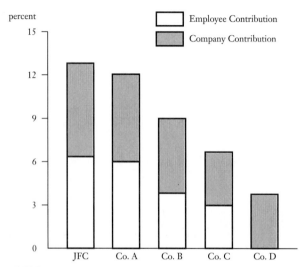

Contributions to Savings Plan
Percent of Total

FIGURE 25-8. **Graphic Shows Comparison More Clearly**

☐ SUMMARY

Using managerial accounting to keep score and direct attention involves both problem solving and communications. Communication is an integral part of the problem-solving process because the report writing or communications phase is frequently the stage at which creative solutions emerge. To communicate effectively, the accountant must first clearly define the purposes of the communication and analyze the audience's needs. The content of the message derives from its purposes and its audiences. When purposes and content have been decided, strategy, organization, and tone must be tailored to the target audience. The communication challenges that follow are designed to provide you with a range of managerial accounting situations requiring effective communications.

☐ COMMUNICATION CHALLENGES

EXERCISE 1

Using the operating report in this chapter as an example, *draw up your own operating report on your miscellaneous expenses for one week.* First you will need to budget for your weekly out-of-pocket expenses, such as meals that you pay for by cash or credit card; do not include dormitory rent, apartment rent, utilities, or meals at a university cafeteria that are paid for on a longer-term basis. Include other expenses such as groceries, laundry and cleaning, gasoline and car maintenance, parking, entertainment, and other miscellaneous expenses. After writing up your budget, keep track of these expenses for the week. At the end of the week, write an operating report comparing your budget to your actual expenses and explaining the major variances. Designate as your audience a spouse, parent, or student affairs department that has asked you to prepare a budget and to record your actual expenses for a week to determine loan needs. Fill out a strategy planner before writing the report to help you plan variance explanations.

EXERCISE 2

a. Using your operating report for exercise 1, *draw a graphic to show the share of your actual expenses for these major items:* groceries, meals out, entertainment, car or transportation expenses (gasoline, parking, maintenance, or fares) and any other expenses. Small expense items may be grouped as "miscellaneous." This graphic will readily illustrate a comparison of these items.

b. Take items that account for the most variance in your operating report and *create a graphic to compare actual expenses to the budget.* In both graphics, provide a title and appropriate labels.

EXERCISE 3

Below is a table that shows the return on a $100 investment over different time periods for a company's employee savings plan. The plan has three investment options. Using the information on the table, *create a graphic that compares the growth of the investment for these options.*

Returns on Investment: Dividends and Earnings Annual Total Rates of Return
$100 Investment

| TIME PERIOD | | | | |
Investment Option	1 year percent/$	3 year percent/$	5 year percent/$	10 year percent/$
Company stock	21.5/$121.50	23.2/$187.00	26.1/$319.20	22.2/$741.50
Equity portfolio	16.6/$116.60	13.3/$145.40	15.5/$205.20	15.6/$427.80
Common assets	8.4/$108.40	8.7/$128.60	9.8/$159.50	10.8/$275.20

CASE: THE DALLAS CONSULTING GROUP

Adapted from Robert Anthony and Glenn Welsch, *Fundamentals of Management Accounting* (3rd ed.). Homewood, IL: Richard D. Irwin, 1980. In *Cost Accounting* (1984), by E. B. Deakin and M. W. Maher. Homewood, IL: Richard D. Irwin (pp. 823–824).

"I just don't understand why you're worried about analyzing our profit variance," said Dave Lundberg to his partner, Adam Dixon. Both Lundberg and Dixon are partners in the Dallas Consulting Group (DCG). "Look, we made $40,000 more profit than we expected (see Exhibit A). That's great as far as I am concerned," continued Lundberg.

Adam Dixon agreed to come up with data that would help sort out the causes of DCG's $40,000 profit variance.

DCG is a professional services partnership of three established consultants who specialize in cost reduction through the use of time-motion studies and through the streamlining of production operations by optimizing physical layout, manpower, and so on. In both of these areas,

DCG consultants spend a great deal of time studying customers' operations.

The three partners each receive fixed salaries that represent the largest portion of operating expenses. They are professors, and each uses his or her university office for DCG business. DCG itself has only a post office box. All other DCG employees, primarily graduate students at the university, are also paid fixed salaries. No other significant operating costs are incurred by the partnership.

Revenues consist solely of professional fees charged to customers for the two different types of services. Charges are based on the number of hours actually worked on a job. Thus, an increase in the actual number of hours worked on a job will cause a corresponding increase in revenue. Since all salaries are fixed, however, DCG's total operating expenses do not change.

Following the conversation with Lundberg, Dixon gathered the data summarized in Exhibit B. He took the data with him to Lundberg's office, and said, "I think I can identify several reasons for our increased profits. First of all, we raised the price for time-motion studies to $35 per hour. Also, if you remember, we originally estimated that the ten consulting firms in the Dallas area would probably average about 15,000 hours of work each this year, so the total industry volume in Dallas would be 150,000 hours. However, a check with all the local consulting firms indicates that the actual total consulting market must have been around 112,000 hours."

"This is indeed interesting, Adam," replied Lundberg. "This new data leads me to believe that there are several causes for our increased profits, some of which may have been negative. . . . Do you think you could quantify the effects of these factors in terms of dollars?" *Write a memo in answer to Lundberg's question.*

Revenue and Nonmanufacturing Cost Variances

Exhibit A: Budget and Actual Results

	Budget	Actual	Variance
Sales revenues	$ 630,000	$ 670,000	$ 40,000
Expenses:			
Salaries	460,000	460,000	
Income	$ 170,000	$ 210,000	$ 40,000

Exhibit B: Detail of Revenue Calculations

Services[a]	Hours	Rate	Amount
Budget:			
A	6,000	$ 30	$ 180,000
B	9,000	50	450,000
	15,000		$ 630,000
Actual:			
A	2,000	35	70,000
B	12,000	50	600,000
	14,000		$ 670,000

[a] Service A = time-motion studies.
Service B = consulting for production operations.

IF YOU WOULD LIKE TO READ MORE

Horngren, C. T. (1982). *Cost accounting: A managerial emphasis* (3rd ed.). Englewood Cliffs, NJ: Prentice-Hall. A leading text in the field. Comprehensive, with good problem materials.

Kohler, E. L. (1983). *Dictionary for accountants* (6th ed.). W. W. Cooper & Y. Ijici, (Eds.). Englewood Cliffs, NJ: Prentice-Hall. This dictionary has been used throughout the profession for years. Communication instructors will find this a valuable help.

Needles, B. E., Jr., & Julius, E. H. (1984). *Principles of accounting* (2nd ed.). Boston: Houghton Mifflin. Needles and Julius offer a full set of teaching materials for a course covering financial and managerial accounting. Materials include a textbook; student's workbook; instructor's manual; readings; quizzes, problem sets, and tests; answers to problem sets, quizzes, and tests; computer disks; and overhead transparencies. Communications instructors (who are so inclined) can teach themselves accounting with this set.

Davidson, S., Maher, M. W., Stickney, C. P., & Weil, R. L. (1985). *Managerial accounting: An introduction to concepts, method, and uses* (3rd ed.). Chicago: Dryden Press.

NOTES

1. Names in this report and a few phrases have been changed to conceal the identity of the company owning the project.

2. M. Harvey, "Three-way path to fair analysis of performance." *Accountancy* (1987, November).

3. G. Zelazny, *Say it with charts: The executive's guide to successful presentations.* New York: Dow Jones-Irwin (1985). Zelazny, who has headed McKinsey and Company's graphics department for many years, has written an entire book based on the idea that all business graphics illustrate messages that involve comparisons.

FINANCE AND FINANCIAL COMMUNICATIONS

OBJECTIVES

This chapter will help you

- communicate the results of financial analysis in a variety of contexts

- understand the general characteristics of financial reports

- integrate knowledge of several disciplines and functions within the firm as you design financial reports

- apply the problem-solving process in creating financial reports

PREVIEW

Financial analysts review the overall operations of a firm and of its various functional departments to reach conclusions about risk and return. Then they transform those conclusions into statements about value and performance. These value and performance statements are the ultimate objectives of financial analysis and financial reporting. Some financial analysts work inside the company and analyze prospective outcomes of various proposed projects, while other analysts operate outside the company, analyzing the company's value and performance for various investors and lenders.

Risk-return statements alone would not mean much to a reader who was unaware of the firm's place in its industry and in the economy. The financial analyst provides this context for the reader by employing a conceptual framework. As the financial framework makes clear, financial analysts must play an integrative role, employing knowledge of the other important disciplines within the firm. The quantitative side of financial analysis converts the actions of all other components of a firm into a common denominator: cash flow. If this conversion process is not accurate, then obviously the analysis will suffer. The analyst must communicate with people in other departments to document his or her understanding of their operations.

The financial analyst can use a sequence of problem-solving steps to obtain information, perform the analysis, and prepare reports. The complete sequence of steps fits the most comprehensive problems, such as valuing a going concern or making a strategic investment decision. For smaller problems, a subset of the complete sequence will be adequate.

Financial analysis is not a substitute for decision making. Instead, it *supports* decision making. Consequently, after financial analyses have been performed, the analyst's results and conclusions must be communicated in a manner that promotes effective decision making. Furthermore, the analyst must reintroduce the qualitative or conceptual issues that may have been eliminated in the process of converting information into cash flows. In addition, the analyst often must convert numerical analyses into persuasive figures and conceptual diagrams.

THE QUESTIONS FINANCIAL ANALYSTS ANSWER

Financial analysts in banking, investments, and corporate finance address fundamental questions that every company asks: "In which assets should a particular company invest?" "How should the company finance these investments?" and "How will investment and financing decisions affect the value of the firm?" A firm's marketing and production objectives, such as the development of a new product or a plan to increase productive capacity at a plant, create the need to invest in assets. The financing question then follows naturally. *Financial analysts within the company* write reports to management. *Financial analysts in banks or other financial institutions* also write reports answering these questions as their firms become involved in the financial affairs of the company. The outside analysts write for audiences within their investment firms or for the public.

Financial analysts can answer a variety of questions related to performance:

- How did the division perform relative to its performance last year?
- Did the firm perform better or worse than other firms in the industry?

As a discipline, finance must provide a conceptual framework that can be used to answer these and other questions that evaluate performance and link it to value, such as

- What is the debt capacity of a new corporate loan applicant?
- What is the underlying value of the firm we are planning to acquire?

KEY POINT

Ultimately, a financial analyst must accept the vulnerability of expressing a professional opinion about value and performance, although analysts consult research results as well as opinions of experts in the field, when they are available. *A professional opinion, communicated orally or in writing, is the analyst's most important work product.* To make statements about value and performance, financial analysts must make *conclusory statements* of *professional opinion* that rely upon *relative comparisons* based on a mix of *fact and opinion.* The meanings of these key terms are illustrated in the examples that follow.

An Example: Analysis of Credit Applications

A credit analyst must review credit applications from companies seeking loans and make a recommendation regarding the applications. He or she must state in the opening paragraph of the memorandum to the credit file (a) whether credit should be extended and (b), the maximum amount of credit to which the customer is entitled (*conclusory statement*). Often, the conclusion will be based in part upon communications with third parties and an evaluation of things both said and unsaid in those conversations. As an experienced analyst, he or she is skilled at making inferences from silence and equivocation as well as from direct, positive replies (*professional opinion*).

Analysts must combine quantitative data and other facts.

Other factors in the credit decision will be determined by standard financial analysis of the applicant and a comparison of the applicant with quantitative credit standards (*relative comparison*). In addition, if there are other facts or opinions to which the analyst assigns importance that do not play a role in the standard credit decision framework, he or she would also state those in the memorandum. For example, assume that the credit analyst discovered that the controller of the applicant previously worked for a similar firm that went bankrupt. What importance should be assigned to this fact? What weight should it be given in the decision (*fact and opinion*)?

The Financial Analyst's Framework

The framework the analyst uses to study business situations enables him or her to identify the kinds of information needed to resolve a problem. The framework guides analyses and identifies benchmarks for comparisons, providing a schema to characterize the critical relationships underlying a business situation.

Financial analysis transforms records of transactions into cash flows.

The framework of the financial analyst is quite simple. Every transaction that a firm executes, no matter how large or how small, has both risk and return consequences for the firm. The financial analyst has standard definitions for risk and return and employs standardized techniques to measure them. After thoroughly examining all aspects of a transaction, the financial analyst characterizes the transaction as a set of cash flows, usually with some type of financial model. If there are several means of accomplishing the same transaction, each will be represented as a different stream of cash flows. Each set of cash flows will be evaluated according to its risk and return characteristics.

An Example: Analyzing Seasonal Demand

A firm that faces a regular seasonal peak in demand will experience certain "frictions" during the peak demand season. The marketing department may see the problem as caused by poor production scheduling and inadequate capacity. The production department may see the problem as caused by the marketing department's inability to spread sales evenly throughout the year and its failure to understand the production constraints during the peak season. The financial analyst will perceive that because the firm has limited means to control the timing of demand, it must either schedule production to match demand or build up inventory during the off-season to meet demand during the peak season.

Management must choose after considering several issues: the riskiness of carrying inventory, the cost of financing more inventory, and the potential return that could be realized by carrying more inventory and reducing production during the peak period. Management may also consider whether additional capacity is available during the peak season from some other source and what that capacity would cost. The financial analyst examines these alternatives and integrates the views of marketing, production, and other disciplines to enable management to make a wise decision.

Understanding the Financial Framework

Performance measures results in one period; *value* is the expected results over several periods.

The financial analyst's objective is to characterize changes in performance and value that are expected to result from changes in production, marketing, financing, or some other operating policy variable. *Performance* is a measure of a firm's results in a single period. Performance may be measured in several ways: level of earnings, growth of earnings, return on equity, or some other return on investment measure. While a number of factors contribute to performance, the financial analyst begins with the return on equity (ROE) as the primary measure. *Value* is a function of expected performance over multiple periods. Thus, to arrive at value, the financial analyst needs some method to transform multiperiod performance into a single measure of value. This transformation role is played by the risk-return tradeoff function mentioned above.

Performance in each period will have risk and return characteristics. *Risk* is defined as the variability of the performance measure. *Return* is the expected or average level of the performance measure. The analyst uses all available, relevant information in performing the analysis. However, the financial analyst cannot rely solely upon observable numerical relationships. Frequently he or she must use judgment as a guide in constructing and interpreting the quantitative analysis. Consequently person.l judgment may color the analyst's final estimate of value.

Analysis is not the same as decision making; analysis supports decisions.

The financial analyst performs a decision support function. Most decisions address a specific fact situation. By testing hypotheses about the relationship between decisions and future performance, the financial analyst helps the decision makers deal with risk. The results of the analysis, tempered by judgment, characterize the risk and return dimensions of possible courses of action. Based on some explicit tradeoff between risk and return, the analyst recommends a best

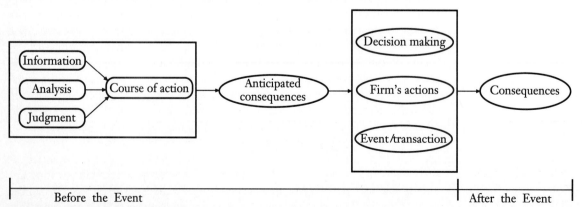

FIGURE 26-1. Financial Model of Analysis

course of action ("best" is defined as the one that results in the greatest incremental increase in the value of the firm).

Financial analysts' techniques and models imply that the analyst has access to a complete set of reliable information. However, he or she never encounters a situation that affords complete and reliable information. Where information is unavailable or unreliable, the analyst's judgment will affect both assumptions and interpretations of results. This common need to employ judgment explains why broad experience benefits the financial analyst. Judgment may seem the antithesis of cold, hard analysis, but successful financial analysts rely on both.

Financial analyses are never made with perfect, complete, reliable information.

This would be a good time to stop and do preliminary exercise 1 in the Communication Challenges.

❑ GENERAL CHARACTERISTICS OF FINANCIAL COMMUNICATIONS

In this section the generic term *report* represents a broad class of communications: oral presentations, memoranda, letters, interviews, and multipage written documents. This section identifies several features financial reports share.

Reports Respond to Questions

Be sure you understand the question your analysis is supposed to answer.

People write reports because managers ask questions. Therefore, reports should answer these questions clearly and concisely. Obvious? Of course, but the sad fact is that people often misunderstand the question underlying the request for a report or simply fail to respond to it. To ensure against such an error, formulate your conclusions as a direct response to the audiences' questions.

New financial analysts are commonly asked to perform ratio analysis of a company's recent financial performance. Why? Because someone else wants to know what the company did during the last period. The verb "did" may seem deceptively simple to the new analyst. Frequently, the analyst will reach such conclusions as: "The return on equity declined while the profit margin on sales increased." This statement simply summarizes some published results. The purpose of ratio analysis is to find out much more. The person requesting the analysis had broader questions in mind: "Why did one ratio go up while the other went down? What actions by the company caused this result? What factors in the environment contributed to these results? What do these actions and events portend for the future performance of the company?" The report should respond to these and other questions that may be answered by observed patterns in the ratios.

The Financial Scenario Will Define Your Role

Your report and your role will be part of a scenario.

Risk and return are at the heart of all financial analysis, because they are at the heart of all financial scenarios. Figure 26-1 provides a general scenario for all financial decisions. Financial reports may address only a portion of the transaction sequence, however, since the actual sequence may cover an extended period of time. Nonetheless, in every situation several roles must be played:

- Someone must gather information and perform analyses that will characterize risk and return factors.
- Someone must quantify the value consequences of risk and return as measured.
- Someone must specify actions to be taken and their financial consequences.
- Someone must anticipate external events that could impact significantly on the outcome of the decision.
- Someone must make the decision.
- Someone must implement the decision.
- Someone must monitor the implementation of the course of action and its consequences.

Every financial report will fall somewhere within this scenario. It is always helpful to know how your report relates to this outline and how it is expected to assist the decision maker. In your work as an analyst, clarify your role in the scenario and identify the purpose of your report in the decision-making process. Are you to gather information only? Are you to analyze information provided by others? With whom will you interact and how?

Reports Reflect Situations

The amount of information included in the report reflects the amount of knowledge held in common by all the participants in the situation.

As you learned earlier in this book, a scenario is a template for a transaction: a general description of activities undertaken in a situation. The scenarios for routine situations will be understood by most participants, and commonly understood information may not be explicitly communicated in the financial reports. The two documents below illustrate these differences. The first (Figure 26-2) is an analyst's report for an in-house group of managers who direct portfolios. It contains almost exclusively numbers, plus a heading that emphasizes the principal message. The report was suitable for posting via electronic mail to others in the group. The second report (shown in the Document Spotlight) is aimed at a wider and more varied audience, who needs more explanation.

In this cryptic memo, the analyst recommends that equity managers sell shares of PLL (Pall Corporation) in their portfolios and buy shares of stock in MILI. The abbreviations stand for the stock exchange symbols for these companies, which serve different end markets. The quarterly earnings per share estimated analysis yields a lower risk and higher reward for MILI.

The second document, shown in the Document Spotlight, is written for distribution to a larger group of people with various backgrounds in a financial services company. It refers to a research abstract published by an analyst at a specific brokerage firm, which would have been distributed to a much larger public audience.

TO: Equity Managers

FROM: B.W.

SUBJECT: Switch from PLL to MILI

PLL (23)			**MILI (32)**		
End Markets			End Markets		
Aerospace	27%		Pharmaceuticals	30%	
Health Care	24		Life Science/Govt	23	
Industrial	15		Chemical Industry	12	
Electronics	8		Health Care	12	
Energy/Utilities	6		Electronics	11	
Food & Beverage	5		Food & Beverage	5	
Other	7				
Foreign	40		Foreign 40% exports, 10% overseas production		

Q EPS ests				Q EPS		
* before	* Oct 1Q	22 vs.	20	Dec 4Q 52–57 vs.	45 for 1.75	
write offs	* Jan 2Q	33	29	Mar 1Q88	45 vs.	35
and cap. gains	* Ap 3Q	45	39	Jun 2Q	50	40
	July 4Q	50	43	Sept 3Q	50	39
		1.50	1.31	Dec 4Q	70	54
					2.15 vs. 1.75	

Valuation: cal 88E 1.65*
       13.9x   rel PE 1.1
    judge rel PE range 1.4–1.0
    reward 27%; risk 9%

Valuation: 88E
14.8 x   rel PE 1.16
judge rel PE range 1.5–1.1
reward 29%, risk 5%

Growth: 15%
       9–10 units, 1–2 prices
       3–4 currency
ROE 20%   15% debt

Secular growth: 20%
units 15%, prices 1–2,
balance margins & currency
ROE 15%   4% debt

*PLL is Pall Corporation

FIGURE 26-2.   Analyst's Report

An Example: Routine Situation

Virtually everyone in a routine situation understands the scenario, which affects report design and content.

Banks are in the business of making loans. Loan officers are employed to identify banking customers and to solicit loan requests from them. Therefore, when a loan officer submits a loan proposal to the bank's loan committee, everyone knows the objective of the presentation, the types of conclusions that the loan officer may have reached, and the kinds of information and analysis contained in

DOCUMENT SPOTLIGHT

A RECOMMENDATION TO SELL

This memorandum, printed on a special piece of paper headed "ACTION REPORT," illustrates many of the ideas in this chapter. Although it contains many of the same types of information as the routine information memo just presented, it also contains explanatory detail, presented in paragraphs with headings. The key message, that the analyst recommends selling shares of Limited Stores, Ltd., is emphasized in the memo's subject heading. As explained in the chapter, this memo presents the analyst's professional opinion, and involves relative comparisons involving a mixture of fact and opinion. For example, the analyst says, "I did not like the fact that other income . . ." and "I think this prepayment . . . could be a 'fudge factor' that has something to do with currency translation. . . ."

She uses judgment when she says, "The odds are . . ." The need to act without complete information is also shown here, when the analyst draws a conclusion about the prepayment, ". . . although I have not been able to get through to the company with my question." The analyst applies her knowledge of the company's business and looks to the broader economy and to the political environment when she says, "*Gross margins may be under pressure going forward* due to LTD's huge quota needs and protectionism as well as the impact of the lower dollar on manufacturing prices." She returns to quantitative data (earnings per share, relative price to earnings ratios, the range of implied stock prices, and the projection for movement) and projections for her third point.

---

the loan proposal. The members of the loan committee are experienced at reading such proposals and in using them to make loan decisions. Both the committee and the loan officer know the factors that are important in deciding to extend credit to a firm. There is no uncertainty in the overall scenario. The uncertainty lies in the specific facts of the situation.

The following comment from a bank loan officer whose bank specializes in serving physicians and health care companies describes a typical prospect call:

> I call on a number of doctors whose offices are in my bank's service area. Believe it or not, I am often more interested in talking to the office manager than the doctor. If the doctor has a good location and the area demographics are good, he or she should succeed in an income statement sense: the doctor will generate enough revenue. I can determine this kind of information very quickly from the income statement.
>
> After I bring the customer's information back to the bank, the credit department will review the applicant's past performance and financial potential. They will calculate the ratios, prepare cash flow projections, and compare the applicant with similar firms. The credit analyst will assign the customer a credit quality score.
>
> When I prepare my loan proposal for the loan committee's review, I focus on critical success factors for the business. For medical practices, the most important success factor is *collections*.

A RECOMMENDATION TO SELL (*continued*)

ACTION REPORT

DATE: 12-10-90

FROM: Sarah J. Babcock

SUBJECT: Recommended Sale of Limited Stores, LTD (51 3/4)
          Possible Swap into MAY   MA (47 7/8) SPAL (334.11)

Reasons for Recommending the Sale of LTD

1. Limited's high absolute P/E [price-to-earnings ratio] makes it subject to a steep decline should the more optimistic consensus outlook prove to be incorrect.

   CIMC is currently using an '88 estimate of $2.10. Consensus is closer to $2.30 (a 36% gain over this year). If analysts bring their estimates down, this $0.20/share difference could result in a $6.00/share drop in the stock if LTD maintains its 30 P/E. Odds are that if estimates come down so will the P/E, thus compounding the problem.

2. Evidence supports our feeling that estimates are too aggressive.

   a. The quality of earnings was not up to LTD's usual caliber in the most recent quarter. Few analysts have mentioned this because they put so much faith in Les Wexner, LTD's Chairman. (The attached report from [brokerage house name] is an exception. This is a new and unknown analyst.) I did not like the fact that other income of 3 mil. helped LTD reach the low end of consensus. I think that this prepayment of accounts payable could in fact be a "fudge factor" that has something to do with currency translation, although I have not been able to get through to the company with my question.
   b. Gross margins may be under pressure going forward due to LTD's huge quota needs and protectionism as well as the impact of the lower dollar on manufacturing prices.
   c. Sales are starting to look weaker than expected. As LTD has built inventories, this problem may be compounded if the company is forced to promote.

3. The valuation is rich at 30x '87 projected eps [earnings per share] and 3x '87 projected sales, regardless of relative multiple targets.

EPS		RELATIVE P/E	IMPLIED PRICE		
'87	'88	RANGE	RANGE	UP	DOWN
$1.64	2.10	1.85 - 1.15	65 - 40	+27	−21

Reprinted with permission; writer's name, and company name concealed by request.

Most medical services are paid for by third-party payers: insurance companies and the government. The working capital needed by the medical practice will be determined by its efficiency in collecting claims for services delivered to patients. Since accounts receivable are the only thing that the practice can provide as collateral for a loan, I look at them carefully. I want to know the practice's success in collecting them and the efficiency with which it collects them; that is, how quickly and at what cost.

I normally also ask for a personal guarantee and for a pledge of additional collateral. That way, the loan committee is more comfortable with the bank's risk level.*

The objective of the loan officer and other participants in the preparation of the loan package is to represent the facts of the situation as accurately and completely as possible. Because the situation is routine, the types of facts needed are already known by all concerned.

Nonroutine reports must describe the data and the analysis in greater detail and justify the analysis thoroughly.

Nonroutine situations place different demands on the communicator and the audience. When a nonroutine situation arises, it may not be clear what information and analysis are required. The participants in the decision must develop a scenario and the report or reports should document that the scenario was followed. If there are changes in the scenario, the changes will be reflected in the reports that ultimately are prepared.

Nonroutine situations place unusual demands on report audiences also. It is quite likely that the audience will have had little or no experience with similar reports. Because both the writer and the audience are inexperienced, reports in a nonroutine situation must describe the data in detail and justify the analysis. The writer must assume that the audience knows relatively little and dedicate greater effort to educating as well as informing readers.

An Example: Nonroutine Situation

Assume that you are the vice president of finance for a regional manufacturing company, Brondex Sprockets. You have worked twelve years of your fifteen-year career for Brondex. At a meeting of the executive committee the president announces that he is considering selling a portion of the company's common stock to the public in an underwritten offering. He appoints you as the chair of a three-person committee that includes the controller and the corporate counsel. The committee is charged with investigating the merits and the mechanics of going public. He also announces that your committee's report will be the number-one item on the agenda of the board of directors meeting scheduled for three months from today.

As the vice president of finance, you have some general knowledge of the scenario and of the situation. You must establish a specific scenario that the committee can employ for the timely preparation of its report. The board of

---

*Quoted by permission. Name withheld by request.

directors, the audience for your committee's report, will not be uniformly familiar with the information you employ or the analysis that you have performed. Indeed, they may know little about the process prescribed by the Securities Act of 1933 or the advantages and disadvantages of having to file reports regularly in fulfillment of the reporting requirements of the Securities Exchange Act of 1934. Unlike the loan proposal situation in which everyone involved at the bank understood the decision-making framework, this situation requires that your committee's report describe a framework the directors can use in making their decision.

Reports Address Risk and Return Issues

At the core of any financial report will be a discussion of the factors that contribute to risk and return. Your textbooks, whether in corporate finance, investments, or commercial banking, describe standard techniques you may use for identifying and measuring risk and return. Many business firms have proprietary approaches. For example, most banks have an internally developed method for grading loan applicants and assigning them a risk score. When presented with a new situation for analysis, ask yourself: "How do we characterize and measure risk in this situation? How do we characterize and measure return?" Normally the risk factors will fall into two categories: those that are subject to management control and those that are not. Always identify clearly the relevant risk factors and the way they have been treated in your analysis.

Managers know that their decisions have significant consequences for the firm and its performance. While they focus their efforts on those decision variables that they can control, they do not ignore the uncontrollables. They discern the potential impact of the uncontrollables, and they prepare contingency plans for responding to them. In preparing a financial report to support management decision making, you must treat the two kinds of factors differently. The embedded assumptions about the uncontrollables must be disclosed, and the importance of maintaining the controllables at assumed levels must be stressed. The following excerpt from an analyst's report illustrates how a writer can make limitations explicit.

This report is the work of an insider, a controller looking at a proposed project. The controller has estimated the future cash flows that will occur over the life of the project and the cost of capital to reach a determination about the prospects for success. The basic objective is to maximize the present value of the firm's net cash flows. A project should be undertaken only if there is an increase in value over the value expected if the project were not undertaken. The method applies a given rate to discounting (and accruing) both of these cash flows. The controller's key test for the project's success, as shown in the following report excerpt, is the determination of this "net present value."

This report analyzes a proposed line of cordless hand tools. The new line should be extremely successful, both in terms of market acceptance and financial results. Several critical assumptions underlie this conclusion. These assumptions should guide our implementation of production and marketing for the new line.

Our marketing analysis indicated several important features of the overall market and the individual customers. First, the market can be split between the home user and the professional user. Second, product reliability is essential. Both of these features were incorporated into the assumptions underlying the financial projections presented in the report. Our sensitivity analysis shows that a change in either of these two variables could substantially reduce the net present value, and hence the success, of the new line of cordless tools.

Previous studies have shown that both segments of the market can be very profitable. However, due to their relationship with the construction industry, sales to the professional segment are more cyclical than home user sales. Both segments have seasonal effects, with the sales to the professionals being in the summer and home user sales peaking at Christmas and Father's Day. It is important to separate the segments from the products. Home users, if satisfied with their first purchase, commonly will step up to the professional quality tools. Therefore, long-term success will depend on the sales of the professional line to both segments. We assume that the professional line is priced accordingly and that its margins are higher.

In the past, competitors tried to earn higher margins on the home user line. To do so, they let quality fall. The most glaring reduction in quality control occurred in the manufacture of the cordless tools' batteries. To reduce unit costs, the competition debased the quality of the batteries. Consequently, home users bought units that rapidly ran out of power. To complete work, they either pulled out their regular electric tools or they waited for the battery to recharge, a clearly inferior choice. This cost-cutting error has created a bad quality image for competitor X's products and has created the opportunity for us to introduce our line.

Our revenue forecasts and the realization of the projected rate of return depend on attracting the handyman segment to the professional product. Two implementation steps were assumed. First, that we aggressively promote the professional tool to the home user. Second, that excellent quality be maintained in both product lines.

We must maintain quality, especially in the manufacture and the testing of batteries. If management is unable to commit itself to these product goals, then the analysis must be revised. Our sensitivity analysis shows that a change in either of these two variables could substantially reduce the net present value, and hence the success, of the new line of cordless tools.

Excerpt from Analyst's Report

Reports Have Deadlines

Don't wait until you have "complete information" to write your report.

Beware the "perfect information" monster. Far too many analysts have failed not because their analyses were flawed (although a surfeit of these cases can be cited), but because they did not respond on time to the question. Such delays are not due to procrastination alone. Instead, some busy people defer writing because they have not completed their analysis or because certain critical pieces of information are absent. While you should seek to obtain the best set of information available, you will never have access to complete information. Accept the fact that you will always be compelled to rely on less than perfect information to perform your analysis. Deadlines are an effective way of thwarting the perfect information monster. Always assume there is an implicit deadline, even if you are not given an explicit one.

The director of research at a regional brokerage firm once told me the following story about a young analyst that he had hired.

> I hired this guy who had outstanding credentials—Ivy League undergraduate, number two in his class at a top-flight graduate school. He worked here three months and never produced a single research report. At that time we had a review, and I expressed my concern that things were not working out. He told me that he thought he was making good progress. While he had not written anything for publication, he was developing his research ideas and had identified several good companies that he was in the process of analyzing. However, since these would be his first recommendations, he was determined that his analysis be as thorough as possible. Three months later, the guy still had not written a single sentence for me to review. I had to let him go after six months with the firm.

Obviously, the failed analyst did not understand the requirements of his job. While his title was "analyst" and analysis was his technical role, his communication role was a big part of his job—he had been hired to communicate with the firm's brokers and clients. While no specific deadlines had been imposed, the analyst had to produce some work product within a reasonable time. When the second "deadline" arrived and he still had produced no communications, the research director had no choice but to let him go.

This would be a good time to stop and prepare preliminary exercise 2 in the Communication Challenges at the end of this chapter.

The Analyst's Role and Knowledge of Other Disciplines

Because finance integrates knowledge of many business specialties, financial positions are often avenues to top management spots.

You may have observed that many CEO's have finance degrees and have risen through the financial side of an organization. These individuals did not, in most instances, rise to the top position because they were knowledgeable about finance. Instead, they succeeded because they employed their financial skills and experience to learn about the company and its core businesses and operations. Because finance performs an integrative function, it affords individuals a great opportunity to learn about a business. Consequently, it can be a very good avenue to the top of an organization. Different business disciplines employ different conceptual models of the firm. These models reflect the types of problems that each discipline addresses and its methods of analyzing them. The financial analyst uses these models from other disciplines in a variety of ways. This section briefly reviews the intersections between finance and the other business disciplines and discusses how the knowledge of other disciplines is used in the preparation of reports and presentations.

Accounting

Financial analysts must understand and use accounting information to construct cash flows.

If you do not have a good understanding of accounting at least at the intermediate level, then your opportunities as a financial analyst will be limited. Analysts in corporate finance, investments, and commercial banking are regularly called upon to make decisions based upon a set of financial statements. You cannot perform the requisite analysis in any finance position if you do not understand, and therefore cannot interpret, the fundamental data upon which the discipline relies. In any business organization, the fundamental business data are always produced by the accounting system.

Often your task will be to reconstruct the transactions that actually occurred, using the accounting information. You must be able to identify situations in which accounting policies have been employed that, although they are permissible and correctly employed, have a tendency to misrepresent reality or to mislead the reader. In other situations, the accounting may faithfully represent a complex transaction that may be quite difficult to understand without a sophisticated accounting background.

The history of the securities industry tells us that in some instances accounting numbers have materially misrepresented facts. These instances of misrepresentation have sometimes been uncovered by financial analysts who examined carefully all of the facts disclosed by the accountants. These discoveries indicate only that the accountant's model of the firm, as reflected by recorded transactions, is imperfect, not that accountants lack integrity.

Marketing

Financial projections and analyses often rely on sales forecasts and marketing studies.

Your knowledge of marketing can affect the accuracy of your analysis, correcting results that are derived from other disciplines. You must use what you learn in one field to supplement other interpretations. *Your reports must present the complex results of multiple viewpoints.* For example, microeconomics teaches that consumers trade quantity against price. On a demand curve, a unique quantity is associated with each price. As price goes up, quantity goes down, and vice versa. Marketing teaches that a host of other factors besides price will determine demand.

Most financial projections, and consequently a great many financial analyses, are based on a sales forecast. If the sales forecast has been derived from sales force estimates, it may fail to consider the impact of variables that do not impinge directly upon the salesman and customer. Whether the analyst makes his or her own forecast or relies upon the corporate planning department or some third party forecasting service, errors in the sales forecast can be fatal to the analysis. I believe that more often than not these errors result from an inadequate understanding and treatment of the marketing variables.

Marketing is concerned primarily with the relationship between the firm and its customers. However, the marketing specialist considers this relationship in terms of the firm's external operating environment. No matter what your analytical task, take some time in the beginning to understand the nature of the customer and of the product. Before you begin to study the accounting information, ask yourself, "Is this a good product? Is there a good match between customer and product? Are any potential customers being overlooked?" Don't accept the opinions of others uncritically. Take the time to form your own opinion.

Production

Production information is needed to evaluate the feasibility of projected changes.

You cannot describe accurately the financial performance of a process that you do not understand. Consequently, you must spend some time observing and understanding how the product or service is produced. The number of inputs, their prices, the number of processing steps, and the time from initial processing until completion, have cash flow implications for the firm. Because most manufacturing firms employ managerial accounting systems, it should be easy to obtain historical data pertaining to the cost of producing a product. In contrast, obtaining reliable production data for services may be difficult.

Management and Other Organizational Considerations

Accounting, marketing, and production knowledge will help you perform necessary quantitative analysis to support a decision. However, very few decisions are reached solely on the basis of quantitative analysis. Instead, management will interject into the decision process a host of nonquantitative, organizational considerations. Every financial report should reflect an awareness of these organizational considerations, including the flow of information, the locus of decision-making authority, the quality of interactions between superior and subordinate, and a host of other "people problems."

In reports the financial analyst may also consider the firm's mission statement or recent strategic decisions. The best way to avoid pitfalls is to be aware of the important strategic considerations before senior management, but do not let this awareness mask facts that need to be stated. Instead, let your awareness help you manage your audience's uncertainties (initial questions, need for information, feelings, and beliefs) so that management can make good decisions.

❑ THE PROBLEM-SOLVING PROCESS IN FINANCIAL COMMUNICATIONS

While the communication of financial information, analysis, conclusions, and decisions may assume a variety of forms, the sequence of steps followed will always be the same (see the earlier discussion of problem solving in Chapter 1,

"Communication and Your Career"). The steps in the financial decision-making process are described below.

State the Problem

Before you begin, state the purposes of your work. This may not seem necessary if you are preparing a routine monitoring report. However, as a writer and as an analyst it is always a good exercise to verbalize your objectives, even if the verbalization does not become a part of the final report. If you are preparing a report that relates to a nonroutine situation, then a purpose statement will be even more necessary. In the initial statement of the problem, you will describe a situation that requires attention of some sort and your reasons for involving the reader in that situation.

Obtain and Review Necessary Information

Your initial task will be to obtain information that will be useful in accomplishing your objective. A clear statement of purposes should help you to avoid wasting time in the collection of unnecessary data. Although the primary source of information will be accounting information, that alone will rarely be sufficient. Depending upon your objective, you may need to obtain information pertaining to other facets of the company's activities. These other types of necessary information will inform you about a variety of factors that impinge upon the company and affect its published financial information.

You should look for information that describes competitive factors in the company's industry and discusses industry trends. You should obtain information about management, primarily information pertaining to their experience and capabilities. If there have been any recent changes in laws or regulations that affect the company and its business, you should obtain information on them. Finally, you may need to investigate relationships between the company and other interested and essential parties: customers, suppliers, employees, bankers, and regulators. In short, a financial analyst must be fully aware of the relationships represented in Figure 26-1.

Perform the Appropriate Analysis

Once you have sufficient data before you, you are ready to begin your analysis. There are several standard methods of analysis in finance, such as ratio analysis, DuPont analysis, and discounted cash flow analysis. Financial ratio analysis takes information that appears in two separate places—the income statement and the balance sheet—and presents that information in a common format. Accountants use the income statement to measure the flow of revenue and expense through the firm; the balance sheet reflects the historical acquisition cost of resources controlled by the firm at a single point in time.

Ratio Analysis   Ratios compare two stock measures, two flow measures, or a flow measure with a stock measure. Return-on-investment measures compare profit numbers from the income statement with investment numbers from the balance sheet. Profit is dependent upon the level of activity (sales), which in turn requires investment in assets. Therefore, activity ratios will compare sales with various categories of investment: current assets, fixed assets, total assets. Ratio analysis provides you with a template. It tells you how to organize financial information in a manner that supports comparisons across firms and directs your inquiry into areas that deserve further investigation.

The results of your ratio analysis may not lead to simple conclusions. Once calculated, ratios must be interpreted, not individually but as a whole, as a single representation of a company's performance. The only absolute judgments to be made from ratio analysis are that the value for a particular ratio differs from an industry average or from last year's value. Such absolute observations serve no analytical purpose. They bear fruit only when you describe the company's activities in a report. To generate that report, you may use several tools, including DuPont analysis, discounted cash flow analysis, and other methods that you will study in your finance courses.

DuPont Analysis   DuPont analysis focuses upon the return that the owners of the business realize and takes into account the three other ratios that are used to determine the owners' return: the firm's return on equity (ROE); the total asset turnover ratio, which tells about the firm's asset structure (its receivables, inventory, and fixed assets); and the debt ratio, which reflects the composition of the firm's capital structure.

Discounted Cash Flow Analysis   When the purpose of financial analysis is the valuation of a security, a piece of equipment, or a firm, you will employ some form of discounted cash flow (DCF) analysis. A DCF analysis has two parts. The first part of the analysis determines the future cash flows to be received by the asset's owner. The second part of the analysis applies a discount rate to transform future cash flows to their present value.

The cash flow analysis in forecasts of financial performance estimates the amount of cash that the firm will receive in future years. Integrating all the information that you have gathered, you can build a scenario that realistically describes the financial performance of the asset or the company as a whole. Your forecast will take the form of accounting forecasts or pro forma statements of cash flows.

You will then supplement the cash flow forecast with additional information. You must form some conclusions with regard to the riskiness of the asset when compared with other available investment opportunities. Then, based upon your evaluation of the asset's riskiness and upon your examination of currently prevailing interest rates, you must determine what rate of return would be necessary to entice investors to purchase the asset. To determine whether a purchaser of the asset would receive the minimum necessary return, you would then use the minimum acceptable rate of return to discount the cash flows in your scenario to present value. This discounted present value represents your view of the asset's value.

Depict a Complete Financial Situation to Support Decision Making

Before you conclude that the value produced by your discounted cash flow analysis is the unequivocally correct one, you should consider other factors. For example, if you are valuing an acquisition candidate, your major concerns will be continued growth in revenues and an ability to control costs. The forecast may assume that these will continue unabated at their current or historical levels, but these two factors introduce uncertainty into the analysis. You must identify the actions and the environmental factors that will determine the firm's ability to grow and to control costs, even if you cannot incorporate them directly into the cash flow model. This model should yield some insight into the acquisition's consequences if growth slowed or costs increased. This type of analysis is often called "What if?" analysis or sensitivity analysis.

Redirect the Report's Focus from Symptoms to Problems

This is also a good time to review the purpose of the report as stated at the outset. If the problem was not specified correctly at the outset, you may realize that you should restate it after some analysis has been performed. The most common discovery is that the problem as first stated addressed a symptom rather than a root cause. For example, a lower than acceptable rate of return on owners' equity is always a *symptom*. After some analysis, the *cause* of the lower profitability—for example, excess inventories, poor marketing effort, or inefficient production methods—will become evident. An analyst will reformulate the problem and will develop courses of action that reduce inventories, increase marketing success, or reduce production costs.

At this time, it is important to remember the earlier discussion about the genesis of problems: Some problems result from controllable factors, while others are produced by factors over which people have no control. Clearly identify the kind of factor you are dealing with, because the two require different strategies. If the problem results from an uncontrollable environmental factor, definition of the problem should make it clear that the source of the problem cannot be eliminated. When faced with such a problem, your best course of action is one that will reduce the sensitivity of your cash flows to this factor. Alternatively, if the problem emanates from a source that you can control, then frame it as such and address it directly.

I regularly use a case that illustrates this process very well. The case ends by asking the students which of two production scheduling alternatives should be adopted by the president of a small manufacturing firm. The director of manufacturing has recommended a change because he perceives the old method to be inefficient. The students initially frame the problem as the need to choose between two production scheduling alternatives. However, the case gives the students little guidance in choosing between the two alternatives. After some analysis, the students discover that the problem involves more than production. Suddenly, the focus of the class discussion changes from production efficiency to financial efficiency. The student analysis shifts to the determinants of cash flow, both controllable and uncontrollable. They discover that while the production scheduling and its associated cash outflows are controllable, the seasonal pattern of sales and its associated cash inflows are not. At that point, the problem is redefined as the potential mismatch between cash inflows and outflows. They realize that adjusting the production schedule is one action that management can take to reduce the risk posed by this mismatch. The redefinition of the problem and the new focus of the analysis would not have been possible at the outset of the discussion. The students simply did not know enough about the situation at that time.

Another redefinition process was illustrated in the nonroutine situation described earlier in the chapter. You will recall that the president appointed the vice president of finance as head of a committee to investigate the merits of going public. After the committee's work was underway, the vice president discovered that the president's reason for taking the company public had been for the company to grow through acquisitions to a size that would enable the company to remain competitive. The company must know whether appropriate acquisition candidates are likely to be available when the company has obtained money through the sale of its stock. The committee's report was not to be limited to the mechanics of the actual sale transaction, but was expected to address such strategic issues as having a liquid "corporate currency" with which to expand through acquisitions.

Develop and Test Alternative Courses of Action

Finance professionals received spreadsheet software enthusiastically because it allowed them to shorten substantially the time required to develop and solve a financial model. Models describe a set of relationships (the situation as perceived by the analyst). The model allows the analyst to test the impact of alternative courses of action on the set of relevant factors. The major benefit of spreadsheets occurs at this stage. Thus, the technological context for financial analysis reports has strongly influenced their contents.

Assuming that you have described the existing situation accurately, you can define alternative courses of action by stating the changes these alternatives will have on the spreadsheet relationships. You can test the course of action by adjusting the spreadsheet to reflect these changes, and examining the model's forecast of performance or value. In a very short period of time, the spreadsheet model enables you to demonstrate for the decision maker the results of a number of alternatives.

In the case involving my students, described earlier, once the students understood that uncertain demand was the problem and that the existing production schedule was only one course of action that reduced the impact of the problem on the firm, they developed a variety of other courses of action. Some of these courses of action involved marketing changes; some involved financing changes. Such analyses are far more creative and useful for the decision maker.

While spreadsheets have changed dramatically our approach to testing alternative strategies, they are not a panacea. The major problem with spreadsheet models is that they become reified; that is, analysts have a tendency to assume that the real world should behave like the model. Make no mistake, business is conducted in the real world. Any change to a model assumes that people perform tasks differently and respond differently to standard business situations. The spreadsheet model should reflect accurately these behavioral changes, and you should not assume that people can or will change their behavior to conform with the model.

For example, if you assume in your spreadsheet analysis that a firm reduces its inventory investment from $0.25 per dollar of sales to $0.20, you must be prepared to explain how such a reduction could be achieved and whether the reduced level of inventory would affect sales. Think about the specific questions that must be answered: What category of inventory—raw materials, work in process, or finished goods—will be reduced? What will prevent stockouts and lost sales if the reductions are made? Will inventories for all product lines be affected? If not, how were the affected product lines selected? How is "inventory production" affected during the transition period from one level of inventory to another? All of these questions must be answered. Consequences for both production and marketing must be identified. The set of actions that leads to the $.05 reduction in inventory for every dollar of sales is indeed complex, and furthermore, unexpected consequences may result. You must consider carefully the set of actions and all of their consequences, then present them in the report.

Select a Course of Action

Having examined the likely consequences of alternative courses of action, you are prepared to evaluate the alternatives and to express a professional opinion. Since we have employed financial concepts to develop the model used in making the decision, the alternatives will be evaluated in terms of their risk and return consequences. Experienced financial analysts discuss these two concepts in both quantitative and qualitative terms. The quantitative aspects of risk and return should be captured by the model. Qualitative risk and return statements about the alternatives will often reflect strategic issues as well as issues that were not incorporated in the financial model.

The objective at this stage is to develop a consensus. There may be no clearly superior course of action. Instead, the "best" alternative may emerge as one becomes dominant. *Dominant* is used in the following sense: If one of the alternatives appears to be clearly superior in one dimension and is not clearly inferior in the other, then it can be said to be the dominant alternative.

The interpretive process described above can employ a variety of analytical frameworks. What makes it uniquely financial is the role played by financial models and by the concepts of risk and return. The major advantage that this process provides to managers is the integrative aspect of financial analysis. If you perform the analysis correctly, all important aspects of the problem will play a role in your discussions, producing a professional opinion and support for a management decision. This process should help you to understand how to make your reports, regardless of where they fit in the scenario, more useful to the audience receiving them and to the ultimate decision maker.

In general, the same fundamental concepts of design, headings, and organization that you have learned in earlier chapters apply to documents presenting financial analysis and conclusions. An examination of the documents produced by your firm will enable you to detect any significant differences in format or style. These you should vary as appropriate in order to meet the needs of your audiences in particular situations.

☐ COMMUNICATION CHALLENGES

PRELIMINARY EXERCISE 1   Select some important non-financial decision that you have made in the past. Then answer the following questions relative to that decision.

a. Use a diagram like Figure 26-1 to outline your decision and the associated events and consequences.
b. What factors gave rise to the risk and return characteristics of your decision?
c. How did you perform the tradeoff between risk and return in making your decision?
d. Were the consequences exactly what you expected? If they were not, what factors did you inaccurately anticipate? What factors did you fail to anticipate?

PRELIMINARY EXERCISE 2   Consumers engage in financial analysis of some form when they purchase a home, a car, or a major consumer appliance. Describe a major purchase that you have made.

a. What questions did you have to resolve in making your decision?
b. What information did you gather and how did you analyze it?
c. How did you characterize risk and return factors in your decision?
d. What controllable and uncontrollable factors did you identify?
e. What external factors, if any, imposed a deadline on your decision?

EXERCISE 1

Preparing to Call on a Customer

Susan Stem is a vice president of Metropolitan Bank, where she manages a portfolio of loans ranging in size from $2 million to $50 million. Her responsibilities include monitoring and servicing existing customers as well as calling on prospects and making new loans. While she is rewarded for making new loans, the worst thing in a loan officer's career is to initiate a loan that ultimately goes into default.

Recently one of Susan's customers gave her the name of an associate who was unhappy with his current banking relationship. Susan has made an appointment with the man, Tom Adams. Prior to the meeting, Susan called Mr. Adams, who gave her a brief description of his business and told her that he had had no prior experience with her bank. Review the comments early in the chapter of the loan officer who called on physicians' offices as loan prospects. While the physician's office is a service company and can offer little in collateral beyond personal guarantees and miscellaneous personal collateral, a manufacturing company will have other sources of collateral: real estate, equipment, inventories, backorders, and receivables.

As one who knows marketing fundamentals, Susan also realizes that a company that has only a few large customers will be more vulnerable to risk than a manufacturing firm with a broad customer base. Her knowledge of production tells her to look for seasonal variation in manufacturing companies, because such companies are likely to need loans to cover the cost of inventory buildups in the off-peak season. Although she is an experienced loan officer, the committee has not made many loans to manufacturing companies because the region has a rather small number of these firms.

a. *What should be Susan's primary objective in her initial meeting with Mr. Adams?*
b. *What does the bank want to know? To what questions does it want answers?*
c. *Prepare a mind map that will help Susan to plan for and structure the initial interview with Mr. Adams.*
d. *What questions should she ask to help her in understanding this prospective client's needs?*

EXERCISE 2

Writing a Call Report

A call report is a short report that Metropolitan Bank requires its loan officers to prepare after visiting with a current or prospective customer. It should be useful for several purposes. First, it should assist the person preparing it in planning future meetings with the same firm. Second, it is a record of things that were discussed that will help create a history of the relationship. Third, it will help the officer to keep track of the customer's needs and ensure that no potential opportunity to develop new business is overlooked. Fourth, it will apprise the officer's superiors of his or her marketing activities. This exercise asks you to plan and write a call report.

Susan Stem, vice president of Metropolitan Bank, visited the offices of Tyrel Manufacturing, Inc. this afternoon. This visit was an initial interview in which she met with the president, Mike Adams, and the controller, Hoyt Jackson. Mike told Susan about the company's growth during its ten-year operating history and described in general terms his growth plans for the next five years. Susan noted that his plans sounded quite ambitious.

Mike had started Tyrel, a manufacturer of valves, after working for fifteen years in the engineering department of a competitor. Hoyt had worked previously for a major accounting firm and had been in charge of the audit for Mike's former employer. Mike observed, "Three years ago I finally convinced Hoyt to leave public accounting. It took me a long time to do it."

Mike mentioned that Tyrel currently banks at the First National Bank and has been there for the last three years. During the relationship, Tyrel regularly has used its maximum line of credit for three or more months. Hoyt noted that while they are not unhappy with their banking relationship overall, there recently have been some problems. What Hoyt considers to be bookkeeping errors on the part of the bank have resulted in a number of returned checks and some substantial service charges for insufficient funds. Mike expressed some concern that the officer currently assigned to the relationship does not understand Tyrel's business. "I really don't think that kid understands the difference between a ball valve and a butterfly valve."

After meeting in his office, Mike gave Susan a tour of his manufacturing and shipping facilities. She noted that both areas were very busy and that few machine stations were idle. When she asked Mike if this reflected a normal day's activity level, he responded, "For now it does. This is our busy season, and we operate two ten-hour shifts, six days a week."

As they walked from the shop back to the office, Mike pointed to a large parcel of land adjacent to the shop. "That's our expansion site over there. We bought it two years ago. It should be sufficient to support our growth for the next ten years." Upon returning to the office, she asked for and received a copy of Tyrel's latest audited financial statements. She thanked Mike for the opportunity to meet with him, and returned to the bank.

Susan Stem would have prepared her report on a form designed for that purpose. *Part of this assignment is designing the call report form as well as writing the report itself.* The call report should display information in places that will make using the form easy. This form will be read by several audiences: the person who supervises the loan officers, people who take over the account later on, people who are looking for prospects that did not become the bank's customers at one time, but who might still be good call prospects. Items of information that would not change from one call to the other should be placed at the bottom of the form. Actions to be taken and the answers to the bank's primary questions should be placed near the top of the form, so that people who are trying to determine progress on the account can do so quickly.

You may want to leave a space for indicating the date when a follow-up step has been completed. Evaluate your initial design to determine whether there are large blank spaces anywhere. You may be able to create a grid to display routine information (obtained from every prospect). You may decide whether you will use the same form for all calls or create a different form for initial calls and follow-up calls.

1. *Prepare a list of questions or a form to be used in preparing call reports.*
2. *Use your form to prepare a call report for Susan's call on Tyrel Manufacturing, Inc.*
3. *Test your form by writing the report using the form.*

Using your form will give you a test of how convenient it is. You may ask a student from another class to pretend to be someone replacing you during your vacation. See how easily the user can figure out what has happened on the account by reading the form.

EXERCISE 3

Memo to the Committee: New Assignment

Assume that you are the vice president of finance for Brondex Sprockets, discussed on pages 700–701, who was appointed the chair of a three-person committee charged with investigating the merits and the mechanics of going public. Your committee includes the controller and the corporate counsel.

After receiving your assignment, you sat down and drew the diagram shown in Figure 26-3.

Obviously, a number of important questions are embedded in the "going public" issue. The committee's report three months from now will have to state each question, assign a level of importance to it, describe the information and analysis employed to answer the question, and outline for the board your answer to the question. Ultimately, the board will use your set of answers in making its decision. The report will be the final communication requirement in the scenario. For now, you must gain the controller's and the legal counsel's cooperation, plan what questions to answer, and decide how to gather the necessary information.

First you must call an initial meeting with the controller and the general counsel. You want to present the questions you think must be answered. By the time of the first committee meeting, they also should have developed a set of questions to be addressed by the committee's report. You must draft a memo outlining an agenda for the committee's first meeting. *Your first task is to draft the memo.*

From the Desk of the Vice President

Mechanics of Transaction	Course of Action: Going Public	Consequences
What underwriter?		Market Value
How many shares?		Liquidity
What price?		For owner
What discount to the		For firm
underwriter?		(cash received)
When?		Legal Liability
How much will be		for managers
"secondary"?		for manager directors
Planning & preparation?		for outside directors
Accounting issues or		
problems?		
Related transactions?		

FIGURE 26-3.   Planning a Report

EXERCISE 4

You are still the chair of the committee reporting on the possibility of going public in Exercise 3, and your committee has had its first meeting.

Redefining the Project

After the meeting, you feel as though the committee has done a good job of establishing the set of questions to be answered. You have assigned each member responsibilities for gathering information and performing analyses sufficient to answer each question. As you expected, both the controller and the general counsel asked questions that you had failed to consider, and each had information regarding the legal and accounting dimensions of the transaction. You are on your way to meet with the president, and you intend to discuss your progress with him.

In your meeting, you are almost through with your presentation when the president asks, "Who is preparing a review of the recent merger and acquisition transactions in our industry?" You reply that you have not asked anyone to answer that question in detail. The president responds, "Damn it, why do you think we are going to all the trouble of selling stock? Our industry has changed. The only people who will be around in five years are large public companies. I intend to be one of them. Once we have publicly traded stock, we can launch an aggressive acquisitions campaign. If we wait too long, the best independent companies will already be gone, acquired by our competitors. I want you to push this thing hard. You have less than two and a half months."

Upon returning to your office, you pull out the diagram that you prepared before writing your memo. What major changes must be made on the diagram? *Mark your changes on the diagram.*

EXERCISE 5

Persuading the President to Adopt a New Procedure

Tom Reynolds is the treasurer of a privately owned company. While he owns 10 percent of the stock, the majority of the stock (63 percent) is owned by Jerry French, the president of the company. The company has recently experienced an upturn in business and is planning to make substantial new capital investments in the next five years.

Current plans include entering a new geographic market. To serve the new market, substantial warehousing and manufacturing facilities would have to be built. The company has no established policy for reviewing capital investment projects. The expansion has never really been analyzed. Jerry remarked one day, "We're making so much money this year, we can finally become a major player in this industry. The fastest way for us to grow is to expand into a new region where several of our competitors currently have manufacturing plants."

When Tom asked if Jerry wanted him to analyze the financial consequences of the expansion, Jerry replied, "What's there to analyze? We are making plenty of money in this area, and we'll make plenty of money when we open up in the new region."

When Tom asked Jerry how he planned to finance the expansion, Jerry replied, "We'll use the cash in our account at Metropolitan Bank for the building and we'll get them to loan us the money for the land. That money in the bank won't cost us anything and the long-term mortgage on the land should be easy for us to repay over fifteen years."

Tom recently had attended a seminar at a local university entitled "The Corporate Treasurer and Modern Financial Theory." The three-day seminar introduced Tom to some challenging ideas. The most significant to Tom was the concept of the cost of capital and the methods that the professors developed for calculating a firm's cost of capital. Clearly, he decided, different financing decisions could strongly affect a company's performance. As a private homework project while at the seminar, Tom made some preliminary calculations of his firm's cost of capital. Tom decided that he was going to prepare a memo to Jerry, first thing, addressing the need to formalize the procedure for selecting and financing new capital investment projects. He felt the planned geographic expansion was the first project that should be subjected to the new procedure.

1. *Prepare an issue analysis tree Tom can use in preparing his memo to Jerry.* Tom wants to propose that the new procedure be instituted and that the geographic expansion be subjected to the new procedure. He intends to attach his preliminary calculations as an appendix.

2. *Draft the memo.*

IF YOU WOULD LIKE TO READ MORE

Copeland, T. E., & Weston, J. F. (1988). *Financial theory and corporate policy* (3rd ed.). Reading, MA: Addison-Wesley. An advanced text in corporate finance. For professionals.

Downes, J. (1985). *Dictionary of finance and investment terms*. Woodbury, NY: Barron's. This basic dictionary is an excellent reference for communications instructors.

Duilio, E. A. (1987). *Theory and problems of money and banking*. Schaum's Outline Series in Economics. New York: McGraw-Hill. Like other books in the series, this one offers a good basic introduction to its subject. This book analyzes money and banking practices as they have developed since the mid-1970s. Communications instructors might also find the *Mathematics of finance* volume in the series useful if they are interested in knowing more about the quantitative side of financial analysis.

Fruhan, W. E., Jr. (1979). *Financial strategy: Studies in the creation, transfer, and distribution of shareholder value.* Homewood, IL: Richard D. Irwin. A basic text in financial strategy that different firms may choose.

Fuller, R. J., & Farrell, J. L., Jr. (1987). *Modern investments and security analysis.* New York: McGraw-Hill. A standard and widely-used text in investments.

Gup, B. E., Fraser, D. R., & Kolari, J. W. (1989). *Commercial bank management.* New York: Wiley. This book provides an introduction to financial analysis as it is practiced in commercial banks. Good for understanding the banking situations companies face.

Haugen, R. A. (1986). *Modern investment theory.* Englewood Cliffs, NJ: Prentice-Hall. This text requires only a minimum level of training in mathematics and statistics. Good coverage of portfolio theory, issues related to capital asset pricing, interest rates and bond management, options, forward and futures contracts. Also has chapter on taxes, investment strategy, and securities prices.

Van Horne, J. C. (1989). *Financial management and policy* (8th ed.). Englewood Cliffs, NJ: Prentice-Hall. A classic introductory text in corporate finance.

☐ STRATEGIC PLANNING COMMUNICATIONS

OBJECTIVES

This chapter will help you

- anticipate the varied scenarios used for strategic planning

- describe concisely a company's goals, mission, and strategy

- organize the discussion of your analyses

- analyze the internal and external audiences for strategic plans

- recognize the relationship between the strategic plan and public relations materials of the firm

PREVIEW

trategic planning is the process wherein a corporation develops and communicates its plans to compete and succeed in the marketplace. A corporation's strategic plan can be as simple as a few pages or as complex as a multivolume report painstakingly assembled by a large task force over a several-month period. The short plan and financial projections would probably be more relevant for a small company or a start-up firm, whereas the large report would more likely be found in a large multinational enterprise such as Nippon Bank, Royal Dutch Shell, or General Electric. Although you will more fully develop your skills at strategic planning in a course on business policy or business strategy, in this chapter you will learn to identify the key variables that affect the selection and execution of a communications strategy related to a strategic plan.[1] Because actual strategic plans vary enormously in length, formality, and audience, the best preparation for writing such plans on the job is to learn how to analyze the critical factors that influence the planning process and how to select communication strategies appropriate in different companies. This chapter will discuss not only the strategic plan itself, but the communications that occur during the planning process.

STRATEGIC PLANNING COMMUNICATIONS:
❏ # DESCRIBING THE FIRM'S GOALS, MISSION, AND STRATEGIES

A Company's Strategic Plan

A strategic plan will typically contain statements about three key elements: the firm's goals, its mission, and its strategy.

Goals

Goals are general targets for the firm.

A firm should identify its goals. Is the firm trying to get the largest market share in its industry? Is it aiming to be the lowest-cost producer? Does it want to be known for the high quality of its service? Does the firm wish to provide consistent dividends to its stockholders? Or is the firm targeted toward other ends? The challenge is to articulate goals with sufficient precision to provide guidance without too many details. Different stakeholders (people with a tangible stake, or interest, in the organization) may have very different goals: employees want stable employment and high wages, lenders want prompt repayment of debt, customers want high-quality products and services at low prices, governmental regulators want safe products emanating from nonpolluting plants, and so on. Balancing these groups' varied interests in a single strategic goal statement is not easy. This statement must lead the firm smoothly through turbulent times, during which the concerns of different subsets of stakeholders will take the lead in directing the firm's affairs.

To see how one company succeeded in balancing the conflicting interests of its stakeholders while producing a useful statement of its strategic goals, consider George A. Steiner's report on the goals of Lockheed Aircraft:

1. To be the major company satisfying in the highest technical sense the national security needs of the United States and its allies in space, air, land, and sea.
2. To employ technical resources in meeting the nondefense needs of governments and the requirements of commercial markets.
3. To achieve continuous growth of profits at a rate needed to attract and retain stockholder investment.
4. To recognize and appropriately discharge our responsibilities for the welfare of our employees, the communities in which we do business, and society as a whole.
5. To maintain a large proportion of sales in advanced technical products bearing the Lockheed name.
6. To maintain continuity of the enterprise by holding relatively low rates of change of ownership, management and employees.*

---

*From *Top Management Planning* (p. 146) by G. Steiner. New York: Macmillan. Copyright 1969 by Macmillan. Reprinted by permission.

Lockheed's goals are so broad that they do not dictate specific management decisions. They do not set priorities, and they will not suffice as standards to judge the achievements of the firm. They do, however, set the general direction for the firm, without causing some important stakeholder groups to take offense at what Lockheed is trying to accomplish.

Mission Statement

A mission statement says who the company is and what distinguishes it from competitors.

The firm's mission statement must describe its business and its sense of identity. For example, one firm might say, "We are in the printing industry, supplying printing services to individuals and small businesses needing quick, low-cost assistance." The mission statement for another firm might be, "We manufacture handcrafted toys that are distributed and sold by brokers; we concentrate on high-quality products with loving attention to detail; innovation in our product line is of paramount importance to our success." The mission statement specifies the products and services offered by the firm and delineates the customers who buy them. Because the economic attractiveness of markets changes, it is not easy to decide upon an optimal mission statement for a firm, one that balances opportunity in the marketplace (present and future) with the capabilities available within the firm.

George Melloan writes about Cray Research, Inc., a manufacturer of supercomputers: "Its corporate mission statement reads, simply: 'Cray Research designs, manufactures, markets and supports the most powerful computer systems available.'"[2] Such a simple, powerful mission statement, an easily understood vision of the firm, lays down an exciting challenge for its employees and announces high standards of excellence to its customers.

Firms sometimes communicate their mission statements through their advertising, as Randall's Food Markets, Inc. did with its television commercials. Figure 27-1 is a script and Figure 27-2 is a storyboard. (A storyboard lays out in print the words spoken and illustrates some of the more important visuals shown during the advertisement.) These thirty-second television commercials manage to communicate that Randall's is both a place to obtain groceries and related items, and that it is a place where store personnel will treat shoppers with friendly concern. Randall's strives as part of its mission to create a store atmosphere where it is pleasant to shop and where the customers are treasured as friends. Its commercials, as portrayed by these storyboards, communicate these messages.

Strategy

A strategy is the way the firm will accomplish its mission.

A firm's strategy states how the firm will execute its mission to realize its strategic goals. Strategy identifies the firm's action plans and programs, which should cover all facets of the company: marketing, operations, finances, human resources, plant and equipment, and so on. A realistic strategy operates within the scope of the firm's mission statement, attains its strategic goals in the face of marketplace competition, and uses resources available to the firm. Needless to say, it is very difficult to devise a workable, realistic strategy for a firm, and this difficulty adds to the complexities of strategic planning.

TELEVISION COPY

CLIENT   Randall's

DESCRIPTION   :30 TV - SPOT #4

AIR DATE

VTR #

DATE PREPARED   November 17, 1989

JOB #

VIDEO	AUDIO
OLDER WOMAN HURRIES INTO STORE AS IT BEGINS TO RAIN. CHECKOUT CLERK SMILES IN UNDERSTANDING.	SINGER: One store understands, we treat you like a friend . . .
EMPLOYEE STOCKING HBA SHELF ON HER KNEES. ENTIRE FAMILY WALKS BY IN IDENTICAL YELLOW GOLASHES AND RAINCOATS.	One store works so hard because we want you back again
FISH CLERK LEANING OVER COUNTER EXPLAINING HOW TO COOK FISH. PULL BACK TO REVEAL ALL THE PEOPLE AT COUNTER ARE LEANING OVER TO LISTEN	One word says it all . . .
WOMAN AND MAN REACHING FOR SAME <u>EXTRA REMARKABLE</u> ITEM BUY ITEM. LOOK UP AND SMILE.	We give you so much more . . .
LITTLE GIRL IN BASKET REACHES OUT TO GRAB FLOWER AS MOTHER ROLLS BY.	That's why we say Randall's is . . .
SACKER HOLDING UMBRELLA FOR OLDER LADY IN PARKING LOT IN RAIN. SUPER: <u>LOGO</u> AND <u>YOUR REMARKABLE STORE</u>	Your remarkable store.

FIGURE 27-1. Television Commercial Script

This and subsequent Randall's television commercial scripts copyright 1987 by Randall's. Reprinted by permission.

FIGURE 27-2. Television Commercial Storyboard

While the Randall's television commercials emphasize the company's mission and seek customers' approval of that mission, a Northwest Industries advertisement in *Business Week* took on a more comprehensive task.[3] Its advertisement presented not only its mission but its strategy to a wide audience. By reaching beyond those already connected with the company, it was partially engaged in creating goodwill for itself, and it doubtlessly was attempting to interest others to buy its stock and corporate bonds, to purchase its products, and to respect the wisdom of its management. While written in a breezy manner suitable for casual magazine readers, the plan covers the three essential elements of a strategic plan: goals, mission, and strategy.

In 1978, a period of high inflation, Northwest Industries' goals were "to produce real growth" (that is, positive growth over and above that due solely from the rate of inflation) and "to maximize the total return to our stockholders" (that is, dividends plus appreciation in the price of common stock). The mission of Northwest Industries is, by inference, to manage a conglomerate, consisting at the time of Acme Boot, General Battery, and Union Underwear, among other operating companies. Their advertisement mentions criteria they use in acquiring and divesting operating companies (for example, avoid "companies subject to unusually large cyclical swings" or that are "dependent on a single customer or supplier" or that are "highly labor-intensive" or that do not have a predominant U.S. base). Their advertisement also discusses the strategies they use in running their operating companies: vertical integration, forward commitments on key raw materials, efficient production, and focusing on higher profit-margin goods.[4] They explain their vertical integration and efficient production strategies in this excerpt from their ad in Figure 27-3.

Scenarios for Formulating the Strategic Plan

Different firms have different scenarios for creating strategic plans.

The strategic plan uniting the three key ingredients (goals, mission statement, and strategy) in a coherent package may be developed through a variety of scenarios. One scenario is for a senior company officer, typically the president or chief executive officer (CEO), to prepare the entire strategic plan. Another scenario is for part of the senior management team (several vice presidents, for example) to create a strategic plan and to report their results for review and refinement to the rest of the senior management team. A third scenario is to assemble a task force from various parts of the organization (a plant manager, a sales manager, a vice president, a representative from the treasurer's office, etc.) to engage in strategic planning for presentation to senior management. Finally, strategic planning may be such a routine way of doing business in some firms that a permanent group is formed solely to do strategic planning.

Whatever technique is used to conduct the strategic planning process, the strategic planner has to keep several factors in mind at the same time. The firm operates in several environments simultaneously; consequently, planning for the firm must go on in each of them. The planner needs to decide upon an appropriate communications strategy for the resulting strategic plan: to whom the results of the planning process will be communicated, how much detail will be

STRATEGIC PLAN FOR NORTHWEST INDUSTRIES (1978)

No company can control or even completely foresee the rate of inflation. But at Northwest Industries we're always trying to lessen its influence on our operations. We do this by sticking with long-standing management strategies that are particularly helpful in uncertain times.

Our goal is to procure real growth. And that means to maximize the total return to our stockholders—including dividend income.

VERTICAL INTEGRATION

One tool we use is vertical integration. It doesn't just provide cost efficiencies. It also helps insulate our operating companies from price volatility in purchased materials and services. For instance, our General Battery Corporation's integrated production processes include everything from secondary lead smelting and plastic case manufacturing to the delivery of batteries by the company's own truck distribution system. This kind of control helps keep our product costs both reasonable and comparatively predictable.

We also have a conscious policy of making forward commitments on key raw materials well into the future—far longer than many of our competitors. Occasionally we guess wrong and miss out on falling prices. But we like the advantage of having known costs for an extended period of time. For instance, by settling now on future cotton costs, Union Underwear Company can stabilize an important cost element. This helps Union plan production and price its goods sensibly. But be sure of this: we are *not* speculators or commodity traders. We are manufacturers.

EFFICIENT PRODUCTION

Efficient production also helps us fight inflation. Almost all of our companies are industry leaders. That allows us advantages many competitors do not have, so we can make good products at lower costs. And when it comes to maintaining or increasing margins in an inflationary environment, our companies frequently do the job through cost reduction rather than by relying simply on price increases.

Another way our companies maintain margins without price increase is by upgrading product mix. They drop lower margin goods to concentrate on more profitable items. This ensures our facilities are utilized for maximum profitability. An example is Acme Boot Company getting out of the manufacturing of golf and dress shoes to make and sell more western boots. A simple move, but effective.

From a Northwest Industry ad, *Business Week* (1978, November 20), 168-169. Copyright 1978 by Northwest Industries. Quoted with permission.

FIGURE 27-3.

communicated, and how the plan will be presented. Finally, the planner needs to decide upon the appropriate methodology to perform the planning—which analytic tools are the right ones to use in light of the firm's environment, the communications target, the format of the results to be presented, and the presentation of the plan. This section of the chapter will lead you through the steps that you might go through in one scenario.

Writing about Multiple Forces in the Firm's Environment

Writers must analyze many aspects of the firm's environment during the planning process.

The firm for which you work operates in an environment that has multiple aspects, as explained in Chapter 2. Among the most powerful are the economic marketplace and a network of social and political relationships. In the marketplace, the firm competes on the basis of economics with other firms for sales of goods and services (through pricing and quality), advertising space and time (through purchases), geographic location (through purchase and rent of real estate and buildings), the right to use other people's money (through interest and dividend payments), and the right to people's labor (through salaries and wages). Decisions made in the marketplace environment are intended to be economically optimal ones.

In the planning process, you must analyze the market conditions, as well as any probable changes (due to one competitor's acquiring another, a new product's being introduced into the marketplace, or a change in the number of prospective customers). As writer, you normally begin by describing the economic conditions for each product or service offered by your firm: perfectly competitive, monopolistic, oligopolistic, and so on. Then, you describe the relative market shares, the bases for customer purchase decisions, and the strong and weak points of each of your firm's products and services.

Social and political groups may limit the firm's business dealings.

Social and political entities of the firm's environment judge the firm's behavior on its consistency with societal mores and norms. If a company chooses to trade with an unfriendly government, its decision may be economically rational but very unwise in terms of its ability to continue its societally-endowed charter to operate. For example, the German firm that had sold to Libya a plant for making chemical weapons suffered severe government penalties after an international conference in late 1988.

Governments, regulatory agencies, and the courts evaluate the firm for its compliance with governmental laws and policies. A firm that consciously chooses to violate equal employment or pollution abatement legislation is asking for trouble, regardless of the economic hardships to the firm caused by adherence to those laws. For example, thanks to recent legislation, firms must now demand proof of citizenship of each employee or prospective employee, via a birth certificate or passport, or run afoul of immigrations laws concerning illegal employment of aliens.

Availability of technology, personnel, or supplies may affect the firm's choices.

Other elements in the external environment may affect firms as well. For some, changes in the prevalent technology (computers, communications, space exploration, etc.) profoundly impact the way the firm goes about its business and the success it may enjoy. For example, during the famed "Black Monday" market crash of October 19, 1987, Fidelity Investments' extensive computer system enabled it to avoid many of the problems its competitors faced. Other firms may be crucially dependent upon some aspect of their business; for example, universities rely upon a steady stream of qualified professors to teach courses. When there are too few, as occurred recently in computer science programs, crisis ensues. Firms that operate mines or drill for oil are similarly dependent upon good relationships with foreign countries possessing valuable mineral resources.

A strategic plan must work equally successfully under all the relevant conditions in a specific firm's environment. Therefore, as a planner and communicator, you must first identify clearly the relevant features of the environment in which a specific firm operates and the stakeholders who will have an interest in its strategy. Knowing that, you next can choose an appropriate communications strategy.

Understanding the Audiences for Your Plan

People inside and outside the company will see various versions of the strategic plan.

Who will see the detailed strategic plan? Typically, two groups of people inside the firm and four groups of people outside the firm see various versions of the strategic plan. (See Linnet Deily's example in the Executives' Perspectives section).

Internal Audiences

Senior managers. They receive an extended synopsis of the plan, long enough and detailed enough that they can devise and monitor actions, but not so detailed as to be cumbersome. Detailed records of the plan are kept on file in the event that senior management needs to refer to them for clarification or elaboration.

Employees. Others within the firm receive versions of the plan varying in degree of detail and specificity, depending upon their level within the firm and how much they need to know in order to make the strategic plan work.

External Audiences

Financial analysts. The finance community likes to be apprised of the general features of the strategic plan (they actually prefer the detailed one, but it should not be released in order to keep competitors ignorant of the firm's specific intentions and timing). Analysts use the plan to prepare earnings estimates and performance forecasts for the firm and the industry it is in.

Owners. Shareholders are usually given the same information afforded to financial analysts, and are usually given the information at the same time. Oftentimes, however, the strategic plan can only be inferred from financial documents such as the Security and Exchange Commission's Form 10-Q, which is read only by sophisticated shareholders. An abbreviated version of the plan frequently surfaces in the shareholder's annual report, but even that document is not read carefully by all concerned. (See Chapter 26.)

The media. A firm's strategic plan may affect the firm's hiring of labor, expansion of plants, introduction of new products or services, or have some other newsworthy dimension. As such, it behooves the firm to prepare news releases of its strategic plan for the print media and to prepare speakers and visuals that will interest the electronic media.

Other stakeholders. A wide variety of other special interest groups may have concerns about the firm's strategic plan. Customers, suppliers, lenders, unions, environmentalists, consumer advocates, community action groups, and others may want to see relevant parts of the strategic plan, as well as how the special interests of the stakeholders fit into the bigger picture that the firm paints with its strategic plan.

Preparing a Written Analysis of a Firm's Environment

Analyze the environment and the company with appropriate tools.

To analyze the firm's environment, you may use several analytical tools. Some widely-used tools, described in the Appendix, include the SWOT (Strengths, Weaknesses, Opportunities, and Threats) analysis, the Porter model of industry competition, stakeholder analysis, and the McKinsey 7-S or Seven-Factor Model for business leadership. If you have not become familiar with these tools in a management class, you may wish to read more about them in the Appendix. Each of these analytical tools will provide you a different picture of a firm's situation. Some of these insights will be more valuable than others in developing your firm's strategy.

Besides these four major analytical tools, a host of other techniques are available. These include computer simulation models of the firm and computer models of industries that were developed to understand the firm's structure, dynamics, and reactions to competitors' actions. Scenario analysis attempts to forecast how the firm would fare in different future environments. Cross-impact analysis attempts to judge how one set of trends may in turn cause others to occur. Mathematical modeling, Delphi forecasting by experts, and expert systems and artificial intelligence techniques are also being applied to the problems of strategy formulation and analysis.

Your Audiences Care about Your Results, Not Your Processes

Organize the report to show the logical relationships among the results of various analyses, not to show all the steps in your analysis.

The audiences for your report are interested primarily in the results of your analysis, not in a story of how you arrived at these conclusions. Many students and new employees sometimes organize their discussion around a series of tests or tools, in effect saying,

> "The industry analysis tells us X"

> "The SWOT analysis produces results Y"

> "The stakeholder analysis shows Z"

and so on. This pattern focuses the reader's or listener's attention on the tools of analysis, not on the interpretation of the firm's situation. Instead of choosing such a naive arrangement, examine closely the relationships between X, Y, and Z—the insights you have developed as a result of your analyses.

Try to describe for yourself, in a series of notes, the kinds of relationships that exist between the results of the various analyses. Does one set of results confirm or tend to disprove a supposed relationship? Does one set provide a guide to specific advantageous steps that another analysis only implied?

An Analysis of the Prospects for a New Hotel

Consider, by way of example, the work of some strategic planners for a hotel chain. Their industry analysis suggested that opportunities for new hotels existed in Houston, a city that had recently built a major convention center. Their stakeholder analysis showed, however, that many urban poor people of a single ethnic minority had been displaced from their residences when the convention center was built, and therefore a new hotel was likely to be opposed by a neighborhood preservation group. On the other hand, their SWOT analysis showed that their hotel company had an excellent record in minority hiring and minority relations. Even though the hotel chain might receive opposition when seeking a building permit, the firm's strategic planners were confident that the prospect of new jobs and the positive record of the firm in building good community relations would reduce the opposition to a manageable level and would result in minimal unfavorable publicity for the firm.

To review, you should organize the discussion of the firm's environment by summarizing clearly the relations among analytic results, and proving each supporting claim by drawing on the evidence from the appropriate analyses. If the writers in the hotel chain example were to follow this advice, they would begin with a statement such as, "Analysis of the sociopolitical environment in Houston, Texas, reveals good opportunities for the firm, coupled with certain manageable problems." Then, the detailed results of each of the analytic tests sketched in the previous paragraph could be used to support that claim.

Planning in Practice

How the Overall Situation Affects the Process

The overall situation that caused planning to begin will affect how you plan and how you communicate.

It is easy to state how strategic planning is supposed to operate in principle; the reality of planning by actual firms immersed in the daily battle for profits can be quite different. The actual situation faced by the organization strongly influences the strategic planning and the way its results are communicated. Why is the strategic planning occurring, and who requested a strategic plan? Is it due to a direct order from the CEO, is it simply a routine annual activity, has it been engendered in response to a crisis situation, is it a preliminary step before seeking more capitalization, or has it been caused by the creation of a new senior management team? Each of these communication contexts will cause subsequent events to unfold differently. Thus, you should be sensitive to what has elicited the request for a strategic plan; once you know that, you also know a lot about the strategic planning process that must follow, as well as a communication strategy for the result.

A direct order from the CEO immediately identifies the CEO as the most important stakeholder in the process. That person's preferences concerning formal versus informal written reports, oral briefings, elaborate multimedia presentations, etc., will dictate the *genre* of the report—its form, its length, its comprehensiveness in documentation, and so on. How detailed and extensive the report is, how quickly it is to be produced, and identities of other possible recipients of the report will hinge on the preferences of the CEO.

But if strategic planning is simply a routine annual activity, then the best guess for next year's report and reporting process will probably be whatever happened last year, adjusted for anticipated events. The planning will probably follow the same process, the report will probably visually resemble previous reports, the same people will probably do the planning and write the report, and it will probably go to the same distribution list. Only if somewhere in the bureaucracy was some complaint registered or some suggestion for improvement noted will the planning and reporting processes be altered in the least.

If a crisis has precipitated the strategic planning process (for example, a major lawsuit, a drastic decline in market share, a competitor's introduction of a vastly improved product, or mounting losses), then the subsequent events tend to be focused both in terms of attention and in time horizon. If a governmental agency is threatening to close a major production plant, the company's strategic planning need not concern the state of the global economy ten years hence. Such crisis-evoked strategic planning efforts tend to be performed by task forces as opposed to standing planning units, and they tend to be composed of senior managers and problem area specialists assembled from throughout the organization. Typically, no formal report is issued, unless some external group requests one as part of the resolution of the crisis, and the recipient of the report is senior management itself, especially that part empowered to take the actions recommended by the report. In this case, the report is typically oral, focused on the crisis, and without visual aids, all owing to the urgency of the scenario.

Sometimes strategic planning is undertaken in order to seek more capitalization for the firm. No "back-of-the-envelope scribbling" will suffice to convince venture capitalists, lenders, financial analysts, or the public to invest their funds in the firm. Instead, the resulting business plan (see Chapter 28) must be an impressive document that effectively "markets" the company and its new initiatives. In most cases, this situation calls for both a slick publication and a very persuasive oral presentation. The resulting strategic business plan must unimpeachably convince wary investors of the present strength and future prospects of the firm with respect to its industry and competition.

If the firm seeks public financing, the U.S. government, through the Securities and Exchange Commission, requires that possible benefits to investors not be overstated and that all risks be fully disclosed. There are stiff penalties, including imprisonment in federal penitentiaries, for failing to comply with these disclosure requirements. Although this potential liability should make strategic planning even more exciting, in practice there are routine "laundry lists" of items to be included in risk disclosure statements.

Different audiences make different media appropriate.

When a company is led by a new senior management team, either because of an outside takeover of the firm or an internal succession of a new CEO who assembles a new cabinet to help run the company, a different type of strategic planning and reporting is called for. Most likely, these people need a quick education about the firm, its prospects, its competitors, and its industry. Once the new senior management team has learned, probably from oral briefings on those topics, the critical factors for survival and success, it will need more detailed information (probably in the form of written reports) about those critical success factors.

How Senior Management Affects the Process

The communication styles of senior managers, in particular their cultural roles within the organization, will strongly affect both the strategic planning process and the ways in which the results of that process are communicated. Broadly, there are three types of senior management, and each configuration affects the planning process differently. In the "great leader" model, there is a single, strong, frequently charismatic leader atop the organization; think of Lee Iacocca at Chrysler, Thomas J. Watson at IBM, Harold Geneen at IT&T, Katherine Graham at *The Washington Post*, or Walter Wriston at Citicorp. Strategic planning does not so much serve these people as it flows *from* these people. Great leaders set strategic goals for the firm and provide the impetus for the attainment of challenging objectives. For them, strategic planning is a way for the firm to identify the means by which it is going to tackle the strategic goals set for it by the leader.

In contrast, the bureaucratized organization consists of a group of people, each carrying out his or her duties according to an agreed-upon set of formal job descriptions. The senior managers are there because they are older, wiser, more experienced, and more competent than the others in the organization. But they are not infallible, nor do they have enormous bases of personal power and influence. Strategic planning in this context is directed more at keeping the organization from making any huge, survival-threatening mistakes. Strategic planning and reporting are simply rational standard operating procedures (SOPs); their form, depth, content, distribution, etc., will conform to organizational norms, as do the other SOPs. In this type of senior management situation, the past most definitely provides the prologue.

The third type of senior management scenario is the politicized organization. In this case, the company may be considered to be structured into a loose set of shifting political coalitions. Such companies have no single great leader to lead them, nor are they led by a faceless bureaucracy concerned with following standard routines. Instead, the senior management team consists of factions vying with one another for power and control of the organization. The coalitions compete with one another for power over the destiny of the organization and its resources. Which coalition is dominant on any one issue will vary from time to time, depending on the particular fortunes of the groups.

Different combinations of stakeholders affect the planning and reporting process.

Strategic planning and reporting in this instance requires careful attention to the most important stakeholders at the moment. The most relevant stakeholders may be the presently dominant senior management coalition (for routine strategic planning and reporting), some external group of individuals (owners, environmentalists, governmental regulators, etc., in the event of a crisis), some parties within the organization (for example, if the strategic plan calls for a retrenchment or major expansion in some subdivision of the organization), or even some competitors or other outside organizations (for example, if the strategic plan calls for an alliance or joint venture or some other compact with organizations external to the firm). Naturally, planning and reporting will have to be responsive to whichever of these particular stakeholders happens to hold the upper hand at the time.

How Corporate Culture Affects Strategic Planning Communications

The culture of an organization—the way things get done, or the "persisting integrated pattern of thoughts, attitudes, actions and artifacts"[5]—affects the way strategic planning is carried out and the way the results are communicated. An organization's culture typically does not affect the targets of strategic planning (what gets planned for), or identify the recipients of the plan. One must develop good antennae for reading correctly the culture in order to play organizational politics successfully.

Corporate culture affects attitudes toward planning and responding to recommendations.

Corporate culture involves social cohesion within the organization. Are people warm and friendly toward one another or cold and impersonal ("professional")? An organization with a strongly cohesive culture will not require the planners to prepare a report that is long on persuasion backed up by lots of formal analysis and data collection. A supportive organizational atmosphere will engender a great deal of trust in the efforts of others in the firm. By contrast, in an organization where there is a great deal of suspicion and mistrust of others, the dissemination of the planning report will be kept tightly controlled, a great deal of attention will be paid to the wording in the report, and the only actions recommended will be those that can be rationally justified.

Finally, attitudes toward innovation form another important element of an organization's culture. Those firms that encourage the development of new products and services, new operational processes, and new ways of looking at the world will likewise support innovative strategic plans, delivered in creative manners and distributed to novel recipients. A plan calling for entry into new markets, a plan appearing on videotape cassettes, and a plan sent to the firm's major customers will be more likely to receive ratification by an organization with such a culture. But a firm that places a premium on maintaining traditional patterns of behavior and that discourages experimentation by responding, "That's just not the way we do things around here," will likely only accept a strategic planning report that uses standard methodology, is structured as previous ones, contains few surprises, and is sent to the same people who received previous plans.

Corporate cultures can be strong, albeit sometimes subtle. They are exceedingly resistant to change, and any successful change to a firm's culture generally takes a long time to bring about. Astute strategic planners and communicators will learn to recognize the important facets of organizational culture in their firms and learn to live with the constraints and permissions entailed in their firm's culture.

As you can now realize, the great number of variables in both the external and internal environments of a firm produces enormous differences in the strategic planning process, in the audiences for strategic planning communications, and in the types of strategic plans (ranging from oral reports or memos to multiple volumes). The best skill you can develop, as a person not yet working in a company, is skill in recognizing and analyzing the critical factors that will affect you in strategic planning, whatever your role in a company.

❏ COMMUNICATION CHALLENGES

EXERCISE 1

Choose an organization with which you are very familiar; for example, your college or university, your church, a store where you regularly shop, or your bank. *Describe that organization's mission*—its business field and the ways in which it differs from its competitors. What are the special characteristics of that firm or organization that help define its identity and cause it to be seen as the unique entity that it is?

EXERCISE 2

Using the same organization whose mission statement you described in answer to the first exercise, or another company with which you are very familiar, *prepare a concise statement describing the strategies it uses to carry out its mission and to compete successfully for customers.*

EXERCISE 3

Using the same organization you chose either for exercise 1 or 2, identify the elements in the firm's environments that influence its operations. If this is a large company, look up articles in your college library about the company. You may use some of the search techniques recommended in Chapter 12, "Research Strategies for Reports," to locate good sources for information. Apply one or more of the analytical tools described in the Appendix (Industry Analysis, SWOT, Stakeholder Analysis, or 7-S) to the information you obtain, and *write an environmental analysis section for your company's strategic plan.*

EXERCISE 4

Prepare a one-page guide for your own future use, comparing the scenario for strategic planning you would expect to find in a company dominated by a great leader with the scenario you would expect to find in a large insurance company (more likely a bureaucratized organization run by standard operating procedures). At the end of the guide, add a paragraph indicating how much experience you have had with either type of firm. Do your experiences agree with the descriptions in the text?

EXERCISE 5

Compare and analyze the additional copy and storyboards in Figures 27-4, 27-5, and 27-6, to determine which of the three best conveys the mission of Randall's food stores.

EXERCISE 6

Choose a store where you shop frequently. This can be any kind of store. Plan storyboards for a 30-second commercial to publicize the store's mission. You need not be able to draw the sketches on the storyboard; just jot down phrases telling what the picture would show. *Write the narrator's script or the characters' dialogue for the commercial.*

TELEVISION COPY

CLIENT   Randall's

DESCRIPTION   :30 TV - (SPOT #3)

AIR DATE

VTR #

DATE PREPARED   November 17, 1989

JOB #

VIDEO	AUDIO
THREE TEENAGED GIRLS IN VIDEO DEPARTMENT. LOOKING FOR MOVIES, CUTE GUY WALKS BY-THEY ALL TURN TO LOOK.	<u>SINGER</u>: One store understands, we treat you like a friend . . .
FATHER AND SON IN FRONT OF DELI COUNTER. BOTH ARE DRESSED IN IDENTICAL "BUSINESS" SUITS.	One store works so hard because we want you back again
YOUNG MAN (FORMER EMPLOYEE) SEES FRIEND SACKER AND "GIVES HIM FIVE".	One word says it all . . .
KID IN PRODUCE DEPARTMENT WITH BASEBALL CAP ON. MANAGER REACHES OUT AND FLIPS CAP UP. LITTLE GIRL LAUGHS..	We give you so much more . . .
MOTHER PUSHING CART, DAUGHTER PUSHING TOY CART.	That's why we say Randall's is . .
TEENAGED GIRLS WALKING OUT OF STORE. SAME BOY WITH SACK AND SKATEBOARD SMILES AT THEM. THEY GIGGLE. SUPER: <u>LOGO</u> AND <u>YOUR REMARKABLE STORE</u>	Your remarkable store.

FIGURE 27-4.

TELEVISION COPY

CLIENT   Randall's

DESCRIPTION   :30 TV - (SPOT #2)

AIR DATE

VTR #

DATE PREPARED   November 17, 1989

JOB #

VIDEO	AUDIO
LITTLE BOY TRYING TO GET BIG DOG TO SIT OUTSIDE OF STORE. SACKER COMES OVER. TAKES HOLD OF LEASH.	SINGER: One store understands, we treat you like a friend . . .
TWO BIG, HUSKY HIGHSCHOOL FOOTBALL PLAYERS GETTING CAKE FOR THEIR COACH, HAPPY BIRTHDAY COACH.	One store works so hard because we want you back again
WORKING WOMAN COMES UP TO SALAD BAR. POPS GRAPE IN MOUTH THEN LOOKS AROUND TO SEE IF PRODUCE CLERK SAW HER. HE GIVES HER A CUTE SMILE.	One word says it all . . .
SACKER PUTTING SACKS IN WINNEBAGO.	We give you so much more . . .
LITTLE GIRL TRIES ON LIPSTICK AT COSMETICS COUNTER AS MOTHER LOOKS ON.	That's why we say Randall's is . .
LITTLE BOY COMES OUT OF RANDALL'S CARRYING SACK. TAKES LEASH, WAVES TO SACKER. SUPER: LOGO AND YOUR REMARKABLE STORE	Your remarkable store.

FIGURE 27-5.

TELEVISION COPY

CLIENT   Randall's

DESCRIPTION   :30 TV - (SPOT #1)

AIR DATE

VTR #

DATE PREPARED   November 17, 1989

JOB #

VIDEO	AUDIO
WIDE SHOT OF BROWNIE TROOP, PUSH IN TO SEE STORE MANAGER HOLDING ONE LITTLE BROWNIE.	SINGER: One store understands, we treat you like a friend . . .
OLD MAN SACKER PUTTING GROCERIES IN TRUNK FOR TWO OLDER LADIES.	One store works so hard because we want you back again
SEE YUPPIE JOGGER WITH EARPHONES CARRYING SMALL BASKET DOWN AISLE.	One word says it all . . .
TWIN GIRLS CHOOSING SAME KIND OF COOKIE IN BAKERY DEPARTMENT.	
FATHER AND SON AT CHECKOUT COUNTER. SON PUNCHING IN PIN NUMBER.	We give you so much more . . .
BROWNIES WAVE TO STORE MANAGER. HE WAVES BACK AS ONE BROWNIE GIVES STORE MANAGER FLOWER. HE SMILES. SUPER: LOGO AND YOUR REMARKABLE STORE	That's why we say Randall's is . . Your remarkable store.

FIGURE 27-6.

APPENDIX

TOOLS OF ANALYSIS FOR STRATEGIC PLANNING

The strategic planner may choose from a wide variety of analytical tools. Four of the more popular ones will be summarized in this section: Industry analysis, an analysis of the firm's environments; strengths, weaknesses, opportunities, and threats (or SWOT analysis); stakeholder analysis, and the Seven-Factor Model of business leadership. (You will develop skill at using these tools by taking your school's business policy or business strategy course.) The planner must choose the tools most relevant for the task at hand.

You can uncover the structure of the industry in which the firm competes by doing an *industry analysis* along the lines suggested by Michael Porter.[6] With this method you characterize the bargaining power of customers, identify the threat of the introduction of substitute products or services, gauge the bargaining power of suppliers, specify threats of new competitors entering the marketplace, and describe the degree of rivalry among existing firms in the market. Answering all those implied questions will produce a clear picture of the kinds of competitive strategies that are more likely and less likely to achieve the strategic goals the firm has set for itself.

For example, Design & Manufacturing Company is a dishwasher manufacturer that sells exclusively to Sears, Roebuck & Company. Obviously, Sears has immense power over the prices D&M can charge, the product features on the dishwashers it sells, and the overall quality of its products. However, since Sears is so dependent on D&M for its supply of dishwashers to sell, D&M can affect Sears' warranty policy, delivery acceptances, and advertising strategy. In the short run, this situation is a bilateral monopoly. Therefore, the range of strategic options open to each of these two firms is extremely limited in the short run. Furthermore, again in the short run, there is not an economic relationship between the two firms, but rather, a political relationship. Whichever firm bargains with the other more successfully is going to enjoy relatively greater profits. Expressed another way, in the short run there is a fixed amount of profit to be obtained from manufacturing, marketing, distributing, and servicing dishwashers, and the negotiations between Sears and D&M will determine how that fixed-size pie is divided up.

As another example of industry analysis, the desirability of opening a professional sports franchise in a city depends in part on other options available for people to spend their entertainment money (for example, college sports, high school sports, movies, theater), the possibility of franchises in other sports being awarded to that city, and the explosive salaries of professional sports players. As a final example, the once-staid watch business has been rocked by first, the entry of the Japanese with low-cost, high-reliability timepieces, and second, the entry of semiconductor firms looking for new outlets for their microchip technology. The industry analysis approach will give you a good feel for the entry and exit patterns of competitors in the marketplace as well as help you understand how intense the rivalry may be among marketplace competitors.

To understand the firm's alignment within its industry, you should perform a SWOT analysis.[7] SWOT stands for *S*trengths, *W*eaknesses, *O*pportunities, *T*hreats. The strengths dimension refers to understanding what the firm is good at, vis-à-vis its competitors. Perhaps it has a good reputation, a loyal low-cost labor force, an enviable location, superior engineering, or some other competence that favorably distinguishes it from its competition. The weaknesses dimension refers to its shortcomings, again vis-à-vis its competitors. Perhaps the firm is not as well known, has brand names too similar to those of others, is packaged in a "me-too" manner, has recently lost a key researcher, or has had a fire at an important plant. The opportunities dimension asks the planner to identify potential market successes for the firm that may exist because of other firms' weaknesses or because of special conditions in the firm's environment. Capitalize upon opportunities quickly, because they generally do not persist for long. Threats are, analogously, risky conditions in the environment or capabilities among competitors that may result in economic damage to the firm unless it takes some corrective action.

For example, consider a SWOT analysis of a pharmaceutical firm. Its strengths may be that it has an extensive product line, mounts a strong R & D force, and enjoys modern, state-of-the-art production facilities. Its weaknesses may be that it is faced with persistent labor problems, finds new capital expensive to raise, and has a weak distribution network in the south central part of the United States. Opportunities open to the firm may include competitors withdrawing from key markets, a foreign government indicating willingness to let the firm sell an entire product line there, and forecasted shifts in consumer demographics indicating higher use of key products in the future. Threats facing the firm may include ever-longer time periods required before the Food and Drug Administration approves new products, the potential for greater product liability insurance and greater legal costs, and the possibility of rivals' technological innovations erasing the advantages presently offered by some key products.

Stakeholder analysis is yet another approach toward assessing the firm's multiple external environments. (This topic is addressed at greater length in Chapter 28.) Stakeholder analysis calls for the planner to identify sets of stakeholders (for example, the financial community, unions, trade associations, suppliers, political parties) and to list specific stakeholders within each one of those broad groups.[8] The planner then judges what the stakes are for each one of the specific stakeholders: Lenders may be interested in economic return, one customer segment may be heavy users of the firm's product with little possibility of substitution, a union may only be interested in pension benefits, owners may be interested in stability of dividends and growth in stock price, a trade association may only be interested in the size of its membership, and so on.

You also should estimate the power each specific stakeholder possesses to influence affairs in its domain of interest. Finally, you should examine the strategic plan to determine the likelihood that stakeholders will respond positively or negatively to different aspects of it, perhaps by assembling small focus groups of people from the same stakeholder set to learn their reaction to it before the plan is broadcast widely. The remaining issue is how to channel the energies of those favorably disposed toward the plan while dispersing the antipathies of those likely to oppose it. Naturally, you may alter the strategic plan in light of the stakeholder analysis.

The 7-S, or Seven Factor Model for business leadership, is used to analyze how well-integrated a company's culture is.[9] The seven Ss (strategy, structure, systems, skills, staffing, style, and shared values) must support and reinforce one another if the company is to be truly excellent. Strategy, here, refers to the ways in which the company pays attention to its customers, constantly develops innovations, and motivates its personnel to accomplish those ends. Structure is the way the firm is organized to deliver its strategy. Systems means the set of administrative routines to keep the firm running smoothly: the reporting procedure, the meeting formats, and the information systems in use. Skills alludes to the distinctive capabilities possessed by the firm and by individuals within it. Staffing denotes the demographic composition of key personnel categories within the firm. Style encompasses both the management style and the cultural style of the company; the feeling one gets as one walks around the company office.[10] Finally, shared values is defined as the set of beliefs that are central to the ethos of the firm; they could range from "caveat emptor" to "the customer is king." The model is illustrated in Figure 27-7.

Besides these four major analytical tools for strategic planning, a host of other techniques are available for use. These include computer simulation models of the firm and computer models of industries that were developed to understand the firm's structure, dynamics, and reactions to competitors' actions. Scenario analysis attempts to forecast how the firm would fare in different future environments. Cross-impact analysis attempts to judge how one set of trends may in turn cause others to occur. Mathematical modeling, Delphi forecasting by experts, and expert systems and artificial intelligence techniques are also being applied to the problems of strategy formulation and analysis.

Any method that promises to assist a company with its strategic planning problem will be examined for its possible utility. Management's problems in understanding the firm, assessing its environments, and planning courses of actions that will take the firm to even greater levels of success are profound, recurrent, and nettlesome.

(continues)

APPENDIX

TOOLS OF ANALYSIS FOR STRATEGIC PLANNING (*continued*)

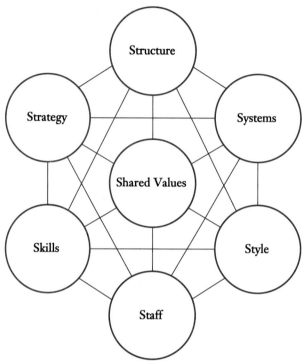

FIGURE 27-7. **McKinsey 7-S Framework** ©

From Peters, T., & Waterman, R. (1982). *In search of excellence: Lessons from America's best-run companies.* New York: Harper & Row, p. 11. Reprinted with permission of McKinsey & Co.

IF YOU WOULD LIKE TO READ MORE

Abell, D. F. (1980). *Defining the business: The starting point of strategic planning.* Englewood Cliffs, NJ: Prentice-Hall. Offers a view of how to understand a company's customers, markets, and products. This is a necessary ingredient in developing and refining a strategic plan.

Christensen, C. R., Andrews, K. R., Bower, J. L., Hamermesh, R. G., & Porter, M. E. (1987). *Business policy: Text and cases* (6th ed.). Homewood, IL: Dow Jones-Irwin. All of the steps needed to develop and implement a corporate strategy are explained in this book, along with a number of cases to test your understanding of the ideas. One of the cases is Continental Airlines (A), which deals with a decision they face concerning the possible purchase of two used DC-10 aircraft.

Deal, T. E., & Kennedy, A. A. (1982). *Corporate cultures: The rites and rituals of corporate life.* Reading, MA: Addison-Wesley. Makes the argument that companies with strong cultures will be more likely to prosper. Some types of cultures are identified and discussed, along with their most important features (values, slogans, heroes, rites, and rituals).

Freeman, R. E. (1984). *Strategic management: A stakeholder approach.* Marshfield, MA: Pitman Publishing. Ways of identifying and dealing with stakeholders and using this approach in setting strategic direction are explained in this book.

Pascale, R. T., & Athos, A. G. (1981). *The art of Japanese management: Applications for American executives.* New York: Warner Books. American and Japanese management styles are contrasted, primarily through the careful examination of International Telephone and Telegraph Co. under Harold Geneen and the Matsushita Electric Co. under Konosuke Matsushita.

Peters, T. J., & Waterman, R. (1982). *In search of excellence: Lessons from America's best-run companies.* New York: Harper & Row. Eight precepts for doing business derived from studying 43 "excellent" companies.

Porter, M. E. (1985). *Competitive advantage.* New York: Macmillan. The factors shaping competition within an industry are lucidly explained in this text.

Sawyer, G. C. (1983). *Corporate planning as a creative process.* Oxford, OH: Planning Executives Institute. A formulaic approach to conducting strategic planning is given in this book; it tends to have a "cookbook" flavor in prescribing how a strategic plan should be developed and communicated.

Steiner, G. A. (1969). *Top management planning.* New York: Macmillan. Among the best books available for describing how senior-level managers engage in strategic planning. It contains many useful illustrations of actual corporate practice.

NOTES

1. A case study of the Texas Air Company available in your instructor's resource guide can illustrate many of those factors as they appear in the "real world," and thus reinforce your understanding and appreciation of the communication process as it relates to corporate strategic planning.

2. G. Melloan, "Staying ahead of the pack at Cray Research." *The Wall Street Journal* (1988, February 23), 29.

3. Northwest Industries Advertisement, *Business Week* (1978; November 20), 168–169.

4. *Vertical integration* is control of all phases of production from raw materials to final product. A firm may want to assume long-term contracts for availability of key raw materials. *Efficient production* reduces cost and improves profit margin (the difference between costs and revenues). Northwest intends to focus on selling goods with higher profit margins.

5. T. E. Deal, & A. A. Kennedy, *Corporate cultures: The rites and rituals of corporate life.* Reading, MA: Addison-Wesley (1982), 4.

6. M. E. Porter, *Competitive advantage*, Appendix B. New York: Macmillan (1980), 368–382.

7. C. R. Christensen, K. R. Andrews, J. L. Bower, R. G. Hamermesh, & M. E. Porter, *Business policy: Text and cases* (6th ed.). Homewood, IL: Dow Jones-Irwin (1987), 227–253.

8. R. E. Freeman, *Strategic management: A stakeholder approach.* Marshfield, MA: Pitman Publishing (1984), 52–80.

9. R. T. Pascale, & A. G. Athos, *The art of Japanese management: Applications for American executives.* New York: Warner Books. T. J. Peters, & R. Waterman, *In search of excellence: Lessons from America's best-run companies.* New York: Harper & Row (1982), 3–26.

10. Deal & Kennedy, "Diagnosis: Learning to read cultures," 129–140.

NEW VENTURE COMMUNICATIONS

OBJECTIVES

This chapter will help you learn to

- draft working papers for a new venture

- apply problem-solving techniques

- interact informally with others to develop ideas

- transform notes and information into structured plans meeting professional expectations

PREVIEW

To gain a competitive footing against larger, established firms, new ventures depend on planning.

Successful planning involves both communication skills and quantitative skills. An emerging company uses communication to develop a scenario for the company's overall success and to secure financing. An emerging company uses quantitative skills to give a measurable dimension to assumptions, expectations, and results of its operations.

This chapter emphasizes the many communications skills needed in preparing the complete business plan for a new venture and the financing plan used to raise money. It explains the working papers used in the creation of the complete plan. The chapter also explains a wide variety of communication activities that are involved in the preparation and use of these plans.

❏ PLANNING A NEW BUSINESS VENTURE

For a time, management theorists expected that giant companies stretching around the globe would completely dominate the world economy. Their advantages of size, organization, and economies of scale seemed likely to doom small firms. While multinational corporations have had an enormous influence over the last two decades, small new businesses—fledgling competitors—still find opportunities. With no slack to spare, emerging companies must use their talents wisely. These firms can fight the big companies' economies of scale with new ideas and efficient allocation of scarce resources. These crucial competitive functions require planning.

Planning is needed at all stages of business development from inception to maturity. Although many firms begin planning only after the firm has advanced beyond the start-up stage, this delay is a serious mistake. In the early stages, the entrepreneur may be overwhelmed with immediate tasks. Planning may seem an impossible luxury; something to be postponed until many hours can be set aside. Unfortunately, unplanned work often isn't efficient. Without planning at the outset, resources can be frittered away.

Planning requires both communication skills and quantitative skills.

Successful planning involves both communication skills and quantitative skills. An emerging company uses communication to develop a plan for the company's overall success and secure financing. An emerging company uses quantitative skills to give a measurable dimension to assumptions, expectations, and the outcomes of its operations. By comparing anticipated outcomes with actual amounts, a company's management can make better choices, evaluate strategy and methods, identify changes in the environment, and adjust to improve performance. Chapter 27, "Strategic Planning Communications," introduced the wide range of processes and document types that may be part of the strategic planning process in mid- and large-size companies. This chapter focuses on communications leading to the *complete business plan* and the related *financing plan* that are crucial for *small business development*.

Business Planning and Communication

Too often, people who want to start new companies think of new venture communication as *only* the final written plan, not realizing the many communications activities that are essential in the development of that plan.

Communication Skills for Business Planning

Planning requires many different communication skills.

Planning involves a wide variety of oral communication, listening, brainstorming, and negotiation skills in the early phases. The entrepreneur, like other creative people, may develop ideas in many ways. Some of the discovery techniques (such as brainstorming, mind mapping, and freewriting) in Chapter 5 or the problem-solving process explained in Chapter 1 can help develop new business ideas. Informal conversations that test the feasibility and explore the implications of an idea can help the entrepreneur extend and refine the business concept. If a business organization has already been established, formal and informal planning meetings with employees can expand the entrepreneur's initial ideas. A new business owner needs more communications than you might expect.

NEW VENTURE PLANNING

Phase	Communications Activities Required
Preliminary Planning	Interviewing
	Summarizing published information about industry, competitors, regulations, market information
	Brainstorming
	Negotiating with others
	Writing and note taking
	Drafting working papers
	Writing the complete business plan
	Preparing the financing strategy
	Document design and formatting
Seeking Financing	Writing letters
	Giving an oral presentation
	Summarizing
	Negotiating
Making Arrangements	Hiring new people
	Training others
	Creating goodwill communications
	Preparing marketing and advertising
Operating and Ongoing Planning	Keeping a log or daily notes
	Monitoring
	Control, comparison of budget vs. actual
	Motivating others to contribute, work hard
	Dealing with new customers

Especially if the person is working alone, notes, diaries, and written preliminary drafts or "working papers" are vital for exploring emerging ideas. Failure to recognize the necessity for working papers prevents many would-be business owners from realizing their dreams. They can't write the complete plan, because they haven't done the preliminary work. "There just isn't enough desk-top space in my brain," one man attending an entrepreneurship conference explained; "I've got to get it down and spread it out on paper so that I can really put all my ideas to use." The new venture owner must make connections between ideas about the product or service and dozens of other ideas, such as market demand, competitors, financing, and people to help with the work.

Notes and drafts capture ideas and allow the planner to make new connections among them.

Communication is essential for making these connections. By talking with friends, business advisors, and consultants, taking notes during these conversations, keeping a diary or log of ideas and issues, and preparing working papers, the vision for the new company can take shape much more easily. Unless the new owner connects all the ideas, the new venture will not achieve the efficiency necessary for competing against established companies. The computer can be very useful in printing out draft copies of different working papers, revising, and recombining or reformatting these working papers to create other documents; efficiency counts here, too. If you do not have a computer available, color-coded index cards may be a handy way to organize your working materials.

The notes and working papers become the basis of the complete plan.

Eventually, the working papers can be transformed into the format of a formal report. Even this formal report should be in a loose-leaf binder, so that parts of the plan can be adjusted as new opportunities or threats to the business arise. The complete business plan will benefit the owner and others who work with the company, both as employees and as investors, lenders, or advisors. Parts of the complete plan will be assembled and presented as a financing plan. Other parts may form the basis of work with advertisers and other suppliers. Preliminary planning sets in motion a continuous planning process that is part of the ongoing work of the firm.

To develop a business plan, you'll have to learn to think as an entrepreneur, to learn the scenario and roles for developing a business plan. Because planning is an abstract subject, we've illustrated the planning process with a case woven throughout the discussion. At the end of the chapter, we've provided another case with exercises that involve a student like you in working with an entrepreneur who wants to open a new funeral home in Wesson, New Jersey. You can participate in the process of preparing the working papers, including brainstorming, summarizing, writing draft statements of the key points of the complete business plan, preparing a graphic for the loan application, writing letters, and writing the introductory summary for your complete plan. Other courses, such as finance, accounting, and marketing, will help you develop the quantitative skills needed for preparing cash flow projections and other elements needed in your business.

Case: Natelson's Marina

The case of Natelson's Marina illustrates the process of communication in planning.[1] A businessperson, Jan Natelson, inherited her elderly uncle's marina, where he had maintained a dock and sold and rented boats. Jan's uncle had in fact been in many businesses. He was in the restaurant business, with a dockside cafe serving meals to boating parties. He was in the real estate business, buying and selling lots. He was in the fuel service business, buying and selling gasoline and oil. He was in the repair business, buying parts and hiring mechanics. He rented dock space to boat owners. He also sold and rented boats and motors. Jan lived in the same town and had been working for several years as an insurance adjuster. She had slim resources, but she felt the marina represented a good opportunity. She did not know which lines of her uncle's business would be profitable and which would not, and she did not understand how the various activities fit together. The communication processes that Jan used to build a plan and put her venture on an even keel will be discussed throughout this chapter.

Written Notes and Working Papers: Accumulating a Wealth of Ideas

Before a person can create a new business plan, he or she must accumulate a wealth of ideas about all the many aspects of the new business. Small but crucial details may be forgotten if they are not captured electronically or in print. Jan Natelson was engaged in many of the communications activities listed in the preliminary phase. She discussed her new business with her financial advisors (her banker, investment counselor, and a consultant), held informal conversations with her uncle's employees, and talked over long-term life objectives with her family. She looked through correspondence in the files from the time when her uncle first started the marina, and she kept a journal of her ideas over a three-week period.

Notes display ideas that cannot be kept in mind simultaneously.

Jan made a list of the things she enjoyed most about work, as well as a list of aggravations and dissatisfactions. She reviewed her strengths, and she looked over the strengths of the employees. She paid a consultant to prepare brief industry reports on the competition in the real estate, restaurant, and boat businesses in the region. In these different forms—all communication—a picture of the best opportunities and the company's strengths began to emerge. Jan captured this picture in her working papers, a series of short summaries pertaining to different aspects of her business, that would help her write her complete business plan.

Exploring the Nature of the Business Enterprise

Explore the nature of your enterprise with plans.

A planner must understand the nature of the proposed business enterprise and represent it in the complete plan. In essence, an enterprise is a social entity that puts together people, capital, and materials to produce products and services (see Figure 28-1). This process results in *costs*, while the sale of the ensuing products and services generates *revenues*. Profits, which are the difference between revenues and costs, usually constitute one of the objectives of the enterprise. The complete plan identifies the sources of the inflows, explains the operations of the enterprise, and supports claims about expected outflows. Good

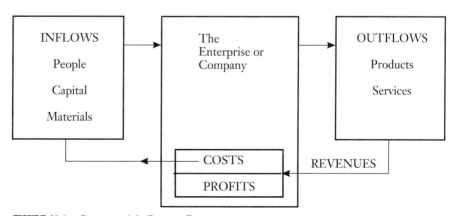

FIGURE 28-1. Dynamics of the Business Enterprise

managers imaginatively plan, organize, staff, direct, and control their businesses in order to achieve profits.

A very real hazard exists in over-formalizing the management process. In any situation, inflexible administration will hurt the ability of an enterprise to respond to changing circumstances. The planner must demonstrate that he or she has understood the nature of the enterprise and has a clear plan for dealing with defined circumstances and the analytical and imaginative abilities to cope with change. The working papers explore the nature of the proposed enterprise.

Preparing the Working Papers

Create eight sets of working papers to explore different aspects of your proposed firm.

Working papers are discovery drafts that express the planner's thoughts on critical aspects of the new company. A working paper may be one or two sentences or several pages. We recommend preparing separate working papers on eight key topics:

1. The mission of the enterprise
2. The definition of the business
3. The opportunity
4. External variables
5. Critical assumptions
6. The determinants of expected success
7. Major strengths and weaknesses
8. Financing strategy

Usually, you will need a succinct explanation of no more than one page to summarize each topic, although your working paper may be the basis for a much longer detailed section (such as the analysis of the industry) in the complete plan. Furthermore, you may create several versions or drafts of each working paper.

The important thing is to have separate places for working on different kinds of ideas. There will be days when you have great marketing ideas, but you don't want to think about other topics. It is easier to pull out a separate folder or call up a separate document on the computer than to face a huge stack of materials. If you are working on a computer, create different "folders" (or directories) or documents for different topics. Eventually, you can combine or merge these files. A collection of manila folders can serve the same purpose. You need to feel organized, but not so rigidly structured that important ideas are closed out.

Working Paper One: Stating the Mission of the Enterprise

Mission: the demand you serve.

The first working paper is also the shortest. It expresses the demand your new business will serve. A one- or two-sentence answer to the question, "What is the mission of your business?" is all that is needed. Nonetheless, these may be the most important fifty words in the life of the business.

The desire to run a business is not sufficient to justify an enterprise. There also has to be an economic demand for a firm. That is, the business must supply products or services that people will buy in sufficient quantity to justify the cost of producing those goods or services. The entrepreneur who says, "I want to be in the television repair business in Westville because I want to do my own thing and I like the climate there," may not be in business long if nobody in Westville wants to hire the entrepreneur to repair television sets. On the other hand, many businesses have been created because an enterprising person detected a real unmet need for specific goods or services and started a firm to supply them. A consulting firm's market analysis report, which would also include key economic, geographic, demographic, and other data, might also identify such a demand.

Writing out why the proposed firm should be started, what unique niche it will fill, and why someone else has not already done the same thing clarifies goals. Jan Natelson planned to address the needs of people who resided permanently and temporarily in her resort community. Jan adopted as her mission:

> Natelson Marina will become the profitable, primary continuing source for boats and high-quality boat services along the bay.

If the businessperson plans to transform an existing business, as Jan Natelson did, he or she should also explain why the goal of the firm should be changed: why the firm was needed originally, what niche it has been filling, and what (if any) competition has arisen. The collection of businesses she inherited, Jan decided, reflected her uncle's personal interests in his semiretired state and were not suited to achieving her goals.

The terms "goals" and "mission" are used inconsistently in books and articles on business. In this chapter, the *mission* of the firm is the broad set of social, economic, and human goals the firm intends to achieve. Later, the small business leader must define specific quantifiable objectives that the firm should accomplish to carry out this mission. Jan Natelson continued her working paper by specifying the particular product lines (types of boats), services (sales, repair, and storage), geographic area, market share, return on investment, profit margins, and asset management objectives that her advisors had helped her define.

Working Paper Two: Defining the Business

Nature of the business: the way you will carry out the mission.

A good plan specifically defines what business the firm is in. The marina operator, Jan Natelson, decided she was not going to be in the restaurant or real estate business any longer. Her consultant's report pointed out that the small resort town in which Jan lived had many restaurants; the competition was keen, and restaurants required a great deal of time in supervising employees. The real estate business no longer offered the kinds of deals that had been attractive when her uncle started buying a few parcels of land. So much of the rural area had been developed as housing tracts and resort homes that developers had turned to draining marshlands. Jan wasn't interested in buying and holding land for a long period, and she wanted to concentrate her resources and her time. After studying the consultant's report, Jan Natelson defined her business as "buying, selling, and servicing boats and motors for older people and upscale clients who do not have the time to manage their boats themselves."

You will want to boil your definition of your business down to a concise statement, as Jan did, but you shouldn't begin by trying to write such a sentence. Your first draft should be a collection of descriptions, different combinations of products and services that interest you. Let your imagination be very visual and specific as you picture what your new company would do and why your customers or clients would be happy. Since at the working paper stage you need not show the document to anyone else, writing a collection of fantasy descriptions of "ideal days" in your new business could unlock a new view of what you would really like to do if you could work for yourself. Later drafts of this working paper may contain many comparisons, as you consider different combinations of services, products, and arrangements. Eventually, you will fix on a concise definition.

Working Paper Three: Identifying the Opportunity

Opportunity: What is the demand, and why does it exist?

If your new business is to compete with an established one, the specific opportunity must be identified in detail. How did this opportunity arise? How long will it last? How stable will it be? How big is it? Why will the present competitors not choose to seize it, or why will they be unable to do so? To answer these questions you will need information on the industry, present competitors, and the prospective market.

In the study the consultant prepared for Jan Natelson, the census data showed that the average age of the population in the region had steadily increased over the past ten years and that people over age 60 made up nearly a quarter of the county's population. Surprisingly, during the same time the average income per household in the county had risen.

All these data confirmed the immediate impression that more and more retired people had bought homes along the bay shore or were living in boats at marinas or at private clubs along the water. These older people were fairly well-to-do, and constituted an important customer base for Natelson's marina. Two yacht clubs and three other marinas offered plenty of competition, but the yacht clubs restricted membership and favored long-time local residents. One of the marinas, located near the beachfront pier and amusement park, appealed more to younger boating enthusiasts. Of the other two, one was serious competition, but the other was located near the docks and warehouses, offering an old, dirty, unattractive place to store boats. The opportunity for Jan Natelson was to serve the unmet needs of this specific group, which she described in as much detail as she could so that she could plan how to reach them.

Working Paper Four: Specifying External Variables

What external variables will affect your success?

Sometimes uncontrollable outside factors will affect the firm's success. Information about many of these variables is now readily available in both print and electronic form. Many economic, demographic, and social statistics important to the average business are often available in reasonably priced government publications available in U.S. Government Book Stores located across the country. These stores have practically everything the government prints, and if they do not have a particular item they will order it. Many other sources (both printed and electronic) are available through public libraries. Chapter 12, "Research Strategies for Reports," explains how to find such information.

Working Paper Five: Making Critical Assumptions

Translate variables into specific estimates.

Once the significant external variables have been determined and the pertinent sources of information have been located, it is necessary to make specific assumptions about each variable and project values for each period in the planning horizon. Ordinarily, this is the most difficult part of planning. To whatever extent possible, the entrepreneur should employ projections that have already been made by experts in the field in question, although these might be tempered with his or her own view of the situation.

As a result of studying such demographic and economic trends, Jan Natelson decided to assume that the proportion of older people in the county would continue to increase, but at a slightly lower rate than it had in the past period. She also decided to assume that income would increase at about 75 percent of the rate that it had increased over the past ten years, since the state legislature was threatening to increase taxes. Assumptions about inflation, interest rates, taxes, and costs of supplies were also necessary.

Working Paper Six: Pinpointing Success Determinants

Which factors have the greatest force in outcomes?

The next step is to pinpoint the important variables within the company that affect successful performance and to write the working papers on your business strategy. For some firms, the growth rate of sales will be the most important element. These enterprises usually have some degree of control over the market in which they participate, and an aggressive advertising and sales promotion program may be the key to success. Other companies face a more competitive situation where they may be unable to secure a larger market share by adopting an aggressive selling strategy. These firms may even have their prices set by a market dominated by larger competitors or customers who may be able to dictate terms. The major success determinants for businesses in these circumstances may be those relating to cost control and efficiency.

Writing about the critical factors will help you express what you know about the causal processes that will go on in your new business. Identifying these processes may help you see how they are interrelated as well. You may find this working paper turning into a network diagram as you recognize various interactions. Working with an accountant or other advisor may enable you to simulate these interactions and create projections.

Each individual firm will have its own set of unique internal variables. For manufacturing firms, turnovers, rejects, machine downtime, and capacity may be quite important. For service entities, labor costs, account collection, and overhead control may be significant. Retail concerns usually must be very aware of mark-ups, inventory management, and promotional techniques. Businesses of all kinds with high fixed cost levels must be knowledgeable of their cost structure and the dollar and unit break-even points. The strategy for the business must account for the effects of these success determinants in the business. You will need to write a working paper of a page or so about each of the strategies related to these determinants: your marketing, production, and other plans.

Jan considered convenience and customer appeal to be the most important determinants of her success. Her strategy for capturing a large share of the business was to offer the Cadillac of marinas: to make the marina clean, beautiful, and comfortable for retired and affluent people. Jan planned to make several improvements to the marina after she disposed of her present speculative real estate. A new parking lot, shaded walkways, a refurbished deck, an indoor lounge area at the entrance of the marina, and an immaculate service bay for the boats next to the showroom would give the place a club atmosphere. A handsome antique phone bearing the sign "Ring for the Butler" would be placed in the lounge.

Jan made arrangements with a new catering firm just a few blocks away, The Butler's Bounty, to answer that phone and provide silver tray catering service to the marina. Butler's Bounty owned an ancient Rolls Royce, polished to the nines, in which the delivery person, dressed in butler's coat and wearing gloves, delivered orders on silver trays or other formal serving pieces. Butler's Bounty guaranteed the butler would arrive within fifteen minutes for beverage orders, twenty minutes for short orders, and thirty minutes for picnic hampers or complete meals. Orders in advance for brunch or luncheon service could be served in the lounge or on the deck. Jan was free of the responsibility of hiring and supervising cooks and waiters, and the food to be served to people coming to and from their boats would match the upscale image her mission requires.

Having decided what her essential commercial activity should be, Jan was able to concentrate on developing the best strategies for selling, renting, and servicing her boats and motors (marketing plan), for buying her products, supplies, and equipment, and employing personnel (production plan), and for efficiently raising and utilizing her capital (financial plan). Each of these plans became a separate working paper in her "success determinants" file.

Working Paper Seven: Outlining Strengths and Weaknesses

Realistic appraisals of strengths and candid admissions of weaknesses underlie solid plans.

A new venture must have strengths that can offset the experience, greater size, and other advantages of established competitors. What are these strengths? Providing a new product that has no competitive alternative, selling a low-priced product, offering a better service than competitors offer, or producing a high-quality product may be major strengths.

Entrepreneurs themselves may be key ingredients in the success of their businesses. Their knowledge, expertise, and overall "get-up-and-go" may fuel their businesses' success. In other cases, weak competitors may be the principal strength of a venture. Typically, established firms become "fat and lazy," thereby opening up an opportunity for zealous innovators. Other strengths may be found in marketing strategies, distributor networks, financial capacity, the ability of the firm to grant credit terms to customers, lack of debt, cost effectiveness and efficiency of the plant and equipment, the employees who work for the firm, the lack of a union among the employees, existing contracts or the promise of contracts from major customers, the financial condition of the clients of the business, and the general economic climate at the time. These strengths must be listed and analyzed. Making notes over time and collecting these in a summary can provide a convincing picture of the firm's prospects when you are presenting your business concept to investors or lenders.

Among the strengths of Natelson's Marina were the employees' experience in running a marina. The two excellent mechanics who repaired the boats could trouble-shoot effectively when people complained about their motors. The bookkeeper, Lynn Hatton, was also a strength, Natelson realized. Her British accent impressed people over the telephone, and customers treated her as a person of status. This perception would enable her to function well in interacting more with the public. The location of Natelson's Marina was clearly better than that of all the marinas but one, and the view from the Natelson's Marina in the early morning was spectacular.

You can't afford to overlook the major weaknesses of the business that may cause it to fail. You will need to be ready to explain how you intend to overcome these weaknesses. In many respects, outlining the weaknesses is the reverse of outlining the strengths. Is the product or service not really very much differentiated from other products or services on the market? Is the competition so severe that it may be difficult to carve out a unique niche in the market? Is it impossible to find just the right location? For a business that sells to the general public, location may be very significant. The newness of the firm causes many weaknesses. People simply do not know the firm is in business. These problems can be remedied, but the firm has to have the financial resources to stay in business meanwhile.

Financial factors are often among the major weaknesses of the new enterprise. The firm may be undercapitalized and the financial needs of the business may have been seriously understated by the optimistic entrepreneur who was positive the firm would cross the break-even point during the second month of operations. The firm may have been started with a lot of borrowed money, and paying interest on the debt may be a problem. It may be difficult for the new business to get credit, and even suppliers may put the new enterprise on a "cash on delivery" basis until it has been in business for awhile. Once again, each situation will be unique. Complete candor in analyzing the possible weaknesses of the new venture idea may be the most important element in preparing the business plan, however.

Working Paper Eight: Financing Strategy

From the initial working papers you will develop detailed plans and pro forma financial statements that will connect your broad goals with specific financial strategies (see Figure 28-2). You must set fairly specific quantitative objectives,

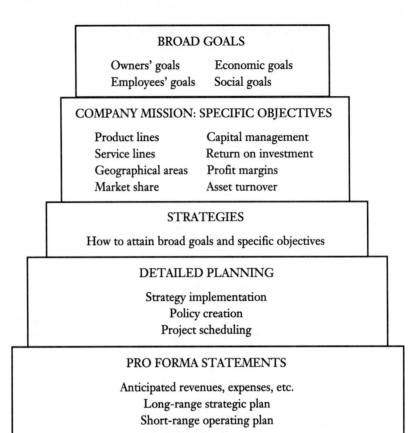

FIGURE 28-2. Hierarchy of Business Plan Components

translating these into anticipated revenues and costs. Some of these steps will require quantitative skills acquired in other business courses or with the help of consultants. Nonetheless, you must be able to understand and explain the quantitative measures, especially the financing strategy. The financing strategy is the plan for raising sufficient capital for your fledgling business. A cogent summary of the financing strategy is necessary for speaking with confidence to prospective investors or lenders.

Financial projections may reveal insights about other aspects of your working plans.

For example, the objective of increasing sales by 10 percent next year might be postulated together with an objective to decrease costs by 2 percent, to increase profits by 15 percent, and to improve return on investment from 14 percent to 16 percent. These percentage objectives can then be translated into dollar amounts and tested for internal consistency. Such queries as this might be made: Is it consistent to increase profits by 15 percent while return on investment advances by 2 percent? You will need to be able to answer such questions in words as well as in numbers.

Obviously, the general objectives should lead to more specific supporting subobjectives. Thus, in order to realize the general sales and profit objectives established, it may be necessary to posit subobjectives such as adding sales personnel, increasing the number of customers, and making certain capital expenditures to improve efficiency. All of these subobjectives must be mutually consistent and should be derived from the overall percentage and dollar objectives. As you begin to test your ideas with quantitative methods, you may gain insights that send you back to your other working papers with new ideas.

In the case of Natelson's Marina, Jan's intention to reach older and affluent people depended on being able to remodel and refurbish her facilities. Jan did not have enough money saved to finance the improvements from cash on hand, partly because her uncle had been doing so many other things and because her inheritance was the property and the company, not other financial assets of her uncle's estate. Remodeling part of the marina to create a lounge and rebuilding the deck were among her subobjectives. Jan already had two excellent mechanics, but she planned to sell all the new boats herself. She decided that to attain her sales goals, she would have to hire a part-time person to help with sales on weekends during the warm weather season.

The financing strategy may call for the entrepreneur to supply part of the funds and for the rest of the money to come from a loan or from venture capitalists. If a loan is needed, the financing strategy might show the source of the entrepreneur's contribution and propose a payback schedule for the loan. If equity capital is needed, venture capitalists will receive a significant share of ownership of the business and perhaps a payment, either monthly or yearly, also. Fortunately for Jan, the marina itself had been her uncle's property and was owned free and clear, so that Jan's financing strategy was to finance improvements through a first mortgage on her property.

Writing the Detailed Plans

Develop a Communication Strategy for Your Plan

A writer-centered plan has limited usefulness.

Although for many entrepreneurs the business plan is a highly personal document, the plan will have many audiences over time. Write the plan to address their needs. Investors, key management personnel, lenders, and others may review the plan. You need to motivate lenders to support the business, to inspire employees with a vision of the firm's mission, and to inform them with precisely worded strategies and estimates. What uncertainties would a lender have about this business? What do employees need to know, think, and feel about the strategy to enable them to carry out the plan? Create a persuasive strategy and consider your audiences carefully as you write. As with other formal reports, different parts of the complete plan will be tailored to the needs of different sorts of readers. Review Chapter 13, "Writing Reports," if you have any questions about this advice.

The Two Plans: The Complete Plan and the Financing Plan

Financing plan = complete business plan, minus the strategic plan, the operating plan, and certain appendices.

The planning process culminates in the preparation of the planning documents, the *complete plan* and the *financing or summary plan*. The complete plan will include both the strategic plan and the operating or short-range plan. The long-range strategic plan takes into account the broad goals of the organization and usually deals in horizons of several years. Typically, the operating plan is done on a one-year basis. The operating plan should be considerably more specific and should provide quarterly, perhaps monthly, and conceivably, weekly budget figures.

Keep the complete report in loose-leaf form, so that you can make changes easily.

Nevertheless, all parts of the complete plan should be considered tentative, even the budget numbers. Planning is a continuous process, and plans may have to change to correspond to an ever-changing environment. If a major assumption is no longer valid, replanning may be necessary, and a new plan formulated. *For this reason, the complete business plan should never be a bound document. It should be placed in a loose-leaf notebook where pages can be substituted as required.*

The results of long-term and short-term planning while preparing the complete plan alert the entrepreneur to the need to raise money and, hence, take a financing plan to investors. The *summary* or *financing* plan is specifically prepared to raise money. It includes all of the complete plan except the strategic plan, the operating plan, and the appendices.

Complete Plan Outline

The complete plan, like other reports, has two major parts: the introductory summary and the discussion.

The following outline summarizes the sections of a complete plan. The starred sections of the outline would also appear in the summary (financing) plan that is presented to bankers, venture capitalists, or other potential investors. The outline is structured to enable the entrepreneur to select key sections for presentation to bankers, venture capitalists, and other investors, who have reviewed so many of these plans that they expect a common form or genre. Presenting the financing plan in a conventional form makes the entrepreneur look more professional and competent to the investors.

OUTLINE OF A COMPLETE BUSINESS PLAN

Introduction*
  I. Presentation of the venture, opportunity, and financing need
     A. A one-paragraph statement about the nature of the business
     B. A one-paragraph rationale for the existence of the business: the opportunity
     C. A brief statement about the financing required
 II. Summary of industry and venture
     A. Key characteristics of the industry
     B. Structure and important features of the company

Discussion

III. Pro forma financial statements*
    A. Balance sheet
    B. Income and cash flow pro forma statements over the planning horizon
IV. Complete analysis of the industry*
 V. Form and organizational structure of the company*
VI. The long-range strategic plan
    A. Enterprise goals
    B. Enterprise mission
    D. Enterprise strategies
    E. Planning assumptions
    F. Strategic long-range plan objectives
        1. Sales, cost, and profit projections
        2. Major capital additions (plant equipment, etc.)
        3. Cash flow and financing
        4. Personnel requirements
VII. The short-term operating plan
    A. Marketing (sales) plan
    B. Production plan
    C. Various expense plans
    D. Operating income plan
    E. Cash flow and funds flow plans
    F. Planned balance sheets
    G. Planned operating and financial ratios
VIII. Appendices*
    A. Pertinent contracts
    B. Technical information
    C. Other support data

*appears in the financing plan

Writing the Introduction

An introduction for a business plan resembles the introductory summary for a report; it contains the foreword and the summary of conclusions and recommendations. The introduction should be brief—three paragraphs. In a business plan, the foreword describes the business, the opportunity it will seize, and the financing strategy (one paragraph for each). The summary of conclusions and recommendations points out the relevant major points about the industry and market and the strengths of the business that fit the industry. This part may be three to five pages.

    Begin with a one-paragraph statement about the nature of the business. Draw on working papers one and two for these paragraphs. Then write a one-paragraph rationale for the existence of the business: the opportunity. Draw on your summary of the opportunity, working paper three, for this second paragraph. Finally, offer a statement about the financing required, a summary of your conclusions based on the pro forma projections, and your financing strategy.

In the second part of the introductory summary, expand on the nature of the opportunity by presenting more facts about the industry and the way that the new company's anticipated strengths will enable it to operate in this industry. Draw on the working papers on the opportunity, the company's strengths, and success determinants in preparing this section.

Some books advise beginning the introduction with a statement about the amount of financing needed (for example, "This is an application for a loan of $42,000"), but the reasonableness of committing a sum to a venture seems much more plausible when the connection between the venture and the opportunity has been set forth. Unless the instructions from the lender require describing the amount of the request in the opening line, place the financing request at the end of the opening part of the introduction.

The second part of the introduction focuses on the industry and explains the market and the strengths of the business. In the case of Lily's Flowers, the owner described the opportunity East Brompton Village presented: an excellent customer base of individuals who value flowers. The suburb's average per-family income was $85,000 and the average residential property value was $195,000. A recent survey of *East Brompton Journal* readers had ranked cut flowers among the ten most-valued personal luxuries. Residents had been driving to Megacity to obtain their flowers because there was no convenient retail business in East Brompton Village specializing in cut flowers. Lily's planned to take advantage of this market by stocking small quantities of many types of cut flowers in a conveniently located setting (between the bank and the grocery) enjoying a steady stream of passing customers. The owner planned the experience to be like walking through a garden with winding brick paths and selecting flowers to be cut with shears, but the flowers would be already cut. A clear picture of the business and the opportunity prepared the banker to hear about the second mortgage and unsecured loan the owner needed to start the shop.

Writing the Discussion Section

Organize parts of the discussion to answer key questions.

Writing the discussion section of a business plan is similar to writing the discussion section of any formal report. The principal components of the discussion section are well known, but the contents of each section must be organized to answer the readers' questions and influence the readers' decisions. You must organize each section to answer the key questions about the industry, the markets, the structure of the company, or other topic. Rely on your communication strategy and your analysis of the audiences in preparing the plan. The discussion section may vary a great deal in length, depending on the size of the new venture, the newness of the business idea, and the complexity of the industry or the market. The discussion section might be as short as ten pages or as long as a hundred and fifty, including the financial projections.

EXAMPLE 1

PARAGRAPHS 1–3 OF MEDATHLETIC INSURANCE COMPANY'S INTRODUCTORY SUMMARY

MedAthletic Insurance Company will offer permanent total disability insurance to athletes and sports clubs. Such insurance protects the earning capacity of individuals and the financial stability of clubs who have multi-year or guaranteed contracts with star players. MedAthletic Insurance Company will enter into contracts with United Insurance Society to issue policies for players under a complete reinsurance arrangement.

Demand for disability insurance for amateur and professional athletes has escalated, while the number of actual claims has remained about the same, creating an unusual profit opportunity in sports insurance. The growing number of players who receive or expect to receive compensation in excess of $200,000 annually has increased the number of potential insureds dramatically. The total annual volume of premiums in the six major sports (baseball, football, hockey, basketball, tennis, and golf) is presently estimated at between $22 and $26 million annually. At the same time, the capacity of underwriters serving this demand has decreased, creating a need for a major U.S. life insurance company as an underwriter in this field.

Financing required for the establishment of the company will be $78,400. The owner will invest $36,000 of savings and retain two-thirds of the common stock. The investors will invest $18,000 and receive one-third of the common stock, and $24,400 will be subordinated debt.

EXAMPLE 2

LILY'S CUT FLOWER SHOP

Lily's will feature fashionable cut flowers by the stalk and decorative containers. Lily's will also create a limited number of floral arrangements and deliver them.

Cut flower shops cater to affluent customers, primarily women, who want to enjoy the pleasure of flowers in the home. Cut flowers replace the decorations once available from personal gardens and the formal arrangements no longer in fashion.

Renovations and financing sufficient for the first nine months of operation will require a loan of $42,000. The owner proposes to invest $30,000 of savings in the business. Other financing will be an unsecured loan of $6,000 and a second mortgage of $6,000 on another of the owner's rental properties.

ONGOING PLANNING FOR THE NEW VENTURE

Planning, Communicating, and Human Relations

Motivating people is central to effective management. Employee participation in establishing company goals, plans, and policies has been recognized as an effective way to ensure productivity improvement at all organizational levels. Communicating with employees, as Jan Natelson did, builds commitment among the people who will carry out the company's strategy, producing the high level of efficiency new firms need.

People involved in planning become committed to the plan's success.

In the meetings and conversations that are part of the planning process, the entrepreneur and the employees can solve problems that may be associated with conflicting goals. As the team develops policies and plans their implementation, they can resolve misunderstandings. The commitment to planning, defining, clarifying, and sharing the firm's vision produces positive attitudes. Furthermore, the lines of communication established in this way develop relationships (see Chapter 3) that can be used when future problems arise. Although employee suggestion boxes and call-in lines may be useful, direct personal communication is usually most effective in a small organization.

As the firm develops, the entrepreneur should spend more and more time evaluating progress and thinking about the future position of the enterprise. What new ideas are available to reduce the cost of operation, to expand into new areas, and to make the company more profitable? It is easy to put off the more loosely defined job of planning in favor of directing daily activities. The entrepreneur must, however, avoid this temptation in order to direct the enterprise toward its goals while assuring long-term survival. Many successful entrepreneurs have dictated notes or kept daily journals to ensure daily attention to this vital function.

People implement a plan they understand better than one they don't understand.

The control and feedback functions are devoted to making sure that planned events happen. Managers spend most of their time implementing and controlling. Nevertheless, every employee plans to some extent, and everyone in the business should be involved in the planning process in some manner. The entrepreneur may use a variety of communication channels to ensure that he or she benefits from employees' planning. If planning becomes a one-person affair—if the entrepreneur plans alone and then orders employees to follow instructions—progress will not be as satisfactory as it would have been if the employees had had some input. Employees have to understand where the firm is moving and why it is moving in that direction. They must feel that they have had some influence on the plan. One characteristic of an effective leader is the degree to which he or she encourages and permits subordinates at various levels to participate in communication about planning.

There are two other reasons for communicating with all employees in the planning process. First, everyone has ideas. Sometimes the most junior employee will come up with ideas that the president has not thought about. Unless the president communicates with these people, good ideas may be lost. Second, if people are excluded, they will not be committed to the plan; if they are not committed to the plan, it is not going to be successful. In a new, small firm, communication is vital to teamwork, efficiency, and survival. When Vista Chemical Company, a firm formed in a leveraged buyout of Conoco Chemicals (described in the Executives' Perspectives section, pp. 783–787), reached its first anniversary as an independent company, the firm published a "Year Book," very much like a high school yearbook, showing department group photos of all the employees. Executives were shown with their departments, not on separate pages. This document reinforced the sense of community and pride among employees who had worked collaboratively to meet the new company's goals.

Of course, what has been said above does not mean that all the employees of a firm should gather around a table and plan for the next year. The chief executive officer and the key people who report to him or her will typically do most of the long-range planning that involves setting goals and objectives for the enterprise. All employees, however, should be involved in the determination of how to operate the business most effectively in the period immediately ahead. Short-range planning should involve every manager in the organization in mapping out his or her part in accomplishing overall enterprise objectives. All employees should be encouraged to give to their immediate supervisors ideas that may affect the objectives to be established and the means of achieving those objectives.

Planning and Accounting

Planning, although related to accounting, is not an accounting procedure but a management technique. The accounting system becomes involved in planning in the following ways:

1. Accounting provides historical data for analysis.
2. The financial part of the profit plan is structured in an accounting format.
3. Actual data used to measure performance are provided by the accounting system.

Similarly, planning is related to budgeting, but a business plan is not simply a budget. Budgets are prepared to define revenue and expense streams. Budgets result from plans. As stated earlier, a business plan is a narrative and quantitative statement depicting what is to be done; why, where, and how it is to be done; and who is to do it. Chapters 24 and 25 on financial and managerial accounting communications discuss in greater detail the kinds of communications that accountants may prepare to assist owners in solving problems and preparing reports for external audiences, such as investors and lenders.

❏ COMMUNICATION CHALLENGES

CASE: JACKSON FUNERAL HOME

In the exercises associated with this case, you will apply discovery methods and problem-solving techniques, interact informally with others to develop ideas, transform notes and information into a structured plan meeting professional expectations, and write a letter to a prospective employee.

Ben Jackson, your mother's younger brother, is a prospective entrepreneur who is contemplating establishing a new business. He is thirty-seven years old and has spent the past eight years as a funeral director in Newark. Given his experience and a strong desire to run his own business, he has begun the preparation of a business plan to determine whether the new venture makes economic sense. You are staying with your uncle Ben and his wife Pat while attending summer school at the local university. You have decided to take two courses this summer that will give you more flexibility in your senior year course schedule. Because he is somewhat younger than your other uncles, you two have always been close, and you have enjoyed staying up in the evenings listening to his ideas.

Your uncle intends to prepare a complete plan to guide the enterprise from its initiation through its first year and then on to the next three years of operations. In the evenings, he talks of little else. Ben has been out of school for several years now, and he welcomes the opportunity to discuss his ideas with someone who is currently in a business administration program. Although you feel pretty confident, the jump from the classroom to the real world, where your uncle and aunt could lose their life savings or become successful business owners, gives new urgency to your studies.

The complete plan Ben hopes to write during your stay will help him and his employees to operate efficiently. It will also be summarized in a financing plan that Ben will use to raise the start-up funds for the first four years of operations.

About a year ago Ben began contemplating opening a business in Wesson, New Jersey, which is located north of Philadelphia just east of the Pennsylvania state line. His choice of location was based partly on his personal desire to live in a smaller town and partly on his belief that a new funeral home could be successful in Wesson. In making the location decision, it occurred to Ben that he was already in the process of planning. In fact, the process had actually started from the point that he decided to establish a new funeral home.

In your evening conversations, you can see that Ben has given serious thought to the mission of his proposed new business. He tells you, "After several years with Evans Funerals, I want to be in business for myself. I want some freedom. Working for Evans, my lifestyle—even what time we get up in the morning and go to bed at night—are in their control. It isn't that I don't like getting up in the morning; Pat and I really enjoy sitting for a few minutes in the early morning sun and reading the *Journal* as we get ready for the day. I love working. I love helping people through what is often the most difficult experiences of their lives. It's that I want to decide these things for myself in the future."

Second, you know that Ben wants to be financially independent. His first personal goal is to reach a net worth of at least $250,000 before he is forty-two years old (five years hence). The figure isn't drawn from out of the blue, he tells you. He has figured what he could save from his present salary and from Pat's income as a buyer for the local department store. By the time they reach retirement age, working in their present positions, they will have to severely curtail their lifestyle in order to make ends meet. Going into business for themselves will be a risk, but it will also offer the potential for a much more enjoyable future.

Over the years, Ben tells you, he has developed a clear picture of what the public wants from a funeral service firm. "No matter how they felt toward the person who has died, the family needs assistance and services of a professional caliber, offered in dignified facilities and a quiet manner. Many people feel very vulnerable when dealing with funeral homes and funeral directors. No matter what their social or economic status, they're afraid of being ripped off. Yet, they wouldn't want to take care of the many unpleasant tasks that are handled by the mortuary establishment. If I'm going to succeed in this business, I've got to build a reputation for honesty and ethical dealings in order to gain the trust of the community. Since people in Wesson don't know us, that part of the venture will be uphill."

EXERCISE 1

Part A. "That part of getting started is still a real question in my mind," Ben tells you. "Why don't *you* do some thinking, and without mentioning any details of my particular plans, talk over with some of your student friends this problem of establishing a personal reputation that can carry over to a funeral business?" In between classes, you sit on one of the benches in the student area patio and make a mind map of the problem and possible solutions (see Chapter 5 if you need more information about how to use this discovery technique).

Part B. With a group of students chosen in class, meet to discuss the ideas each of you has proposed with the mind map for the new funeral company and its leader. During the first part of the session, list all of the possible options on a board or sheet of paper. *Do not evaluate ideas as they are presented.*

In the second part of the meeting, evaluate which of these ideas might work best. What factors would influence the success of these methods? People who die seldom choose the funeral home that handles their services. Are there differences among the people who do choose the services that would affect the success of the techniques for establishing a public reputation?

Part C. Write a one-page summary of your group's discussion, presenting the range of options, the evaluation criteria that emerged, and their primary conclusions about the various options.

EXERCISE 2

You find out that Ben has spent all his free time during the spring analyzing the market for funeral services in the greater Wesson area. Going through old copies

of the Wesson *Guardian* in the Wesson public library, Ben noted which funeral company handled the services for each person whose death was announced in the obituaries and looked up the deceased person's address in the phone book. Using pins of different colors, Ben identified on a map the residence of each deceased person. The pin's color showed which of the existing funeral homes in Wesson handled the service.

Ben also hired a market research firm that prepared a demographic study of the market area. Ben has concluded that there is a definite need for a new funeral firm in Wesson. He believes a minimum of 100 services could be secured (only a 3.3 percent share of the market) with no marketing effort. That figure could double over the next decade if a consistent effort were made to appeal to families who presently employ the services of other funeral directors in the city.

One night Ben explains to you the most important implications of the consultant's report. "The report of Pro Market Analysis, Inc., suggested that five economic, demographic, social, and competitive variables might be significant. These are the median income levels of families living in Wesson, the total population and population movements in Wesson, the mortality rate and absolute number of deaths in Wesson, the religious and ethnic mix of the population, and the number and location of other funeral homes in Wesson. They gave me specific data about these variables for the four previous years. It's a pretty clear picture," Ben concluded.

"Pat and I are willing to give four years to this project," Ben explains, "so that's the planning period I've been using for this new business. She's going to put her experience as a buyer for Dexter Department Stores to work for us. I have two friends in one of Evans' branch mortuaries about twenty miles south of here who would be willing to work for us, and we can hire an assistant in Wesson. Other work, like cleaning services, we will contract out." With this in mind, Ben has reviewed the pertinent data series gathered for him by Pro Market Analysis, Inc. The most important information relates to the expected demand for his services, and population and mortality statistics are those most germane to project this demand.

Ben's basic knowledge of funeral home operations has enabled him to determine the important internal economic variables that will spell success or failure for this new venture. Getting into the role of one of your professors, he relishes giving you an overview of what makes a funeral home tick. "Despite the fact that a funeral home is essentially a service business, the large investment required to operate a funeral establishment means that it will typically have a low variable-cost-to-sales ratio and a high level of fixed costs. Most funeral homes also have substantial excess capacity that must be maintained to meet peak-load periods of demand. Salaries, which for all intents and purposes are a fixed cost for a funeral home, are usually the most significant expense item. Industry sources indicate that about 40 percent of the revenues of American funeral homes are spent on wages and salaries. Facility expenses (rent, taxes, depreciation, interest, utilities, maintenance, etc.) account for another 15 percent, while vehicles (lease costs, depreciation, interest, maintenance, gasoline, etc.) require about 12 percent. The most important variable cost item is casket merchandise, and this expense accounts for about 18 percent of the funeral revenue dollar. When you subtract these total costs from revenues, the profit before income taxes looks pretty good, don't you think?

"Why don't you turn this information into a typical income statement (table) that we could print as a page in a small 8-1/2 × 11 flip chart or print on an overhead transparency? We want them to have a positive view of the funeral industry. That way you could practice what you learned in your communication class and help me get ready to talk with some backers," Ben says. From your classes, you know that an income statement shows the revenue (100 percent) at the top of the table, then divides the category "costs" into "variable costs" and "fixed costs" and subtracts them from the revenue to get the percentage of profits. You could also present the revenues as a "whole to part" graph (consult Chapter 15, "Graphics: Visual Persuasion," if you need help with this task).

Create the income statement as a graphic.

EXERCISE 3

Ben has thought about the possible strengths of his proposed new business. Going to one of his files, he pulls out the following list:

STRENGTHS

1. Location. The Jackson Funeral Home will be conveniently located on Second Avenue in a building that was formerly a reasonably successful funeral home.

2. Service. The Jackson Funeral Home will offer a full line of funeral merchandise (caskets, grave vaults, clothing, etc.) and will strive to offer the best service available in Wesson.

3. Price. The Jackson Funeral Home will price its merchandise and service to offer the best value in Wesson. The principal clientele of the firm will be elderly people with limited wealth. The families of these people should appreciate being able to get the best in quality for a reasonable price.

4. Building. The old Second Avenue Mortuary building will be completely remodeled to reflect an image of quality, yet not opulence.

5. Employees. The Jackson Funeral Home will not be unionized. Employees will be personally selected by Ben Jackson from the most dependable people he has worked with throughout New Jersey and New York.

"Like most entrepreneurs, I don't like to think about the possibility that I won't be successful. Nevertheless, to be honest with myself and my financial backers, I've also outlined the potential problems that will face us," he says. He hands you a second list. "Pinpointing these areas of weaknesses not only gives me a better idea about my chances for success, it also makes it possible to concentrate on curing my weaknesses. This project is not just an ego trip." In order of importance, he has listed the following:

WEAKNESSES

1. Nature of business. It typically takes a long time for a new funeral home to become established in the eyes of the community. Some businesses require months before they handle even a few services, and it may take years for a new location to become profitable.

2. Marketing strategy. It is difficult to market funerals. The nature of the service limits the effectiveness of the usual techniques, such as a grand-opening sales or extensive advertising. Price cutting also does not work ordinarily, since people are not likely to buy a funeral simply because it has been marked down in price.

3. <u>Competition.</u> There are currently twelve funeral homes in Wesson. Although it appears that the market could support another one (particularly in the location that has been selected for the Jackson Funeral Home), competition would remain keen. Two competitors have been in business for over fifty years, and The Wesson Mortuary is clearly thought by almost everyone to be the prestige "carriage-trade" operation in the city. It is also the fastest-growing business. Fortunately, it is located eight miles from the proposed site of the Jackson Funeral Home.

4. <u>Market size.</u> The population of Wesson has been decreasing in recent years and the death rate has been declining. As a result, the overall size of the market has been diminishing slightly.

5. <u>Financing.</u> Ben Jackson has only a limited amount of personal savings to invest in the business. Given what it will take to get the business started and sustained for the first year, additional funds will have to be borrowed or equity partners will have to be found.

Over the Fourth of July holiday, you and your uncle spend a day turning the multiple pieces of information he has collected, along with his own notes and ideas, into a complete plan. You retrieve from your class handout the outline of a complete plan (identical to the one shown earlier in this case). With your uncle, you prepare the working papers, annotating your sources and making notes to yourself. "I'd like you to give me a hand with this," your uncle Ben says. "You'll get a chance to apply some of the things you've been studying in your management classes. While I work on the operating plan, I would like you to draft the introductory summary, parts I and II of the outline.

"The style should be formal without being stuffy. Write in the third person. You know, say, 'The Jackson Funeral Home will . . .' instead of, 'We will . . .' Remember that these people review lots of plans, and they don't spend more than ten minutes on the first reading, when they decide whether they will talk with you at all. You've got to be precise and specific.

"The fireworks tonight can be a celebration for our completing the first step toward an independent

company as well as a tribute to an independent nation," he says with a smile.

Your class handout shows the following outline.

Introduction

I. Presentation of the venture, opportunity, and financing need
   A. A one-paragraph statement about the nature of the business
   B. A one-paragraph rationale for the existence of the business
   C. A brief statement about the financing required
II. Summary of industry and venture
   A. Key characteristics of the industry
   B. Structure and important features of the company

Draft these parts of the outline.

EXERCISE 4

After the fireworks, sitting on the porch with your aunt and uncle, you remember that your roommate two years ago, an upperclassman named Lee Jenkins, was from Wesson. Lee's major was business administration with a concentration in marketing. You remark that Lee might be a good candidate for the assistant's job, a person who related well to others, especially older people. "Lee was the only person I knew who could get the secretaries in the business school to release the key to the photocopying room," you chuckle. "I wonder if Lee went back to Wesson?"

Just before school starts, your uncle calls with the news that the financing plan has been successful. "We hope to open about the first of November, but it would be a big help if we had someone familiar with the town working with us as we take care of all this preliminary stuff. Would you check your address book for Lee Jenkins' home address and write a letter, seeing whether a position with us would be of interest? I'd really appreciate your doing this, because now that we're really going to try it, there are a thousand things to do. Pat's got the house on the market, and we're busy trying to execute all of those items we put on the list this summer. It's a good thing we made that list, because there's scarcely a moment to call my own these days." You check your address book and find that Lee's home address in Wesson was on 1214 Chestnut Street.

Write the letter to Lee Jenkins in Wesson.

IF YOU WOULD LIKE TO READ MORE

Books

Mancuso, J. R. (1978). *How to start, finance, and manage your own small business*. Englewood Cliffs, NJ: Prentice-Hall. A concise work on new venture creation and small business management.

McKeever, M. (1988). *Nolo's small business start-up: How to write a business plan* (3rd ed.). Berkeley, CA: Nolo Press. Contains sample loan applications for a small service business, manufacturing business, and house improvement for resale project.

Moran, P. (1984). *Invest in yourself: A woman's guide to starting her own business*. New York: Doubleday. Contains good exercises for assessing your interests, talents, and resources.

Williams, E. E., & Manzo, S. E. (1983). *Business planning for the entrepreneur: How to write and execute a business plan*. New York: Van Nostrand Reinhold. Contains a complete discussion, with financials, of the funeral home case discussed in this chapter.

Magazines and Newspapers

Inc. 38 Commercial Wharf, Boston, MA 02110. Aimed at fairly large small businesses.

In Business. Box 323, Emmons, PA 18049. A good source for start-up companies. Many articles on taxes, legal matters, hiring and firing, and other topics.

Mother Earth News. Box 70, Hendersonville, NC 28739. Practical advice on "cottage industries"; not the "hot new field" types of businesses.

The Wall Street Journal, available on newsstands, periodically has special issues devoted to new businesses.

NOTE

1. This case is a disguised version of an actual case.

PART SIX

EXECUTIVES' PERSPECTIVES

❑ CREATING EXCELLENCE

When First Interstate Bancorp acquired a group of fifty-nine Texas banks in 1988, the state's economic climate was uncertain. Many banks in Texas had failed, and the collapse of dozens of savings and loan companies had rattled the confidence of both financial service customers and investors. Texas bank employees understandably worried about the future. First Interstate (a California-based corporation) had acquired these banks without government assistance, which meant that their return to profitability would take a bit longer than the return of those the government had "bailed out." Nonetheless, the banks First Interstate acquired had a heritage of excellence in performance, and we were determined to create the best bank in Texas, a solid institution that served its customers, employees, shareholders, and Texas communities. The challenge, in short, was to create excellence.

Although the economic climate of the state might have seemed the most serious threat, our chief obstacle was a lack of communication—employees felt isolated and powerless. Our fifty-nine banks had previously operated almost as

---

Linnet Deily is President and Chief Operating Officer, First Interstate Bank of Texas.

independent companies, but changes in the banking laws now permitted branch banking, allowing much closer coordination of all functions. To make those possibilities a reality, employees had to understand the direction and strategies of the company as a whole, and they had to develop close relationships with others throughout the organization so that banking functions could be integrated. During the first few months, communication became a principal means of ensuring a return to excellence.

THE FIRST PHASE: MULTIPLE FORMS OF COMMUNICATION

The I's of Texas: Knowing the News, Knowing People

To transform employees' isolation, we created a newsletter, *The I's of Texas* (a play on the "eyes of Texas" and "Interstates of Texas"), which disseminated news of products, policies, and people throughout the company every Monday morning. Although securities regulations prevented our releasing significant news to insiders before it was released to the press, we tried to release news simultaneously to employees, issuing special editions when necessary. We didn't want employees learning about their company from the newspapers. Naturally, in addition to corporate news, the newsletter featured individuals, community service projects, and contest winners (as illustrated in Figure 1). To make *The I's of Texas* a trustworthy source, the editor scrutinized drafts to avoid puffery or exaggeration.

Meeting Every Employee

In the first six months, I scheduled a meeting with every employee in his or her office or work location. If leaders are going to be more than anonymous abstractions, they must be real people that employees know. I wanted to know the people in the organization, and I wanted them to know me. As I met our employees, I had the opportunity to receive feedback directly, and I was also able to share with them first-hand the strategic direction of the bank.

The Management Advisory Council Minutes

To reinforce our commitment to answering employees' questions—not just spreading management views—we created the Management Advisory Council. This ten-member group of upper-level managers solicits questions from employees and seeks answers from top management. Three top executives meet with the council every quarter, presenting written answers to all questions and elaborating on these answers orally during the meetings. The written answers and minutes of the meetings are published and widely read throughout the organization as "the MAC Minutes." The only editing occurs as the questions are submitted: Questions targeting a specific individual may be paraphrased in a ge-

First Interstate Bank of Texas | May 7, 1990 | Volume 2, Number 18

FITX Has Outstanding Participation in March of Dimes Teamwalk

Thank you! Over 1,000 FITX employees and their families donned their walking shoes for the 1990 March of Dimes WalkAmerica. Our company has set records in terms of dollars raised for the March of Dimes as well as participation statewide.

Our volunteers walked between 12 and 18 miles in an effort to raise money in the fight against birth defects, and they had a good time doing it. Participation was strong statewide with approximately 550 volunteers in the Houston area, 150 in the Dallas/Ft. Worth area and the remaining 300 coming from our Central and East Texas locations.

We made quite an impression when we stepped off in our prize-winning neon t-shirts and cool palm tree sunglasses. In Ft. Worth and Houston, our neon T-shirts won first place in the "Most Creative" (Houston) and "Favorite T-shirt" (Ft. Worth) categories among our corporate competitors. The Ft. Bend branch also got into the spirit of things by winning the "Spirit Van" award for their enthusiasm and creativity. After the walk, the volunteers got together for picnic lunches, kicked up their feet and enjoyed each others company.

Although the final contribution figures are not in, FITX expects to make a record contribution to the 1990 WalkAmerica. One record breaker is Darleen Austin, Houston Central, who raised $5,626. Darleen was the top fundraiser in the company in 1989 and she doubled her total for 1990. We will share the final results with you as soon as possible.

"I am very proud of the efforts demonstrated by all of our volunteers and coordinators across the state," said Linnet Deily, president and chief operating officer. "The March of Dimes is a worthwhile cause, and I appreciate the personal time, dedication and foot-power you put forth to help others."

Alexander Selected a NACM Credit Executive of the Year

Jim Alexander, vice president, Credit Operations, was recently named as a 1990 Credit Executive of the Year by the National Association of Credit Management (NACM).

Alexander was among five NACM members nationwide to receive this honor. He was nominated by the Houston Association of Credit Management (HACM) and was reviewed at the national level based on local and national involvement, educational and individual accomplishments and promotion of the credit profession.

The Credit Executive of the Year is one of the most prestigious awards presented by NACM, as the winners are some of the leading professionals in the credit management field. We extend our congratulations and appreciation to Jim.

Just a Reminder . . .

Questions for the Management Advisory Council must be submitted by Friday, May 11 in order to be included in the next edition of *MAC Minutes*. Please send your questions to Lisa Wagenfuehr, MS 194 (Fax 713-226-1888). Question forms can be obtained from your branch/department manager or from Lisa at 713-221-4910.

Mortgage Loan Division Highlights Home Loans

The Community Banking Group has completed two weeks of "The Great First Interstate House Hunt," its 1990 Mortgage Loan Campaign, a joint effort of the branches and our new Mortgage Loan division. This eight week campaign is intended to highlight the new permanent home mortgage loan program.

In our third week, our employees have submitted referrals that have resulted in over 40 completed loan applications. These completed applications yielded cash awards to the employees who referred them. Weekly statewide drawings from these referral cards are also being held. The winners for weeks one and two are:

| Week 1 | Jeri Pearson | North Belt |
| Week 2 | Cindy Ramsey | Conroe |

Customers already have positive things to say about our Mortgage division and branch staff. One of our Austin customers recently closed a 15 year home loan for $161,000. After completing the application at our North Austin branch, his loan was submitted to the Regional Loan Center. The Center provided processing of all credit, income and property qualifications as well as providing the legal documents and coordinating the closing. FITX helped the customer in two ways, first we paid off his First Interstate construction loan and secondly, we provided long-term financing for his home.

The customer was very pleased with the quality and responsiveness of our staff from the moment he entered the North Austin branch as well as his communication with the Mortgage staff in Houston. In fact, he cancelled a home loan application at another bank due to poor service, and as a result of the

Continued on next page . . .

FIGURE 1. Sample Page of Newsletter

neric form so that the council meetings cannot become a political forum. About 35 percent of the questions are human resources questions, which suggests the importance employees attach to these matters. The obligation to answer all questions keeps employees' concerns before the executives. As chief operating officer, I join the council at lunch during the day-long meeting, which encourages informal policy discussions of the issues raised.

Forming New Friendships, Grass-Roots Planning

We used one-day meetings to build good working relationships. Very early we brought together about 120 key managers, briefed them on the prospects for the coming era, introduced the management team, and previewed vital projects for 1989. Having concluded that these meetings initiated a dialogue between managers and top executives, we held a two-day session in early 1990, including team building through sports activities. The meetings generated an interest in planning; we asked for feedback from small, break-out groups on ideas for improving the bank, and the ideas generated were so good that we asked the groups to develop detailed recommendations on the "Top Five" ideas.

Cascading the Strategic Plan

As managers began sharing their ideas about vital issues, they needed an expanded understanding of the bank's direction, objectives, and specific strategies. Indeed, people in a branch system must be able to picture the organization as a whole so that they can contribute good ideas consistent with overall goals. Furthermore, they need to see the plan in tangible form.

In 1990 the bank presented its strategic plan to all employees in all branches. The plan defined the bank's mission, which is to serve its four major constituencies: customers, employees, shareholders, and Texas communities. To meet these constituencies' needs, the bank dedicated itself to the highest level of customer satisfaction, ethical business practices, open communication, teamwork, and to an organizational culture that fosters pride and personal satisfaction. In an attractive brochure, the bank set forth the specific objectives associated with each of the four constituencies and the strategies selected in 1990 for achieving these objectives. A card bearing the mission statement alone was inserted in the back cover of this brochure, easy to remove for reference.

The brochure was distributed to and discussed with employees in small group meetings. Beginning with top executives, each group read and discussed the strategic plan, then arranged meetings with the closest associates. In a month, every employee had participated in a strategic plan discussion meeting and had signed a statement that he or she had received and read the plan. The seriousness of this distribution process communicated to all employees, regardless of their positions, that they were expected to understand this plan and to implement it. The strategic plan had to come alive through these employees' informed creativity and cooperation.

Communicating Corporate News to Customers

My remarks so far have described internal communications, but we have also made important strides in communicating with customers. Some of our most effective customer communications have resulted from a "scripting" program that encouraged employees to anticipate their communication with customers. "Scripting" is an informal procedure for planning what one will say as predictable scenarios unfold. For example, as soon as our 1990 first-quarter results confirmed our projections, employees called their customers to tell them the good news. The staff in one office made a list of the ways they could capitalize on the announcement. They decided to place copies of the newspaper article throughout the branch. Employees asked customers, "Did you see the article about our first-quarter earnings?" Copies were also distributed by tellers. The personal communication caused one customer to change his mind about withdrawing $100,000. Tellers in another branch were able to generate 261 referrals in one month as a result of asking customers whether they knew about specific services available in the bank. Furthermore, sharing these success stories has increased the rate of innovation and the level of productivity tremendously.

❑ THE SECOND PHASE OF COMMUNICATING EXCELLENCE

In retrospect, the multiple forms of communication seem like bricks in a pre-designed comprehensive plan, but in many cases the solutions were chosen instinctively. As we saw what the situation required, we developed our own scenarios for creating excellence, taking into account the size of this organization, people's needs, and the fact that our offices were located throughout the state. However, I want to stress that our experience is not a cookbook recipe for someone else; it is not these particular means or solutions that I recommend but an awareness that in creating and implementing a strategic plan, communication will affect nearly every element of a company's success.

In the first 18 months after the acquisition, a high proportion of our communication effort had to be devoted to team building; in 1991, with a highly motivated and thoroughly knowledgeable management in place throughout the banks of the system, we can strengthen the written communication links—the newsletter and the Management Advisory Council minutes—and expand the meetings and conferences to include more employees. We have begun holding meetings each quarter to orient all newly hired or newly promoted managers. These meetings are intended to give these people a more complete macro perspective, to shorten the time it takes for them to become outstandingly productive.

I believe these continued meetings and conferences among top managers in each branch will support the planning process and forge relationships among participants. Old friendships will be strengthened. Knowledge and innovation will increase. As employees throughout the bank see the results of communicating effectively with customers, colleagues, and managers, we expect to develop a corporate culture at First Interstate that ensures high levels of satisfaction among customers and employees. It will doubtless also enhance our profitability, which will gratify our shareholders and our parent company. As First Interstate of Texas grows and expands its community service projects, it can offer more jobs in Texas communities, more capital for Texas business, and generous civic support. We will have started a dynamic, self-perpetuating process: creating excellence.

PHASING OUT CHLOROFLUOROCARBONS: COMPLEX DECISION MAKING AT E. I. DU PONT DE NEMOURS & COMPANY

Two important elements of du Pont's corporate culture came into play as we began to examine the emerging chlorofluorocarbon (CFC) issue. One element was a strong respect for science; the other, an equally strong commitment to health, safety, and the environment.

We are very explicit in saying that we won't produce anything unless it can be made, used, handled and disposed of safely, and in a way that is consistent with appropriate safety, health, and environmental quality criteria. As soon as the first scientific questions about CFCs came to light, these corporate prin-

R. E. Heckert is Chairman, E. I. du Pont de Nemours & Company.

The author spoke at Rice University on November 2, 1988, about du Pont's decision to phase out production of certain chlorofluorocarbons (CFCs), which were suspected of harming the ozone layer. These excerpts from his presentation emphasize the communications necessary to the decision-making process and the communications used in conveying the decision.

ciples were applied to our business decision-making process. In 1972 we convened a "Seminar on the Ecology of Fluorocarbons." In a letter of invitation to CFC producers around the world, we said, "It is prudent that we investigate any effects which the compounds may produce on plants or animals now or in the future." The symposium led to a research program sponsored by nineteen companies under the auspices of the Chemical Manufacturers Association. To date, the group has spent about $20 million on research into CFCs, including support for the recent Antarctic expeditions to gather information on the seasonal ozone "hole" over that region.

The situation at the beginning of the 1980s was dynamic; few of the variables remained constant for very long. Published reports began to suggest conflicting conclusions—at least to the general public. Several analyses of actual measurements found no persistent trend in ozone levels, supporting the belief that there would not be significant changes in ozone in the near term. Then another set of calculations suggested 15 to 20 percent ozone depletion by the end of the next century. If all this sounds confusing, rest assured it was. For several years, there was no clear consensus, and we remained true to our corporate culture, insisting that policies should be based on good science, not speculation.

In early 1985 two British scientists uncovered the first hard evidence—temporary but significant changes in the ozone over Antarctica. Although scientists didn't all agree about the cause of the so-called Antarctic hole, the observation of a real and measurable change focused world attention back on the issue.

Given the growth of CFC use and evidence linking continued growth to probable ozone depletion at some point in the future, du Pont began reexamining its position. After a review group studied the data, senior management announced a new position in September 1986: We favored some mechanism to restrain CFC growth, and insisted that it should be global in scope. While du Pont led the industry effort to limit CFC growth, we were not alone. Much of industry in 1986 had come to accept the need for some kind of limit. That general acceptance contributed to the development of an international process that resulted in the signing of the Montreal Protocol in 1987. No sooner was the ink dry on the Protocol and the ratification process begun when a new development was announced. At the same time, a team of more than 100 scientists sponsored by NASA revealed new findings on the Antarctic hole; these findings tightened the linkage between certain CFCs and ozone depletion.

Dr. McFarland, a member of the NASA team and a du Pont scientist, took action immediately after the announcement. Within three days, he and other du Pont scientists presented the new data to me and other members of our Executive Committee—the highest level of senior management, consisting of the chairman, president, and executive vice presidents. We knew a major change in the company's position was in order.

We quickly mobilized to notify people who needed to know: our customers, competitors, and employees around the world. Less than a week after the NASA study was announced, we made our response public: du Pont would set as

Process development for CFC alternatives is under way at the du Pont Company's alternatives pilot plant in Deepwater, N.J.

a goal an orderly phaseout of production of the CFCs associated with ozone depletion. We would link the phaseout to the introduction of safe alternative chemicals and technologies, and would set as a target a complete phaseout no later than the turn of the century. And we would call for a strengthening of the Protocol to encompass further global limitations on CFC emissions.

What conclusions can we draw from our experience to date? First, our corporate culture proved to be a good compass in the decision-making process. Our determination to act on scientific evidence rather than speculation exposed us to some criticism along the way, but as soon as hard evidence did appear, we didn't hesitate to act on it. Furthermore, our long-standing commitment to safety and environmental protection as a first priority was well understood up and down the line of management. Once the scientific evidence was clear, everyone understood that a phaseout was the right choice, and no one suggested that we turn our back on our commitment to environmental quality.

Second, the CFC case illustrates that business decisions are rarely, if ever, made under static conditions. We didn't have the luxury of knowing all the facts at any point in the process—and many uncertainties remain today. Case studies done as part of the business school curriculum should factor in a large dose of uncertainty, because that's certainly the way it works in the real world.

Third, a company, like an individual, has to have the courage of its convictions, and the courage to change its position when that is called for. We weren't bashful about defending CFCs when we saw evidence that they were not damaging the ozone layer. I don't regret for one minute that we did so. But I'm very proud that we were not intransigent when evidence to the contrary became strong. If we had stubbornly opted for rear-guard battle to oppose the Montreal Protocol or delay action after the March 1988 findings were announced, we would have served neither du Pont's nor the public's interest. And from what I've seen and heard, we earned a lot of respect for being consistently forthright about our views.

WORKING WITH CORPORATE CULTURE TO INSTITUTE CHANGE

In January 1989 Cray Research, Inc., set in motion two events that were to mark the most tumultuous and challenging period in its history. The first of these actions, the reorganization of Cray's U.S. marketing functions, focused on the company's internal operations. The second, the departure of the company's founder, Seymore Cray, to start a rival organization, had far greater implications. Because Cray is the world leader in super-computing, its actions significantly altered the course of an entire billion-dollar-a-year industry.

My responsibility within the Petroleum Marketing group as Regional Human Resources Manager meant that I must communicate these changes so employees would not only understand them but would accept and support them as well. To achieve positive effects in a changing environment would require a well-rounded, two-way communications effort in which people were not just informed but were actively listened to and allowed to become a part of the process.

James Sheehy is Regional Human Resources Manager, Cray Research, Inc.

☐ THE GOLDFISH SWALLOWS THE WHALE

With its reorganization of marketing, Cray eliminated its Central Region operations that had managed marketing and customer support activities in 15 states. Nine of those states were added to the Petroleum Marketing group, which had previously included only Texas and Oklahoma.

Helping employees to accept and support this change was a complex task: From their perspective, it was a case of a goldfish swallowing a whale. Overnight, Petroleum Marketing grew from two states to the entire central U.S. Headquartered in Houston, it now managed a territory that stretched north to Minneapolis, east to Detroit, and south to New Orleans. The customer base expanded to include not only petroleum clients, but also aerospace, university, agri-chemical, defense, and automotive accounts. One hundred and eighty employees were uprooted and moved from one management structure to another. Since Cray's marketing regions functioned autonomously, the changes had a strong impact on how these people were managed and upon their sense of identity within the organization.

Two things were critical at this juncture: to forge an identity for the new organization and to communicate the changes in a continuous and positive way. We chose to communicate in a variety of formats: personal visits with small groups, special newsletters, electronic mail updates, and ceremonial activities, such as achievement awards and anniversary recognitions.

Six weeks after we had announced the reorganization, I had visited fifteen Cray locations to meet with employees and listen to their concerns. Every site was included, from small two- and three-person locations to larger offices where 20 or more employees could gather. The focus of these meetings was simply to provide face-to-face contact and to gauge the overall feelings of employees toward the reorganization. One key element was to make sure employees knew they had a contact for problems and concerns, regardless of their location or work hours. To facilitate this process, I provided my home phone number and offered to be "on call" whenever they had a need that could not be immediately addressed by local management.

The feelings and questions I encountered ran the gamut from curiosity about the new structure and its management team ("How does this affect me? Where do I fit in?"), to anger ("We liked things the way they were. What was wrong with the way it was?"), to fear and uncertainty ("Is this the first of more changes? What happens next?"). Employees were also concerned about how the reorganization would be perceived by our customers, and they wanted to know how they should respond to "outside" questions. Much interest was focused on how things would work on a day-to-day basis: who would approve purchase requests, where to send expense reports, who would handle health care reimbursements, where to call if operational questions came up, and so forth.

I kept a record of all the questions asked, and the most common—along with our responses—were shared with all employees in later editions of the newsletter or through electronic mail. We used weekly electronic mail updates to follow up on the meetings and report the progress of the reorganization. Our bi-weekly newsletter contained information on personnel changes and maps showing the new region and the locations of Cray customers and employees (see Figure 1).

These communication elements helped lay the groundwork for more than the reorganization. By communicating early and establishing a personal link, we created a feeling among employees that there was a resource they could turn to that truly did listen to them and had empathy for what they were going through. This personal channel not only allowed management to get the word out on the reorganization and other future activities, it also served as a barometer of employee morale.

❑ DEPARTURE AND REDEFINITION

Our communication groundwork also proved invaluable in dealing with the second major change: the departure of the company's founder, Seymore Cray, to start another organization. This development was significant, both for Cray and for the super-computing industry as a whole. It marked the departure not only of Cray's founder, but of the person who had almost single-handedly created the industry itself. To compound matters, Seymore Cray was not retiring on his laurels but was leaving to start a rival company that would pursue development of a new-generation super-computer meant to challenge or exceed the performance of machines being designed within Cray Research.

Thus the departure presented a new dimension to the communications challenge because the parting had to be seen as positive to everyone, even when it was creating a formidable rival to the company's future. This turn of events required a heavy sell for what was good about Cray Research without making employees feel that we were detracting from Seymore or his achievements.

Once again, we needed to help people go through a significant change. For some it included a grieving process; for others it meant a transition from a company they closely identified with to something they were unsure of. We had to clarify and redefine organizational objectives to acknowledge the change, while highlighting the intrinsic qualities people wanted and needed in their company.

For example, the culture at Cray valued openness in communications, and employees had been accustomed to decisions being made by a consensus process. The rapid changes, however, required a number of on-the-spot decisions and personnel moves within a very short period of time. These were required to take advantage of opportunities in the marketplace or to position the organization to be more cost effective and profitable.

Considerable effort was spent in explaining these global needs as management saw them, while allowing employees to comment and make suggestions regarding the process. The goal was to prepare and staff the new organization and to make people feel good about these changes. Helping people become a part of the process, by simply listening to them and allowing them a forum for

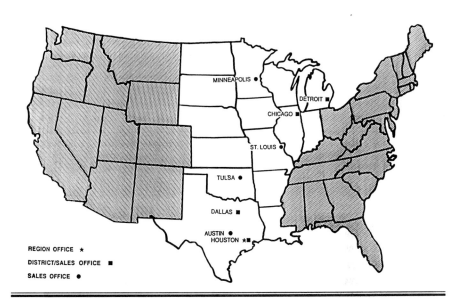

FIGURE 1. Newsletter Map of the New Marketing Group

voicing their concerns, was instrumental to reestablishing the feelings of trust, esprit, and belonging that were highly valued qualities at Cray. It was critical to the success of our strategy that employees felt as if they were a part of a dynamic process and that their contributions were seen as having value and merit.

The most effective single ingredient in making this an effective transition was the personal contact that had developed during the reorganization visits. The personal visits to the employees, no matter where they were located or how few might be at a given location, proved our commitment of availability and willingness to listen. By grieving with them and talking them through the changes, by offering to be available to them—even when at home—and by following up with written detail on a timely basis, we not only communicated an important change, but managed it. There was no significant turnover among employees following Seymore's departure; instead, there was a positive feeling that Cray Research would grow and prosper.

DA WHAT?
INTERNAL AND EXTERNAL
COMMUNICATIONS IN THE FOUNDING
OF THE DA CAMERA SOCIETY, HOUSTON

In 1988 Sergiu Luca, a famous violinist and tireless organizer, envisioned a new chamber music organization, the Da Camera Society, dedicated to the exploration of small ensemble music, "high art that's highly entertaining." Luca explained the new society as follows:

> But what is the Da Camera Society? It is an umbrella organization dedicated to producing and presenting the widest range of small ensemble repertoire. What is meant by small ensemble? Other than "not large," as in symphony or grand opera (and Houston can boast of having amongst the country's finest), a proper definition can be somewhat elusive. My own less-than-perfect attempt reads: "A group of performers each playing or singing an independent part, and achieving a co-

June S. Holly is a consultant in organization effectiveness.

hesive musical statement, usually without a conductor." Clearly, by that definition, the progressive jazz quartet Oregon qualifies, as well as the Juilliard Quartet; the Piazzolla New Tango Quintet, as well as the Schubert "Trout" Quintet; the "Voice of the Whale" by Crumb, as well as the voices in a Josquin des Prez mass. And that is precisely what is so unique and exciting about the Da Camera Society (Sergiu Luca, Da Camera Brochure, 1988).

❏ STEPS IN ORGANIZING DA CAMERA

Watching Luca's dream take shape as I assisted him during a six-month's consulting engagement for fundraising in 1988 and 1989, I noted that in spite of his visionary approach, he did not discount practical communication steps. Da Camera Society's pragmatic necessities were addressed early, even while program ideas emerged. Luca and a small group of enthusiastic advisors selected a board of directors notable for their support of the arts. Luca hired a small but committed and qualified staff to begin the rigorous tasks that give birth to an ambitious premier season. Perhaps most important, Luca also obtained initial sponsorship of two major foundations. This support was gained through meetings between the Da Camera board and the trustees of the foundations, followed by written grant applications and additional meetings.

Staff Motivation and Communications

The staff met weekly in sessions that evaluated the work of the organization, public reaction, logistical matters, and upcoming events. These meetings demanded flexibility and a willingness by the staff to move in new directions and assume additional roles. As a consultant to Da Camera and an accepted ad hoc member of the staff, I often described the *modus operandi* as "catching lightning in a box"—a metaphor for work during opening week. Informal meals together generated camaraderie. Luca's own thoughtful touches—an outdoor party for staff at his home, with champagne to celebrate—helped staff members cope with mounting pressure.

Programs/Music/Musicians

Luca created an organization that closely paralleled the Chamber Music Society of Lincoln Center in New York City. He set his sights high. Seven series of concerts were planned that would entice a wide variety of music lovers (see concert series descriptions). Opening week was set to begin October 1, 1988, with the first concert of each of the seven series. A benefit concert for the AIDS Foundation at The Menil Collection (a new and impressive art museum in central Houston) and an out-of-town concert also initiated Da Camera's introduction. This ambitious opening characterized the organization's energy, creativity, and interest in reaching diverse audiences. It demonstrated Luca's image of the way a fine arts group of superior quality must greet its public for the first time.

Da Camera's Seven Concert Series for Its Premier Season

The Signature Series, Da Camera's flagship series, with eight programs including such composers as Mozart, Mendelssohn, Stravinsky, Janacek, Dvořák, Sandor Veress, Debussy, Ravel, Schubert, Bolcom, Paganini, Johann Strauss, Brahms, and Bartok. Musicians were all highly talented and widely renowned, many internationally.

The Beethoven Quartet Cycle was comprised of six concerts performed by the famed Juilliard String Quartet.

The Crossover Series, advertised as "Adventures in the Unexpected," with three concerts featuring: Oregon (a progressive jazz quartet); Joan Morris and William Bolcom presenting The Classic American Popular Song; and Astor Piazzolla and the New Tango Quintet.

After 1910, with Sandor Veress, "one of European music's most respected elder statesmen," as the featured composer. The four *After 1910* concerts also included other renowned composers of the twentieth century up through the 1950s.

The Discovery Series presented three artists—all new to Houston audiences in recital: Jian Wang, cello; Eric Ruske, horn; and Lucia Lin, violin.

The Connoisseur Series, three concerts—each with a spiritual impact—was so popular that an additional performance for each of the three was added at The Menil to accommodate enthusiastic subscribers. This series included "An Evening of Motets and Masses," by Josquin des Prez, directed by Michael Hammond; "Suites for Cello" by Bach, performed by Anner Bylsma, world-famous Baroque cellist; and "Vingt Regards sur L'Enfant Jesus," performed by Brian Connelly, pianist.

Little Day Music, a free concert held each month in the Wortham Center foyer, featured the same excellent musicians who had just played in a regular concert. School children from all over the city, a different school each month, were invited as special guests. Downtown workers and the general citizenry were encouraged to bring their lunches to enjoy the fifty-minute concert. Continuing Da Camera Society's approach to public appeal and education, the musicians invited children in the audiences to inspect their instruments and to talk with them after the concerts.

FIGURE 1. Da Camera's First Concert Series Descriptions

Promotion and Image: Da Camera as a Winner

Emerging organizations frequently begin their public relations with modest brochures and cost-saving promotional pieces that reveal tentative expectations and a cautious venture. Da Camera's assurance as an important entity in Houston's art scene was vivid in the organization's communications.

From the first, Da Camera was programmed as a winner, with no obvious tentative or negative thoughts about its future. To substantiate his positive projections, Luca told the public from the outset that this new organization was to be imaginative, off-beat, and challenging. The fact that the exciting music would be played in the finest halls and would offer a highly significant opportunity for Houston—and Texas—was communicated in a blitz of publicity through local papers and a regular weekly program on KRTS 92.1 FM radio in Houston. The same assurance and creativity were reflected in the oversized and dramatic brochure circulated throughout the city during late spring and summer, 1988. On the brochure's cover was a line drawing of Alexander Calder's "Two Acrobats" (1929), a sculpture of wire and wood construction in The Menil Collection.

The back cover of the brochure also caught attention through a photo (from Bettmann Archives) of a charming baby with wide, dark eyes and a quizzical expression, and the mere words, "Da What?" The genius of Da Camera was epitomized in that eye-and-mind-catching photo and the two words, raising a question and provoking interest. "Da What?" became a symbol and opened opportunities to explain the newly born Da Camera.

❑ ACCOLADES FROM THE PRESS, PUBLIC, AND PROFESSIONAL MUSICIANS

Music critics and audiences enthusiastically praised performances. In December 1988, Charles Ward of the Houston Chronicle named Da Camera as one of the four "best" classical musical happenings in Houston during 1988. He wrote:

> If that chamber music group [Da Camera] is able to sustain interest and income, it will be the single most important addition to musical life here this decade, in terms of organizations. . . . Sergiu Luca, the concert violinist who teaches at Rice University, has given the city a chamber music society with ambitions and achievements that, so far, match the best series in New York City. (Charles Ward, *Houston Chronicle*, December 25, 1988)

Arts critic Ann Holmes wrote:

> It was a dashing—and at moments thrilling—example of the kind of grand music for intimate ensembles that the city has not seen in several decades. (Ann Holmes, *Houston Chronicle*, October 24, 1988)

Participating musicians also wrote of their delight in playing in a small ensemble with other talented and widely noted musicians. Luca's friend and mentor, violinist Isaac Stern, wrote to him: "Da Camera Society shows your imaginative touch and a certain amount of confidence in miracles—a quality I have always admired in you." Audiences were always invited backstage after each performance to greet the artists and converse with them. This proved to be a popular and engaging way for audiences to feel a part of the concert.

Why Da Camera Is a Success

There are a number of reasons that Da Camera caught the attention and spirit of support that it enjoyed even as a new organization in a city in which dozens of new arts organizations had struggled. These reasons for success largely center on the aura Da Camera has communicated to the public and to potential supporters. It has convinced the public and potential donors that Da Camera will provide music that can be heard nowhere else in Houston. The organization thrives under the verve and inspiration of a dynamic leader; it communicates the image of an entity absolutely essential to the arts in Houston. Nothing in its beginnings communicated anything but success—a winner—a new venture that would vastly enhance and enrich the city's cultural life. Sergiu Luca believes his dream *will* come true and that the question, "Da What?" *will* be answered by an ever-growing and fully satisfied constituency.

FIGURE 2. Sergiu Luca, Director, Da Camera Society

LAUNCHING A LEVERAGED BUYOUT: VISTA CHEMICAL COMPANY

When Conoco, Inc., was acquired in 1981 by E. I. du Pont de Nemours & Company, the new parent organization soon announced plans to sell assets to help pay for the purchase. At the time, I was executive vice president of Conoco Chemicals. Anticipating a divestiture, we senior managers realized that if our division could become an independent company, it would begin its life as the 12th largest chemical company in the industry, equivalent in size to a public Fortune 500 company. So we sought financing and proposed the purchase of our businesses in a management-led leveraged buyout, and in July 1984 a new private company with a 40-year history, Vista Chemical Company, was born. The well-planned communication program that announced the intent to form the company strongly affected our initial success.

John D. Burns is Chairman, President, and Chief Executive Officer, Vista Chemical Company.

Changing the Signs at Vista

☐ THE VISTA ANNOUNCEMENT

Because the sale of a public company's assets is important to many people, such as investors, customers, competitors, creditors, and employees, the Securities and Exchange Commission (SEC) closely regulates the distribution of information to ensure equitable access to all parties. Conoco Chemicals' four-person Communications Department managed the announcement that the letter of intent to sell had been signed. Its efforts, described in the following excerpt from the department's report, won an award from the International Association of Business Communicators.

> Because the investment group involved in purchasing assets of Conoco Chemicals from du Pont included members of Conoco Chemicals' own management, the Communication Department had to deal not only with concerns of du Pont, the parent company, but also with the management of Conoco Chemicals and that of the soon-to-be-formed Vista Chemical Company. Although all parties were committed to the successful execution of the sale, they often had conflicting interests in many aspects of the negotiations. Thus, the Communications Department often had to walk a fine line in both planning and execution of the announcement, and do its part to maintain goodwill among all parties to the pending sale.
>
> Up until just weeks before the announcement, the Communications Department of Conoco Chemicals had functioned as a subordinate organization of the Conoco Public Relations Department. . . . As the announcement date grew close, the Communications Department's role evolved into that of an independent communication counsel for the buyers, and its work with Conoco and du Pont's public

relations and public affairs departments began to take on the quality of "arm's-length" negotiations. Both du Pont and E. F. Hutton [the investment bankers for the transaction] planned separate announcements of the signing.

We needed the Communications Department to reach many audiences with the announcement: employees, customers, suppliers, the financial community, government officials, interested parties in the communities where Conoco Chemicals' offices and plants were located, affiliated companies, and the chemical industry. Conoco Chemicals' 1300 employees, which might seem the most accessible of these audiences, were scattered across the globe, located in Houston, Texas; Lake Charles, Louisiana; Aberdeen, Mississippi; Hammond, Indiana; Baltimore, Maryland; Oklahoma City, Oklahoma; Oak Brook, Illinois; Saddlebrook, New Jersey; and Santa Ana, California. In addition, the employees of affiliated international companies and the international marketing organization that would be part of the new company were officed in Japan and Belgium.

To meet our needs, the Communications Department formed comprehensive goals for the announcement project:

1. To secure Conoco Chemicals' employees' positive acceptance of the circumstances so that they would remain with the company, on the job, without a significant morale problem affecting their work.
2. To persuade union bargaining units not to oppose or obstruct the formation of the new company, but to support an economical transfer of the old Conoco Chemicals' labor contracts to the new Vista Chemical Company.
3. To persuade specific Conoco employees, not directly employed by Conoco Chemicals but who would be essential to Vista's success, to sign letters of intent to work for the new company.
4. To persuade our customers, suppliers, affiliates, and the chemical industry that business with us should continue uninterrupted.
5. To persuade the financial community that Vista would be a good investment.
6. To minimize our audiences' perception of change and to assure them of the new company's similarity to the "old" Conoco Chemicals.
7. To achieve the above while still retaining the goodwill of the du Pont/Conoco management so they would support and not obstruct the negotiations of the final agreements that would create the new company.

After defining goals, the four department members spent several days making up lists of questions and issues that would concern each audience. Finding answers to these questions was a complex process. Those of us who were heavily involved in the negotiations worked with the communications staff when we could, but the answers to many of the questions would not be known at the time of the announcement. Furthermore, some of the parties to the sale wanted to minimize the amount of information released, and the management of E. F. Hutton and du Pont, as well as those of us who would head Vista Chemical Company, had to approve all announcements.

The Vista management's communication philosophy was to provide timely information wherever possible. Where information wasn't immediately available, we intended to acknowledge people's concerns and promise them informa-

Editorial Contacts:
Mike Reynolds
Conoco Chemicals Company
(713) 531-3210

C. Clark Ambrose
E. F. Hutton Group, Inc.
(212) 742-5330
For immediate release

Houston, Oct. 18—An investment group, which includes members of management of Conoco Chemicals, has signed a letter of intent with du Pont Company to purchase certain Conoco Chemicals assets for approximately $600 million in cash, John D. Burns, executive vice president of Conoco Chemicals, said today.

Mr. Burns leads the management group, which includes J. J. Langford and R. E. Lehmkuhl, Conoco Chemicals vice presidents. The investment group was organized by the E. F. Hutton Group, Inc., and Gordon A. Cain, a former Conoco vice president.

The purchasers plan to organize a new company, named Vista Chemical Company, which is expected to have about 1,600 employees. Definitive agreements are expected to be finalized by the end of this year. Closing of the proposed purchase is expected to occur during the first quarter of 1984.

(More)

Conoco Chemicals' Press Release

tion as soon as we could release it. To implement this approach, the communications team planned a strategy combining several media:

1. a press release to be issued by Conoco Chemicals, shown here;
2. presentations by Conoco Chemicals' management to both Conoco and Conoco Chemicals' employees;
3. a videotaped presentation for employees who were not able to attend presentations;
4. an employee "buyout hotline" to provide a continuing flow of information between management and employees during the three to four months of the negotiations;
5. a special edition of *ChemNews*, the employee magazine;
6. a letter to city/regional/state government officials and community leaders;
7. a mail-gram to customers/suppliers;

> The following manufacturing sites and businesses are included in the proposed purchase:
>
> - Lake Charles, LA, ethylene, normal paraffins, methyl chloride, synthetic alcohols, alumina, ethoxylates, vinyl chloride monomer and detergent alkylates;
> - Baltimore, MD and Hammond, IN, detergent alkylate and derivates;
> - Aberdeen, MS and Oklahoma City, OK, polyvinyl chloride resins, compounds, and dryblends.
>
> Also included in the proposed transaction are interests in affiliates in Argentina (Petroquimica Argentina, S.A.), Spain (Petroquimica Espanola S.A.), and Japan (Nippon Aluminum Alkyls, Ltd., and Nissan-Conoco Corp.), and three wholly-owned marketing subsidiaries: Conoco Chemicals Europe N.V., Conoco Chemicals Far East, Inc., and Conoco Chemicals Latin America S.A.
>
> "We are most excited about this opportunity for the employees and the customers involved in these businesses," Mr. Burns said. "The surfactant chemicals, polyvinyl chloride, and feedstock plants have been the backbone of the Conoco Chemicals division for a number of years, and we are committed to their continued improvement. We look forward to continuing the successful relationship we have had over the years with our employees, customers, and suppliers."
>
> Revenues for the new company, based on the businesses involved, were approximately $450 million in 1982.
>
> # # #

8. a telex to affiliated companies and their stockholders, containing essentially the same information as the press release;
9. a letter from management to employees providing a "hard copy" of the information in the management presentations;
10. a press packet for company spokespersons; and
11. a slide show for customers.

Because of the sensitive nature of the issue, all of us who were presenting this announcement had only limited information we could give to the press. Nevertheless, nearly all the goals of the program were achieved. Only four employees chose not to remain with the new company; sales of almost all products increased; no major customer cancelled its business; morale remained high; and a majority of the financial press reports were positive. The effective management of communication with complex, diverse audiences during this period allowed the new Vista Chemical Company to set sail under strongly favorable conditions. The first year began slowly, but turned around in the second quarter. Marshaling resources to repay a substantial portion of the $500 million purchase price, we were able to make Vista a public company again in December of 1986 and to restructure the company financially in 1989.

THE PERSONAL AND LEGAL CONTEXTS FOR COMMUNICATING ABOUT INSURANCE

Operating my own insurance business offered me a personal challenge and an opportunity that being a critical care nurse on a transplant team no longer seemed to offer. Like nursing, insurance gave me the chance to help people. While being at the frontier of medicine had been exciting and often poignant, I wanted greater independence and a chance to help people manage risks more successfully than by braving a last-ditch ordeal.

The key to the insurance business might seem to be the legal contract or policy between the company and the customer, since the policy governs what remedies the customer will have if losses occur. More important than the policy, though, is having the right policy, the one suited to the customer's needs and risk situation. It is more accurate to say that the key to the insurance business is

Jackie McCoy is an agent for State Farm Insurance, Houston, Texas.

communication, because that is how the customer discovers the right policy. In the discussions between agents and clients, people face their needs, often ones they might prefer to ignore, and find good ways to cope with them. Through communication, I help them define their needs. I also provide information they require to make decisions.

The communication that goes on before a policy is purchased, while it is in force and after a loss has occurred, is therefore part of a long-term personal counseling relationship. At the same time, because of the contractual nature of the business, our communication also exists in a legal framework. Agents and insurance companies can be sued or held legally liable if they fail to inform customers about certain provisions in their policies. This dual context, at once personal and legal, affects communication in an insurance company in many ways.

The personal side of communication dominates the initial discussions and the marketing efforts. A mutual affinity between the agent and the client has to develop, because deeply significant issues are at stake: income for the family survivors after the death of a mother or father, restoration of a home after a fire, replacement of a stolen car, or payment of medical expenses. The insurance agent is dealing with the individual's ability to survive some of the worst crises in our civilization and the ability to protect and provide for loved ones. These aren't matters to discuss with just anyone. When someone calls, I try to find common ground with the person, perhaps at first no more than residence in the same part of the city, an interest in boats or golf, if that's the kind of insurance the caller seeks, or some other link that can set in motion the feeling that we share mutual concerns.

As the relationship develops and the conversations continue, the legal aspect of my relationship with the client comes into play. I am legally obliged to bring to the customer's attention the potential for certain kinds of losses and the availability of coverage for them. It might seem that mentioning a full range of services or products is only maximizing a sales opportunity, but legal precedents have created new standards of due care and professional liability. The trends in litigation are too powerful to ignore; agents and companies they represent have been sued when available coverage was not secured by people who later suffered losses. For example, the mother of an accident victim told a State Farm agent she intended to sue after her son was killed in a motorcycle accident because his policy did not cover accidental death. She felt the agent should somehow have forced the young man to buy the additional coverage.

The best way to document that I have offered certain coverage but the client has refused it is to put the offer in writing. Later the agent can prove that he or she acted competently and professionally toward all potential customers. If offering coverage in writing is standard practice in an office, then a judge is likely to accept that routine as evidence that an agent offered coverage in a specific instance being considered by the court.

The ability of written communication to document professional service and to show that all the necessary information was submitted to the client has made written communications about insurance much more standard and uniform, less spontaneous and personal, as shown in the first sample letter. This

Client Conference

uniformity would demonstrate to a court that I always provide information of a particular kind in certain situations. We have to show every reasonable effort to inform the customer about the actual coverage provided by the policy, because people are notoriously unlikely to read their insurance policies until *after* a loss has occurred. We try in several ways to ensure that the client understands policy provisions, explaining them before the policy is chosen, writing a letter at the time we issue the policy (see Figure 1), and sending another letter at renewal time (shown in Figure 2).

Many times we put brightly colored stickers on policies to point out limitations in coverage. Here in the Houston area, people often are unaware that the standard homeowner's policy does not provide coverage for damage from rising water, or flood insurance. We've taken to putting "You do not have flood insurance" stickers on policies in the hope that as customers file their policies, they will at least notice the stickers.

Every three years we send letters to our clients, as in Figure 2, to find out whether changes have occurred that would justify a change in coverage. For example, we ask people whether the liability limits they selected are still adequate. We include all the personal information relevant to the policy, which enables us to make even a form letter sound more like an exchange between friends about a mutual concern.

In addition to supplying information about the provisions of policies and the types of coverage available, insurance agents must educate their clients. We try to include the answers to frequently asked questions in our correspondence.

STATE FARM INSURANCE®

Jackie McCoy
Auto-Life-Health-Home and Business

3642 University
Houston, Texas 77005 Phone (713) 666-3642

August 15, 1990

Ms. Laura Sluder
3949 Rensselaer Drive
Houston, TX 77005

Dear Laura:

Your home is now protected by the enclosed policy. Please review the principal points of coverage, listed below, to make sure the policy suits your needs. Your new policy provides $200,000 coverage on your home, $120,000 on your personal property, $100,000 personal liability, $1000 medical payments, and $500 physical damage to property of others. The annual premium is $1015.

This policy has a $250 deductible. It includes a glass endorsement that covers up to $100 per pane of glass in the event of breakage, and replacement cost coverage that virtually eliminates the depreciation on your personal property in the event of a loss. This policy has a $500 limit on theft of jewelry and furs, $100 on currency, $500 on items such as stamp and coin collections and $2500 on business property or computers used for business. This policy does not cover loss caused by or resulting from flood or rising waters.

In order to serve you efficiently in the event of a loss, we ask that you keep receipts and other records (warranty cards, instruction manuals) of newly purchased items. On older items for which you may not have kept receipts, a picture or video inventory would be helpful. Our claims adjusters will ask for any proof of ownership that you may have.

We certainly do appreciate your allowing us to assist you with your insurance needs, and we look forward to providing you with the best of service. Please take a few minutes to read over this policy. If you have any questions, give me a call. Thanks again for your business.

Sincerely,

Jackie McCoy

Jackie McCoy

JM: ah
encl: policy

FIGURE 1. Sample Letter to Client When Policy Is Issued

STATE FARM
INSURANCE ®

Jackie McCoy
Auto-Life-Health-Home and Business

3642 University
Houston, Texas 77005 Phone (713) 666-3642

August 2, 1990

Mr. Sam G. Wong
3241 Terhune
Houston, TX 77005

Dear Sam:

I wish it were possible to see you each time you have a policy renewing to express personally my appreciation for your business. Since I cannot do that, I depend on this letter to say, "Thank you."

I would like you to look through the provisions of the policy now renewing to see whether the amounts are still adequate. Your homeowner's policy provides $100,000 coverage on your home, $60,000 on your personal property, $100,000 personal liability, $1000 medical payments, and $500 physical damage to property of others.

This policy has a $250 deductible. It includes a glass endorsement that covers up to $100 per pane of glass in the event of breakage, and replacement cost coverage that virtually eliminates the depreciation on your personal property in the event of a loss. This policy has a $500 limit on theft of jewelry and furs, $100 on currency, $500 on items such as stamp and coin collections, and $2500 on business property or computers used for business. This policy does not cover loss caused by or resulting from flood or rising waters.

If these provisions no longer seem sufficient, please call me and we will discuss them. I want you to have exactly the coverage you need. Thanks again for your business.

Sincerely,

Jackie McCoy

Jackie McCoy

JH: jm

FIGURE 2.   Sample Letter to Client at Time of Policy Renewal

For example, people often ask when they should drop collision coverage. In addition, some of the best literature on AIDS is being provided to employers by insurance companies. Health information is often part of the educational materials distributed by insurance companies, especially to older adults. New business owners often do not know what kinds of coverage their fledgling companies need, and insurance agents can provide that basic knowledge. Insurance companies have been at the forefront of support for education generally. Aetna Corporation, for instance, promotes education for the disadvantaged.

Along with communication with customers, a large volume of communication between the agent and the insurance company ensures the processing of purchases and claims. Much of this communication is routine and is submitted on forms. Gradually, communication between agents and the companies they represent is likely to become electronic, reducing paperwork and speeding transmission.

Nevertheless, I'm confident that computers are not going to replace us completely anytime soon. When a hurricane has blown down a fence and the customer calls to ask, "When are you coming out?" that question is a call from one person to another, seeking reassurance that I care about this disaster, about the disruption in the family's life, and the undetermined cost of setting things to rights. The personal side of communication still matters. I send my clients birthday cards each year. I figure that because I love to get cards, they probably do, too. I've heard too often how much caring matters when one of those birthday people says, "Thanks for your card. It was the only one I got."

FIESTA MART: COMMUNICATING WITH CUSTOMERS FROM MANY CULTURES

Houston in the last quarter century has become a multicultural, international city; its public school students speak over seventy native languages and their families value many ethnic culinary traditions. Our company, Fiesta Mart, is a Houston chain of food markets that defy the cookie-cutter sameness of giant retail chain stores. The giant food chains emphasize efficiency and low cost, which leads to prepackaged products and impersonal shopping experiences. Fiesta Mart, in contrast, seeks out sites in ethnic neighborhoods and tries to participate in the cultural blend of those communities. Our stores are located in neighborhoods that may be predominantly Hispanic, Anglo, black, Middle Eastern, or Asian. When I first came to Houston, my intent was to serve Hispanic neighborhoods with a store that imitated the Mexican *mercado*, a wonderful community marketplace where people enjoy selecting and purchasing what is needed for daily life. Twenty years ago, most of the large supermarkets were

Donald Bonham is President of Fiesta Mart, Inc.

located a long way from Hispanic neighborhoods, and Hispanic women were likely to stay at home, either because they lacked transportation or because it was not their custom to go to these efficient but impersonal stores. To encourage people to come to shop and to enjoy their experience, I named our store Fiesta Mart and encouraged people to think of their shopping as coming to a party.

Fiesta Mart offers customers an alternative; its slogan is "Discover the Difference for Yourself." Our basic goal is to provide people with purchasing experiences that enhance their quality of life. These purchases involve food or products usually associated with the surroundings in which food is purchased. The Fiesta Mart environment enhances quality of life by making shopping a pleasure, a positive experience of selecting good values from abundance and being assisted by friendly people who respect themselves and their customers.

In order to create this stable, positive environment, Fiesta Mart trains and retains employees for long-term productivity and personal growth. We hire a high proportion of minorities, and we have a very high proportion of full-time employees. Employees are supposed to help the customer, to make the experience pleasant, and to ensure the high quality of products and the cleanliness and beauty of the store environment. After all, you wouldn't invite your guests to a party without making sure your house looked its best and that everything was ready.

❑ ENHANCING CUSTOMERS' QUALITY OF LIFE

The Shopping Experience

Fiesta Mart responds with sensitivity to the cultures of the communities it serves, and seeks to create a stimulating, colorful business environment and the highest quality products. The customer cannot select good values from abundance unless the products to be selected are of the best quality and attractively displayed. At Fiesta, our food products are piled in high mounds; nothing else so clearly communicates abundance and availability. We avoid prepackaged, plastic-wrapped serving-size portions, except for products that must be prepackaged for health and safety. We want the customer to enjoy the tactile pleasure of handling good produce, the smells of fruits and breads, the decisions of preferring one potato or ear of corn to another. Selecting one's food is an essential and wonderful human experience.

The "Fiesta Club Party" Concept

In addition to creating an atmosphere for shopping that differs from most grocery stores, Fiesta Mart promotes its shopping experience with an unusual program for neighborhoods called "the Fiesta Club Party." A "Fiesta Club Party" is a fund-raising luncheon or dinner combining fun with dining pleasure. Nonprofit organizations in our customer neighborhoods may call one of two home economists and schedule a dinner that the organization will advertise and conduct to make money for its projects. The economists schedule up to ten club party dinners each week.

Here's how the Fiesta Club Party works. The club members plan the dinner with the help of the home economist, who has created several distinctive dinner menus, and the day of the dinner club members shop with the home economist at their neighborhood Fiesta Mart for supplies. The supplies cost the club nothing. Fiesta Mart and food product sponsors, such as Tropicana, Coca Cola, and other companies, bear the cost of supplies. The home economist shows the club members how to prepare and serve the meal, and at the party, a master of ceremonies entertains the dinner guests with stories, jokes, and party games. The local Fiesta Mart manager welcomes the guests and compliments the club. The club takes the proceeds from the dinner or luncheon and uses them for their other projects.

Fiesta Club Parties help charitable organizations raise over $150,000 annually for their projects. The Fiesta Club Parties and the Fiesta shopping experience reflects a philosophy of living dear to Hispanic culture: that celebration is the essence of life, and that human work—whether shopping or earning a living or raising funds for good causes—should be done with a spirit of joy. As Fiesta has grown, communicating that philosophy has become the heart of our relationship with customers.

❏ RESPONSIVENESS TO CULTURES AND COMMUNICATION

Over our nearly two decades of business in Houston, we have branched out of the Hispanic neighborhoods to parts of the city whose inhabitants are from other cultures. Like the Hispanic community, these groups have their own ideas about the experience of purchasing and their own preferred products, but all people love parties; they love celebrating life; and they all enjoy the experience of selecting good values from abundance. In bringing that positive experience to new communities of customers, we had to be responsive to their cultures, which made communication with customers extremely important.

We encouraged store managers to support community projects in their neighborhoods. Our stores have been involved in many types of projects, but the managers always try to make sure these projects serve the communities: youth activities, adult learning centers, scholarship programs, and community festivals. These projects allow Fiesta to communicate that we see ourselves as members of the neighborhoods in which our customers live.

In addition to advertising and community support, other communication was crucial because we had to learn from these new customers how they felt about foods and about shopping. Furthermore, we had to communicate the ways in which Fiesta is distinctive among food markets to new groups. We had to convince them to "discover the difference" for themselves. This challenge meant much more than learning which foods to order for ethnic cuisines. For instance, in Asian communities there is a tradition of formality and mutual respect between shopkeepers and customers; we needed to learn their ways of expressing that respect. In contrast, some ethnic groups assume the relationship between merchants and customers to be adversarial; customers display a great deal of emotion and antagonism. They expect us to be firm. In some communities shoppers expect to treat the employees with disdain or abuse, which could ruin the morale of employees. The types of situations and transactions with each of these new customer groups differed from those we had known in our first stores.

Decentralized management was necessary to give store managers the flexibility to respond appropriately to these new customer groups. And while we needed to appreciate customers' expectations, we could not allow employees to be harrassed—after all, you cannot have a fiesta atmosphere if the guests are berating the hosts. So we promoted respect for employees in some stores with posters that said, "We like our customers, but we love our employees." In different ways the managers at these various stores formed relationships with our new communities, and nearly all of our stores have enjoyed a high degree of client loyalty despite the fierce competition that characterizes the retail grocery business.

Over the years, we have seen changes in customers' expectations. Customers now expect stores to screen products for safety and to enforce local concerns for the environment. We have a huge recycling operation at Fiesta. Some customers demand that the store not sell products that they perceive are produced in offensive ways: they want milk-fed veal and young lamb removed from our product lines. Others want us to refuse to do business with suppliers who do business in South Africa or who represent a particular social policy the customer finds offensive. These nontraditional customer demands will create even greater communication challenges for store managers, who must communicate with one another to find ways of adapting to these new situations. I am confident, however, that our basic business philosophy will continue to serve us well as America becomes an increasingly multicultural society. Communication with these customers will continue to be our number one challenge.

❏ PLEDGING QUALITY

Back in 1984, when Compaq Computer Corporation was two years old, a small group of enthusiastic employees began to discuss the need for communication within the company about the quality of its products and services to its customer base. As Director of Corporate Training and Development, one of my responsibilities was to aid in the communication process. We set about to help employees understand the need for quality. By testing and revising our quality assurance and communication processes over the next five years, we involved every Compaq employee in achieving our goal of creating defect-free products and services.

At the time, we were a fledgling company, but we had been very successful in the introduction of our portable computer line. The three founders of our company were dedicated to creating reliable, visually appealing products that performed the way users wanted them to perform. An advertising slogan based on the quality and reliability of the product announced: "It simply works better."

Lee Murdy is Director of Corporate Training and Development, Compaq Computer Corporation.

The small band of quality enthusiasts convinced the founders that we needed to adopt a programmed approach to implement and maintain quality in our products and services. The Crosby Approach was a 14-step plan that motivated all segments of the organization to "do it right the first time." The Crosby plan called for determining the cost of quality and having everyone in the organization work together to eliminate waste, errors, and non-value-added efforts and expense, thus reducing the cost of quality. In essence, the theme was "Quality Is Free."

❏ DEVELOPING A STATEMENT

Because the corporation was fast growing and lacked established systems and procedures, it was unable to sustain the Crosby approach; however, the program did help us in two ways. It implanted the concept of doing tasks right the first time among many of the early employees, and it also led to the development of a quality statement that we still use. After many wordsmithing sessions, top management, including the founders, was able to agree on the following statement:

> We at Compaq Computer Corporation are absolutely committed to provide defect-free products and services to our customers in cooperation with equally committed suppliers and authorized dealers.

This statement, signed by Rod Canion, President and Chief Executive Officer, was put on plaques and mounted on the walls in strategic locations in conference rooms, factory halls, and office-building common areas. Although the plaques proclaimed a policy, they didn't cause employees to internalize the message.

❏ BACKING WORDS WITH ACTIONS

Interestingly enough, the first plaques sent out were not considered to be a "quality presentation." Therefore, they were retrieved and new plaques were reissued at the company's expense, because the Compaq managers had not specified requirements well to the supplier. Ironically, specifying the requirements of any product was one of the key features of the quality program that had been slated for immediate implementation.

Managers were charged with accomplishing the 14-step quality program. The quality statement hung on the walls for two years. The key decision makers were responsible for ensuring product quality. With very little fanfare and a penchant for listening and doing what made sense, management quietly worked to produce quality products and get them to market on time. However, it is difficult for a few individuals to be responsible for the continuous quality of many other people's work.

❏ ADJUSTING THE APPROACH

As the company grew and grew, reaching 3000, 4000, then 5000 employees, it became apparent that all employees, not just key managers, needed to be involved in ensuring quality. As top management discussed the factory of the future, they decided that the focus had to be on the principles of quality. Working with consultants in 1986, management pondered a very fundamental question: How could the company improve quality, cost, and cycle-time continuously to produce outstanding products and services?

The result of these discussions was "Total Quality Commitment" (TQC). This concept was not invented by Compaq but had been functioning in Japanese businesses for some time. The American wave was just catching on. Compaq designed its own TQC process. Underlying this process were several basic principles: (1) focusing on customer satisfaction, processes, problem solving, and teamwork; (2) involving individuals; and (3) continuously improving quality, cost, and cycle-time. Perhaps not so coincidentally, the quality statement, which had been created two years earlier, fit these principles quite well—so well that we decided to use this statement as a rallying point in training and communication. Management first launched Total Quality Commitment in the manufacturing department, where the most employees were and where the most immediate benefits could be found.

❏ COMMUNICATING VALUES

It might seem elementary, but all employees had to memorize the quality statement during the orientation and training program for Total Quality Commitment. The statement functioned as a pledge, motivating all employees to integrate quality into their everyday thinking and working. Just as in an advertising campaign, we plastered the quality statement throughout our workbooks and had many more plaques made and distributed throughout the company, which had grown six-fold from the time the original plaques were introduced.

We even devised a recognition process whereby employees were recognized and awarded a lapel pin for knowing the statement by heart and reciting it in front of a group of their peers. Employees became very competitive about reciting the pledge, and various positive competitive games emerged. All managers who could say the pledge by heart were given a pin and a supply of pins to give out to their employees. If employees came up to them at any time during work and recited the pledge to them in front of their peers, the managers or supervisors were obliged to give the employees their own lapel pins. Employees also could ask a manager to repeat the pledge. If the manager could not repeat the pledge by heart correctly, then his or her lapel button had to be relinquished; the manager would have to recite the pledge correctly to win it back. This process, which was a lot of fun, communicated the values of the quality statement through the quality pledge in visual, verbal, and interpersonal channels. The quality statement was alive.

Whenever anyone asks why we are using this communication process, one of the answers is the pledge itself: "We at Compaq Computer Corporation are absolutely committed to provide defect-free products and services to our customers in cooperation with equally committed suppliers and authorized dealers." In 1988, the Gordon S. Black survey of the personal computer industry ranked Compaq Computer Corporation number one in overall customer satisfaction and in overall quality of products. Those rankings are a result of the values communicated throughout the company.